Strategy

LAWRENCE
FREEDMAN

Strategy
A History

OXFORD
UNIVERSITY PRESS

Oxford University Press is a department of the University of Oxford.
It furthers the University's objective of excellence in research, scholarship,
and education by publishing worldwide.

Oxford New York
Auckland   Cape   Town   Dar es Salaam   Hong Kong   Karachi
Kuala Lumpur   Madrid   Melbourne   Mexico City   Nairobi
New Delhi   Shanghai   Taipei   Toronto

With offices in
Argentina   Austria   Brazil   Chile   Czech Republic   France   Greece
Guatemala   Hungary   Italy   Japan   Poland   Portugal   Singapore
South Korea   Switzerland   Thailand   Turkey   Ukraine Vietnam

Oxford is a registered trademark of Oxford University Press in the UK and certain other
countries.

Published in the United States of America by
Oxford University Press
198 Madison Avenue, New York, NY 10016

Library of Congress Cataloging-in-Publication Data
Freedman, Lawrence.
Strategy : a history / Lawrence Freedman.
pages cm
Includes bibliographical references and index.
ISBN 978-0-19-932515-3 (hardback)   ISBN 978-0-19-022923-8 (pbk)
1. Strategy—History.   2. Military history.   3. Strategic culture.   4. Strategic planning.   I. Title.
U162.F86 2013
320.6—dc23
2013011944

9 8 7
Printed in the United States of America
on acid-free paper

For Judith

CONTENTS

Everyone has a plan 'till they get punched in the mouth.

—Mike Tyson

EVERYONE NEEDS A strategy. Leaders of armies, major corporations, and political parties have long been expected to have strategies, but now no serious organization could imagine being without one. Despite the problems of finding ways through the uncertainty and confusion of human affairs, a strategic approach is still considered to be preferable to one that is merely tactical, let alone random. Having a strategy suggests an ability to look up from the short term and the trivial to view the long term and the essential, to address causes rather than symptoms, to see woods rather than trees. Without a strategy, facing up to any problem or striving for any objective would be considered negligent. Certainly no military campaign, company investment, or government initiative is likely to receiving backing unless there is a strategy to evaluate. If a decision can be described as strategically significant, then it is obviously more important than decisions of a more routine nature. By extension, people making such decisions are more important than those who only offer advice or are tasked with implementation.

Strategies are now offered not only for the life-or-death, make-or-break decisions of great states and large corporations but also for more mundane matters. There is a call for a strategy every time the path to a given destination is not straightforward or whenever judgments are required on resources needed, their effective application, and their appropriate sequence. In business, chief executives may take responsibility for overall strategy, but there are separate strategies for procurement, marketing, human resources, and so on. Doctors have clinical strategies, lawyers have prosecution strategies, and social workers have counseling strategies. Individuals have their own strategies—for developing a career, coping with bereavement, filling in tax returns, or even potty-training an infant or buying a car. In fact, there is now no human activity so lowly, banal, or intimate that it can reasonably be deprived of a strategy.

For those who want more effective strategies, there are plenty of books offering advice. The multiplicity of audiences shows in the variations of style. Some books rely on a jokey presentation, others on large print or inspirational stories from the successful and victorious. There are learned tomes with graphs and charts detailing many complicated factors to be taken into account. Somewhere between are checklists of activities that, if followed carefully, will at least increase the chances of achieving the right result. There are extended pep talks, encouraging bold thinking and decisive moves and a commitment to victory. These may be no more than collections of clichés, not always consistent, with hints on how to struggle with opponents and bring along prospective allies. Elsewhere there are more philosophical reflections on the paradoxes of conflict and the pitfalls of losing flexibility in the single-minded pursuit of a distant goal. There are even tips on how to be a fantasy strategist while staring at a screen, refighting ancient wars or dominating aliens in imagined universes with complicated rules and extraordinary weapons.

Can the same word apply to battle plans, political campaigning, and business deals—not to mention means of coping with the stresses of everyday life—without becoming meaningless? Columnist Matthew Parris has lamented the ubiquity of the word *strategy* and the ease with which it becomes attached to any desirable end. He commented on demands for a "growth strategy" in the face of a stagnant and indebted economy but wondered who would claim a "rain strategy" as an answer to drought. "Every sinner needs a virtue strategy. Every starveling needs a food strategy." "There exist few modern circumstances," he observed, "where the removal of the word 'strategy' from any passage containing it fails to clarify matters, usually demonstrating the argument's circularity."[1] Yet *strategy* remains the best word we have for expressing attempts to think about actions in advance, in the light of our goals and our capacities. It captures a process for which there are no obvious alternative words, although the meaning has become diluted through promiscuous and often inappropriate use. In this respect *strategy* is not much different from other related words, such as *power* and *politics*. While their exact meanings are explored, rarely to a conclusion, in scholarly texts, their adoption in everyday speech tends to be imprecise, loose, and lazy.

There is no agreed-upon definition of *strategy* that describes the field and limits its boundaries. One common contemporary definition describes it as being about maintaining a balance between ends, ways, and means; about identifying objectives; and about the resources and methods available for meeting such objectives.[2] This balance requires not only finding out how to achieve desired ends but also adjusting ends so that realistic ways can be found to meet them by available means. This process can describe the simplest tasks, but when the ends are easily reached, when inanimate objects rather than other people are involved, and when very little is at stake, this barely counts as strategy. By and large, strategy comes into play where there is actual or potential conflict, when interests collide and forms of resolution are required. This is why a strategy is much more than a plan. A plan supposes a sequence of events that allows one to move with confidence from one state of affairs to another. Strategy is required when others might frustrate one's plans because they have different and possibly opposing interests and concerns. The conflicts can be quite mild, for example, between those within the same organization notionally pursuing the same goals but with distinctive responsibilities. As the quote from boxer Mike Tyson illustrates, a well-aimed blow can thwart the cleverest plan. The inherent unpredictability of human affairs, due to chance events as well as the efforts of opponents and the missteps of friends, provides strategy with its challenge and drama. Strategy is often expected to start with a description of a desired end state, but in practice there is rarely an orderly movement to goals set in advance. Instead, the process evolves through a series of states, each one not quite what was anticipated or hoped for, requiring a reappraisal and modification of the original strategy, including ultimate objectives. The picture of strategy that should emerge from this book is one that is fluid and flexible, governed by the starting point and not the end point.

Strategy is also frequently presented as a duel, a clash of two opposing wills. This reflects the term's military origins and regular comparisons to a wrestling match. It can also be the result of the simple modeling of conflicts encouraged by game theory with the standard two-by-two matrix. Few situations involving strategy are so simple. A boxer in a ring with Mike Tyson might have few options, but his prospects would improve greatly if it was possible to break the rules and bring in a fellow fighter from outside the ring. As we shall see, combining with others often constitutes the most astute strategic move; for the same reason, preventing opponents from doing the same can be as valuable. A duel is also a bad metaphor because it suggests a fight to the finish with only one winner. Yet conflicts can be resolved through building on shared interests or forging a winning coalition with the next available partner. As both types of moves can require complex negotiations, it may be a challenge to convince natural supporters that the necessary concessions have been worthwhile or prudent. So the realm of strategy is one of bargaining and persuasion as well as threats and pressure, psychological as well as physical effects, and words as well as deeds. This is why strategy is the central political art. It is about getting more out of a situation than the starting balance of power would suggest. It is the art of creating power.

For those who start as powerful, strategy should not be too difficult. The sensible application of superior resources tends to be successful. A famous biblical passage observes "that the race is not to the swift, nor the battle to the strong."[3] The American writer Damon Runyon added, "But that's the way to bet." Fighting against superior force may score high on nobility and heroism but normally low on discretion and effectiveness. This is why underdog strategies, in situations where the starting balance of power would predict defeat, provide the real tests of creativity. Such strategies often look to the possibility of success through the application of a superior intelligence, which takes advantage of the boring, ponderous, muscle-bound approach adopted by those who take their superior resources for granted. The exemplars of such an approach are Odysseus but not Achilles, Sun Tzu and Liddell Hart but not Clausewitz and Jomini. They would seek victory at a reasonable cost by means of deceits, ruses, feints, maneuvers, speed, and a quicker wit. There is an undoubted satisfaction by winning through wit rather than brute force. The problems come when opponents turn out to be not only better resourced but also as alert, brave, and clever.

Strategy's etymology goes back to classical Greek. Through the Middle Ages and into the modern era, however, the relevant reference tended to be to the "art of war." The sort of issues that later came firmly under the heading of strategy—the value of alliances, the role of battle, the respective merits of force and guile—were firmly in view. The word *strategy* only began to be used in Britain, France, and Germany in the late eighteenth century, reflecting an Enlightenment optimism that war—like all other spheres of human affairs—could benefit from the application of reason. It also reflected the demands of contemporary warfare, with mass armies and long logistics chains. The employment of force now required careful preparation and theoretical guidance. Before, ends and means might be combined in the mind of the warrior leader, who would be responsible for both the formulation and execution of a strategy. Increasingly, these functions were separated. Governments set objectives they expected the generals to achieve. The generals acquired specialist staffs to devise campaign plans that others would implement.

Given the ease with which military metaphors are taken up in other spheres of activity, including the language of command, it is not surprising that political and business leaders adopted the idea of strategy. References to business strategy were rare before 1960. They started to take off during the 1970s and by 2000 became more frequent than references to military strategy.[4] It is through the literature on management and business that the use of the word has spread. As organizations' plans and policies, at least their most important and far-reaching ones, came to be described as "strategic," it was not too large a jump for individuals to use the term when considering how best to make professional choices. The social and philosophical movements of the 1960s encouraged the "personal" to become more "political," potentially introducing strategy into more basic relationships.

Corporations acquired planning staffs which set targets for others to follow. Politicians hired consultants who advised on how to win elections. And then those with experience in these tasks wrote and lectured on the principles of strategy, offering prescriptions that might bring success in potentially diverse settings. The rise of strategy has therefore gone hand in hand with bureaucratization of organizations, professionalization of functions, and growth of the social sciences. It reflected the hope that the specialist study of economics, sociology, politics, and psychology would make possible a more comprehensible and therefore more predictable world, so that all moves could be better informed and judged, tailored more effectively to the circumstances of the moment.

One response to the advance of the strategists was to challenge their presumptions of control and the centralized power structures they encouraged. Strategy has been presented as a conceit and an illusion, a pretense that the affairs of the multitudes can be manipulated from above by an elite. Instead of the deliberate decisions of a few, critics pointed to the countless moves of innumerable individuals, unable to see the big picture yet coping as well as they can in the circumstances, leading to outcomes that nobody had intended or even desired. This critique has encouraged demands for decentralized decision-making and empowered individuals. In turn, this encouraged strategy as a more personal response to the vicissitudes of everyday life.

This book describes the development of these different approaches, from rigorous centralized planning processes at one extreme to the sum of numerous individual decisions at the other. It shows how in these distinct military, political, and business spheres, there has been a degree of convergence around the idea that the best strategic practice may now consist in forming compelling accounts of how to turn a developing situation into a desirable outcome. The practice of thinking of strategy as a special sort of narrative came into vogue as the 1960s turned into the 1970s, and disillusion set in with the idea that large enterprises and even wars could be controlled by means of a central plan. Developments in cognitive psychology and contemporary philosophy came together to stress the importance of the constructs through which events are interpreted.

As a history, this book aims to provide an account of the development of the most prominent themes in strategic theory—as they affect war, politics, and business—without losing sight of the critics and dissidents. Readers might be surprised by some of the characters that appear, and by chapters that barely seem to mention strategy at all. This is because of the importance of the theories that set the terms for strategy. These establish the problems the strategists must address and the circumstances in which they operate, as well as their forms of political and social action. The result is that this book is not so much about planning for conflict or the application of practical intelligence to forms of uncertainty but rather about relationships between theory and practice, and indeed theories as a form of practice. Strategy provides a way into a whole range of discourses: abstract formulations of what it means to act rationally and postmodern musings on domination and resistance; propositions on causation and insights into the working of the human brain; and practical advice on how best to catch enemies in battle, undermine rivals in elections, and launch a new product into the market. Strategists have addressed the efficiency of various forms of coercion as well as inducements, human nature under stress, the organization of large groups of people on the move, negotiating techniques, visions of a good society, and standards of ethical conduct.

The approach I have adopted here does not follow any particular school of social science. In fact, I have sought to show how the ascent of certain schools can be explained by academic strategies. Toward the end I develop the idea of strategic scripts as a way of thinking about strategy as a story told in the future tense. I believe this follows from the lines of analysis developed during the course of the book, but I hope readers enjoy the history even if they do not accept the analysis. What fascinates me about strategy is that it is about choice and because these choices can be important the reasoning behind them is worthy of careful examination. It is about decisions that matter to those making them, dealing with personal advancement and group survival, but also views and values that are deeply held, businesses that affect the livelihoods of many, the opportunity to shape a nation's future course. To study strategy in this way is potentially subversive of those forms of social science which must control for the random and the disorderly, the anomalous and paradoxical, the exceptional and eccentric as awkward outliers. With strategy, these cases must be given special attention precisely because the actors have challenged expectations by either falling short or beating the odds. This might not make for great deductive theory, but it can allow the student to appreciate the thrill and drama of some of the most challenging forms of decision-making without worrying about mathematical proofs.

To keep the topic manageable I have focused largely on Western thinking about strategy, and for recent times, I have particularly examined American approaches. Because I wanted to link the main themes in the book with developments in broader political and social theory, greater geographical comprehensiveness would have been impossible. I fully understand that different cultures would yield different insights, but the United States has been not only the most powerful but also the most intellectually innovative country in recent times. In classical times Athens set the pace; in the late nineteenth century it was Germany. The advantage of staying within the bounds of Western culture is that it is possible to draw out the influences and the shared themes over time and across apparently different areas of activity. Selectivity has also been essential. I touch on the classic texts—the writers to whom regular reference is made—and those now forgotten (often deservedly so) who made an impact in their time. I have also sought to put trends and tendencies in strategic thinking in context. To keep the discussion grounded I have kept in mind Raymond Aron's observation about how strategic thought "draws its inspiration from each century, or rather at each moment of history, from the problems which events themselves pose."[5] To make sense of the key theorists, and to provide a critical edge, it is important to consider the events to which these thinkers were responding. One does not, however, need to go as far as George Orwell who, reviewing a book on strategy, observed that "there is something unsatisfactory in tracing an historical change to an individual theorist, because a theory does not gain ground unless material conditions favor it."[6] The history of ideas is fascinating in part because ideas developed in one context live on and take on new meanings in another.

As a theme of this book is the growing importance of stories as a means of thinking about and communicating strategies, I have tried to show where the most important strategic stories came from, the intent behind their construction, and how their meanings were changed over time. In keeping with this narrative theme I have also used a number of examples from literature—including the Bible, Homer, Milton, and Tolstoy—to illuminate core issues and the treatment of strategic behavior.

The book begins by treating the "prehistory" of strategy, addressing the two major sources of the Western cultural tradition—the Hebrew Bible and the great texts of the classical Greeks—and authors who have been most enduring in their influence—Thucydides, Sun Tzu, and Machiavelli. The first main section of the book looks at military strategy. The second section is concerned with political strategy, particularly efforts on behalf of underdogs. The third section considers the development of strategies for managers of large organizations, especially businesses. This section is the shortest, but only because it covers half a century of literature rather than two centuries. The last section considers the contemporary contribution of the social sciences and seeks to draw the main themes together.

Research for this book has taken me into unfamiliar territory. It has proved to be an opportunity to explore issues dimly remembered from undergraduate days and many that had previously passed me by. I was taught in political theory to read the original texts and not just the commentaries, and I have tried to do so, but it would be misleading to suggest that I have not relied extensively on the interpretations of others. I have drawn—I hope with full attribution—from the insights and ideas of a wide range of specialists. Part of the enjoyment of writing this book has come from my exposure to some wonderful scholarship, in social science and fields supposedly distant from my own. Despite the best efforts of colleagues I have undoubtedly overreached in a number of areas. Nonetheless, the exercise has reinforced my conviction that academics worry too much about making a good impression within their own disciplinary boundaries while not paying enough attention to what is going on beyond them. While the stance is often critical, I hope it is not disrespectful. These are issues worth arguing about and I look forward to those who feel that I have missed significant points arguing back.

My own expertise and the origins of the subject mean that much of the book is concerned with war, but I have also sought to do justice to revolutionary, electoral, and business strategies and explore how they have influenced each other. I have no practical experience of war, although I have met many warriors. I was very politically active as a student and engaged in many energetic debates about reform, revolution, and violence. In later years, while at King's College London, I have had a variety of managerial roles for some three decades (even ending up with "strategy" in my title). In this respect, I have in my time tried to think strategically as well as think about strategy.

PART I | Origins

CHAPTER I | Origins 1: Evolution

Man is descended from a hairy, tailed quadruped, probably arboreal in its habits.

—Charles Darwin

IN THIS CHAPTER I argue that there are elemental features of human strategy that are common across time and space. These include deception and coalition formation, and the instrumental use of violence. These features are so elemental that traces of them can be found among chimpanzees. Chimps are self-aware, understand others well enough to deceive them, and show gratitude or retribution according to whether they have been given or denied support. They have forms of communication, think through difficult problems, and plan ahead.

Years of careful observation of chimpanzees, first in the wild and then in special colonies at zoos, challenged the previous view that their social bonds were limited. It became apparent that individual chimps in the same area came together regularly and developed complex relations. They not only worked together but also had fights. Of particular interest for students of strategy, chimpanzees were political in their behavior. They built up coalitions, offering grooming, sex, and food to potential supporters—all in order to prevail in conflicts. But they also appreciated the importance of limiting their conflicts so that they could live cooperatively thereafter. They kissed and made up after a violent quarrel. By showing their vulnerability they invited trust.[1]

During the 1970s, Frans de Waal observed the chimpanzee colony at Arnhem Zoo, making copious notes as a remarkable series of dramas began to unfold. In his 1982 book, *Chimpanzee Politics*, he drew some startling conclusions about the complexity of chimpanzee society. In his view, the evidence of coalition formation and power struggles among the chimps deserved the label "political."[2]

Raw strength could only take chimps so far. When dominant males asserted power, their hair stood on end to make them appear larger and more ferocious than they actually were. They charged at groups of subordinate apes—who immediately scattered—and then received due respect through some submissive greeting or by being groomed in an elaborate fashion. De Waal realized, however, that as the hierarchy changed, those gaining power were not necessarily the strongest. Social maneuvers were of even greater importance as other chimpanzees joined in on one side or the other and shifted their allegiances. Changes in the hierarchy were not abrupt, but orderly.

The first change charted by de Waal began with the established dominant male, Yeroen, initially enjoying the support of most of the females but appearing unsure of how to respond to a conspicuous challenge to his authority by another male, Luit. In a definite affront, Luit mated with a female right in front of Yeroen. Then Luit got another male, Nikkie, to join him to tilt the balance of power in his favor. During the course of the power struggles, the tactics deployed involved not only displays of strength and determination but also measures designed to encourage females to defect, such as grooming them and playing with their children. Yeroen's angry tantrums, which might once have made subordinates wary of defecting, gradually lost their impact as they became more frequent. He eventually gave up. This struggle led to another. With Luit now dominant, Yeroen was prepared to work with Nikkie to regain some of his past prestige, even though he would not become dominant again.

Actual fighting played only a small part in this process. Biting, the most dangerous act of aggression, was rarely used. De Waal concluded that rather than changing the social relationships, the fights tended to reflect the changes that had already taken place. The apes appeared to know that they should limit violence among themselves, for they might have to unite against external rivals. They also seemed to understand the need for mediation and reconciliation. Once a goal had been achieved, the patterns of behavior changed—for example, both the winners and losers became less aggressive.

According to de Waal, the core elements of this strategic activity were the ability to recognize each other individually and to perceive social relationships, including how others might combine to form coalitions and how these coalitions might then be broken up. To make choices, the chimpanzees needed to grasp the potential consequences of their actions and be able, to some extent, to plan a route to their goal. As chimpanzees exhibited all these attributes, de Waal concluded that "the roots of politics are older than humanity." His later work built upon these original insights, pointing to evidence that primates can show tolerance, altruism, and restraint, meaning they have a capacity for empathy. Empathy involves at least emotional sensitivity to others and at most an ability to understand another's point of view. This, de Waal argued, is "essential for the regulation of social interactions, coordinated activity, and cooperation toward shared goals."[3]

Deception also turned out to be a vital strategic quality. It involved deliberately sending untrue signals with a view to changing another's behavior. Apes tricked other members of their group out of food or sneaked off for some furtive courtship when alpha males were not paying attention. Again, this required a degree of empathy with other apes. It was necessary to understand the normal behavior of others if only to appreciate how they might be misled.

What we might call "strategic intelligence," for both chimps and humans, evolved through interactions in a complex social environment as much as from the demands of survival in a harsh physical environment. Consider the human brain. The brain consumes 20 percent of the body's energy, far more than any other organ, while making up only 2 percent of an adult's body weight. Something so costly to maintain must have developed to meet a vital need. Richard Byrne and Nadia Corp studied eighteen species from all the major branches of primates and correlated the size of the neocortex to the amount of deception the species practiced. They established a link between the size of the brains and general social intelligence, including the ability to work together and manage conflict, as well as trickery.[4] In evolutionary terms, the value of these skills was not hard to imagine in the face of challenges from other species that might be stronger but also more stupid. If neocortex size set the limits on the mental world of a particular animal, then it would also set limits on those with whom relationships could be formed, and therefore the number of allies available at times of conflict. So, the larger the brain the greater the ability to maintain substantial social networks. The concept of "Machiavellian intelligence," as promoted by Byrne, established a link between strategy and evolution. The sort of basic survival techniques identified by Niccolo Machiavelli for sixteenth-century Italy turned out to be similar to those necessary for survival in the most primitive of social groups.[5]

The concept developed as part of a conjunction of research on the physical development of the brain, close observations of both primates and humans, and considerations of the influence of ecological and social factors. The early intellectual challenges facing our ancestors would have involved thinking through how to get up high trees without falling down and constructing safe places to sleep once there, or the sequence of manual actions necessary to acquire and eat particularly nutritious but hard-to-get-at foods with spines or thick skins. Physical tasks required a sequence of activities, and so it became necessary to plan ahead. Whatever the ecological imperatives and physical demands that increased brain size, at some point the key driver became the need to maintain sizable and coherent social groups. Working effectively in groups required understanding the particular characters of other members of the groups, how they were ranked in the hierarchy and with whom they had attachments, and what all this might mean in specific situations.

Strategies of Violence

One important complexity was the need to take on other groups with whom there were no social bonds, what Charles Darwin called "the struggle for existence." A sense of the potential for cooperation and the limits to conflict might shape social relations within the "in" group, but different imperatives come into play once there is a confrontation with an "out" group. Individual aggression is common in animals, but warfare—groups fighting each other— is less so. Ants are among the most warlike of creatures. Their foreign policy has been described as "restless aggression, territorial conquest, and genocidal annihilation of neighboring colonies whenever possible. If ants had nuclear weapons, they would probably end the world in a week."[6] As ant warfare is conducted by specialized warriors with no capacity for reproduction, the population of the colony is not threatened by their loss in battle. Warfare among ants has a clear purpose: a struggle for food and territory. When one colony defeats another, stored grain is taken to the victors' nests and the other colony is killed off or driven away. Ant warfare is in no sense strategic. It relies on relentless and ruthless attrition through brute force. The ants stick together; build up a superior mass; and wear down the enemy defenses by constant, vicious, and no-holds-barred attacks. There is no scope for bargaining and negotiation.

By contrast, studies of chimpanzees demonstrated a strategic intelligence at work. Males of other species might fight each other one-on-one for the opportunity to mate with females. What was noteworthy about the chimps was that on occasion one group would take on a neighboring group, and some chimps would die in the conflict. This was not a routine feature of chimpanzee life. It became more likely under certain conditions, again suggesting strategic behavior rather than mere aggressive instinct.

Some of the most notable observations of chimpanzees at war come from Jane Goodall, the pioneering student of the social lives of chimpanzees. She began watching them in 1960 in Tanzania's Gombe Stream National Park, and found a number of occasions when individual apes had been murdered by males from neighboring colonies. A particularly dramatic conflict occurred at Gombe after a community split as the result of a falling out between two alpha males. Hostility continued between the two communities, known as the Kasekala and the Kahama. It led to a protracted conflict between 1973 and 1974 which concluded with the extinction of the Kahama. The males of the Kasekala took over both the Kahama's territory and their females.[7] Goodall observed that, when acting defensively, the chimpanzees would call each other to a fight and move rapidly toward where they were needed. Border patrols would also be mounted to explore potentially contentious territory. Because of the risk of being caught by a superior group, these patrols were conducted with great caution, avoiding unnecessary noise and checking regularly for signs of the other, hostile community. Normal boisterous behavior was saved for when they returned to familiar territory. What was most striking about these patrols was that on occasion they turned into something more predatory as the chimps moved away from the borders and quite far into neighboring territory. There would be long and silent waits until there was an opportunity to attack a vulnerable victim. After catching their victims by surprise, the attacking chimps would leave their enemies dead or dying.

It has been argued that it would be unwise to generalize from this study because of the artificial conditions created by the reduced habitat and Goodall's influence over the food supply. She used feeding stations to draw the apes out of the forest, which encouraged competition among concentrated groups. By contrast, de Waal was able to observe chimpanzees by manipulating the distribution of food to reduce conflict levels. Goodall acknowledged—and regretted—that her intervention prompted more aggressive behavior but pointed out that it did not invalidate the finding that in certain conditions chimpanzees acted in particular ways. Moreover, her findings are not unique. Close observation of communities elsewhere also showed a capacity for warfare, albeit occasional.

Why did they fight? Richard Wrangham identified the sources of conflict as "improved access to resources such as food, females, or safety." Power relationships between neighboring communities mattered because of the chimps' need for ripe fruit, which was in turn a consequence of their digestive systems. When fruit was scarce, individual chimpanzees traveled alone or in small groups to find more; because of the uneven distribution of fruit supplies, the territory of one community could be well endowed while another was bereft. This was a recipe for conflict, and an explanation for why a stronger community would seek to take advantage of a weaker one. Wrangham argued that adult male chimpanzees "assess the costs and benefits of violence" and attack when the "probable net benefit is sufficiently high." A consequence of a kill was that the relative position of one community was significantly enhanced (as these communities were often not large, the loss of one member made a real difference.). He called this the "imbalance-of-power hypothesis, which stated that coalitionary kills occurred because of two factors: inter-group hostility, and large power asymmetries between rival parties."[8] This explained why killing took place but not the origins of the underlying conflict—the struggle for a scarce and vital resource.

More striking than the incidence of extreme violence was the calculating attitude to conflict. Goodall observed that "a small patrol will turn and flee if it meets a larger party, or one with more males, even *within* its own range; whereas if a large party, travelling out of its range, meets a smaller party of neighbors, it is likely to chase or attack." When there was greater symmetry among the numbers of adult males, the typical result was "visual and auditory display exchanges without conflict."[9] The important point, therefore, was that the apes were astute when it came to working out power balances. They tried to avoid a fight if they were weaker, readily retreating in the face of superior force, but moved in when they were stronger. Thus it is no surprise that no instances of one of the attacking pack getting killed were recorded. What made the difference was not strength in battle but "the relative size and composition of parties when they encounter each other."[10] This pragmatic attitude to violence underlined its instrumentality.

The evolutionist, therefore, saw strategy as a natural consequence of scarce vital resources and the struggle for survival. But it was not just a question of the survival of the fittest, in terms of raw strength and instinctive aggression. The survivors would also need to have outthought their opponents, to have shown a better grasp of social relationships and how to manipulate them. From the start of time, success could come as much from being smart as being strong, and it was especially smart to get others to help overpower opponents.

Similar patterns have been discerned in so-called primitive warfare among humans, although what passed for strategy appears to have been "customary and unspoken" and can now be inferred only "from the conduct and effects of warfare."[11] The strategies appear to have been largely attritional, with the enemy being worn down by regular battles and raids, normally with low casualties but also surprise massacres on occasion. Victory would be total: wealth and food plundered, houses and fields destroyed, women and children killed or captured. As logistic support was minimal, it was not possible to engage in prolonged combat or extended maneuvers because either food or ammunition would soon be exhausted. Raids had a number of advantages. They were hard to guard against, as security was normally poor and small groups moving at night were hard to detect, and it was possible to withdraw if the odds looked unfavorable. There was, according to Azar Gat, every incentive to avoid open warfare. Before attempting a killing it was best if the victims were "caught helpless, relatively defenseless, and, above all, little capable of effectively harming the attackers." These factors led to a "remarkably uniform" pattern of warfare, manifested within "any society of hunter-gatherers and primitive agriculturalists studied."[12]

From the study of these societies and those of chimps we can identify some of the elemental features of strategic behavior.[13] These features emerge out of social structures that invite conflict. They require some recognition of the distinctive attributes of individuals who are potential opponents or allies, and sufficient empathy with these individuals' situations to make it possible to influence their behavior, including by impressing or misleading them. The most effective strategies do not depend solely on violence—though this can play an instrumental role, by demonstrating superiority as much as expressing aggression—but benefit instead from the ability to forge coalitions. Little in the rest of this book will suggest that this list should be expanded. The elements of strategic behavior have not changed, only the complexity of the situations in which they must be applied.

CHAPTER 2 | Origins 2: The Bible

For by now I could have stretched out my hand and struck you and your
people with a plague that would have wiped you off the earth. But I have
raised you up for this very purpose, that I might show you my power and
that my name might be proclaimed in all the earth.

—Exodus 9:14–16

A N ALTERNATIVE ACCOUNT of the origins of strategy—indeed, of the origins of everything—comes from the Hebrew Bible. There is no suggestion in the Bible that strategy is in any sense unnatural. Many of the stories
revolve around conflicts (sometimes internecine and often with the enemies
of Israel) in which trickery and deception are regularly employed. Some stories (David and Goliath being the most obvious example) still influence the
way we think and talk about strategy. The best strategic advice in the Bible,
however, is to always trust God and obey his laws. God might allow others
to shape the game, but he was always the biggest player. When he withheld
support the result was often disaster. When he came in on the side of his
people the result was never in doubt.

The questions of the literalness of the Bible and the issues it raises about
free will and causation have long been at the heart of theological debate. If
everything can be put down to God's intent, what role is there for distinctive
human desires? Is human intent a product of God's intent, or can it develop

independently? For the student of strategy, the Bible makes for frustrating reading. Its stories display evident human frailties, with a pronounced tendency for deception as a vital strategic practice. When an individual was in a tough spot and there was a crafty way out, it tended to be taken. For example, Jacob, with his mother's connivance, tricked his blind father into giving him the blessing intended for his elder brother, Esau. Jacob was tricked in turn by his prospective father-in-law, so he ended up with two wives rather than one. And finally, Jacob was deceived by his sons into believing that his favorite son, Joseph, had been killed rather than sold into slavery. The Bible acknowledges the moral ambiguity involved in trickery, and the outrage of the deceived, yet also accepts its value in the face of superior but unworthy power. In a world of flawed human beings, deception comes naturally and often.

There are two possible explanations for the latitude allowed by God in human behavior. The first is that there is nothing in the end to be learned from all of this because all actions are subject to a higher manipulation. The second is that humans are able to make their own calculations, but in the end only one strategic judgment matters: whether or not to obey God. After recasting biblical stories using game theory, Steven Brams concluded that God was a "superlative strategist."[1] Given his starting advantages, anything less than superlative would appear something of a disappointment. But Brams noted that God enjoyed omniscience but not omnipotence. He was not a mere puppetmaster but rather was affected by the choices of the other players. To help explain God's purpose and his later strategy, Brams drew on the philosopher Leszek Kolakowski. God created the world for "His own glory," but this would be pointless unless it could be appreciated. "He needed a setting in which to be great." This was only possible after the creation of the world, "for now He had someone who could admire Him and to whom to compare Himself—and how favorably."[2] On this reading, God created strategy by allowing choice, because he wanted people to choose obedience through an act of will rather than because they were programed to do so. Even if individuals were part of a divine plan that had been set out at the moment of creation, they were allowed the sensation of choice and the ability to calculate and plan. The Bible tells of human choices regularly being manipulated by God to create the situations in which his greatness would become apparent.

The issue came up as soon as man and woman were formed to take control of the new world that God had created. After placing Adam and Eve in Eden, God immediately set a test. In his first words he explained that they could "eat from any fruit in the garden." One critical exception was fruit from the Tree of Knowledge of Good and Evil. "If you eat its fruit," God warned

Adam, "you will be doomed to die." We must assume that Eden was created with these tests in mind. If God really did not want Adam and Eve to lapse, it would have been simple not to put the fruit there in the first place. The test was soon failed. Eve tasted the forbidden fruit and then persuaded Adam to do the same. In the face of God's anger, Adam blamed his own ignorance but also Eve—the "woman whom you gave me"—and so pushed the blame back to God.

The source of the Fall was the serpent who persuaded Eve to disobey. The translations of the serpent's strategy vary from "subtle" to "crafty" and "cunning." He convinced Eve that there was no risk and much to gain. The reason the fruit was forbidden was not because of death but because of power. "God doth know that in the day ye eat thereof, then your eyes shall be opened, and ye shall be as gods." The serpent was accusing God of deception. Perhaps he had a point. Once the fruit was eaten, God did consider Adam and Eve to have become "like one of us" because they could now differentiate good from evil. If they had also taken from the Tree of Life, they would have avoided death. It was precisely for this reason that God expelled them from Eden; had they managed to eat of this tree, God's threat would have been neutralized and they could have anticipated everlasting life.[3] Instead, Adam and Eve became mortal and were now doomed to die (though Adam managed to struggle on until he was 930 years old). Banishment from Eden consigned man to extracting a living from the soil and woman to suffering in childbirth. The serpent was condemned to slither around on his belly and eat dust.[4]

The Ten Plagues as Strategic Coercion

The point at which God asserted his greatness to his chosen people was when he arranged the escape of the Jews from Egypt, where they were kept as slaves. One reading of the story of Exodus is that it was not so much about freeing the Israelites from slavery as about asserting God's greatness by establishing a people beholden to him and ensuring that they—and others—were in awe of his power. Under this interpretation, the Exodus story becomes a gigantic manipulation. The Israelites were encouraged to leave a country they were in no hurry to leave. Not surprisingly, they moaned thereafter when they were stuck in the desert, while God used the plagues to drive home the message of his power and superiority over Egyptian gods.

Diana Lipton has suggested that the Exodus reflected less a concern that the Israelites were being oppressed and more one that they were being seduced by Egyptian life and were in the process of being assimilated.[5] The

Israelites had entered Egypt because of Jacob's son Joseph, who had risen to high rank in Egyptian society. They were led out by Moses, an Israelite who had grown up among the Egyptians but was persuaded by God to assert the distinctive identity of the Israelites. Moses acted largely as God's agent in all his dealings with Pharaoh.

The favored strategy was coercive, using threats to persuade the target—in this case Pharaoh—to yield. The challenge was to influence the target's calculations, so that the potential cost of not complying exceeded the potential cost of losing what was currently held. The Israelite slaves were valuable to Egypt, so the threat had to be substantial. Coercive threats must be credible to be effective, yet those issued by Moses depended on a god not worshiped by Egyptians. There was no immediate reason to take him seriously. The first challenge was therefore how to change this perception. That was not difficult. The greater challenge was to get Pharaoh to respond. The strategy, a standard form of coercion involving a progressive "turning of the screw" in an attempt to find the target's threshold of pain, led to regular promises of compliance upon which Pharaoh equally regularly reneged.

Moses initially demanded that Pharaoh "let my people go" in relatively modest terms. He asked that the Hebrew slaves be allowed to go into the wilderness for a three days' journey to pray and sacrifice. If not, Pharaoh was told, then "the Lord our God [might] fall upon us with pestilence, or with the sword." The first people to be coerced in this story, therefore, were the Jews themselves. Moses presented them as caught between the power of Pharaoh and an even more powerful God. Pharaoh's response was to deny any knowledge or respect for this god and to make the Hebrews' lives even more miserable by telling them to find their own straw for their bricks. This extra suffering immediately undermined Moses's confidence and credibility.

Pharaoh was not punished at first. Instead, to persuade him to take God more seriously, he was treated to a demonstration of God's power. Moses's brother Aaron cast down his rod before Pharaoh and it became a serpent. Surprisingly, Pharaoh's magicians performed the same trick, but then Aaron's rod swallowed up all the other rods. This had no impact on Pharaoh. Tricks involving rigidified snakes were quite common in Egypt. So Moses tried but failed to make his point in a non-punitive manner. Pharaoh remained unconvinced of God's power.

There then followed the ten plagues. First the river turned to blood. This made little impression either. Pharaoh's magicians claimed they could also transform water into blood. Then out of the river came an abundance of frogs. Pharaoh hesitated and said that the Hebrews could go, but changed his mind when the frogs were removed. After a plague of gnats, the court magicians were stumped. At last a trick that they could not reproduce. They acknowledged the "finger of God," but Pharaoh was still unmoved. With swarms of flies Pharaoh weakened but again reneged when the plague was lifted. Next was the killing of Egypt's cattle, followed by everyone being covered in boils. Moses was told by God to go to Pharaoh and say on his behalf:

> Let my people go that they may serve me. For I will at this time send all my plagues upon thine heart, and upon thy servants, and upon thy people; that thou may knowest that there is none like me in all the earth. For now I will stretch out my hand, that I may smite thee and thy people with pestilence; and thou shalt be cut off from the earth. And in very deed for this cause have I raised thee up, for to shew in thee my power; and that my name may be declared throughout all the earth. As yet thou exaltest thou myself against my people, that thou wilt not let them go?[6]

Then came a threat of hail and advice that Pharaoh tell everyone to get themselves and their beasts home before the hail lest they die. This started to make the Egyptians uneasy. Some took the advice and sought shelter; others did not. Only the former survived the subsequent hailstorm.

Pharaoh, now anxious, agreed he was wicked and that the Hebrews could go, once the thunder and lightning stopped. Again he reneged, raising the stakes: by breaking a promise, Pharaoh had become a sinner on his own terms. After a plague of locusts, with the deadline for compliance the next day, Pharaoh's servants had a go at him: "How long shall this man be a snare unto us? Let the men go, that they may serve the Lord their God: knowest thou not yet that Egypt is destroyed?" Pharaoh relented and called in Moses and Aaron. He started to bargain. Who would go? Moses said everyone, with their flocks and herds. Pharaoh was only prepared to let the men and children go. He knew the women were irrelevant to acts of worship, and the only reason to take flocks and herds was if there was no intention to return. Moses's demands were now getting complex. The modest initial demand, an opportunity for the Hebrew men to leave for a while to pray, was being transformed into something much more complete.

After the eighth plague, locusts devouring all the fruits and herbs that had survived the hail, negotiations soon resumed. Pharaoh was contrite, but only until the locusts were blown away. The ninth plague, three days of complete darkness, was most alarming for a kingdom that worshiped the sun and dreaded a persistent eclipse. Like the third and the sixth, this plague was quite unannounced. It was a warning that the time for negotiation was over. Once the darkness lifted, Pharaoh agreed that everyone could go—other than the flocks and herds. Moses said it had to be everyone and everything. It was now evident that this would be no excursion for prayer and sacrifice but a permanent departure from Egypt. Furious, Pharaoh broke off negotiations: "Take heed to thyself, see my face no more; for in that day thou seest my face thou shalt die." Moses agreed he would not return.

God said there would be one more plague and this would be successful. The Hebrews, spared all the previous plagues, were told to prepare. By daubing their houses with blood from sheep or goats God would know to pass over them when he smote the firstborn of the Egyptians. At midnight on the fourteenth day of the month there was not a house in Egypt "where there was not one dead." This caused great misery and consternation. Moses and Aaron were summoned and told to leave. So eager were the Eyptians to be rid of them that all the Israelites and their livestock were allowed to depart, with jewelry and raiments and what else they required.

The loss of the slaves was a serious blow to Pharaoh. He changed his mind one last time and decided to chase after them with chariots, horsemen, and his army. Once again, his memory was remarkably short. A regular victim of God's power, he only seemed to believe in it while the pressure was actually upon him and his people. Initially it appeared that the Hebrews had been caught. They cowered on the edge of the Red Sea, fearing that they were to die in the wilderness, with the Egyptians about to come upon them. There was no time for threats to coerce Pharaoh. This time God's intervention was more direct. The Red Sea divided and the Hebrews escaped as the waves were held back in suspended animation. The Egyptians followed the same route but the "host of Pharaoh" was drowned as the walls of water engulfed them.

The actual methods employed in this case were quite unique, but the strategic logic reflected a turning of the screw. Commentators have even noticed the pattern of graduated escalation—the first four plagues were mere nuisances, the second four caused real pain, and the last two took the Egyptians into the realm of absolute dread. Others have noted that the escalation progressed in pairs—the first pair connected with the Nile, the second involving insects, the third attacking life, the fourth destroying crops in a two-stage assault, and the last two conveying the full extent of God's power. Still others have stressed the significance of every third plague arriving without warning. We may note the importance of subtle variations in the way the pressure was applied, playing on the psychology of Pharaoh and his court.

The most striking feature of this story, however, lies in the difficulty of persuading Pharaoh to respond positively to threats of such palpable credibility and potency. Why did he take so long to let the Israelites go? Threats might fail because they are not believed or are suspected to be bluff. Initially

Pharaoh may have assumed he was witnessing just an unusually accomplished version of the sort of magic produced in his own court. A critical turning point came when his magicians realized this magic was beyond theirs. But this point was reached quite early on in the escalatory process. Moses could always demonstrate that he was not bluffing.

Another problem might have been that Moses increased his demands with the pressure. At the start, he asked only for a chance to pray, but this turned into a chance to escape. Once the Egyptians were desperate to see the backs of the Israelites, the demand was for sufficient animals and other goods to ease the privations of the coming journey. A threat that might have been sufficient to obtain compliance with modest demands became inadequate as the stakes were raised.

A superficial reading—and certainly the telling of the Passover tale—suggests that Pharaoh's obstinacy had a simpler explanation: he was a most unpleasant man, whose continuing deceit and double-dealing contrasted with the courtesy and dignity exhibited by Moses at all times. He was so sure of his own power that he was prepared to engage in this disastrous trial of strength. There is, however, a more intriguing explanation: Pharaoh was set up. Before the plagues started, God told Moses:

> I will harden Pharaoh's heart, and multiply my signs and my wonders in the land of Egypt. But Pharaoh shall not hearken unto you, that I may lay my hand upon Egypt, and bring forth mine armies, and my people the children of Israel, out of the land of Egypt by great judgments.[7]

Sure enough, every time Pharaoh hesitated in the face of the onslaught of plagues, the Bible reports that the Lord hardened Pharaoh's heart. God explained this to Moses, after the hail, when Pharaoh acknowledged God's power for the first time but still reneged on a promise.

> I have hardened his heart, and the hearts of his servants, that I might shew these my signs before him: and that thou mayest tell in the ears of thy son, and of thy son's son, what things I have wrought in Egypt, and my signs which I have done among them; that ye may know how that I am the Lord.[8]

God needed an obstinate Pharaoh because the only way he could demonstrate the full range of his power, and its superiority over all other powers on earth, was to put on the most awesome display. If Pharaoh had crumbled at the first plague there would have been no wondrous reports to pass down to future generations. Others would not appreciate the extent of his formidable power.

This was problematic for Talmudic scholars and later for Christian theologians, for it raises fundamental questions of free will. If punishment comes because we have made the wrong moral choices, then what are we to do about an agent who continues to be immoral despite recognizing the folly of his ways? It was not that God wanted an excuse to destroy the Egyptians—witness his rebuke to the Jews when they rejoiced at the destruction of the Egyptian army. As noted, relations between ordinary Egyptians and the Hebrews do not appear to have been bad, yet the loss of innocent life in the final plague—even the sons of maidservants were struck down—only seems to make moral sense if the stubbornness of Pharaoh could be blamed for the suffering of his people. Strategy as well as morality depended on choice, and if the players in this drama were merely acting out a preordained script from which no deviation was permitted, then the only strategist at work here was God.

A Coercive Reputation

One act of successful coercion facilitates future acts. God's threats now had credibility. The reputation of his extraordinary power made it far easier to coerce the inhabitants of the land of Israel, which had been promised to the Jews. Just before entering this land, Moses died and Joshua became the leader of the Israelites. The first obstacle to occupying the new land was the old walled city of Jericho, at the center of fertile land and in control of the water source.[9] Joshua sent two spies to discover the lay of the land. They lodged with Rahab, who is normally described as a prostitute but who may have been more of an innkeeper (an inn was always a good place to pick up gossip). When the king of Jericho demanded that the spies be handed over, Rahab hid them instead. Having heard what had happened to the Egyptians, she explained, "All the inhabitants of the land are quaking before you." They had all lost heart, and "no man had any spirit left because of you." She made a deal. In return for her family being spared whatever was going to befall the rest of the city, she agreed not to disclose the spies' mission. This deal was not based on the moral worthiness of the Hebrew God—just his superior power. When it came to actually taking Jericho, there was no need for a prolonged siege. Around the walls the Israelites marched for six days, until it became such a routine that the guardians of the city took little notice, and then they struck as God brought the walls (weakened through a recent earthquake) tumbling down.

As the invasion progressed, those on its line of advance had every reason to be afraid. There was no mercy shown to those occupying the land God had promised to the Israelites, although mercy could be shown to people who lived far away. Aware of this, the Gibeonites pretended to Joshua that they were not from the next city but rather a distant people. They engaged in a careful deception, appearing disheveled and claiming to have traveled from a faraway place, drawn by the fame of God. When Joshua doubted this claim, they drew attention to their "dry and crumbly" bread, their cracked wineskins, and their worn-out clothes and sandals. Joshua was sufficiently taken in that he promised not to harm the Gibeonites in return for their servitude. Soon the Israelites realized they had been duped. Joshua was furious. He could not break an oath made in God's name even if obtained by deceit. Instead he cursed the Gibeonites, telling them that they would be slaves forever. "Why did you deceive me?" he asked. The answer was honest. Once they knew of God's promise "to give you the whole land and to wipe out all the inhabitants of the country on your account," they were in great fear. Joshua had only himself to blame if he had been deceived. Convinced by the Gibeonites' appearance, he "did not inquire of the Lord." What is the point of having access to omniscience if it is not used to check out a potentially dubious story?[10]

The book of Judges relates a regular pattern of Israelites turning away from God, who then used a hostile tribe, the Midianites, to punish them. The liberating figure of Gideon appeared after the Midianites had been allowed to enter the country and impoverish the people. The Israelites were suffering for their idolatry and begged for deliverance. God chose Gideon for the mission. When he gathered a large army of some thirty thousand men, God deemed this too many. If they thought victory came by superior numbers, God judged, they might "vaunt themselves against me, saying, 'Mine own hand hath saved me.'" The numbers had to be reduced. First, those who were "fearful and afraid" were asked to depart. This cut the numbers by about two-thirds. Then a curious test was set, involving seeing how the men drank at a lake. Those who went on their knees were sent home; those who put their hands to their mouths were kept, perhaps because this showed that they were staying alert. The numbers were now only 1 percent of the original army—just three hundred men. Against them were ranged their enemies, lying "along in the valley like grasshoppers for multitude; and their camels were without number, as the sand by the sea side for multitude." Gideon divided his three hundred men into three companies and put a trumpet in every man's hand. They were then told to watch him and do as he did when they got to the outside of the enemy camp. "When I blow with a trumpet, I and all that are with me, then blow ye the trumpets also on every side of all the camp, and say, 'The sword of the LORD, and of Gideon.'" This they did.

And the enemy "ran, and cried, and fled."[11] This reinforced the basic lesson in all these stories. The best—indeed the only—strategy was to obey God and then do as he told you.

David and Goliath

One of the most iconic of all the Bible's stories is that of David and Goliath. It is invariably invoked by an underdog, yet the underdog status was illusory because David had God on his side. The basics of the story are well known. On opposite sides of a valley were the armies of the Philistines and the Israelites. Out of the Philistine camp emerged a giant of a man, Goliath of Gath, dressed in heavy brass armor, protected by a shield, and wielding a large spear with a large iron head. He dared the Israelites to send out a champion to fight him. If he was killed in the fight then the Philistines would serve the Israelites. If he prevailed it would be the Israelites who served. The challenge, repeated daily for forty days without a response, appeared to paralyze the Israelites, including their king, Saul. They "were dismayed and greatly afraid." The only one not afraid was a young shepherd, David, who had been sent to the camp by his father with some bread and cheese for the army. He heard Goliath's challenge, saw the fear around him, and noted a promise of great riches should anyone actually manage to kill Goliath. David presented himself to the dubious king. David was still young, yet Goliath had been "a man of war from his youth." David offered as his credentials a tale of how he had killed both a lion and a bear who were after his lambs.

Saul relented and gave David his armor and sword, dressing him for a gladiatorial fight with Goliath. But David discarded these accoutrements, saying he could not take them as he had not "tested them." Instead he took his staff, five smooth stones from the brook, and his sling. Not surprisingly, Goliath found the challenger that the Israelites had eventually produced unimpressive, even insulting. "Am I a dog that thou comest to me with staves?" Their encounter was brief. Goliath promised to feed David's "flesh unto the fowls of the air and to the beasts of the field." The young man replied that he came in God's name and then ran toward the Philistine. As soon as he was in position, he took a stone out of his bag "and slung it and smote the Philistine in his forehead, so that the stone sunk into his forehead. And he fell upon his face to the earth." David then took the giant's sword to kill him and cut off his head. When the Philistines saw their champion was dead, they fled.[12]

David's success depended on surprise and accuracy. He knew he could not defeat Goliath on the giant's terms, which is why he rejected Saul's armor and with it the conventions of this form of combat. Unencumbered, he had speed and so could unleash his secret weapon before Goliath had a chance to respond. He had one chance with his sling. If he had missed, or if the stone had pinged off Goliath's armor or not stunned him so effectively, there would have been no second shot. As vital as the first shot was quick action to prevent any recovery. Not only did David bring Goliath down but by killing him he prevented him getting up again. He also depended on the Philistines accepting the result, and not trying to recover honor in the face of such a sneaky attack by turning the individual contest into a full battle. If they had done so, David's prowess with the sling would have been of no value. Indeed, this was a trick he could never use again. David had no plan B. If his plan A had failed, he would have been left defenseless.

The story is rarely given any context. This was one of a complex set of encounters between the Israelites and the Philistines. The Philistines controlled the territory west of the Jordan River. In earlier clashes, the Israelites fared very badly and lost four thousand men. Having apparently learned their lesson and returned to the laws of God, they regained God's protection, so that at one point a loud noise was sufficient to send the Philistines running away in panic. They were chased and subdued. The Israelites recaptured lost land. All this took place while the prophet Samuel was still leading the country as a Judge.

Saul was the first king of the Israelites, anointed by Samuel. This constitutional innovation was intended to meet the Israelites' desire to be led in the same way as other nations. Their king was chosen on the grounds that he looked the part—handsome and tall—was humble, and had shown military prowess. He was not, however, always obedient to God. Hostilities resumed with the Philistines after a provocative raid by Saul's son Jonathan in which a Philistine officer was killed. The Philistines mobilized and the Israelites were once again overwhelmed. Saul turned out to be a poor general (for example, forbidding his men food on the eve of a major battle) and cautious (reluctant to go out and face Goliath himself). Given that God was supposed to be the best defense, this lack of confidence—and therefore faith—was itself an act of disobedience. Though David's sling gained the headlines, Goliath's fate was sealed by David's faith.

Through the Bible we are allowed to see the factors at work that determined the history of the Israelites, but to the subjects of these stories it would have been challenging to work out what was going on. God's objectives were clear enough, but his methods were invariably deceptive, leading his victims into traps under the erroneous impression that they were masters of their destinies. As a result, deception became a strong biblical theme. Cunning was accepted as a natural method for an underdog who must use wits to succeed. The trickster appeared defiant, employing "wit, wile, and deception and assum[ing] that no victories are final and neat." Yet to the extent that they did this without God's help, the tricks often rebounded and any success was "unstable."[13] David's success resulted from combining an unreliable trick with a much more reliable faith.

The stories of the Exodus and David have both been used to give hope to underdogs. Indeed, reference to David is almost de rigueur whenever an underdog strategy is discussed. Seldom noted, however, is that success did not solely depend on the initial blow but also on the second blow, by which David ensured that Goliath had no chance to recover, as well as the Philistines' readiness to accept the result. In both stories, the key to success lay in the opponent's response. Both the Pharaoh and Goliath failed to appreciate the traps they were entering. Only Pharaoh had the opportunity to consider what he was up against and adjust his strategy accordingly. But as God was hardening his heart, any momentary understanding that he was leading his country into further hardship soon disappeared. Moses was following God's orders and so was Pharaoh. In the end, the drama—and therefore the evidence of true strategy—was artificial.

The core message of the Bible was evident to those who read it for guidance and inspiration over the centuries. God's subjects asserted their faith and their obedience as part of their standard preparations for war, even when they were fighting each other. They might have been sure that this was a necessary condition for victory. Few found it sufficient.

CHAPTER 3 | Origins 3: The Greeks

Do not trust the Horse, Trojans/ Whatever it is, I fear the Greeks even
bearing gifts.

—Laocoön in Virgil's *Aeneid*

O**UR THIRD SOURCE** for the origins of strategy is ancient Greece. In
terms of its subsequent influence, this was the most important. At
first the stories told about power and war shared with the Bible the complication of divine intervention, which implied that the best strategic advice
was to stay on the right side of the gods, but by the fifth century BCE a
Greek enlightenment, a combination of intellectual open-mindedness and
rigorous political debate, had taken place. This resulted in an extraordinarily rich philosophical and historical literature that has had an enduring
influence. Homer's heroes were masters of both words and actions, although
the differences between Achilles and Odysseus showed the potential tension
between the two. The man of action could either be admired for his courage or dismissed as a fool for his sole reliance on strength, while the man
of words could be celebrated for his intelligence or treated warily because
words could deceive.

One of the curiosities of this literature is that some of its most interesting reflections on what it might mean to think as well as act strategically—
not only in a military sense—were later played down and lost their impact.
We can attribute this to the intervention of Plato. He was determined that

philosophy should break decisively with the tendencies he lumped together as sophistry, which he saw as a diversion from a disinterested search for truth into a mercenary means of persuasion. There is some irony in that Plato's method for disposing of sophistry, using exaggeration and caricature, was intensely strategic. Given the care with which he was studied by later generations, the importance of Plato's success in this enterprise should not be underestimated.

From Homer came the contrasting qualities, represented respectively by Achilles and Odysseus, of biē and mētis (strength and cunning), which over time—for example, in Machiavelli—came to be represented as force and guile. This polarity continued to find expression in strategic literature. Outsmarting the opponent risked less pain than open conflict, although winning by cunning and subterfuge was often deplored for a lack of honor and nobility. There was also the more practical problem that reliance on deception was apt to suffer diminishing returns as opponents came to appreciate what they were facing. As the previous two chapters demonstrate, there was nothing unnatural or surprising in efforts to get the better of stronger opponents by catching them by surprise or tricking them in some way. Other ways of coping with superior strength, however, were combining with others or disrupting an opponent's coalition.

A preference for force or guile might reflect a temperamental disposition, but it could not be a strategy in itself. That must depend on how best to turn a complex and developing set of affairs to advantage, which in turn must depend on an ability to persuade those who must implement the strategy that it is wise. The master of casting a strategy in its most compelling form, at least according to Thucydides, was the Athenian statesman Pericles. The ability to persuade not only one's people but also allies and enemies was a vital attribute of the successful strategist. In this way, strategy required a combination of words and deeds, and the ability to manipulate them both.

Odysseus

Mētis described a particular notion of a strategic intelligence for which there is no obvious English equivalent. In Greek it was related to mētiaō: "to consider, meditate, plan," together with metióomai, "to contrive," conveyed a sense of a capacity to think ahead, attend to detail, grasp how others think and behave, and possess a general resourcefulness. But it could also convey deception and trickery, capturing the moral ambivalence around a quality so essential to the strategist's art. According to the mythology, the goddess Mētis was chosen by Zeus as his first wife. Fearful that a son combining his strength with his mother's intelligence would become too powerful, Zeus employed her own methods of deceit and surprise to avoid that risk and so ate her. He intended to control the source of all mētis forever when he swallowed Mētis. What he did not know was that Mētis was already pregnant, with a daughter Athena, who was born—fully formed—through Zeus's head. Athena, the goddess of both wisdom and war, came to be associated with mētis more than the other divinities. She developed a close association with the mortal who most embodied mētis, Odysseus, the hero of Homer's *Odyssey*. Athena described him as "far the best of all mortals in thought and word, and I'm renowned among all the gods for my wisdom and my cunning ways."[1]

Odysseus exhibited an agile and expedient intelligence. He could evaluate situations quickly, think ahead, and stay sharply focused on the ultimate goal even when caught in ambiguous and uncertain situations. More concerned with success than glory, he was indirect and psychological in his methods, seeking to confuse, disorient, and outwit opponents. But Odysseus also suffered from the challenge of the known deceiver. After a time, he became a victim of the liar's paradox: it became hard to get anyone to believe him, even when he was telling the truth. His greatest triumph was the wooden horse left outside the gates of Troy, which ended a decade of siege and opened up the city for utter destruction and mass slaughter. Virgil, the Roman who took a less generous view of Odysseus than did Homer, described how the Greeks made a show of giving up on their struggle to seize Troy. A large horselike construction, filled with up to fifty soldiers, was hauled to a position just outside the city walls. It carried the inscription: "For their return home, the Achaeans dedicate this thank-offering to Athena."[2]

The Trojans, hoping that the decade-long siege had been lifted, came out to inspect this strange horse. King Priam and the elders debated what to do. The choice was simple. They could treat it as a threat and either burn it or break it up to see what was inside, or haul it inside and use it as an opportunity to honor Athena. But Athena was known to have favored the Greeks and be prone to trickery. After all that had happened, was it really wise to trust either her or the Greeks? Odysseus always knew that the Trojans would need some persuasion. This was accomplished by Sinon, an expert liar. He claimed to the Trojans that he was a defector. His story was that he had escaped the Greeks after falling out with Odysseus. He was about to be offered up as a sacrifice to persuade the gods to provide favorable winds for the Greek ships to get home. The Trojans were half persuaded. Priam asked whether the "huge monster of a horse" was for religious purposes or "some engine of war." Sinon explained that it was indeed designed to placate Athena, whom the Greeks had offended. It was not meant for the Trojans, he added. In fact it had been built so large because the Greeks were worried that if the Trojans got the horse into the city they would never again be vulnerable to invasion.

Sinon had arrived on the scene as the priest Laocoön was warning that this apparent offering was a fraud, a "trick of war." When Laocoön threw a spear at the horse, the frightened soldiers inside had moaned. This might have been something of a giveaway, were it not for the intervention of Athena, who sent sea serpents to strangle Laocoön and his two sons. This suggested he was being punished for sacrilege—a good reason not to follow his advice. The other warning came from Cassandra, Priam's daughter, who told the people they were fools and faced an "evil fate." Alas, Cassandra had been granted the gift of prophecy by the god Apollo but was then cursed for not returning his love. Unlike Sinon, who could lie and be believed, Cassandra would make accurate predictions and never be believed. And so the decision was made. The Trojans decided to take the horse through the gate. During the night, the hidden Greek soldiers got out. On a signal from Sinon, the Greek army advanced and the gates of Troy were opened for them. The city was sacked and the people massacred.

Homer mentioned the wooden horse only in passing in *The Odyssey*, as a special example of the sort of craftiness that distinguished Odysseus from his more pedestrian peers. He had a talent for getting out of predicaments that might have led others to succumb to fatalism or lash out with hopeless bravado. Homer's indulgent view of Odysseus's escapades was not shared by Virgil. He thought such behavior deplorable and unfortunately typical of untrustworthy Greeks. In later centuries, Sinon was placed with Odysseus in Dante's Eighth Circle of Hell, a place for those guilty of fraudulent rhetoric and falsification. Proper heroes would be guided by virtue and truth rather than opportunism and trickery.

In his epics, Homer contrasted mētis with biē, or brute force. Biē was personified by Achilles, famed for his exceptional physical strength, bravery, agility, and mastery of the spear, but also his great rages. While *The Odyssey* was about mētis, *The Iliad* was largely an exploration of biē. Achilles demonstrated not only the limits to what force could achieve but also how it could become associated with a certain wildness, a bloodlust that led to terrible deaths and slaughter. Yet it was hard to do without force. When Achilles gave up on the war against the Trojans after being slighted by King Agamemnon, it was Odysseus who led the delegation sent to plead with him. Achilles's response was to denounce Odysseus and his methods: "I hate like the gates of Hades, the man who says one thing and hides another inside him." Just as pointedly, Achilles drew attention to the failure of mētis to stop the Greeks being pushed back to the sea by the rampaging "man-killing" Hector, the equivalent Trojan superhero.

Hector was also described as a man of mētis, the only Trojan with Zeus-like qualities and therefore the man in whom the Trojans invested their greatest hopes. On crucial occasions, the strategic good sense associated with mētis deserted him. This was attributed to the malign influence of Athena, who the poor Trojans believed was still protecting the city at a time she was doing anything but. At the council of the Trojans, an opportunity for a negotiated peace was missed when Hector was guided more by hatred for the Greeks and enthusiasm for battle than a shrewd understanding of what the future might hold. He advocated an offensive course. When the offensive began, he went on the rampage, driving the Greeks back. One casualty was Patroclus, a close friend of Achilles. His death led Achilles to turn his considerable rage away from Agamemnon and against Hector. Having reentered the fight, Achilles cut down many Trojans, while all the time searching for Hector. Eventually, tricked again by Athena, Hector found himself facing Achilles, something he had understandably hoped to avoid.[3] He was soon killed with a single blow to the neck. Achilles then tied Hector's body to his chariot and dragged it round the battlefield.

As this is close to the end of *The Iliad*, we are led to think that Achilles's victory sealed the fate of Troy. Yet the Greeks could not press home their advantage. Achilles was soon killed by Paris, the man who had caused the war in the first place by taking Helen from King Menelaus of Sparta. Paris struck Achilles with an arrow from a distance. According to one account—though not Homer's—the arrow had to hit him in his heel. In this legend, his mother had dipped the newly born Achilles in the river Styx. He gained invulnerability where the waters touched him but not on his heel, where his mother's hand had gripped him. Achilles's heel served as a reminder that even the strongest have their points of weakness which, if found, can be used to bring them down. Hector killing Patroclus and Achilles killing Hector could also be taken as salutary warnings of the dangers of overreaching, of using force without intelligent restraint. Brute force is not enough. "In the final analysis," notes Jenny Strauss Clay, "the humane heroism of Odysseus, based as it is on intelligence and endurance, is set above the quicksilver glory of Achilles."[4]

After the war had been decided by the ruse of the wooden horse, the Greeks began their journey home. It was as challenging as the original siege. Terrible storms caused their ships to sink or crash against rocks.

Odysseus was blown off course and took another ten years to get home. His adventures along the way provided ample opportunity to apply mētis. A striking test came when Polyphemus, a giant one-eyed Cyclops, devoured a number of his men. Odysseus and his surviving men were trapped by a boulder that only Polyphemus could move. The first stage of Odysseus's plan was to get Polyphemus to drink more than was good for him. Then Odysseus told the drunk Cyclops that his name in Greek was Outis, made up of *ou tis*, meaning "not anyone."[5] This allowed Odysseus to conceal his identity and set up Polyphemus for a later piece of deception. Next, Odysseus blinded the giant by drilling a stake into his eye. As Polyphemus cried out in agony, his fellow Cyclopei asked, "Is any man stealing your flocks and driving them off? Is any man trying to kill you through cunning or superior strength?" When he replied, "Noman (*Outis*) is trying to kill me through his cunning," they took this literally and so thought no more about it.[6] Polyphemus removed the boulder to let out his sheep. He tried to feel to see if Odysseus and his men were escaping on top of the animals, but they had tied themselves underneath the animals. Unwisely, Odysseus then decided to boast. No longer Outis, he identified himself as one "known for his cunning." Polyphemus's father, the sea god Poseidon, then determined to make Odysseus's life miserable on his long journey home.

The Method in Mētis

For Odysseus, the ends justified the means. The trickster was always prepared to be judged by results. The moral unease that this approach generated was evident in Sophocles's play, *Philoctetes*. This was the name of a Greek warrior en route to the Trojan War. His advantage was a bow given to him by the god Heracles; his disadvantage, a painful and smelly wound resulting from a snake bite. Odysseus found the smell and Philoctetes's cries of pain intolerable and left the poor man angry and in agony—but with his bow—on an island. A decade later, Odysseus realized that the bow was essential in the fight against Troy and set off with Neoptolemus, the son of Achilles, to acquire it. Given his past treatment of Philoctetes, Odysseus knew neither brute force nor persuasion would get the bow, so Odysseus encouraged Neoptolemus to trick Philoctetes. The young man, however, had his father's "natural antipathy/ to get [his] ends by tricks and stratagems." He would prefer to "fail with honor" than to win by cheating. Did not Odysseus find the lying "vile"? No, came the reply, putting scruples above the common good placed the whole war effort at risk.

In the play, the matter was resolved by the favored device of the deus ex machina. The god Heracles told Philoctetes to join the battle. The response was immediate: "Voice for which I have long yearned, Form, long visioned, now discerned! Thee I cannot disobey."[7] So craven obedience to a god quickly solved the dispute in a way that cunning could not. All ended happily. Odysseus succeeded in his mission, Neoptolemus maintained his honor, and Philoctetes gained glory and healing of his wound. The play underlined the difficulty of relying on deception and then expecting to be trusted. Those who knew Odysseus's reputation rarely trusted him even when he was being straight.[8] The impact of the best story was diminished when the teller lacked credibility.

Odysseus has been described as exemplifying "a particular idea of practical intelligence." According to Barnouw, he was able to consider "intended actions in the light of anticipated consequences." He kept his main purpose in mind and thought "back from that final goal through a complex network of means (and obstacles) to achieve it." The contrast therefore was not just with brute force but the recklessness of those who were not so well tuned to the signs of danger and who failed to think through the potential consequences of their actions. When Odysseus decided not to succumb to some short-term impulse for revenge, it was because he remembered how much more he wanted to achieve his long-term goals of returning safely to his wife Penelope and his kingdom in Ithaca. Rather than seeing reason and passion in opposition to one another, practical intelligence was about finding the appropriate relations between competing ends, each with an associated bundle of passions and reasons. Odysseus's understanding of how others viewed the world allowed him to manipulate their thought processes by giving out signs that he knew they would read in a particular way. He was not playing pranks on others just because he enjoyed their discomfort. Rather, his craftiness and capacity for deception were geared to his ultimate objectives. Mētis was therefore forward-looking, with elements of anticipation and planning, as well as guile and trickery. Barnouw described this intelligence as being as much "visceral as intellectual," less an "impassive weighing of alternatives," and more a prioritizing of aims or impulses that are most desired. It reflected more "the strength and depth of passion as the work of reason."[9]

Marcel Detienne and Jean-Pierre Vernant similarly argued that mētis as exemplified by Odysseus was a distinctive form of practical intelligence. More than being shrewd and crafty, it was also forward-looking, locating current actions as part of a longer-term plan, grasping the potential of situations so as to be able to manipulate others into error. This suggested a cast of mind as much as a plan of action, a way by which the underdog could triumph over the notionally stronger. Despite the association between mētis and the "disloyal trick, the perfidious lie, treachery," it could also be "the absolute weapon, the only one that has the power to ensure victory and domination over others, whatever the circumstances, whatever the conditions of the conflict." Whereas strength could be defeated by superior strength, mētis could defeat all strength.

Mētis was of most value when matters were fluid, fast moving, unfamiliar, and uncertain, combining "contrary features and forces that are opposed to each other." It was suited to situations when there could be no formulaic or predictable behavior, benefiting from a "greater grip" of the present, "more awareness" of the future, "richer experience accumulated from the past," an ability to adapt constantly to changing events, and sufficient pliability to accommodate the unexpected. This practical intelligence operated in circumstances of conflict and was reflected in such qualities as forethought, perspicacity, quickness and acuteness of understanding, as well as a capacity for trickery and deceit. Such a person was elusive, slipping through an "adversary's fingers like running water," relying on ambiguity, inversion, and reversal.[10] All this described a strategic intelligence, able to discern a way through complicated and ambiguous situations and then come out on top. But it was also largely intuitive, or at least implicit, and at moments of sudden danger and crisis, this might be all that could be relied upon. There was no reason, however, why the same qualities could not come into play when there was time to be more deliberative and calculating.

Thucydides

Atē, the daughter of Eris, the goddess of strife, spent her time encouraging stupidity in both mortals and immortals. She was banished from Mount Olympus to earth. Barbara Tuchman described her as the goddess of infatuation, mischief, delusion, and folly. Atē was said to blind her victims to considerations of morality or expedience and render them "incapable of rational choice." Such gods, lamented Tuchman, provided humans with an excuse for their folly. Homer has Zeus, the king of the gods, insisting that if mortals had suffered "beyond that which is ordained" it was not because of the gods but because of the "blindness of their own hearts." It was not fate that led to disaster, but bad strategy.[11] Yet appeals to the gods continued to be made regularly in Athenian affairs. Omens were sought and oracles consulted.

Then, during the Athenian enlightenment of the fifth century BCE, an alternative approach developed that rejected explanations for events based on the immortals and instead looked to human behavior and decisions. In addition, warfare became too complicated to be left to the heroic deeds of individual warriors; more coordination and planning was needed. The Athenian War Council consisted of ten *strategoi* who were expected to be able to lead from the front, fight with the best, and show total commitment. In this respect the origins of strategy lie with generalship, that is, the qualities that made for effective leadership.[12] Thucydides, who lived from around 460 to 395 BCE, was a *strategos*. After he failed to prevent a Spartan occupation of Amphipolis, he was exiled for twenty years, which provided opportunities to get to know Spartans as well as Athenians. "I had leisure," he recalled, "to observe affairs somewhat particularly."[13] This leisure was used to write what he considered to be the definitive history of the war between Athens and Sparta, known as the Peloponnesian War. This was fought from 431 to 404 BCE between the Peloponnesian League, led by Sparta, and the Athenian empire, known as the Delian League. Sparta was the clear victor. Before the war Athens had been the strongest of the Greek city states. By the war's conclusion, Athens was much diminished.

As a historian, Thucydides exemplified the enlightenment spirit, describing conflict in unsentimental and calculating terms, posing hard questions of power and purpose, and observing how choices had consequences. He dismissed explanations for human affairs that depended on capricious fate and mischievous gods and concentrated instead on political leaders and their strategies. He insisted on a dogged empiricism, seeking an accurate account of events backed up where necessary and possible by diligent research. His narrative illuminated some of the central themes of all strategy: the limits imposed by the circumstances of the time, the importance of coalitions as a source of strength but also instability, the challenge of coping with internal opponents and external pressures simultaneously, the difficulties of strategies that are defensive and patient in the face of demands for quick and decisive offensives, the impact of the unexpected, and—perhaps most importantly— the role of language as a strategic instrument. The headlines from Thucydides were often taken to be the descriptions of the irresistibility of power and the imperviousness of the strong to the complaints of the weak or considerations of morality. On this basis he has been cast as one of the founders of realism, a temperament to which strategic theorists have been presumed to be susceptible because of their relentless focus on power and their presumption that self-interest best explains behavior. According to the more doctrinaire realism, the lack of a supreme authority governing all international affairs has always rendered states inherently insecure. If they dared not trust in the good intentions of others, they must make provisions for their own defense—though these provisions in turn made others insecure.[14] The significance of Thucydides from this perspective was that he demonstrated its timelessness.

In a non-doctrinaire sense, Thucydides was indeed a realist, describing human affairs as he found them rather than how he might wish them to be. But he did not suggest that men were bound to act on the basis of a narrow self-interest or that they actually served their broader interests if they did. The picture he presented was much more complex and fluid, one in which momentary strength could hide an underlying weakness, and political leaders were addressing a range of actors—some internal and others external—realizing that new combinations could create new forms of advantage and disadvantage.

He put into the mouths of key actors, however, statements which suggested that they were following the unavoidable imperatives of power, from which there could be no reprieve. The Athenians, for example, explained at one point that they were not holding on to their empire "contrary to the common practice of mankind" but "under the pressure of three of the strongest motives, fear, honor, and interest." They did not set the example: "It has always been the law that the weaker should be subject to the stronger."[15] The same point was put most memorably in the Melian dialogue when the Athenians point out that "the strong do what they can while the weak must suffer what they must."[16] They had no choice but to suppress the Melians, not only to extend their rule but because not doing so when they had the chance would show them to be feeble and damage their reputation. Law and morality were fragile restraints, as the powerful could make laws and define morality to suit their purposes. Yet because Thucydides quoted arguments in favor of crude exercises of power did not mean that he endorsed them. He also reported alternative, even idealistic, views as well as the unfortunate consequences of always worrying about appearing weak, for this led later to disastrous gambles when caution would have been prudent.

The most important direct assertion of a realist philosophy comes in his most famous observation, considering the origins of the Peloponnesian War: "What made the war inevitable was the growth of Athenian power and the fear which this caused in Sparta." He acknowledged other explanations, based on the "causes of complaint," but seemed to be displacing them by a more systemic analysis.[17] One challenge to this interpretation of Thucydides's views lies in questions of translation. A more subtle translation suggests that while Thucydides undoubtedly saw the shifting power balance between the two powers as being of great—and previously understated—importance, the origins of the war lie in its combination with the disputes of the moment.[18] That still leaves a question of whether the systemic factor deserved the prominence given it. Thucydides may have stressed it for the sake of the reputation of his hero Pericles, the ruler of Athens for some thirty years from 460 BCE.

The power and prestige of Athens had grown as a result of its leadership of the successful Greek resistance to Persia, although it was not particularly growing prior to the war. It had turned the loose collection of mutually supportive city states that worked with Athens into a more controlled alliance. This, however, created its own vulnerability as Athenian hegemony became increasingly unpopular. Pericles, who consolidated his authority as Athens's statesmen in 461 BCE, had concluded that it was a sufficient challenge to manage the existing empire without seeking to expand the League further. Sparta had acknowledged this restraint. After a war that lasted from 460 to 445 BCE, the two had agreed to the Thirty Years' Peace. Since that treaty, Pericles had avoided provoking Sparta, a fact noted and accepted by Sparta. It had neither taken an aggressive stance nor made exceptional preparations for war.

The reason why the question of the relationship between the two had come back into play was because of the complications of alliance. A coalition was an obvious benefit for a weaker power wishing to get stronger, but an alliance for a power that was already strong could be a mixed blessing because it could raise expectations and generate obligations while adding little in return. The members of the coalition might agree on a common enemy but little else. Furthermore, the measures taken by Athens to make sure that it did benefit from the Delian League, including contributions to the Athenian treasury and navy, generated resentment. As the Persian threat declined, the resentment increased and Athens became tougher, demanding that their allies become more Athenian, including more democratic. The Spartans, by contrast, showed little interest in the internal affairs of their allies. The position Pericles was trying to sustain was therefore precarious. The empire was of great value to Athens, but the city states were restless.

For different reasons, the Peloponnesian League was also restless. Sparta was being pressed by one of its most substantial allies, Corinth, to take a harder line with Athens. Corinth had its supporters, including Megara, which had its own grievance as a result of the "Megarian Decree" that denied its produce access to Athenian markets. The reason Megara was demanding a push against Athens was because it was in dispute with Corcyra, which had become an obstacle to its own expansion. Corcyra had sought to protect its position by seeking naval support through alliance with Athens. If Athens had resisted, war might have been avoided, but instead an awkward compromise emerged. An alliance would be formed but it would only be defensive. Donald Kagan notes the curiosity in Thucydides's presentation of the issue to his fellow Athenians. He was probably present at these debates, yet he abandoned his normal practice of providing full reports of speeches presenting alternative points of view.[19] Kagan concludes that he did so because further elaboration would have made it clear that the decisions on war were not so much inevitable but the result of Pericles's persuasive powers.[20] Those who took controversial decisions on war tended to portray their decisions as acts of necessity and play down the exercise of discretion.

It was decided to send emissaries to Sparta to explain Athenian policy, although Thucydides suggested that the presence of authoritative Athenians in Sparta at the time of the key deliberations was almost accidental. He therefore did not explain who was sent or the nature of their instructions. In a fuller account of the Spartan debate, Thucydides had Corinth, thwarted by Athens, demanding Spartan support. The demand carried a threat. If Sparta exhibited supine passivity, their allies would be put at risk and would then be driven "in despair to some other alliance."[21] This raised the stakes. Sparta would not want to acquire a reputation for weakness or be weakened in practice by the loss of substantial allies. This was what created the crisis for Sparta. To be sure, Corinth portrayed Athens as grasping with limitless hegemonic ambitions. But to the extent Sparta took note of Corinth, it was not because such fears were shared but because of concern about the defection of a key ally. Indeed the "war party" in Sparta was somewhat dismissive of Athenian power. King Archidamus was much warier, and more anxious to keep the peace, but his advice was ignored and in August 432 BCE, the Spartan assembly voted for war.

Yet even after voting for war, Sparta still sent diplomatic missions to Athens, and these almost resulted in a compromise. In the end it came down to the Megarian Decree. Notably, the emissaries did not push the cause of Corinth but identified the Decree as an unambiguous violation of the Thirty Years' Peace. Thucydides records that many speakers came forward with different views, some favoring war and others revoking the Decree for the sake of peace.[22] This time he reported Pericles's decisive intervention in detail, which focused on Sparta's rejection of arbitration. He accused it of relying on coercion rather than discussion. Such demands demonstrated a refusal to treat Athens as equal. He used an argument still often heard when warning of a larger ambition behind an opponent's apparently modest and reasonable demand. This was not a "trifle," Pericles insisted: "If you yield to them you will immediately be required to make another concession which will be greater, since you will have made the first concession out of fear."[23] Even then, there was restraint in his strategy. It put the onus on Sparta to strike the first blow and refuse arbitration.

In the most extreme version, Thucydides's proposition about the inevitability of war does not stand up. There were a number of points where alternative views might have prevailed and made possible an alternative history. As Richard Ned Lebow has argued, far from being inevitable, war was "the result of an improbable series of remarkably bad judgments made by the leaders of the several powers involved."[24] These started with the lesser powers whose rivalries and entanglements drew in Sparta and Athens. The Athenians might have rejected Corcyra's bid for alliance; Sparta might have rejected Corinth's urgings to take a strong stand; Athens might have abandoned the Megarian Decree; Sparta might have agreed to arbitration.

Yet there were structural factors at play here. The relationship between the two alliances was unstable. There was sufficient residual distrust to create space for those lesser powers who wanted to pursue their own interests. Athens and Sparta had managed to make the Thirty Years' Peace work because there were leaders on both sides who were prepared to moderate any urges to action and aggrandizement in order to keep the peace, but each side also had hawkish factions that disliked moderation and made the case for war. Just as the Corinthians told the Spartans that Athens was inherently aggressive, so the Corcyreans told Athens that they should be welcomed as allies because of the strength of their combined navies. This would be needed when war came, for Sparta and its allies were "eager for war out of fear of you, and . . . the Corinthians have great influence with them and are your enemies."[25] Thus decision-making was unsettled by the developing fluidity in allegiances. Athens saw a choice between alliance with Corcyra or seeing its navy being taken by the Peloponnesians; Sparta saw a choice between backing Corinth's ambitions or risking its defection.

The leadership in both camps, however, was the same that had preserved the peace in the past. Now their ability to follow conciliatory, restrained strategies was circumscribed. Instead they tried to mitigate the effects of the harder line by presenting it in its most restrained version. Thus Pericles accepted an alliance with Corcyra but insisted it should be defensive, which was a novel concept intended to find the least provocative way forward short of rebuttal. When ships were dispatched to affirm this new alliance, it was only a small squadron, insufficient to embolden Corcyra to go on the offensive but also unfortunately insufficient to deter Corinth, so in the end Athens ended up with a more forward commitment than intended. When Sparta wanted to find a diplomatic alternative to the war it had already decided upon in principle, it did not push hard on behalf of Corinth but concentrated on what might have seemed to be a minor issue, the Megarian Decree. By then the room for maneuver on both sides was narrowing. Pericles saw danger in backing down in the face of any direct Spartan demand, but he promised to accept the verdict of arbitration.

The strategy Pericles then followed for the war also contained elements of restraint. It made sense if it was supposed that there was still a peace party in Sparta whose hand would be strengthened once it could be shown that the war party had embarked on a futile course. It also reflected another asymmetry between the two leagues. The Peloponnesian League was largely continental, while Athens—although itself on the mainland—presided over a largely maritime empire. Aware of the strength of the Spartan army, Pericles sought to avoid a land battle and rely instead on Athens's superior naval strength. Pericles did not see the possibility of inflicting a decisive blow against Sparta, so instead he sought a stalemate. His calculation was that Athens had the reserves to outlast Sparta even if the war dragged on for a number of years. In the language of later centuries, he sought victory through enemy exhaustion rather than annihilation.

Politically this strategy was brave in its restraint, but it represented an enormous gamble, and probably only someone with the prestige of Pericles could have carried the day with this proposition. The gamble did not come off. There were annual Spartan attacks on Attica—a source of produce near Athens—to which no response was made other than to send raiding parties around the Peloponnesus. The regular loss of crops from Attica drained the treasury's ability to import essential produce from elsewhere. It also left Athens looking helpless in the face of Spartan aggression. Then came a calamity. A plague in 430 BCE, aggravated by the overcrowding in Athens caused by displaced Atticans, resulted in immense distress. For once Pericles lacked good arguments. Eventually he was removed from office and peace was offered to Sparta. Sparta insisted on draconian terms, effectively asking Athens to abandon its empire, which completely undermined the peace party. Pericles returned as leader, but in 429 BCE he was struck by the plague (which almost killed Thucydides) and died. His efforts to find a course between excessive aggression and appeasement had led him to seek a combination of firmness and restraint. In the end, this increased rather than eased the risks to Athens. The strategy had a limited coercive effect on Sparta, was excessively costly to Athens, and encouraged the colonies to become rebellious. After Pericles died, Athens adopted a more aggressive strategy. This reaped some rewards, and even peace terms from Sparta, but it was then the Athenians' turn to overextend themselves.

Language and Trickery

Thucydides admired Pericles because of his ability to manage the Athenian political system by using his authority and eloquence to appeal to reason and persuade the crowd to adopt sensible policies rather than pandering to the demagoguery and mass irrationality that was an ever-present possibility in a democracy—and to which Athens succumbed after he died.[26]

Athenian democracy required that all the city's key decisions follow intense public deliberations. Strategy could not stay implicit but had to be articulated. It was essential not only to have the foresight to see how events might unfold if the right action was taken but also the ability to convince others that this was so. Assembly and courtroom debates involved opposing speeches—antilogies—that put a premium on the ability to develop strong arguments. There was an interest in the development and application of the persuasive arts.[27] Gorgias, who arrived in Athens during the early stages of the Peloponnesian War (427 BCE) and lived to a great age, offered displays of rhetorical virtuosity. He showed how it was possible to make a weak argument stronger through careful construction, and taught his art to willing pupils. He saw words as equivalent to physical force. They could cause pain and joy: "Some strike fear, some stir the audience to boldness, some benumb and bewitch the soul with evil persuasion." One of his surviving discourses demonstrated why Helen could be excused for triggering the Trojan War by running off with Paris. Protagoras, another influential figure, was notable for his explorations into the proper use of language. He somewhat uniquely described himself as a sophist (from *sophistes*, meaning "wise man"), a term that became significant retrospectively when Plato used it to define a whole group of thinkers. There was a market for a specialist education in public discourse. Litigants could learn how to plead effectively; candidates for office could broaden their appeal; active politicians could be more persuasive.[28]

Pericles enjoyed the company of the intellectuals, including Protagoras. He dismissed the idea that there was distinction to be made between men of action and those of words: "We are lovers of wisdom without sacrificing manly courage." Persuasion required compelling words: those with knowledge but not the "power clearly to express it" might as well have had no ideas at all. He presented himself to the people of Athens as "one who has at least as much ability as anyone else to see what ought to be done and explain what he sees." The importance of the persuasive arts explains why speeches and dialogues were so important in Thucydides's account. This is how Pericles presented strategic arguments, probably described by Thucydides with more coherence than they had in reality.

Pericles's success lay in his authority and ability to convince the people to follow strategies developed with care and foresight. He sought to control events through the application and expression of intellect. As Parry put it, the creativity of his speeches lay in his ability to describe a future that could be achieved if his advice was followed. This concept of the future was drawn from existing reality but moved beyond it. Its plausibility derived from its practicability but also its "discernment of the strongest and most lasting forces in the outside world." Pericles then needed to ensure that events conformed to this vision. He therefore had to be much more than a persuasive orator. His speeches were strategic scripts, offering a satisfactory way forward that reflected his grasp of what might be possible in the light of the forces at work in the world. More than most, he could make reality correspond with his vision by setting out ways of acting that the Athenians could follow successfully. But it always also depended on how foes acted as well as factors of chance. In the end, the integrity of the script could be undermined by events. The deeper meaning of Thucydides's account was tragic, because it revealed the limits of strategic reasoning in the face of a contrary world:

> But actuality in the end proves unmanageable. It breaks in upon men's conceptions, changes them, and finally destroys them. Even where men's conceptions are sound and reasonable, where by their own creative power and their discernment of actuality they *correspond* to things, actuality in its capacity as Luck, will behave in an *unreasonable* way, as Pericles says, and overturn conceptions of the greatest nobility and intelligence.

For Pericles it was the plague in its terrible suddenness, symbolizing "the destructive and incalculable power of actuality," that undermined his vision and denied the control he sought over the historical process. Once he could not convince the Athenian people, he was undone. The tragedy for Thucydides, in offering Pericles as his hero, was that he could not accept an alternative approach. Words as action, analyzing reality and showing how it could be reshaped, were the only hope of controlling actuality. When conceptions and language struggled to keep up with reality, they became almost meaningless and turned into slogans, devoid of true meaning.[29]

Another character, Diodotus, provided a critique. When the oligarchs of Mytilene revolted unsuccessfully against Athens, Diodotus persuaded his fellow citizens not to impose a harsh punishment as demanded by the demagogue Cleon. In doing so, Diodotus reflected on the role of speech-making in a democracy. It was essential, he argued, that decent citizens should make cases based on rational arguments honestly expressed, but the hostile environment of the assembly was putting a premium on deception.

> It has become the rule also to treat good advice honestly given as being no less under suspicion than the bad, so that a person who has something good to say must tell lies in order to be believed, just as someone who gives terrible advice must win over the people by deception.[30]

He then illustrated his point by making his case for leniency on the basis of Athenian interests rather than justice and by drawing attention to the limited deterrent effect of harsh punishments.[31]

An even more striking example of Thucydides's concern with the corruption of language was found in his description of the uprising in Corcyra, which resulted in a bloody civil war between the democrats and the oligarchs. As he described the breakdown of social order, he also described the corruption of language. Recklessness became courage, prudence became cowardice, moderation became unmanly, an ability to see all sides of a question became an incapacity to act, while violence became manly and plotting self-defense. The advocate of extreme measures was to be trusted and those who opposed them suspect.[32] The language followed the action. As restraint collapsed so did the possibity of sensible discourse.

Plato's Strategic Coup

By the end of the century, Athens was diminished and entering a period of political turbulence, during which it was brutally run for a while by Spartan sympathizers. Intellectuals—once such an active, positive force—became objects of suspicion, and they withdrew from political affairs. One figure became cast in the role of a martyr for philosophy. Socrates had said positive things about Sparta and negative things about democracy, took a constantly critical attitude, and was considered to look and act strangely. He was sentenced to death in 399 BCE for corrupting the young. Although Socrates left no writings, he did have devoted students, including Plato, who was about twenty-five when Socrates died. Plato created an idealized version of his teacher, developing his own philosophy by recording many of Socrates's supposed conversations. Plato left a rich series of dialogues on an extraordinary range of issues, but no definitive and systematic account of his views. Nonetheless, certain themes emerged strongly. The most relevant for our purposes concerned the political role of philosophy, including damning those that had gone before for the very qualities that had made their intellects strategic. It was Plato who labeled this prior philosophy as sophism, for which he developed a formidable charge sheet.

According to Plato, the sophists were not serious in their philosophical endeavors. They had given up on the search for truth in order to play rhetorical games, using their persuasive powers on behalf of any case—however unworthy the cause or perverse the logic—in return for payment. Based largely on his own testimony, Plato bequeathed an enduring and demeaning image of the sophists as the "spin-doctors" of their day, rhetorical strategists, relativist in their morality, disinterested in truth, suggesting that all that really mattered was power. They were hired hands, traveling wordsmiths who sold their skills to the highest bidder without any view of right and wrong. They displayed an appalling capacity to defeat a just argument by an unjust one and so use their cleverness to confuse ordinary people. An art put up for sale lost its worth. By serving a variety of masters, the sophists lacked a moral core and encouraged forms of competitive demagogy. The demands of conscience and sense of collective responsibility, shared values and respect for tradition, were all put at risk by their relentless skepticism, disdain for the gods, and promotion of self-interest. Tricks with language allowed the foolish and ignorant to appear wise and knowledgeable. For Plato, virtues were universal and timeless, and it was only through philosophy that they could be described and defined.

This charge sheet has now been discredited: the sophists were not a coherent group, and their views were complex and varied. It was not a collective name they chose for themselves, and it only acquired a pejorative connotation because of Plato. A number may not even have been that interested in persuasion but were instead experimenting in discourse and also providing a form of intellectually mischievous entertainment.[33] The artificiality of Plato's exercise is attested to by his deliberate attempt to rescue his teacher Socrates from this despised group of imposters, despite the fact that Socrates shared many of their characteristics, not least his skeptical, questioning approach to all forms of inquiry. In contemporary terms that Chapter 26 further explores, we might say that Plato engineered a "paradigm shift," and he did this by lumping together those with whom he disagreed into an old paradigm that failed to meet the tests of truth-seeking, to be compared to the new paradigm, developed around a distinct, specialized discipline and profession of philosophy. To use another contemporary term, he "framed" the issue as being a choice between the ethical search for the truth on the one hand and the expedient construction of persuasive arguments as a form of trade on the other. Pericles saw intellectual cultivation as something to which all Athenians aspired; Plato saw philosophy as an exclusive vocation with pure objectives.[34]

Plato believed that true philosophers would be so special that they should be rulers. This would not be because they were skilled in argument and could get people to support their preferred course of action, for Plato did not believe in democracy. It was because they could acquire the highest form of knowledge, grasping with clarity and certainty the essential quality of goodness, which they could then employ to watch over and care for the citizenry. Plato was no enthusiast for intellectual pluralism or the complex interaction of ideas and action that characterized a vibrant political system. The rulers must have supreme power to decide what was wise and just. This vision has had an occasional appeal to would-be philosopher-kings and has been identified as a source of totalitarianism.[35]

Apparently contradicting his insistence on truth as the highest goal was his advocacy of a foundational myth, a "noble lie" that would keep the people "content in their roles." The advocate was Socrates: "We want one single, grand lie which will be believed by everybody—including the rulers ideally, but failing that the rest of the city."[36] No issue demonstrated more the tension inherent in combining the role of philosopher and ruler, with their respective commitments to the truth and civic order. Plato seems to have reconciled the two by a notion of truth that was not merely empirical but also moral, an insight into the higher virtues. Not everyone could have this sort of insight and this created responsibilities when dealing with lesser minds, the lower classes whose grasp of the world was always bound to be limited and illusory. The noble lie was therefore one for good purpose, introduced by Socrates as charter myths for his ideal city. These must be lies that produce harmony and well-being, compared to those of Homer, for example, whose fictions were all about killing and disputes. The noble lie was a white lie on a grand scale. Just as children might be tricked into taking medicines or soldiers encouraged into battle, so communities had to be educated into a belief in social harmony and a conviction that the existing order was natural. The class structure was therefore the result of the different metals the gods had put into individual souls—gold for rulers, silver for auxiliaries, and iron and bronze for farmers and artisans.

Plato's main legacy was not in the character of rulers but in the establishment of philosophy as a specialist profession. Later we will see how something similar happened with the post-enlightenment social sciences in modern times. What started as a set of puzzles about knowledge and its practical application, engaging directly with large and contentious social and political questions, became an assertion of a specialist expertise and claims to a higher "scientific" truth. Strategy, which had to be about conflict—not just between and within the city states but also between the claims of words and the reality of deeds, between the virtue of honesty and the expedience of deception—was always far from a Platonic ideal. Part of Plato's legacy was the sharp distinction between theoretical and practical knowledge, in place of a tradition which appreciated the constant interaction between views of the world and the experience of coping with its complexities.

| Sun Tzu and Machiavelli

All warfare is based on deception.

—Sun Tzu

THE MOST POWERFUL dichotomy in all strategic thought was the one first introduced by Homer as the distinction between biē and mētis, one seeking victory in the physical domain and the other in the mental, one relying on being strong and the other on being smart, one depending on courage and the other imagination, one facing the enemy directly and the other approaching indirectly, one prepared to fall with honor and the other seeking to survive with deception. Under the Romans the pendulum swung away from mētis and toward biē. Homer's Odysseus morphed into Virgil's Ulysses and became part of a story of deceitful and treacherous Greeks. Even the Athenians, as they found themselves on the losing side in their war with Sparta, began to have some sympathy for the Trojans and saw Odysseus's cruel trick in a new light. Heroes were sought who were more plain-speaking, honorable as well as brave in battle, less reliant on cunning and cleverness.

Thus the Roman historian Livy wrote of the more traditionally minded Senators' distaste for a tendency toward "an excessively cunning wisdom." This was akin to "Punic tricks and Greek craftiness, among whom it was more glorious to deceive an enemy than to conquer by force." Romans would not wage war "through ambushes and nocturnal battles, nor through feigned flight and unforeseen returns upon a careless enemy." On occasion there might be "more profit in trick than courage." The spirit of an enemy, however, could only be truly suppressed by "open hand-to-hand combat in a just and righteous war," rather than by "craft or accident."[1]

Despite this stance, the attraction of trickery remained strong. Valerius Maximus, writing not long after at the time of Tiberius, described stratagems positively and offered the first formal definition. "Truly that aspect of cunning is illustrious and far removed from all reproach, whose deeds are called by the Greek expression *strategemata*, because they can scarcely be suitably expressed by a (single Latin) term." The examples he gave were a *salubre mendacium* ("a white lie") to lift morale (effectively persuading one part of your force to attack on the grounds—not necessarily true—that another part was advancing effectively); a false refugee (such as Sinon) who corrupts the enemy from within; a psychological ploy of the besieged to demoralize their besiegers; deceiving one enemy army of your presence, while striking another of their armies with double strength; maneuvers to confuse the enemy, followed by a surprise attack; and besieging the foe's city when he makes an attempt against yours. All this captured the basic psychological aspect of deception: unsettling the enemy or at least reassuring your own side. A stratagem would permit more to be accomplished than by arms alone.[2]

In *Strategemata*, composed by the Roman Senator Frontinus between 84 and 88, the traditions of Roman warfare were passed on. The book was widely disseminated and retained a long influence, including Machiavelli for example. Frontinus made a distinction, possibly of his own invention, in the introduction. "If there prove to be any persons who take an interest in these books," he asked, "let them remember to discriminate between 'strategy' and 'stratagems,' which are by nature extremely similar." Strategy or strategika referred to "everything achieved by a commander, be it characterized by foresight, advantage, enterprise, or resolution." Stratagems, or strategemata, the subject of the book, rested "on skill and cleverness." They were "effective quite as much when the enemy is to be evaded as when he is to be crushed."[3] Frontinus's stratagems certainly included elements of trickery and deception, but they also included more practical matters and efforts to sustain the morale of troops. So stratagems were a subset of strategy. Frontinus did write a general treatise on military matters, but this unfortunately was lost.

In other cultures, stratagems and cunning were considered much more appealing—especially to get out of a tight spot—and commended as essential features of an effective strategy. Lisa Raphals, picking up on Detienne and Vernant's discussion of mētis, made the comparison with the Chinese term zhi. This had a wide variety of meanings from wisdom, knowledge, and intelligence to skill, craft, cleverness, or cunning. The individual who demonstrated *zhi* appeared as a sage general, whose mastery of the art of deception allowed him to prevail over an opponent of stronger physical force, just like those with mētis.[4] Winning against a weak opponent required nothing special. Real skill was shown by getting into positions that did not allow for defeat and would ensure victory over enemies. Deception was crucial: conveying confusion when there was order, cowardice instead of courage, weakness instead of strength. It also required the ability to determine when the enemy was attempting to deceive. Spies, for example, could help understand enemy dispositions and then judge when to be crafty or straightforward, when to maneuver and when to attack directly, when to commit and when to stay flexible.

Sun Tzu

The enduring model of the sage warrior was Sun Tzu, as represented by the short book on strategy known as *The Art of War*. Little is known about the author, or even if there was a single author. According to tradition, he was a general who served the king of Wu in Eastern China around 500 BCE, toward the end of China's Spring and Autumn period, although no contemporary references to him have been found. *The Art of War* seems to have been written or at least compiled over the subsequent century during the Warring States period. The context was a competition for influence among a set of individually weak kingdoms at a time when central authority in China had collapsed. Over time the text acquired important commentaries which added to its significance. There are other Chinese military classics from this period, but Sun Tzu remains the best known.

Sun Tzu's influence lies in the underlying approach to strategy. Influenced by Taoist philosophy, *The Art of War* covers statecraft as well as war. As with any ancient text, the language could seem quaint and the references obscure but the underlying theme was clear enough. Supreme excellence in war was not found in winning "one hundred victories in one hundred battles." Rather, it was better "to subdue the enemy without fighting." The great strategist had to be a master of deception, using force where it was most effective: "Avoid what is strong to strike what is weak."[5] Defeating the enemy's strategy (or "balk the enemy's plans") was the "highest form of generalship." Next came preventing "the junction of the enemy's forces," followed by attacking "the enemy's army in the field," and—worst of all—besieging walled cities.

In Sun Tzu's formulaic aphorisms, the key to deception was simply a matter of doing the opposite of what was expected—look incapacitated when capable, passive when active, near when far, far when near. This required good order and discipline. Simulating cowardice, for example, required courage. It also required an understanding of the opponent. If the enemy general was "choleric," then he could be easily upset; if "obstinate and prone to anger," insults could enrage him and cause him to be impetuous; if arrogant, he could be lulled into a false sense of superiority and a lowered guard. A dangerous commander, according to Sun Tzu, would be reckless, cowardly, quick-tempered, too concerned with reputation, and too compassionate.

What really made the difference was "foreknowledge." This could not be "elicited from spirits, nor from gods, nor by analogy with past events, nor from calculations. It must be obtained from men who know the enemy situation" and could acquire information about dispositions, the character of the troops, and the identity of the generals. The enemy's political relationships could also be a target. "Sometimes drive a wedge between a sovereign and his ministers; on other occasions separate his allies from him. Make them mutually suspicious so that they drift apart. Then you can plot against them."

For East Asian generals, Sun Tzu became a standard text. He was an evident influence in the writings of the Chinese communist leader Mao Zedong. Napoleon was said to have studied a French Jesuit's translation of *The Art of War*. Though not available in English until the early twentieth century, it came to be taken increasingly seriously as a source of military and—during the 1980s—even business wisdom. The book's approach was most relevant for those facing complex struggles, in which encounters were expected to be indecisive and alliances and enmities were shifting.

The Art of War did not provide a single route to victory and recognized that while battles were best avoided they sometimes had to be fought. Sun Tzu described relatively simple conflicts, in which bold moves left an enemy helpless or dissolving into disorder. A possible weakness, in a "strong tendency to point out what one should strive for, rather than explain how one should achieve one's aim," was also a source of strength. Any such explanations would now seem arcane and overtaken by massive changes in military methodology; if Sun Tzu had offered detailed advice on tactics, the book would now tend to be passed over. Instead, students of Sun Tzu are "merely given specific pointers as to what to ponder, but the solution, or the way one chooses to tread, must be one's own."[6]

His approach worked best when followed by only one side: if both commanders were reading Sun Tzu, the maneuvers and deceptions could lead to no decision at all or else an unexpected collision that caught them both unaware. A reputation for deception would lead to a lot of double-guessing, just as one for avoiding battle could turn into a presumption of weakness. In the face of a strong and coherent adversary, clever mind games could take you only so far. If both sides were doing everything possible to avoid a frontal confrontation, then the victor would be the one who could avoid commitment the longest, eventually reaching a point where the enemy had nowhere else to go and so had to fight at a disadvantage or surrender. There was, at any rate, only a limited amount of mystery and subtlety that a leader could cultivate without confusing those being led as much as the opponent. In the end, the point about Sun Tzu was not that he offered a winning formula for all situations but that he offered an ideal type of a particular sort of strategy, based on outsmarting the opponent rather than overwhelming him with brute force.

François Jullien developed an intriguing line of thought by demonstrating the similarities between the Chinese approach to war, as exemplified by Sun Tzu, and the Chinese use of language. He argued that the disinclination to engage in high-risk, potentially destructive direct confrontations in war was also followed in rhetorical conflicts, which were similarly indirect and implicit. Circuitous, subtle forms of expression, both allusive and elusive, could be the equivalents of armies dodging and harrying. By refusing to be pinned down or make an argument with sufficient clarity to be refuted, the initiative could be kept—although this could make for potentially infinite "games of manipulation."[7] Following an indirect approach to discourse would raise the same problems as with battle: when both sides were using identical ploys the contest could be indefinite and it would be hard to reach any sort of closure.

Jullien offered a contrast with the Athenians. They saw the advantages in decisive action that brought both war and argument to a quick close, thereby avoiding the expense and frustrations of prolonged confrontation. Warfare was direct and battle based, with troops organized into phalanxes to ensure maximum impact against the enemy, and victory coming to those with the requisite strength and courage. The generals were capable of deception and understood the advantages of surprise, but they did not want to waste time in games of dodging and harassment. In the same way, the Athenians were straightforward in argument. Whether in the theater, the tribunal, or the assembly, orators would make their cases directly and transparently, with points open to refutation, within a limited time period. There could therefore be decisive arguments as there were decisive battles. In these battles of persuasion in which—as Thucydides put it—arguments were "hurled forcefully against each other," the decision would come from a third party such as a jury or the electorate.

This was an appealing contrast, and it may be that the approach to battles of persuasion reflected broad and enduring cultural preferences that affected attitudes to any confrontation. The suggestion, however, of a strong Greek preference for "decisive" battle came from Victor David Hanson's controversial argument that the terms for a continuing Western way of war were set in classical times.[8] Critics have challenged this theory on the basis of the analysis of Greek warfare and the subsequent history.[9] Beatrice Heuser has demonstrated emphatically that at least one strong strand in Western military thought up to the Napoleonic wars was to avoid pitched battles: "Few believed either in the inevitability or the unconditional desirability of battle."[10] Quintus Fabius Maximus, who gave his name to the "Fabian strategy," was initially derided as the "delayer" because of what seemed to be a cowardly strategy in the face of the pillaging advance of Hannibal's Carthaginian army. But after the Roman defeat at Cannae in 216 BCE, the wisdom of the approach was acknowledged. For some thirteen years thereafter, the Romans avoided pitched battles, while harassing Hannibal's supply lines, until he finally gave up and left Italy.

The Roman treatise on warfare best known through the Middle Ages, when the vital lessons were all still believed to be contained in classical texts, was the *De Re Militari* of Vegetus. Because similar constraints of resources, transport, and geography were faced during the Middle Ages, the key issues were logistical and an offensive army unable to forage and pillage would get into trouble. The relevant line from the *De Re Militari* stated that battle was the "last extremity" and should only be followed when all other plans had been considered and expedients tried. Where the odds were too great, battle should be declined. Better to employ "stratagem and finesse" to destroy the enemy as much as possible in detail and then intimidate them. Vegetus expressed, in terms similar to Sun Tzu, a preference for starving enemies into submission rather than fighting them ("famine is more terrible than the sword"), and spoke of how it "is better to beat the enemy through want, surprises, and care for difficult places (i.e., through maneuver) than by a battle in the open field."[11] There has been a debate on whether medieval warfare was really so battle averse. Clifford Rogers argued that commanders were more prepared to seek battle—at least when on the offensive—but he was far from insisting that the decisive battle was the dominant mode of warfare.[12]

The Byzantine emperor Maurice's *Strategikon* had a similar take at the start of the seventh century: "[I]t is well to hurt the enemy by deceit, by raids or by hunger, and never be enticed to a pitched battle, which is a demonstration more of luck than of bravery." To indicate that there was another view, Heuser quoted Henri, duke of Rohan, writing during the Thirty Years' War that "of all actions of war the most glorious and the most important is to give battle," and regretting that wars were then "made more in the fashion of the fox than of the lion, and . . . based more on sieges than on combat." But Heuser then noted that he saw no combat and that those who had experience of war were much more cautious. Maurice de Saxe, who led the French forces in the early eighteenth century, saw pitched battles as best avoided:

> Nothing so reduces the enemy to absurdity as this method: nothing advances affairs better. Frequent small engagements will dissipate the enemy until he is forced to hide from you.[13]

Using armies for occasional raiding, assaulting the economic life of the enemy, and threatening and demoralizing the enemy's population provided an alternative form of coercion to battle. Most importantly, when accounting for success—for example, with regard to the Hundred Years' War—"political elements were always more significant than military ones," even with talented strategists in command and after victory in pitched battle.[14] The English made the most of their local allies in France just as the French sought to encourage the Scots to distract the English at home.

As the retrospective label "Hundred Years' War" indicates, conflicts might move through distinctive stages but lack decisiveness because the underlying disputes were never fully resolved. In this respect, the role of battle was quite different at this time from how it later became understood. Commenting on the strategic considerations behind one of the most famous battles of this war, when the English under Henry V beat the French at Agincourt in 1415, Jan Willem Honig urged that battle be viewed in terms of the complex conventions of the time, in which sieges, hostages, political demands, and even massacres all had their allotted place. Both sides moved warily toward battle, appearing to both seek and fear it at the same time, and worked their way through an elaborate script, before the two armies confronted each other for the vital encounter. Behind all of this, argued Honig, was the "metaphysical mystique" surrounding battle, for it reflected a view of war as litigation with God as the judge and battle as decisive as a divine judgment. It came when all other forms of dispute settlement had been exhausted.

> The result was a competition in risk which was tempered by the mutually shared fear of appealing to God, the ultimate judge. This fear, and the doubt that any good medieval Christian had regarding the justice of his cause and the strength of his faith, produced an incentive to

develop and adhere to a set of conventions which kept the armed inter-action between opponents within certain bounds.

This meant that warfare could follow relatively predictable paths, and face-saving ways of avoiding battle were available. There was still uncertainty over whether the opponent would follow the rules or offer a self-serving interpretation, but shared norms nonetheless influenced conflict and strategy.[15] Despite its dangers, battle had a special role as an occasional means of resolving disputes by reference to chance. It was a form of contract, a way of agreeing on who had won and what victory meant. It required accepting that since a peaceful settlement was unavailable, this was how a dispute was best resolved. Battle was a "chance of arms," a form of consensual violence out of which would emerge a victor. The battles were limited in time and space, fought on a defined field within a single day (tension at dawn, exhaustion by dusk). Within those confines they would be bloody and vicious, but at least they might produce a conclusion without spilling over into the rest of the country. The minimum required to declare victory was to hold the field of battle at the end of the day, as the enemy fled. A battle could only be decisive if both sides agreed who had won and the practical value of victory. This was not the self-restraint derived from either aristocratic codes of chivalry or a concept of limited strategy but a function of law. Battle was considered an enforceable wager. It was precisely because so much could be at stake and fortune could play such a large part that it was approached with such caution.[16]

Machiavelli

I'll drown more sailors than the mermaid shall;
I'll slay more gazers than the basilisk;
I'll play the orator as well as Nestor,
Deceive more slily than Ulysses could,
And, like a Sinon, take another Troy.
I can add colors to the chameleon,
Change shapes with Proteus for advantages,
And set the murderous Machiavel to school.[17]

Whether rules for acceptable behavior were always followed strictly, they certainly shaped the discourse of the time. This helps explain the dramatic impact of Niccolo Machiavelli's sharp explanations for political behavior based on the self-interest of rulers. He went beyond tolerance for ruses and subterfuge in war to the heart of the conduct of all the affairs of state. He came to be placed on the line of cunning and thus untrustworthy operators that began with Odysseus. It was not long before "Machiavellian" came to describe anyone with a talent for manipulation and an inclination to deceit in the pursuit of personal gain, fascinated with power for its own sake rather than with the virtuous and noble things power allows one to do. Machiavelli's amorality was denounced by the Church, so that the "Machiavel," the embodiment of this theory, could be presented as almost an instrument of the devil (Niccolo fitting neatly the pre-existing Satanic moniker of "old Nick"). In the Duke of Gloucester (later Richard III), whose words are quoted above, Shakespeare identified a man who epitomized the worst defects of such a character.

Niccolo Machiavelli himself was a Florentine bureaucrat, diplomat, political adviser, and practical philosopher. His most famous book, *The Prince*, was written as a handbook for rulers and asserted Machiavelli's own qualifications to serve as an adviser at a time of great turbulence and danger in Italian affairs. There was urgency in his prose that reflected the desperation of his times and a fear of the political consequences of weakness for Florence in particular and Italy in general in the face of French and Spanish strength. For the same reason, Machiavelli also wrote intelligently and persuasively on military affairs. He sought a more enduring form of military capability, based on conscription, that could provide a more reliable base from which to defend the state and extend its power. Unfortunately, the Florentine militia he helped establish was defeated in battle with the Spanish at Prato in 1512. As with Thucydides, Machiavelli's exclusion from actual power gave him the time to write about how power might be exercised by others.

It also gave him a detached perspective, adding to his sense of the difference between the ideal world, in which the truly noble would always be rewarded for their virtue, and the less uplifting reality. Machiavelli's method was empirical, which is why he is considered the father of political science. He did not consider himself to be offering a new morality but rather a reflection on contemporary practical morality. Political survival depended on an unsentimental realism rather than the pursuit of an illusory ideal. This meant paying attention to conflicts of interests and their potential resolution by either force or trickery. But guile and cunning could not create their own political legacy: the foundation of states still lay in good laws and good armies.

Machiavelli's interest in political methodology reflected the same challenge that stimulated most strategists, including Sun Tzu: how to cope with the potentially greater strength of others. Machiavelli did not exaggerate the scope of strategy. There would always be risks. It was therefore not always possible to identify a safe course. Anticipating the "minimax" outcome in twentieth-century game theory, he observed that: "In the nature of things you can never try to escape one danger without encountering another; but prudence consists in knowing how to recognize the nature of the different dangers and in accepting the least bad as good."[18] What could be done depended on circumstances. "[F]ortune governs one half of our actions, but even so she leaves the half more or less in our power to control." Even in this area of apparent control, it would be necessary to adapt to circumstances. Free will suggested the possibility of fitting events to an established character; Machiavelli suggested that the character would be shaped by events.

Machiavelli's *Art of War* was the only book published during his lifetime. This might have been the inspiration for the title given to Sun Tzu's work. Indeed, almost all disquisition on the subject—from that of Raimondo Montecuccoli in the seventeenth century to Maurice de Saxe in the eighteenth to Baron de Jomini in the nineteenth—was called *The Art of War*. This was a generic title, often covering largely technical matters. Machiavelli's contribution to the genre was extremely successful and was translated into many languages. He addressed the potential value of a standing army and how one could be properly formed to serve the true interests of the state. He struggled with the practical issues of the day, from fortresses to the advent of gunpowder. Because the book took the form of a conversation between individuals debating the key issues, and it cannot be assumed that one always represented Machiavelli's thoughts, exactly where he stood on some issues remained ambiguous. But the broad thrust of his concerns was evident, particularly the importance of a competent and loyal army in providing for security and creating diplomatic freedom to maneuver. He understood the relationship of war to politics and the importance of making sure an enemy was clearly defeated even after it left the field of battle, so there was no chance to regroup. He understood that battle might be a place where Fortuna had a large hand and for that reason was wary of leaving her too much of a role. Hence the need to engage all forces in battle rather than make a limited commitment. Not surprisingly, he also showed regard for deception, trickery, and espionage, the advantages that could come through being better informed than the enemy, and an occasionally stated preference for winning without battle if possible.

The most interesting aspects of his work, however, were less about dealing with an external enemy and more about sustaining loyalty and commitment internally. This concern was reflected in his preference for a local militia rather than professional soldiers motivated only by money. He was unsure about appeals to patriotism and more confident in tough discipline, including practical measures to make sure that deserters could not take their possessions with them. "To persuade or dissuade a few of a thing is very easy. For if words are not enough, you can use authority or force." Convincing the multitude was more difficult: they had to be persuaded en masse. Because of this, "excellent captains need to be orators." Speaking to the army "takes away fear, inflames spirits, increases obstinacy, uncovers deceptions, promises rewards, shows dangers and the way to flee them, fills with hope, praises, vituperates, and does all those things by which the human passion are extinguished or inflamed."[19] The sort of orations that might make men want to fight would encourage indignation and contempt toward enemies and make the soldiers ashamed of their sloth and cowardice.

In *The Prince*, Machiavelli offered notoriously cynical advice on how to gain and hold on to power, by being ready to indulge in all manner of private dealings while appearing publicly beyond reproach. The underlying message was that if you sought to be virtuous in both word and deed you would suffer badly. Survival must be the highest objective; otherwise nothing could be achieved. This required the prince to vary his conduct according to changing circumstance, including a readiness to act immorally whenever necessary. In one of his most famous passages, Machiavelli posed the question

> whether it be better to be loved than feared, or the reverse? The answer
> is that one would like to be both the one and the other: but because
> it is difficult to combine, it is far better to be feared than loved if you
> cannot be both. One can make this generalization about men: they are
> ungrateful, fickle, liars and deceivers, they shun danger and are greedy
> for profit; while you treat them well, they are yours. They would shed
> their blood for you, risk their property, their lives, their children, so
> long, as I said above, as danger is remote; but when you are in danger
> they turn against you.[20]

This negative view of human nature was central to Machiavelli's approach. At one point he contrasted the lessons to be learned from the lion and the fox, the first representing strength and the second cunning. One needed to be a fox "in order to recognize traps, and a lion to frighten off wolves." As "men are wretched creatures who could not keep their word to you, you need not keep your word to them." It was, however, no good to be caught in displays of bad faith. That was why it was useful to be a fox: "One must know how to color one's actions and to be a great liar and deceiver. Men are so simple, and so much creatures of circumstance, that the deceiver will always find somebody ready to be deceived." As much as possible it was best for the prince to appear to be "compassionate, faithful to his word, guileless, and devout," and even to act that way so long as it was prudent to do so. It could be helpful to be seen to be harsh, for that helped maintain order, but not to be considered entirely without virtue. "Everyone sees what you appear to be, few experience what you really are... The common people are always impressed by appearances and results."[21] A capacity to mislead—and on a large scale—was an essential attribute. At some point the appearance of virtue could not be wholly detached from practice. Machiavelli understood that to hold on to power it was necessary to reduce the reliance on harsh, cruel methods and to behave in more moderate, graceful ways.

Princes, he warned, should avoid being hated and despised. He was not against the use of cruelty but thought it should only be employed when essential and then "once and for all" so that it was possible to turn to "the good of one's subjects." He advised strongly against the sort of cruelty "which, although infrequent to start with, as time goes on, rather than disappearing, becomes more evident." This was based on his assessment of human psychology. If the prince got his harsh behavior over right at the start, and then refrained from repetition, "he will be able to set men's minds at rest and win them over to him when he confers benefits." Otherwise, the prince "is always forced to have the knife ready in his hand and he can never depend on his subjects because they, suffering fresh and continuous violence, can never feel secure with regard to him." Though violence should be inflicted once and for all, for "people will then forget what it tastes like and so be less resentful," benefits by contrast should be conferred gradually because "they will taste better."[22] Machiavelli understood that even if power was obtained by force and guile and consolidated with cruelty, it required consent to be secured. The best power was that which had to be exercised least.

Although *Machiavellian* has become synonymous with strategies based on deceit and manipulation, Machiavelli's approach was actually far more balanced. He understood that the more the prince was perceived to rely on devious methods, the less likely it would be that they succeeded. The wise strategist would seek to develop a foundation for the exercise of power that went beyond false impressions and harsh punishments, but on real accomplishments and general respect.

| Satan's Strategy

The will is a beast of burden. If God mounts it, it wishes and goes as
God wills; if Satan mounts it, it wishes and goes as Satan wills. Nor
can it choose its rider . . . the riders contend for its possession.

—Martin Luther

MACHIAVELLI'S INFLUENCE on subsequent political thought was profound. His candid appreciation of the realities of power provided new
ways to talk about politics, whether offered as guidance to those prepared
to be flexible and adaptable—as he advocated—or taken to the extremes
personified in the sinister and amoral stage villain Machiavel. One striking
illustration of his influence on discussions of political conduct is found in the
writings of John Milton. In his epic poem *Paradise Lost*, published in 1667,
Milton's Satan is the embodiment of Machiavellianism. Evaluating Satan's
strategy allows us to consider the limits and possibilities of the attributes
associated with Machiavelli, as well as the continuing constraints imposed on
strategic freedom by the presence of God.

Milton's core project was to address the most perplexing of theological
issues about free will as first introduced by the story of Adam and Eve. If
everything was preordained, Adam and Eve had no choice in the matter.
Their original sin was not their fault. If it was their fault, God still needed
to have some reason to allow it to happen. If the choice was between good

and evil, then God must have created evil. If human beings could be tempted in this way, then they must have been created imperfect. Yet if this was a consequence of the original design, did they deserve to be punished? If there was no flaw, then how were they able to sin, and from where did they find a concept of sin? How could there be two falls, as Eve was the only one actually tempted by the serpent before she went on to persuade Adam. What was the serpent's motive?

In *Paradise Lost*, John Milton tried to make sense of all of this. At one level, his story was about a rebellion within a kingdom, the defeat of the rebels, and the consequences of the rebels' attempts to reverse their defeat. At another level, it was—as Milton put it in his introduction—about how to "justify the ways of God to man," particularly how to reconcile God's omnipotence with man's free will. And at yet another level, it was about earthly relationships between kings and men. Milton wrote during the restoration of the monarchy following a civil war in which he had been a devoted republican. It was a time of suppression of dissenters; at one point, Milton himself was close to being executed for treason.

The concept of free will raises questions about God's role in human affairs. If God does not intervene, then what is the purpose of prayer and repentance? If he does intervene, then why do bad things happen to good people? Contemporary theologians may have come up with formulations to answer these questions, but in seventeenth-century Europe when Milton was writing, they were hot topics—politically as well as religiously.

The century began under the influence of a rigorous Calvinism preaching a God of such power that little could be done to thwart his will. Divine grace had been allocated in advance. Everything was set in motion by the original grand design. "God orders and ordains all things," observed Augustine of Hippo. He worked in the "hearts of men to incline their wills withersoever He wills." He "freely and unchangeably ordained whatsoever comes to pass," echoed the Calvinists. Nothing could happen that reflected any will other than his. Humankind was just playing out a drama according to a script set down by God at the moment of creation, with no later need for improvisation. It was beyond the comprehension of mere men. This view went even beyond omnipotence, which merely presumed that God could intervene in human society if and when he wished to do so, and assumed that history was set on an unalterable course. If all events were predetermined, and choice was merely an illusion, then the only response was fatalism. Any attempt to change the course of history was pointless.

Against the Calvinists, the followers of Jacobus Arminius argued that humans are able to make their own histories through the exercise of free will and that God's strength was manifest in acts of love in response to humans' obedience and repentance for their sins. The God of the Calvinists was arbitrary and beyond explanation. The God of the Arminians would allow no arbitrary exclusion from his grace and insisted on the human ability to distinguish good from evil, in order to demonstrate their obedience to God.

By the time of *Paradise Lost*, and after an early Calvinism, Milton was with the Arminians. His view was that "God made no absolute decrees about anything which he left in the power of men, for men have freedom of action." To hold the opposite position would be absurd and unfair. If God turned "man to moral good or evil just as he likes, and then rewards the good and punishes the wicked, it will cause an outcry against divine justice from all sides."[1] The best answer to the conundrum posed by Genesis was that without evil there would be no way to test the faith of humans and allow them to realize their potential for goodness. Milton has God explain that he made man, "just and right/ Sufficient to have stood, though free to fall."[2]

One way to think about evil was as a function of human weakness, a constant readiness to be tempted and knowingly disobey God's word. Another way, common by Milton's time, was to consider evil as a living, active force, deliberately trying to subvert God and tempt man. Evil acquired the personality of Satan, and the serpent in Genesis was therefore really Satan in disguise, although there was no basis in Genesis for this notion. In a number of ancient civilizations, serpents have signified evil, but also fertility. Satan did not appear until late in the Bible and then not in opposition to God but as a loyal angel. Satan had an adversarial role and took a harsh line in disputations before God in heaven, but he was always loyal in the end. The best-known example of this is in the book of Job, when he is introduced as returning "from going to and fro in the earth, and from walking up and down in it."[3] His role was one of challenging men in their sinfulness. It was Satan who urged God to test Job, and when God agreed, Satan was sent to make Job's life miserable. Nonetheless, Satan did this not as a rebel but as a member of the heavenly court.

Eventually Satan, acting not merely as a harsh angel but also as one who had fallen, came to be blamed for all forms of division and misery. The early Church had attempted to challenge the influence of Manichaeism (another eastern religion which explained matters in terms of the contrast between the forces of good and evil), but its insistence that evil was not constituted as a live being failed to convince. The idea of a demonic force constantly seeking to lure humankind away from obeying God took hold. The main difference for Manicheans was that in the end this had to be an unequal struggle. Hell could be no sanctuary where Satan reigned supreme. God was always superior.

Evil could therefore imperil the world but also be sufficiently containable and vulnerable to defeat.[4] The Bible closes with the book of Revelation, in which Satan represents the forces of evil. An extraordinary scene is described, a war in heaven between Michael and "the dragon," each with their own cohort of angels. "And the great dragon was thrown down, that ancient serpent, who is called the Devil and Satan, the deceiver of the whole world—he was thrown down to the earth, and his angels were thrown down with him."[5] Biblical scholars consider this to refer to a vision of a tremendous upheaval at the end of time. Milton was not alone, however, in taking this to refer to the start of time. It was Satan's rebellion against God that led to his exile to earth where he became a troublemaker, gaining his first victory as the serpent persuading Eve to eat of the Tree of Knowledge.

Heavenly Battles

Milton's narrative gained force not only because of his mastery of language and sense of drama but also because of his intense commitment to the notion of free will. To square the circle of faith, he sought to demonstrate that the true exercise of free will leads to a decision to obey God completely and without reservation. So while God allows free will, he knows how individuals will decide. Milton also distinguished between a challenge to the authority of a secular king—a good thing—and a challenge to the heavenly king—a bad thing. Indeed, the secular king's authority needed to be challenged because it was tantamount to a challenge to God's authority. The arguments that might be used to justify disobedience in one context should not work at all in another. Yet rhetorically this did not quite work, as the arguments against both types of kings sounded very similar. As many commentators have observed, when Satan makes the case against blind obedience to God, Milton gives him the best lines. William Blake observed that Milton was "of the Devil's party without knowing it."[6] Milton's portrayal of Satan as a leader matched a Machiavellian prince. Satan had the appropriate character—a blend of the courageous and cunning—was able to adapt to changing circumstances, had the confidence to take risks, and was aware of the respective merits of force and guile ("Our better part remains/ To work in close design, by fraud or guile/ What force effected not").[7]

The narrative structure humanizes the main characters, with the effect of diminishing God and elevating Satan. Milton undermined God's aura and left him appearing defensive and pedantic. As we have seen in Exodus, God could be deceptive and manipulative as part of his mysterious ways, but his approach in *Paradise Lost* was less subtle. Satan comes across as a much more rounded character, altogether more interesting.[8] Though at times he appeared regretful of his fallen status, he still followed his chosen path. His ambivalent character and claims meant that he was not always so easy to resist. For Milton, Satan was Machiavel, using fraudulent rhetoric and force to manipulate the fallen angels while also attempting to attribute exactly these corrosive tendencies to God.[9] Satan adopted the republican claims of free choice, merit, and consent in describing his rule, while asserting that God depends on coercion and fraud.

There are many themes and ideas developed in *Paradise Lost*, of which the most important is the link between the events at the start of time and the eventual crucifixion and resurrection of Jesus. My focus is solely on the conflict between God and Satan and what this might tell us about their respective strategic calculations. There are two key episodes in this story. In *Paradise Lost*, they do not appear in chronological order, but here they do. The first is the story of the great battle in heaven, which is told by Rafael, one of God's loyal angels, to Adam to warn him about the nature of Satan and his potential for evil. Unfortunately, by the time this story has been told, Eve has already been tempted. The second episode, the opening scene of the book, depicts the deliberations among Satan's followers as they work out how to respond to their defeat in the first battle.

In the beginning, according to Milton, Satan—then known as Lucifer—was one of the great angels among the heavenly host. The crisis came when God proclaimed his Son to be his equal. Satan was greatly affronted. He had been given no warning of this development and now felt that his position in the hierarchy was undermined. Satan urged the other angels to join him in rebellion: "Will ye submit your necks and choose to bend/ The supple knee?" He then provided a powerful case for political rights:

> Who can in reason then or right assume/ Monarchie over such as live by right/ His equals, if in power and splendor less/ In freedome equal? or can introduce/ Law and Edict on us, who without law/ Erre not, much less for this to be our Lord,/And look for adoration to th' abuse/ Of those Imperial Titles which assert/ Our being ordain'd to govern, not to serve?[10]

A third of the angels rallied to Satan's side, and heaven was attacked. But heaven was ready. Curiously, rather than a place dedicated to peace, beauty, and tranquility, heaven was already geared up for battle and organized on martial lines. Milton had been an admirer of Oliver Cromwell's New Model Army, with its organization and discipline. This seems to have given him the idea for a New Model Heaven.[11] This struggle was more than hand-to-hand combat. The rebels were pushed back on the first day, but they countered on the second day with cannon, only to be countered in turn by having hills and mountains hurled at them. The rebels' resort to gunpowder, a material linked to treason in the Catholic plot of 1605, is not without significance. At the time, it was often described as the devil's invention, calculated to remove honor and glory from war.

God watched this chaos and at last intervened on the third day. Why did he let it continue? The reasoning was consistent with that used to interpret the basic message of the Hebrew Bible. He was creating the conditions in which his glory and wonder would be appreciated. In this case, it was the Son whose decisive role had to be noticed. He explained to the Son that this was in order "that the Glory may be thine/ Of ending this great war, since none but Thou/ Can end it." He commanded him to lead out all the heavenly forces and drive the rebel angels down to hell. The Son accepted the command willingly, again demonstrating a clear contrast between his obedience and Satan's rebellion. For the Son, "to obey is happiness entire." Satan's forces also regrouped, "hope conceiving from despair." They made themselves ready for a battle they knew must be final. The Son told his forces to stand aside for this was his battle: "Against me is all their rage."[12]

Leaving aside the odd ideas of a civil war in heaven, the use of artillery (somehow mountains as projectiles are more fitting), or even the earthly tendency to stop fighting for the night, there was an added twist that resulted from the immortality of the angels on both sides. No wound was ever fatal, although they did cause pain. Despite his admiration for martial virtues, Milton was also demonstrating that some matters could never be truly solved by battle. Perhaps he was also reflecting on his experience of victory for the parliamentary side in the civil war followed by the return of the monarchy. Even in this particular contest, it was the special strength of the Son rather than weight of numbers that made all the difference.

Pandemonium

When the enemy is able to recover from initial blows, it is difficult to inflict a decisive defeat. Immortal combatants gave an added twist to this classic dilemma. As *Paradise Lost* opened, the fallen angels were meeting to regroup and consider their next steps in their new home. Despite being expelled from heaven, Satan was undaunted. He remained a dedicated opponent of "the tyranny of Heav'n." "Here at last," he proclaimed from hell, "We shall be free. [. . .] Better to reign in Hell than serve in Heaven!"

A strategic debate then took place in hell among the leaders of the fallen angels—Moloch, Belial, Mammon, Beelzebub, and Satan himself. The setting was a special place called Pandemonium (literally a house of devils), where the rebels gather to consider their next steps. God presumably had the option of preventing them ever causing trouble again, but he still allowed them to decide their own course of action. Satan was determined to raise his comrades out of their miserable sense of weakness and work to oppose everything that God was trying to do. "To do aught good never will be our task, But ever to do ill our sole delight." He used a parade, with accompanying brass band, to raise the spirits of his followers and demonstrate that they were still a force of great strength, greater "than the forces on both sides in the Trojan War, greater than any forces King Arthur or Charlemagne could command." While this may have raised the morale of his followers against God, it could not serve as the basis of a credible strategy.[13]

A set of options was described that might have been put to any group trying to respond to a major setback. Anthony Jay noted that "in every important respect the situation is that of a corporation trying to formulate a new policy after taking a terrific beating from its chief competitor and being driven out of the market it had previously depended on."[14] Satan, who knew what he wanted, nonetheless followed good practice and opened proceedings by asking for proposals.

Moloch was the first to step forward, recommending "open war." His appeal was based on emotion and drive, aggression and fatalism, while contemptuous of attempts to use wiles: "Let us rather choose/ arm'd with hell flames and fury, all at once/ O'er Heaven's high towers to force resistless way." He could not, he admitted, promise victory, but at least a form of revenge.

Compared with Moloch's unsubtle aggression, Belial offered more realism, but the effect was defeatist: "ignoble ease and peaceful sloth." He doubted they could achieve even revenge. "The tow'rs of heaven are filled/ With armed watch, that renders all access/ Impregnable." He made a fundamental point about the impossibility of both "force and guile" that his fellow devils seemed ready to ignore. God saw "all things at one view" and so saw and derided the devil's council even while it was in progress. Belial's alternative was therefore to wait until God relented. "This is now/ Our doom, which if we can sustain and bear,/ Our supreme foe in time may much remit/ His anger."

Mammon ridiculed both of the previous options. He had little taste for war or expectations of God's forgiveness: "With what eyes could we/ Stand in his presence humble, and receive/ Strict laws imposed, to celebrate his throne/ With warbled hymns, and to his Godhead sing/ Force hallelujahs, while he lordly sits/ Our envied Sov'reign." His idea was to develop the possibilities of hell: "This desert soil/ Wants not her hidden lustre, gems and gold: Nor want we skill or art, from whence to raise/ Magnificence: and what can heav'n show more?" So he urged the fallen angels "to found this nether empire, which might rise/ By policy and long process of time/ In emulation opposite to heav'n." As he had helped construct Pandemonium, Mammon's ideas had some credibility. For the first time the audience saw something they liked. Mammon "scarce had finished when such murmur filled/ The assembly, as when hollow rocks retain/ The sound of blustering winds."

But like any clever chairman, Satan had worked out his preferred outcome before the debate had begun. Everything had been structured to produce the desired conclusion. His second-in-command, Beelzebub, "Pleaded his devilish counsel, first devised/ By Satan and in part prospered." First, he undermined Mammon by warning that God would not allow hell to become equivalent to heaven. Beelzebub proposed taking an initiative but not the direct strategy of Moloch. Satan spoke of a "place/ (If ancient and prophetic fame in heaven/ err not) another world, the happy seat/ Of some new race called Man." This new race was supposedly equal to angels, perhaps created to fill the gap left by the exiled rebels. This was a way of getting at God without the futility of a direct assault. Perhaps men might be tricked into joining the rebellion. As a strategist Satan had identified one possible explanation for the defeat in heaven. It was simply a lack of numbers. There were twice as many loyal angels as rebels. Instead of trying to reverse the outcome of battle through a direct assault, which would be futile, why not trick men into joining the rebellion? After Satan praised Beelzebub's plan, it was adopted. Having come up with the strategy, Satan set off to implement it. First he needed good intelligence. "Thither let us bend all our thoughts, to learn/ What creatures there inhabit. Of what mould/ Or substance, how endued, and what their power,/ And where their weakness, how attempted best,/ By force or subtlety."[15]

He journeyed seven times around the earth to avoid the vigilance of the angels guarding Paradise. He tricked his way into Eden, appearing to the guard as a cherub. His aim was to conquer Eden and then colonize it with his fallen angels. But, coming upon Eve in Eden, he was enraptured by her beauty and for a while was "stupidly good, of enmity disarmed,/ Of guile, of hate, of envy, of revenge," until he pulled himself together and reminded himself that he was about "hate, not love." He considered Adam and Eve now more cynically as he recalls his aim of malign coalition: "League with you

I seek,/ and mutual amitie so streight, so close,/ That I with you must dwell, or you with me,/ Henceforth."

In the form of a serpent, which Milton compared to the Trojan Horse, Satan tempted Eve to eat fruit from the Tree of Knowledge. Satan argued that he, a beast, received the gift of speech after eating it and God had not killed him. Eve later explains to Adam that she doubted he would have "discern'd/ Fraud in the Serpent, speaking as he spake." Even if she had been aware of the possible deceptiveness of appearances, why should she have been suspicious? "No grounds of enmity between us known,/ Why he should mean me ill or seek to harm."[16]

After eating the fruit, Eve persuaded Adam to eat some as well. This set up a potential contest for the allegiance of men. Should they give themselves over to Satan, the balance of power might tilt in his direction. For Adam and Eve, this was the moment of decision. No longer innocent, they must choose. Satan's cause was defeated when Adam and Eve made their choice; they repented and aligned themselves with God. Michael's prophecy was "so shall the World goe on,/ To good malignant, to bad men benigne,/ Under her own waight groaning" until Christ's second coming. The lesson, as Adam came to understand, was that even the few must oppose the unjust and the wicked, for "suffering for truth's sake/ Is fortitude to highest victorie." God's accomplishments would not always be the obvious route. They came "by things deem'd weak/ Subverting wordly strong."[17]

By that time, a less-confident Satan, away from his home ground and supporters, had his own "troubl'd thoughts," acknowledging the omnipotence of God and the error of his revolt, as well as the evil within him. His pride would not allow him to contemplate submission. The problem was not with the strategy Milton attributed to Satan. With all involved enjoying immortality, brute force was never going to be decisive. Satan's best hope was to turn humans so that they joined the ranks of the fallen. In this effort deception was essential, and initially Satan was successful in removing Adam and Eve as allies of the angels. What he failed to do was win them over to his cause, for here God had the ultimate weapon in his Son.

Although Milton put sentiments about freedom—in words he might have used against his own king—into the Satanic speeches, he was not necessarily of the devil's party. Milton's heaven, while odd in its apparent militarism, was never described in tyrannical terms. The angels obeyed God as a result of his inherent authority rather than fear of punishment, and individual angels were given latitude when acting on God's behalf. They came together naturally and joyously to defend heaven against the rebels. Moreover, there was every difference between using such republican rhetoric to denounce an earthly king, who had usurped the power of God and claimed to be his agent, and the denunciation of God himself. In 1609, James I spoke to Parliament about how "kings are justly called Gods, for they exercise in a manner or resemblance of Divine power upon earth...Kings are not only God's Lieutenants upon earth, and sit upon God's throne, but even by God himself they are called Gods." Milton's political project from the start was to challenge this presumption and the associated claim that disobedience to a king was tantamount to disobedience to God. Such a presumption was idolatrous. Milton's hell was a developing monarchy "with royalist politics, perverted language, perverse rhetoric, political manipulation, and demagoguery."[18] Despite the language Satan employed as a rebel leader, he acted as a supreme king once he got to hell. He appeared as a great sultan and addressed Pandemonium "high on a throne of Royal State." He took his command for granted. He did not offer the rebels republican self-government but rather servitude to himself, a usurping king. His feigned commitment to political rights was no more to be believed than the vivid description of a serpent's life he gave Eve while tempting her—or his other imaginative deceptions, for that matter.

The real puzzle is why Satan ever believed he could succeed. The problem was not predestination but God's omnipotence and omniscience. Not only did God have superior power, but he could not be tricked either. Whatever was being planned, God saw it coming. As a former archangel, Satan should also have seen it coming. This is why, despite appearing to be modeled on Machiavelli's ideal prince, Milton's Satan fell short in key respects. In confrontation with God he made elementary mistakes and lacked the prudence Machiavelli advised when dealing with a stronger power. Machiavelli's prince was "above all a pragmatist." Machiavelli did not admire "those who oppose insurmountable odds or persist in lost causes." In *Paradise Lost*, Satan acknowledged that while in heaven he underestimated God's strength, and once in hell he made no effort to reconsider the logic of his initial rebellion. He stuck with a strategy that had already brought him failure, in part by claiming that it was almost successful. He learned nothing that could truly make God vulnerable. His boasting that he could do so was, to quote Riebling, "a mockery of strategic wisdom." He was ready to use force or guile, but not to gain true advantage—only to wage "eternal Warr." Against an omnipotent foe, this hardly betrayed pragmatism. "Satan may seem to be a free agent, boldly innovating his future," but "he is instead a slave to his own nature."[19]

In Milton's fiction, Satan's task was to allow God to make a point. Satan was "cast in a poem with an axiomatically omniscient and omnipotent God." This meant, according to John Carey, "that every hostile move he makes must be self-defeating. Yet his fictional function is precisely to make hostile moves: he is the fiend, the enemy."[20] If, having seen the possibility of redemption, Satan had taken it, then the plot would no longer work. But that still left the flaw. Milton provided God with a truly evil opponent who was sufficiently clever to develop a challenge substantial enough to demonstrate God's glory but not so clever that he could conclude that he should surrender to God's mercy. By exploring the relative merits of force, guile, conciliation, and fatalism, *Paradise Lost* illuminated strategic debates, but as with all debates in which God was involved, in the end the deliberations were all futile. The players in these dramas could act to serve their own purposes only to the extent that these conformed to God's overarching plan.

The Limits Of Guile

Although the regular references to deception in the Bible are by no means always disapproving, the serpent's cunning, which gets humankind off to such a poor start, did not set an encouraging precedent. Milton further confirmed the link between cunning and wickedness by identifying the serpent as Satan in disguise. When Milton referred to "guile," he connoted fraud, cunning, and trickery. From a strategic perspective, these still could seem preferable to violence—and certainly to defeat—but such methods were underhanded, certainly lacking in nobility and bravery. Those who won by such guile would forever have a stain on their character. Even now, it is complimentary to describe a person as being "without guile." What such a person says can be taken at face value; there is no need to search for hidden meanings. Or else we speak of a victim "beguiled" by a seductive personality or idea as one detached from normal composure and rationality. A comparable word is *wiles*, which the philosopher Hobbes employed as an alternative "to master the persons of all men he can."[21] The Oxford Dictionary definition conveys the distasteful flavor of wiles: "a crafty, cunning, or deceitful trick; a sly, insidious, or underhand artifice; a stratagem, ruse. Formerly sometimes in somewhat wider sense: A piece of deception, a deceit, a delusion."

Stratagems, as described by Frontinus, involved deceit, surprise, contrivance, obfuscation, and general trickery. A stratagem is still defined as an "artifice or trick designed to outwit or surprise the enemy." There were examples in Shakespeare in which resorting to stratagem appeared as less than wholesome, a way of gaining an unfair advantage by surprising the enemy. The mad Lear's suggestion of a "delicate stratagem" to "shoe a troop of horse with felt" was not to be taken seriously. The preference for acting without trickery was made most clear in *Henry V*, in which the king boasted of a victory achieved "without stratagem" but rather "in plain shock and even play of battle."[22]

The word *plot* also acquired negative connotations during the seventeenth century. Its association with dangerous mischief or malevolent scheming was sealed once the failed attempt by Catholic conspirators (including Guy Fawkes) to blow up the House of Commons while King James visited on November 5, 1605, became known as the Gunpowder Plot. *Plot* has thereafter implied treachery and conspiracy—a perverted plan, hatched by a few, dependent on secrecy, geared to overthrowing the established order. Yet, the etymology of *plot* resembles that of *plan*. Both originally referred to a flat area of ground, then to a drawing of an area of land or a building, then to a drawing to guide the construction of a building, and eventually to a set of measures adopted to accomplish something. A plan became a detailed proposal setting out how a goal would be attained. The military had their "plan of attack" or "plan of campaign," and these moved from their literal meanings to become metaphors for going on the offensive or embarking on a challenging mission in any context. When matters progress smoothly, they were going "according to plan." Eventually, a plan implied much more than a sensible way of thinking through how to complete some difficult or complicated task. *Plot* morphed into something similar but less wholesome. The fine distinction between the two was found in Dr. Johnson's 1755 dictionary. A plan was a "scheme," while a plot was also a "scheme" but a "conspiracy, stratagem, contrivance" as well.[23]

There was always a double standard when it came to cunning, trickery, deception, and stratagem. Against your own people—with whom deception should be much easier because you understood them and they were more likely to trust you—it was generally reprehensible, but against enemies, it could be acceptable and even admirable if the trick was a good one. The closer the social bond, the more distasteful were attempts to exploit the bond through deception; the weaker the bond, the more difficult it was to deceive successfully. Either way, reliance on cunning was subject to a law of diminishing returns. Once the reputation was acquired, then others would be watching out for tricks. Such tricks were therefore vulnerable to problems in execution or exposure when an opponent had good intelligence. For all these reasons, the influence of cunning and trickery tended to be most evident when small scale and personal. It was possible to trick governments and armies, but this was always a gamble and might not gain more than a temporary and limited advantage. Once warfare moved to mass armies with complex organizations, there would be limits to what could be achieved by means of guile. The emphasis would be on force.

PART II | Strategies of Force

| The New Science of Strategy

When I have learnt what progress has been made in modern gunnery,

When I know more of tactics than a novice in a nunnery—

In short, when I've a smattering of elemental strategy

You'll say a better Major-General has never sat a-gee.

For my military knowledge, though I'm plucky and adventury,

Has only been brought down to the beginning of the century.

—Gilbert and Sullivan, *The Pirates of Penzance*

IN THE FAMOUS patter song from their light opera of 1879, Gilbert and Sullivan have their "modern major general" parading his knowledge of all things historical, classical, artistic, and scientific. Only at the end does he admit that the gaps in his knowledge are those exactly relevant to his trade. When he admits that his military knowledge has yet to reach the start of the nineteenth century, he is saying that it is pre-Napoleonic, therefore belonging to a quite different age and unfit for contemporary purposes.

Martin van Creveld has asked whether strategy existed before 1800.[1] From the perspective of this book, of course, it existed from the moment primates formed social groupings. Van Creveld accepted that there were always some informed notions of the conduct of war and how to achieve victory. Commanders had to work out their approach to battle and organize their forces accordingly. What van Creveld had in mind was a step change that occurred around this time. Before 1800, intelligence-gathering and communication systems were slow and unreliable. For that reason, generals had to be on the front line—or at least not too far behind—in order to adjust quickly to the changing fortunes of battle. They dared not develop plans of any complexity. Adopting measures such as splitting forces in order to attack the enemy from different directions or holding back reserves to reinforce success was likely to lead to command and logistical nightmares. Roads were poor and movement was bound to be slow. Although it was no longer necessary to live off the land, logistical support required that magazines be moved along supply lines. This entailed a serious vulnerability if the enemy managed to cut the lines. Modest maneuvers or nighttime marches were the best options for catching an enemy by surprise. Armies that lacked passion and commitment, whose soldiers were easily tempted to desert if food was in short supply or conditions too harsh, did not encourage confidence in sustainable campaigns. Prudence suggested concentrating on pushing enemies into positions where they would feel vulnerable or struggle to stay supplied. All this limited the impact of wars on the apparently stable European balance of power. Then, as transport systems were improving and lands were becoming properly mapped, along came Napoleon Bonaparte, self-proclaimed emperor of France. Napoleon embodied a new way of fighting wars: a combination of individual genius and mass organization, and objectives far more ambitious than those of his predecessors.

The French Revolution of 1789 was a source of great energy, innovation, and destruction. It unleashed political and social forces that could not be contained in their time and whose repercussions continued to be felt in the succeeding centuries. In military affairs, the Revolution led to large, popular armies whose impact was enhanced by the developing means of transporting them over long distances. There was a move away from limited wars of position, bound up with quarrels between individual rulers and shaped by logistical constraints and unreliable armies, to total wars engaging whole nations.[2] With Napoleon, wars became means by which one state could challenge the very existence of another. No longer were they an elaborate form of bargaining. The high stakes removed incentives to compromise and encouraged a fight to a bloody conclusion. Military maneuvers were no longer ritualistic—their impact reinforced by the occasional battle—but preludes to great confrontations that could see whole armies effectively eliminated and states subjugated.

This section opens with the introduction of the modern concept of strategy and then describes the views of its two key exponents, Baron Henri de

Jomini and Carl von Clausewitz. They developed their ideas at a time of great political turbulence, a time when individual battles redrew the maps of Europe and new challenges were thrown up by the need to mobilize, motivate, move, and direct mass armies. The focus was on battle and the possibility of inflicting such a defeat that the enemy would be left in a politically hopeless position. This was when the idea of the battle of annihilation was firmly implanted in military minds. Lost in this process was a view of battle as the "chance of arms" which until then had been accepted by the belligerents as an appropriate form of dispute resolution.

This view survived well into the nineteenth century, and arguably only collapsed in that century's second half. It was, however, always tenuous and its days were numbered. It was the product of a monarchical system in which the causes and outcomes of war were bound up with matters of most interest to rulers, such as dynastic succession or sovereignty over particular pieces of territory, and so it was vulnerable to the rise of nationalism and republicanism. It was part of a normative framework that was always subject to interpretation at its edges. In the most restrained version, victory was the agreed outcome of a day's fighting, which would leave one army triumphant on the field of battle, looking for booty and stripping enemy corpses. It still depended on the enemy accepting the result. Certain victories appeared to have more legitimacy than others, for example, those achieved without recourse to gross deceptions. But the notionally defeated sovereign could challenge his predicament by observing that while retreat might have been necessary, the other side took more casualties; or the retreat was in sufficiently good order so another battle could be fought. The victor had to calculate whether sufficient damage had been done to convince the enemy to now negotiate sensibly. This depended in part on what was at stake, as well as on whether the enemy had any capacity to fight back or else might be coerced through sieges and rampages through the countryside, which he was helpless to prevent.

Even a badly bruised opponent might find a way to continue resistance, regroup, or acquire an external ally. Given the uncertainties and explosive tendencies connected with war, was it wise to assume that this was no more than a form of violent diplomacy? If it was bound to end with a compromise, why not settle the matter with diplomacy before blood was shed, or look for alternative—possibly economic—forms of coercion? Forming alliances and undermining those of the enemy—evidently a matter of statecraft—could be of as much or even greater importance to a war's outcome than a display of brilliant generalship.

The starting point for nineteenth-century strategic discourse, however, was the expectation of a decisive battle, from which exceptions might be found, rather than the demands of statecraft, for which battle might be the exception. Military circles encouraged the characterization of the international system as extensions of the battlefield, as constant struggles for survival and domination.

Strategy as Profession and Product

If we consider strategy to be a particular sort of practical problem-solving, it has existed since the start of time. Even if the word was not always in use, we can now look back and observe how personalities engaged in activities that would later be called strategy. Did the arrival of a word to capture this activity make an important difference to the actual practice? Even after its introduction, *strategy* was not universally employed as a descriptor even by those who might now be considered accomplished strategists. What was different was the idea of strategy as a general body of knowledge from which leaders could draw. The strategist came to be a distinctive professional offering specialist advice to elites, and strategy became a distinctive product reflecting the complexity of situations in which states and organizations found themselves.

We noted earlier the role of the *stratēgos* in 5th-century Athens. According to Edward Luttwak, the ancient Greek and Byzantine equivalent to our *strategy* would have been *stratēgike episteme* (generals' knowledge) or *stratēgōn sophia* (generals' wisdom).[3] This knowledge took the form of compilations of stratagems, as in the *Strategematon*, the Greek title of the Latin work by Frontinus. The Greeks would have described what was known about the conduct of war as *taktike techne*, which included what we call tactics as well as rhetoric and diplomacy.

The word *strategy* only came into general use at the start of the nineteenth century. Its origins predated Napoleon and reflected the Enlightenment's growing confidence in empirical science and the application of reason. Even war, the most unruly of human activities, might be studied and conducted in the same spirit. This field of study at first was known as *tactics*, a word that had for some time referred to the orderly organization and maneuver of troops. *Tactics* defined as "the science of military movements" could, according to Beatrice Heuser, be traced back to the fourth century BCE. There was no corresponding definition of *strategy* until an anonymous sixth-century work linked it explicitly with the general's art. "Strategy is the means by which a commander may defend his own lands and defeat his enemies." In 900, the Byzantine emperor Leo VI wrote of *strategía* to provide an overall term for the business of the *strategos*. A few centuries later there was some knowledge of Leo's work, but when in 1554 a Cambridge professor translated the text into Latin, which lacks a word for strategy, he used "the art of the general" or "the art of command."[4]

In 1770, Jacques Antoine Hippolyte, Comte de Guibert, published his *Essai général de tactique*. Then only 27, Guibert was a precocious and extravagant French intellectual who had already acquired extensive military experience. He produced a systematic treatise on military science that captured the spirit of the Enlightenment and gained enormous influence. At issue was whether it was possible to overcome the indecisiveness of contemporary war. Guibert's view was that achieving a decisive result with a mass army required an ability to maneuver. He distinguished "elementary tactics," which became "tactics," from "grand tactics," which became "strategy." Guibert wanted a unified theory, raising tactics to "the science of all times, all places and all arms." His key distinction was between raising and training armies, and then using them in war.[5] By 1779, he was writing of "la stratégique."[6]

The sudden introduction of the word is attributed by Heuser to Paul Gédéon Joly de Maizeroy's translation of Leo's book into French in 1771. Joly de Maizeroy identified Leo's "science of the general" as being separate from the subordinate spheres of tactics. In a footnote, he observed: "*La stratégique* is thus properly said to be the art of the commander, to wield and employ appropriately and with adroitness all the means of the general in his hand, to move all the parts that are subordinate to him, and to apply them successfully." By 1777, a German translation of the work used the term *Strategie*. Joly de Maizeroy described strategy as "sublime" (a word also used by Guibert) and involving reason more than rules. There was much to consider: "In order to formulate plans, strategy studies the relationships between time, positions, means and different interests, and takes every factor into account...which is the province of dialectics, that is to say, of reasoning, which is the highest faculty of the mind."[7] The term now began to achieve a wide currency, offering a way of inserting deliberate, calculating thought into an arena previously remarkable for its absence.

In Britain from the start of the nineteenth century, a plethora of words emerged: *strategematic, strategematical, strategematist, strategemical*. All sought to convey the idea of being versed in strategies and stratagems. Thus, a strategemitor would devise stratagems, while a stratarchy referred to the system of rule in an army, starting with the top commander. This word was once used by British prime minister William Gladstone to refer to how armies would go beyond hierarchy to require absolute obedience to superior officers. Then there was stratarithmetry, which was a way of estimating how many men you had by drawing up an army or body of men into a given geometrical figure. An alternative word for strategist was strategian, which goes neatly with tactician—though this did not catch on.

The distinction between strategy and tactics was of acknowledged importance as a means of distinguishing between different levels of command and contact with the enemy. Thus strategy was the art of the commander-in-chief "projecting and directing the larger military movements and operations of a campaign," while tactics was "the art of handling forces in battle or in the immediate presence of the enemy."[8] Soon the word migrated away from its military context and into such diverse areas as trade, politics, and theology.

The speed with which the word *strategy* gained currency meant that it came to be used without a generally agreed upon definition. There was a consensus that strategy had something to do with the supreme commander and that it was about linking military means to the objects of war. It involved making connections between all that was going on in the military sphere beyond the more intimate and small-scale maneuvers and encounters handled at the lower levels of command. But the activities that came under the heading of strategy were also understood to be intensely practical, a consequence of the sheer size of the armies of the new age, the extraordinary demands posed by their movement and provisioning, and the factors that would govern how enemies should be approached. Much of this might be subject to forms of practical knowledge and principles that could be described in a systematic and instructive way, with checklists of considerations to be taken into account by the more forward-looking commanders. It is not surprising therefore that strategy became closely associated with planning. Questions of supply and transport limited what could be achieved, and calculations of firepower and fortification influenced decisions on the deployment of troops. Put this way, strategy covered all those aspects of a military campaign that might properly be determined in advance.

Improved maps made an enormous difference to planning of this sort. Developments in cartography meant that it was possible to consider how a campaign might develop by plotting its likely course on sheets of paper, representing base camps and lines of supply, enemy positions, and opportunities for maneuvers. A start had been made on the reconceptualization of war in spatial terms by a Henry Lloyd, who had left Britain because of his participation in the Jacobite rebellion of 1745 and then fought with a variety of European armies. Having observed that those who embraced the profession of arms took "little or no pains to study it," he claimed to have identified fixed principles of war that could vary only in their application.[9] Lloyd is credited with inventing the term *line of operations*, which remains in use to this day and describes an army's path from its starting point to its final destination. Lloyd influenced subsequent military theorists, including the Prussian Heinrich Dietrich von Bulow, who went to France in 1790 to experience the Revolution first hand. Having studied Napoleon's methods, he wrote on military affairs, including a *Practical Guide to Strategy* in 1805. He got somewhat carried away by the possibilities of geometric representations of armies preparing for battle. His reliance on mathematical principles led to him to offer proofs on how armies might constitute themselves and move forward, according to distances from their starting base and enemy objective. The approach can be discerned from his definition of strategy as "all enemy movements out of the enemy's cannon range or range of vision," so that tactics covered what happened within that range.[10] His observations on tactics were considered to have merit, but much to his chagrin his description of the "new war system" was ignored by Prussian generals.

Whatever the scientific method might bring to the battlefield, when it came to deciding on the moment, form, and conduct of battle, much would depend on the general's own judgment—perhaps more a matter of character, insight, and intuition than careful calculation and planning. When battle was joined, the theory could say little because of the many variables in play. At that point, war became an art form. Strategy could be considered a matter of science, in the sense of being systematic, empirically based, and logically developed, covering all those things that could be planned in advance and were subject to calculation. As art, strategy covered actions taken by bold generals who could achieve extraordinary results in unpromising situations.

Napoleon's Strategy

Napoleon preferred to keep the critical ingredients behind his approach beyond explanation. The art of war, he insisted, was simple and commonsensical. It was "all in execution...nothing about it is theoretical." The essence of the art was simple: "With a numerically inferior army" it was necessary to have "larger forces than the enemy at the point which is to be attacked or defended." How best to achieve that was an art that could "be learned neither from books nor from practice." This was matter for the military genius and therefore for intuition. Napoleon's contribution to strategy was not so much in his theory but in his practice. Nobody could think of better ways of using great armies to win great wars.

Napoleon was not creating new forms of warfare completely from scratch. He was building on the achievements of Frederick the Great, the most admired commander of his time. Frederick was king of Prussia from 1740 to 1786 and a reflective and prolific writer on war. His success was the result of turning his army into a responsive instrument, well trained and held together by tough discipline. Initially he preferred his wars to be "short and lively," which required accepting battle. Long wars exhausted a state's resources as well as its soldiers, and Frederick's country was relatively poor. His seizure of Silesia early in his reign, during the War of Austrian Succession, made his reputation as a tactical genius. Whitman uses this campaign as a prime example of how a "law of victory" could ensure restraint, so long as both sides accepted battle as a form of wager. Frederick observed that battles "decide the fortune of states" and could "put an end to a dispute that otherwise might never be settled." As kings were subject to "no superior tribunal," combat could "decide their rights" and "judge the validity of their reasons."[11]

Over time, however, Frederick became more wary of battle due to its dependence upon chance. Success might need to come through the accumulation of small gains rather than a single decisive encounter. Unlike Napoleon, Frederick preferred to avoid fighting too far from his own borders, did not expect to destroy the opposing army in battle, and avoided frontal attacks. His signature tactic was the "oblique order," an often complex maneuver requiring a disciplined force. It involved concentrating forces against the enemy's strongest flank while avoiding engagement on his own weak flank. If the enemy did not succumb, an orderly retreat would still be possible; if the enemy flank was overrun, the next step was to wheel round and roll up his line. What Frederick shared with Napoleon—and what later theorists celebrated in both—was the ability to create strength on the battlefield, even without an overall numerical advantage, and direct it against an enemy's vulnerabilities.

As a young officer, Napoleon also read Guibert and took from him some basic ideas which he made his own. In particular, he noted the need to launch attacks at the key points where superiority had been achieved, and to reach these points by moving quickly. Although Guibert had observed that "hegemony over Europe will fall to that nation which...becomes possessed of manly virtues and creates a national army," he had not seen conscription as the means to this end. He assumed the duties of a citizen and a soldier to be opposed. At most, a militia might be raised as a defensive force. The actual creation of the mass army can be credited to Lazar Carnot, a key figure in the French Revolution, who had an uneasy relationship with Napoleon but served him until 1815. It was Carnot who as minister of war used conscription to create the *levée en masse* and turned it into a formidable, trained, and disciplined organization. Carnot also showed how a mass army could be used as an offensive instrument by separating it into independent units that could move faster than the enemy, enabling attacks against the flanks and creating opportunities to cut off communications. Most of Napoleon's generals learned their trade under Carnot.

Napoleon's contribution was to grasp how the potential of the mass army could be realized. He imbibed the military wisdom of the Enlightenment and took advantage of the system created by Carnot in such a way as to upset not only traditional thinking about war but also the whole European balance of power. His genius lay not in the originality or novelty of his ideas on strategy but in their interpretation in context and the boldness of his execution. His focus was always on the decisive battle. He was prepared to embrace the inherent brutality of war and sought to generate sufficient concentrated violence to shatter the opposing army. This was the route to the political goal. An enemy with a broken army would be unwilling to resist political demands. As this required a comprehensive defeat, Napoleon had little interest in indirect strategies. When a point of weakness was found, extra forces would be poured in to break through. They could then move against the enemy from the rear or to the flanks. This required taking risks, for example, accepting vulnerabilities to his own rear and flanks as he concentrated strength. But Napoleon was not reckless. He would wait until the right moment to make his move. Since he put a priority on ensuring that he had the maximum strength, his great battles were often fought in obscure places where he saw an opportunity to strike with guaranteed superiority and utter ruthlessness. By combining political and military authority in one person, Napoleon was also in a position to act boldly without extensive consultations. His optimism, self-confidence, and extraordinary run of victories earned him the loyalty of his troops and kept his enemies apprehensive. This created a sense of irresistibility which he was always keen to exploit.

Napoleon never provided a complete account of his approach to war. He did not write of strategy, although he did refer to the "higher parts of war." His views were recorded in a number of maxims. They were often practical reflections on the standard military problems of his day and lack the universal quality of Sun Tzu's writings. Yet they capture the essence of his approach: bringing superior strength to bear at crucial moments ("God is on the side of the heaviest battalions"); defeating the enemy by destroying his army; viewing strategy as "the art of making use of time and space"; using time to gain strength when weaker; and compensating for physical inferiority with greater resolve, fortitude, and perseverance ("The moral is to the physical as three to one"). Many of his maxims revolved around the need to understand the enemy: by fighting too often with one enemy, "you will teach him all your art of war"; never do what the enemy wishes "for this reason alone, that he desires it"; never interrupt an enemy making a mistake; always show confidence, for you can see your own troubles but you cannot see those facing your enemy.[12]

Borodino

We now turn to a battle which was neither an exemplary success nor a notable defeat but acquired importance because it raised doubts about Napoleon's method. The battle of Borodino, some eighty miles from Moscow, was fateful in its consequences. Fought between the French and Russian armies on September 7, 1812, it involved some quarter of a million men. Of these, about seventy-five thousand were killed, wounded, or captured. Although the French came out on top, the Russians did not consider themselves beaten. Moscow was occupied following Borodino, but the Russians refused to agree to peace terms and Napoleon found that he lacked the capacity to sustain his army for any length of time. After five weeks, he began the famous and harsh retreat from Moscow.

It was not that Napoleon lacked a strategy when he began the campaign in the summer of 1812. He expected to follow his past practice of keeping the enemy guessing, finding a point to concentrate overwhelming superiority, and then attacking. Once Russian forces were destroyed, he could dictate peace terms to Tsar Alexander. To keep the war short and avoid being sucked into the Russian heartland, he wanted to fight his battle in the frontier regions. He was confident against Russian armies, since he boasted such stunning victories as Austerlitz in 1805. Russian leadership had generally been abysmal, and Napoleon assumed that the spineless aristocracy would oblige the Tsar to concede once French superiority had been made clear.

Tsar Alexander had a far better, although politically controversial, strategy. It drew on Russia's excellent intelligence network in France. Alexander knew from 1810 that a war was almost inevitable. This gave him time to think about a response and to make preparations, taking a candid view of Russia's weakness, including a lack of reliable allies. One option was to fight at the first opportunity before the French could advance far on sacred Russian soil, relying on the superior spirit of Russian troops and what might be achieved by catching the French by surprise. But Alexander knew the numbers were against him and saw the danger in pitting his main armies, without reserves, against a well-supplied and fully formed French army. A defeat would leave the country unprotected. This led him into a defensive strategy, although this meant giving up on an alliance. Austria and Prussia were reluctant to join an anti-French coalition involving a Russia that planned to retreat, but Alexander doubted that he could rely on them even if he embarked on an offensive strategy. Most importantly, he understood that Napoleon wanted battle. If that was what he wanted, that was exactly what he should not have.

The Russian plan therefore was to fall back, to the chagrin of many senior officers whose instincts were offensive. By trading space for time, they would gain strength. As the French advanced away from their supply lines, the Russians would get closer to theirs. Since Napoleon's system depended on big battles and rapid victories, the Russians would retreat, raid enemy communications with their much superior light cavalry, and wear down Napoleon's forces. "We must avoid big battles until we have fallen right back to our supply lines."[13]

The Russians knew what they needed to do, but they had no actual plan of retreat. That depended on when and how Napoleon made his first move. When it came, the retreat had a degree of improvisation, but it was managed better than Napoleon's advance. The emperor was prepared for an early battle but not for a long advance into unforgiving terrain in the face of inclement weather. As Napoleon chased the Russians in search of a battle, he exhausted his men and particularly his horses. Only as he got close to Moscow could he be confident that he would at last get his battle. Despite his tired and depleted force, Napoleon stuck with his original plan on the assumption that the Russians would not give up Moscow without a fight.

Facing him in charge of the Russian forces was General Mikhail Kutuzov, a shrewd officer with a good understanding of the attitudes of ordinary soldiers and the Russian people, as well as considerable experience in war. But Kutuzov was now 65, physically and mentally slower than before, and surrounded by flatterers. When the battle came, his deployments and command arrangements were haphazard: he delegated his powers of command to subordinate generals to act as they saw fit in the circumstances. His passivity left the impression that he had no idea what was going on or what to do next.

Yet the revelation at Borodino was how much Napoleon was off form and off maxim. The advance into Russia had been unexpectedly challenging and costly in men and materiel. By the time of the battle, the Grand Armée had already lost a third of its original 450,000 men—without a proper fight. Although much is made of the terrible impact of the Russian winter on the retreat from Moscow, the initial and critical damage was done by the Russian summer. The Russians enjoyed a notional numerical advantage at the time of the battle, although this evaporated when some 31,000 Russian militiamen without much by way of weapons or training were subtracted, leaving around 130,000 French facing 125,000 Russians.[14] The emperor himself had put on fat, having enjoyed the good life to excess, and had lost the energy of his earlier years. On the day of the battle he was also unwell, suffering from fever and a painful inability to urinate. He barely seemed in charge.

Napoleon's subordinate generals conducted the battle almost independently of each other and without the cohesion he would once have imposed. Instead of his forces being committed against one particular line of attack, there were a series of uncoordinated probes against the Russian positions. Although his superior firepower blasted holes in the Russian defenses, the enemy fought doggedly and did not surrender—much to Napoleon's consternation. When breakthroughs were possible he dithered, bothered by practicalities when bold maneuvers were proposed to him. With little left of his army to spare at a critical moment, he held back the Imperial Guard out of concern that he would have little left for his next battle.

In past battles he had been an evident presence, riding around to make his own assessments of the situation at the front and to enthuse his troops. On this day, he was absent. A French officer observing the emperor's indecision in the face of contradictory reports about Russian strength, described Napoleon's "suffering and dejected face, his features sunk, and a dull look; giving his orders languishingly, in the midst of these dreadful warlike noises, to which he seemed completely a stranger." Mikaberidze adds that Napoleon was "unrecognizable and his lethargy may have been the most decisive factor in the battle, as he rejected proposals that could have delivered victory."[15]

The emperor took comfort in the fact that at the end of the day he occupied the battlefield and had inflicted greater harm on the enemy than his own forces had suffered. But the Russian army was not annihilated, and those that were not killed or wounded largely escaped. Napoleon had expected to take many prisoners, but the actual haul was small. He now lacked the capacity to finish the Russians off in another battle. A large country with a large population could absorb the losses.

Kutuzov managed to withdraw his forces in an orderly fashion. His one important, absolutely critical, decision was to encourage Napoleon to enter Moscow instead of chasing his army in order to inflict what might have been a decisive defeat. This had not been his original intent. Prior to Borodino, he had resisted the idea that Moscow was just another town that might have to be sacrificed for the greater good of saving the Russian empire. Now Kutuzov acknowledged that he could not save both Moscow and the army and that if the army was lost, then Moscow would go anyway. "Napoleon," he observed, "is like a torrent which we are still too weak to stem. Moscow is the sponge which will suck him in." Napoleon allowed himself to be sucked in. As the city was being occupied, fires began and ultimately destroyed two-thirds of it.

Napoleon expected the Tsar to sue for peace. Soon he realized that with the Russians unwilling to either fight another battle or negotiate a settlement, he was stranded, unable to sustain his forces through hunger and cold. He had no choice but to return to France. The journey home was bitter and crippling. When the Russians eventually advanced, the Tsar was able to realize the ultimate goal of his own strategy, which was to revive the anti-Napoleon coalition in Europe.

After this debacle and a first exile, Napoleon made one further attempt at glory, which came to grief at Waterloo in 1815. This master of war had been defeated and those writing the textbooks were left to ponder not only the sources of his original success but the causes of his ultimate failure. For present during the Russian campaign, though playing minor roles, were the two greatest nineteenth-century theorists of war: Carl von Clausewitz and Baron Antoine Henri de Jomini.

*{W}ar is not an exercise of the will directed at inanimate matter, as
is the case with the mechanical arts, or at matter which is animate but
passive and yielding, as is the case with the human mind and emotions in
the fine arts. In war, the will is directed at an animate object that reacts.*

—Clausewitz, *On War*

CARL VON CLAUSEWITZ, born 1780, learned his military craft in the
Prussian army as it failed to resist Napoleon's mass army. Dismayed at
Prussia's craven subordination to victorious France, Clausewitz joined the
Russian army (hence his appearance at Borodino) before returning to the
Prussian army for the campaign that culminated at Waterloo and the final
defeat of Bonaparte. Along with the bulk of the European officer class, he had
been mesmerized by Napoleon. In 1812, he saw at close quarters the great
man's fallibility: his loss of the killer instinct at the critical moment, the limits to his genius. Clausewitz wrote a full account of the campaign, though his
own role—and his account—was hampered by his lack of Russian. He did
help organize the Convention of Tauroggen, whereby the Prussian contingent
that had been obliged to march with Napoleon came to the Russian side.

Clausewitz did not think Borodino a classic of strategy. In the whole battle he found "not a single trace of an art or superior intelligence," the result
coming "less from a carefully considered decision than from indecision and

circumstance." His initial, and not unreasonable, conclusion was that the "vastness" of Russia made it impossible "to cover and occupy strategically." A "large country of European civilization" could not "be conquered without the help of internal discord."[1] Later he was harsher on Napoleon for not chasing the Russian army and described Borodino as a battle that was "never completely fought out."[2] Both judgments had important implications: the first that the degree of popular support for the state made a difference when dealing with external threats; the second that a victory that did not leave the enemy fatally wounded was of limited value.

Clausewitz's military reputation in Prussia was modest, and when he was sent to direct the war school it was in an administrative capacity. He did not teach, but he did have the time to collect his thoughts about this remarkable and transformational period of warfare and pull them together for a masterwork, *On War*.

War's tendency toward the absolute both thrilled and appalled the younger Clausewitz. The more mature Clausewitz appreciated the reasons why wars in practice still fell short of the absolute and that, post-Napoleon just as pre-Napoleon, they might be fought for more modest ends than the survival of states. It was this that led to his determination to engage in a major revision of his whole text, a project that was only partly completed when he died. According to one interpretation, this moment of truth came upon Clausewitz gradually; by another view, 1827 was more of a crisis as he realized that his theory of war failed to account sufficiently for the various forms in which it had actually occurred.[3] He was still in the process of revising *On War* when he was struck down by cholera in 1832. His widow did the best she could with the book's posthumous publication, but the final version inevitably left commentators guessing about what might have been found had he lived to complete the work to his satisfaction.

Jomini

While Clausewitz was seeking to advise the Russians in 1812, Jomini was on the French side. In the retreat from Moscow, he lost his papers at a river crossing as the remnants of the French army were harassed by Russian partisans. Although Clausewitz is now considered to be the greater of the two and Jomini is rarely read, it was Jomini who for most of the nineteenth century was taken to be the foremost interpreter of the Napoleonic method. Napoleon was said to have remarked that Jomini betrayed the innermost secrets of his strategy. Jomini certainly claimed, based on his observations of the master, to have discerned basic principles of warfare. This earned him the "dubious title of founder of modern strategy."[4]

Jomini was born in Switzerland in 1779. Though he started work as a banker in Paris, he joined the French army in 1797 and came under the patronage of then General and eventually Marshal Michel Ney. Jomini wrote a treatise on the campaigns of Frederick the Great in 1803. This work contained those core beliefs which sustained him until his death in 1869 at the age of 90. He held staff positions for both Napoleon and Ney, but was a difficult egotist and a serial resigner. By 1813 he had risen to become Ney's chief of staff, but after he was denied promotion to *general de division* he offered his services to Russia, where he became a full general. His core ideas were published in his *Art of War* (always a popular title), which was first published in 1830 and then in a revised form in 1838.[5] His book has been described as "the greatest military textbook of the nineteenth century."[6] By elucidating the enduring principles of strategy, Jomini sought to "make instruction easier, operational judgment sounder, and mistakes less frequent." *The Art of War* was published widely. This meant that opposing armies might well have been following the same precepts, and so the advice would become self-neutralizing, unless one side dared to seek advantage by breaking Jomini's rules.

To Jomini, strategy was the sphere of activity between the political, where decisions were made about who to fight, and the tactical, which was the sphere of actual combat. By saying that strategy was the art of making war upon the map, he was interested in how the theater of operations as a whole was conceived by the commander and the moves against the enemy formulated, while taking advantage of the spatial awareness made possible by modern cartography. "Strategy decides where to act; logistics brings the troops to this point; grand tactics decides the manner of execution and the employment of the troops."[7]

Politics and tactics were governed by different principles, and Jomini had surprisingly little to say about either. According to John Shy, the only aspect of war that "truly interested him concerned the supreme commander, the Frederick or Napoleon who played the great bloody game, who by sheer intellect and will dominated the men who served him and used them to defeat his enemies." Jomini's armies appeared as "faceless masses, armed and fed in mysterious ways." Their commanders would show their greatness by massing force against weaker enemy forces at some decisive point.[8] Both Frederick the Great and Napoleon had demonstrated the importance of following this core principle, though it was by no means straightforward in application. Focusing on one point to the exclusion of others, and leaving your own flanks vulnerable, required a degree of boldness and an ability to weigh risks. Ways had to be found to mass the army for the attack and to identify the main point against which to direct the attack.

Jomini failed to test the historical cases which did not conform to his precepts. He also assumed that military units of equivalent size were essentially equal in how they were armed, trained, disciplined, supplied, and motivated. Strategy was therefore important because only the quality of the commanders and their decisions really made a difference. This was why he could conceive of it as following timeless principles, which required him to assert during his long life that major material shifts, such as the use of railways, were matters of detail. If the principles really were timeless, why was Napoleon such a revelation? Jomini's answer was that the growing maturity in military thought meant that the principles were properly appreciated.[9] He was not the last to use this argument.

Before Jomini went out of fashion during the twentieth century he was the first port of call for any aspiring strategist and a model of lucidity and intelligibility. Jomini might not always have been a scintillating read, but he was much easier to follow than Clausewitz.

The relationship between the two was complex. The younger Clausewitz clearly borrowed from Jomini, and the second edition of the *Art of War* took into account Clausewitz's criticisms.[10] The two men never met and did not speak warmly of each other. On many operational issues, the differences were not great. Jomini claimed to be aware of the dangers of theoretical pedantry, while Clausewitz grasped the importance of operational techniques. Jomini's prime purpose was instruction and he found Clausewitz's theorizing overblown. As Clausewitz developed his ideas, he differentiated himself from von Bulow's mathematical approach, but his criticisms might also be taken to apply to Jomini. He observed that efforts to "equip the conduct of war with principles, rules, or even systems" failed because they could not "take an adequate account of the endless complexities involved." "Pity the soldier," wrote Clausewitz, "who is supposed to crawl among these scraps of rules, not good enough for genius, which genius can ignore, or laugh at. No; what genius does is the best rule, and theory can do no better than show how and why this should be the case."[11] Clausewitz came to be celebrated as a greater theorist of war, but Jomini had enduring appeal to military planners. Because he developed his theories while Napoleon was at his peak, Jomini's writing showed an optimism that is lacking in Clausewitz. Hew Strachan notes how Jomini's confidence in his principles, his "rational and managerial," "prospective and purposeful" theory of war and self-contained view of battle appealed to generations of American generals and admirals.[12]

Clausewitz's Strategy

In *On War*, Clausewitz was attempting something very ambitious. More than a textbook for an aspiring general, this was a whole theory of war. His achievement was to develop a conceptual framework that captured war's essence sufficiently for subsequent generations to return to it when seeking to make sense of the conflicts of their own time. The ambiguities and tensions in *On War* allowed Marxists, Nazis, and liberals to claim it as authoritative support for their own theories and strategies.[13] Even those who considered *On War* wrongheaded and out of date entered into direct competition, as if their own credibility depended on undermining Clausewitz.[14] Contributing to the advanced scholarship on Clausewitz now requires discussing the adequacy of the available translations, the interaction of biography and intellectual development, what might be read into occasional phrases that are suggestive of larger thoughts, and the dual meanings carried by key concepts and their application in particular cases.[15]

With this in mind, we can explore the theory of strategy that emerged from Clausewitz's theory of war. Clausewitz's most famous dictum, that war is a continuation of policy by other means, is a charter for strategists. The choice of the word *policy* in the translation by Michael Howard and Peter Paret reflected their view that the reference needed to be something above everyday "politics," a word which they saw as having negative connotations in Britain and the United States. Bassford has argued that policy sounds too settled, unilateral, and rational, while politics has the virtue of conveying interactivity, binding rivals together in their conflict.[16] Both meanings can be made to work. The key point is that insisting on political purpose takes war away from mindless violence. This dictum does not propose that war is always a sensible expression of policy, or that the movement from politics to war is from one defined state to another. The difference lies in the violence and the sharpness of the confrontation between two opposed wills. This in turn exacerbates the influence of those factors of emotion and chance that are evident in the political sphere but become so much more significant in the military, and constantly complicate war's conduct. So while Clausewitz by no means rules out an effective strategy, for this would render *On War* a pointless exercise, his stress was on the limits to strategy, the constraints that make it unwise to try to be too clever.

The challenge for politics, and therefore strategy, was to impose a semblance of rationality, in terms of the dogged pursuit of state objectives. Although his dictum came to be regularly cited as an authority for civilian primacy over the military, Antulio Echevarria cautions that many of

Clausewitz's thoughts on politics and international conflict, especially in the unrevised sections, were circular and deterministic. The key to Clausewitz's greatness as theorist of war lay instead in the observation that was at the heart of his mature thought, that war was shaped by a

> remarkable trinity—composed of primordial violence, hatred, and enmity, which are to be regarded as a blind natural force; of the play of chance and probability within which the creative spirit is free to roam; and of its element of subordination, as an instrument of policy, which makes [war] subject to reason alone.[17]

His theory depended on the dynamic interplay of these three factors. The trinity superseded the dictum, for it suggested that politics was not in command but one factor among three. With respect to the survival of the state in a challenging international system—which was how Clausewitz understood the concept—politics must always set the terms for war, but politics could not challenge the "grammar of war" lest it reduce the chances of success and so the achievement of the ultimate objective. This could in turn lead to military actions with great political consequences. Despite the apparent subordination of the military to politics, the dynamic quality of the trinity helped explained why the relationship was not so simple.[18]

As a clash of opposing wills, a duel on a grand scale, war in the ideal sense tended to absolute violence. Having posed this possibility, Clausewitz pointed to the other two parts of the trinity to explain why it was unlikely to be realized. Politics was one source of restraint, but friction was another. This was one of Clausewitz's most significant contributions to military thought. Friction helped explain the difference between war as it might be—that is, absolute and unrestrained—and actual war. He explained the phenomenon in one of his most celebrated passages:

> Everything in war is simple, but the simplest thing is difficult. The difficulties accumulate and end by producing a kind of friction that is inconceivable unless one has experienced war...Countless minor incidents—the kind you can never really foresee—combine to lower the general level of performance, so that one always falls short of the intended goal.

The result was "effects that cannot be measured, just because they are largely due to chance." Friction thus caused delay and confusion. Action in war became like walking in water, and vision was regularly obscured. "All actions take place in something virtually akin to dusk, which in addition, like fog or moonlight, gives objects an exaggerated size and a grotesque view."[19]

Generals in charge of military organizations were doomed to disappointment. Everything would take longer than it should, and it would be hard to generate the flexibility needed to keep up with events.

Within the paradoxical trinity, violence and chance could still be subordinated to politics and the application of reason. If the strategist did not apply reason, war would become progressively chaotic and unpredictable. The challenge for the intelligent strategist was to anticipate both the enemy and all those elements of friction and chance that got in the way. The correct approach was not to give up and assume that chaos and unpredictability would mock all plans and overwhelm best efforts but rather to prepare for such eventualities in advance. The test of a great general was making a plan that he could see through. Clausewitz wrote about the need for the commander to be a military genius, but he did not necessarily mean an exceptional, once-in-a-generation individual such as Napoleon. Genius required a grasp of the demands of war, the nature of the enemy, and the need to stay cool at all times. Indeed, Clausewitz was wary of the general who tried to be too smart. He preferred those who kept their imaginations in check and a firm grip on the harsh realities of battle.

So while his description of war suggested that the wise course would be to retain maximum flexibility and prepare to seize opportunities as they arose, he came to the opposite conclusion, arguing for a clear plan of conduct based on a series of connected, sequential steps. He preferred a stress on careful planning without distractions. The strategist must "draft the plan of the war, and the aim will determine the series of actions intended to achieve it."[20] A war should not be started without a plan for its conduct firmly in mind. Once implementation had begun, it should only be amended at times of unavoidable necessity.[21] Clausewitz's definition of strategy as "the use of the engagement to achieve the objectives of the war" translated political goals into a military aim. The strategist would "shape the individual campaigns and, within these, decide on the individual engagements."[22] Preferring to enter war with a plan for victory was understandable. But why the confidence that any plan could be implemented?

Clausewitz offered three reasons. First, despite all the talk of unpredictability, not everything was a mystery. Certain actions had known effects. An enemy attacked from behind or caught in an ambush would exhibit lower morale and less bravery. Most importantly, it was possible to make relatively objective assessments of the opposing sides, taking into account their experience and their "spirit and temper." While the enemy's own plans and responses to situations could not be known exactly, the laws of probability could be applied. Confronting an excitable visionary would require a different plan than that for an enemy known to be hard and calculating. The bold would be granted more respect than the cautious, the active more than the passive, and the clever more than the stupid.

A second factor was the unreliability of intelligence. Without a robust starting plan, occasional reports might cause an undue deviation: "Many intelligence reports in war are contradictory; even more are false, and most are uncertain." Furthermore, intelligence tended to have a pessimistic bias. The exaggeration of bad news led to gloomy and despondent commanders who conjured up landscapes of imagined perils: "War has a way of masking the stage with scenery crudely daubed with fearsome apparitions." These vivid impressions overwhelmed systematic thought, and so "even the man who planned the operation and now sees it being carried out may well lose confidence in his earlier judgment." He must therefore exorcise false appearances by trusting instead in "the laws of probability" and in his own judgment gained from "knowledge of men and affairs and from common sense."[23] With improved information gathering, Clausewitz's advice to ignore timely intelligence now appears as more of a recipe for disaster than a means of avoiding unnecessary panic.

Third, both sides were subject to friction, so it was a poor excuse for defeat. The question was who could cope with it better. The essence of good generalship was to triumph over friction, to the extent possible, through both careful planning and maintaining a presence of mind when the unexpected happened.[24] "The good general must know friction in order to overcome it whenever possible, and in order not to expect a standard of achievement in his operations which this very friction makes impossible."[25] This important qualification warned against excessive strategic ambition.

So size mattered. Armies were "so much alike" that there was "little difference between the best and the worst of them." The most reliable means to success, in both tactics and strategy, was therefore superiority in numbers: "The skill of the greatest commanders may be counterbalanced by a two-to-one ratio in the fighting forces." Clausewitz could see the attraction of cunning, indirect strategies, which could confuse the enemy and lower morale. He noted that it might be thought that "strategy" took its name from "trickery," but he saw little historical evidence that tricks (stratagems) could be effective and considered it dangerous to make a false impression by deploying large forces, which might be left in the wrong position when they were really needed. At the tactical level, surprise was important and attainable, but at the strategic level the mobilization and movement of forces were likely to give the game away. Friction was also a major factor, holding up the sort of movements necessary to catch the enemy unawares. So when it came to the choice of force or guile, Clausewitz opted for the former. The "strategist's chessmen do not have the kind of mobility that is essential for stratagem and cunning...accurate and penetrating understanding is a more useful and essential asset for the commander than any gift for cunning." His advice was to keep the plan simple, especially against a capable opponent. A simple plan would require the excellent execution of each engagement; for this reason, tactical success was vital. In this respect, the strategic plan survived so long as successive engagements were being won.

This put a premium on knowing when to stop. An enemy willing and able to redouble his efforts put a final victory out of reach. Another important Clausewitzian concept was the "culminating point of victory," the point at which further attack could lead to a reversal of fortunes. It was "important to calculate this point correctly when planning the campaign."[26] This was about the developing balance of advantage as a campaign progressed. After being wounded, would the enemy collapse with exhaustion or be enraged? What were the distractions to be avoided, the opportunistic but diverting targets away from the main line of advance? There would be temptations to capture "certain geographical points" or seize "undefended provinces," as if they had value in themselves as "windfall profits," but that could put the main aim at risk. A consistent, focused approach should discourage disruption. Here were the reasons for Napoleon's failure in 1812.

The Russian campaign and lack of confidence in strategies based on surprise and complex maneuvers led Clausewitz to the view that the advantage lay with the defense. The forward movement necessary to occupy enemy territory taxed the attacker's energies and resources, while the defender was able to use this time to prepare to receive the attacker. "Time which is allowed to pass unused accumulates to the credit of the defender." Surprise could work as much in favor of the defense as the offense. It was about catching the enemy unawares with regard to "plans and dispositions, especially those concerning the distribution of forces." The attacker was "free to strike at any point along the whole line of defense, and in full force," but could still be surprised if the defender was stronger than expected at the spot chosen. The defender operated on familiar ground, could choose his position carefully, and enjoyed short supply lines and a friendly local population, which could be a source of intelligence and even reserves. Even if the offensive succeeded, the occupying force might be ground down through insurrectionary or partisan warfare, as Napoleon discovered in Spain. Moreover, so long as the defending state could avoid surrender, other states might join in on its side. According to prevailing notions of the "balance of power," other states were likely to intervene against a determined aggressor in order to prevent it becoming too powerful. Even the strongest individual state could be defeated by an organized coalition ranged against it and determined to restore equilibrium to the international system. This too Napoleon discovered to his cost. But while Clausewitz described defense as the stronger form of fighting, he also noted that its purpose was negative. It was limited, passive, concerned only with preservation. Only attack could secure the objectives of war. Defense was unavoidably preferred by the weak, but once there was a favorable balance of strength, the incentives were to move to the attack. "A sudden powerful transition to the offensive—the flashing sword of vengeance—is the greatest moment for the defense."[27]

When it came to the offense, another important Clausewitzian concept was the "center of gravity" (*Schwerpunkt*). Along with a number of his other concepts, including friction, this was taken from the physics of the day. A center of gravity represented the point where the forces of gravity could be said to converge within an object, the spot at which the object's weight was balanced in all directions. Striking at or otherwise upsetting the center of gravity could cause objects to lose balance and fall to the ground. For a simple, symmetrical shape, finding the center of gravity was straightforward. Once an object had moving parts or changes in composition, the center would be constantly shifting. Clausewitz never quite got to grips with the metaphor. "A center of gravity," he explained, "is always found where the mass is concentrated the most densely. It presents the most effective target for a blow; furthermore, the heaviest blow is that struck by the center of gravity." The *Schwerpunkt* was "the central feature of the enemy's power" and therefore "the point against which all our energies should be directed." This required tracing back the "ultimate substance" of enemy strength to its source and then directing the attack against this source. The target might not be a concentration of physical strength but possibly the point where enemy forces connected and were given direction. Any disruption would maximize effects beyond the immediate point to the larger whole.

Though he did not fully follow this through, Clausewitz recognized that the critical point might be a capital city or the coherence of an alliance. With respect to alliances, which had been central to the ebb and flow of the Napoleonic Wars, Clausewitz understood that individual members would always have their own interests at the fore and that joining an alliance could carry risks (for example, by attracting force away from a partner or by having to aid a much weaker partner). If the alliance was to prosper, it needed a unity of political purpose or at least "the interests and forces of most of the allies" must be "subordinate to those of the leader." This offered a center of gravity that an opponent could challenge, disrupting the alliance by encouraging disunity.[28] Not all peacetime alliances even turned into a joint enterprise against a common foe, as the matter became akin to a "business deal" and actions were "clogged with diplomatic reservations."[29]

From this it can be seen that the identity of a center of gravity was not obvious. The concept only made any sense if it was assumed that the enemy could be viewed holistically, as a unity, so that an attack on the point where it came together could throw it off balance or cause collapse. But there might be no obvious single focal point, if the enemy did not present itself in that way. On this basis, a loose coalition might be harder to disrupt than a tight alliance, although it might fight less effectively for the same reason.[30] If the enemy was not totally committed—for example, in a limited war—there might be even less reason to expect that a blow against its army would have an impact much beyond the area in which it was committed. Yet it was this concept, as much as any other of Clausewitz's, that came to be embedded in Western military thought, although often as a source of confusion rather than clarity.

The Sources of Victory

As Clausewitz described the nature of war, strategy became a sustained act of will, required in order to master its terrible uncertainties and resulting from human frailties and the capricious impact of chance. Since the enemy faced the same problems, it was still possible to prevail by bringing superior force to bear against the enemy's center of gravity. Clausewitz was of the view, almost taken for granted in his time, that once the enemy army was defeated in battle, the route to victory was clear. Without an army a state was helpless. It could either be eliminated, gobbled up in its entirety, or forced to accept whatever terms the victor might impose. Because of this, states would do everything possible to avoid defeat and carry on the fight in some way. In the new post-1789 era, this was as much a matter of popular enthusiasm as governmental judgment.

Clausewitz understood how policy linked the statesman and the general: policy gave the general his objectives and the resources available to meet them. As for these objectives, Strachan refers to a creed of 1815, "For me the chief rules of politics [or policy] are: never be helpless; expect nothing from the generosity of another; do not give up an objective before it becomes impossible; hold sacred the honor of the state."[31] In giving direction to strategy, therefore, policy was essentially an expression of national interests in relations with other states. Clausewitz acknowledged, but did not really explore, the impact of the internal politics of the state on strategy, as a particular form of friction. It was important that the commander-in-chief be part of government, in order to be able to explain the strategy being followed and help assess its relationship with policy. Clausewitz could not but be aware of how strong, popular national feelings created their own pressures for war and a determination to fight to the bitter end. It was, however, largely through a growing sense of the limits of what could be achieved through war that he began to consider the possibility of war pursued for limited ends, as it had been in the eighteenth century.

Though a state that had lost its army was effectively beaten, "victory consists not only in the occupation of the battlefield, but in the destruction of the enemy's physical and psychic forces, which is usually not attained until the enemy is pursued after a victorious battle."[32] If enemy armed forces were destroyed, whatever was wanted from the enemy could be seized and its public opinion would be cowed. Yet, as at Borodino, total destruction of the enemy army might not be possible. Even if achieved, the result might only be temporary. A defeated enemy might rise again. It would harbor thoughts of revenge, of reversing the setback. As victory might be temporary rather than durable in its effects, it might be prudent to negotiate a settlement under the most favorable terms when the optimum position has been reached.

Napoleon's career warned of the consequences of relying on military victory as the sole means of achieving political objectives. He wanted complete hegemony in Europe. There was a notion, still to be found among some international relations theorists, that this was an entirely natural goal for a great power. In practice, because victory could never be complete, it was a recipe for continuing war and eventually a friendless defeat. Napoleon's stunning victories over the Austrians and Russians in 1805, and then the Prussians the next year, did not take them out of the picture. Having supinely accepted the result of battle, they re-entered the fight, this time understanding France's methods better. As Napoleon discovered, the obvious counters to a regular army seeking a decisive battle were guerrilla warfare or reconstituted armies combining in a formidable coalition to ensure numerical superiority. He had relied on battle to achieve his objectives but did not have a clear notion of how these objectives could result in a new European political order with any sort of stability. It was hard to dominate the continent on the basis of methods that others could copy. Undoubtedly a genius in battle, Napoleon lacked political subtlety. He inclined toward punitive peace terms and was poor at forging coalitions.

If the aim of war was a favorable peace, then military operations were a means to this end. War that was "a complete untrammeled, absolute manifestation of violence (as the pure concept would require)" would "usurp the place of policy the moment policy had brought it into being." Policy would be driven away and war would rule by its own laws "very much like a mine that can explode only in the manner or direction predetermined by the setting."[33] In accepting that war could be fought for limited objectives and was not inevitably absolute in means or ends, there were still perplexing problems. The more ambitious the objectives, the more a state would commit to war and the more violent it would become. But the corollary could not be guaranteed. A war begun with limited objectives might not be fought by correspondingly limited means. Combat might be infused with the purposes of war but was shaped by armies in opposition. This created a reciprocal effect that could generate explosive forces from within, whatever the attempts to establish controls from without. We now tend to call this process "escalation." Popular engagement could aggravate the effect. "Between two peoples and states such tensions, such a mass of hostile feeling, may exist," Clausewitz observed, "that the slightest quarrel can produce a wholly disproportionate effect—a real explosion."[34]

In this tension we find the clue to Clausewitz's enduring influence. He understood that rational policy could impose itself on war, but it was always competing with the blind natural forces of "violence, hatred and enmity," as well as probability and chance. He linked policy, chance, and hatred to government, the army, and the people, respectively, although the link perhaps gave a restrictive, institutional form to these attributes. Each state had its own trinity, in tension within itself as well as with that of the opposing side. "Where policy is pitted against passion, where hostility ousts rationality, the characteristics of war itself can subordinate and usurp those of the 'trinity.'"[35] This broader political context underlined the basic point. Clausewitz accepted that the military task should be set by the politicians. Once that had been accomplished, the military could expect the politicians to use a military victory to best advantage. At the time, the normal assumption was that a political victory would naturally follow a military victory. If the assumption was wrong, then strategy's focus on military affairs was insufficient. It was about the clash of opposing forces when the real issue concerned the clash of opposing states.

The Roman origins of the word *victory* located it firmly in the military sphere. Jomini and Clausewitz understood that the objective of war came from outside the military sphere. Their basic instinct, however, was that with the "retirement of the enemy from the field of battle," terms could be imposed. There was some proportion between ends and means. But the problem remained that while a military victory was measurable, a political victory was not necessarily so. The forms of resistance and disaffection a defeated people might show could soon compromise the apparent achievements on the battlefield. If the broader political consequences of war were difficult to anticipate, then the military was likely to be left exploring its own tangible goals without regard to the broader context. Moreover, as Napoleon's career demonstrated, simply taking the same approach to military strategy in a series of repeat performances was unlikely to sustain a high level of results. Opponents would see the pattern and work out the counters. Brian Bond noted how this raised a fundamental problem: "If strategy was a science whose principles could be learnt what was to prevent all the belligerents learning them? In that case stalemate or attrition must result."[36]

CHAPTER 8 | The False Science

Tell me how the Germans have trained you to fight Bonaparte by this
new science you call 'strategy.'

—Tolstoy, *War and Peace*

THE MISERIES AND privations associated with the Napoleonic Wars
led to the development of an international peace movement. Over the
course of the nineteenth century, this movement encouraged the formation
of "peace societies" and the convening of humanitarian conferences. War was
denounced as not only uncivilized, wasteful, and destructive, but also fundamentally irrational. In particular, it was an offense against economics. This
was put most succinctly by John Stuart Mill in 1848: "It is commerce which
is rapidly rendering war obsolete, by strengthening and multiplying the personal interests which act in natural opposition to it." The eager proponents
of free trade saw how this could create forms of international intercourse that
would render resort to war self-evidently foolish as well as awful, producing
a formidable combination of morality and utilitarianism.[1]

The British proponents of free trade might have thought this a far more
efficient way of managing international affairs than one based on nationalism
and war, with peace dependent on a tenuous balance of power. From the perspective of those less well placed, this appeared as a self-serving claim. The
Prussian economist Friedrich List observed, in an argument that many still

find compelling, that free trade would result in "a universal subjection of the less advanced nations to the supremacy of the predominant manufacturing, commercial, and naval power."[2] A far greater problem was to ignore the factor that had so stunned Clausewitz during his early military career, a force that "beggared all imagination." The French Revolution had brought the people, with all their passion and fervor, to the fore. Napoleon had turned this into a source of his power, using it to develop his own personality cult and draw on popular enthusiasm to create an army with high morale and commitment, convinced of an inextricable, patriotic link between their own well-being and the success of the state. Clausewitz's grasp of the significance of this new factor, which led him to make it part of his trinity, helped make his theory so durable. He understood the impact of popular passion on how wars were fought, by undermining attempts at restraint, and he recognized nationalism as a source of war. As France became seen as a threat, people elsewhere rallied behind their own flags. The people identified not with each other but with the nation. "Between two peoples," Clausewitz observed, "there can be such tensions, such a mass of inflammable material."[3]

This went against notions of progressive civility in international affairs and added a cautionary note to demands for greater democracy. It undermined the claims of liberal reformers that war was an elite conspiracy. The speed and ease with which a belligerent nationalism could be tapped could therefore come as a rude shock to the radical, anti-war free-marketeers. The Crimean War that began just after the century's midway point demonstrated the strength of popular enthusiasm (even in Britain) for war-making. Not for the last time would liberal reformers find themselves caught between dispassionate utilitarianism and passionate democracy. This chapter discusses how this issue of war and politics was considered by two very distinctive personalities, neither of whom were liberals: the Russian writer Count Leo Tolstoy, who disputed that mass armies were ever truly controlled by their generals, and the German Field Marshal Helmuth von Moltke, who explored to the full the possibilities and limitations of command.

Tolstoy and History

The experience of Crimea had a very personal impact on Leo Tolstoy, a young, aristocratic Russian officer posted to Sebastapol during the war. Tolstoy was attracted to the good life but preoccupied with religion. He began to acquire fame as a writer by sending commentaries back from the front. They were filled with his sharp observations of how individuals were caught up in the arbitrariness of conflict. Tolstoy witnessed Russian soldiers cut down by enemy fire and their bodies left behind as the army retreated. He became increasingly annoyed at the insensitivity and incompetence of Russia's elite and explored how literature could express the experiences of the peasantry as well as the nobility. In 1863, he began six years of work that would lead to his masterpiece, *War and Peace*. Though a diligent researcher who studied documents, interviewed survivors, and walked around the battlegrounds of 1812, his approach was antipathetic to that of professional historians, just as it broke with conventions of fiction in its approach to plot. The book was, he explained, "what the author wanted and was able to express, in the form in which it is expressed." Part of the mixture, introduced during the book's later revisions, included short essays challenging conventional views of history and, by extension, a Clausewitzian view of strategy.

Clausewitz represented much of what Tolstoy opposed. He even made a minor appearance in *War and Peace*. Prince Andrei Bolkonsky (assumed to be representing Tolstoy's views) overheard a conversation between two Germans, Adjutant General Wolzogen and Clausewitz. One said, "The war must be extended widely," and the other agreed that "the only aim is to weaken the enemy, so of course one cannot take into account the loss of private individuals." This left Andrei cross. The extension would be in an area where his father, son, and sister were staying. His judgment was scornful. Prussia had "yielded up all Europe to him [Napoleon], and have now come to teach us. Fine teachers!"[4] Their theories were "not worth an empty eggshell."

Tolstoy was hostile to the conceits of political leaders who mistakenly considered themselves to be in control of events, as well as historians who believed that they understood them. As even sympathetic readers found it hard to get to grips with his views—which were never likely to find much favor with political, military, or intellectual elites—it is not surprising that his ideas had no influence on the actual practice of strategy in his time. But Tolstoy's wider political influence spread during the rest of the century and affected attempts to develop nonviolent strategies. His general critique had its echoes over the next century.

Making sense of Tolstoy's philosophy of history is no easy task. Indeed the erudition deployed by Isaiah Berlin in his attempt to do so was considered a small masterpiece in itself.[5] Tolstoy deplored the "great man theory of history," the idea that events were best explained by references to the wishes and decisions of individuals who through their position and special qualities were able to push events in one direction rather than another. His objection went beyond the normal complaint about such theories, that they underplayed the importance of broader economic, social, and political trends. Tolstoy appeared to distrust all theories that attempted to put the study of human affairs on a quasi-scientific basis by imposing abstract categories and assuming an inner rationality. General Pfühl would have attributed success to his theory of "oblique movement deduced by him from the history of Frederick the Great's wars" but blamed failure on imperfect implementation.

Tolstoy stressed the "sum of men's individual wills" rather than just those of the senior but ultimately deluded figures who believed that their decisions had significant effects. He saw a dualism in man, in whom could be found both an individual life—free in its own way—and a "swarm-life" by which he "inevitably obeys laws laid down for him," living consciously for himself but also as an "unconscious instrument in the attainment of the historical, universal, aims of humanity." Here Tolstoy joined those who sought to reconcile the ability of individuals to choose and act independently with a conviction that humanity as a whole was following a distinct path, whether set down by a divine hand, historical forces, collective emotions, or the logic of the marketplace. At some point in this reconciliation, Tolstoy supposed, individual possibilities would become submerged by the whole. The challenge in this philosophy was not to those low in the social structure but to those at the top, the elites who believed that they were making history.

One clear difficulty with this thesis, even when Tolstoy was telling the story, was that the leading actors on the political stage did make a difference, and their decisions had consequences. It would be odd to assert that European history would have been exactly the same had Napoleon not been born. Accepting that history could not be a pseudo-science did not require denying the possibility of systematic thought and conceptualization. It was also odd to use Napoleon's performance at Borodino to debunk the great man theory of history. This was, as Gallie notes, "one of the strangest, least typical, of campaigns known to history," yet Tolstoy uses it to make points of universal validity to be applied to matters far less strange and atypical.[6] Tolstoy showed the emperor pretending to be master of events over which in practice he had no control. He was all bustle and activity, beguiled by an "artificial phantasm of life," issuing orders of great precision too far from the battlefield to make a real difference: "none of his orders were executed and during the battle he did not know what was going on." Instead, he played out a role as "representative of authority." According to Tolstoy, he did this rather well. "He did nothing harmful to the progress of the battle, as he inclined to the most reasonable opinions, made no confusion, did not contradict himself, did not get frightened or run away from the field of battle, but with great tact and military experience carried out his role of appearing to command calmly and with dignity." The orders he sent out rarely made sense to those receiving them, and what he heard in return was often overtaken by events by the time it reached him. This was not, however, Napoleon's problem that day: he was unwell and, unusually for him, uncertain about where to put his main effort. Then, when he had his opportunity to scatter the enemy, he lacked the reserve strength to take it. Tolstoy hardly chose this particular great man at the height of his power. When describing Napoleon at Austerlitz, Tolstoy recognized those qualities which made his contemporaries treat the emperor with awe and admiration, however grudging.

By contrast, Tolstoy was kind to Kutuzov, who was portrayed as having an inner wisdom despite his apparent stupidity, because he grasped the logic of the situation. When it came to knowledge of the supposed military sciences, Napoleon had the advantage over Kutuzov, but the Russian understood something deeper and more profound, and could see how the situation was bound to develop. Kutuzov told Prince Andrei that "time and patience are the strongest warriors." The young man concluded that the old man could grasp "the inevitable march of events" and had the wisdom to avoid meddling. In this way, Kutuzov's passivity during the battle reflected wisdom more than inertia, a reliance on the army's spirit rather than a commander's orders. The only time he issued an order was at the point of defeat. It was to prepare for a counterattack, impossible in the circumstances. The aim was to give heart to his men rather than convey a real intention. In Tolstoy's account, the French offensive floundered because they lacked the moral force to press on, while the Russians had the moral force to resist.

Tolstoy's contempt for the "new science" of strategy was a warning against the "erroneous idea that the command which precedes the event causes the event." Though thousands of commands would be issued, historians focused only on the few executed that were consistent with events while forgetting "the others that were not executed because they could not be."[7] This was a challenge to a strategic approach that generated plans and issued orders for actions that could affect few of the many factors in play and was based on ignorance about the actual state of affairs. Tolstoy described chaotic deliberations in July 1812, when Russian commanders wondered how to cope with the advancing Napoleon. At issue was whether to abandon the camp at Drissa. For one general, the problem was that the camp had a river behind it; for another, that was what constituted its value. Prince Andrei listened to the cacophony of voices and opinions and all these "surmises, plans, refutations, and shouts" and concluded that "there is not and cannot be any science of war, and that therefore there can be no such thing as a military genius." In these matters, the conditions and circumstances were unknown and could not be defined. Not enough was understood about the strength of Russian or French forces. All depended "on innumerable conditions, the significance of which is determined at a particular moment which arrives no one knows when." The attribution of genius to military men reflected no more than the pomp and power with which they were invested, and the sycophants who flattered them. Not only were there no special qualities that made for a good commander, but a commander seemed to function most effectively without "the highest and best human attributes—love, poetry, tenderness, and philosophic inquiring doubt." The success of military action depended not on such people but rather "on the man in the ranks who shouts, 'We are lost!' or who shouts, 'Hurrah!' "[8]

Battle was inherently confusing, and there was unlikely to be a clear link between orders as cause and actions as effect. But part of strategy was to understand what battle could and could not achieve. In this regard, Russia's fate was determined by strategy as much as any elemental forces beyond human comprehension. As Lieven notes, Tolstoy failed to credit the clarity of the Tsar's strategy and the extent to which events unfolded according to plan, as the Tsar anticipated. Nonetheless, more than "all the history books ever written," *War and Peace* shaped popular perceptions of Napoleon's defeat. "By denying any rational direction of events in 1812 by human actors and implying that military professionalism was a German disease Tolstoy feeds rather easily into Western interpretations of 1812 which blame snow or chance for French defeat."[9] It was one thing to acknowledge that military organizations would not always be responsive to the demands of the center. Orders would be misinterpreted; intelligence would be faulty; original campaign plans would need to be modified and at times supplanted. It was entirely different to insist that commands could never be effectual and change the course of a battle or to deny the potential of leadership; the relevance of intelligence, advice, and orders; and the influence of professional experience, training, and competence. Perhaps for Tolstoy, developing his anarchist philosophy, less important than whether some were able to shape events more than others was whether they should ever be able to do so. In objecting to the very idea of the exercise of power, the arrogance of those who claimed to control the lives of others, he sought to minimize its impact.

The issue for Tolstoy was not that events lacked causes but that there were so many. Historians picked the most obvious and thus missed out on so many more. As Berlin put it, "No theories can possibly fit the immense variety of possible human behavior, the vast multiplicity of minute, undiscoverable causes and effects which form that interplay of men and nature which history purports to record."[10] One sympathetic interpreter has sought to show how Tolstoy effectively punctured the pretensions of not only the philosophers of his time but also subsequent social scientists who took advantage of hindsight by seeking only evidence or a singular factor that supported their theories and ignoring anything contradictory. Historians also focused on decisive moments, but such moments were rare because outcomes were the produce of many separate moments, each containing its own contingent possibilities. Their explanations missed significant aspects that remained hidden from view while giving undue prominence to others. This is why historical interpretations were regularly challenged and revised. On this basis, Gary Morson identified with Tolstoy's belief that true understanding only existed in the present and events were decided "on the instant." This is why Kutuzov's best advice before the battle was to get a good night's sleep: immediate attentiveness to unfolding possibilities was going to be more valuable than forward planning.[11]

Salutary warnings about the limits to central control or grand theory were one thing; suggestions that everything came down to small, immediate decisions—as if some were no more important than others and past decisions had no consequences whatsoever for those which came later—were quite another. Historians might struggle to capture the totality of the processes they sought to explain, but there was always a possibility of reinterpretations. Historians looked to the past, while strategists addressed the future. The challenge was how to respond in unpredictable situations in which only certain factors were subject to influence but something still had to be done, such that inaction was also a portentous decision. With the benefit of hindsight, the historian might see how it all might have been different. But choices had to be made at the time in the face of unknowns. Most seriously, there was a fundamental contradiction in this line of argument. Under the charge of irrelevance, the generals and their theories were left off the hook, perhaps looking foolish but no longer dangerous. If they were relevant they should be answerable for their follies.

Von Moltke

The year after *War and Peace* was published there was a fateful demonstration of the strategist's art that showed how consequential it could be, as well as its limitations. The occasion was the 1870 Franco-Prussian War, and the commanding figure was Field Marshal Helmuth Karl Bernhard Graf von Moltke. Von Moltke was a self-proclaimed follower of Clausewitz and one of his most effective promoters. He was even a student at the Prussian War College when the master was in charge. Although the two do not appear to have met, Clausewitz marked von Moltke's report "exemplary." Von Moltke read *On War* after it appeared in limited circulation in 1832.[12] He was born in the nineteenth century's first year and lived until its ninety-first. He was chief of staff of the Prussian army for thirty years and can claim to be one of the century's greatest and most successful military strategists.

Although born into the nobility, his family was poor. His army career began at the age of 11 when he was sent to cadet school in Denmark. Cultured and well read, he would have been classed as a liberal humanist until the revolutions of 1848 caused him to move abruptly to the right and become a tough patriot and uncompromising anti-socialist. He became chief of staff in 1857 and created the system that set the standards for military professionalism for the next hundred years. He addressed all aspects of military organization, armament, training, and logistics. The first war in which he made his mark was one against the Danes in 1864, but it was the campaigns that led to German unification under Prussia and the supplanting of France as the strongest power in Europe that made his name.

Von Moltke wrote little about strategy. Gunther Rothenberg describes him as a "grammarian" who "engaged in very little abstract speculation."[13] His most important contributions, which were written before and after his most spectacular success in the 1870 Franco-Prussian War, betray the influence of Clausewitz. Yet in two critical respects he moved beyond Clausewitz and the Napoleonic model. By the 1860s far more could be done with armies than had been possible at the start of the century, as a result of the arrival of the railways as well as improved road networks. Von Moltke was unusually alert to the logistical potential of these developments, appreciating what could be achieved once it was possible to move mass armies with relative ease. He also recognized the potential for deadlock if both sides mobilized large human reserves and a war carried on without either side quite being able to bring it to a conclusion.

The second factor influencing von Moltke's approach was that he internalized Clausewitz's dictum about war being a continuation of politics. He happily served his monarch and less happily shared influence with Chancellor Otto von Bismarck. He acquired as a result a sense of the uncertain fit between political ends and military means, but also of the possibilities of limited war and the value of allies. While, à la Clausewitz, he believed the object of war was to "implement the government's policy by force," he grumbled that politicians (read Bismarck) might demand more from war than it could realistically deliver. Once objectives were set, it was up to the military to realize them. "Political considerations can be taken into account only as long as they do not make demands that are militarily improper or impossible." Yet if some ends could not be met, a dialogue between the military and political spheres was unavoidable: they could not work in splendid isolation from each other, one setting the ends and the other the means. This was evident in von Moltke's definition of victory: "the highest goal attainable with available means." His attitude toward battle was close to that of Clausewitz, but firmer in his conviction that victory was the best means to decide a war.

> The victory in the decision by arms is the most important moment in war. Only victory breaks the enemy will and compels him to submit to our own. Neither the occupation of territory nor the capturing of fortified places, but only the destruction of the enemy fighting-power will, as a rule, decide. This is thus the primary objective of operations.

This did not really help with wars fought for limited objectives when the effort required to destroy the enemy fighting power would not be commensurate.

More innovative in von Moltke's approach to strategy was his refusal to be locked into any system or plan. He was responsible for the famous observation that "no plan survived contact with the enemy." He told his commanders that war could not be "conducted on a green table" and was prepared to delegate authority so that they could respond to situations as they found them rather than how the high command expected them to be. He distrusted generalities and fixed precepts. The important thing was to keep the objective in view while accepting the need for "practical adaptation." He was wary of abstractions and attempts to establish general principles. For von Moltke, strategy was instead a "free, practical, artistic activity" and a "system of expediencies."[14] The choice of strategy might be based on common sense: the test of character was to find this in situations of extreme stress. Because of Prussia's challenging strategic position, there was always a risk of others joining in once a war had begun. Victory therefore had to be swift and conclusive, and that meant there was no option but to get on the offensive as soon as possible. At the same time, von Moltke was conscious of developing battlefield conditions, in particular the impact of increasingly deadly firepower, so he was also anxious to avoid frontal assaults. Although he saw strategy as playing on the unpredictable aspects of conflicts and the unexpected opportunities this could create, at this point the task was handed over to tactics as strategy became "silent." In this he took a different view from Clausewitz, who saw the completion of battle as a task for strategy. Von Moltke saw the tactical task as conceptually simple—destroying as much of the enemy force as possible—but practically challenging, which was why his preparations for battle were meticulous. Once battle was done strategy came back into play.[15]

His approach, described as "strategic envelopment," was based on concentrating superior forces faster than the enemy and came to be a feature of German strategy thereafter. As with Napoleon and Clausewitz before him, von Moltke was in no doubt about the importance of numbers. Prior to war, size could be bolstered through coalition, and one of the consequences of the war of 1866 with Austria was to acquire allies among the smaller German states. During war, superior force could be brought to bear at a particular point, irrespective of the broader balance of power. To achieve this it was necessary to mobilize quickly, and this was the area where careful planning could make a difference. Under von Moltke, the general staff, which had long had a role in Prussian military preparations, was expanded and elevated. It became not only the source but also the custodian of military plans, responsible for design and then execution.

Von Moltke's most radical innovation as a commander, which went against the textbooks of the time, was to divide his army so that both parts could be kept supplied until they would combine for the battle ("march divided; strike united"). The risks were that they might be caught separately and be overwhelmed, or brought together too quickly, thus putting a strain on supplies. In the 1866 war with Austria he used the railways to get his troops into position first, even though Austria had been the first to mobilize. Observers were staggered when he allowed his two armies to be separated by some one hundred miles. If the Austrian commanders had been more alert, this could have proved disastrous for von Moltke. In the end, the Austrians were caught by two armies arriving from different directions.

This victory set up a war with France for which von Moltke prepared carefully. This time he divided his army into three, giving him maximum flexibility so he could react quickly as the French plan became apparent. He kept his options open until it was time to strike.

> It is even better if the forces can be moved on the day of the battle from separate points against the battlefield itself. In other words, if the operations can be directed in such a manner that the last brief march from different directions leads to the front and into the flank of the enemy, then the strategy has achieved the best that it is able to achieve, and great results must follow.

This could not, however, be guaranteed. Factors of space and time might be calculated, but not the variables where decision-making would also depend upon "the outcome of previous minor battles, on the weather, on false news; in brief, on all that is called chance and luck in human affairs."[16] Concentrate too early or too late and it might be impossible to recover.

In the critical war with France in 1870, von Moltke's victory was complete, at least in terms of the conventional phase of the war. He caught out the French army first in Metz on August 18 and then two weeks later at Sedan. Not all of his commanders followed the plan, but their lapses were more than compensated for by the numerous mistakes and outdated methods of the French side. Although the French army was defeated after seven weeks, the war was not over. Irregular and regular forces came together in France to form a government of national defense. This was a vivid demonstration of how political victory did not always follow automatically from battlefield victory. As the Germans moved toward Paris, von Moltke was aware of the potential vulnerability of extended lines of communication and the continuing ability of the French navy to keep the country supplied. There was an argument with Chancellor Otto von Bismarck over whether to bombard Paris. Von Moltke was worried this would only stiffen French resistance and preferred a siege. Bismarck worried that a slow conclusion to the campaign might prompt Britain and Austria to enter the war on France's side. The Kaiser agreed with his chancellor and the bombardment began in January 1871. The French government lacked the stomach for a fight and began to negotiate. It was still not over, for then there was a popular revolt, in the form of the Paris Commune. An improvised, irregular army animated by popular passions but lacking in discipline appalled von Moltke.[17] Nor was he much pleased with losing the debate over strategy. Bismarck had confessed, to his "shame," that he had never read Clausewitz, but he had a clear view on the continuing role of politics once war had begun. "To fix and limit the objects to be attained by the war, and to advise the monarch in respect of them, is and remains during the war just as before it a political function, and the manner in which these questions are solved cannot be without influence on the conduct of the war."[18]

Von Moltke accepted that the aims of war were determined by policy. Once fighting began, however, the military must be given a free hand: "strategy" must be "fully independent of policy." This belief went back to the formation of the Prussian general staff after the defeat at Jena in 1806, in order to guard against princely incompetence. Von Moltke judged this role to be as essential as ever. Surround a commander in the field with "independent and negative counselors" and nothing would ever get done. "They will present every difficulty, they will have foreseen all eventualities; they will always be right; they will defeat every positive idea because they have none of their own. These counselors are the spoilers; they negate the Army leader."[19] There was an unavoidable tension at the heart of von Moltke's position. It was illuminated by his reported conversation with crown prince Frederick William at the height of the crisis. Von Moltke explained that after Paris was taken the army would "push forward into the south of France in order to finally break the enemy's power." When asked about the risks of Prussian strength being exhausted so that battles could no longer be won, he denied the possibility. "We must always win battles. We must throw France completely to the ground." Then "we can dictate the kind of peace we want." "What if," wondered the crown prince, "we ourselves bleed to death in the process?" Von Moltke replied : "We shall not bleed to death and, if we do, we shall have got peace in return." He was then asked whether he was informed about the current political situation, as this "might perhaps make such a course seem unwise." "No," the field marshal replied, "I have only to concern myself with military matters."[20]

Out of these highly charged debates emerged a concept of crucial importance for subsequent military thought. Stressing his delegated powers from the Kaiser to issue operational commands, von Moltke identified the operational level of war as the one within which the commander must expect no political interference. The episode over Paris might have just demonstrated the fantasy of this political exclusion, but for commanders in the field this became an article of faith, essential to the proper and successful implementation of strategy.

CHAPTER 9 | Annihilation or Exhaustion

Git thar fustest with the mostest.

—General Nathan B. Forrest, *quoted (probably incorrectly) on strategy*

A T THE START of the twentieth century, the military historian Hans Delbrück argued that all military strategy could be divided into two basic forms. The first, conforming to the majority view of the day was *Niederwerfungsstrategie*, the strategy of annihilation, which demanded a decisive battle to eliminate the enemy's army. The second drew on Clausewitz's note of 1827 which recognized the possibility for another type of war when the available military means could not deliver a decisive battle.[1] This Delbrück described as *Ermattungsstrategie*, the strategy of exhaustion, sometimes translated as attrition. Whereas with a strategy of annihilation there was just one pole, the battle, with exhaustion there was another pole, involving a variety of ways to achieve the political ends of war, including occupying territory, destroying crops, and blockading. In the past, these alternative approaches, for want of better options, had often been used and could be effective. What was important was to be flexible when deciding upon a strategy, to attend to the political realities of the time, and to not rely on a military strategy that might be beyond practical capacity.

Delbrück did not intend to imply that the strongest was bound to be attracted by annihilation whereas the weak were fated to do what they could through exhaustion. Exhaustion was not about a single decisive battle but about an extended campaign that would wear the enemy out. He mocked the idea of a "pure maneuver strategy that allows war to be conducted without bloodshed." There was always a possibility of battle. His view of a strategy of exhaustion was more operational than an anticipation of the later concept of attritional war. This placed more emphasis on how underlying economic, industrial, and demographic factors would sustain warfare.

Delbrück's analysis led him into furious arguments with the historians of the German general staff, especially when Delbrück argued that Frederick the Great had practiced limited war rather than decisive battle. The history was on his side, in that Frederick had become wary of battle and careful in his ambition, but there was still a problem with the dichotomous presentation of complex options.[2] The problem was to suggest that a fundamental choice had to be made in advance about how to comport an army for a coming war, a tendency that remained evident in strategic debate over the coming century. The challenge for Delbrück at this time, however, was to get German generals to contemplate anything other than a swift offensive leading to the annihilation of the enemy army in a decisive battle.

The American Civil War

The complex relationship between theory and practice in strategy was revealed by the American Civil War (1861–1865). At one level, the outcome of the war was the result of the North enjoying twice the population and far greater industrial strength than the South. For much of the war the Confederacy could claim more imaginative generals. As the weaker side it might have been tempted to rely on defensive tactics, but instead often took the military initiative, perhaps in the hope that the North would respect the outcome of a truly decisive battle. President Lincoln saw clearly that the Union's strategy required an offensive, but to his exasperation his generals seemed to be unable to mount one successfully until quite late in the war.

Clausewitz had no discernible influence on these events. That was not so with Jomini. The leading teacher at West Point, Dennis Mahan, had spent time in France studying the Napoleonic Wars and was an avowed Jominian, while his star pupil, Henry "Old Brains" Halleck, who became President Lincoln's general-in-chief, had gone so far as to translate Jomini's *Life of Napoleon* into English. Mahan celebrated Napoleon's military art,

by which an enemy is broken and utterly dispersed by one and the same blow. No futilities of preparation; no uncertain feeling about in search of the key point; no hesitancy upon the decisive moment; the whole field of view taken in by one eagle glance; what could not be seen divined by an unerring instinct; clouds of light troops thrown forward to bewilder his foe; a crashing fire of cannon in mass opened upon him; the rush of the impetuous column into the gaps made by the artillery; the overwhelming charge of the resistless cuirassier; followed by the lancer and the hussar to sweep up the broken dispersed bands; such were the tactical lessons taught in almost every battle of this great military period.[3]

Halleck was a senior general at the start of the war and soon became general in chief. His specialty as an engineer, however, was fortification, and that gave him a regard for defenses that was never wholly in keeping with Mahan's call for "vigor on the field and rapidity of pursuit." A combination of expertise in defensive methods, including digging trenches and deadly rifled muskets, was bound to inhibit frontal assaults. This caution was also evident in the Union's first general-in-chief, George McLellan.

Jomini's influence among the generals is evident in their focus on lines of communication and their opposition to Lincoln's proposals to mount a series of concurrent attacks against the South, including coastal operations. This they judged to be an affront to the principles of war as it would require divided forces. It was just the sort of proposal to be expected from an untutored civilian.[4] Lincoln, who never doubted that this would be a long, wearing battle, was reluctant to press his own views but was ready to replace his generals in the hope of finding someone who would take the fight to the enemy. The generals were wary of the defense's potential and were so enamored with the idea of a decisive battle that they were reluctant to risk their forces in anything else. As General McClellan put it: "I do not wish to waste life in useless battles, but prefer to strike at the heart." Lincoln became increasingly frustrated by a preference for maneuvers over assaults. This he described disparagingly as "strategy." "That's the word—strategy!" he exclaimed in 1862, "General McClellan thinks he is going to whip the rebels by strategy."[5] It described a form of warfare that did everything with an army but fight. Feints, maneuvers, and other clever moves might win the occasional battle, but it was brute force, relentlessly applied, that made the difference. When the South was eventually penetrated, exposing the limits of the Confederacy's defenses, Lincoln was prepared to accept the benefits: "Now, gentleman, that was true strategy because the enemy was diverted from his purpose."[6]

Robert E. Lee of the Confederacy had made his own studies of Napoleon and was totally convinced of the need to go on the offensive to annihilate enemy forces. He knew that he could not mount a successful passive defense and so had to take the initiative, using maneuvers to get into the best position but then accepting battle. But this involved high casualties, and the Union side did at least understand defenses. Lee had set a goal for victory that he could not realize, and he suffered the consequences. The rival armies were "too big, too resilient, too thoroughly sustained by the will of democratic governments" to be destroyed "in a single Napoleonic battle." Ulysses Grant saw the logic clearly and brutally. The terrible loss of life in both armies had achieved little, observed Grant, but he understood that the North could survive the losses better than the South and so he decided to embark on "as desperate fighting as the world has ever witnessed," locking Lee's forces in constant combat until he barely had an army left.[7] Meanwhile, Grant sent General Sherman to make life miserable for the people of the South, bring home the costs of the war, and make it harder to sustain an army in the field.

Lincoln's own contribution was to press ahead in January 1863 with the Emancipation Proclamation that freed slaves in the areas under rebellion, a move described as a "necessary war measure for suppressing said rebellion." This not only further unsettled the South but reinforced the Union army. By 1865, former slaves counted for 10 percent of its army. In the end this was a war of exhaustion. The leader of the Confederacy, Jefferson Davis, observed how the war's "magnitude" had exceeded his expectations. "The enemy have displayed more power and energy and resources than I had attributed to them. Their finances have held out far better than I imagined would be the case...It is not possible that a war of the dimensions that this one has assumed, of proportions so gigantic, can be very long protracted. The combatants must soon be exhausted."[8]

The Cult of the Offensive

Industrialization was expanding the numbers of men who could be organized for war, while steam and electricity were making it easier to mobilize and transport them. Firepower was also steadily improving in its range and lethality. All this challenged commanders. The geographical scope of operations and the numbers involved were expanding, while the limitations of weather were easing. The implications for logistics and the actual conduct of battle were uncertain. The politics of war was also changing. Because it drew on whole societies and national sentiments it was much harder to separate the military from the civilian spheres.

The fact that individual battles in the American Civil War were not decisive and that the French continued to resist even after the apparently decisive battle of Sedan in 1870 warned of the limits to the established view of how to achieve victory in war. Yet so ingrained was the idea of a decisive battle that the urge was still to find ways to force a satisfactory conclusion. Even those who sensed their own weakness in the face of superior numbers did not look so much to guile as to superior spirit. After the defeat of 1870–1871, French theorists glorified the "offensive" and celebrated moral strength as the key to persuading their men to charge against enemy firepower.[9] If the material balance of power was not going to guarantee victory, then the vital factor had to be found in something more spiritual—what British field marshal Douglas Haig called "morale and a determination to conquer." The key text was that of Ardant du Picq, who argued that everything depended on the emotional and moral state of the individual soldier. He was killed in the 1870 war but his work was published posthumously in 1880 as *Etudes sur le combat* (Battle Studies). Its influence reached the French high command. Ferdinand Foch, who became supreme allied commander during the Great War, was convinced that the question of losing was about a psychological state of mind. Du Picq insisted that the physical impulse was nothing, the "moral impulse" everything. This lay "in the perception by the enemy of the resolution that animates you." By the time the attack arrived, the defenders could be "disconcerted, wavering, worried, hesitant, vacillating."[10] The doctrine of the offensive became official French policy. It later came to be described as a "cult."

German policy started from a different basis. Von Moltke had no doubt that if Germany could not achieve a quick victory in a future war, its position would soon become dire. The key premise accepted by all German strategists was that if the country was subjected to attack from both east and west it could soon be squeezed, unless one of the belligerents could be removed from the fight early on. After 1871, von Moltke became progressively more pessimistic about Germany's ability to achieve this. As plans were developed for a war against both France and Russia, he realized the need to scale down political expectations even as the military demands became greater. He wanted to get Germany into the optimum position from which to negotiate a political settlement. That required going on the offensive (so as to acquire territory to be used in the eventual bargaining) rather than absorbing the offensives of others.

The intensity of the debate reflected von Moltke's successors' determination to avoid exhaustion. They could not bring themselves to prepare for an inevitable stalemate. They held to the conviction that when it came to the crunch, the new political order could and should be created through force of arms. As chief of the German general staff at the turn of the century, Alfred von Schlieffen epitomized this view. The secret, he believed, was to be found in combining a grand and compelling concept with meticulous attention to detail. In 1891, he described the "essential element in the art of strategy" as bringing "superior numbers into action. This is relatively easy when one is stronger from the outset, more difficult when one is weaker, and probably impossible when the numerical imbalance is very great."[11] In the most probable contingencies for Germany, facing France from the west and Russia from the east, one enemy must be destroyed before the other was engaged. A frontal assault would cause excessive casualties, leaving insufficient capacity for future battles. It would therefore be necessary to take the initiative, first outflanking the enemy force and then destroying it. Von Schlieffen sought to address the challenge of friction and anticipate the enemy counterstrategy by insisting on careful planning. The whole campaign was choreographed from mobilization to victory. The enemy would have no choice but to follow the German script rather than its own. Contrary to the precepts of von Moltke, this allowed little scope for individual initiative or for much going wrong. Von Schlieffen was aware that there were few margins for error. He was therefore prepared to take political risks, in particular by violating the neutrality of Belgium and Luxembourg, in order to reduce the military risks.

An intense debate has developed among military historians as to whether there really was ever a Schlieffen Plan, prepared just before von Moltke's nephew (known as the Younger) took over as chief of the general staff in 1906. The German records are incomplete and whatever was bequeathed undoubtedly was amended as circumstances changed.[12] At times the general staff looked to the east rather than the west and adjusted force levels. The thinking in 1914, nevertheless, did follow an ingrained strategic concept, using envelopment to remove one enemy from the war at maximum speed with minimum losses. This strategy was outlined by von Moltke the Younger in December 1911, when he recommended that in all circumstances, Germany should open the campaign by directing all available resources against France.

> In the battle against France lies the decision in the war. The Republic is our most dangerous enemy, but we can hope to bring about a rapid decision here. If France is beaten in the first great battle, this country, which possesses no great manpower reserves, will hardly be in a position to conduct a long-lasting war. Russia, on the other hand, can shift her forces into the interior of her immeasurable land and can protract the war for an immeasurable time. Therefore, Germany's entire effort

must be focused on ending the war, at least on one front, with a single great blow as soon as possible.[13]

The German offensive of August 1914 was the culmination of a century of developments in military thought and practice, updating the received wisdom of the Napoleonic period for recent developments in communications and logistics. It broke from the Clausewitzian model by assuming, without evidence, that the offense could be the stronger form of warfare. As Strachan notes, the war plans of all European armies in 1914 were Jominian: "operational plans for single campaigns, designed to achieve decisive success through maneuver according to certain principles."[14] The enemy defenses would be circumvented and then engaged with a strength and momentum that would leave them reeling. This assumed high levels of commitment, skill, élan, and willpower; and an enemy that would fail to rise to the challenge.

This was a strategy that had been decided upon well in advance and to which all planning had been geared. To ensure that the plan was properly executed, troops who could follow commands obediently and precisely were required. Instead of a Tolstoyan army of individuals shaping outcomes through numerous individual choices, this was a group turned by discipline and drill into instruments of the commander's will. Where latitude was required for local initiatives in the face of unforeseeable developments, these would still reflect the commanders' intent, conveyed not only through direct communications but indirectly through a shared institutional culture and agreed doctrine. The systems of hierarchy and control, of specialized functions and their coordination, appeared as the highest stage of modern bureaucratic development. The general staff had the pick of the brightest military brains. It set the standards for comprehensive planning and preparation of individuals to follow straightforward commands in trying conditions.

But none of this could guarantee success. Ensuring victory required that military imperatives take precedence over any diplomatic considerations. Most seriously this entailed violating Belgian neutrality, which made it more likely that Great Britain would enter the war and crush any actual or potential civilian resistance. Even then, promises of success depended on the assumed superiority of the army, whose resolute will would crush weaker nations that had inferior plans, poorer tactical grasp, and less-disciplined troops. Besides, there was no obvious alternative: there was neither the appetite nor the resources for a prolonged war of exhaustion, and there could be no other way of executing a war of annihilation. Other than the one most feared by the military, a progressive demilitarization and softening of the state, the only alternative was to use threats of war to get a better diplomatic settlement. As so much depended on getting in an effective first blow, once mobilization began the political situation was soon out of control.

After Napoleon's fall, the presumption that the great issues that divided states could be resolved through force of arms was taken for granted yet only tested on a few occasions. Though these occasions left the presumption reinforced they also pointed to reasons for caution: the huge developments in transportation, in particular the railroads, which facilitated complex movements to encircle opponents and catch them unawares also made it possible to get fresh reserves to the front; industrialization had led to improvements in the weight, range, and accuracy of both artillery and small arms, making it possible to blast holes in defensive lines but also to make defending fire against an onrushing army quite murderous. The basic lesson from the Napoleonic Wars, that there was only so much one country's army, whatever the brilliance of its operations, could do against a much stronger alliance, remained in place. So was the lesson of 1871 that the stresses of war on a country could lead to popular anger and revolutionary surges. War was a radical instrument. It threatened to upturn the international order and unleash wild political forces at home. It was one thing to have a strategy for swift military action that would deal the enemy a knockout blow. But if the enemy survived then there were no compelling strategies for what came next.

Mahan and Corbett

While these debates about land offensives and decisive victories preoccupied continental powers, Great Britain, was content to rely upon its maritime strength. Naval strategy was a minority interest and was largely concerned with whatever Britain had done and was still doing to maintain its sprawling empire and its intercontinental trade. The dominant concept was command of the sea, which could be traced back to Thucydides. This essentially meant being able to move men and materiel wherever you wished without interference while being able to prevent the enemy's attempt to do the same. In the nineteenth century, Great Britain enjoyed the command of the sea. It had managed to extract the maximum benefit out of its naval assets, creating an aura of irresistible strength, despatching warships to remind lesser powers of the country's interests, conveying menace, providing assurance, and creating a bargaining position or inflicting blows on an upstart, all the while ensuring that the imperial lines of communication could be sustained and reinforced.

This had not required consideration of how to beat an equivalent power in battle, the main preoccupation of land warfare, because for much of the nineteenth century, Britain did not face such a power. The French might once have mounted a challenge, but British naval superiority had been reasserted at Trafalgar in 1805. Since then, there had been no shortage of naval actions but also no serious challenge to Britain's naval predominance. To maintain this happy state, the British concluded that they must always have a navy twice the size of any other. Only at the turn of the century, with the conversion to steam underway and Germany growing in industrial strength, was this standard threatened. Prior to the Great War, Britain maintained its top position, but only with a considerable effort.

It was late in the nineteenth century when naval power gained a theorist with a compelling thesis. Alfred Thayer Mahan, after an unhappy and indifferent naval career, found himself unexpectedly in charge of the new U.S. Naval War College in 1886. There he developed a series of lectures on the influence of sea power in history. This turned into his two most important books, the first concluding with the French Revolution and the second in 1812. His writings were both prolix and—once retired from the Navy in 1896 until his death in 1914—prolific.[15] His focus was not so much on principles of strategy but on the relationship between naval and economic power, particularly how Britain's ascent as a great power had depended not "by attempting great military operations on land, but by controlling the sea, and through the sea the world outside Europe."[16] As an American he was seeking to encourage his country to follow the British example, not to challenge Britain but to provide extra support so that the two countries could keep the seas open for trade.

His work was acclaimed in Britain. His central thesis, focusing on the failure of France to become a naval power while Britain succeeded, was congenial. Aspiring powers accepted the premise that the British experience told of the necessity for countries dependent on the sea to have large navies composed of large ships. While it has been argued that Mahan's historical and geopolitical judgments deserve serious consideration, his views on the actual deployment of naval power were far less developed.[17] He repeatedly insisted that the principles of land and sea war were essentially the same, and for illumination of these principles he turned to Jomini, from whom he claimed to have "learned the few, very few, leading considerations in military combination." His father, Dennis, had been instrumental in ensuring that Jomini had such a positive reception in the United States.[18] This led to the stress on the decisive battle. The organized forces of the enemy must be the "chief objective." This was "Jomini's dictum," piercing "like a two-edged sword to the joints and marrow of many specious propositions" and demanded a concentration of force (the "ABC" of any strategy) in preparation for battle. By following these principles, naval officers could achieve the same level of strategic maturity as their army counterparts.[19] Unfortunately, the "development of the Art of War at sea has been slower, and is now less advanced, than on shore," Mahan observed. In "the race for material and mechanical development, sea-officers as a class have allowed their attention to be unduly diverted from the systematic study of the Conduct of War, which is their peculiar and main concern."[20] He was, however, primarily a historian. When he tried to pull together his ideas on naval strategy into a single volume he confessed that it was the worst book he had written.[21]

While Mahan was a great booster for naval power and gained countless admirers among American and British naval circles for doing so, his lasting theoretical contributions were limited. As with others who believed that history offers timeless principles, he was unable to accommodate into his basic framework the massive changes in naval power resulting from the new technologies exemplified by steam power. As with others who sought to promote the virtues of one type of military power, he was nervous about it being seen as subordinate to another type, and so he dismissed the idea of using the navy to guard shore positions, to prevent it becoming a branch of the army. The role of navies was to compete with other navies for the command of the sea. As with others who were focused on decisive battles, Mahan showed little interest in more limited forms of engagement and was dismissive of engaging in commerce destruction until after the decisive naval battle, for victory would put enemy commerce at your mercy.

Very similar ideas were being developed in Germany by Admiral Alfred von Tirpitz, who was responsible in the late nineteenth century for turning the navy of the recently unified Germany from a second-rate force into a serious challenger to British naval supremacy. His vision was both ambitious and unimaginative. It was similar to Mahan's except that while Mahan took his inspiration from Jomini, Tirpitz took his from Clausewitz. He was preparing for a future war at sea that would look very much like war on land, the "combat of fleets against fleets" to gain command of the sea. The model was explicitly derived from land warfare—he even wrote of the "battle of armies on water." He argued that the navy's "natural mission" was a "strategic offensive," to seek victory in an "arranged mass battle." Other possibilities, such as coastal bombardments and blockades, were impossible so long as "the opposing fleet still exists and is ready for battle." All this was despite the evident difficulty of imposing on an enemy a naval battle he wished to avoid.[22]

While Mahan and Tirpitz sought to promote their countries as rising naval powers using remarkably similar concepts of the likely objectives and methods of war at sea, Britain lacked a naval strategist of note. As Winston Churchill observed after the Great War, the Royal Navy had made "no important contribution to naval literature." Its "thought and study" were devoted to the daily routine. "We had brilliant experts of every description, brave and devoted hearts; but at the outset of the conflict we had more captains of ships than captains of war." The standard work on seapower had been written by an American admiral. The best that Britain had to offer was written by a civilian.[23] The civilian in question was Sir Julian Corbett. Measured and moderate in his analysis and prose, he provided the most substantial critique of the dominant ethos of the time, asserting the possibilities of limited war, raising questions about the focus on concentrating forces for a decisive battle on land, and suggesting why this was an inadequate way to think about war at sea. An occasional novelist with a background in law, Corbett lacked practical naval experience. This was often held against him, along with his skepticism regarding decisive battles and naval offensives and his readiness to challenge the great myths of British naval history (for example, those surrounding the 1805 Battle of Trafalgar).

Yet despite all of this, he was given a central role in naval education as a lecturer at the staff college. He also played a role in policymaking as an Admiralty insider, even during the Great War. He was then given the responsibility for overseeing the official histories of the naval war. He was on the side of the reformers, trying to modernize the attitudes and culture of the Royal Navy. This made him a natural target for conservative elements in the maritime community. Although he was actively consulted during the war, the impact of his broad theories has been doubted.[24] During the Great War, one senior figure commended Corbett for having written "one of the best books in our language upon political and military strategy" from which all sorts of lessons, "some of inestimable value, may be gleaned." But no one had time to read it. "Obviously history is written for schoolmasters and arm-chair strategists. Statesmen and warriors pick their way through the dark."[25]

His efforts to accommodate the views of those he was challenging made his work at times unnecessarily convoluted. Whereas Mahan was in some respects a polemicist writing for a receptive audience, Corbett was in a trickier position, a civilian writing for a skeptical audience. While Mahan sought to apply Jomini, Corbett began with Clausewitz, but with greater subtlety than Tirpitz.[26] Like Delbrück, Corbett picked up on those aspects of *On War* that allowed for the possibility of something other than decisive battle in an absolute war. The wisdom of Britain's naval strategy, demonstrated by achieving so much with limited resources, was the result of a succession of limited engagements for limited purposes. It had managed to combine "naval and military action" to give the "contingent a weight and mobility that are beyond its intrinsic power."[27] The potential of limited war at sea was compared to the potential for absolute war in continental Europe. There compact, nationalistic, and organized states bordered each other. If war came, popular feeling was apt to be high and it was possible to commit extra resource into the campaign if battles went badly. The further away from borders, the lower the political stakes and the greater the logistical problems. This made limitation and restraint more likely. The destruction of the enemy's armed forces was a means to an end and not an end in itself. If the end could be achieved by different means, so much the better.

The vital question for strategy was not how to win a battle but how to exert pressure on the enemy's society and government. This argued for consideration of blockade and attacks on commerce ("guerre de course") as much as seeking out the enemy fleet. Major or grand strategy was about the purposes of war, taking into account international relations and economic factors, to which the strategy for the actual conduct of war should be subordinate. As it was highly unlikely that a war would be decided solely by naval action, except possibly over time as a result of blockade, armies and navies should not be considered separately. "Since men live on the land and not upon the sea, great issues between nations at war have always been decided—except in the rarest cases—either by what your army can do against your enemy's territory and national life, or else by fear of what the fleet makes possible for your army to do." The relationship between land and sea forces was the business of maritime strategy, from which the fleet's specific tasks would emerge. That would be the business of a purely naval strategy.

The key to success on land was control of territory; at sea it was control of communications. This was because the sea did not lend itself to possession. Offensive and defensive operations would tend to merge into one another. Because of this, the loss of command of the sea, which meant that passage might be opposed, did not necessarily imply that another power enjoyed command. "The command is normally in dispute. It is this state of dispute with which naval strategy is most nearly concerned." Corbett could see why it would be desirable to seek out and destroy the enemy fleet to gain command of the sea—the equivalent of a Napoleonic decisive battle—but he also understood why it might not be possible. Trafalgar, he noted, was "ranked as one of the decisive battles of the world, and yet of all the great victories, there is not one which to all appearance was so barren of immediate result . . . It gave England finally the dominion of the seas, but it left Napoleon dictator of the continent."

By exalting the offensive "into a fetish," the defensive was discredited. Yet at sea the defensive was stronger because of the ease with which battle could be avoided. A fleet that knew it was weaker would have every incentive to avoid the stronger. Unlike Mahan, Corbett saw great advantages in dispersal, such as avoiding a stronger fleet, luring a weaker fleet into danger under the illusion that it enjoyed local strength, and producing a winning combination of ships. In this respect, the "ideal concentration" was "an appearance of weakness that covers a reality of strength." The worst concentration, by the same token, would limit the area of the sea that could be controlled, leaving other parts vulnerable for any use. "The more you concentrate your force and efforts to secure the desired decision, the more you will expose your trade to sporadic attack."[28] The Great War gave far more support to Corbett's views rather than Mahan's. The one great naval battle, at Jutland in 1915, was inconclusive and in Corbett's eyes unnecessary, because the Royal Navy was still able to sustain a blockade that would have weakened Germany over time. Meanwhile, submarine warfare against British merchant shipping found Britain unprepared and only belatedly able to cope after adopting a convoy system.

Geopolitics

It may well be that other great powers would have followed Britain into building large navies if Mahan had never written a word, but he certainly gave these efforts legitimacy and credibility. They were bound up with what was essentially a mercantilist vision of economic strength, protected and enhanced through the exertion of military power. Presenting the oceans as containing their own sea lanes, pathways for commerce that could be guaranteed by a naval hegemon, Mahan introduced a concept that took hold among maritime enthusiasts. His thesis was vigorously championed by President Theodore Roosevelt, who was something of a naval historian himself in an earlier life, and led to a major expansion in the U.S. fleet after 1907.

Perhaps because the British were aware that their days of naval superiority were numbered, it was not only Corbett who provided an important qualification to Mahan's thesis. A quite different perspective was provided by the geographer, adventurer, and politician Sir Halford Mackinder. Mahan was addressing what he assumed to be a real choice for the United States: whether to be a continental or a maritime power. For that reason he bemoaned the fascination with developing the country's interior to the detriment of its sea-boards. Mackinder did not accept this dichotomy. In an essay delivered to the Royal Geographical Society in 1904, he explained why it was possible for a land power to acquire strength from the interior which could then be applied to create a navy.[29] A maritime power, and certainly a small island such as Britain, lacked this option. New forms of transport, particularly rail, would make it possible to exploit interior resources in a way that would have been impossible when movement depended on horses. He looked at the great Eurasian landmass and saw how either Germany or Russia (or the two in combination) could come to control it all, from which they would gain such economic power that it would be a comparatively small matter to project it out to sea. Mackinder explained in 1905: "Half a continent may ultimately outbuild and outman an island."[30] On this basis he saw an increasing vulnerability, which Britain could only address by closer integration with her empire.

His theory was given a more mature expression in a book published just after the First World War in which he gave the Eurasian interior its name, the "heartland." This was the "region to which under modern conditions, sea-power can be refused access."[31] He divided the world into a core "World-Island"—which was potentially self-sufficient, comprising Eurasia and Africa—with the rest of the islands—including the Americas, Australia, Japan, the British Isles, and Oceania—around the "periphery." These smaller islands required sea transport to function. Despite Germany's defeat in 1918, Mackinder saw the basic danger remaining of "ever-increasing strategical opportunities to land-power as against sea-power." This resulted in the advice to keep "the German and the Slav" apart. Three maxims flowed from his analysis: "Who rules East Europe controls the heartland; Who rules the heartland commands the World-Island; Who rules the World-Island commands the World."[32] The importance of distance, which Mackinder saw being transformed by railways and motorized transport, was eventually affected even more by the ability of aircraft to fly over both land and sea. Surprisingly, Mackinder paid little attention to the possibilities of air power though it was only a few weeks before he gave his seminal paper in 1904 that the Wright brothers made their historic first flight.

There was much that Mackinder shared with Mahan. International relations were understood in terms of relentless competition among naturally expansive great powers. What Mackinder introduced was a way of thinking about the geographical dimension that showed how the land and sea could be understood as part of the same world system, and as a source of continuity even as political and technological change affected its relevance. He was not a geographical determinist, accepting that power balances would also depend on "the relative number, virility, equipment, and organization of the competing peoples."[33] What Mackinder offered was a way of rooting the higher-level strategic discourse in the interaction between states and the enduring features of their environment.

Mackinder never used the term "geopolitics." It was coined by the Swede Rudolf Kjellén, who was a student of Friedrich Ratzel, the first geographer to focus on political geography. Kjellén's works were translated into German and picked up by Karl Haushofer, a former General who founded the German geopolitical school.[34] Although he was not a Nazi, Haushofer reflected a world view that thought naturally in terms of distinctive ethnic groups occupying sufficient space to exercise economic independence (autarky). The logic of "lebensraum" (the need to expand living space) became part of Nazi ideology. Such associations left geopolitics discredited.[35] Mackinder's more nuanced approach provided a context for the parochial concerns of individual states but also reinforced anxieties that there might be a route for a hostile power (for this option was not available to Britain) to eventual world domination. This idea influenced the titanic struggles of the coming century. It encouraged the view that there were a number of timeless imperatives arising out of the structure of international politics that states ignored at their peril. These encouraged a focus on the more conservative notions of nationality and territory and played down considerations of ideology and values, though these might well have been the most important factors when it came to deciding what was worth fighting for and with whom it was desirable to forge and maintain alliances. So, while geopolitics appeared to move strategy to a higher plane than one which concentrated solely on the operational art, it suffered from the same defect of failing to attend to the wider political context.

CHAPTER 10 | Brain and Brawn

Quiet people go out in the morning, and see air-fleets passing overhead—
dripping death—dripping death!

—H. G. Wells, *The War in the Air, 1908*

FEW EPISODES REVEALED the limitations of military planning more than
the German offensive of August 1914. The general staff controlled what
they could, but their plans had paid insufficient attention to what France
might do to disrupt these plans—especially as logistics and communications
lines became extended. The plan's schedule soon proved impossible to meet,
especially as Belgium put up some resistance. This led to brutal dealings
with civilians (a pattern which continued through the war), including forced
labor, denial of food supplies, and wanton destruction.[1] Within weeks, the
offensive had been halted. Yet the failure to knock France out of the war
and the need to then cope with the Russians and the British (because of the
attack on Belgium) did not lead to a fundamental reappraisal of war aims or
strategic principles. The search was still on for a decisive victory, relying on
superiority in temperament, refusal to countenance a hint of timidity, and
faith in some new technique that could turn the tide. The first of these was
the use of gas warfare. The next drastic move was unrestricted submarine
warfare, reflecting optimistic views about the inability of civil shipping to
cope with the threat. This had the predictable effect of bringing the United

States into the war. The final gamble was the offensive of March 1918 that left the army extended and exposed.

Delbrück had applauded the initial offensive and thought it would succeed, but once it stalled he quickly revised his thinking. If Germany could not annihilate it would have to exhaust the enemy, although Delbrück struggled to assess the relative economic impacts on the belligerents. He argued for a deal with Britain and France in order to concentrate on Russia. The uncompromising political and military stance led him to despair. Germany had "in a sense the whole world leagued against us," he wrote in 1917, adding that "fear of German despotism is one of the weightiest facts with which we have to reckon, one of the strongest factors in the enemy's power."[2]

In the middle of this great stalemate, when there seemed to be few obvious means of breaking the deadlock other than by persevering with the costly and futile combination of artillery bombardment and infantry charges, plans began to be drawn up for more daring strategies. In each case the intention was to realize the potential of a new technology—the tank on the ground or the airplane in the air—to break the will of the enemy. In both cases the presumed impact of the new weaponry was assumed to be psychological as much as physical. The aim was to cause what would in effect be a collective nervous breakdown on the enemy side. This directly challenged the assumption that a decisive victory had to involve the annihilation of the enemy army. In neither case were the plans realistic: the technologies were still in their infancy, the production capacity limited and the tactics underdeveloped. Nonetheless, in both cases these early plans set the terms for the intense postwar debates about future strategy.

Air Power

The Germans were early converts to the value of long-range bombardment and to the view that its success would lie less in the amount of physical injury caused and more in the enemy's willingness to continue to prosecute the war. When the first Zeppelin raids occurred in 1915, the actual results were meager, though in London the ability of the Zeppelins to fly overhead was considered humiliating in itself and bad for morale. As the British learned to deal with the Zeppelins, German aircraft took over with greater effect. In the summer of 1917, a time when morale was already fragile, the first attack on London killed 162 people and injured 432. Up to this point, the British had concentrated their own aircraft in support of the army in France. This remained the priority, but after the London raids the government promised revenge and a degree of protection to the public. At the time, the Royal Flying Corps' main interest beyond the French trenches was the German lines of supply that fed the front. The commander General Hugh Trenchard was trying to develop a vision of how best to use a still scarce resource as an independent force that could mount concentrated attacks against chosen targets in sufficient numbers and with sufficient continuity to make a decisive impact. Although he judged that bombers of greater range could eventually target Berlin, the only initial response to the attacks on England was some very limited and rather indiscriminate bombing of Germany.

Trenchard's vision had a strong influence on the group of American airmen who arrived just after the German raids, as their country entered the war. Captain Nap Gorrell, one member of this team whose task was to set out requirements for American aircraft production, began to develop a plan for an air campaign. In line with Trenchard's thinking, Gorrell argued that "a new policy of attacking the enemy" was needed. This he described as "strategical bombing" geared to impeding the flow of supplies from Germany to the front. The assumption was that there was a linked industrial complex, involving a limited number of vital targets, upon which Germany's war effort depended. Gorrell also assumed that civilians would be demoralized and reluctant to return to work in the aftermath of such attacks. They might even find air attack so unendurable that they would pressure their governments to seek terms. To achieve this he envisaged a massive armada of thousands of aircraft, flying night and day, moving systematically from one set of targets to another. The plan did not prosper. It was too visionary in the light of the pressing demands to protect and support the armies at the front, and far too ambitious in terms of production capability.[3]

The importance of Gorrell's plan was that it drew upon the views of the key figures who were all to become vociferous advocates of strategic airpower after the war. These included not only Trenchard but also the American General Billy Mitchell, whose campaigning for an independent air corps would lead to his court-martial, and Giulio Douhet, then struggling to get the Italian military to accept his futuristic views of air power. The connection with Douhet was through his friend, the Italian aircraft designer Gianni Caproni. It was Mitchell's stridency in pursuit of institutional independence more than his innovative ideas that got him into trouble with his superiors. Against the backdrop of America's industrial strength, he was less worried about "tactical" missions distracting from the "strategic." Douhet reported for the Italian army on the first known combat use of aircraft, in Libya in 1911, and published his landmark book *Command in the Air* in 1921.[4] The ideas he expressed were by no means unique to him, but he provided the most systematic—and the most strident, especially by the time of the book's second edition in 1927—presentation of the apparent strategic logic of air-power.[5] This logic was really a continuation of Mahan's, which was in turn a continuation of Jomini's. Mahan assumed a decisive naval battle would allow for command of the sea; Douhet applied this to the air and assumed that decisiveness there would produce command of the air.

As Azar Gat has demonstrated, behind the enthusiasm for the new engines of war, whether on land or in the air, was a modernist fascination with the possibility of a rationalist, technocratic super-efficient society built around machines, linked to elitism in political theory and futurism in art, and feeding naturally into fascism.[6] This did not mean, however, that those who developed new strategic theories around these weapons adopted the whole package. Many did not. They were imagining a future not necessarily far away but still well beyond current capabilities. Their theories developed around a combination of optimism about technology and pessimism about humanity.

With some variations, postwar airpower advocates relied on five core propositions. First and most important was the conviction that appropriately deployed airpower provided an independent route to victory. The corollary of this was that it needed its own independent command and should not be subordinate to the needs of either armies or navies. This was reflected in the references to "strategic" aviation, which suggested that long-range bombard-ment missions were superior to merely "tactical" auxiliary applications. They could on their own attain the purposes of war.

Second, the defense was likely to remain dominant in land warfare, which meant that defeating the enemy army in battle—the classical route to victory—was now prohibitively expensive in terms of blood and trea-sure. Fortunately, it would no longer be necessary to defeat the enemy army because aircraft could fly right over the front lines to reach the heart of the enemy. Trenchard explained: "It is not necessary, for an air force, in order to defeat the enemy nation, to defeat its armed forces first. Airpower can dis-pense with that intermediate step."[7]

Third, in contrast to surface warfare, in the air the offense would be stron-ger than the defense. As Douhet put it, the aircraft was "the offensive weapon par excellence." This thought was later most graphically expressed in 1932 by British Prime Minister Stanley Baldwin when he warned the "man in the street" that there was "no power on earth that can protect him from being bombed. Whatever people may tell him, the bomber will always get through." As late as 1937, Air Chief Marshal Hugh Dowding, commander of the Royal Air Force fighter command, stated that bombing attacks on

London would cause such panic that defeat could occur "in a fortnight or less."[8]

Fourth, these potentially decisive effects would be achieved less by the actual destruction of people and property than by the consequences of this destruction on the ability of governments to function and prosecute a war. Popular pressure would oblige the enemy to sue for peace. Trenchard wrote in 1928 how the goal of air action was "to paralyse from the very outset the enemy's production centres of munitions of war of every sort and to stop all communications and transportation." More could be achieved by attacking the enemy's "vital centres" than attacking the forces that sought to protect them.[9] In this, the more people-friendly version, it was the loss of vital infrastructure that would make it progressively difficult to feed the nation's war machine. In the less people-friendly version, it was assumed that the effects would come through popular demoralization, demotivation, and even panic on such a scale that the government would have to abandon the war.

Fifth, the advantage would go to the side that attacked first. For Douhet, the "command of the air" would come when it was possible to "prevent the enemy from flying while retaining the ability to fly oneself." This would be achieved by aggressively bombarding the enemy's air bases and factories ("destroying the eggs in their nest"), a tactic that favored attacking as soon as possible—even preemptively, before the enemy air force was already on its way. There would be no time for a formal declaration of war. As we have seen with land warfare, the main reason to take this sort of risk would be the expectation that the first blows could be translated into a decisive victory.

There were practical issues connected to all these propositions. Offensive long-range bombers would have to carry fuel as well as ordnance and could be vulnerable to faster, more agile fighter aircraft. If they flew in daylight these bombers were more likely to be spotted en route to their targets. They might be safer flying at night but would find it harder to hit targets with accuracy. Then there was the risk of retaliation. Douhet assumed that a war would start with a competition to inflict as much as damage as possible on the enemy society, and the victor would be the first to pound the other into submission. That was a dire prospect, especially if neither side managed a decisive blow. The logic of this prospect of mutual destruction was mutual deterrence, since both sides would presumably be anxious to protect their people from revenge attacks. Even during the Allied discussions of a long-range bomber offensive in 1917, French enthusiasm waned as they contemplated their own vulnerability to German retaliation. Unless it was assumed that first blows could lead to the physical collapse of the war economy, which was unlikely, a lot was resting on the assumption that an early victory would result from the impact on civilian morale.

Unlike soldiers who were trained to deal with attack, Douhet assumed that civilians would be helpless.

> A complete breakdown of the social structure cannot but take place in a country being subjected to...merciless pounding from the air. The time would soon come when, to put an end to horror and suffering, the people themselves, driven by the instinct of self-preservation, would rise up and demand an end to the war.[10]

Douhet was dismissive of anything that detracted from the most massive early offensives—there was no point in investing in air defenses or keeping anything in reserve, let alone preparing for auxiliary missions in support of the army or navy. He recognized that this would put a premium on getting the targeting right, yet he was strikingly vague on targeting priorities. There could be no "hard and fast rules" because much would depend on the "material, moral, and psychological" circumstances.[11]

Nor did he or the other advocates have much evidence upon which to base their claims, other than extrapolations from the first responses of Britain and France to German bombs. This led to some curious social theory on the general softness of the lower classes, the respective resilience of British and German workers, and the consequence of the presence of panicky aliens. Prior to the war there had been a lot of interest in crowd psychology, inspired in particular by the Frenchman Gustave Le Bon. He provided a quasi-scientific basis, taken extraordinarily seriously at the time, for those who feared the entry of the masses into political life and also those who became excited by the possibility of harnessing popular emotions. Chapter 22 considers this more carefully. For the moment all that is important to note is Le Bon's claim that individuals lost their distinctive personalities in crowds, and that this collective was highly suggestible. There was no particular reason, however, why an essentially irrational crowd would demand surrender. The mood might push in the opposite direction. In 1908, the British author H. G. Wells, who was well aware of Le Bon's work, wrote *War in the Air*. His assumption was that the crowd (in this case, New Yorkers) would not so much panic as turn extremely belligerent. The authorities in his novel wanted to surrender but the people, roused to anger, disagreed. With the head "conquered and stunned," the body was "released" from its rule.

> New York had become a headless monster, no longer capable of collective submission. Everywhere it lifted itself rebelliously; everywhere

authorities and officials left to their own initiative were joining in the arming and flag-hoisting and excitement of that afternoon.

The result was that the Germans were forced to make good their threats. New York was wrecked "because she was at once too strong to be occupied and too undisciplined and proud to surrender in order to escape destruction."[12]

The actual mechanisms through which a government would be forced to abandon a war were left unexplained by Douhet and his colleagues. In this respect, the advocates of this approach suffered from combined psychological and democratic fallacies by which they assumed that elites would be obliged to respond to hysterical mass opinion. There were always a variety of possible scenarios short of a panicked surrender. As the Second World War demonstrated, a population might be stunned into fatalism with no options other than resigned stoicism, adjusting to the new conditions, turning anger against the enemy. If they truly wished to stop the war they would need an effective political opposition. Otherwise they were likely to be cowed into silent suffering by a repressive regime. Basic factors of social cohesion and political structure, as well as more specific ones relating to the extent of the understanding of and support for the war policy and its execution, were just as crucial. To replace a government or get an existing one to change its mind required both political means and an alternative policy.

These issues illustrated a feature of any approach to conflict that did not attempt to achieve its objectives by physically occupying the enemy society. Such an approach required a construct of the enemy's socioeconomic and political system that provided reliable indicators of its vulnerabilities and potential pressure points. If this was going to lead to a decisive act, rather than contribute to a form of deadly bargaining, the assumption had to be that if the right points could be found—whether in industrial production, political control, or popular morale—the system as a whole could be brought down. This hypothesis continued to have an influence, but its foundations were speculative at best.

Armored Warfare

A possible theoretical basis for the assumption was developed by a British army officer, John Frederick Charles "Boney" Fuller. Fuller joined the Tank Corps in 1916, at the start of what he immediately recognized to be a revolutionary development. At the time armored vehicles were having an impact, but they were too cumbersome and unreliable to be the basis of an offensive.

During 1918, Fuller developed a plan for a war-winning offensive, known as "Plan 1919." The plan depended on a new tank coming into large-scale production the next year. As with Gorrell and his proposed air campaign, Fuller was overly optimistic about the capabilities becoming available to support his ambition. The real importance of his ideas, like Gorrell's, lay in their relevance for the conduct of future wars.

Although Fuller played no role in the development of the tank and was not the first to conceive of it developing an offensive role, he was the pre-eminent figure in formulating the new Tank Corps doctrine. Once convinced that tanks offered much more than support to the infantry, Fuller began to describe what might be achieved when tanks could be deployed in larger numbers, at greater speeds, and over longer ranges. Mechanical warfare, he observed, was about to replace muscular warfare. The days when firepower would have to be carried by men or pulled by horses into battle were passing. The petrol engine was going to revolutionize land warfare just as surely as steam had revolutionized naval warfare. He knew that the first steps would be tentative, perhaps not much more than raids against German lines, but he envisioned a future army of one thousand tanks, dividing for a standard attack on enemy defensive lines and another attack directed at the enemy's command structure. His ideas were refined following the Allied retreat during the German offensive of spring 1918. He attributed the retreat to the paralysis of the high command. As "the potential strength of a body of men lies in its organization," he concluded, "if we can destroy this organization, we shall have gained our object." Fuller became an advocate of "brain warfare," that is, attacks aimed at disorganizing the enemy's mental processes and ensuring the collapse of the enemy's will to resist. There was no need to target the enemy army; better to target the command structure. In his plan, the German army headquarters was the major objective. The aim was to shoot the enemy through the head rather than force death through many wounds to the body. Literally brainless, the enemy would be confused and its forces would turn into a rabble. Later in his life he reflected that Plan 1919 promised victory with a "stupendous drama, the only satisfactory way to win a war."

In this metaphor of the army as a body, the headquarters was the brain and the lines of communication the nervous system, leading into the muscular forward forces. The whole system required constant supply. It was, however, still an analogy. As Brian Holden Reid noted, the army was not the same as an organism because the component parts could exist independently of each other. "Brains, courage and fighting power are not compartmentalized, and a crisis can throw up a relatively junior officer who can provide the guidance formerly given by higher authority." It was the case that the German collapse in 1918 was accelerated when the divisional headquarters was overrun by tanks, but this was at the end of a long and exhausting war, when morale on both sides was fragile. This encouraged the view that shock always resulted in a form of panic, and a tendency emerged to play down the other factors that might wear down an enemy. Again we can see the similarities with the early air power theorists, with whom Fuller had an affinity. He wrote in 1923 about an air attack that would transform London into a "vast raving Bedlam" so that the government at Westminster would be "swept away by an avalanche of terror."[13] Fuller had also read Le Bon closely. His innovation was to use notions of crowd psychology to consider how not only civilians but also armies might buckle under pressure.

The odd thing about Fuller's military theories was that they drew upon and developed a wider set of ideas that had been gestating for some time and reflected his wide but idiosyncratic reading. Fuller dabbled in mysticism and the occult, had an enthusiasm for modernism and a contempt for democracy, and eventually developed a commitment to fascism. His readiness to challenge conventional religion led naturally, he judged, to a readiness to challenge conventional military thinking. In addition to Le Bon, social Darwinism and philosophical pragmatism had also influenced his thinking. He made the familiar claim that his approach to the study of war was scientific. His actual method belied this but did reflect his belief that he had identified patterns that would recur irrespective of time and place. He had little doubt that his analysis compared more than favorably with what he considered to be exasperating, amateurish, and doltish senior British officers. Their incompetence, fully demonstrated during the Great War, was now revealed fully in their failure to appreciate Fuller's insights. Yet his approach was based on grandiose claims and a romantic urge to find a form of battle that avoided the mass slaughter he had witnessed in France. Somehow this flawed and unappealing, arrogant and authoritarian character, whose theorizing beyond military matters was eccentric and often barely intelligible, hit upon an original conception of armored warfare that turned what was widely viewed as an interesting but limited specialist tool into the basis of a new type of warfare. Fuller became one of the first to focus on the possibility of disorienting the enemy's "brain" rather than eliminating his physical strength.[14]

After the war, reflecting on the fate of what he described as "pot bellied and pea brained" armies fixated on firepower, Fuller sought to develop further the possibility of using tanks and aircraft in a battle that would be decisive as a result of psychological dislocation rather than physical destruction. As with many of the technological optimists of the time, he underplayed the logistical difficulties inherent in his vision and overplayed the extent to which it would not require the enormous armies of the Great War or the vast resources of industrial societies.[15] His theories depended on a dim view of humanity. His first major book, *The Reformation of War*, made a crude elitist distinction between the masters (super-men) and the slaves (super-monkeys), with the latter mentally challenged, naturally fearful, and tending to the feminine (a common reference of the time to emotional, hysterical personalities). In his next major theoretical statement, *The Foundations of the Science of War*,[16] he ruminated more on the nature of crowds. This was central to his view of an army and society at large as an organism which could be swayed by strong leadership. Fuller saw a grasp of crowd psychology as the "foundation of leadership." Crowds, whether they started as heterogeneous or homogeneous, tended toward a single "mind" controlled by a "soul" which was in itself dominated by instincts. It was Le Bon's story of a crowd acting like an irrational individual rather than a mass of separate rational individuals. Fuller's crowd was "a mere automaton under the will of the suggester, and, through lack of intellect, its acts [were] always unbalanced and extreme-lower or more exalted than the individual's, according to the nature of the suggestion it has received."

To Fuller, crowds were pathologically mad, credulous, impulsive and irritable, and ruled by sentiments. To challenge the crowd, the "man of genius," refusing to "swim with the stream," must instead divert "the stream from its course by compelling it to swirl forward in his own direction." If, as Napoleon put it, the moral was superior to the physical by three to one, the genius was more important than the normal by ten to one. A normal man should be considered a piece of machinery. Fuller urged that it was necessary to devise for such a man an "accurate system" that could be presented in "so simple a form, that without thinking, without perhaps knowing what we intend, he with his hands will accomplish what our brains have devised."[17] In this he was probably influenced by Frederick Taylor, whose system of scientific management is discussed in Chapter 32.

Fuller described a "military crowd" by reference to Le Bon's "mass of men dominated by a spirit which is the product of the thoughts of each individual concentrated on one idea." Hopefully this would be the will to win, but should it become disorganized by surprise or some calamity, then an urge to self-preservation would take over. An army was an organized crowd, held together and directed through training and common purpose, but it was a crowd nonetheless and so could turn when stressed. With strong "mind" and "soul," an army could endure, but once it faced heavy losses, morale could suffer and fear take over.

> As the battle bursts into flame, creative reason holds control or is lost; imagination rattles the dice of chance and the man obeys, or, like an animal hunting another, acts on his own intuition. Self-sacrifice urges men on; self-preservation urges men back; reason decides; or, if no decision be possible, sense of duty carries the will to win one step nearer to its goal. So the contest is waged, not necessarily by masses of surging men, but rather by vacant spaces riddled by death.[18]

In battle, an army shocked and bereft of leadership could lose its discipline and readiness to go forward. In civilian life, there was no real contest. The emotional, impulsive crowd was doomed to panic.

CHAPTER 11 | The Indirect Approach

A strategist should think in terms of paralyzing, not of killing.

—Basil Liddell Hart

S IR BASIL LIDDELL Hart was also shaped in his thinking by his experiences in the Great War (he had been gassed and wounded at the
Somme[1]) and his determination that future wars should avoid the sort of
mindless slaughter he had witnessed. Fuller was the more original and
powerful thinker, but not always the most accessible. His friend Liddell
Hart had a crisper style, and despite some poor calls in the run-up to the
Second World War, his reputation grew after that war. This was partly
because he gave unstinting support to a new generation of civilian strategists and military historians, who were able to develop their craft in the
comparative security of the universities rather than through continual free-
lancing like Liddell Hart. In addition, Liddell Hart's ideas about limited
war gained traction as thermonuclear weapons gave new meaning to the
idea of total war. He was also a relentless propagandizer on his own behalf,
to the point of suggesting that the tragedy of the Second World War was
that British generals neglected his ideas on armored warfare, while German
generals turned them into the blitzkrieg. After his death in 1970, his history was challenged and his self-promotion rebuked,[2] but the central idea
of the "indirect approach" continued to gain adherents in business as well
as military circles.

Initially Liddell Hart's work was wholly derivative. Before he sought to claim a remarkable parallel development between Fuller's ideas and his own, he had pronounced *The Reformation of War* to be "the book of the century." He had read T. E. Lawrence's early presentation of his ideas in *The Army Quarterly* in 1920 and appears, although this is less easy to document, to have drawn on the work of Julian Corbett as well. Liddell Hart was never challenged by those from whom he had borrowed so liberally. Lawrence kept no records and so was only impressed later by the similarity between his views and those of his good friend, Liddell Hart.[3] In 1922 Corbett died. Fuller did not care about the plagiarism, although his wife did. Following Fuller, Liddell Hart adopted the analogy of the brain controlling the body to call for attacks on the enemy's communications and command centers. His appeal for an "indirect approach" as the "most hopeful and economic form of strategy" struck a chord with those who believed that cleverness was preferable to brute force. Moreover, unlike Fuller, he asserted his own originality by comparing the indirect approach to the more direct, which he claimed to be Clausewitz's terrible legacy.

Liddell Hart blamed Clausewitz, or at least his followers, for their conviction that everything must be geared to decisive battles with the sole aim of destroying the enemy army through frontal assaults. Everything he hated about the futile mass offensives and horrific bloodshed of the Western Front in the First World War he seemed to blame on Clausewitz, the "evil genius of military thought." His presentation tended to caricature, as if Clausewitz was gripped by some sort of bloodlust, unable to view war except in absolutist terms, anxious for battle at the first opportunity, and seeking to win through overwhelming numbers rather than proper strategy. He wrote furiously in one of his earliest books about "the Ghost of Napoleon."[4] The approach he deplored was mechanical and a-strategic. Clausewitz's "gospel deprived strategy of its laurels."

Eventually Liddell Hart acknowledged that the differences between Clausewitz's view of war and his own were not large—they both understood that it was an extension of politics and influenced by psychology as much as brute force.[5] He could point to the density and philosophical complexity of *On War*. This made it more likely that Clausewitz would be read as an incitement to early battle at the first opportunity rather than at a more advantageous moment. The view that Clausewitz's disciples extracted simplistic slogans and applied them crudely was clearly expressed late in his career when Liddell Hart wrote the introduction to Samuel Griffith's popular translation of *The Art of War*. Sun Tzu's "realism and moderation," he wrote, formed a contrast to "Clausewitz's tendency to emphasize the logical ideal and 'absolute'" that had led these disciples to develop "the theory and practice of total war beyond all bounds of sense." Interestingly, Liddell Hart recorded that he was first made aware of Sun Tzu by a contact in China in 1927. "On reading the book I found many other points that coincided with my own lines of thought, especially his constant emphasis on doing the unexpected and pursuing the indirect approach. It helped me to realize the agelessness of the more fundamental military ideas, even of a tactical nature."[6] According to one biographer, there was no direct influence of Sun Tzu when Liddell Hart was developing his approach in the 1920s because he did not actually read the book until the early 1940s.[7] This makes his specific mention of 1927 curious, especially since he started to develop his "indirect approach"—so close to Sun Tzu in many clear elements—over the next two years. There was certainly no mention of Sun Tzu in the first version of his constantly refined presentation of his core ideas, *The Decisive Wars of History*, but the last version, *Strategy: The Indirect Approach*, included extensive quotes at the front of the book. The Giles translation of Sun Tzu, the one most in use at the time, includes the line: "In all fighting the direct methods may be used for joining battle, but indirect methods will be needed in order to secure victory." Later translations from the Chinese, however, contrasted the straightforward with the crafty, the normal with the extraordinary, or the orthodox with the unorthodox.

Liddell Hart followed Sun Tzu by prescribing an ideal form of strategy as it should be rather than how it often turned out in practice. Liddell Hart judged Clausewitz's definition too narrow, too battle-focused, as if this was the only means to the strategic end. Instead, he defined strategy as "the art of distributing and employing military means to fulfill the ends of policy." The ends of policy were not a military responsibility. They were handed down from the level of grand strategy, where all instruments of policy were weighed, one against each other, and where it was necessary to look beyond the war to the subsequent peace. At the other end of the spectrum, tactics came into play when "the application of the military instrument merges into actual fighting, the dispositions for and control of such direct action."

In an age of total war, Liddell Hart was seeking limitation, a search that became even more urgent after the invention of nuclear weapons. He was an advocate of limited aims as a means of ensuring limited means, although this urge to proportionality between the two contained an important fallacy: that military means could be geared to the political stakes rather than the strength of the opposition. Large wars could start for small stakes. To this Liddell Hart would reply that if prospective costs were wholly disproportionate to likely gains, the value of the whole enterprise should be questioned.

The art of strategy required not only finding means to achieve a fixed end but also identifying realistic and desirable ends. His method was to define the ideal against which actual performance would be judged. Thus the aim of war was "to subdue the enemy's will to resist, with the least possible human and economic loss to itself." Avoiding loss meant avoiding large battles, though the basic principles would apply even if battle had to be joined. The link with Sun Tzu was clear: "The perfection of strategy would be, therefore, to produce a decision without any serious fighting."

Instead of the direct approach, taking the obvious route into a confrontation with a prepared enemy, the indirect approach would "diminish the possibility of resistance." The vital impact would be in the psychological rather than the physical sphere. This required calculating the factors affecting the will of the opponent. So while movement might be the key to catching the enemy out physically, surprise was the key to influencing the enemy's psychology. "Dislocation is the aim of strategy; its sequel may either be the enemy's dissolution or his easier disruption in battle. Dissolution may involve some partial measure of fighting, but this has not the character of a battle." It is important to note that although Fuller and Liddell Hart are often seen as intellectual twins, on this they disagreed. Fuller certainly sought the psychological dislocation of the enemy, but he saw no problem in taking the direct route if that would have the desired effect. An indirect approach was "usually a necessary evil," and "weapon power" would determine which to choose. Where Liddell Hart was dogmatic, Fuller was pragmatic. Liddell Hart wanted to avoid battle; for Fuller, it was the likely source of victory.[8]

In the physical sphere, avoiding battle required upsetting the enemy's dispositions by means of a sudden "change of front." This could be achieved by separating enemy forces, endangering supplies, menacing routes of retreat, or combining several of these moves. In the psychological sphere, dislocation required that these physical effects be impressed on the commander's mind, creating a "sense of being trapped." Moving directly against an opponent would not throw him off balance. At most it would impose a strain, but even if successful, the enemy would retreat to his "reserves, supplies, and reinforcements." The aim was therefore to find "the line of least resistance," which translated in the psychological sphere into "the line of least expectation." It was also important to maintain a number of options. Having alternatives kept the enemy guessing, putting him on the "horns of a dilemma," and allowed for flexibility should the enemy guard against your chosen route. "A plan, like a tree, must have branches—if it is to bear fruit. A plan with a single aim is apt to prove a barren pole."[9]

Liddell Hart claimed that his theory developed through a careful examination of the whole of military history. Unfortunately, his approach to history was intuitive and eclectic rather than, as he liked to believe, "scientific." There were always elements of subtlety, surprise, or innovation in military victories, and indirectness could be "strategic, tactical, psychological and sometimes even 'unconscious.'" As Bond noted, Liddell Hart came extremely close to a circular argument: by his definition, a "decisive victory" was an event which is secured by an "indirect approach."[10] As with Sun Tzu, Liddell Hart's attraction was that he celebrated the subtle intelligence over brute force. But also like Sun Tzu's, it raised the questions of how matters would be resolved if both sides were following an indirect approach, the practical problems of coordination, and the impact of chance and friction. Although Liddell Hart later became celebrated as an apostle of maneuver, the campaigns he admired were often attritional, in that they required wearing down the opponent.

The ideal indirect strategy created conditions in which the enemy was forced to conclude that defeat had become inevitable before battle was joined. This strategy relied upon the intelligent maneuver of forces to create a relationship that, once apparent, encouraged the adversary to become more conciliatory. The logic pointed to deterrence. If the likely outcome of battle was known, the best advice would be to avoid the original provocation or—at the other extreme—go for complete, preemptive surprise. Liddell Hart was addressing situations which lacked this clarity and were harder to predict or control, by indirect or direct means. If battle was to be avoided, the role of land war must be limited and sea and air power relied on instead. Blockade from the sea or bombardment from the air might undermine enemy power by damaging the morale and logistical system of the armed forces and perhaps the underlying economic and social structure which sustained the state. Not surprisingly, therefore, Liddell Hart advocated both types of warfare during his career, although his enthusiasm for both naval blockades and air raids waxed and waned. The difficulty was that unless territory was taken the enemy could continue to resist.

Liddell Hart's advocacy of strategic air power was quite short-lived, although it included a flirtation with crowd psychology when he warned how ordinary people subjected to attack from the air could be "maddened into the impulse to maraud."[11] When it came to following the indirect approach on land, his analysis—following Fuller—focused on the impact of mechanization. Here too he concluded (on the eve of the Second World War) that the potential of a well-organized defense was probably more potent than that of a maneuvering offensive. He hoped that this would reduce the likely aggressor's readiness and ability to disrupt the status quo. Thus, despite his enthusiasm for the indirect approach, Liddell Hart came up constantly against the very real constraints on its implementation, especially when confronting an opponent of equivalent—let alone greater—raw power and tactical intelligence. An indirect approach represented a strategic ideal but one only likely to be realized in very special circumstances. Societies and their armies could prove to be extremely resilient. Getting in a position to mount sustained pressure in a resolute manner requires effective military dominance—whether at sea, in the air, or on land. This in turn was likely to require very direct and decisive contact with enemy forces. This led Liddell Hart to eventually conclude that very little useful purpose could be served by war.

Churchill's Strategy

The maneuver which brings an ally into the field is as serviceable as that which wins a great battle. The maneuver which gains an important strategic point may be less valuable than that which placates or overawes a dangerous neutral.

—Winston Churchill, *The World Crisis*

We shall discuss later the reality behind the blitzkrieg story. There is no doubt that the Wehrmacht's mastery of armored warfare gained Germany some great victories in the early stages of the Second World War that led to virtual domination of Europe. But the domination was never complete and in the end Germany lost. It was settled by the logic of alliance as much as military prowess. Germany was consistently superior in the field but in the end could not cope with the combined weight of the United States, the Soviet Union, and the British Empire. That this would be the eventual outcome was hardly apparent in the spring of 1940, when only one of the "big three" was actually at war, and its situation appeared to be parlous. On May 10, 1940, the German army began an offensive that in ten days saw it move through Belgium and Holland to the French coast. Soon France fell and Britain was alone. Yet Britain continued to fight when its position appeared hopeless and eschewed the possibility of a deal with Hitler that might have left it a diminished but still independent power.

Richard Betts has used this example to query the role of strategy. The British government's decision to continue to fight was one of the most "epochal" decisions of the last century, yet at the time it made little strategic sense.[12] For it to make sense, Betts argued, Churchill would have had to know in advance and with confidence that the Germans would be unable to cross the English Channel, lose the Battle of Britain, and eventually lose the Battle of the Atlantic. Most importantly, Churchill would have had to assume that by the end of 1941 Britain would be fighting alongside the Soviet Union and the United States.

This is, however, the wrong way to look at the decision in terms of strategy. A better approach was that adopted by Ian Kershaw in his analysis of the decision-making among the great powers during the Second World War. He did not pose the question of strategy in terms of how to best meet ultimate objectives but how the available options come to be defined and what considerations influenced the choices. His starting point was where political leaders found themselves rather than where they wished to be.[13]

As Germany advanced toward France, and Britain's close ally teetered, Winston Churchill became prime minister. His first days in office were taken up with whether France could stay in the war and what might be done if she could not. His own reputation as a war leader had yet to be made: he was still viewed with suspicion for a career marred by regular lapses of judgment. Now he had to address the arguments of his foreign secretary, Lord Halifax, that there was no point in accepting unnecessary suffering if a compromise deal with Hitler could be found that would preserve Britain's independence and integrity. There appeared to be an option using Italy, who had yet to join the war, as a mediator. Churchill convinced his colleagues that this was not worth pursuing.

The choice they faced was not about alternative means of winning but about how best to avoid defeat and humiliating terms. It was not about refusing to negotiate under any circumstances but whether there was anything to be gained by trying to negotiate when circumstances were so dire. The option of a negotiated outcome was not rejected because of Churchill's pugnacity but because the arguments in favor of it were unpersuasive. It depended on Benito Mussolini, who was becoming an increasingly unlikely mediator because of his pro-German stance and lack of influence over Hitler. On examination, possible peace terms appeared to be unacceptable. In an effort to appear reasonable during taxing cabinet discussions, Churchill professed himself willing to consider concessions in areas of British influence or the transfer of a few spare colonies to "get out of the mess," but demands which went to the heart of the country's constitutional independence, involving a different sort of government and enforced disarmament, would be intolerable.[14] Available terms might be better than those following military defeat, but this was not self-evidently the case. It was possible that matters would get even worse and Britain would be subjugated. But it was also possible that this would not happen. Any deal would be better for Britain if the Germans assumed they were dealing with an opponent that had some fight left. In addition, the very act of exploring a settlement would be viewed abroad as weakness and cause demoralization at home. For the moment, the country was not beaten and the armed forces felt that they could organize strong resistance to a German invasion. These discussions took place before the "miracle" of Dunkirk. The initial expectation had been that, at best, tens of thousands would escape to Britain from defeated France. When a third of a million troops were rescued from the beaches where they were suffering relentless air attacks, this provided an early vindication of the decision to fight on.

Churchill could have no idea at the time about the likely course of the war. According to Eliot Cohen, Churchill did not think of strategy as a blueprint for victory. He knew that the course of a war could not be predicted and that steps to victory might not be discerned until they were about to be taken. He distrusted "cut and dried calculations" on how wars would be won. For him, strategy was very much an art and not a science—indeed so art-like as to be close to painting. "There must be that all-embracing view which presents the beginning and the end, the whole and each part, as one instantaneous impression retentively and untiringly held in the mind." With a few key themes always at the fore and a grasp of context, there was a framework for taking in new developments exploiting new opportunities. This was not, as Cohen notes, a machine built "to narrow tolerances and an exact design," nor was it "a chaotic welter of unconnected and opportunistic decisions."[15]

While Churchill's approach to purely military affairs could be impetuous, he had a natural grasp of coalition warfare. Coalitions were always going to be central to British strategy. The empire contributed significantly to the war effort in terms of men and materiel, and its special needs had to be accommodated. The United States had the unequivocal potential to tip the scales when a European confrontation reached a delicate stage. Almost immediately after taking office, Churchill saw that the only way to a satisfactory conclusion of the war was "to drag the United States in," and this was thereafter at the center of his strategy. His predecessor Neville Chamberlain had not attempted to develop any rapport with President Franklin Roosevelt. Churchill began at once what turned into a regular and intense correspondence with Roosevelt, although so long as Britain's position looked so parlous and American opinion remained so anti-war, little could be expected from Washington. His first letter was if anything desperate, warning of the consequences for American security of a British defeat. If Britain could hang on, something might turn American opinion. Churchill was even prepared to believe that this might happen if the country was invaded.[16]

At the time, Hitler's choices appeared more palatable and easier. German victories had confirmed his reputation as a military genius with unquestioned authority. Yet he recognized the difficulty of following the defeat of France with an invasion of Britain. A cross-channel invasion would be complicated and risky. There were also other options for getting Britain out of the war. The first was to push it out of the Mediterranean, further affecting its prestige and influence and interfering with its source of oil. Whether or not this would have had the desired effects, Hitler was wary of his regional partners—Mussolini's Italy, Franco's Spain, and Vichy France. They all disagreed with each other, and none could be considered reliable. Mussolini, for example, used German victories to move a reluctant country into war. He then demonstrated his independence from Hitler by launching a foolhardy invasion of Greece. This left him weakened and Hitler furious. Germany had to rescue the Italian position in Greece and then North Africa, leading to a major diversion of attention and resources from Hitler's main project, the invasion of the Soviet Union.

He considered a war with the Soviet Union to be not only inevitable but also the culmination of his ambitions, allowing him to establish German dominion over continental Europe and deal once and for all with the twin—and, in his eyes, closely related—threats of the Jews and Communism. If he was going to go to war with Russia anyway, it was best to do so while the country was still weak following Josef Stalin's mass purges of the army and communist party in the 1930s.[17] A quick defeat of Russia would achieve Hitler's essential objective and leave Britain truly isolated. But Hitler also had a view about how the war was likely to develop. Britain, he assumed, only resisted out of a hope that the Russians would join the war. Of course, without a quick win, Hitler faced the dreaded prospect of a war on two fronts—something good strategists were supposed to avoid—as well as increasing strain on national resources. He needed to conquer the Soviet Union to sustain the war and to gain access to food supplies and oil. With the Soviet Union defeated, he reasoned, Britain would realize that the game was up and seek terms. If Hitler had accepted that the Soviet Union could not be defeated, his only course would have been to seek a limited peace with Britain that would have matched neither the scale of his prior military achievements nor his pending political ambition.

Another reason for acting quickly was that the Americans were likely to come into the war eventually, but not—he assumed—until 1942 at the earliest. Getting Russia out of the way quickly would limit the possibility of a grand coalition building up against him. In this Stalin helped. The Soviet leader refused to listen to all those who tried to warn him about Hitler's plans. He assumed that the German leader would stick to the script that Stalin had worked out for him, providing clues of the imminence of attack. Churchill's warnings were dismissed as self-serving propaganda, intended to provoke war between the two European giants to help relieve the pressure on Britain. Unlike Tsar Alexander in 1812, Stalin compounded the problem by having his armies deployed on the border, making it easier for the German army to plot a course that would cut them off before they could properly engage. The result was a military disaster from which the Soviet Union barely escaped. Yet a combination of the famous and fierce Russian winter and some critical German misjudgments about when and where to advance let Stalin recover from the early blow. Once defeat was avoided, industrial strength slowly but surely revived and the vast size of the Russian territory was too much for the invaders. The virtuoso performances of German commanders could put off defeat, but they could not overcome the formidable limits imposed by a flawed grand strategy.

Germany's first blow against the Soviet Union depended on surprise (as did Japan's against the United States), but it was not a knockout. The initial advantage did not guarantee a long-term victory. The stunning German victories of the spring 1940 and the bombing of British cities that began in the autumn approximated the possibilities imagined by Fuller, Liddell Hart, and the airpower theorists, but they were not decisive. They moved the war from one stage to another, and the next stage was more vicious and protracted. The tank battles became large scale and attritional, culminating in the 1943 Battle of Kursk. Populations did not crumble under air attacks but endured terrific devastation, culminating in the two atomic bombs dropped on the Japanese cities of Hiroshima and Nagasaki—the war's shocking finale. Our discussion of American military thought in the 1970s and 1980s will demonstrate the United States' high regard for the German operational art and recall that this was not good enough to win the war.

When it came to victory, what mattered most was how coalitions were formed, came together, and were disrupted. This gave meaning to battles. The Axis was weak because Italy's military performance was lackluster, Spain stayed neutral, and Japan fought its own war and tried to avoid conflict with the Soviet Union. Britain's moment of greatest peril came when France was lost as an ally, but started to be eased when Germany attacked the Soviet Union. Churchill's hopes rested on the United States, sympathetic to the British cause but not in a belligerent mood. It was eighteen months before America was in the war. As soon as America entered the fray, Churchill rejoiced. "So we had won after all!... How long the war would last or in what fashion it would end, no man could tell, nor did I at this moment care... We should not be wiped out. Our history would not come to an end."[18]

CHAPTER 12 | Nuclear Games

We may be likened to two scorpions in a bottle, each capable of killing the
other, but only at the risk of his own life.

—J. Robert Oppenheimer

WARS NORMALLY CONCLUDE with calls for a new era of peace and justice, and the Second World War was no exception. Unfortunately,
the developing tensions between the United States and the Soviet Union and
their ideologically opposed blocs provided few grounds for optimism. The
possibility of a third world war became apparent almost immediately as the
underlying antagonism between Britain and the United States on the one
hand and the Soviet Union on the other surfaced over the fate of the territories liberated from German occupation. Soon there was talk of a "cold war,"
a term popularized in 1947 by Walter Lippmann in a book with that title.[1]
Lippmann recalled the term from the late 1930s when "la guerre froide" had
been used to characterize Hitler's war of nerves against the French.[2] A cold
war was therefore one in which two states weighed each other up, viewing
each other warily like two boxers circling each other in the ring before the
proper fight began. It was not used with any optimism, as if anticipating
decades of antagonism that would never quite tip over into a hot war.[3]

The British essayist George Orwell actually used the term before
Lippmann, in October 1945, as he tried to assess the impact of atom

bombs on international affairs. He described the prospect "of two or three monstrous super-states, each possessed of a weapon by which millions of people can be wiped out in a few seconds, dividing the world between them." He saw, however, that while such a war was possible, this might be avoided as a result of "a tacit agreement never to use the bomb against one another." Use would only be threatened against those unable to retaliate. So this new form of supreme power might not only lead to an uneasy standoff between states but also to even more effective ways of keeping the exploited classes down. An end to large-scale wars perhaps, but instead "a peace that is no peace" between "horribly stable...slave empires."[4] The idea that atom bombs would rob the exploited "of all power to revolt" may not have appeared so far-fetched at the time, given recent evidence of the readiness of regimes to use instruments of mass slaughter against subject peoples.

The question of what strategic purposes these new weapons could serve was first addressed seriously by historian Bernard Brodie, who had previously specialized in maritime strategy. On hearing of the atom bomb, Brodie told his wife, "Everything that I have written is now obsolete."[5] Established forms of strategic theory were inadequate. "Everything about the atomic bomb," he observed, "is overshadowed by the twin facts that it exists and its destructive power is fantastically great. Thus far the chief purpose of our military establishment has been to win wars. From now on its chief purpose must be to avert them. It can have almost no other useful purpose."[6] From the start, therefore, Brodie recognized the dissuasive character of the "absolute weapon." Political communities would be wary about using a weapon against others that could also wipe them out if used against them.

The New Strategists

By his own career, Brodie defined the possibility of a field of strategy in which civilians took the lead. He already had a low opinion of the quality of military thinking—and made little effort to hide this—and regretted the extent to which the study of war had lagged behind other fields of human activity. "The purpose of soldiers is obviously not to produce books," he remarked in a 1949 article, "but one must assume that any real ferment of thought could not have so completely avoided breaking into print." Military training, he suggested, discouraged contemplation, was anti-intellectual, and focused excessively on practical matters and command issues. To the extent strategy was discussed it was with reference to the supposedly unchanging principles of war, along the lines first set down by Jomini. These were at best "a pointed injunction to use common sense."

With military problems growing not only in complexity but also in the potential for utter disaster, Brodie insisted that strategy needed to be taken altogether more seriously. As an example of how this might be done, he pointed to economics. Just as the economist sought to utilize the total resources of the nation to maximize its wealth, the strategist sought to use the same resources to maximize the total effectiveness of the nation in war. As all military problems were about economy of means, a "substantial part of classical economic theory is directly applicable to problems of military strategy." In particular "a science like economics" could show the way to a "genuine analytical method."[7] The idea that the resolution of strategic problems depended on intellect and analysis rather than character and intuition fit in with the trend to subject all human decisions to the dictates of rationality and the application of science. It was given more urgency by the potentially catastrophic consequences of misjudgment in the nuclear age.

The scientific method as a means of interpreting large amounts of disparate data had proved itself in Britain in the Second World War. It first made a mark when used to determine the best way to employ radar in air defense. As one of the key figures in the British program noted, the methodology used was closer to classical economics than physics, although economists were not directly engaged.[8] During the course of the war, operations research—as the new field came to be known—made major strides in support of actual operations, including working out the safest arrangement for convoys in the face of submarine attack or choosing targets for air raids.[9] Mathematicians and physicists made more of an impact in the United States, notably those who became involved in the Manhattan Project, the organization which had led to the production of the first atomic bomb.

The center for the postwar application of such methods to practical, and particularly military, problems was the RAND Corporation, which became the prototypical "think tank." The organization was set up under an air force grant to develop operational research. It soon became an independent nonprofit corporation addressing defense issues and other aspects of public policy using advanced analytical techniques. RAND began by recruiting natural scientists and engineers who expected to deal with hardware. Sharon Ghamari-Tabrizi describes RAND as fashioning itself as a cold war avant-garde, self-consciously exploratory and experimental, with an "insouciant disregard" for traditional forms of military experience.[10] Soon it was hiring economists and other social scientists. The steady improvements in computational power made mathematical approaches to complex problems more practical. Even economics up to this point had been more literate than numerate. Now quantitative analyses grew in strength and credibility. It is hard to overstate the importance of RAND, especially during its early years, in transforming established patterns of thought not only in the military sphere but throughout the social sciences. The resources and tools it had available, including the most advanced computers of the day, provided it with a capacity to innovate, which it did with a remarkable sense of mission and confidence.

The new universe that was explored at RAND was simulated as much as observed. Philip Mirowski describes what he calls the "Cyborg sciences." These reflected the new interactions between men and machines. They broke down the distinctions between nature and society, as models of one began to resemble the other, and between "reality" and simulacra. The Monte Carlo simulations adopted for dealing with uncertainty in data during the Manhattan Project, for example, opened up a range of possible experiments to explore the logic of complex systems, discerning ways through uncertainty and forms of order in chaos.[11] RAND analysts saw these new methods as supplanting rather than supplementing traditional patterns of thought. Simple forms of cause and effect could be left behind as it became possible to explore the character of dynamic systems, with the constantly changing interaction between component parts. The models of systems, more or less orderly and stable, that had started to become fashionable before the war could take on new meanings. And even in areas where intense computation was not required, there was a growing comfort in scientific circles—both natural and social—with models that were formal and abstract, not just based on direct observations of a narrow segment of accessible reality but on explorations of something that approximated to a much larger and otherwise inaccessible reality. Types of systems and relationships could be analyzed in ways that the human mind, left on its own, could not begin to manage.

As one of the first textbooks on operations research noted, work of this sort required an "impersonal curiosity concerning new subjects," rejection of "unsupported statements," and a desire to rest "decisions on some quantitative basis, even if the basis is only a rough estimate." Although this approach started with a focus on problems of national defense, its most far-reaching impact was elsewhere. Because in the military, particularly the nuclear sphere, there were practical and consequential decisions to be taken, the research and analysis had to remain grounded in evidence even when it was conceptually innovative.

When faced with the possibility of nuclear war, an event for which there could be neither precedent nor experiment and which in its enormity challenged imagination, only simulation was possible. In areas which seemed to be wholly unique ("How many nuclear wars have you fought, general?"), experience counted for less than a sharp and disciplined intellect. When in 1961, Hedley Bull, a young Australian with a skeptical but discerning eye, considered the state of strategic thought, he observed how much of it assumed the "rational action" of a kind of "strategic man." This man, Bull observed, "on further acquaintance reveals himself as a university professor of unusual intellectual subtlety."[12] The reason for the ascent of strategic man, he suggested, was nuclear weapons. Strategy could no longer be solely concerned with how to fight war as an instrument of policy but also had to understand how to threaten war. Studies of actual violence had to be supplemented by discussions of deterrence and the manipulation of risk. It was because of this that strategic thinking was no longer a military preserve. Civilian experts, Bull noted, overwhelmed the military with their publications and were the obvious people to consult on questions of deterrence and arms control. Now that John F. Kennedy had become president, civilian strategists had "entered the citadels of power and have prevailed over military advisers in major issues of policy." Neither the military nor the civilians had any experience of the conduct of a nuclear war, so inevitably much strategic thinking was of an "abstract and speculative character," which suited the civilians. They demonstrated "sophistication and high technical quality" in their work.[13]

The key people in this new approach had largely come from RAND. They were led at the Pentagon by a secretary of defense, Robert McNamara, who had pioneered the use of quantitative analysis while at the Ford Motor Company. He challenged the armed services to justify their budgets and programs in the face of intensive questioning. His agents in this were young analysts gathered in the Office of Systems Analysis. They were smart, brash, confident, and dismissive of the faltering attempts of military officers to block their ascent. McNamara's right-hand man in the Pentagon, Charles Hitch, who was recruited from RAND, had observed with a colleague in 1960: "Essentially we regard all military problems as, in one of their aspects, economic problems in the efficient allocation and use of resources."[14] McNamara demanded data and insisted on quantitative analysis as the best way to assess the costs and benefits of alternative programs. Disregarding the preferences of the armed services, McNamara canceled favored programs and challenged cherished beliefs.

It became a truism that McNamara's methods were inappropriate for fighting a war, especially one as politically complex as Vietnam, and failure here sullied his reputation forever. Yet for the first part of his tenure in the Pentagon, McNamara was considered to be the most gifted and effective member of the cabinets of Kennedy and then Lyndon Johnson. The military floundered in his presence, looking amateurish even when discussing operational issues. McNamara was described as an "IBM on legs." Decisive and articulate, he was the epitome of the rational strategic man in his mastery of the evidence and analytical techniques.[15] The mythology surrounding McNamara, and the opposition he faced, exaggerated the difference his methods had made. The military had not dominated Eisenhower's budgetary process, nor had the civilians controlled Kennedy's as much as was claimed. Nonetheless, senior officers viewed with alarm the civilians who lacked combat experience yet pontificated on military tasks. The arrogance that the civilians had nurtured at RAND, never doubting their intellectual superiority over their military paymasters, had left resentments that were now aggravated as programs and budgets were put at risk. One tirade, from a former chief of the air staff, was joyously quoted in a book by two members of McNamara's staff against whom it was directed. General White complained about the "pipe-smoking, tree-full-of-owls" types, doubting that "these over-confident, sometimes arrogant young professors, mathematicians and other theorists have sufficient wordliness or motivation to stand up to the sort of enemy we face."[16]

While Bull defended the new strategists against various charges of being uncritical, amoral, or pseudoscientific, he noted a conceit. Many were of the view that previously "military affairs escaped scientific study and received only the haphazard attention of second-rate minds." He also noted an aspiration among the civilians to turn strategy into a science by "eliminating antiquated methods and replacing them with up-to-date ones." If only, as some hoped, these new methods could get closer to economics they could help "rationalize our choices and increase our control over our environment." Brodie also doubted the exaggerated ambition. Though White's comments confirmed the stereotype of a narrow-minded and prejudiced military, Brodie also found the new analysts and their methods a mixed blessing. They improved decision-making in the Pentagon on such matters as the procurement of new weapons, but there remained limits to what could be achieved by applying economics to strategy. Economists tended to be insensitive to and intolerant of political considerations that got in the way of their theories. More worrying than their weakness in diplomatic or military history, and in contemporary politics, was their lack of awareness of "how important a deficiency this is for strategic insight." The quality of the theoretical structures adopted by economists led to a disdain for other social sciences as "primitive in their techniques and intellectually unworthy."[17]

Game Theory

The presumed signature methodology of the new strategy was game theory. As Chapter 13 demonstrates, the actual influence on nuclear strategy was slight. Nonetheless, game theory represented a way of thinking about strategic issues that was abstract and formal. Its influence on the social sciences eventually became significant. It emerged as the result of collaboration between two European émigrés working at Princeton during the war. From Hungary came John von Neumann. As a child he could astound with feats of memory and computation, and he was soon recognized as one of the mathematical geniuses of his age. He had developed the basic principle of game theory in the 1920s by contemplating poker. When Oskar Morgenstern, an economist from Vienna, got to know von Neumann at Princeton he saw the broader significance of his ideas and helped give them structure. Their formidable joint work, *The Theory of Games and Economic Behavior*, was published in 1944.

Why poker and not chess, which had always been seen as the strategist's game? The scientist Jacob Bronowski records von Neumann's reply:

> "No, no," he said. "Chess is not a game. Chess is a well-defined form of computation. You may not be able to work out all the answers, but in theory there must be a solution, a right procedure in any position. Now real games," he said, "are not like that at all. Real life is not like that. Real life consists of bluffing, of little tactics of deception, of asking yourself what is the other man going to think I mean to do. And that is what games are about in my theory."[18]

In chess both sides are working with exactly the same, perfect information, besides what is going on in the head of the opponent. Chance is a factor in poker, but the game is not pure chance. It is possible to apply probabilities to assess the likely hands of other players. As there will always be a degree of uncertainty, the same hand can be played in different ways according to judgments about whether other players are bidding out of strength or weakness. It is possible to outthink the competition. Game theory was therefore about intelligent strategies in inherently uncertain situations.

Von Neumann watched how in poker all the players encouraged uncertainty about the quality of their cards. Bluff was essential and unpredictability in their play helpful. He identified the optimum outcome for one rational poker player playing against another as the "minimax" solution, the best of the worst outcomes. His 1928 proof of this solution gave game theory its mathematical credibility, moving it away from a representation of how a game might be played to a suggestion of how it should be played. By showing how to proceed rationally in an irrational situation, game theory demonstrated why it might be logical to bluff for both offensive and defensive purposes, and how the occasional random move could make it difficult for an opponent to discern a pattern of play, thereby adding to his uncertainty.[19]

The book von Neumann co-authored with Morgenstern was described as "one of the most influential and least-read books of the twentieth century." At 641 pages of dense mathematics, it barely sold four thousand copies in its first five years in print.[20] After extensive but mixed reviews, and though some enthusiasts began to spread the word, the economics profession gave every impression of being underwhelmed. Where it initially took root was in the operations research community, to the point that it was described in an early postwar survey as a branch of mathematics special to this field. Here von Neumann appears to have been particularly influential. As one of the government's top scientific advisers until his premature death from cancer in 1959, he encouraged all means, including linear programming and the increased use of computers, of raising the quality of the scientific input. He saw RAND as an institution that could showcase the new techniques.[21]

Von Neumann and Morgenstern also found their popularizer. John McDonald's *Strategy in Poker, Business and War* is curiously neglected in the histories of game theory. In 1949, McDonald came across von Neumann and Morgenstern when researching an article on poker for *Fortune Magazine*. Then McDonald wrote another article on game theory for the same magazine, before turning both articles into a book. The reason for the neglect of McDonald's book may be that it did not take the theory forward and was geared to a popular exposition. But the author had extensive conversations with the academics and provided a clear statement of what they thought they might achieve. McDonald acknowledged that the mathematical proofs would challenge any lay reader, but he promised that the underlying concepts could be readily grasped. Game theory offered insights not just into military strategy but strategy in general. It was relevant whenever relationships involved conflict, imperfect information, and incentives to deceive. Because the theory was "formal and neutral, non-ideological," it was "as good for one man as for another." It would not help with assessing values and ethics, but "it may be able to tell what one can get and how one can get it."

In terms of the shift in strategic thinking prompted by game theory, the critical insight was that acting strategically depended on expectations about the likely actions of others over whom one has no control. The players in a game of strategy do not cooperate, yet their actions are interdependent. In such restrained circumstances the rational strategy was not to attempt to maximize gain but instead to accept an optimal outcome. Minimax, McDonald observed, was "one of the most talked about novelties in learned circles today." When he moved on to consider its applications, paying particular attention to the importance of coalitions, he saw a number of possibilities. "War is chance," he concluded, "and minimax must be its modern philosophy." Yet he also described this as a theory with "imagination but no magic." It involved "an act of logic with an unusual twist, which can be followed to the borderline of mathematical computation."[22]

The presumption behind the pioneering work on game theory, enthusiastically encouraged at RAND, was the conviction that there could be a scientific basis for strategy. Past endeavors to put these matters on a properly scientific basis had supposedly faltered because the analytical tools were not available. Specialists in military strategy lacked the mathematics, and the mathematics lacked the concepts and computational capacity. Now that these were available true breakthroughs could be made. Game theory was exciting because it directly addressed the problems posed by the fact that there was more than one decision-maker and then offered mathematical solutions. It was soon generating its own literature and conferences.

In 1954, the sociologist Jessie Bernard made an early attempt to consider the broader relevance of game theory for the softer social sciences. She also worried about an inherent amorality, "a modernized, streamlined, mathematical version of Machiavellianism." It implied a "low concept of human nature," expecting "nothing generous, nothing noble, nothing idealistic. It expects people to bluff, to deceive, to feint, to withhold information, to play their advantages to the utmost, to make the most of their opponent's weaknesses." Although Bernard acknowledged the focus on rational decision, she misunderstood the theory, presenting it as a mathematical means of testing rather than of generating strategies. The misunderstanding was perhaps not unreasonable for she assumed that different qualities were required to come up with strategies: "Imagination, insight, intuition, ability to put one's self in another person's position, understanding of the wellsprings of human motivation—good as well as evil—these are required for the thinking up of policies or strategies."[23] For this reason, the "hardest work, so far as the social scientist is concerned, is probably already completed by the time the theory of games takes over." In her grasp of the theory's claim, she missed the point, though in her appreciation of the theory's limits she was ahead of her time. The theory assumed rationality, but on the basis of preferences and values that the players brought with them to the game.

Prisoners' Dilemma

The values attached to alternative outcomes of games were payoffs. The aim was to maximize them. Players were aware that in this respect they all had the same aim. In card games they accepted that their choices would be determined by the established rules of the game. As the application was extended, the choices could be shaped not only by mutually agreed upon and accepted rules but by the situation in which they found themselves. The theory progressed by identifying situations resembling real life that created challenging choices for the players. For the theory to move on, it was necessary to get beyond the limits of the von Neumann and Morgenstern analysis involving two players and "zero-sum payoffs," which meant that what one won the other must lose. The normal approach for a mathematician having solved a comparatively simple problem was to move on to a more complex case, such as coalition formation. But this process turned out to be difficult in the case of game theory, especially if mathematical proofs were going to be required at each new stage.

The key breakthrough came in the exploration of non-zero-sum games, in which the players could all gain or all lose, depending on how the game was played. The actual invention of the game of prisoners' dilemma should be attributed to two RAND analysts, Merrill Flood and Melvin Dresher. The most famous formulation, however, was provided in 1950 by Albert Tucker when lecturing to psychologists at Stanford University. Prisoners' dilemma involved two prisoners—unable to communicate with each other—whose fate depended on whether or not they confessed during interrogation and whether their answers coincided. If both remained silent, they were prosecuted on a minor charge and received light sentences (one year). If both confessed, they were prosecuted but with a recommendation for a sentence below the maximum (five years). If one confessed and the other did not, then the confessor got a lenient sentence (three months) while the other was prosecuted for the maximum sentence (ten years). The two players were left alone in separate cells to think things over.

		B	
		1 Silence	2 Confess
A	1 Silence	-1 a1b1 -1	-0.25 a1b2 -10
	2 Confess	-10 a2b1 -0.25	-5 a2b2 -5

FIGURE 12.1 *The figures in the corners refer to expectation of sentence.*

It should be noted that the matrix itself was a revolutionary way of presenting strategic outcomes and remained thereafter a fixture of formal analysis. This matrix demonstrated the prediction for prisoners' dilemma (see fig. 12.1). They both confessed. *A* was unable to conspire with *B* and knew that if he remained silent he risked ten years' imprisonment; if he confessed, he risked only five years. Furthermore, if *B* decided on the solution that would be of the greatest mutual benefit and so remained silent, *A* could improve his own position by confessing, in a sense double-crossing *B*. Game theory predicted that *B* would follow the same reasoning. This was the minimax strategy guaranteeing the best of the worst possible outcomes. A key feature of this game was that the two players were forced into conflict. They suffered a worse result than if they could communicate and coordinate their answers and then trust each other to keep to the agreed strategy. Prisoners' dilemma came to be a powerful tool for examining situations where players might either work with or against each other (normally put as "cooperate" or "defect").

Game theory gained a boost during the early 1960s because it was presumed to have shaped nuclear strategy, although its actual influence was fleeting. It seemed to be of value because the core conflict could fit into a matrix as it was bipolar and between two alliances of roughly equivalent power. The conflict was clearly non-zero sum in that in any nuclear war both sides were likely to lose catastrophically. Thus they had a shared interest in peace, even while pursuing their distinct interests. There was no obvious way that the conflict would end, as the two alliances reflected opposing world views. There was a degree of stability in the relationship in terms of both the underlying antagonism and a fear of pushing matters to a decisive confrontation.

The theory helped clarify the predicament facing governments. The challenge was to use it to generate strategies for dealing with the policy dilemmas it created. Formal methodologies were favored by some analysts as a means of engaging in systematic thought in the face of the otherwise paralyzing contingency of nuclear war. It was easier to cope with the awful implications of any move if the discussion was kept abstract and impersonal. Yet when contributing to policy, analysts had to move beyond the theory. It soon reached its limits when it came to addressing such questions as to how vital interests could be defended without disaster when war was so dangerous, or whether it was possible to fight wars limited to conventional capabilities without escalation.

| The Rationality of Irrationality

This is a moral tract on mass murder: How to plan it, how to commit it,
how to get away with it, how to justify it.

—James Newman, review of Herman Kahn, *On Thermonuclear War*

D ESPITE BRODIE'S NOMENCLATURE, the first atomic weapons were not
"absolute." They were in the range of other munitions (the bomb that
destroyed Hiroshima was equivalent to the load of some two hundred B-29
bombers). Also, at least initially, the weapons were scarce. The key development introduced by atomic bombs was less in the scale of their destructive
power than in their efficiency. By the start of the 1950s, this situation had
been transformed by two related developments. The first was the breaking of
the U.S. monopoly by the Soviet Union, which conducted its first atomic test
in August 1949. Once two could play the nuclear game, the rules had to be
changed. Thought of initiating nuclear war would henceforth be qualified by
the possibility of retaliation.

The second development followed from the first. In an effort to extend
its effective nuclear superiority, the United States developed thermonuclear
bombs, based on the principles of nuclear fusion rather than fission. This
made possible weapons with no obvious limits to their destructive potential.
In 1950 the American government assumed that the introduction of thermonuclear weapons would allow the United States and its allies time to build
up conventional forces to match those of the Soviet Union and its satellites.

When Dwight D. Eisenhower became president in January 1953, he saw things differently. He wanted to take advantage of American nuclear superiority while it lasted, and also reduce the burden of spending on conventional rearmament. By this time, the nuclear arsenal was becoming more plentiful and more powerful. The strategy that emerged from these considerations became known as "massive retaliation," following a speech made by Secretary of State John Foster Dulles in January 1954, when he declared that in the future a U.S. response to aggression would be "at places and with means of our own choosing."[1]

This doctrine was interpreted as threatening nuclear attack against targets in the Soviet Union and China in response to conventional aggression anywhere in the world. Massive retaliation was widely criticized for placing excessive reliance on nuclear threats, which would become less credible as Soviet nuclear strength grew. If a limited challenge developed and the United States had neglected its own conventional forces, then the choice would be between "suicide or surrender." Dependence upon nuclear threats in the face of an opponent able to make threats of its own sparked a surge of intellectual creativity—later described as a "golden age" of strategic studies.[2] At its core was the key concept deterrence, to be explored with a range of new methodologies designed to cope with the special demands of the nuclear age.

Deterrence

The idea that palpable strength might cause an opponent to stay his hand was hardly new. The word *deterrence* is based on the Latin *deterre*—to frighten from or away. In its contemporary use it came to reflect an instrumental sense of seeking to induce caution by threats of pain. It was possible to be deterred without being threatened, for example, one might be cautious in anticipation of how another might respond to a provocative act. As a strategy, however, deterrence involved deliberate, purposive threats. This concept developed prior to the Second World War in contemplation of strategic air raids. The presumption of civilian panic that had animated the first airpower theorists retained a powerful hold on official imaginations. The fear of the crowd led to musings on the likely anarchy that would follow sustained attacks. Although the British lacked capabilities for mass long-range attacks prior to the war, they doubted the possibility of defense and believed that only the threat of punitive attacks could hold Germany back. Ultimately, Britain had to rely on defense, which it did with unexpected success thanks to radar. The raids against Britain, and those mounted in return against Germany with even greater ferocity, resulted in terrible civilian pain but had limited political effects. Their main effect was on the ability to prosecute the war by disrupting production and fuel supplies. The surveys undertaken after the war demonstrated the modest impact of strategic bombing compared with the pre-war claims. But this did not really matter because the atom bomb pushed the dread to a new level. As Richard Overy put it, with air power the "theory had run ahead of the technology. After 1945 the two reached a fresh alignment."[3]

Deterrence answered the stark exam question posed by the arrival of nuclear weapons: What role can there be for a capability that has no tactical role in stopping armies or navies but can destroy whole cities? Answers in terms of war-fighting, though explored by the Eisenhower administration, appeared distasteful; answers in terms of deterrence promised the prevention of future war. It sounded robust without being reckless. It anticipated aggression and guarded against surprise but could still be presented as essentially reactive. The difficulty was whether deterrence could be expected to hold if it was self-evidently based on a bluff. Credibility appeared to depend on a readiness to convey recklessness, illustrated by another of John Foster Dulles's comments about the need to be ready "to go to the brink" during a crisis. Thus the residual possibility of use left a formidable imprint, precisely because it would be so catastrophic.

This reinforced the view that the main benefit of force lay in what was held in reserve. The military capacity of the West must never be used to its full extent, though for the sake of deterrence the possibility must exist. As decades passed, and the Cold War still did not turn hot, deterrence appeared to be working. At times of crisis there was a welcome caution and prudence all around. War was avoided because politicians were all too aware of the consequences of failure and the dangers of preparing to crush enemies with overwhelming force. The dread of total war influenced all considerations of the use of force, and not just those directly involving nuclear weapons. It was never possible to be sure where the first military step, however tentative, might lead.

The impossibility of a fight to the finish affected all relations between the American and Soviet blocs. There developed "a predominance of the latent over the manifest, of the oblique over the direct, of the limited over the general."[4] If, as it seemed, there was no way of getting out of the nuclear age, then deterrence made the best of a bad job. While it was often difficult to explain exactly how deterrence had worked its magic—and historians can point to some terrifying moments when catastrophe was round the corner— yet a third world war did not happen. The fact that the superpowers were alarmed by the prospect of such a war surely had something to do with its failure to materialize.

The importance of deterrence meant that considerable efforts were devoted to exploring the concept and examining its policy implications. Deterrence succeeded if nothing happened, which led to a problem when working out cause and effect. Inaction might reflect a lack of intention or an intention once present that had lapsed. Deterrence of an intended action could be due to a range of factors, including some unrelated to the deterrer's threats and some related in ways the deterrer did not nececessarily intend. According to the most straightforward definition, that deterrence depended on convincing the target that prospective costs would outweigh prospective gains, it could be achieved by limiting gains as much as imposing costs. Preventing gain by means of a credible ability to stop aggression in its tracks became known as deterrence by denial,[5] while imposing costs became deterrence by punishment. Denial was essentially another word for an effective defense, which if recognized in advance would provide a convincing argument against aggression. Thus the main conceptual challenges concerned punishment, especially the most brutal punishment of all: nuclear retaliation.

As deterrence became wedded to a foreign policy of containment, interpreted as preventing any Soviet advances, both major war and minor provocations had to be deterred, not just those directed against the United States but also those directed against allies, and even the enemy's enemies. Herman Kahn, an early popularizer of some of the more abstruse theories of deterrence, distinguished three types: Type I involved superpower nuclear exchanges; Type II limited conventional or tactical nuclear attacks involving allies; and Type III addressed most other types of challenges.[6] At each stage, the requirements in terms of political will became more demanding, especially once both sides had acquired nuclear arsenals. It was one thing to threaten nuclear retaliation to deter nuclear attack, quite another to threaten nuclear use to deter a non-nuclear event. Because it was always unlikely that the United States would be directly attacked by a major power with anything other than nuclear weapons, the most likely non-nuclear event to be deterred would be an attack on an ally. This requirement came to be known as "extended deterrence." Because of the development of Soviet capabilities, U.S. methods of deterrence became less confident, moving from disproportionate to proportionate retaliation, from setting definite obstacles to aggression to warnings that should aggression occur the consequences could be beyond calculation, from assured and unconstrained threats of overwhelming force to a shared risk of mutual destruction.

Schelling

The theorist who did more than any other to explore the conundrums of deterrence and nuclear strategy was Thomas Schelling. He was one of a number of figures in and around RAND during the 1950s—including Bernard Brodie, Albert Wohlstetter, and Herman Kahn—who despite their differences contributed to a developing framework for thinking about these weapons that acknowledged their horrific novelty yet tried to describe their strategic possibilities. At the time, Kahn—ebullient and provocative, and one possible model for Stanley Kubrik's *Dr. Strangelove*—was the best known. His book *On Thermonuclear War* forged a link with Clausewitz, at least in its title, although his biographer doubted whether he had ever even done more than skimmed Clausewitz: "He never showed a smidgen of interest in any strategic theorist."[7] Wohlstetter described his prose as "dictated through a public address system."[8]

He was nuclear strategy's "first celebrity," with his "physical mass and somewhat geeky cast" confirming myths that the ultimate war would be the product of the imaginings of "mad geniuses." A mass of statistics on the likely character of nuclear war would be qualified by breezy and hardly comforting statements, such as "barring bad luck and bad management," and led to policy options that were evaluated in terms of possible losses of units of humanity measured in the millions.[9] Kahn's fellow nuclear strategists objected as much to his showmanship and the bad name he gave their new profession as to his claims about emerging victorious from the apocalypse. An enthusiastic advocate of civil defense, Kahn was convinced that control was possible in all types of conflict, even nuclear war.

Schelling was a more substantial theorist, developing ways of thinking about conflict that illuminated nuclear issues while remaining relevant to broader strategic questions. After the mid-1960s, when he felt he had said much of what he wanted to say about nuclear matters, he turned his attention to other issues, ranging from crime to cigarette smoking, but still applied the same essential approach. His achievement was underlined by the award of a Nobel Prize in economics in 2005 for "having enhanced our understanding of conflict and cooperation through game-theory analysis."[10] Yet Schelling's relationship to game theory was equivocal. He did not describe himself as a game theorist but rather a social scientist who used game theory on occasion. He hit upon his big idea before he came across game theory as a means through which it could be expressed. He preferred to reason through analogy in ways that purists found maddening. Schelling's reputation depended on his gifts as a brilliant expositor who wrote with elegance and lucidity, traits for which this particular field of endeavor were not well known.[11]

Schelling did not claim to have achieved the "science" that had long been sought in strategy or that formal logic could in principle lead to a mathematical solution. He shared the view, growing among the operational research community, that advanced mathematics and abstract models were making their work less accessible to potential users,[12] and he always opposed the suggestion that strategy was or should be "a branch of mathematics."[13] He confessed to having learned more "from reading ancient Greek history and by looking at salesmanship than studying game theory." The greatest achievement of game theory, as far as he was concerned, was the payoff matrix. It was extraordinarily useful to be able to put together in a matrix a "simple situation involving as few as two people and two choices."[14]

His equivocation on game theory was not unique. Other nuclear strategists who worked at RAND during the 1950s tended to talk of following the "spirit" of game theory rather than its rules. In a 1949 article, Brodie referred to game theory in a footnote as a source of "mathematical systematization," adding that "for various reasons" he did not share the authors' "conviction that their theory could be directly and profitably applied to problems of military strategy."[15] Later, while finding its "refinements" of little use, he acknowledged the value of the "constant reminder that in war we shall be dealing with an opponent who will react to our moves and to whom we must react."[16] Few of the books on nuclear strategy made much, if any, mention of game theory. This absence was notable in a book by one of the founders of game theory, Oskar Morgenstern.[17] Bruce-Briggs suggests that the close association between nuclear strategy and game theory was a consequence of the reception of Kahn's *On Thermonuclear War*. Although Kahn had used neither game theory nor mathematics, he was accused of being the most extreme example of a game-theory-wielding militarist, a moniker implying great technical capacity but no moral sensibility. Schelling was also included in this category.[18] Schelling observed at the time, "I don't see that game theory is any more involved than Latin grammar or geophysics; but its quaint name makes mysterious and patronizing references to it an effective ploy."[19]

Schelling had little background in military issues. Trained as an economist, he worked on the implementation of the postwar Marshall Plan for economic reconstruction in Europe. This led to his general interest in negotiations of all types, particularly the process of finding points that could support an agreed solution, possibly through tacit as much as explicit bargaining. After publishing an article demonstrating the possibility of arriving at common solutions without direct communication,[20] he read Luce and Raiffa's *Games and Decisions* and saw the potential of game theory.[21] His interest in how "nations, people, or organizations go about committing themselves to threats and promises in bargaining positions" led him into contact with RAND in 1956 and he spent a productive year there from 1958 to 1959.[22] Schelling was able to test his developing theories in the company of other key thinkers from a variety of disciplines, all trying to make sense of the nuclear age. Although he was offered jobs in the Kennedy administration, he preferred to keep his independence. He did work as a consultant, however.

Many of the ideas and concepts Schelling developed along with his colleagues at RAND became familiar and entered the strategic vernacular, but it is important to note just how novel and radical they were. Critics complained, with some justice, that the methodology allowed talk about dreadful possibilities in dispassionate terms and contemplated moves that should never be countenanced by a civilized people. Their models did not offer a way of transcending the Cold War conflict and failed to accommodate the ideological and geopolitical issues. These were important limitations, but they should not hide the achievement of developing a way to think about conflict that could also accommodate cooperation.

Schelling started with the special features of a game of strategy, compared with those of chance or skill: "Each player's best choice depends on the action he expects the other to take, which he knows depends, in turn, on the other's expectation of his own." Strategy was all about interdependence, "the conditioning of one's own behavior on the behavior of others." This could cover any social relationships in which there was a mixture of conflict and cooperation. All partnerships were to some degree precarious, just as all antagonisms were to some degree incomplete. The combination of conflict and cooperation was at the heart of the theory. It became irrelevant when there was an absence of either. Schelling noted that the theory "degenerates at one extreme if there is not scope for mutual accommodation, no common interest at all even in avoiding mutual disaster; it degenerates at the other extreme if there is no conflict at all and no problem in identifying and reaching common goals."[23]

On this basis the role of force could be rethought. Traditionally it had been used by countries to take and hold what they wanted: "Forcibly a country can repel and expel, penetrate and occupy, seize, exterminate, disarm and disable, confine, deny access, and directly frustrate intrusion or attack. It can, that is, if it has enough strength. 'Enough' depends on how much an opponent has."[24] In setting up an alternative to brute force, Schelling made one of his most startling assertions: "In addition to weakening an enemy militarily it can cause an enemy plain suffering." Contrary to prevailing views—and established international law, for that matter—that stressed the importance of avoiding unnecessary suffering, Schelling claimed that the ability to hurt was "among the most impressive attributes of military force." Its value lay not in actually doing so, which would constitute a gross failure of strategy, but in what opponents might do to avoid it. So long as the violence could both be anticipated and avoided by accommodation, it had coercive value. "The power to hurt is bargaining power. To exploit it is diplomacy—vicious diplomacy, but diplomacy." Under this proposition, strategy moved from considerations of conquest and resistance to deterrence, intimidation, blackmail, and threats.

Coercion was therefore at the heart of the theory. The hurt did not have to be nuclear. The same framework could work with less punitive forms, for example, economic sanctions. It could also take in the traditional distinction between offense and defense, although not in the sense of being able to be certain of either conquering territory or stopping any invasion at the borders. The point about coercion was that it involved influencing through threats rather than controlling the opponent's behavior. The defensive equivalent was deterrence, persuading an enemy not to attack; the offensive equivalent was "compellence," inducing withdrawal or acquiescence. Deterrence demanded an opponent's inaction; compellence demanded action or ceasing adverse actions. Deterrence was about the status quo and had no obvious time limits; compellence projected forward to a new place and could be urgent. Deterrence was easier because all that was required was that an action be withheld. The target could deny that one was ever contemplated. Compliance was more conspicuous with compellence, more evidently "submission under duress," less "capable of being rationalized as something that one was going to do anyhow." The two could merge. Once an initial deterrent threat had failed and an opponent was acting in a hostile way, the next threat must be compellent. In a conflict in which both sides could hurt each other but neither could forcibly accomplish its purpose, and in which the balance of advantage kept changing hands, the requirement to deter and to compel could shift, depending on who was on top at any time.[25]

Nuclear threats had a special character. Executing them would be an unusually horrible thing to do, but a state with a nuclear monopoly might feel that it was not too difficult to gain strategic advantage by threatening others. What made the difference was that something equally horrible might come back in return. How could one benefit from threats that lacked credibility because of the risk of retaliation and could thus be exposed as bluff at the first challenge? Again, Schelling addressed this conundrum by turning traditional concepts upside down. The aim of strategy, it had been supposed, was to exert the maximum control over the course of an unfolding conflict.

Schelling asked a different question: could there be strategic advantages in accepting a loss of control? Coercive threats worked by influencing an opponent's choices. Perhaps their choice could be made more difficult by limiting one's own. To inject credibility into an apparently irrational stance, why not work to create an essentially irrational situation?

The idea was to shift the onus of decision onto the other side, so that it was the opponent who was obliged to choose between continued combat and backing down. Only "the enemy's withdrawal can tranquilize the situation; otherwise it may turn out to be a contest of nerves."[26] There were precedents: the Greeks burning their bridges to show they would stand and fight against the Persians; the Spanish conqueror Cortez conspicuously burning his ships in front of the Aztecs. By removing retreat as an option, your men had no choice but to fight, while the enemy would be discouraged by an apparent display of confidence.

In the nuclear sphere, at one extreme, choice could be wholly conceded to the opponent by making the threatened action automatic, beyond recall unless stopped by an act of compliance. That was the notion of the "doomsday machine": pass a line and nothing could be done to stop the detonation and the shared calamity. Removing all choice was unacceptable, so Schelling posed the problem in terms of progressive risk. The opponent would know that even if the threatener had second thoughts, the threat might still be implemented. This set up the possibility of a "competition in risk-taking" which could turn war into a contest of "endurance, nerve, obstinacy and pain." This would be not quite a doomsday machine, but the threatened would know that the threat could not be wholly bluff because the threatener was not completely in control. Schelling called this "The Threat That Leaves Something to Chance." The feature of such threats was that "though one may or may not carry them out, *the final decision is not altogether under the threatener's control.*"[27] In his version of Clausewitz's friction, Schelling emphasized the ubiquity of uncertainty that gave this type of threat credibility:

> Violence, especially in war, is a confused and uncertain activity, highly unpredictable depending on decisions made by fallible human beings organized into imperfect governments depending on fallible communications and warning systems and on the untested performance of people and equipment. It is furthermore a hotheaded activity, in which commitments and reputations can develop a momentum of their own.[28]

Whereas Clausewitz saw friction as undermining all but the most dogged of strategies, Schelling saw how these uncertainties might be used creatively, if recklessly. The uncertainty would grow as a crisis turned into a limited conflict and then moved toward general war, getting out of hand "by degrees."[29] Skillful tactics would exploit this fact, not shrink from it. The assumption was that it was worth letting a "situation get somewhat out of hand" because the opponent would find such circumstances intolerable. Deterrence was possible because of a situation in which terrible things *might* happen (which was credible because of human irrationality) rather than a specific threat to do those things (which was incredible because of human rationality).

The potential rationality of irrationality was illustrated using the game of "chicken." Two cars were driven toward each other by delinquent teenagers, Bill and Ben, anxious to prove their toughness. The first to swerve lost. If both swerved, nothing was gained; if neither swerved, everything was lost. If Bill swerved and Ben did not, then Bill suffered humiliation and Ben gained prestige. The matrix appeared as shown below.

TABLE 13. 1

		Bill	
		1 Swerve	2 Don't Swerve
Ben	1 Swerve	0 a1b1 0	+20 a1b2 -20
	2 Don't Swerve	-20 a2b1 +20	-100 a2b2 -100

The figures in the corners refer to values attached to alternative outcomes.

The minimax strategy dictated that they both swerved as the best of the worst outcomes. This represented the natural caution displayed by both sides during the Cold War. Timing, however, made a difference. Bill was prepared to swerve, but Ben swerved first. Bill won because he delayed his commitment. He kept his nerve longer. Perhaps he was confident that Ben would swerve because he knew him to be weak-willed. Suppose that Ben was aware of this impression and sought to correct it. He wanted Bill to think him reckless or even a bit crazy. A number of ruses might reinforce such an impression: swaggering, boasting, or feigning drunkenness. Irrationality became rational. If Ben could persuade Bill that he had taken leave of his senses, Ben might just prevail.

This illuminates the basic problem with this line of argument. Even if one was apparently committed to a patently irrational course to impress the opponent, a foot would still hover close to the brake pedal and hands would stay firmly on the steering wheel. What might work for two individuals was less likely to work for governments who needed to convince their own people that they knew what they were doing. Even if the internal audience was tolerant of ruses designed to suggest a loss of control, such stunts could not be a regular feature of crisis management. Whether the game involved individuals or states, it was difficult to pretend irrationality consistently, in one game after another. Like deceptive strategies, pretended irrationality would be difficult to repeat as it would affect perceptions of behavior next time round. Indeed it could be counterproductive if the other side overcompensated. The more often the game was played, the more dangerous it could become. The full importance of any strategic encounter lay not only in the implications for the matter at hand but also in the long-term impact on the relationship between the two adversaries. The results of strategies adopted in a particular game would affect their potential success if used in subsequent games. Game theory presented simultaneous decisions by players. Schelling understood that the moves often took place sequentially, so that the structure of the game changed each time.[30]

The mutual learning process was important to Schelling's schema. It was almost a mission to reorient game theory to take account of the fact that "people *can* often concert their intentions or expectations with others if each knows that the other is trying to do the same." Unlike theorists who argued that equilibrium points could be found using mathematics, Schelling insisted that points would suggest themselves as being obvious or natural. This required "some common language that permits them to hold discourse." Communication of this sort between adversaries would not allow for great subtlety or sophistication, especially if the language did not emerge through formal negotiations or declarations. It could be tacit as much as explicit, dependent on prominent symbols and values in a shared culture, guided by tradition and precedence, with mutual understandings created and reinforced through deeds as much as words. It would draw "on imagination more than on logic; it could depend on analogy, precedent, accidental arrangement, symmetry, aesthetic or geometric configuration, casuistic reasoning, and who the parties are and what they know about each other."[31] Certain focal points would become salient. They would need to be simple, recognizable, and conspicuous. In *Arms and Influence*, Schelling gave examples of features that might suggest themselves to opposing forces who could not communicate directly:

> National boundaries and rivers, shorelines, the battle line itself, even
> parallels of latitude, the distinction between air and ground, the

distinction between nuclear fission and chemical combustion, the distinction between combat support and economic support, the distinction between combatants and non-combatants, the distinctions among nationalities.[32]

Once proper communication was possible, and the players could use direct speech and overt bargaining, the "pure-coordination game," Schelling suggests, "not only ceases to be interesting but virtually ceases to be a 'game.'"[33]

Yet for all the possibilities of indirect communication, the influence of norms and conventions of behavior, or the focal points thrown up by nature, it was hard to see how they could be more reliable than direct communications. In circumstances where the opportunities for direct communication were sparse, as was the case between the two ideological blocs for much of the Cold War, Schelling's insight about the possibility of still finding shared focal points by indirect means was valuable. But it could not be taken too far. It did not necessarily mean that these points would be found when they were really needed. Moreover, when two sides were working with such different sets of values and beliefs, what was salient for one might not be so salient for the other. Without direct communication to verify that an agreed point had been found, it was possible to miscalulate by assuming that the other side attached the same salience to the same point or by assuming that agreement on such matters was impossible. It could seem, as Hedley Bull observed in a review of *Arms and Influence*, that the superpowers would be "sending and receiving messages and ironing out understandings" with "scarcely as much as a nod or a wink."[34]

First and Second Strikes

Schelling argued that not only was it possible to think of nuclear strategy in terms of bargaining and coercion but it was unwise to think of it in any other way. This challenged the idea of a decisive victory directly by claiming that at least in the nuclear area it made no sense. That did not mean that there was no concept of what a decisive nuclear victory would look like. To ensure success it would have to take the form of a knockout blow that left the opponent no chance to retaliate. This was not a possibility that either side in the Cold War ever felt able to dismiss entirely. It provided part of the dynamic of the arms race between the two sides and governed calculations of risk. A "first-strike capability" came to refer to the potential ability to disarm the enemy in a surprise attack. No military operation ever conceived could be as fateful. It would be the first and only time it would be attempted and would be launched in secret, using untried weapons against a range of disparate targets in a wholly unique scenario, using equally untried defenses to catch any retaliatory weapons. Whether such a capability was in reach depended on evaluations of the developing capabilities of offensive and defensive weapons.

In a celebrated RAND study of the mid-1950s, a team led by Albert Wohlstetter demonstrated that the air bases of the U.S. Strategic Air Command could be vulnerable to a surprise attack. Retaliation from such an attack would be impossible, thereby exposing the United States and its allies to Soviet blackmail.[35] This challenged the prevailing view that nuclear weapons could be used solely in "counter-value" strikes against easily targeted political and economic centers. A "counter-force" strike against military targets would potentially be strategically decisive because it would leave the opponent without any way of retaliating. If, however, the attacked nation was able to absorb an attempted first strike and retain sufficient forces to hit back then it would have a "second-strike capability." Wohlstetter believed that this study, drawing on "the tradition of operations research and empirical systems analysis," far more than Schelling's musings, discovered the "vulnerabilities of strategic forces."[36]

Suppose both sides had a first-strike capability. Brodie set out the alternative possibilities in a 1954 article in which he observed that in a world in which "either side can make a surprise attack on the other" it would make sense to be "trigger-happy." As with the "American gunfighter duel, frontier style," the "one who leads on the draw and the aim achieves a good clean win." If neither side had the capability, however, trigger-happiness would be suicidal, and restraint only prudent.[37] Depending on how the technology developed, there would either be powerful pressures to preempt at times of high political tension, which could lead to a dangerous dynamic, or there would be considerable stability, as no premium would be attached to unleashing nuclear hostilities. Thus, confidence in stability depended on expectations with regard to the opponent's attitude and behavior. In a compelling example of his mode of analysis, Schelling described a "reciprocal fear of surprise attack" to show how an apparently stable system of deterrence could suddenly be destabilized even when there was no "fundamental" basis for either side to strike first: "A modest temptation on each side to sneak in a first blow—a temptation too small by itself to motivate an attack—might become compounded through a process of interacting expectations, with additional motive for attack being produced by successive cycles of 'He thinks we think he thinks we think . . . he thinks we think he'll attack; so he thinks we shall; so he will; so we must.'"

To reduce any chance of such thoughts, nuclear systems should be unequivocally geared to a second strike: relatively invulnerable and relatively inaccurate. In practice this meant that cities would be threatened, not weapons.

The logic became even more uncomfortable and paradoxical. Nothing should be done to diminish the murderous consequences of a nuclear war because nothing should be done to encourage any thought that it was worth starting. "A weapon that can hurt only people, and cannot possibly damage the other side's striking force," Schelling explained, "is profoundly defensive; it provides its possessor no incentive to strike first." The danger lay with weapons intended to "seek out the enemy's missiles and bombers—that *can* exploit the advantage of striking first and consequently provide a temptation to do so."[38] The aim was to stabilize the U.S.-Soviet nuclear relationship. On this basis, Schelling noted, missile-carrying submarines were admirable for second-strike purposes. They were extremely hard to find and destroy at sea, but it was also hard (at the time he was writing) to use them for accurate strikes against the enemy forces. For this reason, Schelling argued that Americans should not want a monopoly on these submarines, for if they "have either no intention or no political capacity for a first strike it would usually be helpful if the enemy were confidently assured of this."

If such reasoning led to conclusions that seemed quite bizarre to the military mind, the same was true for those on the other side of the argument, campaigning for radical measures of disarmament. The more weapons one had, the more difficult it was for the adversary to wipe them out in a surprise attack. An agreement designed to stabilize the nuclear relationship would be easier to maintain at higher rather than lower levels, for it would be much more difficult to prepare to cheat by hiding extra missiles if the starting numbers were high.[39] Neither the military nor the disarmers were at all sure that their activities should be mutually reinforcing. The term "arms control" was in fact coined in the 1950s precisely to identify forms of mutual understanding that were compatible with the new imperatives of military strategy.[40] It meant that the military had to get used to the idea that while opposing the enemy's force they must

> also collaborate, implicitly if not explicitly, in avoiding the kinds of crises in which withdrawal is intolerable for both sides, in avoiding false alarms and mistaken intentions, and in providing—along with its deterrent threat of resistance or retaliation in the event of unacceptable challenges—reassurance that restraint on the part of potential enemies will be matched by restraint of our own.[41]

In line with Schelling's general interest in how productive agreements could be reached without direct communication, arms control could involve "induced or reciprocated 'self-control,' whether the inducements include negotiated treaties or just informal understandings and reciprocated restraints."[42]

In any event, technological developments supported the second strike. Attempts to develop effective defenses against nuclear attack proved futile. By the mid-1960s, fears eased of a technological arms race that might encourage either side to unleash a surprise attack. For the foreseeable future, each side could eliminate the other as a modern industrial state. Robert McNamara, as secretary of defense, argued that so long as the two superpowers had confidence in their capacity for mutual assured destruction—an ability to impose "unacceptable damage" defined as 25 percent of population and 50 percent of industry—the relationship between the two would be stable. These levels, it should be noted, reflected less a judgment about the tolerances of modern societies and more the point at which extra explosions would result in diminishing marginal returns measured by new damage and casualties, the point at which—to use Winston Churchill's vivid phrase—"all you are going to do is make the rubble bounce."

If serious fighting did begin, the incentives would shift. Assuming no rush into nuclear exchanges, it would still be possible to shape the development of the conflict by drawing on the potential of what could happen. So long as cities were spared there was some hope of establishing a new bargain, even in the midst of war. But once cities were destroyed there was nothing else to lose. Attacks on cities would be "a massive and modern version of an ancient institution: the exchange of hostages." Keeping something of value vulnerable was a way of enforcing good behavior.[43] Like Clausewitz, Schelling saw how raw and angry passions could also undermine restraint.

The process by which a conflict intensified and became more dangerous came to be described as "escalation." This word (not one that Schelling favored) came into vogue to describe a tragic process as a limited war became total. It was based on the metaphor of the moving staircase that once started could not be stopped, however much the original decision might be regretted. The term—initially interchangeable with words like *explosion*, *eruption*, and *trigger*—was first used to challenge the idea of a limited nuclear war. Henry Kissinger, for example, defined escalation in 1960 as "the addition of increments of power until limited war insensibly merges into all-out war."[44] Schelling was aware of opportunities to use the process for bargaining purposes as well as how these would become fewer as control over events was progressively lost. To get the aggressor to stop and preferably go back to the starting point, relinquishing captured territory, the threat would have to be credible and serious, yet the circumstances would be those in which a previous deterrent threat had not been taken sufficiently seriously. The function of limited war therefore had to be understood less in terms of ensuring that war stayed limited and more in terms of posing "the deliberate risk of all-out war" and keeping the risk of escalation "within moderate limits above zero."[45] The role of the first nuclear exchanges would not be "solely or mainly to redress a balance on the battlefield" but primarily "to make the war too painful or too dangerous to continue."[46]

Schelling developed his ideas before it became apparent that the superpower confrontation would become dominated by thoughts of mutual destruction. The possibilities that Schelling explored did not materialize because the consequences of any nuclear use would be so horrendous that they did not lend themselves to subtle and clever maneuvers. Crisis behavior became careful, cautious, and circumspect. So much of Schelling's framework can be considered in retrospect as a mind-clearing exercise, exploring a range of possibilities that never moved beyond speculative hypotheses but at least demonstrated the inadequacy of conventional strategic thought. During the 1950s, with memories of past lurches to war still strong, few were confident that a third world war could be indefinitely postponed. The exploration of the logic of deterrence, and why it made sense to accept this logic rather than attempt to circumvent it, was important enough to justify the effort.

Existential Deterrence

It might have even been possible to imagine a major war between the two superpowers in which nuclear weapons were not used, although few would have been prepared to rely on continuing restraint. The core problem which niggled away at America's strategists was that of extended deterrence, the commitment to bring nuclear means to the aid of non-nuclear allies. Once a stalemate was reached, it seemed reckless to consider nuclear war on behalf of allies. But the Europeans were assumed to have insufficient conventional strength to hold back a determined assault by the Soviet-led Warsaw Pact. If Europe was not to be overrun, there at least had to be a possibility that the United States would initiate nuclear war. Were it not for this basic political commitment, reflecting a vital interest, there would have been no need to worry about Schelling's "threats that left something to chance." This idea was best captured by so-called tactical nuclear weapons whose military value could never be properly explained but conveyed the risk that once entangled in a land war in Europe, they could trigger nuclear war in a way that was beyond rational consideration.

By the start of the 1960s, there was a developing view in the United States that the best way to ease this problem was to reduce dependence upon nuclear threats by increasing conventional forces—to create deterrence by denial. The difficulty was that a conventional build-up would be expensive and such obvious efforts to reduce their nuclear liabilities would suggest to European minds that the Americans might consider European security a less than vital interest. Behind this there was a disjunction between the formal strategic analysis emerging from the American think tanks and the politics of Europe, divided between two hostile ideological blocs, yet enjoying some stability. The Europeans did not view the continent as being on the edge of war. They understood that nuclear threats might not be credible, but deterrence could still work because of the residual possibility that in the irrational, intense circumstances of another European war, nuclear weapons might be used. The possibility did not have to be very large for political leaders to decide to stick with a manageable status quo. On this basis, the key to deterrence was alliance, the close link between American power—including its nuclear arsenal—and European security. The threat to deterrence was anything which undermined that link.

Here was a clash of strategic frameworks. One was top down, the classical, grand strategic perspective which focused on the formidable reasons not to risk war when it was possible to imagine catastrophe for all involved. The other was bottom up, an operational analysis which considered where the advantage might lie in a conflict, should the politicians decide the stakes were worth the fight. This pointed to an inability to match Soviet conventional strength. Only increasingly incredible nuclear threats were available should Moscow take advantage of this vulnerability, raising the possibility that it just might.

This issue came to a head in 1961 when newly elected President Kennedy was faced with a major challenge over the status of Berlin. The old German capital was firmly in communist East Germany, yet as part of the postwar settlement it had been divided into two. West Berlin, connected uneasily to West Germany, offered an easy route out for East Germans seeking to escape communism. This was a major irritant to Moscow. There were threats that summer of a Soviet move to cut off West Berlin and bring it into communist control. As the city was indefensible by conventional means, any effort to prevent this carried a risk of nuclear war. Ultimately this risk was sufficient for the communists to limit the provocation, and they built a wall which divided Berlin and so kept their people hemmed in.

During that summer's crisis, a paper by Schelling setting out his ideas on limited nuclear conflict was passed to Kennedy. The paper stressed the importance of heightening the risk to the enemy rather than making a futile bid to win a decisive victory. "We should plan for a war of nerve, of demonstration and of bargaining, not of tactical target destruction." This paper apparently made a "deep impression" on Kennedy. Schelling had been talking with McGeorge Bundy, Kennedy's national security advisor. They shared a concern that the military seemed unable to think through the "hideous jump between conventional warfare and a single massive all-out blast."[47] His main contribution to policy at this time, however, was to help set up a "crisis game" that sought to simulate, as closely as possible, the confused and stressful conditions decision-makers might face and the questions to be addressed should tensions over Berlin escalate. Schelling's game explored how the Berlin crisis might unfold. This had the advantage of being a contained scenario, in which the dimensions and core views of the protagonists were known. In September 1961, a number of rounds of this game took place in Washington designed to impress on the participants the "bargaining aspect of a military crisis." The games forced senior policymakers—military and civilian—to work out responses to various contingencies. The conclusions, which had an effect on both official thought and Schelling's future theorizing, emphasized the pressure of events. It was far harder to communicate efficiently than was often assumed, as the enemy saw only the actions and not the intent behind them, and there would be far less time for diplomacy to operate than had been hoped.

Yet it also became extraordinarily difficult in the games to trigger a large-scale conventional war, much less a nuclear conflict. According to Alan Ferguson, Schelling's collaborator, "our inability to get a fight started" was the "single most striking result."[48] The games also highlighted a problem with Berlin: "Whoever it is who has to initiate the action that neither side wants is the side that is deterred. In a fragile situation, good strategy involves leaving the overt act up to the other side."[49] The game therefore gave little support to the idea that any nuclear use, even for signaling purposes, provided realistic options for NATO in the event that the Berlin crisis worsened but it did reinforce the size of the gap between conventional and nuclear war. Reporting back to Kennedy, an aide highlighted the difficulty of using "military power flexibly and effectively for tactical purposes in the conduct of the day to day political struggle with the Soviet Union."[50]

The next year Kennedy faced an even greater crisis prompted by the discovery that the Soviet Union was building missile sites in Cuba. Many of the conversations of leading players on the American side were recorded as they debated potential moves and counter-moves. The president spent much of the crisis trying to determine the effect of a particular course of action on Moscow, and to do this he tried to put himself in Nikita Khrushchev's shoes. In doing so, Kennedy supposed that the Soviet leader was cast in the same mould, responding to the same stimuli and facing the same sort of pressures from his own hard-liners, finding it as hard as Kennedy would to back down from public commitments. He was fearful that a missile strike against Cuba would lead to a Soviet attack against Turkey, where American missiles of equivalent range and targeting were based; a blockade of Cuba would revive the issue of a blockade of West Berlin.

Kennedy formed an in-group of key officials—known as ExComm— to debate the alternatives. One option was to launch air strikes against the offending bases in Cuba to take them out before they became operational. This option had to take into account whether it might be possible to get away with a small "surgical" strike or whether the risk could only be removed by continual and heavy strikes, possibly followed by an invasion. Another option involved a more gradualist approach, demonstrating resolve through a blockade to prevent military equipment getting to Cuba. ExComm's decisions in part depended on the practicalities: the air force's confidence in their ability to find and destroy the bases, the quality of the air defenses they would face, and the risk that some of the weapons were already operational. When confronting the possibility of air strikes, especially without warning, a number of members of ExComm felt uneasy. The United States had, after all, been the victim of a surprise air strike on December 7, 1941. The president's speechwriter, Ted Sorenson, noted that he had no trouble writing the speech announcing the blockade but great difficulty writing one to report an air strike. The other advantage of the blockade was it did not preclude tougher action if it failed to produce immediate results. It kept options open and the opponent guessing.

There was still anxiety over whether the blockade could be enforced. Robert Kennedy wrote of his brother as he waited to see how Soviet ships would respond.

> I think these few minutes were the time of greatest concern for the President. Was the world on the brink of a holocaust? Was it our error? A mistake? Was there something further that should have been done? Or not done? His hand went up to his face and covered his mouth. He opened and closed his fist. His face seemed drawn, his eyes pained, almost gray.

From the other side, consider a long, impassioned private letter to Kennedy that arrived two days later from the Soviet leader Nikita Khrushchev:

> If people do not show wisdom, then in the final analysis they will come to a clash, like blind moles, and then reciprocal extermination will begin. . . . we and you ought not to pull on the ends of the rope

in which you have tied the knot of war, because the more the two of us pull, the tighter that knot will be tied. And a moment may come when that knot will be tied so tight that even he who tied it will not have the strength to untie it, and then it will be necessary to cut it, and what that would mean is not for me to explain to you, because you yourself understand perfectly of what terrible forces our countries dispose.[51]

On Saturday, October 27, 1962, tensions were at their height after mixed messages from Moscow—one conciliatory, the other tough—and the added tension of an American spy plane getting shot down over Cuba. The presumed response was to retaliate against Soviet surface-to-air missile sites in Cuba. While this might be held back, at some point surveillance would need to start again, putting U.S. aircraft at risk and making a response unavoidable. Robert McNamara set out a possible script. If surveillance aircraft were fired upon, the United States would have to respond. There would be losses of aircraft, and "we'll be shooting up Cuba quite a bit." This was not a position that could be sustained for very long. "So we must be prepared to attack Cuba—quickly." This was going to require an "all-out attack" involving air strikes, with "sorties every day thereafter, and I personally believe that this is almost certain to lead to an invasion, I won't say certain to, but *almost* certain to lead to an invasion."

The next stage assumed a tit-for-tat reprisal from Khrushchev: "If we do this, and leave those missiles in Turkey the Soviet Union *may*, and I think probably will, attack the Turkish missiles." This led inexorably on to the proposition that "*if* the Soviet Union attacks the Turkish missiles, we *must* respond. We *cannot* allow a Soviet attack on the—on the Jupiter missiles in Turkey without a military response by NATO." He continued

> Now the minimum military response by NATO to a Soviet attack on the Turkish Jupiter missiles would be a response with conventional weapons by NATO forces in Turkey, that is to say Turkish and U.S. aircraft, against Soviet warships and/or naval bases in the Black Sea area. Now that to me is the absolute minimum, and I would say that it is *damned dangerous* to—to have had a Soviet attack on Turkey and a NATO response on the Soviet Union.[52]

McNamara took this sufficiently seriously, even though he was assuming in this script that his own government would take choices that he clearly thought unwise, to suspect that a nuclear war would be set in motion the next day. In reality, neither Kennedy nor Khrushchev were prepared to contemplate such a calamity and they found a way to draw back from the brink: withdrawal of Soviet missiles in return for an American promise not to invade Cuba. During the crisis there were many examples of how poorly the two sides understood each other, yet on the most fundamental issue they had a shared view. They were determined to avoid a nuclear tragedy.

Although the outcome of the missile crisis was shaped by a shared fear of nuclear war, one conclusion drawn was that with a clear head and a strong will, such crises were possible to manage. In particular, the successful outcome was used to challenge the notion of escalation. This had been not so much a strategy as something to be avoided. After the crisis, the metaphor was challenged for failing to recognize the potential for graduated moves, especially during the early stages of a conflict before serious battle had been joined. Albert and Roberta Wohlstetter observed that "there are down-escalators as well as up-escalators, and there are landings between escalators where one can decide to get off or get on, to go up or down, or to stay there; or to take the stairs. Just where automaticity or irreversibility takes over is an uncertain but vital matter, and that is one of the reasons a decision maker may want to take a breath at a landing to consider next steps."[53]

Herman Kahn sought to show that even once nuclear exchanges had begun there were ways of conducting operations that might keep the pressure on the other side while avoiding Armageddon. He saw escalation as a dragon to be slain: not so much a phenomenon operating independent of human action but a possible product of inadequate intellectual and physical preparation. He introduced the idea that escalation might be a deliberate act. The noun acquired a verb when he referred to "people who wish to escalate a little themselves, but somehow feel that the other side would not be willing to go one step further."[54] Escalation was transformed from a hopelessly unruly process to one that might be tamed and possibly manipulated. In his 1965 book *On Escalation*, he introduced the "escalation ladder" with sixteen thresholds and forty-four steps. For most, the striking feature of the book was the possibility of anyone coming up with almost thirty distinct ways of using nuclear weapons following their first use at rung fifteen.[55] The escalation up the ladder concluded, when all semblance of control had been lost, with a "wargasm." Kahn declared himself innocent of the Freudian connotations. Luigi Nono, the radical Italian composer, used Kahn's ladder as the theme for a musical composition dedicated to the National Liberation Front of Vietnam, which moved from (1) "crisi manifesta" to (44) "spasmo o guerra insensata."[56]

McGeorge Bundy, former national security advisor to both Kennedy and Johnson, also reacted strongly to analyses such as these. He concluded that the arms race had become largely irrelevant in terms of actual international political behavior. Once both sides acquired thermonuclear weapons, there was a stalemate. The "certain prospect of retaliation" meant that there had been "literally no prospect at all that any sane political authority, in either the United States or the Soviet Union, would consciously choose to start a nuclear war." He wrote of the "enormous gulf between what political leaders really think about nuclear weapons and what is assumed in complex calculations of relative 'advantage' in simulated strategic warfare." In the think tanks, levels of "acceptable" damage could involve the loss of tens of millions of lives, so that the "loss of dozens of great cities is somehow a real choice for sane men." For Bundy, in "the real world of real political leaders" a "decision that would bring even one hydrogen bomb on one city of one's own country would be recognized in advance as a catastrophic blunder; ten bombs on ten cities would be a disaster beyond history; and a hundred bombs on a hundred cities are unthinkable."[57]

Bundy's belief that the more esoteric strategic debates had lost touch with reality led in 1983 to the argument that because both sides would be able to retaliate with thermonuclear weapons even after the "strongest possible pre-emptive attack," there was in place a form of deterrence which he described as "existential," resting on "uncertainty about what could happen."[58] This removed the strategic effect from particular weapons programs, preparations for employment, or doctrinal pronouncements. So long as any superpower war carried a high risk of utter calamity, it was best not to take risks. This notion proved to be extremely seductive not only because of its intuitive plausibility but because it solved all those perplexing problems of nuclear policy by rendering them virtually irrelevant, so long as they did not stray too far into the realms of recklessness and foolishness. Although in policymaking circles it was still extremely difficult to think of ways to assess the size and composition of nuclear arsenals except by reference to the assumed requirements of actual exchanges, as evidenced in numerous debates in Washington over new weapons systems, these debates eventually acquired a routine quality. The scenarios became drained of credibility. Nuclear deterrence worked for the United States because it warned of the severe dangers of disrupting the status quo. The sense of danger depended not on the rationality of a nuclear response but on the residual doubt that once the passions of war had been unleashed no reliance could be placed on a rational response.

CHAPTER 14 | Guerrilla Warfare

The power of Armies is a visible thing,

Formal and circumscribed in time and space;

But who the limits of that power shall trace

Which a brave People into light can bring

Or hide, at will,—for freedom combating

By just revenge inflamed? No foot may chase,

No eye can follow, to a fatal place

That power, that spirit, whether on the wing

Like the strong wind, or sleeping like the wind

Within its awful caves

—William Wordsworth, *1811*

IF NUCLEAR WEAPONS pulled military strategy away from conventional warfare in one direction, guerrilla warfare moved it in another. With nuclear weapons the issue was about threatening society with extreme force. Guerrilla warfare was about the response of an enraged society to illegitimate military force. Although it later acquired an association with radical political movements, its basic attraction was as a method that could help weaker sides survive. Although as a form of warfare it was not at all new, and had recently been adopted in the American War of Independence, guerrilla warfare gained its name from the tactics of ambush and harassment used during the "little war" fought by Spaniards against French occupation forces at the start of the nineteenth century. Wordsworth's poem refers to this campaign.

Guerrilla warfare was therefore defensive, fought on home territory with the advantages of popular support and local knowledge. It was geared to a strategy of exhaustion, gaining time in the hope that the enemy would tire or that something else would turn up. Such warfare was unlikely to be successful on its own. Irregular forces worked most effectively when providing a distraction to an enemy also facing regular forces in a more conventional campaign. Napoleon suffered in Spain because he also faced the British army. Similarly, Russian peasants made life additionally miserable for French forces in 1812. Clausewitz, who experienced the French occupation of Prussia and was in a position to observe the Spanish insurrection and the French debacle in Russia, made guerrilla warfare the subject of his early lectures and writing. In *On War*, it was considered a form of defense. By the 1820s, when Clausewitz wrote most of *On War*, it had become an uncommon strategy. Popular energies appeared to have been played out and conservative states were in command.

Guerrilla warfare could cause an occupying force trouble, but it was the "last and desperate resort" of an otherwise defeated people. A general uprising against an occupier would need to be "nebulous and elusive," because as soon as it became concrete it could be crushed. Though a strategically defensive concept, the tactics of guerrilla warfare had to be offensive, aiming to catch the enemy unawares. Guerrilla warfare would most likely be effective when conducted from rough and inaccessible terrain in a country's interior. Clausewitz did not see irregular militias as being of much value in the absence of regular forces.[1] Jomini had a similar response. He understood the challenges militias could pose for occupying forces, and how difficult they might make wars of expansion if popular opinion could readily be excited, but he recoiled from the prospect. Wars in which entire peoples had become animated by religious, national, or ideological differences he considered deplorable, "organized assassination," arousing "violent passions that make them spiteful, cruel, and terrible." He acknowledged that his "prejudices were with the good old times when the French and English guards courteously invited each other to fire first" rather than the "frightful epoch when priests, women, and children throughout Spain plotted the murder of isolated soldiers."[2]

During the 1830s, the possibility that guerrilla warfare might serve an insurrection was raised by Mazzini's failed Young Italy campaign, with the red-shirted Giuseppe Garibaldi emerging as a gifted guerrilla commander. Despite this example, the main models for revolutionary violence remained a sudden uprising of the masses that would catch authorities by surprise. The idea that they might be worn down gradually in a prolonged campaign did not catch on. Frederick Engels, in an article drafted for Karl Marx, saw the emergence of the guerrillas in Spain as a reflection of the failure of the Spanish army. Engels presented them as more of a mob than an army, motivated by "hatred, revenge, and love of plunder."[3] He tended to think in terms of conventional military formations, even when contemplating revolution, and assumed that after a revolution a socialist republic would need a proper army for its defense. The presumption that a revolution would need a disciplined fighting force of class-conscious proletarians continued to influence socialist thinking, so that guerrilla warfare was seen as the domain of anarchists and criminals, of drunken riffraff indulging their violent tendencies. Though somewhat sympathetic to this view in Russia, Lenin refused to dismiss guerrilla warfare entirely. But he believed it could only be a subordinate form of struggle, not the main method, and would benefit from proper party discipline to keep it under control. Once the mass movement had reached a certain stage of development, guerrilla warfare was not out of the question during the "fairly large intervals" that would occur between the "big engagements" in the revolutionary civil war.[4]

When, after the 1917 uprising, the Bolsheviks found themselves caught up in a civil war, military commissar Leon Trotsky also saw guerrilla warfare as a useful but subordinate form of fighting. It was demanding, so it required proper organization and direction and must be free from amateurish and adventurist influences. It could not "overthrow" an enemy but could cause difficulties. Whereas the stronger force would seek annihilation of the enemy using large-scale, centrally directed mass armies, the weaker force—Trotsky argued—might seek to disorganize the stronger using light, mobile units operating independently of one another. This followed Delbrück's distinction between annihilation and exhaustion. Trotsky was clearly in favor of annihilation. "The Soviet power has been all the time, and is still, the stronger side." Its task was to crush the enemy "so as to free its hands for socialist construction." It was the enemy, therefore, that was attempting guerrilla warfare. This reflected the shift, for the proletariat was now the ruling class and the tsarists were the rebels. Trotsky denied that his strategy was too ponderous and positional, and lacked mobility.[5] The Red Army had begun with "volunteers, rebels, primitive, inexperienced guerrillas" and turned them into "proper, trained, disciplined regiments and divisions." Nonetheless, as the civil war became more challenging, Trotsky sought to form mobile guerrilla detachments, supplements to "the weighty masses of the Red Army," that would cause problems for the enemy on its rear.[6] Guerrilla warfare was therefore viewed, even by radicals, as a lesser strategy, a defensive expedient but not a source of victory.

Lawrence of Arabia

The expansion of the European empires during the nineteenth century prompted regular uprisings and rebellions, which put their own demands on regular forces. The British army put these tasks under the heading of imperial policing. The classic discussion was C. E. Calwell's *Small Wars*, published in 1896, which observed that as a general rule, "the quelling of the rebellion in distant colonies means protracted, thankless, invertebrate war."[7] It was Thomas Edward Lawrence, an archaeologist who made his name during the Great War seeking to foment an Arab rebellion against Ottoman rule, who did the most to develop principles about how guerrilla warfare should be fought rather than how it could be contained. Lawrence had not only a startling story to tell but also impressive literary gifts. His vivid metaphors and aphorisms help explain his influence. His memoir of the campaign, *The Seven Pillars of Wisdom*, remains a classic. His basic philosophy of guerrilla warfare, with a brief history of the revolt, was first published in October 1920.[8] After the war, he struggled with the myth he had helped to create about himself, as well as with the failure of the Allied government to honor the promises of independence Lawrence had made to the Arabs.

The campaign against the Turks had begun in 1916 with operations against the long railroad between Medina and Damascus, a key supply line. The regular loss of trains frustrated the Turks, for whom fully protecting the railroad appeared impossible against the Arab enemy, Eventually, this turned into a full-scale Arab revolt—a major distraction for the Turks. Lawrence described a moment early in 1917. He had been wrestling with the limitations of irregular forces. They could not do what armed forces were supposed to do: "seek for the enemy's army, his centre of power, and destroy it in battle." Moreover, they would not effectively attack a position nor could they defend one, as he had recently discovered. He concluded that their advantage lay in "depth, not in face" and that the threat of attack could be used to get the Turks stuck in defensive positions.

Lawrence then became ill and contemplated the future of his campaign while he recovered. He was "tolerably read" in military theory and impressed by Clausewitz. Yet he was repelled by the idea of an "absolute war" that was concerned solely with the destruction of enemy forces in "the one process battle." It felt like buying victory in blood and he did not think the Arabs would want to do that. They were fighting for their freedom ("a pleasure only to be tasted by a man alive"). While armies were like plants, "immobile as a whole, firm-rooted, nourished through long stems to the head," the Arab irregulars were more "a thing intangible, invulnerable, without front or back, drifting about like gas." The Turks would lack enough men to cope with the "ill will of the Arab people," especially as they were likely to treat the rebellion in absolute terms. They would not realize "to make war upon rebellion is messy and slow, like eating soup with a knife." Attacking the Turks' supply lines would keep them short of materiel. Instead of a war of contact there was the possibility here of a war of detachment. This would involve becoming known to the enemy only when there was an opportunity to attack and avoiding being put on the defensive by "perfect" intelligence. There was a psychological aspect to this. Lawrence spoke, in the commonplace of the time, of the "crowd" and the need to adjust the "spirit to the point where it becomes fit to exploit in action, the prearrangement of a changing opinion to a certain end." The Arabs not only had to order their own men's minds but also those of the enemy ("as far as we could reach them") and of supporting and hostile nations, as well as the "neutrals looking on."

To this end Lawrence developed a small, highly mobile, and well-equipped force, which could take advantage of the Turks having distributed their forces thinly. The Arabs had nothing to defend and excellent knowledge of the desert. Tactics were "tip and run, not pushes, but strokes." Having made their point in one place, they would not hold it but would instead move on to strike again elsewhere. Victory depended on the use of "speed, concealment, accuracy of fire." "Irregular war," Lawrence observed, "is more intellectual than a bayonet charge." These tactics reduced the Turks to "helplessness." Yet he conceded that this irregular war was not the main event in the defeat of the Ottoman Empire, which came as a result of a much more conventional push by British forces under General Allenby. In this respect, Lawrence's campaign was a "side show upon a side show," though significant in a supporting role. In his acknowledgment of Allenby's role there was a tinge of regret that this deprived him of an opportunity to see whether war could be won without battles. It had been a "thrilling experiment" to "prove irregular war or rebellion to be an exact science." He noted the advantages: an unassailable base (in his case the Red Sea ports protected by the Royal Navy), an alien enemy unable to manage the space it was occupying, and a friendly population ("Rebellions can be made by 2 per cent active in a striking force, and 98 per cent passive sympathetically."). Lawrence offered the following synopsis:

> In fifty words: granted mobility, security (in the form of denying targets to the enemy), time, and doctrine (the idea to convert every subject to friendliness), victory will rest with the insurgents, for the

algebraic factors are in the end decisive, and against them perfection of means and spirit struggle quite in vain.

It is not surprising to find that Liddell Hart was enamored of Lawrence, for he was the epitome of the indirect approach in action. The two men had brief correspondence after the war, and Liddell Hart borrowed Lawrence's insights. They later became friends when Liddell Hart summarized the main themes of Lawrence's thought for an article in the 1929 edition of the *Encyclopaedia Britannica*, for which he was military editor. Lawrence's exploits served a didactic purpose in illustrating the indirect approach, and Liddell Hart was impressed by this man who was both a thinker and doer and had found himself with such an influential command without have passed through the military system. Thereafter, Liddell Hart wrote an admiring biography in which he put Lawrence on a plinth.[9] He was intrigued with Lawrence's observation that the Arabs hankered after bloodless victories. Otherwise he had little interest in irregular warfare for radical purposes. If anything, Liddell Hart disapproved of it because it normally led to brutality and terrorism. What enthused him was the possibility that regular warfare could develop along the lines Lawrence had shown to be possible with irregular warfare.[10]

Mao and Giap

This same resistance to the idea that guerrilla warfare could be a separate route to victory was evident in the strategy of Mao Zedong, who led the Chinese communists to victory over their nationalist opponents in 1949. Mao saw guerrilla warfare as an acceptable strategy when on the defensive but not as an independent route to victory. He relied on it whenever his immediate need was simply to survive. As this was often the case, his writings on guerrilla tactics have a certain authority, but his preferred form of warfare involved mobile, regular forces. Reliance on guerrilla warfare was dictated not only by the fact that for some twenty years Mao's forces were facing stronger armies in the former of the nationalist Kuomintang and Japanese occupation forces (from 1937–1945) but also because he made his base in rural areas and came to see the peasants rather than the urban proletariat as the source of revolution.

Although Mao came from a rural family, his initial work as a Communist Party activist in the 1920s focused on labor struggles. This was required by the Party's urban leadership, but Mao could not see how the working classes in such a vast, populous, and agrarian country as China could act as agents of change. After witnessing peasant uprisings in Hunan, he observed in 1927 that the peasants, properly mobilized, could be "like a mighty storm, like a hurricane, a force so swift that no power, however great, will be able to hold it back," sweeping away "all the imperialists, warlords, corrupt officials, local tyrants and evil gentry into their graves." That year a fragile united front between the nationalists and the communists collapsed. In the ensuing confrontation, Mao's army was defeated and he was forced to flee. He concluded quickly that it was only by means of guerrilla warfare in the expanses of rural China that survival was possible.[11] The next stage in his thinking, following the party leadership's disastrous forays against nationalist cities in 1930, was to conceive of the countryside not so much as a base from which to attack cities but as the place where the revolution could be made. He built up a new power base—the Kiangsi Soviet—but another failed conventional offensive against nationalist strongholds in 1934 led to a counterattack which put this base under pressure. He escaped by a mass evacuation, known as the Long March, which succeeded to the extent that he evaded capture—at an extremely high cost. The communists marched some six thousand miles for a year, until a new safe haven was found in Shensi province in October 1935. By then, Mao's force had been much reduced, to barely ten thousand men. According to Chang and Halliday, the nationalists actually allowed the communist army to escape—as Stalin was holding the son of nationalist leader Chiang Kai-shek hostage—and then Mao took an unnecessarily long route to avoid joining a rival's larger force.[12] With the old leadership discredited and a reputation, whether or not deserved, as a military commander and expert on rural China, Mao became Communist Party leader.

In July 1937, Japan invaded China. Mao had already proposed a united front against the Japanese. Though agreed upon the previous December, it was always tenuous in practice, not least because it suited Mao more than the nationalists as he was able to gain time. The nationalists were on the defensive, their leaders and officials pushed out of significant parts of the country. Meanwhile the Japanese were unable to establish effective authority, so the communists were given an opportunity to fill the political vacuum. They were accepted as the representatives of the anti-Japanese united front and given a hearing for the economic and social reforms they sought. The peasantry were given a chance to transform local power structures. At the same time Mao was extremely cautious when it came to taking on the Japanese. He concentrated on survival, especially once the United States entered the war in December 1941. Even after the war, when the civil war resumed in China, Mao remained cautious, expecting at best a negotiated peace with the Kuomintang.[13] By 1947, he had begun to appreciate that although the nationalists notionally occupied large parts of the country, their roots were not deep and were at last vulnerable to a communist offensive. He seized power in 1949.

Mao's ideas had taken shape a decade earlier. In their early formulations they diverged from received wisdom. As he was not then the Party leader, these ideas were formulated in more pragmatic and conditional terms than their more dogmatic later expressions suggested. The most authoritative presentation of the theory of people's war was a series of lectures in 1937, in the aftermath of the Long March and the Japanese invasion. These formed the basis of Mao's treatise on guerrilla warfare.[14] They reflected his conviction that the peasantry could be an agent of revolutionary change. Because he was not working with the urban proletariat, who were supposed to acquire political consciousness as a matter of course, he put political education and mobilization at the heart of people's war. This required the masses to understand the politics of the struggle, the objectives for which it was being fought, and the program which would be implemented when it was won. The time gained by guerrilla tactics, therefore, had to be used productively "to conduct propaganda among the masses" to help them gain revolutionary power. Politics, therefore, always had to be in command.

Mao played down material factors, such as economic and military power, in which he was evidently deficient, in favor of human power and morale: "It is people, not things that are decisive."[15] Given the armed struggle in which he had been engaged for over a decade, it was not surprising that he insisted in another famous aphorism that "power grows out of the barrel of a gun," reflecting the twists and turns of the armed struggle that had shaped his life. Mao had read Clausewitz and Lawrence.[16] John Shy judged him to be in some respects closer to Jomini, with "similar maxims, repetitions, and exhortations," and the same "compounding of analysis and prescription" and "didactic drive."[17] The influence of Sun Tzu was clear in his observations on how to wear down a superior enemy while avoiding battle ("The enemy advances, we retreat; the enemy camps, we harass. The enemy tires, we attack; the enemy retreats; we pursue") and the importance of intelligence and a better grasp of the situation ("Know the enemy and know yourself and you can fight a hundred battles without disaster").[18]

While guerrilla warfare had by necessity loomed large in his scheme, Mao was well aware of its limits. He described the basic principle of war as to "preserve oneself and to annihilate the enemy." Guerrilla warfare was only relevant to the first of these tasks, although this happened to be the one which preoccupied him for all but the last few years of his military struggles. He relied on its defensive properties—popular support and local knowledge—against an occupying force. In a well-known metaphor, he described how the people mobilized would be "a vast sea in which the enemy will be swallowed up" but in which their army would thrive like fish.[19] The importance of keeping unity between the guerrilla army and the local people was stressed in his three rules ("All actions are subject to command; Do not steal from the people; Be neither selfish nor unjust") and eight remarks ("Replace the door when you leave the house; Roll up the bedding on which you have slept; Be courteous; Be honest in your transactions; Return what you borrow; Replace what you break; Do not bathe in the presence of women; Do not without authority search the pocketbooks of those you arrest").[20]

Unlike Lawrence, whose fighters could go out and attack the enemy at vulnerable points, Mao was wary of venturing too far from his base. His strategy was to lure the enemy into his areas of strength. Here he could go on the tactical offensive, but there were limits to the possibilities of a strategic offensive. His expectation of the war with Japan was that it was likely to be protracted. As he contemplated its likely course he identified an optimum strategy in terms of three stages. The first stage was defensive. Eventually a stalemate would be reached (second stage), and then the communists would have the confidence and capabilities to move on to the offensive (third stage). Although at the time the Chinese were on their own, Mao was aware that at some point external factors that would undermine Japanese superiority might come into play. He saw a role for both guerrilla and positional (defense or attack of defined points) warfare, but the best results would require mobile warfare. Only that could lead to annihilation of the enemy defined in terms of loss of resistance rather than complete physical destruction. Mao was fighting an enemy with whom there might be a stalemate, but never a compromise. So the third stage demanded regular forces. Until these could be developed, guerrilla units would be crucial. In the third stage they would play no more than a supporting role.

The most assiduous follower of Mao after his revolution was General Vo Nguyen Giap, a schoolteacher from Vietnam who fought against colonial France and then the U.S.-supported anti-communist government in the south. He immersed himself in Maoist theory and practice in China in 1940 and then returned to Vietnam to lead the fight against the Japanese and later the French. He is also reported to have described Lawrence's *Seven Pillars of Wisdom* as his "fighting gospel" that he was "never without." Giap took Mao's three stages seriously, but his major innovation was his readiness to move between the different stages according to circumstances, whereas Mao had seen these as sequential steps. Vietnam was a relatively small country compared to China and so required greater flexibility. In particular, Giap was prepared to use regular forces before the third stage, to hold space, for example.

His description of guerrilla warfare captured the best practice of the Asian communist struggle of the mid-twentieth century. Guerrilla war served the broad masses of an economically backward country standing up to a "well-trained army of aggression." Against the enemy's strength was poised a "boundless heroism." The front was not fixed but was "wherever the enemy is found" and sufficiently exposed to be vulnerable to a local concentration of forces, employing "initiative, flexibility, rapidity, surprise, suddenness in attack and retreat." The enemy would be exhausted "little by little by small victories." Losses were to be avoided "even at the cost of losing ground."[21]

In the communist mainstream, from Engels to Giap, guerrilla warfare was therefore never seen as sufficient in itself. It was a way of holding out until it was possible to develop a true military capacity. At any time it might be all that could be done to stay in the game. But if the aim was to seize power, the regular forces of the state would have to be defeated.

Counterinsurgency

Two books published in the 1950s sought to capture the American struggle to come to terms with communist insurgencies. Graham Greene's *The Quiet American*, based on the author's experiences in Vietnam in the early 1950s, focused on the earnest but naïve American, Alden Pyle, who had a theoretical concept of what Vietnam needed but no true understanding. He was "sincere in his way," but as "incapable of imagining pain or danger to himself as he was incapable of conceiving the pain he might cause others." Eugene Burdick and William Lederer, a professor and military officer, respectively, intended to write a nonfiction book about the mistakes being made by the Americans in confronting communism in southeast Asia. But they decided, correctly, that they could make their point more effectively through fiction. In *The Ugly American*, there was more of an American hero. Colonel Edwin Hillendale helped run successful campaigns in South Vietnam and the Philippines. The message of this book was that Americans seeking to influence events in these societies should live among the people and get to know their language and cultures. "Every person and every nation has a key which will open their hearts," observes Hillendale. "If you use the right key, you can maneuver any person or any nation any way you want."[22]

The main characters in both books were often assumed to have been inspired by General Edward Lansdale. Greene always denied this was the case for his book, but Hillendale evidently was modeled on Lansdale. In 1961, Lansdale became an adviser to President Kennedy after being introduced to him as one of the few Americans who really understood the demands of counterinsurgency. Lansdale understood that without popular support there was "no political base for supporting the fight." People had to be convinced that their lives could be improved through social action and political reform, as well as by the physical protection that came with sensitive military operations. This required a responsive, non-corrupt government; well-behaved armed forces; and a cause in which they could believe.

John Kennedy endorsed *The Ugly American* as a senator, attracted by its central message that people in desperate situations could be as inspired by the ideals of American liberalism as those of Soviet communism. One of Kennedy's first acts as president was to demand that the American military take counterinsurgency far more seriously.[23] Kennedy encouraged all those around him to read Mao and Che Guevara, the theorist of the Cuban revolution, and took a personal interest in special forces and their training manuals and equipment. Groups were established to coordinate what was described as "subterranean war," with South Vietnam soon the main area of concern. The challenge was seen to be less with the diagnosis—drawing attention to the problems with development, weak governmental institutions, and militaries that were more instruments of repression than sources of security for ordinary people—than in working out what to do about it. There was considerable study of Maoist doctrine, which meant that American policy became reactive in the sense of trying to determine whether the North Vietnamese communists were moving from the second to the third stage, or focusing on countering communist propaganda and tactics.

The Americans were influenced by the successful British experience in Malaya as described by Robert Thompson.[24] Under the leadership of Sir Gerald Templer, a communist insurgency had been contained. "The shooting side of the business is only 25 percent of the trouble," observed Templer, "and the other 75 percent lies in getting the people of this country behind us." The answer was not "pouring more troops into the jungle." It was instead, in a phrase Templer made famous, "in the hearts and minds of the people." He understood the importance of civic action but also the need to show a determination to win. This required a readiness to be ruthless.[25] Templer was successful, but he enjoyed favorable conditions. In Malaya, the communists were largely associated with the minority Chinese population, their resupply routes were poor, and economic conditions were reasonable.

The unsuccessful French experiences in Vietnam and Algeria were reflected in the writings of David Galula who provided one of the more lucid texts on how to counter communist tactics, and who popularized the concept of "insurgency." He also stressed the importance of the loyalty of the population. A successful counterinsurgency must ensure the people felt protected so they could cooperate without fear of retribution. Victory would require pacifying one area after another, each serving as a secure base from which to move to the next.[26] Galula's actual experience in Algeria was mixed. His efforts to treat local people positively were not matched by many of his fellow officers. When it came to propaganda, he judged the French "definitely and infinitely more stupid than our opponents." Like other counterinsurgent specialists, Galula found that his theory fitted neither the local political structures nor army culture.[27] The main effect of the attempt by the French officer class to develop a counterinsurgency doctrine that matched the communists in its political intensity and ruthlessness was that they began to turn their ire on Paris for not supporting their efforts with sufficient vigor—even attempting a coup.[28]

An awareness of the need to give the anti-communist South Vietnamese government more legitimacy and turn its forces into agents of democracy and development reflected a theoretical objective that was far removed from the realities on the ground. It was understood that any fighting should be done by indigenous forces, but that left open the question of what should be done when these forces could no longer cope. It was one thing if the insurgency was a response to local conditions cloaked in the rhetoric of international communism; if it truly was being pushed from outside by communists, that was another. The U.S. military was doubtful that this was really a new type of insurgency and preferred to treat it as old-fashioned aggression. Counterinsurgency theory suggested that the role of military action was to create sufficient security to introduce programs to improve the social conditions of the people, thereby winning over their "hearts and minds" and denying the insurgents bases, recruits, and support. Against this the military argued that wars were won by eliminating enemy armed forces and frustrating their operations. This supported a policy of "search and destroy" through shelling and bombing areas where the enemy was believed to be hiding, though the enemy had often moved on and the attacks led to civilian deaths and popular resentment.

One of those involved in the internal discussions later commented ruefully on the "somewhat simplistic" assumptions about a monolithic form of threat, following the script of a "war of national liberation." Under this mindset, sight of the "domestic origins and root causes of internal turmoil" was lost, which meant that the insurgency was treated as if it was "a clearly articulated military force instead of the apex of a pyramid deeply embedded in society."[29] Another official questioned the very description of opponents as "insurgents" instead of revolutionaries or rebels because this denied the possibility that they might be champions of a popular movement. It was hard to accept that the opponents were often local and popular and that their victims were associated with repression.[30] The basic problem was that ameliorating the "worst causes of discontent" and redressing "the most flagrant inequities" would require positive action—and in some cases, radical reform—by the local government, yet the measures being proposed threatened to undermine the government's position because they would involve altering the country's social structure and domestic economy.[31] It is also important to note that the original formulations of counterinsurgency doctrine assumed that the main work would be undertaken by local forces, assisted by American resources and advisors. The use of American forces on a large scale was to be avoided.[32] There were many examples of this during the 1960s. In this respect, South Vietnam was the exception, but it was an exception that clouded all later thoughts on counterinsurgency theory and practice.

By the start of 1965, it was apparent that it was going to be very difficult to deal with the domestic sources of insurgency. Instead, American attention switched to dealing with the supply lines coming from the north. The conflict was firmly framed in terms of a fight with the communist leadership in North Vietnam and beyond rather than as a power struggle within South Vietnam. At this time, Tom Schelling's concepts of bargaining and coercive diplomacy were particularly influential. This can be seen even in discussions of Vietnam, a situation far removed from the one to which Schelling had most applied himself—a superpower confrontation over a prized piece of real estate in the center of Europe and directly linked to a possible nuclear war.[33] The figure in the U.S. Government most influenced by Schelling during the 1960s was John McNaughton, an academic lawyer from Harvard who died in an air crash in July 1967. He had worked with Schelling on the Marshall Plan in the late 1940s, and the two remained good friends. When McNaughton spoke of arms control, for example, he showed interest in the notion of the "reciprocal fear of surprise attack" and "non-zero-sum games."[34] He is said to have remarked that the Cuban missile crisis demonstrated the realism of Schelling's games.[35] McNaughton was a key figure in the development of the U.S. policy on Vietnam, working closely with Secretary of Defense Robert McNamara and National Security Advisor McGeorge Bundy. One of his memos was famously described by a colleague as the reductio ad absurdum of the planner's art, combining realpolitik with the hyper-rationalist belief in control of the most refined American think tank.[36] In a report of a working group McNaughton chaired in February 1964,[37] one suggestion was pure Schelling: it would be possible to influence Hanoi's decisions by action designed "to hurt but not to destroy."[38] Also drawn from Schelling was the proposition that "a decision to use force if necessary, backed by resolute and extensive deployment, and conveyed by every possible means to our adversaries, gives the best present chance of avoiding the actual use of such force." The basic principle was that "a pound of threat is worth an ounce of action—as long as we are not bluffing."[39]

The main threat his group had in mind was the use of American air power. At the time, the government was still trying to avoid using ground forces. But that could not achieve much of direct military value, as the supply lines were hard to disrupt and mass air attacks on civilian populations were considered unacceptable. McNaughton came up with the idea of coercive air strikes with a political purpose, which he described as "progressive squeeze-and-talk," orchestrating diplomatic communications with graduated military pressure. Even if the United States eventually gave up, it was important to show that it had been "willing to keep promises, be tough, take risks, get bloodied, and hurt the enemy badly."[40] McNaughton was thus trying to find ways of giving the impression of commitment without being truly resolute, of following one course while not closing off others.

At the start of 1965, McNaughton consulted Schelling on exactly how the North could be coerced in these unpromising circumstances. According to one account, the two men wrestled unsatisfactorily with the question of "what could the United States ask the North to stop doing that they would obey, that we would soon know they obeyed, and that they could not simply resume doing after the bombing had ceased." Kaplan comments, with some satisfaction: "So assured, at times glibly so, when writing about sending signals with force, inflicting pain to make an opponent behave and weaving patterns of communication through tactics of coercive warfare in theory, Tom Schelling, when faced with a real-life 'limited war,' was stumped, had no idea where to begin."[41] In fact, Schelling was highly skeptical about the likely value of a bombing campaign against the North. He noted the weak diplomacy accompanying the bombing and hoped that there had been private communications to Hanoi of a less ambiguous nature.[42] Schelling's reasoning, while suggestive and provocative, could not by itself generate strategies because that required the introduction of levels of complexity that his theoretical structure could not handle.

The new civilian strategists had some influence on the early stages of the U.S. policy regarding Vietnam, but the overriding influence was American military preferences. In some respects, the two came from the same starting point: a focus on techniques and tactics separate from political context.

Counterinsurgency theory, like nuclear strategy, developed as a special body of expertise geared to discussing special sorts of military relationships as if they were special types of war. As discussed, Mao and Giap never saw guerrilla tactics as more than expedients for when they were weak. They did not think they could win a "guerrilla war"—success at this level would allow them to move on to the next stage defined by the familiar clash of regular armies. What they thought was truly distinctive to their type of warfare was the attention paid to political education and propaganda.

Vietnam, a war for which the civilian strategists had not prepared and on which they had relatively little of value to say, marked the end of the "golden age" of strategic studies. Just as the arrival of mutual assured destruction and a period of relative calm took the urgency out of the Cold War, Vietnam "poisoned the academic well."[43] Colin Gray charged the civilian "men of ideas" with being overconfident about the ease with which theory might be transferred to the "world of action." The prophets had become courtiers, living off their intellectual capital. Their "dual-loyalty" to the needs of problem-oriented officials on the one hand and the disinterested "policy-neutral" standards of scholarship on the other "had tended to produce both irrelevant policy advice and poor scholarship."[44] In response to this criticism, Brodie praised policy engagement and defended the small group of civilian strategists who had accepted the burden of making sense of the new nuclear world, because the military were incapable of doing so. Yet having left RAND in 1966 bemoaning the "astonishing lack of political sense" and ignorance of diplomatic and military history among the engineers and economists, he readily accepted Vietnam as a consequence of these tendencies.[45]

CHAPTER 15 | Observation and Orientation

Strategy without tactics is the slowest route to victory. Tactics without
strategy is the noise before defeat.

—Sun Tzu

WITH THERE APPARENTLY being little more to say on nuclear strategy and Vietnam having turned into such a bruising experience, the
civilian strategists in the United States withdrew from the field. The think
tanks began to dwell more on immediate issues of policy and more technical
matters. The civilians had never had much to say about the classic questions of regular warfare, though this was a natural focus for the professional
military. It was the one area that had been left relatively untouched by the
literature of the 1950s and 1960s due to the preoccupation with the unconventional areas of nuclear and guerrilla warfare.

One exception was a retired French general André Beaufre. Whereas the
tendency in the United States was to turn strategy into a series of technical
and practical issues, Beaufre's approach was broader and more philosophical.
This was reflected in his definition of strategy as "the art of the dialectic of
two opposing wills using force to resolve their dispute."[1] This put strategy at
the highest level of policy, taking in not just a clash of arms but all possible
elements of power. Strategy appeared as the supreme function of the state,
requiring choices between different forms of power and their coordinated

employment to ensure that their effects were maximized. Success could be achieved by means other than physical force. The target was the enemy's will to start or continue a fight. Psychological effects were therefore critical.

The dialectic was composed of three interconnecting parts—nuclear, conventional, and cold-war. As a friend of Liddell Hart, Beaufre picked up on the possibilities of an indirect approach but gave it a broader frame, looking to actions in fields other than the military to make an impact. He therefore had a traditional view of conventional warfare as being about a victory but also assumed that in an age of nuclear deterrence this had become less interesting. By contrast, the cold war intrigued him, because it was a new but apparently permanent phenomenon. It was pushing the conflict out into all areas, including the economic and cultural, where the two sides might encounter each other. In this respect, stirring up discontent in colonies or making humanitarian appeals could be part of the same strategy. The risk in this formulation was that events that had quite other causes were explained by this particular "dialectic of opposing wills."

American readers found Beaufre's philosophical approach, with its Cartesian and Hegelian influences, hard to follow. Bernard Brodie, with his pragmatism and view of strategy as "the pursuit of success in certain types of competitive endeavor," described himself as uncertain of Beaufre's meaning. Brodie also found it hard to take Beaufre's dismissal of military history and his disinterest in the collection of technical data as a distraction. This went against the "general consensus that awareness of technological and other types of change is a top-level requirement among strategists."[2]

Brodie's reaction to Beaufre may help explain the limited attention paid to a contribution by James Wylie. Wylie was an American admiral who wrote a short but lucid guide to contemporary strategy in the 1960s. His approach was compared at the time to Beaufre's.[3] James Wylie's *Military Strategy* retains a following, but its impact has been marginal.[4] Wylie first began to set down his ideas in the early 1950s, partly as reflections on his Second World War experience. He worked in concert with another admiral, Henry Eccles, whose thoughts followed a similar path. Both of them put questions of power at the heart of their analyses. Both wondered what that meant in terms of an ability to assert "control." As naval officers in the Mahan tradition, they believed that control was the objective of strategy.

Eccles recognized that the issue of control went beyond the purely military sphere and was both inward and outward. The distinctive sources of power that had to be addressed internally included not only politicians and the public but also logistics and the industrial bases. The external sources, not only adversaries but also allies and neutrals, were even harder to control.[5]

In these circumstances, control could clearly not be absolute and had to be considered as a matter of degree. Wylie understood strategy as being about ends and means; it was "a purpose together with a some measures for its accomplishment," and war in terms of competing patterns of activity, in which one side would gain advantage by imposing a pattern on the enemy. This did not require actual battle. It could work through shows of coercive force, which could progressively constrain the enemy.

Wylie's main claim to originality lay in a distinction between two types of strategy. The idea was prompted by a comment from the German-American historian Herbert Rosinski in 1951 distinguishing between "directive" and "cumulative" strategies. Rosinski was certainly aware of Delbrück, and he may well have been thinking about updating the distinction between wars of annihilation and exhaustion. Wylie developed his ideas first in a 1952 article. "It landed with no splash at the time," he lamented, "and has lain on the deck ever since."[6] He tried again in his book. The distinction he drew was between a linear sequential strategy, tending to the offensive, and a cumulative strategy. A sequential strategy would involve discrete steps, each dependent upon the one before, which together would shape the outcome of the war. This offered the possibility of forcing the enemy to a satisfactory conclusion, but it also required an ability to plan ahead and anticipate the course of a conflict. The risk, of which Wylie was well aware, was that once one step turned out differently, the remainder of the sequence must follow a different pattern likely to lead to less satisfactory outcomes than the one originally sought. By contrast, a cumulative strategy was more defensive. It involved "the less perceptible minute accumulation of little items piling one on top of the other until at some unknown point the mess of accumulated actions may be large enough to be critical." These items would not be interdependent, so a negative result in one area need not put the whole effort into reverse. This strategy could counter a sequential strategy, denying an enemy control, but it could not offer a quick, decisive result. In practice, Wylie did not consider the two to be exclusive. He did see a cumulative strategy as providing a useful hedge against a bold plan going wrong.[7]

Although this distinction was potentially richer than others that became more prominent in strategic debate in the United States, it is not hard to explain Wylie's limited influence. The concepts were abstract and did not particularly address the preoccupations of the 1960s. It was well into the 1970s before serious debate revived on regular warfare. By then, the classic questions were ripe for reappraisal. Regular warfare was still the area of greatest military expenditure and effort, and new technologies were starting to challenge established doctrine.

The starting point for the revised interest was one of the most elemental and iconic encounters of contemporary warfare. The aerial dogfight combined the hunt and the chase with advanced technology. Colonel John Boyd, an American fighter pilot with experience going back to the Korean War, wrote the definitive manual on the subject. As he did so he hit upon an insight which he developed into a formula of considerable influence. Boyd began with the premise that the U.S. air force had become too preoccupied with speed. This became apparent during the early stages of the air war over Vietnam when apparently obsolete Soviet-built MiGs were prevailing in dogfights because they were more maneuverable. After an intensive analysis of the competing aircraft, Boyd concluded that the key quality was not absolute speed but agility. In a series of moves during the course of a dogfight, the most responsive fighter would be able to get on to the opponent's tail, ready for the kill.

The OODA Loop

Boyd summed all this up as the "OODA loop." OODA stands for observation, orientation, decision, action. The sequence started with observation, as data concerning the environment was collected. This was analyzed in the orientation stage, leading to a decision and then to the execution of an action. The loop became more complex as it developed, especially as Boyd came to appreciate the pervasive importance of orientation. It was a loop because the action changed the environment, which required that the process be repeated. Ideally, the progressive improvement of the orientation and the consequential action would result in getting closer to reality. For the fighter pilot, this brought home the importance of getting to the action part of the loop faster than the opponent. Boyd felt the OODA loop applied to any situation in which it was necessary to keep or gain the initiative. The aim was always to disorient the opponent, who would be unable to grasp a situation developing more quickly than anticipated and in unexpected ways and thus paralyzed into indecision.

Eventually books were written to explain, and in some cases apply, Boyd's theories. He never produced a definitive text of his own. His basic ideas are contained in several hundred slides entitled *Discourse on Winning & Losing.*[8] They formed the basis of briefings given over almost two decades to numerous audiences, including most of the senior figures in the American defense establishment. Their impact was accentuated because they were spread by enthusiastic acolytes who shared Boyd's commitment to a combination of hard cost-benefit analysis and broad strategic vision, as well as disdain for the bureaucrats and careerists who by definition lacked both. In addition, at least at first sight, the OODA loop had a compelling simplicity and sustained the gathering complexity of Boyd's theories. After retiring from the air force, the autodidactic Boyd read widely and moved from his engineering background into mathematical theory and on into history and the social sciences.

His later reading reinforced his views about the difficulty of sustaining the initiative. The enemy might be able to move faster than anticipated; observations might result in more uncertainty than clarity. In one remarkable paper he drew on the work of mathematicians Kurt Gödel and Werner Heisenberg to demonstrate the greater risk of disorientation when attempts were made to fit observations into preconceptions.[9] He then used the second law of thermodynamics to argue that closed systems led to increases in entropy, that is, internal confusion and disorder. Boyd was showing that instead of searching for "laws" to match those developed by Newtonian physics, it was now necessary to make sense of new forms of theory which challenged concepts of systems tending to equilibrium and pointed instead to chaos. The basic conclusion was the need "to deny the adversary the possibility of uncovering or discerning patterns that match our activity, or other aspects of reality in the world."[10]

Because human beings must cope with a constantly changing reality, it was therefore necessary to challenge rigidities in thought. Then these new thoughts would rigidify in their time and so would need dissolving in turn. The lasting importance of Boyd's work lay in the focus on disrupting the enemy's decision-making, encouraging uncertainty and confusion. Under his influence, established notions of command and control were amended to take account of how information was collected, interpreted, and then communicated. By the time he died in 1997, the revolution in information and communication technologies was well underway. Boyd had set the terms for its military exploitation.

Boyd was widely read in the scientific literature of the time and picked up easily on developing theories which used simple propositions to explain complex phenomena. From these he drew language and insights to describe the sort of conflicts that interested him. From Norbert Wiener's cybernetics to Murray Gell-Mann's complexity theory emerged some core themes about the interaction of parts within systems, adaptation to changing environments, and outcomes that seemed indeterminate but were not beyond explanation. The conclusions for practical strategists that emerged from these theories rarely did justice to the elegance of the originals, and could lead to the suspicion that the main result was to develop more impressive language for matters that were already well understood. Many of the emerging themes were present, for example, in Schelling's writings. The most important contribution of complexity theory was to underline the importance of considering individual actors as part of complex systems, so that they must always be assessed in relation to their environment, which was adapting to them as they adapted to it. Problems arose with an inability to adapt.

"Chaos theory" explained how systems in which cause and effect were supposedly known, and in which strategic calculations might be assumed to be reliable, could nonetheless turn into disorderly systems marked by apparently random effects. This underlined the point that micro-causes could have unexpected macro-effects, and that initial conditions determined later outcomes, even though the resultant dynamic interactions meant that they could not be predicted. Effects always had causes even though the processes were obscure. One basic conclusion was that mistakes in the short term would be hard to reverse over the long term.[11]

This challenged the underlying presumption of rationality underpinning bureaucratic organizations and routine planning. Those looking for stability and regularity could find themselves having to cope with the opposite. If effects were uncertain, especially in more complex settings and longer conflicts, how could a responsible strategist think through the consequences of actions. Along with the sociological "laws" of unanticipated consequences and self-fulfilling expectations came the cybernetic concepts of feedback loops and non-linearity. If inputs and outputs were proportional then variables could be plotted along a straight line, as in a linear equation, but with non-linear equations there could be no such plot because the relationships were complex and outcomes would be disproportionate to effects.[12]

The first thought that might be drawn from this was that all strategy was doomed to failure. The second might be that the process could only truly be managed during its early stages, so the best option was to concentrate on getting the initial advantage. This was fine if the conflict could actually be concluded quickly, but once the early stages were passed situations might be expected to move out of control. There was considerable historical evidence to support this proposition, for example, the failure of the Schlieffen Plan.

Attrition and Maneuver

Boyd's writings led to the evaluation of strategies in terms of their ability to cause uncertainty and confusion in the enemy's mind. This could be achieved by undermining the will to fight ("moral warfare"); encouraging distorted perception of reality, by either deception or attacks on means of communication ("mental warfare"); and using the advantages gained to attack war-making capacities so the enemy could not survive ("physical warfare").[13] The prescriptions that flowed from analysis of the first strategy were largely derivative of the post-Napoleonic classics and of Fuller and Liddell Hart.

One of Boyd's key examples was the 1940 Battle of France, which prompted his "Blitzkrieg vs. Maginot Line mentality." French decision-making was paralyzed as the Germans worked out how to operate inside their OODA loops.[14] One key to German success was the readiness to delegate. Tactical commanders could realize the mission in their own way. This depended on a shared understanding of what needed to be done. Boyd distinguished between attrition warfare, focused on the physical domain and using firepower as a destructive force, and maneuver warfare, focused on the mental domain where the aim was to generate "surprise and shock" by using ambiguity, mobility, and deception. Blitzkrieg could also lead to effects in the moral domain, which Boyd saw as being related to menace and uncertainty.

The example was not chosen at random. It played into a major debate then underway on the future of American military policy. The setting of the 1970s was one in which the armed forces of the United States were still licking their Vietnam-imposed wounds and coming to terms with the implications of an all-volunteer army. The generals believed that they could rebuild the army best by focusing on the priority task of securing NATO's central front. This had the added advantage of returning to the comfort zone of preparations for major war and away from insurgencies. In addition, since the 1960s American policymakers had indicated a wish to reduce dependence on nuclear deterrence, as it involved increasingly incredible threats. In this respect the later stages of Vietnam and the 1973 Arab-Israeli War had indicated that there might be new possibilities, notably technologies that allowed conventional munitions to be delivered with extraordinary precision, offering opportunities to rethink land warfare doctrine. At the same time there were concerns that the European challenge had become greater than before: the Warsaw Pact was presumed to still enjoy substantial numerical superiority but also to have revamped its doctrine and built up its strength while the Americans had been preoccupied with Vietnam.

The resentment of McNamara's managerialism at the Pentagon still ran deep, and was reflected in much of the critical literature of the time. He was taken to embody the stifling introduction of conformist practices and the risk-averse culture of large corporations into a business that should really honor warrior virtues and cultivate mavericks. This became another version of the romantic lament against bureaucratization and scientific rationality, although the trends in scientific thinking around complexity encouraged the view that it was the rationalists who were now being overtaken. It also challenged a military elite who had bought into the corporatist culture. Desk bound and far from the scenes of actual conflict, they were as proud of their degrees in business administration and economics as they were forgetful of the ways of military strategy.

The first fruits of the army's post-Vietnam reappraisal of doctrine came with the 1976 publication of *Field Manual 100-5: Operations*, the army's main doctrinal manual.[15] The manual drew on the lethality of modern weaponry, bringing all forms of firepower—land and air—to bear in a combined arms approach in order to generate an "active defense." It was a traditional approach, dependent on the most advanced equipment and professional training to produce a force capable of holding lines against a determined offensive and inflicting crippling damage on the enemy until they were so weak they could not cope with a counterattack.

It did not take long before this manual was subjected to a searing critique. This was as much about reforming the whole military establishment as addressing a difficult conundrum about how to think about NATO's central front. The criticism originated not from within the military establishment but from a group of largely civilian defense specialists, though many had military backgrounds and were influenced by Boyd. To the fore in the attack was William Lind, intensely conservative though he was working as a legislative aide to a democratic senator. Boyd's dichotomy between attritional and maneuver warfare, using the Maginot Line versus Blitzkrieg analogy, was picked up with some vigor by Lind, who had a keen interest in German fighting methods. In contrast to attrition, which has the objective of killing enemy troops or destroying enemy equipment, the blitzkrieg-based alternative of maneuver would have as its "primary objective" breaking "the spirit and the will of the opposing high command by creating unexpected and unfavorable operational or strategic situations."[16]

Within five years the reformers had apparently won the argument, with the adoption of the doctrine of Air Land Battle in 1982 and a revised army field manual. This was intended from the start to set broad principles for any war, not just one in Europe. The battlefield was to be seen in the round, and the critical attributes of successful operations were stressed as "initiative, depth, agility and synchronization."[17] For *Field Manual 100-5*, maneuver was the dynamic element of combat, allowing the concentration of forces to use surprise, psychological shock, position, and momentum to enable smaller forces to defeat larger ones. It was seen as "the employment of forces through movement supported by fire to achieve a position of advantage" from which they could then destroy or threaten to destroy the enemy. The aim was to move fast, probe defenses, and exploit success, carrying the battle deep into the enemy's rear.[18] The spirit was offensive and in line with Boyd's determination to get inside the enemy's OODA loop:

> The underlying purpose of every encounter with the enemy is to seize or retain independence of action. To do this we must make decisions and act more quickly than the enemy to disorganize his forces and to keep him off balance.[19]

By 1986 the *Field Manual 90-8 Counterguerrilla Operations*, dealing with action directed against armed antigovernment forces, claimed that the "basic concept of Air Land Battle doctrine can be applied to Counterguerrilla operations."[20] In 1989 the Marine Corps issued *FMFM-1* which insisted that its doctrine was based on "warfare by maneuver," which would provide a means to defeat a "physically superior foe" by rendering the enemy "incapable of resisting by shattering his moral and physical cohesion."[21]

Operational Art

"Maneuver" displaced "attrition" remarkably quickly. This all took place within a cold-war context, in which the enemy was both well known and substantial, and the problem to be solved was deterring and if necessary resisting aggression across the inner German border. The focus was therefore on a classic great power confrontation between large armies in the center of Europe. It was one which made it possible to draw on the classic texts of military strategy updated for the information age.

Edward Luttwak, a Romanian-born polymath with an unerring eye for a controversial argument, synthesized the various strands of critical thinking around U.S. military policy with a series of articles and books. He challenged the Department of Defense's bloated command structures and fascination with weapons procurement at the expense of strategic thought.[22] Military strategy, he argued, required different ways of thinking than did normal civilian life. The interaction of opposing forces meant that war was a realm "pervaded by a paradoxical logic of its own, standing against the ordinary linear logic by which we live in other spheres of life." This normal logic was violated by "inducing the coming together and even the reversal of opposites." As a result, paradoxical conduct tended to be rewarded while straightforwardly logical action was confounded, "yielding results ironical if not lethally self-damaging."[23] Those who understood how to manage the large civilian bureaucracies presiding over the armed forces could not, therefore, grasp strategy because it involved a quite different way of thinking. They would look for standardized solutions, failing to understand how much easier this made the enemy's task. Luttwak also acknowledged that even if national leaders somehow acquired this paradoxical turn of mind they might not dare display it lest they alarm their constituents and colleagues. Any deviation from the "commonsensical conventions of the time and place" would risk a "loss of authority."[24] The linear planning model, which Robert McNamara had taken to the Pentagon, was flawed precisely because it could not anticipate everything and so was likely to produce perverse outcomes. This led Luttwak into arguing, in effect, for confusion or at least against attempted coherence, for "only policies that are seemingly contradictory can circumvent the self-defeating effect of the paradoxical logic." Luttwak overdid this point: war did not require a different logic, just a recognition of a different context, one in which it would make perfect sense to follow a different path to one followed in peace.[25]

Luttwak focused attention on the importance of what he identified as the "operational level." This had been neglected, and with it the classical traditions of European war. Jomini, Liddell Hart, and John Boyd had referred to this level as one for grand tactics. Jomini described these as "the maneuvering of an army upon the battle-field, and the different formation of troops for attack." Luttwak believed that the operational level was the critical sphere for generalship and for that reason deplored its absence in contemporary American military thought. It was there that "schemes of warfare such as blitzkrieg or defense in depth evolve or are exploited." Americans had neglected this because of their dependence on an "attrition style of war."[26]

The idea of an operational level of war as a politics-free zone where commanders could demonstrate their mastery of managing large forces over wide areas in a series of complex engagements with the enemy was an inheritance from von Moltke. It was given added salience because of its prominence in Soviet military thought. From the formation of the Soviet Union, its military leadership had been engaged in theoretical debates about the operational level as an intermediate stage between tactics and strategy, and which way they should turn when faced with the choice between decisive annihilation or more defensive attrition. In the build-up to the Second World War, Marshal Mikhail Tukhachevsky's reflections on the impact of motorization and airpower had led him to come out firmly in favor of mass, mechanized forces able to conduct deep operations in a war of annihilation. His opponents were castigated not only for poor strategy but for poor theory, which was much more dangerous. This helped seal the fate of many in Stalin's purges, although it did not spare Tukhachevsky a similar fate. After the war, the initial Soviet focus had been on the impact of thermonuclear weapons, which led to a reduced conventional army, but by the late 1960s the numbers were rising again. Reflecting the view that the best chance of victory was early in a war, before American reserves could get across the Atlantic to Europe, the general staff stressed the importance of being able to mount maneuvers deep in NATO territory with minimal prior mobilization, maximum surprise, and combined forces. This tradition, as reflected in the military doctrines of the Warsaw Pact, was another reason for NATO countries, led by the United States, to get on the same wavelength.[27]

Luttwak encouraged the view that attrition based on firepower and maneuver based on movement were almost polar opposites. Attrition was presented as not so much a regrettable response to a challenging predicament but a deliberate choice reflecting a particular mindset. For Luttwak it involved an "exaggerated dependence on firepower as such to the detriment of maneuver and flexibility." This style, he acknowledged, had the "great attractions of predictability and functional simplicity." All military effort could be geared to attacking sets of targets in a systematic fashion. Under its misleading aura, war would be "governed by a logic analogous to that of microeconomics." The "conduct of warfare at all levels" would be "analogous to the management of a profit-maximizing industrial enterprise." In the end, superior resources should win, even though applied with routine and repetitive tactics and procedures. The greater the input, the greater the output. The costs would lie in absorbing the enemy's reciprocal attrition and the calculation could be upended should the enemy attract an ally to achieve a superior balance of power. Against this dull, methodical, bureaucratic linearity Luttwak promoted imaginative flair and operational paradox. Against attritional science he sought a maneuverist art.[28] Relational-maneuver warfare sought to avoid enemy strength in order to attack enemy weakness. It was, Luttwak suggested, an almost compulsory approach for the resource-weak side.

In posing the issue in these terms, Boyd, Luttwak, and their contemporaries were urging a return to the military classics of the modern era, but with a postmodern twist resulting from their heightened sensitivity to cognitive processes. On the critical issues of military strategy, the classics offered less clarity than was often supposed, and so the net result was often to update for a new audience the muddle of earlier times. The starting point was inevitably Clausewitz. But as was well known, *On War* was not a finished work and Clausewitz was in the process of revising his ideas at the time of his death. The resultant ambiguity had affected all those who had taken this work as their starting point, and further distortions had arisen in the responses of key figures such as Delbrück and then Liddell Hart to what they believed Clausewitz had said. Complications of language and translation easily added to the confusion, which meant that the return to the classics led to some intense debates about what they really meant—as if that could help sort out the conceptual confusion that was developing around the attempted application of their ideas to contemporary problems. While these debates were gathering steam, an important new English translation of Clausewitz by Peter Paret and Michael Howard was published and an English edition of Delbrück became available for the first time.[29]

Behind all of this there was one large issue, which was whether there was an alternative to large-scale battle as a route to victory. There was a further and more difficult issue about the meaning (and possibility) of victory itself. Limited war had been prominent in the eighteenth century and there were examples of it from the nineteenth. If a war was to end without one state subjugating another, there was going to have to be some sort of negotiation. The bargain struck could be assumed to have some relationship to the balance of power at the conclusion of hostilities. Clausewitz had recognized this possibility, but he had not explored it fully. His main focus was the use of battle to eliminate the enemy army as a fighting force and thus render the enemy state helpless.

This became known as the strategy of annihilation, a term used by von Moltke and then compared by Delbrück with a strategy of exhaustion. Delbrück saw exhaustion as persuading the enemy to abandon the fight even though its army had not been annihilated. Exhaustion suggested that the enemy had been worn down to the point that it could not face further war. This was most likely to occur if its survival was not at issue and the stakes were limited and susceptible to compromise. Confusion then entered with regard to method, because there was no reason why exhaustion could not result from a series of inconclusive battles. Delbrück also used the term "bipolar strategy" to capture the idea of a commander deciding from moment to moment whether to achieve a goal by battle or maneuver.

The choice between annihilation and exhaustion could not just be a matter of strategic preference but had to reflect the material situation. If battle was unavoidable, there must be sufficient strength to prevail but also, even after a decisive battle, enough residual capability to go on and occupy enemy territory. It might be possible to gain an initial advantage through maneuver, but this might not be sufficient if despite the loss of one army the enemy could field another. Unless one was confident of possessing ultimate military superiority, a push for annihilation was unwise. If force had to be conserved for a long haul, set-piece battles were best avoided other than in the most favorable circumstances. For this reason an association developed between exhaustion and maneuver, as ways of avoiding direct battle.[30]

It was Liddell Hart who took the idea of maneuver and developed it to a new stage by contrasting it much more sharply with major battle. To further add to the confusion, frontal assaults had now become associated with attrition since the Great War, although not as Delbrück understood the term (to the extent that was the term he had in mind). Battle of this scale and intensity went well beyond anything envisaged by Clausewitz, however much he might have recognized the underlying strategic principles in play. Liddell Hart kept open the possibility of defeating an opponent by leaving them confused and disoriented, caught by surprise rather than buckling under heavy casualties. What was less clear was whether something that could work well when one army caught another off guard could work with whole states. Even after stunning setbacks in the field, some states might be able to play for time to bring in reserves or move to civil resistance. There was therefore one issue about whether it was possible to defeat opponents in the field by means other than frontal assault, and another about how military victories could be translated into substantial political gains.

Which brings us back to Clausewitz, because these two issues—which go to the heart of his unfulfilled interest in deviations from the strategy of annihilation—were captured but not resolved in one of his enduring but most unsatisfactory concepts: the center of gravity or *Schwerpunkt*. This was a concept which came to be adopted by Western military establishments, although in ways that aggravated its inherent problems. So familiar did the concept become that it started to be referred to by its acronym COG. Clausewitz's focus was on the enemy army, but as the center of gravity was identified as the source of the opponent's power and strength, it could also refer to an alliance or national will.

By the late 1980s, these various strands had come together to form a distinct doctrinal form embedded in Western military establishment. There should be a military focus on the operational level of warfare. Here forces should be directed against the opponent's center of gravity. This would be that point or set of points where the application of military force would be most likely to result in the enemy's surrender. The new thinking encouraged the belief that the most important centers of gravity would be those that led to the enemy's brain, using shock and disorder to produce mental dislocation and therefore paralysis rather than blasting away at the enemy's physical strength.

This distinction between the two forms of warfare was sharpened, almost to the point of caricature. The maneuverists presented attritionists in an unflattering light, seeing the "enemy as targets to be engaged and destroyed systematically. Thus the focus is on efficiency, leading to a methodical almost scientific approach to war." Everything depended on the efficiency with which firepower was employed, encouraging centralized control rather than local initiative. Progress would be defined in quantitative terms, with battle damage assessments, "body counts," and terrain captured. Relying on inflicting punishing attrition meant being prepared to accept it in return. Victory would not "depend so much on military competence as on sheer superiority of numbers in men and equipment." The implication was that lives were being sacrificed because of a lack of imagination and skill. Here the maneuverist, relying on intelligence, scored. The maneuverist would

> circumvent a problem and attack it from a position of advantage rather than meet it straight on. The goal is the application of strength against selected enemy weakness. By definition, maneuver relies on speed and surprise, for without either we cannot concentrate strength against enemy weakness.

The objective was "not so much to destroy physically as it [was] to shatter the enemy's cohesion, organization, command and psychological balance."[31] To do this required superior skill and judgment. Who would not want to be associated with such a strategy?

The key elements of this approach were all problematic, however. The idea of distinct levels of strategy was rooted in established hierarchies. The underlying principle was that at each level the objectives would be passed down from the higher. At the level of grand strategy, a conflict was anticipated, alliances forged, economies geared, people braced, resources allocated, and military roles defined. At the level of strategy, the political objectives were turned into military goals; priorities and specific objectives were agreed upon and allocations of men and equipment made accordingly. At the level of grand tactics or operations, judgments were made as to the most appropriate form of warfare to achieve the goals of that particular campaign in the light of the prevailing conditions. At the level of tactics, military units attempted to push forward the goals of the campaign in the specific circumstances in which they found themselves.

These levels reflected hierarchical command structures geared to regular warfare between great powers as much as sharp distinctions in contemporary practice. What was striking, given the contemporary fascination with systems theory and information flows, was that these were generally considered to challenge such structures. Under the influence of similar ideas, business practice was moving to flatter hierarchies. Too many chains in the command structure were likely to lead to unresponsive organizations. Information up the chain about what was going on at ground level would be slow and subject to distortion, while initiative could be dampened if new orders always had to come down the chain.

This assumption continued to be reflected in discussions of tactical issues as short term, immediate, and not necessarily of lasting importance; while strategic issues were the big ones, long term and fateful, potentially existential in their implications. Yet in limited wars, single engagements could be decisive and so local tactical factors would become matters of grand strategy and subject to the highest political control. During the 1990s, as local factors became more important, the Americans began to talk of a "strategic corporal," able to "make well-reasoned and *independent* decisions under extreme stress—decisions that will likely be subject to the harsh scrutiny of both the media and the court of public opinion." The strategic corporal would be aware that his actions would "potentially influence not only the immediate tactical situation, but the operational and strategic levels as well," and thus the "outcome of the larger operation."[32]

There was also an operational dimension at work at the strategic and tactical levels. British historian Michael Howard identified three other dimensions of strategy in addition to the operational. These were the logistical, social, and technological. He warned of the danger of a preoccupation with operations in isolation from the logistical effort which made them possible, the social context in which they were being conducted, and the forms of technology which they exploited.[33] The attraction of the focus on an operational level where all the critical decisions on the employment of forces took place was that they would be taken away from the civilian-military interface. That was at the notionally more important strategic level. In practice, limiting the focus to a distinct operational level had the effect of keeping actual combat under professional military purview and away from interfering civilian amateurs. In this it reflected one of the military's explanations for failure in the Vietnam War: civilian "micromanagement."

The second set of problems occurred with the notion of the center of gravity. Even as the concept was adopted there was little agreement about what commanders should be looking for and the methodology required to find it. It all might have been simpler if they had adopted Jomini's concept of the decisive point, against which the greatest possible force should be directed. This at least would have avoided the burdens of inappropriate metaphor.[34]

The army, for example, with access to a large force of its own, took the view that this was not about pitting "strength against strength" as originally supposed but more about an indirect approach, applying "combat power against a series of decisive points that avoided enemy strengths."[35] The Marine Corps, with a smaller capability, initially also took the view that it was best to attack not the enemy's strengths but its critical vulnerabilities. The Corps even observed dangers in speaking of a center of gravity, because Clausewitz was about "daring all to win all" in a climactic test of strength.[36] Critical vulnerabilities appeared to be no easier to identify than centers of gravity. The recommendation was to exploit "any and all vulnerabilities" until uncovering a decisive opportunity. This somewhat random process led Joe Strange of the Marine Corps War College to focus on critical capabilities and requirements leading to a process opening with the exploitation of critical vulnerabilities, which would have the cumulative effect of undermining the enemy's center of gravity.[37]

One influential version was developed by John Warden for the air force. He accepted Clausewitz's basic proposition but sought to relate it to air power. The enemy's center of gravity was "that point where the enemy is most vulnerable and where an attack will have the best chance of being decisive." The evidence of decisiveness would be that the enemy leadership could then be convinced "to do what one wants to do." Warden presented the enemy (any enemy) as a system made up of a several interrelated parts held together by a number of nodes and links, some of which were critical. The centers of gravity could be found in each of the five component parts (or rings)—leadership, organic essentials, infrastructure, population, and fielded forces—that described any strategic entity. The point of this was that air power was uniquely qualified to strike at these points simultaneously through parallel, as opposed to sequential or serial, attacks in order to overwhelm and thereby paralyze an opponent. The effect, he argued, would be decisive.[38] The presumption was that the centers were founded on physical structures and their loss would lead the enemy to accept that the game was up. Warden thus sought to demonstrate how employing the sort of firepower that might be associated with attrition could, with careful analysis of targets, be used to achieve the sort of disorientation sought by the maneuverists.

There was, therefore, no consensus on what these concepts meant. After two decades of various formulations it was observed that "the lack of doctrinal guidance on developing and employing COGs wastes planners' time and provides few tangible benefits." It was reported that planning teams could "take hours—if not days—arguing over what is and is not the enemy's COG," with the outcome often decided by the strongest personality rather than the best analysis.[39] This was, however, written in the belief that with a better methodology the task would be manageable and the results worthwhile. The real problem was that concept of a center of gravity had been expanded to the point of meaninglessness. It could refer to a target or a number of targets. The center might be identified because it constituted a source of enemy strength and/or a critical vulnerability. It could be found in the physical, psychological, or political spheres. If all went well once the center was attacked, the result would be decisive or else have consequences with potentially decisive effects, though this might depend on being combined with other significant events. It had become totally detached from the original metaphor, yet the terminology encouraged the expectation that there could be a very specific set of operational objectives that would produce the desired political effect if attacked properly. This reflected Clausewitz's original notion that the key to victory lay in the defeat of the enemy's military system, but if the sources of the enemy's political resilience lay somewhere else, attacks on this supposed center would be bound to disappoint. If it was not a physical location or set of capabilities, but instead a political ideology or an alliance, it would be harder to work out what was supposed to be targeted.

The third set of problems was that military history gave little support to the dichotomous view of attrition and maneuver, or that maneuver could serve as an overall doctrine rather than an occasional opportunity. Carter Malkasian complained that "no commander or theorist who has purposefully implemented attrition or developed the concept was ever cited by advocates of maneuver warfare."[40] Though attrition was presented as a bloody slogging match with troops being sacrificed in mindless exchanges of firepower, Malkasian demonstrated that it could include "in-depth withdrawals, limited ground offensive, frontal assaults, patrolling, careful defensive, scorched-earth tactics, guerrilla warfare, air strikes, artillery firepower, or raids." There had been many examples of successful attritional campaigns, of which Russia's defense against Napoleon in 1812 was "perhaps the grandest."[41] The key characteristic of attrition was that it was about wearing down the enemy, which meant the process was likely to be protracted, gradual, and piecemeal. While it could end with a decisive battle, it could also lead to a negotiation when both sides had decided that they had had enough. This meant that it suited coercive strategies with moderate aims. The danger was that attrition could turn into a contest of endurance, and it was hard to know in advance when the enemy would be worn down.

Hew Strachan trenchantly warned of the danger of the operational level as "a politics-free zone" speaking in a "self-regarding vocabulary about manoeuvre, and increasingly 'manoeuverism,' that is almost metaphysical and whose inwardness makes sense only to those initiated in its meanings."[42] He traced the preoccupation with the operational level back to General Erich Ludendorff. Prior to the First World War, the German army rigidly focused on the problems with its own military domain, excluding civilians from its deliberations and appearing largely indifferent to the political consequences of its actions, on the assumption that whatever was desired could be obtained politically following a successful war of annihilation. Ludendorff preferred to blame his country's defeat in 1918 on a civilian "stab-in-the-back," not his own battlefield failures. He became a proponent of total war by which the complete resources of society must be devoted to victory. Rather than war serving politics, politics should serve war. His view of strategy itself was therefore a continuation of von Moltke's and reflected the sharp operational focus he had adopted during the past war. He would not accept that this perspective had let his country down. This view accounted for the lack of innovative strategic thought in interwar Germany. The initial success of the blitzkrieg in Western Europe in 1940 did not reflect a pre-war doctrine but the old doctrines of envelopment that had shaped the Schlieffen Plan. This time it succeeded through a combination of inspired improvisation and mistakes by the French High Command, which employed neither its strategic army reserve nor tactical air power to deal with the German threat before it gathered momentum.

The successes of 1940 did convince Hitler that blitzkrieg was the way to win wars, so he adopted it as the basis for the attack on the Soviet Union. Soviet mistakes again helped with early progress, but the offensive soon faltered and the economic demands of the campaign were inadequately addressed. While celebrating blitzkrieg as a doctrine, its proponents paid inadequate attention to this experience in the East—not only its failure but the objectives of conquest, plunder, and racial domination that shaped its course.[43] In the end, the experience of the Second World War followed that of the First. The Germans found themselves fighting an attritional campaign after attempting to force a result with a winning maneuver. The blitzkrieg model was therefore flawed, taking little account of the historiography of the Second World War.

Moreover, in terms of NATO's central front at the start of the 1980s, the possibilities of maneuver were oversold. The language of rapid and unexpected moves was appealing but also vague and, when applied to large and cumbersome modern armies, hard to envisage in practice. It reflected an essentially romantic and nostalgic view of strategy, unhampered by the normal constraints of politics and economics, over-impressed by both Soviet doctrine and its supposed vulnerability to maneuver warfare, as well as over-optimistic about the Western ability to implement it successfully.[44] The maneuver strategies advocated were often impractical. They would be high-risk options in European conditions, with its urban sprawl and complex road and train networks, and place enormous strain on good intelligence and effective command and control. A faulty maneuver could lead to absolute disaster and leave the rear exposed. Furthermore, a new offensive doctrine could unsettle American allies in Europe, notably the Federal Republic of Germany, which was wary of association with anything that could be considered an aggressive strategy or a defensive strategy that involved turning its territory into a battleground. The failure to consider the geopolitical context illustrated the problem with considering operational art in isolation from a broader strategy in which holding together an alliance might be more important than developing clever moves for a hypothetical war.

Although an advocate for a maneuverist approach, Luttwak provided the theoretical reasons for caution. He had taken from Liddell Hart the indirect approach, the need to follow the line of least expectation. The obvious route, the most direct with the most favorable terrain, would be the one for which the enemy was best prepared. Taking the most complicated and uncomfortable route would therefore be the best way to catch an enemy out. Unfortunately, once a preference for an indirect approach was known, enemies would be alert for the unexpected, which meant that either an even more unlikely and difficult route had to be found, or perhaps there could be a double bluff, with the original, expected route being adopted as the last place the enemy would look. The test as to which way to go was one of surprise. Without surprise the extra effort required by an awkward route would be pointless and probably dangerous. Surprise made possible "the suspension, if only brief, if only partial, of the entire predicament of strategy, even as the struggle continues."[45] The advantage of surprise was that, for a moment, the enemy would be unable to react and so would be vulnerable. His decision-making cycle would be disrupted.

There were practical reasons why this logic did not lead to a totally confusing sequence of paradoxes. Movement might be restricted such that only necessary fuel and supplies could be carried and barely any space was available for weapons and ammunition. Unless the original engagement was extraordinarily successful there would be no capacity to continue a fight for any length of time. In addition, surprise depended on secrecy and deception. There was no point in embarking on elaborate maneuvers only to be spotted en route and then caught in an ambush. Therefore, an indirect strategy involved "self-weakening measures," and thus costs and risks. To these could be added friction, so sharply identified by Clausewitz. This was the cumulative impact of all the grit that interfered with the smooth implementation of the basic plan: broken down vehicles, misunderstood orders, misdirected supplies, unseasonal weather, and impassable terrain. One aim of strategy would be to aggravate the enemy's propensity to friction by forcing them to adopt an indirect strategy, making sure the direct routes were well protected, and then interdicting supply lines.

Luttwak noted a further paradox, drawn from Clausewitz: the greater the success of the original strategy the greater the risk of friction as an army moved further away from home base. Supply lines became attenuated as the enemy fell back closer to its own home bases where it could replenish and bring forward fresh reserves as the advancing force moved into unfamiliar territory. Victorious armies were apt to overreach themselves, pushing their luck. If they went beyond the "culminating point," the most advantageous position vis-à-vis the enemy, the balance of advantage would start to shift. An enemy in disarray would be unable to regroup, so the attacker would be well advised to press home the advantage. This raised the problem of the indecisive battle. Without full surrender terms, the enemy would look for ways to regroup and return to the fight, even as an insurgency if the country was occupied. Thus the ultimate test of strategy was not whether surprise was achieved. In the end this was a tactical matter. The test was whether the desired political outcome was reached. The basic point was that sticking with any formula allowed the enemy a chance to adjust and respond.

Lastly, there was behind all of this a presumption of cause and effect, that combinations of "ambiguity, deception, novelty, mobility, and actual or threatened violence" would generate sufficient surprise and shock to cause enemy confusion and disorder. The essence of moral conflict, Boyd insisted, was to

> create, exploit, and magnify *menace* (impression of danger to one's well-being and survival), *uncertainty* (impressions, or atmosphere, generated by events that appear erratic, contradictory, unfamiliar, chaotic, etc.), and *mistrust* (atmosphere of doubt and doubt and suspicion that loosens human bonds among members of an organic whole or between organic wholes).

The evidence that this would be working would be "surface *fear*, *anxiety*, and *alienation* in order to generate many non-cooperative centers of gravity."[46]

While comparative morale and coherence undoubtedly made a difference, and confused commanders could watch helplessly as their armies fell apart, this story was told in excessively stark terms of headquarters tipping over in collective nervous breakdowns, organized troops turning into a disorderly rabble, and apparently disciplined and intelligent individuals suddenly reduced to helpless fools thrashing around in the dark. Boyd saw "courage, confidence, and esprit" as constituting a form of "moral strength" that could counter such negative effects. If the enemy did indeed enjoy such moral strength, the imaginative physical effects designed to cause a moral breakdown would fail. Alternatively, individuals and groups would vary in their responses, with some being able to absorb the implications of events and adapt quickly. Their responses might be suboptimal, but sufficient to regroup and cope with the new situation.

One famous example of a commander thrown into mental confusion by a shock military move (although one about which he had been warned) was Stalin in June 1941 as the German offensive began and made rapid gains. For a few days the Soviet people heard nothing from Stalin as he struggled to make sense of the situation. While he was doing so, individuals at the front responded as best they could, some retreating and some throwing themselves into the fight with great bravery. Eventually Stalin rallied himself, broadcast a stirring message to his people, and took command of the fight. The size of his country and his population meant that a quick victory for the Germans was essential, and Hitler was sufficiently contemptuous of the Slav mentality to believe that a hard push by his forces would see the enemy crumble. When the moral collapse failed to materialize to the degree necessary, Hitler's forces were stuck and eventually pushed back. The shock effect wore off as the Soviet leadership steadied itself.

It was one thing to argue that because minds controlled bodies disrupting the workings of minds was preferable to eliminating their bodies, but quite another to assume that just as physical blows could shatter bodies, so mental blows could shatter minds. It was one thing to recognize the importance of the cognitive domain, but quite another to assume that it was susceptible to straightforward manipulation. Human minds could be capable of remarkable feats of denial, resistance, recovery, and adaption, even under extreme stress.

CHAPTER 16 | The Revolution in Military Affairs

{T}he revolution in military affairs may bring a kind of tactical clarity
to the battlefield, but at the price of strategic obscurity.

—Eliot Cohen

THIS "OPERATIONAL" APPROACH to war was never tested in the circumstances for which it was designed. At the end of the 1980s, Soviet communism imploded and the Warsaw Pact soon evaporated, taking with it the
possibility of another great power war in the middle of Europe. The American
military soon came to be preoccupied with a quite different set of problems.
Because circumstances had changed so much this might have provided good
reason to challenge the operational approach, but instead it became even
more entrenched, now spoken of as a revolution in military affairs.

There was no need to worry about an extremely large and capable enemy.
The efforts the Americans had put into new technologies had created a quality gap with all conceivable opponents, while the greater stress on operational
doctrine made it possible to take advantage of superior intelligence and communications to work around opponents. Almost immediately, there was a
demonstration of the new capabilities. Iraq occupied its neighbor Kuwait
in August 1990; early the next year, a coalition led by the United States
liberated Kuwait. Up to this point the impact of improvements in sensors,
smart weapons, and systems integration were untested hypotheses. Skeptics

(including Luttwak) warned of how in a war with Iraq the most conceptually brilliant systems could be undermined by their own complexity and traditional forms of military incompetence.[1] Yet in Operation Desert Storm the equipment worked well: cruise missiles fired from a distance of some one thousand kilometers navigated their way through the streets of Baghdad, entered their target by the front door, and then exploded.

This very one-sided war displayed the potential of modern military systems in a most flattering light. The Iraqis had boasted of the size of their army, but much of its bulk was made up of poorly armed and trained conscripts facing professional, well-equipped forces with vastly superior firepower. It was as if they had kindly arranged their army to show off their opponent's forces to best advantage. A battle plan unfolded that followed the essential principles of Western military practice against a totally outclassed and outgunned enemy who had conceded command of the air. A tentative frontal assault saw the Iraqis crumble, yet General Norman Schwarzkopf went ahead with a complex, enveloping maneuver to catch them as they retreated, but did not quite cut them off quickly enough. The Americans still announced a ceasefire, deliberately eschewing a war of annihilation. This reflected a determination to keep the war limited and not allow success in reaching the declared goal—liberation of Kuwait—to lead to overextension by attempting to occupy all of Iraq. This made good diplomatic and military sense, yet the consequence illustrated the arguments favoring decisive victories. Saddam Hussein was able to survive and the outcome of the war was declared at best incomplete.[2]

The idea that this campaign might set a pattern for the future, to the point of representing a revolution in military affairs, can be traced back to the Pentagon's Office of Net Assessment (ONA), led by Andrew Marshall, a redoubtable veteran of RAND. He was aware that during its last years there had been talk in the Soviet Union of a "military technical revolution" that might bring conventional forces up to new levels of effectiveness. Marshall became convinced that the new systems were not mere improvements but could change the character of war. After the 1991 Gulf War, he asked one of his analysts, Army Lieutenant Colonel Andrew F. Krepinevich, who had been working on what had become the non-issue of the military balance between NATO and the Warsaw Pact, to examine the combined impact of precision weapons and the new information and communication technologies.[3]

By the summer of 1993, Marshall was considering two plausible forms of change in warfare. One possibility was that the long-range precision strike would become "the dominant operational approach." The other was the emergence of "what might be called information warfare."[4] At this point he began to encourage the use of the term "revolution in military affairs" (RMA) instead of "military-technical revolution" to stress the importance of operational and organizational changes as well as technological ones.[5] Krepinevich described the RMA in 1994 as

> what occurs when the application of new technologies into a significant number of military systems combines with innovative operational concepts and organizational adaptation in a way that fundamentally alters the character and conduct of conflict . . . by producing a dramatic increase—often an order of magnitude or greater—in the combat potential and military effectiveness of armed forces.[6]

Although the origins of the RMA lay in doctrine, the driver appeared technological, a consequence of the interaction between systems that collected, processed, and communicated information with those that applied military force. A so-called system of systems would make this interaction smooth and continuous.[7] This concept was particularly appropriate in a maritime context. At sea, as in the air, it was possible to contemplate a battlespace empty of all but combatants. Even going back to the Second World War, air and sea warfare offered patterns susceptible to systematic analysis, which meant that the impact of technical innovations could be discerned.

By contrast, land warfare had always been more complex and fluid, subject to a greater range of influences. The promise of the RMA was to transform land warfare. The ability to strike with precision over great distances meant that time and space could decline as serious constraints. Enemy units would be engaged from without. Armies could stay agile and maneuverable, as they would not have to move with their own firepower, except for that required for self-defense. Instead, they could call in what was required from outside. Reliance on non-organic firepower would reduce dependence upon large, cumbersome, self-contained divisions, and the associated potential for high casualties.[8] While enemy commanders were still attempting to mobilize their resources and develop their plans, they would be rudely interrupted by lethal blows inflicted by forces for whom time and space were no longer serious constraints. The move away from the crude elimination of enemy forces could be completed by following the Boyd line of acting more quickly and moving more deftly, thus putting enemy commanders in a position where resistance would be futile. Enthusiasts hovered on the edge of pronouncing the "fog of war" lifted and the problem of friction answered.[9] At the very least, warfare could move away from high-intensity combat to something more contained and discriminate, geared to disabling an enemy's military establishment with the minimum force necessary. No more resources should be expended, assets ruined, or blood shed than absolutely necessary to achieve specified political goals.

All of this created the prospect of relatively civilized warfare, unsullied by either the destructiveness of nuclear war or the murky, subversive character of Vietnam-type engagements. It would be professional war conducted by professional armies, a vision, in Bacevich's pointed words, "of the Persian Gulf War replayed over and over again."[10] The pure milk of the doctrine is found in a publication of the National Defense University of 1996 which introduced the notion of "shock and awe." The basic message was that all efforts should be focused on overwhelming the enemy physically and mentally as quickly as possible before there was a chance to react. "Shock and awe" would mean that the enemy's perceptions and grasp of events would be overloaded, leaving him paralyzed. The ultimate example of this effect were the nuclear strikes of Hiroshima and Nagasaki, which the authors refused to rule out as a theoretical possibility, though they were more intrigued by the possibility of disinformation, misinformation, and deception.[11]

The influence of such ideas was evident in the 1997 paper "Joint Vision 2010." It defined information superiority largely in war-fighting terms as "the capability to collect, process, and disseminate an uninterrupted flow of information while exploiting or denying an adversary's ability to do the same."[12] By means of "excellent sensors, fast and powerful networks, display technology, and sophisticated modeling and simulation capabilities," information superiority could be achieved. The force would have "a dramatically better awareness or understanding of the battlespace rather than simply more raw data." This could make up for deficiencies in numbers, technology, or position, and it could also speed up command processes. Forces could be organized "from the bottom up—or to self-synchronize—to meet the commander's intent," leading in turn to "the rapid foreclosure of enemy courses of action and the shock of closely coupled events." There would be no time for the enemy to follow Boyd's now-famous OODA loop. Arthur Cebrowski and John Garstka argued that a form of "network-centered warfare" could make battles more efficient in the same way that the application of information technology by businesses was making economies more efficient.[13] In discussing the move from platform-centered to network-centered warfare, the Pentagon largely followed this formulation (Garstka was one of the authors) and recognized that, following the physical and information domains, there was a cognitive domain. Here was found

the mind of the warfighter and the warfighter's supporting populace. Many battles and wars are won or lost in the cognitive domain. The intangibles of leadership, morale, unit cohesion, level of training and experience, situational awareness, and public opinion are elements of this domain. This is the domain where commander's intent, doctrine, tactics, techniques, and procedures reside.[14]

This form of warfare suited the United States because it played to U.S. strengths: it could be capital rather than labor intensive; it reflected a preference for outsmarting opponents; it avoided excessive casualties both received and inflicted; and it conveyed an aura of almost effortless superiority. Those ideas were deeply comforting, and not entirely wrong. Information and communication technologies were bound to make a difference in military practice, although the RMA agenda understated the extent to which American predominance was dependent on not only the sophistication of its technology but also the sheer amount of firepower—particularly air-delivered—at its disposal. Furthermore, while the United States' evident military superiority in a particular type of war was likely to encourage others to fight in different ways, that military capacity would also constrain opponents' ambitions. As a regular conventional war against the United States appeared to be an increasingly foolish proposition, especially after its convincing performance in the 1991 Gulf War, one form of potential challenge to American predominance was removed, just as the prospect of mutual assured destruction had earlier removed nuclear war as a serious policy option.

Nonetheless, the presentation of the RMA was shaped by political preferences about the sort of war the Americans would like to fight. It offered a neat fit between a desire to reduce the risks of high casualties or Vietnam-style campaigns and a Western ethical tradition that stressed discrimination and proportionality in warfare. It assumed professional conventional forces, as high-quality weaponry reduced the relative importance of numbers and put a premium on extremely competent troops. Intolerance of casualties and collateral damage meant targeting military assets rather than innocent civilians. It also precluded resort to weapons of mass destruction. The military would be kept separate from the civil, combatants from noncombatants, fire from society, and organized violence from everyday life. Opponents would be defeated by means of confusion and disorientation rather than slaughter because they could never get out of their OODA loop. If this trend could be pushed far enough, it was possible at some point to envisage a war without tears, conducted over long distances with great precision and as few people as possible—preferably none at all—at risk. The objective was to reduce the role in war-fighting of anything recognizably approaching "battle." The ideal would be one-sided and highly focused engagements geared to causing cognitive confusion. Far from representing a real revolution, the RMA harked back to the earlier, idealized prototype of a decisive military victory settling the fate of nations—indeed of whole civilizations—except that now the accomplishment could be virtually painless for the greatest military power the world had ever seen.

There was an unreal quality to this view of future warfare. It was for political entities that were not fearful, desperate, vengeful, or angry; that could maintain a sense of proportion over the interests at stake and the humanity of the opponent. It was a view that betrayed a detached attitude to the wellsprings of conflict and violence, the outlook of a concerned observer rather than a committed participant. It ignored the physicality of war and war's tendencies to violence and destruction. It would hardly be a revolution in military affairs if those who embraced it only took on conflicts which promised certain and easy victories. The 1991 Gulf War vindicated this vision, but that was helped by Saddam Hussein's ignorance of the real military balance. In this respect, the vindication carried its own refutation. Future opponents were bound to take more care when inviting battle with the United States given the proven vulnerability of second-rate conventional forces to attacks by first-rate powers. After 1991 it was unclear who would fight such a war. The American military literature referred to "peer competitors" with comparable military endowments to those of the United States, but it was unclear exactly who these might be. In addition, for a war to be fought along these lines, the belligerents must not only have comparable military capabilities but also inhabit the same moral and political universe. The model was geared to American strengths and for that very reason was unlikely to be followed by opponents who would seek to exploit the presumed American weaknesses of impatience and casualty intolerance. Enemies would be inclined to cause hurt in an effort to encourage a sense of disproportion in the population and unhinge multilateral coalitions.

Precision warfare made it possible to limit but also to maximize damage. Just as high accuracy made it possible to avoid nuclear power plants, hospitals, and apartment blocks, it also made it possible to score direct hits. Even in the American model there were always dual-use facilities that served both military and civilian purposes—for example, energy and transportation. Targeting them as part of a military purpose still led to the disruption of civilian life. In other respects the new technologies encouraged a progressive overlap between the civilian and military spheres. High-quality surveillance, intelligence, communications, and navigation became widely available as consumer gadgets, which could be exploited by crude, small organizations with limited budgets. Lastly, nuclear weapons and long-range missiles (whose arrival had also been described at the time as a "revolution in military affairs") had expanded the means of destruction and extended the range of its potential application. Attempts to mitigate their effects—for example, through improving anti-missile defenses—had been unimpressive. The capability to destroy hundreds of thousands of human beings in a nuclear flash had not disappeared.

Asymmetric Wars

When a country was in desperate straits and facing defeat in conventional war, attacking the enemy's society might appear to be the only option left. That is why the history of the twentieth-century war had been so discouraging to those who believed that military power could be contained in its effects. There were a series of measures that the weak could adopt against the strong: concentrating on imposing pain rather than winning battles, gaining time rather than moving to closure, targeting the enemy's domestic political base as much as his forward military capabilities, and relying on an unwillingness to accept extreme pain and a weaker stake in the resolution of the conflict. In short, whereas stronger military powers had a natural preference for decisive battlefield victories, the weaker were more ready to draw the civilian sphere into the conflict while avoiding open battle.

The optimal strategies for those unable to match America's conventional military capabilities (almost everyone) would be to attempt to turn the conflict into what came to be described as an "asymmetric war." This concept had been around since the 1970s, as a reflection of the Vietnam experience.[15] Its resurrection began in the mid-1990s, when it began to refer to any engagement between dissimilar forces. All conflicts were between forces that varied in some respects, in geography or alliance as well as in force structure and doctrine. Part of strategy would always be identifying aspects of those differences that generated special opportunities and vulnerabilities. Even when the starting points were relatively symmetrical, the aim would be to identify and describe a critical asymmetry as the vital advantage to secure a victory. The only reason symmetry had worked in the nuclear sphere as mutual assured destruction was because it had resulted in a degree of stability. In the conventional sphere, symmetrical forces were potentially a recipe for mutual exhaustion.

As with so many of these concepts, inconsistent and expansive definitions of asymmetry began to drain it of meaning. The 1999 Joint Strategy Review defined asymmetric approaches as those that attempted "to circumvent or undermine US strengths while exploiting US weaknesses using methods that differ significantly from the United States' expected method of operations." These could be applied "at all levels of warfare—strategic, operational, land tactical—and across the spectrum of military operations." Put this way, the approach became synonymous with any sound strategy for fighting the United States and lost any specificity.[16] The real interest in asymmetrical warfare was in situations where the two sides would be seeking to fight completely different sorts of war, particularly when Americans persevered with regular warfare while opponents either escalated to weapons of mass destruction or adopted forms of irregular war.

The greatest dangers were associated with an enemy that had weapons of mass destruction, but the most likely scenario was being drawn into irregular war. Since Vietnam, the U.S. military had taken the view that rather than make better preparations for irregular war it was best to stay clear of potential quagmires. This tendency had been reinforced by the most celebrated account of Vietnam to emerge out of the army. Harry Summers, an instructor at the Army War College, invoked Clausewitz in explaining how the American focus on counterinsurgency distracted them from the essentially conventional nature of the war. Summers made his point by working backwards from the final victory in 1975 of the North Vietnamese army over the South. This possibility was always inherent in the North's strategy, but that did not mean that the prior insurgency in the South had somehow been irrelevant. For one critic, who had been closely involved in the counterinsurgency during the 1960s, the problem was that the U.S. army paid insufficient attention to the demands of guerrilla warfare and not that they had neglected the enemy's "main force."[17]

The persistent resistance to Vietnam-type engagements was reflected in a distinction between war defined in terms of "large-scale combat operations," to which U.S. forces were geared, and "operations other than war," which included shows of force, operations for purposes of peace enforcement and peacekeeping, and counterterrorism and counterinsurgency, which had a much lower priority.[18] Wariness of irregular wars meant reluctance to develop doctrine and training to accommodate them. It was assumed that forces optimized for large-scale conventional war would be able to accomplish other, supposedly less demanding tasks if absolutely necessary. The relatively small-scale contingencies that became common in the 1990s were in effect dismissed as secondary and residual, an inappropriate use of armed forces, apt to tie them down and catch them in vicious crossfire while conducting marginal political business that did not even touch on the nation's most vital interests.[19]

On September 11, 2001, the United States suffered a unique and unexpected attack, which took the notion of asymmetry to the extreme. A low-budget plan hatched by a small band of Islamist radicals camped in one of the poorest parts of the world was directed against the icons of American economic, military, and political strength. Two planes crashed into the World Trade Center in New York, one into the Pentagon in Washington, and another would have hit the White House or Capitol Hill had it not been for passenger action which forced the plane to crash. It did not take long to identify the group responsible—al-Qaeda, an extreme Islamist group based in Afghanistan and protected by its ideological soul-mates in the Taliban government.

The government's response was to declare a "war on terror" and launch a military campaign designed to overthrow the Taliban and break up al-Qaeda. Although the provocation was on al-Qaeda's terms, the response was on America's. The Taliban was defeated in a quasi-regular war because the Americans were able to come in on the side of the Afghan opposition (the Northern Alliance), who provided the infantry while the United States supplied communications, airpower, and the occasional bribe to help encourage the factions on the enemy side to defect. On this basis, President George W. Bush concluded that the campaign had shown that "an innovative doctrine and high-tech weaponry can shape and then dominate an unconventional conflict." It was a triumph of information-age warfare, with commanders "gaining a real-time picture of the entire battlefield" and then being able to "get targeting information from sensor to shooter almost instantly." There were romantic images of U.S. Special Forces riding on horseback calling in air strikes. Bush claimed that the conflict had "taught us more about the future of our military than a decade of blue ribbon panels and think-tank symposiums,"[20] suggesting that this approach had a wider application beyond the special conditions of Afghanistan in late 2001. The next stage reflected this perception. Instead of devising a plan to deal with radical Islamist movements, the United States embarked on a campaign to topple the regime of Saddam Hussein in Iraq, because Saddam was suspected of possessing weapons of mass destruction and was thus a potential source for any terrorist group that wished to inflict even more terrible damage upon the United States. Again the United States was able to demonstrate convincing superiority in conventional military capabilities as the Iraqi regime was overthrown in short order.

The Afghan and Iraqi campaigns were both apparently decisive; hostile regimes were toppled quickly after their forces were overwhelmed. In neither case, however, did this settle the matter. Secretary of Defense Donald

Rumsfeld had been seeking to make a point about how a war could be fought and won with far fewer forces than would hitherto have been thought prudent. This point was made, although against an enemy barely able to resist.[21] The lack of numbers soon appeared imprudent as U.S. forces struggled to cope with an insurgency. The transition from old to new regime was further complicated by the fact that the political claim that justified the invasion— that Iraq was illicitly developing weapons of mass destruction—was shown to be in error. This encouraged the development of a new rationale based on helping Iraq make the transition to democracy, a task made even harder by the U.S.-led coalition's lack of troops to manage what soon became a deteriorating security situation. Out of the minority Sunni community, which had provided the key figures in the old elite, came the hardest resistance. The Sunnis gained support from those humiliated by Iraq's occupation and fearful of the loss of their power. Their numbers swelled with disbanded military members and volunteers from the many unemployed young men. It included "former regime elements" and a strong al-Qaeda group led by the Jordanian Abu Musab al-Zarqawi, who was as keen to foment civil war with the majority Shiites as he was to expel the Americans. Although Shiites were the natural beneficiaries of the toppling of the Iraqi regime, radical elements from within this community, led by Muqtada al-Sadr, also turned on the Americans. The struggles faced by American forces after such apparently effortless victories demonstrated that victory in battle did not necessarily result in a smooth political transition. It also demonstrated that whatever strengths the Americans had in regular warfare, they coped poorly with irregular warfare.

With U.S. authority under constant challenge and its troops being caught by ambushes and roadside bombs, there were contrary pressures to both reduce profile and put on forceful displays of strength. The coalition was soon militarily stretched and lacking in political credibility. A poor security situation hampered economic and social reconstruction, the lack of which contributed to security problems. Having ignored counterinsurgency for over three decades, American forces struggled. They would move through towns and villages and clear them of insurgents in a show of strength, but without sufficient American troops left behind, the enemy could soon return. This meant that the local population had no incentive to cooperate with the Americans. Attempts were made to build up local security forces, but these were often infiltrated by the militias. U.S. troops had not been trained to withhold fire, avoid rising to provocations, and find ways to reach out to wary local people. They found it hard to separate insurgents from innocent civilians and soon became suspicious of everyone, which added to the sense of mutual alienation.

More effort was going into intimidating opponents than winning over the undecided. An analysis of operations conducted from 2003 to 2005 suggested that most were "reactive to insurgent activity—seeking to hunt down insurgents." Few operations were "directed specifically to create a secure environment for the population."[22] The strategy of "cordon and sweep" put the onus on holding territory and killing the enemy. Whatever the military effects of this approach, the political effects were invariably detrimental.

The perplexing situation in which American forces found themselves resulted in a resurgence of thinking about counterinsurgency, led by officers frustrated by the institutional barriers that had been set up to deny the relevance of irregular forms of warfare. *Military Review*, the house journal of the Combined Arms Center at Fort Leavenworth, barely covered the issue before 2004. Soon it was averaging about five articles on the topic per issue.[23] The old classics of guerrilla warfare—from T. E. Lawrence to David Galula—began to be rediscovered. Officers with a knowledge of past counterinsurgency practice (for example, John Nagl) began to advise on their application to Iraq.[24] David Kilcullen, an Australian officer on loan to the U.S. military, became one of the first postcolonial counterinsurgency theorists, updating the more timeless lessons by incorporating the efforts by al-Qaeda and like-minded groups to establish a form of global insurgency that ignored national boundaries. Kilcullen explored the extent to which ordinary people turned into "accidental guerrillas" less because of their support of extremist ideologies than their resentment at foreign interference in their affairs. To prevent al-Qaeda turning itself into a global insurgency, it had to be disaggregated into separate, manageable pieces. To prevent it prospering within the information environment, the counterinsurgents needed to recognize this to be as important as the physical environment.[25]

The leader of the new counterinsurgency effort was General David Petraeus. He noted the problems that had arisen because the United States had become embroiled in a war for which it had not prepared, and he stressed the political dimension of the problem, emphasizing that it was not just a matter of military technique. "Counterinsurgency strategies must also include, above all, efforts to establish a political environment that helps reduce support for the insurgents and undermines the attraction of whatever ideology they may espouse."[26] At the start of 2007, when the United States appeared to be on the brink of abandoning Iraq to civil war, President Bush decided on one last push. Petraeus was put in charge of what became known as the "surge," although this overstated the importance of numbers as opposed to a new strategy.[27] Over the course of the year, there were definite signs of improvement, and this came to be seen as a turning point in the conflict in terms of mitigating the push to civil war if not meeting the early American aspirations of turning Iraq into a liberal democracy.

The improvement was not so much the result of extra troops and the intelligence with which they were deployed, although these were important, but more due to the extent to which the Iraqis turned away from the logic of civil war, notably with a strong reaction among the Sunnis to the brutality of al-Qaeda. As the number of attacks on Shiite sites declined, there was less excuse for revenge attacks on Sunnis. Using American military strength to reinforce these trends required a more subtle approach to Iraqi politics than simply handing responsibility for security back to the Iraqi government as soon as possible, whether or not they were able to cope. This meant that the Americans were working with the grain of Iraqi politics rather than against it.

War into the Fourth Generation

To what extent did the experience of the 2000s represent a trend or a set of unusual circumstances, unlikely to be repeated? For those who took the former view, there was a theoretical framework that had some credibility because it could easily accommodate international terrorism. It came under the broad heading of "fourth-generation warfare." Like the RMA, this framework had parentage in in OODA loops and maneuver warfare, but it had taken a quite different turn, away from regular war.[28] Its origins lay in an article by a group led by William Lind, a follower of Boyd and energetic reformer.[29] According to this scheme, the first three generations had developed in response to each other (line and column, massed firepower, and then blitzkrieg). The new generation began in the moral and cognitive spheres, where even physically strong entities could be victims of shock, disorientation, and loss of confidence and coherence. This principle was then applied to society as a whole. In the fourth generation, attacks would be directed at the sources of social cohesion, including shared norms and values, economic management, and institutional structures. This was a move from the artificial operational level to a form of upside-down grand strategy, bringing in questions of rival ideologies and ways of life, and forms of conflict that might not actually involve much fighting.

With cataclysmic great power clashes apparently things of the past, the idea that new wars were wholly to be found in and around weak states persisted. A growing amount of international business appeared to involve states suffering from internal wars.[30] The engagement of Western powers in these conflicts was, however, considered discretionary (they were often described as "wars of choice") and undertaken on a humanitarian basis to relieve distress. Though they raised issues outside of military operations, such as economic reconstruction and state-building, they had only a loose fit with the fourth-generation theory. If anything, they were distractions to the more tough-minded of the fourth-generation theorists.

Although the RMA shared the same origins, it could only point to a singular form of regular warfare, which was unlikely to be fought because it suited the United States. Fourth-generation warfare, on the other hand, pointed to almost everything else, which is why there were so many versions of the theory. One strand, most associated with Lind, focused on an eating away of American national identity as a result of unconstrained immigration and multiculturalism. He argued this was less a reflection of social trends and more the result of a deliberate project by "cultural Marxists." Cultural damage appeared as the product of deliberate and hostile moves, by enemies aided and abetted by naïve and wrong-thinking elements at home, rather than of broader and more diffuse social trends or economic imperatives. Another, more influential strand, most associated with Marine Colonel Thomas X. Hammes, concentrated on irregular war, especially the forms of terrorism and insurgency which caused the United States such grief during the 2000s.[31]

There were five core themes in the fourth-generation literature. First, it followed Boyd's focus on the moral and cognitive domains as where wars are won or lost. Second, there was a conviction that the Pentagon was mistaken in its focus on high-technology, short wars. Third, tendencies toward globalization and networks were presented as blurring established boundaries between war and peace, civilian and military, order and chaos. War could not be contained in either time or space. It spanned the "spectrum of human activity" and was "politically, socially (rather than technically) networked and protracted in duration." Fourth, the enemies were not easy to find or pin down. Chuck Spinney, another former associate of Boyd, described the fourth-generation warriors as presenting

> few, if any, important targets vulnerable to conventional attack, and their followers are usually much more willing to fight and die for their causes. They seldom wear uniforms and may be difficult to distinguish from the general population. They are also far less hampered by convention and more likely to seek new and innovative means to achieve their objectives.[32]

Fifth, because these conflicts were played out in the moral and cognitive domains, any military action must be considered as a form of communication.

Lind argued in the original formulation: "Psychological operations may become the dominant operational and strategic weapon in the form of media/information intervention."[33]

As a coherent theory it soon evaporated, not only because of the different strands but also because it depended on a historical schema which did not work. War had never been solely based on regular battle, supposedly at the center of the three previous generations. Moreover, even virtuosos of irregular warfare, such as T. E. Lawrence and Mao Zedong, still accepted that only regular forces could seize state power. The fact that there might be a number of groups relying on irregular forms, from terrorism to insurgency, was a function of their weakness rather than a unique insight into the impact of new technologies and socioeconomic structures in the modern world. There was also a tendency to assume that unwelcome developments had one guiding cause.

In a similar vein, Ralph Peters argued that Western forces must prepare to face "warriors," whom he characterized colorfully as "erratic primitives of shifting allegiances, habituated to violence, with no stake in civil order." He described their approach to war in terms familiar to students of guerrilla warfare. They only stood and fought when they had an overwhelming advantage. "Instead they snipe, ambush, mislead, and betray, attempting to fool the constrained soldiers confronting them into alienating the local population or allies, while otherwise hunkering down and trying to outlast the organized military forces pitted against them."[34] This overstated the problem. Some might enjoy fighting for its own sake, but the most fearsome warriors were likely to be fighting for a cause or a way of life they held dear. The performance of guerrilla bands, militias, and popular armies was mixed to say the least.

Information Operations

A key element in the discussion of asymmetric warfare focused on what were unhelpfully known as "information operations." The term was unhelpful because it referred to a series of related but distinctive activities, some concerned with the flow of information and others with its content. Its potential range was indicated by an official U.S. publication, which asserted as a goal achieving and maintaining "information superiority for the U.S. and its allies." This required an ability "to influence, disrupt, corrupt, or usurp adversarial human and automated decision-making while protecting our own." The mix of the automated and the human was reflected in references to electronic warfare and computer networks as well psychological operations and deception.[35] All this reflected two distinct strands. The first was the traditional concern with changing the perceptions of others, and the second was the impact of digitized information.

When information was a scarce commodity it could be considered in similar ways as other vital commodities, such as fuel and food. Acquiring and protecting high-quality information made it possible to stay ahead of opponents and competitors. Such information might include intellectual property, sensitive financial data, and the plans and capabilities of government agencies and private corporations. This provided intelligence agencies with their raison d'être. While Clausewitz may have dismissed the importance of intelligence, it came to be of increasing value as improved means were found to gather information that opponents intended to keep secret. At first this depended on spies, and then the ability to break codes. As telegraphic communications came into use, their interception could provide evidence on enemy locations as well as messages. Breaking German signal codes during the Second World War gave the Allies a valuable advantage in a number of encounters. Then came the ability to take photographs from the air and later from space. It became progressively harder to stop opponents from picking up vital details about military systems and dispositions.

As more information began to be digitized—so that it became simpler to generate, transmit, collect, and store—and communications became instantaneous, the challenges became those of plenty rather than scarcity. There were large amounts of material that could be accessed, both openly and illicitly. Outsiders sought to hack their way through passwords and firewalls to acquire sensitive material, steal identities, or misappropriate funds. Another challenge was maintaining the integrity of information despite attempted disruption or tampering via the insidious forms of digital penetration known as viruses, worms, trojan horses, and logic bombs, which were often launched from distant servers for no obvious purpose—though there was sometimes a clear and malign intent. The bulk of this activity was criminal and fraudulent, but there were examples of large-scale downloading of government and corporate secrets by state-funded hackers, attacks that closed down governmental systems, mysterious viruses that affected weapons development programs, and damaged software that meant military equipment failed to work properly. Might an army of software wizards use insidious electronic means to dislocate the support systems of modern societies, such as transport, banking, and public health?

There was no doubt that attacks could cause inconvenience and irritation, and on occasion make a real difference. In the midst of operations, the military might find air defense systems disabled, missiles sent off-course, local commanders left in the dark, and senior commanders confused as their screens went blank. If they had bought in to the idea that fast-flowing data streams could eliminate the fog of war, they could be in for a rude shock. Even without enemy interference, a fog could be caused by a superfluity of information—too much to filter, evaluate, and digest—rather than the paucity of the past. Certainly the new information environment posed problems to governments in terms of what they could hope to control and their efforts to influence the news agenda. Ordinary people could spread images with cell phone photos and news, often inaccurate and half-digested, could spread on social networking sites, while governments were still trying to work out what was going on and shape a response.[36]

Did this amount to the danger identified by John Arquilla and David Ronfeldt in 1993, when they warned that "Cyberwar is Coming!"[37] Their claim was that future wars would revolve around knowledge. They distinguished between "cyberwar," which they limited to military systems (although it became expanded in later use) and "netwar," which was more at the societal level. The issue was the same as for any new form of warfare: could it be decisive on its own? Or, as Steve Metz put it, could a "politically usable way" be found to damage an "enemy's national or commercial infrastructure" sufficiently "to attain victory without having to first defeat fielded military forces?"[38]

The presumption that there might be a decisive cyberwar attack assumed that the offense would dominate and that the effects would be far-reaching, enduring, and uncontainable. The threat gained credibility from the frequency with which companies and even high-profile networks, including the Pentagon, were attacked by hackers. Protecting and managing privileged information against sophisticated foes who probed persistently for the weakest links in networks became a high priority. But effective attacks required considerable intelligence on the precise configuration of the enemy's digital systems as well as points of entry into their networks. The possible anonymity and surprise of the attack might have its attractions, but any proposal to mount one would raise obvious questions about the likelihood of success against an alert opponent, the real damage that might be done, the speed of recovery, and the possibility of retaliation (not necessarily in kind). An opponent that had been really hurt might well strike back physically rather than digitally. Thomas Rid warned that the issue was becoming dominated by hyperbole. The bulk of "cyber" attacks were nonviolent in their intent and effect, and in general were less violent than measures they might replace. They were the latest versions of the classic activities of sabotage, espionage, and subversion. "Cyber-war," he concluded, was a "wasted metaphor," failing to address the real issues raised by the new technologies.[39]

Arquilla and Ronfeldt described "netwar" as "an emerging mode of conflict (and crime) at societal levels, short of traditional military warfare, in which the protagonists used network forms of organization and related doctrines, strategies, and technologies attuned to the information age." In contrast to the large, hierarchical stand-alone organizations that conducted police and military operations, and which extremists often mimicked, the protagonists of netwar were "likely to consist of dispersed organizations, small groups, and individuals who communicate, coordinate, and conduct their campaigns in an internetted manner, often without a central command."[40] Terrorists, insurgents, or even nonviolent radical groups would not need to rely on frontal assaults and hierarchical command chains but could "swarm," advancing in small groups from many different directions using different methods in a network held together by cellphones and the web. In practice, the more visible manifestations took the form of "hacktivism," a way of making political or cultural points rather than threatening the economy or social cohesion. Even if more determined adversaries were prepared to mount substantial attacks, the result would likely be "mass disruption" rather than "mass destruction," with inconvenience and disorientation more evident than terror and collapse.[41]

The use of social networking, such as Facebook and Twitter, during the early days of the Arab Spring of 2011 illustrated how swarming could leave governments uncertain about how to cope with a rapidly developing public opinion. Such tactics followed well-established principles from before the information age. Radical groups, especially during their early stages, were often based on loose networks of individuals. To avoid attracting the attention of the authorities, they found it safer to operate as semi-independent cells, communicating with each other and their shared leadership as little as possible. To be sure, the Internet and the other forms of digitized communication made it easier to keep in touch, but the number of security breaches attributed to calls or electronic messages being traced still left them hesitant to talk too openly or too specifically. Moreover, radical networks required an underlying social cohesion or an attachment to a clear campaign objective to bring diverse individuals together. In order to prosper they needed to move beyond the cellular form. This required a leadership able to mobilize and then direct sufficient force to strike significant blows. It was difficult to move beyond being a nuisance and harassing the enemy to seizing control without an authoritative point of decision. As the Arab revolts of 2011–2013 demonstrated, regimes facing serious opposition did not reply with social networking of their own but with repression and force, and in the end, it was the possibility of armed rebellion and the readiness of the military to defend the regime that were crucial.

The initial focus was on the role of information flows in sustaining standard military operations, facilitating faster decision-making and ensuring more precise physical effects. The irregular warfare in the 2000s soon brought into focus the more traditional forms of information warfare, and the Americans appeared to be losing ground to apparently primitive opponents regarding how these conflicts, their stakes, and their conduct were perceived. Their opponents lacked physical strength but seemed to know how to turn impressionable minds. Superiority in the physical environment was of little value unless it could be translated into an advantage in the information environment. As this was the "chosen battlespace" of its foes, the United States was now required to learn to conceptualize its victories in terms of shaping perceptions over time rather than in terms of decisive engagements that annihilated the enemy.[42] The issue was not so much the flow of data but the way that people thought.

The counterinsurgency struggles in Iraq and Afghanistan led to an almost postmodernist embrace of pre-rational and embedded patterns of thought that allowed individuals, and broad social groups, to be caught up in a particular view of the world. Major General Robert Scales sought to explain the contrast between the failure of Islamic armies when fighting conventional battles Western style and their far greater success in unconventional war. He developed the concept of "culture-centric warfare."[43] In facing an enemy that "uses guile, subterfuge, and terror mixed with patience and a willingness to die," he argued, too much effort had been spent attempting to gain "a few additional meters of precision, knots of speed, or bits of bandwidth" and too little to create a "parallel transformation based on cognition and cultural awareness." Winning wars required "creating alliances, leveraging non-military advantages, reading intentions, building trust, converting opinions, and managing perceptions—all tasks that demand an exceptional ability to understand people, their culture, and their motivation." This would be a "dispersed enemy" communicating "by word of mouth and back-alley messengers" and fighting with simple weapons that did "not require networks or sophisticated technological integration to be effective."

One reflection of the growing recognition of cultural factors was that the Pentagon employed an anthropologist, Montgomery McFate, to consider the interplay between military operations and Iraqi society. Among the mistakes she identified were failures to appreciate the role of tribal loyalties as the established civilian structure of power collapsed, the importance of coffee shop rumors compared with official communications, and the meaning of such small things as hand gestures.[44] The growing recognition of the importance of the ability to influence another's view of the world was evident in the frequent references to "hearts and minds" in warnings about what was lost politically by indiscriminate and harsh military operations. The phrase came to be used whenever there was a need to persuade people through good works and sensitivity that security forces were really on their side, as part of a broader strategy of cutting militants off from their potential sources of support, including recruits, intelligence, sustenance, weapons and ammunition, and sanctuaries. The counterargument went back to Machiavelli—that it was better to be respected than loved, that opponents could be intimidated and demoralized by physical strength but encouraged in their opposition by concessions.

The problem was more an over-facile approach to the hearts-and-minds concept. In other contexts, "heart" and "mind" were pitted against each other—strong emotions versus cool calculations, appeals to values and symbols versus appeals to the intellect. This is reflected in an early use by the British General Sir Henry Clinton when facing a similar problem with the upstart Americans in 1776. The British, Clinton argued, needed to "gain the hearts and subdue the minds of America."[45] In practice, in discussions of countering both insurgency and terrorism, those opposed to brute force tended to stress gaining hearts more than subduing minds, as if provisions of goods and services could win the support of a desperate population.

There were three difficulties. First, as noted, local political loyalties would depend on local power structures and any measures would have to be judged in terms of their effects on these structures. Second, while there were undoubted benefits to repairing roads and building schools, or securing power and sanitation, these efforts wouuld not get very far if security was so poor that foreign troops and local people were unable to interact closely and develop mutual trust. They were the sort of policies that might help prevent situations deteriorating but were less likely to help retrieve it once lost. A more minds-oriented approach might establish that trust by addressing questions about who was likely to win the continuing political and military conflict and the long-term agendas of the various parties. The insurgents could sow doubts about who among the local population could be trusted, about what was real and what was fake, about who was truly on one's side and who was pretending. As the insurgents and counterinsurgents played mind games to gain local support, they could be as anxious to create impressions of strength as of kindness, to demonstrate a likely victory as well as to hand out largesse. In terms of the cognitive dimensions of strategy, this was as important as any feel-good effect from good works. Both would depend on the actual experiences of the local population and local leaders, and the mental constructs through which it was interpreted.

Third, this strategy required greater subtlety than just an awareness that different people had different cultures. It was hard to argue against an improved sensitivity about how others viewed the world and the need to avoid ethnocentrism. *Culture* was itself a slippery term, often being used as something that envelops individuals and shapes their actions without them being able to do much about it. The term could include almost anything that could not be explained by reference to hard-nosed matters of interest. Attempts to define another's strategic culture often then came up with something remarkably coherent, without contradiction and almost impervious to change. At least among academics, this approach was largely giving way to a practice of referring to some received ideas that help interpret information and navigate events but which were subject to regular modification and development. We shall return to some of these ideas in the last section of this book when we develop the idea of "scripts."[46] The importance of an exaggerated view of culture was that it could lead to the assumption that alien attitudes and uncooperative behavior reflected the persistence of an ancient way of life, untouched by modern influences, asserting itself whatever the conditions.

Against the suggestion that individuals were socialized into hard cultures sharing assumptions, norms, patterns of behavior, and forms of mutual understanding that could be implicit, unspoken, or taken for granted—that were all but impenetrable to an outsider—was the possibility that in a dynamic situation where communities were being subjected to new influences and challenges, cultures were likely to develop and adjust, and become less effective in binding people together. Thus, observed Porter, in the literature on reconstructed Islamists, warrior peoples, and insurgencies fed by cultural difference, it was as if the people encountered did "not act but are acted upon by impersonal historical forces, taking orders from the culture; or that modes of warfare are singular and fixed by ancestral habit." People were able to learn and accommodate within their cultures new types of weapons and forms of conflict. References to the durability of hatreds and the evocation of cultural symbols could encourage stereotypes of the primordial and the exotic as harmful as those that assumed that all people were seeking to remake themselves in a Western image. Explaining problematic behavior as a consequence of people being set in their ways was not only condescending but also let off the hook those in the intervening forces, whose actions might have prompted a hostile reaction, and underestimated the extent to which opponents in a prolonged conflict would interact and pick up ideas, weapons, and tactics from each other.[47]

The need to have convincing stories impressed itself on officers trying to cope with a vicious enemy while staying on the right side of the people they were supposed to be helping. Kilcullen observed the insurgents' "pernicious influence" drew on a "single narrative"—simple, unified, easily expressed— that could organize experience and provide a framework for understanding events. He understood that it was best to be able to "tap into an existing narrative that excludes the insurgents," stories that people naturally appreciate. Otherwise it was necessary to develop an alternative narrative.[48] It was not so easy for a complex multinational force to forge a narrative that could satisfy a variety of audiences. A British officer saw the value of one that not only helped explain actions but also bound together "one's team, across levels of authority and function; the diplomatic head of mission, the army company commander, the aid specialist, the politician working from a domestic capital, for instance." He recognized that this might lead to variations in the story, but so long as there was an underlying consistency this need not be a problem. But liberal democracies found it hard to generate consistent stories, or to appreciate the needs of the local front line as against those of the distant capital.[49]

A generally rueful collection of essays put together by the Marine Corps suggested that the United States had proved inept at "quickly adapting the vast, dominant, commercial information infrastructure it enjoys to national security purposes."[50] It was perplexing to have been caught out so badly by al-Qaeda, who seemed to be as brazen in their message as they were outrageous in their attacks. Yet in an apparent war of narratives the United States was on the defensive, preoccupied with challenging another's message rather than promoting their own. Attempts were made to fashion notionally attractive communications without being sure how they were being received. In addressing their new target audiences, the Western communicators had to cope with rumors and hearsay, popular distrust of any reports from official sources, a reluctance to be told by foreigners what to think, and competition with a multitude of alternative sources. People filtered out what they did not trust or what they found irrelevant, or they picked up odd fragments and variants of the core message, interpreting and synthesizing them according to their own prejudices and frameworks.

Most seriously, there could be no total control over the impressions being created by either the actions of careless troops or the policy statements of careless politicians. There might be a group of professionals working under the label of information operations, but the audiences could take their cues from whatever caught their attention. The United States might have invented mass communications and the modern public relations industry, but these were challenges that went beyond normal marketing techniques. Those with backgrounds in political campaigning or marketing who were asked to advise on getting the message out in Iraq and Afghanistan often opted for short-lived projects that had no lasting effect. Moreover, these individuals knew that they would be judged by how their products went down with domestic audiences; thus, those were the groups to which they tended to be geared. Not only did this miss the point of the exercise but it could also blind policymakers, who often fell into the trap of believing their own propaganda. Jeff Michaels developed the idea of a "discourse trap" whereby the politically comfortable and approved language used to describe campaigns led policymakers to miss significant developments. By refusing to acknowledge that early terror attacks in Iraq could be the responsibility of anybody other than former members of the regime, for example, they missed the alienation of moderate Sunnis and the growth of Shia radicalism.[51]

Attempts to persuade individuals to see the world in a different light and change their views were difficult enough and required insight into their distinctive backgrounds, characters, and concerns. It was far harder to do this for a whole category of people from an unfamiliar culture with extremely significant internal currents and differences that would be barely perceptible to outsiders. It was important when conducting military operations to understand that their effects went well beyond the kinetic to influencing the way that those caught up in conflicts understood their likely course and what was at stake. This affected the way that allegiances and sympathies might be broken and put together. Understanding this could help avoid egregious errors that might alienate important sections of the population. But because it was hard to measure and pin down effects on beliefs, it was not surprising that commanders trusted the surer results of firepower.[52] If the challenge was to reshape political consciousness to produce an alignment of views with powerful foreigners, there were bound to be limits to what could be done by the military. Favorable images, let alone whole belief systems, could not be fired directly into the minds of the target audience as a form of precision weapon. If there was a consolation, the success of al-Qaeda was also exaggerated. Modern communications media undoubtedly created opportunities for the almost instantaneous transmission of dramatic and eloquent images, and to any modern-day Bakunin there were extraordinary opportunities for "propaganda of the deed."[53] The same factors, however, that worked against successful official "information operations" could also work against the militants—random violence, irrelevance to everyday concerns, and messages that grew tedious with repetition.[54] As Ben Wilkinson observed in a study of radical Islamist groups, the real problem was not the lack of a simple message but the implausibility of the cause and effect relationships they had to postulate if they were to convince themselves and their supporters of eventual success. This led them astray, caught by "bad analogies, false assumptions, misinterpretations and fallacies," overstating the role of human agency, with little room for the accidental and the unpredictable. All this made for a bad case of "narrative delusion."[55] Radical strategists might be at special risk of narrative delusion, because of the size of the gap between aspirations and means, but it is one to which all strategists are prone.

CHAPTER 17 | The Myth of the Master Strategist

*... in 1793 a force appeared that beggared all imagination. Suddenly
war again became the business of the people—a people of thirty millions,
all of whom considered themselves to be citizens.... The resources and
efforts now available for use surpassed all conventional limits; nothing
now impeded the vigor with which war could be waged.*

—Clausewitz, *On War*

THE FRAMEWORK FOR thinking about war and strategy inspired by
Napoleon and developed in its most suggestive form by Clausewitz was
not easily displaced. So shrewd were Clausewitz's insights and so compelling his formulations that it was hard to think of alternative ways to study
war effectively. Those who drew attention to their greater knowledge about
past wars and developments that he could not have imagined missed the
point. The enduring power of his analytical framework lay in the dynamic
interplay of politics, violence, and chance. It was because of this that writers
on military strategy continued to assert their fealty to the great master. One
of these, Colin Gray, wondered why modern strategic thought compared so
poorly with *On War*. There were no war leaders comparable to Napoleon able
to inspire great interpretative theory. He also pointed to a lack of military
practitioners comfortable with theory or civilian theorists familiar with practice. The complexity of modern warfare challenged the lone theorist, while

those concerned with national strategy had become too focused on immediate policy issues.

Gray had an exalted view of the strategist as someone who could view the system as a whole, taking account of the multiple interdependencies and the numerous factors at play in order to identify where effort could be most profitably applied. In his *Modern Strategy*, he identified seventeen factors to take into account: people, society, culture, politics, ethics, economics and logistics, organization, administration, information and intelligence, strategic theory and doctrine, technology, operations, command, geography, friction/chance/uncertainty, adversary, and time. Proper strategy required that these be considered holistically—that is, both individually and in context with the others.[1]

This was picked up by Harry Yarger, a teacher at the U.S. Army War College, who went even further: "Strategic thinking is about thoroughness and holistic thinking. It seeks to understand how the parts interact to form the whole by looking at parts and relationships among them—the effects they have on one another in the past, present, and anticipated future." This holistic perspective would require "a comprehensive knowledge of what else is happening within the strategic environment and the potential first-, second-, and third-order effects of its own choices on the efforts of those above, below, and on the strategist's own level." Nor would it be good enough to work with snapshots and early gains: "The strategist must reject the expedient, near-term solution for the long-term benefit." So much was expected of the true strategist: a student of the present who must be aware of the past, sensitive to the possibilities of the future, conscious of the danger of bias, alert to ambiguity, alive to chaos, ready to think through consequences of alternative courses of action, and then able to articulate all this with sufficient precision for those who must execute its prescriptions.[2] This was a counsel of perfection. There was only so much knowledge that an individual could accumulate, assimilate, and manipulate; only so many potential sequences of events that could be worked through in a system that was full of uncertainty, complexity, and chaos.

Gray also concluded that this was too much, accepting that he had also been too ambitious. Yarger, he observed, "appeared to encourage, even demand, an impossibility."[3] Even making a start on these factors required a considerable technical and conceptual grasp. Nonetheless, Gray still described a strategist as someone rather special, with an "exceedingly demanding" job description, able to see the "big picture," and familiar with all of war's dimensions. He quoted with approval Fred Iklé's observation that good work on national strategy required a "rotund intellect, a well-rounded personality."[4] Similarly,

Yarger had described strategy as "the domain of the strong intellect, the lifelong student, the dedicated professional, and the invulnerable ego."[5]

Could there be such a master strategist with this unique grasp of affairs? If ever found, this person would be a precious resource and in great demand, torn between hard looks into the future and the need to take time to communicate conclusions in an intelligible form to those who must follow them. As such systematic and forward thinking would open up numerous risks and possibilities, any value to a practitioner would require sharpening the focus. An all-encompassing view of the environment might be welcome by a government before embarking on a major initiative where it could expect to take the first move, but could also be a luxury when coping with sudden developments that had unaccountably been missed. Then strategy might be more improvised and ad hoc. In such circumstances, the master strategist might feel a tad unprepared.

The supposed holistic view of the master strategist would also be problematic. There were good reasons to pay attention to "systems effects," the unanticipated results of connections between apparently separate spheres of activity. The likelihood of unexpected effects was a good reason to take care when urging bold moves and then to monitor closely their consequences once taken. Exploring the range and variety of relationships within the broader environment could help identify creative possibilities by generating indirect forms of influence, targeting an opponent's weakest links, or forging surprising alliances.[6] This did not, however, require a view of the whole system. There had to be some boundaries. In principle everything was connected to everything else; in practice the repercussions of a localized action might fade away quite soon. In addition, a holistic view implied an ability to look at a complete system from without, whereas the practical strategist's perspective was bound to be more myopic, focusing on what was close and evidently consequential rather than on distant features that might never need to be engaged. Over time the focus might change. That was not an argument to attempt to anticipate everything in advance but to recognize the unreality of insisting on setting out with confidence, certainty, and clarity a series of steps that was sure to reach long-term goals.

The idea that societies, and their associated military systems might be comprehended as complex systems encouraged the view, reflected in the perplexing searches for enemy centers of gravity, that hitting an enemy system in exactly the right place would cause it to crumble quickly, as the impact would reverberate and affect all the interconnected parts. The frustration of the search was a result of the fact that effects would not simply radiate out from some vital center. Societies could adapt to shocks. As systems, they could break down into more viable subsystems, establish barriers, reduce dependencies, and find alternative forms of sustenance. Feedback would be constant and complex.

Clausewitz did present war as a dynamic system but it was also remarkably self-contained. He was a theorist of war and not of international politics.[7] He looked backward to the political source of war but that was not where he started. At the level of national policy, what eventually became called grand strategy, questions had to be asked about how goals were to be best met. The answers might exclude the armed forces or assign them only a minor role. It was only at this more political level that the success of any military operations could be judged and claims of victory assessed. The quality and timelessness of Clausewitz's analysis of the phenomenon of war left behind the context from which it sprang, that is, the upheavals set in motion by the French Revolution. His focus on decisive victory required reassessment in the light of changes in the political context. Even when it was pointed out that Clausewitz had begun to reappraise limited war, the concept of a decisive battle retained its powerful hold over the military profession. The attraction was not hard to see: it gave the armed forces a special role and responsibility. The fate of the nation was in their hands, a point to be emphasized when seeking additional resources or political support. If affairs could be settled without decisive battles, then the general staffs could lose their importance and clout. Battle, however, became increasingly problematic as firepower became more ferocious over greater ranges and more men could be mobilized to pour into a fight. To retain the possibility of decisiveness, some critical new factor had to be found. Prior to the First World War it was detected in the motivating effects of high morale and a brave national spirit. Afterwards the focus was on the possibilities of surprise and maneuver to overcome the devastating effects of enemy firepower by disorienting them. This interest was revived in the United States during the later decades of the twentieth century though the outcomes of the regular military campaigns could be predicted as much by reference to the raw balance of military power as to any superior operational cleverness.

Even then, apparent victory could be compromised as regular wars turned into irregular struggles. This need not have been news. Clausewitz had noted the effectiveness of the first guerrillas in Spain against Napoleon. Occupying armies regularly faced harassment from a sullen and resistant population. This phenomenon was evident in the challenges to colonialism. When regular battles seemed to lead to stalemate, governments could well try to break the deadlock by seeking to coerce civilian populations, whether through naval blockades or air raids. Popular morale became as important if not more so than military morale. So from the micro-level of counterinsurgency as well as the macro-level of nuclear deterrence, the key effects were not those posed by one armed force against another but those posed against the adversary's political and social structures.

Once the civilian sphere was acknowledged to be so important then questions of perceptions and how they might be influenced came to the fore. Deterrence required influencing the expectations of those who might be contemplating aggressive action to remind them of why this might be a bad idea; irregular warfare required separating the militants from their possible supporters by demonstrating this was a cause doomed to failure and offering few rewards if successful. There was little science in this. A sense of the danger of nuclear war did not require subtle messaging, while attempts to shape the views of people caught up in a war in which they were reluctant to take sides could easily be undermined by a single dramatic event or a lack of understanding of local concerns. Unless the message was very strong, as with nuclear war, it was easier in retrospect to explain the behavior of others than in prospect to influence that behavior through "information operations." The counterinsurgency campaigns of the early twenty-first century reflected a keen appreciation of narratives, but they were more relevant when illuminating problems than as sources of solutions. Looking back, it was possible to discern the processes by which the predominant views within a community had begun to shift, but that was not the same as providing the basis for a forward-looking strategy.

The practical difficulties of this complex interaction between the civilian and military spheres were aggravated by the political separation of the two spheres in terms of the higher command structures. The traditional military view, affirmed by von Moltke, was that once the purposes of war had been set by the political leadership, the war's subsequent conduct was the military's responsibility. The civilians must then take a back seat. It was enough to have to cope with a resolute and wily enemy without having to deal with panicking civilians as well, especially once modern communications constantly put temptation in their way. When an immediate connection could be made between the head of state and the most junior front-line commander, the considered judgments of a whole chain of command might be swept away by a few inexpert and clumsy sentences. Under any circumstances, abrupt shifts in political direction combined with amateurish attempts at playing the great commander were bound to irritate the professionals.

This was the blind spot resulting from the focus on battle, expressed in the belief that the operational art was something best left to military commanders.[8] This model of civil-military relationships whereby the actual deployment and employment of armed force was a largely military responsibility was wholly inadequate. The two spheres needed to be in constant dialogue. Political ends could not be discussed without regard for military feasibility. Diplomatic activity would be shaped by military options and risks. Whether or not to offer diplomatic concessions, seek resources or bases from third parties, or construct alliances, depended on military assessments. These assessments in turn led to assumptions on the shape of the rival coalitions and their ability to withstand long wars or extend their reach through bases. The idea of a military strategy separate from a political strategy was not only misleading but also dangerous.

Civilians could not ignore the supposedly operational issues associated with military strategy. They needed to consider whether the way a war was being fought was consistent with the purposes for which it was being fought, and to look beyond coming battles to the following peace. They needed to keep the public and allies, potential or actual, on their side. This required consideration of the burdens a society could accept and the harm it could legitimately impose on others, and of how to lead a polity toward these limits or away from them. When it came to operations, most military organizations had to improvise at some point, whatever the "lessons" they believed they had learned from previous wars. As they did so, the generals and admirals would often quite properly disagree among themselves on how the enemy would best be defeated. The single military view was the exception rather than the rule, and the differences regularly turned on assessments that were essentially political. The military would need regular political guidance as circumstances changed and old plans became redundant.

The attempt to develop a science of strategy was thus thwarted by the inherent unpredictability of military affairs and compounded by the even greater unpredictability of political affairs. Wars were not won through applying some formula that only seasoned military professionals could grasp, for example, by insisting on a maneuverist rather than an attritional philosophy, clever ways of catching the enemy by surprise versus the single-minded delivery of firepower. Military campaigns had to be designed according to circumstances, and successful commanders would show flexibility in their operational decisions. In explaining success and failure in war it would be wrong to discount the operational art, but as often as not the key to a successful strategy was the political skill necessary to deny the enemy a winning coalition while forging one's own.

The origins of a distinctive concept of military strategy lay in the urge to control, and as we shall see in the next two sections, a similar urge was influential in the origins of both political (even revolutionary) and business strategy. This urge shaped strategies to control the battlefield through the complete elimination of enemy armies. It was also evident in a determination to maintain the operational sphere as the privileged domain of the military. Pure control was always an illusion, at most a temporary sensation of success, which would soon pass as the new situation generated its own challenges. Extracting a state from an attritional conflict would require awkward negotiations, while even impressive victories involved a concept of a sustainable peace and the question of how to deal with the defeated. The idea of a master strategist was therefore a myth. On the one hand, it demanded an impossible omniscience in grasping the totality of complex and dynamic situations or an ability to establish a credible and sustainable path toward distant goals. On the other hand, it failed to take account of what were often the real and immediate demands of strategy-making. This was to bring together a variety of disparate actors to agree on how to address the most pressing problems arising out of the current state of affairs and plot a means of advance to a much better state.

The attempt to control the course of battle came at a time of growing logistical complexity, mass armies, and political upheaval. As we have seen this led to two core principles that proved to be very resilient even as their limitations should have become evident and the circumstances in which they had to be implemented became even more challenging. The first, which had unassailable logic, was that complete control could only reliably be achieved through elimination of the enemy army. The second was that this required maintaining the operational sphere as the privileged domain of the military. This gave debates on military strategy a sharp but also narrow focus. The political dimension was seen as something separate, a source of goals and eventual peace terms but irrelevant to operational conduct.

A military goal of annihilation went naturally with a political goal of subjugation, though that was not always achievable. When the structure of a conflict was examined more broadly, it was likely that the ability to impose a degree of political control on situations would depend on not only the capabilities of the enemy armies but the extent of the popular determination to resist subjugation and what sort of measures could be taken against a hostile population, sources of finance and essential commodities, and the strength and cohesion of the competing alliances. Clausewitz accepted the potential importance of these factors. In his concept of "centers of gravity," he suggested that they could be addressed through a targeted military effort. In practice, however, they were often best addressed on their own terms, raising issues of concessions and bargaining, access to markets and propaganda. The great strategists therefore tended to be those who were able to identify the most salient features of a conflict, political as well as military, and how they might be influenced. Their gifts lay in an ability to convince others of their insights and what this implied by way of action (for example, Lincoln and Churchill). They often came to be viewed as great because of elements of luck and the mistakes of their opponents. Sometimes their luck ran out and their fallibilities were exposed (for example, Pericles).

Master strategists, as described by Gray and Yarger, were therefore a myth. Operating solely in the military sphere, their view could only be partial, and however well-funded their proposals, they would still depend on good luck and a foolish enemy. The only people who could be master strategists were political leaders, because they were the ones who had to cope with the immediate and often competing demands of disparate actors, diplomats as well as generals, ministers along with technical experts, close allies and possible supporters. Even the best of these in the most straightforward situations could not begin to comprehend all the relevant factors and the interactions between them. They would therefore have to rely on the quality of their judgment to identify the most pressing problems arising out of the current state of affairs, plot a means of advance to a better state, and then improvise when events took an unexpected turn.

PART III | Strategy from Below

CHAPTER 18 | Marx and a Strategy for the Working Class

Philosophers have only interpreted the world... the point, however, is to change it.

—Karl Marx, *"Theses on Feuerbach"*

THE LAST SECTION had the United States puzzling out how to cope with irregular warfare, with the concept of decisive victory no longer seeming so relevant and a focus on intense local struggles taking center stage. As it sought to try to cope with terrorist atrocities and ambushes, the United States was aware that it was in a competition to obtain the acquiescence if not the active support of the ordinary people in whose name war was being waged. The armed forces were encouraged to reach out to these people, to find ways of talking to them, and to persuade them that they were truly on their side. These efforts, however, kept on coming up against barriers to comprehension set down by language and culture, as well as past actions, policies, and pronouncements that made the job of persuasion even harder. This question of how minds can be turned, especially in large numbers and in a shared direction, looms large in this section, because that has long been a preoccupation of radicals and revolutionaries determined to upend the existing structures of power on behalf of the masses—though the masses were reluctant participants, if not actively hostile to the whole endeavor.

This section looks at strategy from the perspective of the underdogs, or at least those claiming to act on their behalf, who faced a large gap between desired ends and available means. These were the people for whom strategy was most challenging. They had to mobilize support in ways that would not invite suppression. If suppression was likely, they needed to consider clandestine survival and even violent responses of their own. They asked whether all could be persuaded to rally around the same goals or whether compromise would be necessary, and if so how much would be acceptable. Radical groups with distant goals could find comfort in an isolated purity, while those who tasted success saw the value of accommodating the views of others. As they devised plans of campaign, the issues that dominated the military discourse—endurance and surprise, annihilation versus exhaustion, direct battle or indirect pressure—all made their appearance, often in forms that revealed their military origins.

Theories loom larger in this section, especially those which address the big questions of power and change in industrial societies. Radicals offered theories which described a better world and the historic forces that might make it happen; conservative theories explained why this new world might never materialize and how it might not be any better if it did, warning of the delusions of change and the likely emergence of new elites who would display the same traits as the old. Proponents of violence had theories about how it could be a source of personal as well as social liberation, sweeping away decrepit states whatever their notional strength, while advocates of nonviolence spoke not only of prudence but also the advantages of the moral high ground. Because of the fear the masses roused and the frustrations of those who felt that the masses should be more roused than they were, there were theories of consciousness (lots of them) bemoaning the malleability of belief, the suggestibility of crowds, the impact of propaganda, and the entrenched paradigms and narratives of domination.

Theories charted and also exemplified the processes of bureaucratization and rationalization, offering strategies of efficient design and implementation, explaining why even revolutionary politics required professionalization and sound organization. This became one of the touchstone issues of political life, especially on the left, for it posed sharply the issue of whether it was possible to avoid the bad habits of the powerful while staying effective. There were regular denunciations of the party apparatchiks atop disciplined organizations from those who believed this to be denying the authenticity of the human spirit. By and large, strong organization triumphed over the integrity of spontaneous action. We will nonetheless conclude with the management of presidential campaigns, in the mainstream rather than fringes of political life, but still drawing on theories of social change and political beliefs. Not only did politics become more professional, but so did theory. Occupying an important role in this story is the rise of the social sciences, yearning to be taken as seriously as the natural sciences, with findings of universal validity untainted by partisan interests. In this section and the next, we will see social science—though never wholly value free—represented at times as a source of public policy that, once accepted by an enlightened state, could render politics, and therefore strategy, unnecessary.

The Professional Revolutionaries

We start with would-be insurrectionists developing strategies to overturn the existing social order. This requires us to return almost to the starting point of the last section, for the development of professional revolutionaries was, along with the Napoleonic Wars, a consequence of the great French Revolution of 1789. Though this became the inspiration and benchmark for all revolutions that followed, it was not the result of a plot or the culmination of any deliberate strategy. It was a response to the rigidity and ineptitude of the *ancien regime* and shaped by the Enlightenment, a revolution in ideas and modes of thought. The actual events took everyone by surprise, including those who were propelled to its leadership. The Jacobin Club, which promoted the core ideas of citizenship and the rights of man, and then the terror, was formed just after the actual revolution. Initially moderate, it became increasingly radical in its program and methods. Then the revolution turned in on itself and fell in behind Napoleon. In both international and national affairs the theories of power, violence, and change inspired by this period exercised a continuing hold over revolutionary as well as military strategy.

The ruling conservative elites met at the 1815 Congress of Vienna determined to prevent further outbreaks of revolutionary fervor and battlefield carnage. Some were prepared to permit greater democracy, but most were convinced that only paternalistic monarchies could maintain order. But this was a time of great social and economic upheaval. European societies seethed with discontent. Peasants despaired at the disruption to their traditional patterns of life; workers began to organize, sometimes tenuously and sometimes forcefully; the liberal middle classes railed against the barriers to their freedom, influence over affairs, and ability to make money; the ruling elites, drawn from the land-owning aristocracy, fretted about their hold on power. During the 1840s, economic recession and harvest failures combined to create a widespread view that this was a pre-revolutionary time, that something was about to break. It was time for those who yearned for revolution to make plans.

This was the epoch, as Mike Rapport has noted, that introduced the "professional revolutionary, who plotted tirelessly for the violent overthrow of the conservative order."[1] The professionals believed that revolutions were events that could be started deliberately and did not have to wait until unanticipated surges of popular feeling overwhelmed rotten state structures. Because of 1789, the idea of revolution was not a fantasy. There was no need to be cowed by claims of an established order divinely inspired and beyond human interference. What had happened once could happen again. The revolutionaries schemed and argued about how to turn popular demonstrations and discontent into a proper insurrection. Animated by a sense of huge possibility, they debated strategy and on occasion tried to turn their theories into practice.

Eventually many of these ideas became stale, as a result of both familiarity and futility. They became the slogans of distinct, and often sectarian, mass political organizations. In the first decades of the nineteenth century, however, they were fresh, fluid, and exciting, reflecting intellectual and political ferment. This was a time of innovation in radicalism. Political positions described in terms of "Left" and "Right" followed the seating arrangements in the chamber of the post-Revolution French Legislative Assembly. "Socialism," referring to the need to address the "social question," was first used in 1832, and "communism," referring to a belief in complete equality and common ownership of land and property, entered the lexicon in 1839.

The theorists of revolution drew on the theorists of war. They embraced the same metaphors: they struggled, they attacked, and they fought. They looked for the insurrectionary equivalent of the decisive battle, a moment when it was clear who was going to come out on top. "Clausewitz's emphasis on decisive action and on the tactical offensive even in the strategic defensive became," according to Neumann and von Hagen, "the stock-in-trade of revolutionary strategy."[2] Power would have to be wrested from the ruling elites. That would require defeating the organized violence of the state. Preferably the army would capitulate in the face of just demands and the horror of being asked to fire on their own people, but if necessary they would have to be defeated in direct combat. Insurrections, therefore, were a form of battle and subject to similar rules. But in the face of superior firepower, numbers were all-important to the revolution. Somehow the broad mass of ordinary people, the poor and the dispossessed, peasants and workers, had to be mobilized and directed. They would fight not only to overcome their present misery but also for a new and better society, altogether more admirable and noble, righteous, harmonious, and prosperous.

So while the new class of professional revolutionaries might present themselves first as militants, organizers, and commanders, they also had to make their names as thinkers, articulating the inchoate aspirations of the masses, analyzing what had gone wrong and offering a vision of how all could be put right. The revolutionaries acquired their notoriety by the power of their ideas and their ability to spread them through newspapers, pamphlets, and books. Not surprisingly, the reconciliation of meager means to glorious but somewhat distant ends often required considerable intellectual gymnastics and heroics of belief. This led to rancorous disputes as to the relative merits of a range of impossible strategies. It was one thing to define a good society, quite another to explain how it would be the natural outcome of a great popular movement. It was one thing to develop an intellectually consistent narrative to explain how the revolution could work itself through to the desired outcome, quite another to follow its lines when the moment for revolution came. These great dramas would allow the revolutionaries a glimpse of everything they had been trying to achieve. The question was whether there would be anything more than a glimpse. They were unlikely to get many opportunities to find out.

Most of these professional revolutionaries were born well after 1789, in the first decade of the nineteenth century. Almost two centuries later, many still retain their reputations as defining figures of the left. At the extreme was Louis-Auguste Blanqui, an irrepressible French activist, imprisoned for much of his life, with a predilection for highly organized conspiracies. Though revolution would be undertaken on behalf of the masses their actual participation would neither be expected nor welcomed. He gave his name to "Blanquism," which came to refer in leftist circles to the idea that revolution was best achieved through a putsch or coup d'état. Pierre-Joseph Proudhon was the first to promote anarchy, which he defined in 1840 as "the absence of a master, of a sovereign." He posed the question "What is property?" to which he famously answered "Theft." Anarchism was later given a quite different tinge by the Russian Mikhail Bakunin, whose revolutionary convictions and ideas were still gestating during the 1840s. A more nationalist theme came with the Italian Giuseppe Mazzini, working to unify his fragmented country, which he wished to be republican and socialist. He insisted that patriotism was not incompatible with internationalism. In Hungary, Lajos Kossuth took a similar view as he led the struggle against Austrian domination.

And then there was Karl Marx, a man respected for his formidable intellect by his fellow revolutionaries, but actively disliked, not least for the scorn that he heaped on them. Born in 1818 in Trier in Prussia to a Jewish family converted to Christianity, Marx was supposed to become a lawyer. Instead, at university he became attracted to philosophy, especially to the radical group known as the Young Hegelians. They took the core themes of the great philosopher, Georg Wilhelm Friedrich Hegel, particularly his celebration of reason and freedom, while rejecting his idea that history had reached a satisfactory conclusion in the contemporary Prussian state. Marx's own break with the Young Hegelians came as he stressed the importance of looking at the material causes of historical change. Marx moved to France in 1843, where there was less censorship, and worked as a journalist. There he met his lifetime collaborator, Friedrich Engels, the son of a German industrialist, who was based in Manchester, a center of the industrial revolution. Engels had just published his own book, *The Condition of the Working Class in England in 1844*. They soon became partners. Engels provided Marx with financial support but also drafts for his articles, particularly on military history and theory, in which he had considerable expertise. They established their basic philosophy in *The German Ideology* (written in 1845–1846, although only first published in 1932), which denied the possibility of independent "morality, religion, metaphysics, all the rest of ideology and their corresponding forms of consciousness." Their claim was avowedly materialist. "Life," they insisted, "is not determined by consciousness, but consciousness by life."[3] In practice, as they would discover, the most perplexing problems for the revolutionary strategist could be found in the interplay between the two.

Marx's role in the revolutionary sphere was comparable to Clausewitz's in the military sphere. As Clausewitz provided a theory of war, Marx provided a theory of revolution, though not in quite so abstract a form. The actual influence of Clausewitz on Marx was slight. Engels read him more carefully, but not until the 1850s. If there was an influence it was because they were all operating in the same historicist tradition. In this respect, they shared—though not intimately—"historical and intellectual family ties."[4] Marx's theory demonstrated the role of revolutions in the dynamics of historical change, a consequence of the class struggles that accompanied the changing forms of production. While the theory gave hope to revolutionaries, it was less helpful in telling them what to do. Unlike Clausewitz, who worked out his theory as a result of the experience of war, Marx developed his theory prior to his experience of revolution, and then at once found its application problematic.

Nonetheless, his extraordinarily powerful theory impressed even his opponents during his lifetime and continued to exercise a hold over the socialist imagination. Revolutionaries of the twentieth century almost invariably traced their strategies and political programs back to Marx. His writings ranged from serious journalism to deep philosophy. Some important pieces were not published during his lifetime. Scholars and activists alike have explored the meanings and implications of key passages, searching for guidance in his commentaries on dimly remembered events and otherwise obscure philosophers. Appropriate quotes from the master gave legitimacy to otherwise dubious proposals, while the potential for competing claims about what Marx "really meant" caused numerous splits among those claiming to carry his banner. The problem with the interpretation of Clausewitz was that he was revising his only major work when he died. The problem with the interpretation of Marx was that he completed many works without ever suggesting that he was revising anything.

1848

Marx dismissed all the competing radical notions of the time. Religious imperatives, patriotic appeals, claims to civilized values and assertions of human rights, reactionary politics, and reformist gradualism were all illusions, reflecting either the crude interests of the current ruling class or the ideological residues of those that had gone before, leading the masses to rationalize their own enslavement. For Marx his theory was a vital weapon in itself, a source of confidence in the proletariat, a means of explaining to working people their potential and their destiny.

Strategy had to be grounded in class struggles. There was no point in trying to reconcile the irreconcilables through appeals to goodwill, justice, equality, or the boundless possibilities of the human will. The revolutionary process was about taking power according to prevailing economic and social conditions. Marx's theory inclined toward economic determinism which could argue for waiting for the historical process to reach its inevitable conclusion. But Marx was an activist and anything but fatalistic. At all times his aim was to develop the power of the working class. He cast himself as a strategist for the proletariat and viewed other classes as potential allies or opponents according to their ability to help or hinder its onward march.

On the eve of the revolutionary year of 1848, Marx, not yet 30, was asserting himself as a political leader with a distinctive approach, evidently a cut above the pamphleteers of his time. His forceful writing, combining intellectual rigor with heavy sarcasm, took on acknowledged leaders of socialist thought, especially those of the dreamier sort, and gained converts to his more scientific approach. He was not, however, a natural leader. Instead, he lacked charisma and empathy, and he never gained a huge popular following.

A lecturer more than an orator, argumentative rather than conciliatory, he preferred analysis to emotion. As so often on the left, the message of proletarian unity was combined with disdain for anything other than the course he advocated. He had no fear of splits. Better to have revolutionary clarity and vigor than an artificial accommodation with wrong-headed and muddled notions. Neither Marx nor Engels had any aptitude for coalition building at a personal level.

His first political association was with a traditional group of the left known as the League of the Just, which had all the clandestine affectations of a secret society. Marx and Engels, with the help of others, turned this into a more open association known as the Communist League in 1847, opening branches in Germany, France, and Switzerland. The former slogan "All Men are Brothers!" was replaced by "Proletarians of All Lands, United." The two men sought and gained a commission to provide a definitive communist manifesto. After six intensive weeks of writing, largely by Marx, it was finished in February 1848. Its famous opening statement—"A specter is haunting Europe, the specter of communism"—was meant to be ironic. Communism was not a specter, a ghostly apparition, but a real power and now in the open, calling for the "forcible overthrow of all existing social conditions." The particular list of demands, the sort with which political manifestos tend to be associated, was something of a rag-bag, put together in a great hurry as the publication deadline approached. Most important was the coherent presentation of the theory. "The history of all hitherto existing society," the manifesto explained, "is the history of class struggles." In the current epoch, class antagonism was being simplified "into two great hostile camps, into two great classes directly facing each other—bourgeoisie and proletariat." The unique advantages of communists was that they were the most "advanced and resolute" with the clearest understanding of "the lines of march, the conditions, and the ultimate general results of the proletarian movement." This was not a strategy for a state, nation, party, or institution— and certainly not for an individual. Rather it was for a class, defined in terms of the relationship to the means of production.

During 1848, revolution spread like an epidemic across Europe, with the most important outbreaks in France, Germany, Poland, Italy, and the Austrian Empire. Although the contagion began in Sicily, it was France that led the way in the intensity and seriousness of its own uprising. After the fall of Napoleon, France had returned to a monarchy, supposedly constitutional. As Charles X sought to acquire real power in 1830, he provoked a successful popular revolt, giving further support to the view that this was the one country in Europe where taking to the streets invariably made a difference. Charles's replacement, Louis Philippe, however, was not much better and maintained rule by a privileged elite. The barricades went up again in 1834, providing the backdrop for Victor Hugo's *Les Misérables*. This uprising was suppressed, but in February 1848, after soldiers had fired into a crowd and the mob converged on his palace, Louis Philippe abdicated and fled to England. Soon a provisional government proclaimed the Second French Republic, along with universal male suffrage and relief for the poor.

The revolution, however, soon suffered from both economic and political chaos as the wealthy fled, businesses closed down, and the members of the new government argued with each other. The French socialists were in their language and aspirations creatures of 1789, idealists rather than materialists, concerned with rights and justice rather than capitalism. In rural France, Paris was seen to be selfishly imposing new taxes to support a better city life. Soon demands were heard for more order. Conservatives gained control of the government and with the army began clearing out the barricades. The middle classes were content, but the working classes were left seething. By June, feeling abandoned, the workers of Paris once again put up the barricades. The government forces were ruthless and effective. For four days the workers fought, but in the end it was a massacre and they were defeated.

In Germany, the main arena for Marx and Engels during these heady months, the situation was complicated by the national question. Under the Congress of Vienna, with its stress on an orderly balances of power rather than disruptive self-determination, there was a loose German Federation, which brought together Austria, at its head, along with Prussia and 38 smaller states. To confuse matters further, the Hungarian territories were part of the Austrian Empire but not the German Confederation. The whole top-heavy arrangement, when combined with the authoritarian quality of the individual states, was designed to cause aggravation. The cause of German unity based on national sovereignty went hand in hand with demands for greater democracy.

The revolutions followed a general pattern. An upsurge of broadly based anger resulted in large demonstrations. Stones got thrown. Troops responded. Some demonstrators died. The anger swelled and barricades went up. Where streets were narrow and crowded, the barricades provided real barriers to state control though they were useless in wide thoroughfares and squares. Having lost control of the populated parts of their city centers, the authorities were caught between further bloodshed and political concessions. Divided among themselves, they made enough concessions to satisfy the crowds and then retired to regroup. At first, therefore, the revolutionaries had the "unity of purpose, across social and political divisions" and prevailed.[5] But insurrection was not the end of the story. There might have been opportunities to create new state institutions, including armed forces, to protect the revolution and take it forward, but the uncertainties in the new situation instead created tensions between radicals and moderates. The middle classes wanted reform but were petrified of revolution and persistent disorder. The left overreached itself and played to middle-class fears. There were debates about whether demands went too far or not far enough. Meanwhile the monarchs and their governments rediscovered their ruthlessness and organized their forces. In often bloody battles, the radicals were defeated, their leaders were thrown into prison or escaped into exile, and the population was cowed. In France it was different because of the abdication of Louis Philippe. But it was the exception that proved the rule—in revolution as in war, the quality and cohesion of the contending coalitions made a critical difference.

The initial stance of Marx and Engels for Europe in general and Germany in particular, following the logic of the recently published *Communist Manifesto*, was that workers should support a democratic revolution in preparation for the struggle for socialism. The larger the coalition challenging the old order the more likely it was to be successful. With universal suffrage and freedom of speech, the working classes would be better able to organize their own revolution. At the very least, a move to the next historical stage—even if it took time to complete—would allow the working class to grow in numbers, consciousness, organization, and militancy.[6] The risk was that the triumphant bourgeoisie would immediately move to suppress communist activity. To counter this, communists had to be constantly reminding the working class that even while working on a democratic revolution, relations with the bourgeoisie were bound to be hostile and antagonistic. Out of this came the idea of "permanent revolution," suggesting that there would be no time to relax after stage one of the democratic revolution before moving on immediately to the proletarian stage two.

The speed of events excited them. France was the country where the revolutionary tradition was strong and class struggles were sharp and decisive. As the first news came from Paris in February, Engels exclaimed: "By this glorious revolution the French proletariat has again placed itself at the head of the European movement. All honor to the workers of Paris!"[7] The subsequent disappointment was followed by more excitement with news of the June uprisings. Marx concluded that the great moment had come. "The insurrection [is] growing into the greatest revolution that has ever taken place," he wrote, "into a revolution of the proletariat against the bourgeoisie."[8] Even the crushed uprising was judged to be a sort of advance. By exposing the harsh reality of class struggle, it would forge a more complete communist consciousness. Whereas February had been the "beautiful revolution, the revolution of universal sympathy," June was "the ugly revolution, the repulsive revolution, because reality took the place of the phrase." Marx was not unique among revolutionaries in assuming that failure would make the working class more ferocious and determined rather than despairing and fatalistic.

By this time Marx and Engels were in Cologne. This was an area Marx knew, with a relatively substantial working class and an intense political situation. He established, using a timely inheritance, a campaigning newspaper, the *Neue Rheinische Zeitung* (New Rhenish Newspaper), to promote the radical cause. The paper began publication on June 1 and soon gained some six thousand subscribers. It reflected Marx's belief that the proletariat was too small to move alone and so must unite with the peasants and lower middle classes (petit bourgeoisie) against the bourgeoisie. This unity was unlikely to be achieved by urging socialism on small property holders. So weeks after publishing the *Communist Manifesto*, Marx and Engels made comparatively tame demands—a standard democratic program of a unified republic and universal male suffrage with some additional measures to address social issues. The first rally Marx organized was in a rural area where he brought workers and peasants together.[9]

At the time the main workers' organization was the Cologne Workers Council, with some eight thousand members. Its founder Andreas Gottschalk concentrated on improving social and working conditions rather than wider political action.[10] He judged Marx too extreme in his ultimate goals yet too moderate in his method. He had little sympathy for an orderly progression through revolutionary stages and scant interest in a democratic revolution. Marx argued for support of democratic candidates in elections. The alternative was "to preach Communism in a small corner magazine and found a small sect instead of a large party of action."[11] Gottschalk was for boycotting elections and pushing at once for socialism.

When Gottschalk was arrested in July 1848, Marx and Engels took over the council and redirected it to support the democratic movement. This new stance was not particularly popular, especially when coupled with a request for dues from members. Membership declined sharply. The revolution was turning out to be hard work. The workers were not necessarily progressive. They might be concerned about social conditions and annoyed with big business, but they also yearned for preindustrial days of work and had no appetite for deep class conflict. This lack of revolutionary fervor depressed Marx. He later observed wryly that if German revolutionaries ever stormed a railway station, they would buy a platform ticket.[12] He hoped that the news of the

June events in Paris would galvanize the German revolution. Instead it was the counterrevolutionaries who were emboldened.

As the German governments cracked down, Marx became more radical. From early 1849, he emphasized purely proletarian demands for a socialist republic. As 1850 began, he took heart from deteriorating economic conditions. His spring 1850 essay on "Class Struggles in France" raised the prospect of the proletariat imbued with a new revolutionary consciousness, matured by its defeats, and ready to accelerate the historical process. The events of the previous year meant that "different classes of French society had to count their epochs of development in weeks where they had previously counted them in half centuries."[13] The revolutionary process could create its own momentum, its ferocity shattering idealistic illusions and forging a sense of class interests and destiny in the face of the desperate measures of the ruling class. Prior to this time, Marx had backed demands for workers' rights; now he mocked them for leaving capitalism in place.

His optimism was premature. The mood was against more uprisings and bloodshed. Caution prevailed. The European economy recovered and the revolutionary moment slipped away. Marx and Engels were left politically isolated, with time to reflect on their disappointment. Then it got even worse. In December Louis-Napoleon Bonaparte, nephew of the Emperor, managed to get himself elected as the first president of the new republic, on a vaguely progressive platform. As president, Bonaparte worked with the conservative assembly, but an impasse developed over his continuing interest in social reform. In November 1851, he mounted a coup d'état and a year later he abolished the Second Republic and established himself as emperor.

Engels remarked to Marx how Louis-Napoleon's coup d'état was a travesty of the Eighteenth Brumaire (the date in the French Revolutionary Calendar when the first Napoleon seized power in a coup). This was a re-enactment, "once as grand tragedy and the second time as rotten farce."[14] Marx picked up on this theme in one of his most brilliant and sardonic pieces of historical writing, *The Eighteenth Brumaire of Louis Napoleon*. The proletariat had allowed itself to be tempted by revolutionary activity and so ran "ahead of itself, positing solutions which under the circumstances, degree of education and relations could not be immediately realized." It had lost its way, abandoned by the fearful petit bourgeoisie while the peasantry was still besotted with the Napoleonic legend. Only the conservatives acted on their true interests. Prior to the uprisings, Marx and Engels had recognized the fear of disorder as the wedge that might divide the revolutionary working classes from the rest. But having broken with old-style social democracy, Marx was now inclined to blame the failure on the leadership of the radical movements.

"Men make their own history," he observed in a famous passage from the *Eighteenth Brumaire*, "but they do not make it as they please; they do not make it under self-selected circumstances, but under circumstances existing already, given and transmitted from the past." This was a profound though simple strategic insight. Individuals worked to shape their own destinies but their choices were conditioned by the situations in which they found themselves and the way that they thought about the situation. "The tradition of all dead generations weighs like a nightmare on the brains of the living." At the moment when men started to engage in revolution, "creating something that did not exist before," they suffered from a failure of imagination, looking back rather than forward. They "anxiously conjure up the spirits of the past to their service, borrowing from them names, battle slogans, and costumes in order to present this new scene in world history in time-honored disguise and borrowed language." The original French Revolution appeared first in the image of the Roman Republic and then the Roman Empire, while the Revolution of 1848 could only parody that of 1789. Somehow Marx urged the "social revolution of the nineteenth century" to find its "poetry" from the future rather than the past.

Marx himself was also guilty of this. As MacGuire notes, "it is difficult to escape the all-pervading influence of the French Revolution of 1789 on Marx's thought."[15] It set a benchmark against which all else was judged: the drama of the storming of the Bastille, the subsequent revolutionary justice, and the readiness to rethink everything including the calendar and forms of greeting—to reconceive the world from the bottom up rather than the top down. This was both the prototype and archetype for a contemporary revolution. While trying to lead Cologne workers in 1848, Marx called the Jacobin Convention the "lighthouse of all revolutionary epochs." During this period he constantly referred to the images and lessons of 1789, from the role of peasants to models of leadership and the likelihood of a European War. His strategy for the German revolution in 1848 was encapsulated by the phrase "the French Revolution radicalized."[16] The *Eighteenth Brumaire* itself depends on the comparison.

Marx was also trapped by a theoretical construct developed prior to the revolution that turned out, at first test, to be a poor guide to political practice. His theory offered a compelling narrative with which to address the proletariat and explain its true interests and historical role, on the ascendant and destined to outlast all others, but failed when considering the proletariat of 1848, small and politically immature, one class in a wider configuration, needing allies if it was to make any progress. There were four basic problems with his construct.

First, class had to be more than a social or economic category but an identity willingly accepted by its members. The proletariat had to be not just a class *in* itself, but also a self-aware political force, a class *for* itself. This was the problem of consciousness. The Manifesto referred to the eventual "moment of enthusiasm ... in which this class fraternizes and fuses with society." But would this class identity develop purely as a result of shared experiences and suffering, or depend on constant prompting by communists, or be forged, as at times Marx seemed to think in 1848, through the actual experience of revolution?

Second, consciousness-raising as a class required undermining the competing claims of nation and religion, yet for many workers there was no inconsistency with being a socialist, a patriot, and a Christian. Some of the most important revolutionary figures of the time, such as Mazzini and Kossuth, based their appeals first on nationalism. The cause of Polish emancipation from Russia was widely embraced, including by Marx. The Manifesto insisted on "the common interests of the proletariat independently of nationalism" but Marx was also well aware of national differences in terms of economic and political structures. Indeed he could generalize about national character in ways that would now be considered outrageous. Engels was even more prone to ethnic stereotypes.

Third, despite the Manifesto's claims of a developing polarization the class structure in 1848 was extremely complex. It contained groups who might be historically doomed but for the moment were very much alive. They made possible a wide range of political configurations and outcomes. Marx assumed that "the small manufacturers, merchants and rentiers, the handicraftsmen and the peasants, all these classes fall into the proletariat."[17] But these groups did not necessarily identify with the urban working classes and had their own interests. The petit bourgeoisie were exasperating to Engels: "invariably full of bluster and loud protestations, at times even extreme as far as talking goes" but "faint-hearted, cautious and calculating" in the face of danger and then "aghast, alarmed and wavering" when matters became serious.[18] The peasants were particularly hard to call. Were they as nostalgic as the aristocrats for the old feudal order that was now slipping away, or were they being radicalized by new forms of rural ownership? The tension was evident in the Manifesto which presented the peasantry as reactionary and obsolete but then called for an alliance between workers and peasants in Germany. The artisans, petit bourgeoisie, shop-keepers, and landlords were also all present in significant numbers and with their own political views. Even the working classes in 1848 were a mixed grouping, far more likely to be found in small workshops than large factories, and so viewing mechanization as part of the problem rather than a mark of progress, as a source of further misery more than a necessary stage in economic development. After the failed revolutions Marx blamed the degenerate lumpenproletariat for providing the militia to defeat the June uprising (although actually the mobile guard's social composition was representative of the wider working class).

Fourth, the greatest confusion came from the Manifesto's presumption that a bourgeois revolution must precede the proletarian. This would create the conditions for the growth of the proletariat and their consciousness of their capacity to take control of industrial society. But that was some way down the line. The immediate strategic implication was to urge the working classes to back the middle classes in their revolution. For the bourgeoisie, the course was clear. They could subvert and circumvent the established order through their entrepreneurial creativity. Eventually political affairs would catch up and find space for this dynamic class. There might be gain in this for the proletariat in the form of greater democracy. The promise, however, was not of opportunities for an evolutionary working-class advance but, if the theory was correct, further exploitation and immiseration. As Gottschalk put it when accusing Marx of finding the misery of the workers and the hunger of the poor a matter of only "scientific and doctrinaire interest," why should the "men of the proletariat" make a revolution and spill their blood, to "escape the hell of the Middle Ages by precipitating ourselves voluntarily into the purgatory of decrepit capitalist rule in order to arrive at the cloudy heaven of your Communist Credo."[19]

The Strategy of Insurrection

After the economic distress, so eagerly anticipated in 1849, failed to materialize, Marx and Engels judged that uprisings were unlikely to succeed so long as the army remained loyal to the state. If one did succeed, possibly in France, then it could only survive if it triggered a response elsewhere and, most importantly, could put together a coalition of revolutionary countries to defeat the armies of the reactionaries. As Marx settled down to study political economy, Engels concentrated on military affairs in an effort to assess the potential balance of forces between revolutionary and counterrevolutionary countries. His approach was unsentimental and mechanical. "The more I mug up on war, the greater my contempt for heroism—a fatuous expression, heroism, and never heard on the lips of a proper soldier."[20] Engels doubted that a single country could reproduce Napoleon's early successes. The modern art of war, based on mobility and mass, was now "universally known." Indeed the French were no longer the "pre-eminent bearers" of this tradition. His conclusion was not encouraging. Superiority in strategy and tactics, Engels concluded, would not necessarily favor the revolution. A proletarian revolution would have its own military expression and give rise to new methods of warfare, reflecting the elimination of class distinctions. But this was likely, Engels assumed, to intensify rather than diminish the mass character and mobility of armies and was, at any rate, many years away. In the first instance, when it came to defending the revolution from internal enemies, the bulk of the army would still need to come from "the mob and the peasants." In such a case, the revolution would adopt the means and methods of modern warfare. And so "the big battalions [would] win." Marx respected Engels for his military knowledge but was far less inclined to stress the military factor over others. This became apparent during the American Civil War. Although both were frustrated with the North, Marx was always more confident that its superior material strength would win out in the end, while Engels worried about the Confederacy's superior mastery of military arts. In the summer of 1862, Engels was convinced that "it is all up," but Marx disagreed, observing that "you let yourself be swayed a little too much by the military aspect of things."[21]

In June 1851, Engels wrote to Joseph Weydemeyer, a former military officer and close friend who later that year emigrated to the United States, explaining that he needed the "elementary knowledge... necessary to enable me to understand and correctly evaluate historical facts of a military nature." This included maps and manuals. He asked for an opinion of Clausewitz and also of "Monsieur Jomini, of whom the French make such a fuss?"[22] He read Clausewitz but found Jomini more reliable. In 1853, again writing to Weydemeyer, Engels described Prussian military literature as "positively the worst there is," noting in particular that "despite many fine things, I can't really bring myself to like that natural genius, Clausewitz."[23] By 1857, he had warmed to Clausewitz despite his "strange way of philosophizing," noting with approval Clausewitz's suggestion that fighting is to war what cash payment is to trade.[24]

The interest in military matters also reflected the split which ended the short life of the Communist League. This came in 1850 as a result of Marx's doubts about the imminence of revolution. The opposition was led by August von Willich, a former military officer described by Engels as a "brave, cold-blooded, skilful soldier" though a "boring ideologist."[25] In London, where the émigrés now congregated, Willich was more popular among exiles, sharing tavern life and optimistic talk of returning to liberate Germany. He presented himself as an impatient man of action compared to the elitist and patronizing "literary characters" like Marx and Engels. Whereas they seemed more interested in reading than revolution, confining their work to education and propaganda, and were prepared to support a democratic push, Willich's followers had no interest in supporting bourgeois elements to power but aimed immediately for supreme power. Preparations for revolutionary war began, with drills, shooting practice, and a hierarchical, military-style organization.

Marx was always hostile to the view, most associated with Blanqui, that revolution was a matter of will and military skill as much as material conditions. There was no point urging people to fight against hopeless odds.[26] "While we say to the workers, you have fifteen or twenty of fifty years of civil and national wars to go through, not just to alter conditions but to alter yourselves and qualify for political power," Marx explained to Willich, "you on the contrary say: we must obtain power at once or we might as well lay ourselves down to sleep."[27] In September 1851, Marx wrote to Engels, reporting comments by Willich's colleague Gustav Techow on the lessons of the events of 1849.[28] According to Techow, revolution could not work if confined to a single faction or even nation. It had to become general. Barricades could only signal popular resistance and test a government. Far more important was organization for proper war, which required a disciplined army: "This alone makes an offensive possible and it is only in the offensive that victory lies." National constituent assemblies could not take responsibility because of their internal divisions, arguing about matters that could only be truly decided after victory and foolishly expecting an army to be democratic. Enthusiastic volunteers would stand little chance against disciplined and well-fed soldiers. The revolutionary army would need compulsion, "Iron rigor of discipline." In Engels's dismissive assessment, Techow was postponing the struggle between different classes and perspectives until after the war. A military dictator would suppress internal politics. Yet Techow had no idea about how to recruit such a large army.[29] A revolution in 1852 would be stuck on the defensive, confined to "empty proclamations" or doomed military expeditions.

In September 1952, Engels looked back to the Frankfurt-based German National Assembly from May 1849, which—with leftists and democrats largely in charge—had effectively challenged the three largest states of Austria, Prussia, and Bavaria. There was a strong movement for mass action, including insurrections in Dresden and Baden (in which Engels and Willich participated). The National Assembly might have called upon people to take up arms in its support. Instead it allowed the insurrections to be suppressed. These events prompted Engels to observe:

> Now, insurrection is an art quite as much as war or any other, and subject to certain rules of proceeding, which, when neglected, will

produce the ruin of the party neglecting them. . . . Firstly, never play with insurrection unless you are fully prepared to face the consequences of your play. Insurrection is a calculus with very indefinite magnitudes, the value of which may change every day; the forces opposed to you have all the advantage of organization, discipline, and habitual authority: unless you bring strong odds against them you are defeated and ruined. Secondly, the insurrectionary career once entered upon, act with the greatest determination, and on the offensive. The defensive is the death of every armed rising; it is lost before it measures itself with its enemies. Surprise your antagonists while their forces are scattering, prepare new successes, however small, but daily; keep up the moral ascendancy which the first successful rising has given to you; rally those vacillating elements to your side which always follow the strongest impulse, and which always look out for the safer side; force your enemies to a retreat before they can collect their strength against you; in the words of Danton, the greatest master of revolutionary policy yet known, DE L'AUDACE, DE L'AUDACE, ENCORE DE L'AUDACE![30]

The message was that once a revolutionary process had begun, it had to be sustained. It needed momentum and to stay on the offensive. Hesitate and all would be lost. The initial uprising would not be sufficient. The fight would have to be seen through to the complete defeat of the counterrevolution, which, of course, could require full-scale war with reactionary countries. Engels accepted the full logic of the war of annihilation, should the military course be chosen.

The question this raised, however, was what to do if this course led to certain defeat. If revolutionary strategy was a matter for cool calculation, this would argue for prudence and patience. But if revolutionary strategy was a matter of temperament, reflecting a deep commitment to transformational change as a matter of urgency, restraint could feel unbearable. Either way, as we shall see in the next chapter, radical politics could be intensely frustrating, either living with injustice while waiting for a moment when change might become possible, or else striking out against injustice even when the cause was hopeless.

| Herzen and Bakunin

People don't storm the Bastille because history proceeds by zigzags.
History proceeds by zigzags because when people have had enough, they
storm the Bastille.

—Alexander Herzen

ALEXANDER HERZEN WAS a rare combination of a commitment to radical change with a fear of the consequences of reckless action. He is the hero of playwright Tom Stoppard's remarkable trilogy, *The Coast of Utopia*, in which Stoppard portrays the circle of mainly Russian radical émigrés who moved in and out of Herzen's life during the middle of the nineteenth century. Herzen was born in 1812 in Moscow, just before Borodino. An illegitimate child of the aristocracy, he became a brilliant writer and conversationalist, a shrewd observer of the human condition, and—while in exile—an influential agitator for change in Russia.[1] Stoppard's plays were held together by the interaction between the personal and public dramas of Herzen's life, including his wife's tempestuous affair with a German revolutionary. The intellectual meat came from the constant question about how to stimulate and direct radical political change. In Stoppard's plays the great revolutionary figures of this time look forward with enthusiasm and without qualms to a coming revolution that in reality filled Herzen with deep foreboding.

Stoppard draws on the philosopher Isaiah Berlin, also a fan of Herzen, in portraying a man who "favored the individual over the collective, the actual over the theoretical," and could not accept that "future bliss justified present sacrifice and bloodshed." For Herzen, according to Stoppard, "there was no libretto or destination, and there was always as much in front as behind."[2] When a radical spoke of the "Spirit of History, the ceaseless March of Progress," Herzen exclaimed, "A curse on your capital letters! We're asking people to spill their blood—at least spare them the conceit that they are acting out the biography of an abstract noun."[3]

With his liberal skepticism and general distrust of intellectuals on a mission, Stoppard did not do full justice to Herzen's libertarian socialism.[4] Until the emancipation of the serfs in 1861, Herzen was playing an important role in generating pressure for change in Russia. His paper, *The Bell*, was required reading among intellectual and elite circles in Russia. He produced this in conjunction with his close friend, the poet Nicholas Ogarev. Many readers, even from the elite, shared his sense of humiliation that Russia was the backward country of Europe, still mired in feudalism and unable to join in the economic, social, and political dynamism of the time. Herzen's method was to expose scandals, mock censorship, and reveal abuses, concentrating on the reasons why reform was necessary and not on how it should be achieved. He was even prepared to invest hopes in Tsar Alexander, to whom he made direct appeals. At first this was politically astute, making it possible to condemn the government vigorously without appearing to call for revolution.

This stance led to disputes with revolutionaries who could see no reason to trust the Tsar and accused him of lacking a program. He particularly quarreled with the nihilists. This was a group described by another member of Herzen's circle, the novelist Ivan Turgenev, in his 1862 book *Fathers and Children*. A nihilist "does not bow down before any authority, and accepts no principles on trust, however much respect they may enjoy." The nihilists were resolutely materialist, refusing to believe anything that could not be shown to be true. All abstract thought and aesthetics were decried. Their sole interest was to create a new society. One of their intellectual leaders was Nicholas Chernyshevsky. His novel *What Is to Be Done?*, written while in prison in 1862 and escaping the censor only by mistake, was generally given low marks as literature. It nonetheless became a handbook for young zealots, demonstrating how revolutionaries should steel themselves for the struggles ahead. Whatever Herzen's personal views, his press in London was responsible for the covert publication of many of the key nihilist texts.

Stoppard staged his version of a real encounter between Herzen and Chernyshevsky in 1859. Chernyshevsky had once been an admirer but now found Herzen an irritating "dilettanti of revolutionary ideas." His wealth and social position allowed him a disengaged approach to the struggle and to embrace the delusion of reform, that authority might undermine itself. For Chernyshevsky, "only the axe will do." Herzen considered such arguments divisive. He could not endorse a stance that would serve the government by driving the reformists into the arms of the conservatives. "[A]re we ridding the people of the yoke so that they can live under a dictatorship of the intellectuals?" Better to move forward by peaceful steps than have blood flowing in the gutters.[5]

The Tsar's Emancipation of the Serfs of March 1861 was the turning point. Herzen made this an occasion for a big party at his London home, but the celebration was soon muted. Not only were the details of the declaration a deep disappointment, revealing it to be something of a fraud, but it was followed almost immediately by a massacre in Warsaw by Russian troops. Herzen's sympathy was with the peasants and the Poles, and his anger ran deep. Having worked to hold together a reforming coalition, he could now no longer do so. The betrayal was too great. He broke with the liberals, who feared both restlessness at home and an uprising in Poland. He wrote in *The Bell* in November 1861 that "a moan is growing, a murmur rising—it is the first roar of the ocean waves, which seethe, fraught by storms, after the terrible wearisome calm. *To the people! To the people!*"[6] This may have been more exasperation than a political program, but it was interpreted as a call to revolution. Momentarily Herzen did wonder about whether to support revolution, but he could not bring himself to back leaders who claimed to speak for a people they so evidently disdained. He refused to accept talk of the backwardness of the peasants and so moved toward populism, coming to trust more in the wisdom of ordinary people than that of the intelligentsia. "Manna does not fall from heaven," he observed, "it grows from the soil." Unable to abandon either his radical beliefs or his reluctance to back a self-appointed revolutionary elite, despised by both moderates and extremists, he saw with great clarity and poignancy the gap between ends and means:

> Like knight-errants in the stories, who have lost their way, we were hesitating at the cross-roads. Go to the right, and you will lose your horse, but you will be safe yourself; go to the left and your horse will be safe but you will perish; go forward and everyone will abandon you; go back—that was impossible.[7]

Bakunin

In Stoppard's trilogy, Marx made a cameo appearance as rude and boorish. In a dream sequence, Marx was shown delivering choice epithets for the other leading revolutionaries of 1853 ("flatulent bag of festering tripe," less use than the "boil on my arse," "unctuous jackass," "impudent wind-bag").[8] Certainly at this time Marx and Engels had become disenchanted with many of their fellow revolutionaries. Late in his life Engels described how after a failed revolution, "party groups of various shades are formed, which accuse each other of having driven the cart into the mud, of treason and of all other possible mortal sins.... Naturally, disappointment follows disappointment ... recriminations accumulate and result in general bickering."[9]

Looming larger in Stoppard's account, as in Herzen's life, was Mikhail Bakunin, appearing as a lovable rogue, a poseur full of contradictions, always asking for money, in a fantasy world of his own yet of undoubted charisma. Having been an insurrectionary tourist in 1848, Bakunin was imprisoned in Russia and then sent to exile, from which he escaped. Thereafter he moved from one promising revolutionary setting to another, elaborating a distinctive anarchist doctrine as he did so. He shared much with Marx: rebels from comfortable backgrounds, drawn to Hegelian philosophy during their formative years, engaged with the stirrings of 1848, and enthusiasts for a working class neither knew well. They both studied philosophy in Berlin in 1840 but did not meet until 1844. Their paths crossed a number of times over the following years, including during the heady days of 1848.[10] Bakunin distrusted German intellectuals and their tendency for pedantry, but not as much as Marx distrusted Russians, which is one reason he refused to have anything to do with Herzen.

Bakunin could be an original and penetrating theorist, but he was impatient, often left work unfinished, and was prone to contradictory statements. When it came to political economy, he was a disciple of Marx's. He even contemplated (and received an advance for) a Russian translation of *Capital*. At times Marx appreciated Bakunin's energy and commitment. Though Bakunin believed that Marx had denounced him in 1853 as a Russian agent, they patched over their differences. In the end their effective political careers concluded as they rowed furiously over the direction of the revolutionary movement. "He called me a sentimental idealist and he was right," acknowledged Bakunin, "I called him vain, treacherous and cunning, and I too was right."[11]

Herzen's most quoted description of Bakunin conveys a formidable physical impression, how his "activity, his laziness, his appetite and everything else, like his gigantic stature and everlasting sweat he was in, everything, in fact, was on a superhuman scale ... a giant with his leonine head and tousled mane."[12] In a telling description of the professional revolutionary of the time, Herzen refers to a "passion for propaganda, for agitation, for demagogy, if you like, to incessant activity in founding and organizing plots and conspiracies and establishing relations and in ascribing immense significance to them" but also to a "readiness to risk his life, and recklessness in accepting all the consequences."[13] His supporters objected, both then and now, to the idea that he was borderline deranged and attributed his wild destructive urges to his curious upbringing in an aristocratic idyll.[14] Herzen, who liked and admired Bakunin, pointed to a different sort of tension, an intense version of one facing all revolutionaries caught between ambitious ends and meager means. The stage was far too small for the role Bakunin wanted to play, and he filled it too easily. "His nature was a heroic one," observed Herzen, "left out of work by the course of history." Bakunin "incubated the germ of a colossal activity for which there is no demand." He admitted to "a love for the fantastic, for unusual, unheard-of-adventures, for undertakings that open up a boundless horizon and whose end no one can foresee."[15] Opposing all states, and believing in the wholesome spontaneity of the unfettered masses, he could still concoct plans for clandestine societies organized on hierarchical lines. In practice a poor conspirator, he could still imagine himself as a "secret director," working upon the masses and then on post-revolutionary society as an "invisible force."

The First International and the Paris Commune

Neither Marx nor Bakunin was responsible for the formation of the International Workingmen's Association (IWA), which eventually became known as the First International. It was set up in 1864 to encourage cooperation among workers' associations with the aim of promoting "the protection, the rise, and the complete emancipation of the working class." It was non-sectarian and broad-based, drawing in the numerous refugees based in London and the kaleidoscope of philosophies prevalent at the time, including democrats and anarchists, internationalists and nationalists, idealists and materialists, moderates and extremists.

For Marx this was an opportunity to return to actual politics. He approved of the international links and the focus on the proletariat. This created opportunities to develop a more acute class consciousness and meant that it was worth putting to one side misgivings about the IWA's narrow popular base and ideologically suspect comrades. Marx soon became the International's wordsmith, managing to stay sensitive to its diverse currents of opinion. He observed to Engels how he had "to phrase matters" so as to incorporate his opinion in a form "acceptable to the present point of view of the labor movement." It would take time "before the re-awakened movement will be in a position to use the bold language of yore." When drafting the association's Address to the Working Classes, he even used phrases about "duty" and "right" or "truth, morality, and justice," though they were "placed in such a way that they can do little harm."[16] The final product was therefore measured and cautious, quite different from the assertiveness of the Manifesto. His natural inclination to collectivism and centralization was toned down. Rather than lead from the front, for the moment he was pushing from behind.

Bakunin's years of prison and exile meant that he was unaffected by the post-1848 gloom among émigrés, and he did not really engage with the IWA for four years after its foundation. Over this time his position became more explicitly anarchist. He made his entry into the association at a congress in Basel, with Marx absent. The powerful impression he created led Marx to see him not so much as an errant comrade but as a dangerous rival. Marx had been arguing with anarchists since the 1840s when he took on Proudhon, thereby ensuring a rift between two wings of the same movement that was never healed. Proudhon's strength lay in his writings, as his strategic judgment was always problematic. He had thrown himself into the uprisings in Paris in 1848, as a writer and speaker, but also briefly entered the National Assembly. This unhappy experience, after which he complained about the isolation and fear of the people that marked his fellow representatives, left him more enthusiastic about economic than political progress. In 1852, he had decided that Louis-Napoleon could lead France down a revolutionary road, a position he later abandoned. Although he retained a following in France, Proudhon drifted to the right in his views, becoming increasingly xenophobic, loathing direct action while recoiling from strikes and elections. Rather than wrestle with how to mobilize the masses to topple the state, he urged withdrawal from organized politics of all forms to concentrate on educating people in the ways of mutual support among free men.[17] "The Workers, organized among themselves, without the assistance of the capitalist, and marching by Work to the conquest of the world, will at no time need a brusque uprising, but will become all, by invading all, through the force of principle."[18] So he dealt with the problem of strategy by not advocating any course that needed one.

Bakunin represented a quite different strand of anarchism. He rejected all forms of collectivism but enthusiastically embraced revolution, asserting the creativity of destruction. "Only life itself, freed from all governmental and doctrinaire fetters and given the full liberty of spontaneous action, is capable of creation." A compelling orator, he was a much more charismatic figure than Proudhon. He also had his own international network of activists. Marx accused Bakunin of maintaining a clandestine organization independent of the IWA. There was some truth to the charge: Bakunin was maintaining his network in order to give the movement as a whole a surreptitious push in the preferred direction. At the same time, Marx's campaign was tendentious and spiteful. The net result was to finish off the IWA. Eventually in 1872, Marx was able to get both Bakunin expelled and the seat of the association's general council moved to the United States, which effectively led to its demise.

Their differences were brought to a head by the Paris Commune of 1871, a defining event for revolutionaries, comparable in significance to 1848 and just as unsuccessful. It followed the Franco-Prussian War. As Louis-Napoleon was defeated, radicals took over in France, declared the Third Republic, and continued to resist. After five months, Paris fell in January 1871. The drama was still not over. The city was in a fevered state. The people were well armed and the radicals took control. Prime Minister Adolphe Thiers from the Center-Right government fled to Versailles, where he regrouped with those of his troops, police, and administrators who had not gone over to the radicals. In Paris, a central committee arranged elections for a commune. Sundry radicals and socialists stepped forward, some looking back to the glories of 1789 while others looked forward to the new communist utopia. Louis Blanqui's election as president was largely symbolic as the government had already arrested him. The red flag was flown, the old Republican Calendar reinstated, church and state separated, and modest social reforms introduced. Feminist and socialist ideas were actively canvassed. In the leadership, anarchists, revolutionary socialists, and sundry republicans worked reasonably well together. It did not last. Thiers's new army eventually found a way into the city and overwhelmed a brave but hopeless defense, conducted with little central coordination and direction. Paris was retaken and reprisals began, with estimates of initial executions as high as twenty thousand.

Neither Marxists nor Bakuninists played a major role in the Commune. "They owed more to the commune than the commune owed to either of them."[19] Marx's *The Civil War in France* claimed the Commune as a prototype for a revolutionary government, the "dictatorship of the proletariat," a term that later acquired more sinister overtones. The Commune demonstrated that the working class could hold power but also the difficulty of using the established state machinery for its own purposes. The Communards had "lost precious moments" organizing democratic elections rather than instantly finishing off the Versailles government once and for all. This, Marx thought, might have been achieved by conscripting the able-bodied and having a centralized command. Bakunin's view was quite different. The whole meaning of the Commune lay in its spontaneity and decentralization to workers' councils. Marx's idea of a hard state under strong central direction appalled him.

He warned of the "ruling of the majority by the minority in the name of the alleged superior intelligence of the second." In retrospect, Bakunin's warnings about the rise of a new elite and the oppressive role of the state under socialism looked prescient.[20] They flowed naturally from his conviction that the state was the root of all evil, and from his opposition to anybody setting themselves up as a power over others.

Marx denied that he considered a strong coercive state necessary for the indefinite future. It would eventually, as Engels put it, "wither away." According to the theory the emancipation of the proletariat would be the emancipation of all humanity. As a means of class domination, the state would become redundant. The theory offered comfort, but Marx was never sentimental about the exercise of political power or under any illusions about how vicious class struggle could become. The bourgeoisie would not hand over power willingly and they would fight to get it back if it was taken from them. That could, and probably would, involve war with reactionary states. So, in the short term, Marx did not doubt for one minute that the proletariat would have to fight to hold on to power. This was the lesson of the Commune. To believe that the revolution could survive without central direction and coercive capacity was naïve. For Engels, revolution was "certainly the most authoritarian thing there is; it is the act whereby one part of the population imposes its will upon the other part by means of rifles, bayonets and cannon—authoritarian means, if such there be at all."[21]

For his part, Bakunin considered Marx naïve to believe that a state so forged would ever wither away. States could be expressions of any sectional interests and not just classes. Even well-intentioned revolutionary elites were capable of authoritarianism and deploying state power to maintain and develop their own position. "I am not a communist," he explained, "because communism concentrates and absorbs all the powers of society in the state; it necessarily ends with the concentration of property in the hands of the state." Instead, Bakunin argued for "the abolition of the state, the radical elimination of the principle of authority and the tutelage of the state." He sought "free association from the bottom up, not by authority from the top down."[22] The challenge was not to those who wielded political power but to the very idea of political power. He acknowledged that the revolution must contend with "a military force that now respects nothing, is armed with the most terrible weapons of destruction." Against such a "wild beast," another beast was needed, also wild but more just, "an organized uprising of the people; a social revolution which, like the military reaction, spares nothing and stops at nothing."[23]

Though this approach "allowed power to be studied in its own right,"[24] it assumed that revolutions could be conducted in a way that abolished political power rather than transferred it. Power to Bakunin was an artificial construct, an unnecessary and therefore immoral imposition on humanity. Without power, humanity would be in a more authentic state, with laws reflecting its essentially harmonious nature. Only this optimism could deny anarchy its connotations of chaos and disorder, with less potential-fulfilling liberation and more chronic insecurity. But if the revolution was against power how could it succeed? Bakunin solved the problem for himself by describing a restricted role for a professional revolutionary, though he still left himself open to charges of hypocrisy. Though objecting to power in principle, he seemed to fancy it for himself, as he was always at the heart of these conspiracies. In 1870, for example, he contemplated the "creation of a secret organization of up to 70 members" who would aid the revolution in Russia and form the "collective dictatorship of the secret organization." This organization would "direct the people's revolution" through "an invisible force—recognized by no one, imposed by no one—through which the collective dictatorship of our organization will be all the mightier, the more it remains invisible and unacknowledged, the more it remains without any official legality and significance."

Bakunin was, of course, operating in a milieu infested by government agents, where survival depended on concealing intentions and networks. The conspiracies were also largely products of Bakunin's lively imagination. Few of his plans came close to serious implementation. Nonetheless, Bakunin put some effort into defining the special role for professional revolutionaries. True, they must be exceptional, constituting a "sort of revolutionary general staff composed of individuals who are devoted, energetic, intelligent, and most important, sincere and lacking ambition and vanity, capable of serving as intermediaries between the revolutionary idea and popular instinct."[25] The metaphor of the general staff was revealing in itself: this was after all the strategy-making body of a conventional army. Moreover, Bakunin's critique of orthodox political activity always warned how "the best, the purest, the most intelligent, the most disinterested, the most generous, will always and certainly be corrupted by this profession [of government]." This is why he opposed participation in elections. Good people were not enough.

The way out of the logical morass was to stress how limited a role professional revolutionaries could play, whatever their intentions. For Marx, revolutions were positive, constructive events, arising naturally out of shifts in underlying economic conditions. Bakunin described them as supremely unpredictable affairs, with deep causes that could neither be manipulated nor necessarily recognized by those encouraging or opposing them. Revolutions "make themselves, produced by the force of affairs, by the movement of the masses—then they burst out, instigated by what often appear to be frivolous causes." They emerged out of "historical currents which, continuously and usually slowly, flow underground and unseen within the popular strata, increasingly embracing, penetrating, and undermining them until they emerge from the ground and their turbulent waters break all barriers and destroy everything that impedes their course." In this respect they were not set in motion by individuals or organizations. Instead, they "occur independently of all volition and conspiracy and are always brought about by the force of circumstances."[26]

It is interesting to note how close this view of history was to Tolstoy's. Both conveyed a sense of events emerging out of the individual responses of many people to their circumstances in ways that could neither be predicted nor manipulated. The influence was quite possible. Tolstoy's *War and Peace* was written during the 1860s, appearing first in a serialized form and then in its final version in 1869. Both men were also influenced by Proudhon. Proudhon showed Tolstoy his own new book, *War and Peace*, when the two met in Brussels in 1861. Tolstoy borrowed the title as an act of homage.[27] His own brand of Christian anarchism, which took inspiration from the simple faith of the peasantry, was close to Proudhon's vision of a new society developing from the bottom up.

Unlike Tolstoy or Proudhon, Bakunin did see even modest scope for human agency in providing direction to revolutions. There was a role for bringing together the popular instinct—the people were socialist without realizing it—with revolutionary thought. If they did not, then they might be taken in by those who sought a dictatorship, using the people as "a stepping-stone for their own glory." As one biographer put it, "the intellectual should play the junior role in this process, acting, at best, as helpful editor while the writing of the script was the work of the people themselves."[28] This was a comforting hypothesis but as much of a fudge as Marx's claim that the proletarian dictatorship would be no more than a transitional phase. The idea that there were forms of authority and influence so pure and natural that they could be distinguished from artificial and oppressive forms depended on an extremely simplistic view of power. Politicians always claimed to be no more than servants of the people, listening as much as leading, but in practice—as Bakunin observed—things often turned out differently.

A contrast between the two approaches can be found in their responses to the events of September 1870 as Prussia occupied France. Marx, writing for the IWA, used contemptuous language but his analysis was tight, well informed, and subtle, describing the maneuvers which led to the end of the Second Empire and the German war of conquest. He wanted the German working class, which had supported the war, to insist on an honorable peace with France, while the French working class must escape their fascination with the past. He noted presciently that if the working classes stayed passive, "the present tremendous war will be but the harbinger of still deadlier international feuds." The overall perspective was that of a caring spectator.

Bakunin's *Letters to a Frenchman on the Present Crisis*, addressed to no one in particular, was long and rambling but deeply engaged. One core theme was that the German army could be defeated and another was that this required an alliance between the working class and the peasants. Together, the French people could not be conquered by any "army in the world, however powerful, however well organized and equipped with the most extraordinary weapons." If the bourgeoisie had not been so pathetic, there could already have been "a formidable insurrection by guerrillas or, if necessary, by brigands" against the Germans. Much now depended on the peasants. Though they could be ignorant, egoistic, and reactionary, they retained "their native energy and simple unsophisticated folkways" and would react badly to the "ideas and propaganda which are enthusiastically accepted by the city workers." Yet the gulf between the two was really only a "misunderstanding." The peasants could be educated away from their religion, devotion to the emperor, and support for private property if only the workers made the effort.

As the actual moment of revolution had arrived, it was too late for organization-building or the "pretentious scholastic vocabulary of doctrinaire socialism." Instead, this was a time to "embark on stormy revolutionary seas, and from this very moment we must spread our principles, not with words but with deeds, for this is the most popular, the most potent, and the most irresistible form of propaganda." Once stirred up the peasants could be incited "to destroy, by direct action, every political, judicial, civil, and military institution, and to establish and organize anarchy through the whole countryside." At such times it "is as though an electric current were galvanizing the whole society, uniting the feelings of temperamentally different individuals into one common sentiment, forging totally different minds and wills into one." Alternatively it might be one of those "somber, disheartening, disastrous epochs, when everything reeks of decadence, exhaustion, and death, presaging the exhaustion of public and private conscience. These are the ebb tides following historic catastrophes."

Propaganda of the Deed

This notion of the "propaganda of the deed" reflected Bakunin's growing impatience with theory and a conviction that only dramatic action could penetrate the dim consciousness of the befuddled masses. Here the aim was to show how the peasants could be rid of their shackles. If only they could see the vulnerability of the existing order, their best instincts would kick in and the uprising would follow. Because the sort of deeds chosen by anarchists to stir up the masses often involved assassination, Bakunin came to be viewed as the intellectual father of radical terrorism. A key part of Marx's indictment against Bakunin was his association with Sergei Nechayev. Bitter, ascetic, and militant, Nechayev took nihilism to destructive extremes, claiming the right and obligation to do anything in the name of the cause (a conclusion he did not solely reserve for revolutionary business). On meeting Bakunin in Switzerland in late 1868, he claimed to have escaped from prison and to represent a Russian revolutionary committee. This led Bakunin to proclaim him a member of the Russian Section of the World Revolutionary Alliance (number 2771).[29]

The next few months were disastrous for Bakunin. Later he rejected Nechayev's brutal philosophy. Despite allegations to the contrary, he probably did not coauthor some of Nechayev's starker publications, which celebrated the role of "poison, the knife, the noose" and spoke of the purifying effects of "fire and sword." The "massacre of personages in high places," Nechayev claimed, would create a panic among the ruling classes. The more the mighty were shown to be vulnerable the more others would be emboldened, leading eventually to a general revolution. Nechayev's most notorious publication was the *Catechism of a Revolutionary*, which opened: "The revolutionary is a doomed man. He has no interests of his own, no affairs, no feelings, no attachments, no belongings, not even a name. Everything in him is absorbed by a single, exclusive interest, a single thought, a single passion; the revolution."[30] It was the revolution alone which distinguished between good and evil. In the end Bakunin, beguiled by a young man whose energy and militancy offered hope for the future, did not break with Nechayev because of his philosophy but because of an abuse of hospitality. Nechayev took off with his money, issued gruesome threats to a publisher on his behalf, attempted to seduce Herzen's daughter, and murdered a fellow student to protect his own reputation.

Bakunin died in 1875, exhausted and disillusioned, his revolutionary energy sapped and his dreams dashed. Though he left behind substantial movements in Italy and Spain, as well as Russia, the immediate legacy lay in the pursuit of the "propaganda of the deed." This focus on deeds as a spur to revolt demoted words, and resulted in even less attention being paid to the arts of persuasion. For example, the Italian Errico Malatesta, who discovered the writings of Bakunin in 1871, was explaining five years later how "the revolution consists more in deeds than in words...each time a spontaneous movement of the people erupts...It is the duty of every revolutionary social-ist to declare his solidarity with the movement in the making." Although Malatesta later argued against anarchist terror, at the time the language was forceful. A "river of blood" separated the movement from the future as they sought to destroy all existing institutions.[31] Having urged an insurrectional approach on the Anarchist International, he then went off to make his pro-paganda through deeds, turning up in villages in Campania with an armed band, burning tax registers, and declaring the end of the monarchy. Malatesta and his followers were soon arrested. Yet Malatesta was noted for his analyti-cal and debating skills, evident when it came to influencing juries in political trials. A police informer described him as seeking to "persuade with calm, and never with violent language." He deliberately avoided "the pseudoscien-tific phraseology, violent and paradoxical turns of phrase or verbal abuse that were the stock-in-trade of so many of his fellow anarchists and socialists."[32]

Thereafter he moved around Europe as well as Argentina, Egypt, and the United States, fomenting rebellion where he could and debating the char-acter of the good society and how to overthrow the old order without using power or creating a new power in its place. Later in his long life he deplored indiscriminate terror, insisting that only justifiable violence would support liberation. "One thing is certain," he wrote in 1894, "that with a number of blows of the knife a society like bourgeois society cannot be overthrown, being built, as it is on an enormous mass of private interests and prejudices and sustained, more than it is by force of arms, by the inertia of the masses and their habits of submission."[33]

The heated language of revolution, however, never encouraged a sense of limitation when it came to force. The International Anarchist Congress, held in London in 1881, urged exploring all means for the "annihilation of all rul-ers, ministers of state, nobility, the clergy, the most prominent capitalists, and other exploiters," with special attention to be paid to the study of chemistry and the preparation of explosives. The German anarchist Johann Most argued in the spirit of the Jacobins for the extermination of the possessing classes. In his pamphlet entitled "The Science of Revolutionary Warfare: a manual of instruction in the use and preparation of Nitro-Glycerine, Dynamite, Gun Cotton, Fulminating Mercury, Bombs, Fuses, Poisons, etc, etc.," he wrote: "In giving dynamite to the downtrodden millions of the globe, sci-ence has done its best work. A pound of this stuff beats a bushel of ballots all hollow." Assassinations became regular. Starting with Tsar Alexander II in 1881, the assassins took out a French president, a Spanish prime minister, an Italian king, and a U.S. president (McKinley), failing with the German kaiser. The murder of Archduke Ferdinand of Austria in August 1914 provided the trigger for the First World War. An association between anarchism and terror was established and endures to this day, despite the best efforts of its adherents to stress its gentler and more humane aspects.

The novelist Joseph Conrad wrote perceptively about the anarchists and the circles in which they operated. In his note to *Under Western Eyes*, he commented on how the "ferocity and imbecility" of autocratic rule provoked the "no less imbecile and atrocious answer of a purely Utopian revolutionism encompassing destruction by the first means to hand, in the strange conviction that a fundamental change of hearts must follow the downfall of any given human institution."[34] His most famous characterization of the futile revolutionaries of his time was in *The Secret Agent*, published in 1907. The most notorious character was the bomb-maker known as the Professor (in fact a reject technician from a chemistry department) who lusted after the perfect detonator. By wiring himself up to explode, the Professor concluded that he had rendered himself untouchable by the police. Yet behind his "sinister loneliness" was a "haunting fear" that the people were too feeble to overthrow the established order. He was frustrated by the "resisting power of numbers, the unattackable stolidity of a great multitude." He bemoaned the fact that the "social spirit of this people is wrapped up in scrupulous prejudices, and that is fatal to our work." To break the "worship of legality," he sought to trigger repression.

The most sinister figure in the book agreed. This was not an anarchist, but Vladimir, from an unnamed embassy clearly meant to be Russia's. To Vladimir, England was a weak link in the fight against terror. "This country," he complained, "is absurd with its sentimental regard for individual liberty." What was needed, he concluded, was a "jolly good scare" for which this was the "psychological moment." What would be the best sort of scare? Attempts on monarchs or presidents were no longer so sensational while attacks on churches, restaurants, and theaters could easily be explained away. He wanted "an act of destructive ferocity so absurd as to be incomprehensible, inexplicable, almost unthinkable; in fact, mad? Madness alone is truly terrifying." And so by this reasoning he identified his target as "the first meridian." The hapless Adolf Verloc was told to blow up the Greenwich Observatory. The book was based on a real incident of 1894, in which the building was not touched but the bomber was blown to pieces. Conrad described this episode as "a blood-stained inanity of so fatuous a kind that it was impossible to fathom its origin by any reasonable or even unreasonable process of thought." In his book neither the Professor nor Vladimir are able to trigger the repression they sought and the story becomes one of individual tragedy.[35]

Anarchism was not solely about individual terror. Notably, a genuinely popular mass movement was developed in Spain during the first decades of the twentieth century. Anarchism was a formidable presence on the Left in Spain, more so than communism. It came in a variety of forms, including strong syndicalist tendencies among the workforce. The Confederación Nacional del Trabajo (CNT) was formed in 1911 and a decade later it had over a million members. It shunned politics and committed itself to direct action in the economic sphere, denouncing all forms of power. Politics was never far away, however. There was sufficient organization to have all members agreeing that after appropriate branch discussion they were bound by the majority view. Unsurprisingly for a movement of such a size, it soon had an extremist wing, ready to engage in violent insurrection, and a moderate wing, prepared to do deals with employers and the state. In the early 1930s, the extremists, having organized themselves into an effective Bakunin-type conspiracy within the CNT, supplanted the moderates. This was a time of growing social unrest, and the movement began to face real choices. The consequences of their actions were evident and not merely theoretical.

Having abstained in the 1933 election, and let in a right-wing government, many members voted in 1936 in support of the leftist Popular front. Then came General Franco's coup against the Republic. The resistance was led by the CNT, with its members to the fore in running areas on collectivist principles controlled by the Republic. The harsh realities of power began to intrude. The first choice was whether to dissolve the local government in Catalonia and set up what would be in effect an anarchist dictatorship or work with the sort of institutions they had always denounced. The leadership chose collaboration. As Franco's forces gained ground, the CNT leadership accepted the need for a united front with the socialists and was soon requiring its members to follow a party line. On entering government, the CNT paper observed that because anarchists were now ministers, the state was no longer oppressive. There was conscription and demands for strict military discipline, while the social experiments (some of which had been successful) were halted. In practice, an army composed of militias, each with their own political sponsor, was always likely to lead to factional in-fighting. As the more disciplined force, and with the Republic increasingly reliant upon Soviet support, communists soon dominated the officer corps.[36] Eventually the communists, with Soviet backing, turned on the anarchists and a civil war within the civil war began. To anarchism's association with terror, the experience of Spain added an association with futility and ineffectuality.

Anarchists might see with great clarity the temptations and perversions of power, as well as its incompatibility with their ideal society, but they were unable to demonstrate how to function effectively without it. When an opportunity came to exert influence over human affairs, they either had to forget their past strictures against accepting positions of power or let others who were less squeamish about power take their chance. The anarchists understood how the means employed shaped the ends achieved, but by ruling out all effective means as potentially corrupting, they were left waiting for the people to take an initiative that they could support. There was, as Carl Levy has noted, something paradoxical about this reluctance to take power because the anarchists, more than most, "relied on its leaders (local, national and international) to help preserve institutional continuity."[37] But leaders who had to pretend that they were not leading could not provide strategic direction. Indeed, a refusal to address directly the possibilities of power precluded the possibility of a serious strategy leaving them only the role of angry critics. The question of leadership thereafter continued to divide the Left, with two extremes on offer. On the one hand were the purists who dared do little more than nudge the masses in the right direction; at the other extreme were those who put themselves firmly in the vanguard of change and insisted that there was no other way forward than the one which they set.

CHAPTER 20 | Revisionists and Vanguards

The time of surprise attacks, of revolutions carried through by small
conscious minorities at the head of masses lacking consciousness is past.

—Frederic Engels, *1895*

NGELS'S LAST PUBLISHED work, which appeared a few months before
his death in 1895, is sometimes known as his "testament." That was not
how he viewed it, but it was nonetheless a reflective piece, using the republi-
cation of Marx's 1850 *Class Struggles in France* to comment on the changing fortunes of the working-class movement during the second half of the
century. The political significance of the piece was that it was used by the
leadership of the German Social Democratic Party (SPD) to justify the parliamentary strategy they had been following, with some success, and to warn
against violent revolution. Because of Engels's singular authority, those who
continued to yearn for a more militant approach to revolution found it troubling. They could argue, with some justice, that Engels had been put under
pressure by the SPD hierarchy to tone down his language because a new
antisubversion law was under consideration. Yet despite insisting that he
was not ruling out force, and that the more optimistic aspects of his analysis
only truly applied to Germany, he acknowledged that his views on socialist
strategy had changed significantly since 1848. Then revolution was seen as
a "great decisive battle," that once commenced would continue, no doubt

at length and with many vicissitudes until it concluded with the "final victory of the proletariat." Almost fifty years on, however, a street-fighting insurrectionary victory over a regular army could only be envisaged as a rare exception.

The influence of the military debates of the past decades was evident as he tried to think of ways in which insurrectionists could operate as a successful army. The only way the balance of forces could be tilted in favor of the revolution was by playing on the doubts of troops about the cause for which they were fighting and encouraging them not to fire on their own people. In all other circumstances, the superior equipment and discipline of the regulars would prevail. It was always likely that poorly armed demonstrators would be outnumbered, but now army reserves could use the railways to rush to any trouble spot. Their arms would also be far more effective. Even city planners had been working against the revolution. Cities were now "laid out in long, straight, broad streets, tailor-made to give full effect to the new cannons and rifles."

It would be difficult for the revolution to defend a single borough, never mind a whole town.

> Concentration of the military forces at a decisive point is, of course, out of the question here. Hence passive defense is the predominant form of struggle; an attack will be mounted here and there, by way of exception, in the form of occasional thrusts and assaults on the flanks; as a rule, however, it will be limited to the occupation of positions abandoned by retreating troops.[1]

The only value of the barricade was in its moral rather than material effect, as a means of shaking the "steadfastness" of the military. This was another reason why revolutions could not be undertaken "by small conscious minorities at the head of masses lacking consciousness." If the masses were not directly involved there was no chance.

By contrast, universal male suffrage had created real opportunities and the working classes, via the SPD, had taken full advantage. If the steady rise in the party's vote continued, "we shall grow into the decisive power in the land, before which all other powers will have to bow, whether they like it or not." The risk to the rise of socialism in Germany therefore would be "a clash on a grand scale with the military, a blood-letting like that of 1871 in Paris." To avoid that, resources should be conserved. So Engels saw it as ironic that the "revolutionaries" and "overthrowers" were thriving far better on legal methods. It was the "parties of order" that were "perishing under the legal conditions created by themselves." If the movement was "not so crazy as to let ourselves be driven to street fighting in order to please them," it would be their opponents who would have to contemplate illegal action.

Engels privately was adamant that he could not advocate complete abstinence from force. He was annoyed at being presented as "a peaceful worshipper of legality at any price."[2] He was of the view that when socialists acquired the sort of electoral strength that would justify them taking power, the government would clamp down. It might then be necessary to take to the streets. A couple of passages in his testament, which the party hierarchy feared were too inflammatory, referred to the need to avoid frittering away strength in "vanguard skirmishes" but to "keep it intact until the decisive day." Rather than start the revolutionary process on the streets as a way of stimulating support, his view was that it would only be taken when the masses were fully behind the revolution, for this would be the time when the resolve of the government troops would be at its lowest. A few years earlier he had explained that he doubted that the SPD would be allowed to take power as a majority party. He gave ten to one odds that well before that point "our rulers" would "use violence against us, and this would shift us from the terrain of majority to the terrain of revolution."[3]

Revisionism

Marx's theory implied economic determinism, but as an activist he never denied the possibility of consequential action within the political sphere. Works such as *The Eighteenth Brumaire* made little sense unless it was recognized that the links between class interests and political action could be diffuse and distorted, and that poor choices caused revolutionary opportunities to be lost. Marx would not dismiss any setting, including parliamentary elections, where the cause of the working class might be promoted. His political judgments could be quite pragmatic even while he remained dogmatic in his underlying theory.

By insisting on the scientific basis of socialism, not a mere act of imagination but a causal theory, everything had to turn on how the working classes came to understand their situation and struggle against it. The key moment would come when the proletariat moved from being a class *in* itself to one *for* itself, grasping their full power and potential. One reading of Marx was that this should, somehow, happen naturally—almost spontaneously—as collective eyes were opened to the reasons for their misery and how all could be transformed. But what role did this leave for the party? Surges of popular anger and yearnings for a better life so often resulted in dashed hopes and more persecution and misery. Radical movements either petered out or suddenly took a turn toward respectability, becoming part of the system rather than a means to its overthrow.

This was the curse of Marx, from which he personally suffered: a theory of inevitable, progressive change but one that could doom the activist to frustration. If the politics could never be right without the correct material base, what was the revolutionary politician to do? One answer was to wait until the conditions were right, building up strength until the moment eventually arrived and the working class was ready. The alternative was to find a way of accelerating the pace of change, creating conditions in which class consciousness could develop faster. The SPD as the most substantial and confident of all Marxist parties presented itself as having found the happy medium. The rise in class consciousness could be measured in the growth of party membership and steady successes in elections. There would be no mystery about when the moment of transition to socialism would come: the party would have majority support among the electorate. The risk was that successes in achieving improvements in workers' conditions would drain the movement of its revolutionary fervor, while the party would develop a stake in the system.

Marx and Engels had always put a far greater stress on a correct socialist program rather than a particular strategy. When the SPD was founded in 1875, they were furious with their acolytes, August Bebel and Wilhelm Liebknecht, for merging with Ferdinand Lassalle's General German Workers' Association, which they disapproved of as reformist and unscientific. Marx accepted cooperation between the two parties but not the joint program, which he saw as an attempt to find common ground with the bourgeoisie, as if conflict was based on an unfortunate misunderstanding. It was vital not to "expunge the class struggle from the movement" or even hint at the possibility that workers were too uneducated to emancipate themselves and could only be freed by the bourgeoisie.[4] Three years later, Engels published a critique of the gradualist notions of the blind socialist philosopher, Eugen Dühring, who argued against the determinism of Marx and Engels and for self-governing cooperatives. This tract, known as *Anti-Dühring*, played a significant role in transmitting Marxism in an accessible form to a new generation of socialists. It urged the working class not to settle for second-best, not to rely on philanthropy when they deserved power.

In 1891, following the repeal of an antisocialist law, the SPD adopted the Erfurt Program, written by Karl Kautsky and Eduard Bernstein. This still anticipated the end of capitalism but was prepared to pursue socialism through peaceful means. After Engels died it was Bernstein, his literary executor, who began the process of adjusting revolutionary theory to reformist practice. He noted, contrary to Marx's predictions, that working-class conditions were not declining but improving. In 1898, he published *Evolutionary Socialism*, which, as the title suggested, concluded that revolution was unnecessary and that combinations of cooperatives, unions, and parliamentary representation allowed the progressive and benign transformation of society. He contrasted an intelligent, methodical, but slow process of historical development, depending on legislative activity. While revolutionary activity offered faster progress, it was based on feeling and depended on spontaneity. For Bernstein, "the movement [was] everything, the goal nothing."

His erstwhile collaborator Karl Kautsky disagreed, presenting himself as a keeper of the true faith. As the leading exponent of Marxism in the leading party which embraced Marx, Kautsky was extraordinarily influential in shaping views about scientific socialism. His approach was plodding and unreflective, betraying no doubts about the essential correctness of Marxism and its broad application. Even after the turmoil of the Great War and the Bolshevik Revolution, he never deviated from a set of views acquired at an early age. The science told Kautsky that socialism would develop as capitalism matured and classes polarized. He argued against Bernstein that the issue was not so much the increasing poverty of the workers but the sharpening of class antagonism. Eventually capitalism would be ripe for destruction and the proletariat could take power. Premature action could not lead to the destruction of capitalism. Exactly how the right moment could be properly recognized he never quite explained, nor how the seizure of power would actually occur. It would be a revolution, but its form was hard to judge in advance. His hope was that the more the working class prepared during the prerevolutionary struggles, the more likely the great event would pass peacefully. This left him claiming that SPD was a revolutionary party that saw no point in actually making a revolution.

In principle this made little sense. A party preparing for a long haul of gradual acquisition of power had educational and organizational tasks quite different from one geared to a "once-and-for-all act of violence."[5] Yet in terms of political strategy it made perfect sense. As the party's chief theoretician, Kautsky had hit upon a formula that followed Engels: dogmatic Marxism combined with cautious politics. It kept the revolutionaries in the fold but gave the authorities no excuse for repression. It was hard to argue with success. From 10 percent in the 1887 Reichstag elections, the social democrats polled almost double in 1890, getting up to over 30 percent by 1903. To understand the maturity of the class consciousness of the proletariat, one only had to observe the SPD's developing support.[6]

Rosa

Rosa Luxemburg was a ferocious critic of the revisionists, but she was also wary about the complete identification of the worker's cause with the party. Though born in Russian-ruled Poland, she moved to Zurich after her radical politics got her into early trouble. There she gained a doctorate and then moved to Germany, soon establishing a reputation as brilliant but extreme in her views. She provided a unique link between the Russian and German parties and at different times was active in both, although that meant she also could be an outsider in both. She described herself as "thrice stigmatized: as a woman, as a Jew, and as a cripple." As an intellectual, she introduced a complex proof of why capitalism was doomed economically. Her main impact, though, was as a theorist of socialist strategy and tactics. She was a lively writer, with a vivid turn of phrase, reflecting her conviction that readers must be enthused and inspired and her despair at the language of party articles: "The style is conventional, wooden, stereotypical...just a colorless, dull sound like that of a running engine."[7]

Luxemburg's starting point was that workers would become increasingly socialist through struggle and experience. The task for a party was to help draw this out, but there was no need to impose the ideology from above. She was opposed to the very idea of a centralized, bureaucratic party. The real tactical innovations were not the organizational inventions of party leaders but the "spontaneous product of the movement in ferment." Where there had been upsurges, "the initiative and conscious leadership of the Social Democratic organizations played an insignificant role." She was aware of the potentially troubling implications of Engels's preface to *The Class Struggles in France*. This supported the legal struggle and rejected a rush to the barricades. She insisted, however, that Engels was referring to how the proletariat would struggle while confined by the capitalist state, not to the actual seizure of power. He had been "giving directions to the proletariat oppressed, and not to the proletariat victorious." When the moment came, the proletariat would do whatever was necessary to secure the future of socialism. Only by falling for "Blanquism," or a coup d'état, was there a risk of a premature seizure of power. So long as reliance was placed on the "great conscious popular mass," then the moment would be right for power because, by definition, this could only have come about as a result of the "decomposition of bourgeois society." It was impossible to believe that "a transformation as formidable as the passage from capitalist society to socialist society can be realized in one happy act." The struggle would be a long one, no doubt with setbacks. What she found difficult to imagine was how the struggle could proceed, or the point of victory be identified, without attacks on state power.[8]

She hit upon the idea of the mass strike as the best way to avoid the pitfalls of parliamentary reformism without risking all in a premature insurrection. Her inspiration came not from Germany but from Russia. In January 1905, there began in Russia the first serious uprising in a European country since the 1871 Commune. Against the backdrop of Russia's defeat in the war with Japan, and with the shooting of unarmed workers marching on the Winter Palace to deliver a petition to the Tsar as the trigger, years of economic and political anger spilled over onto the streets. Numerous organizations, from workers' committees to trade unions, sprang up, reflecting the unrest and giving it expression. Soldiers and sailors mutinied, peasants seized land, and workers put up barricades. Luxemburg returned to Warsaw to play her part and emerged convinced that the true revolutionary method was the strike. This would be the spontaneous expression of an objective revolutionary condition, a deeply radicalizing process from which appropriate organizations would emerge. Class feeling would be awoken "as if by an electric shock." Once a real, earnest period of mass strikes began, all calculations of cost would become "merely projects for exhausting the ocean with a tumbler."[9]

There was nothing particularly new in the idea of the mass strike, but it was not normally associated with Marxists. Its potential had been demonstrated by the General Strike in Britain in 1842, which involved some half a million workers. This was a response to wage cuts during tough economic times but then picked up on the political demands associated with the Chartists. Even then the Chartist leadership was equivocal about the connection and in Britain, as elsewhere in Europe, strikes had come to be associated with trade unions and economic demands. Only anarchists adopted the idea of political strikes as a reflection of the sort of mass spontaneity celebrated by Bakunin. For that reason alone, the tactic was treated skeptically by Marxists. In 1873, Engels had mocked the Bakuninist idea that

> one fine morning all the workers in all the industries of a country, or even of the whole world, stop work, thus forcing the propertied classes either humbly to submit within four weeks at the most, or to attack the workers, who would then have the right to defend themselves and use this opportunity to pull down the entire old society.

According to Engels, a mass strike required a "well-formed organization of the working class and plentiful funds." Before that was achieved, the workers would have achieved power by other means. And if they did have the organization and the funds "there would be no need to use the roundabout way of a general strike to achieve its goal."[10]

Luxemburg therefore needed to explain how her idea met Engels's objections. She argued that 1905 had demonstrated something new about the tactic and that it had nothing to do with anarchism. However, her enthusiasm for the idea of change coming about as a natural, organic response of the working classes to their conditions rather than as a device of party strategy was not far away from Bakunin. In her treatise, she thus went out of her way to demonstrate her contempt for anarchism. Still, her distrust for party bureaucrats was evident in the polemics against those who treated tactics as if a "board of directors" could decide on them for an appointed day, and against those who respected only "orderly and well-disciplined" struggles that ran "according to plan and scheme." In Russia in 1905 there was "no predetermined plan, no organized action." The parties were almost left behind by the "spontaneous risings of the masses." Here she was careful to argue that the events were not wholly spontaneous but reflected years of agitation by social democrats.

Nor did she agree with those, such as the German trade unions, who saw strikes in a separate category of economic actions. The economic and political spheres could not be separated. One fed off the other. The advantage of the mass strike was that this was where they came together. The strikes could start with economic demands and then the combination of socialist agitation and government responses would turn them into something more political. Above all, they would be consciousness-raising events: "The most precious, lasting, thing in the rapid ebb and flow of the wave is its mental sediment: the intellectual, cultural growth of the proletariat, which proceeds by fits and starts, and which offers an inviolable guarantee of their further irresistible progress in the economic as in the political struggle." Her aim was to assert the role of the mass strike in Germany as the "first natural, impulsive form of every great revolutionary struggle." The more developed the antagonism between capital and labor, the more effective the mass strikes. They would not replace "brutal street fights," for at some culminating point the armed power of the state would have to be faced. This would be no more than "a moment in the long period of political struggle."[11]

In his memoir, Leon Trotsky described being present at an encounter between Luxemburg and Kautsky in 1907. The two had been close friends but since 1905 had diverged. Trotsky described Luxemburg as small and frail but intelligent and courageous, with a "precise, intense and merciless" style. Kautsky, by contrast, Trotsky found "charming," but with an "angular and dry" mind lacking in "nimbleness and psychological insight." He was caught up in the reality of reform: revolution was just a "misty historical prospect." Together they went to a demonstration, and the exchanges between the two intensified: "Kautsky wanted to remain an onlooker, whereas Rosa was anxious to join the demonstration."[12] The antagonism between the two came out in 1910 over Luxemburg's continued advocacy of the mass strike.

We noted in the last section the influential distinction, introduced by the military historian Hans Delbrück, between a strategy of annihilation, which demanded a decisive battle to eliminate the enemy's army, and a strategy of exhaustion, which drew on a range of alternative means to wear down the enemy. These could also be understood respectively as strategies of overthrow or attrition—terms that might be more helpful in the context of political strategy. In 1910, responding to Luxemburg, Kautsky drew explicitly on Delbrück's work. While overthrow depended on drawing "forces rapidly together in order to go to meet the enemy and to deal decisive blows by means of which the enemy is overthrown and rendered incapable of struggle," with attrition

> the commander-in-chief initially avoids any decisive battle; he aims to keep the opposing army on the move by all sorts of maneuvers, without giving it the opportunity of raising the morale of its troops by gaining victories; he strives to gradually wear them out by continual exhaustion and threats and to consistently reduce their resistance and paralyze them.[13]

Kautsky was all in favor of attrition. Luxemburg's mass strike was an attempt at overthrow, imprudent because it would provoke the state repression and antisocialist legislation he was so anxious to avoid. What if a mass strike was called and few turned up? All the gains from the parliamentary strategy would be lost.

Lenin

Kautsky's distinction between overthrow and attrition was also adopted by Vladimir Ilyich Lenin, the leader of the Bolshevik faction of the Russian Social Democrats. He was arguing about the meaning of 1905 with the opposing Menshevik faction who had used Kautsky's formulation.[14] Later, Kautsky and Lenin would fall out, but for the moment Kautsky was the leader of European socialists and Lenin had his own disagreements with Luxemburg.

Lenin's extraordinary appetite for factional struggle reflected his top priority, which was to get the right form of party organization—with him in control. It was for this reason that while the 1905 revolution was getting started, he was locked in battle in a party congress in London, vying for control of the party newspaper. His approach to all revolutionary matters betrayed a single-mindedness acquired at an early age. Lenin's formative political experiences included his brother Aleksandr being executed for an attempted assassination attempt against the Tsar and expulsion from university for participation in demonstrations. In 1891, having spent two years studying Marx, he was drawn into more active politics (as were others of his generation) by the terrible famine that overtook the country that year, which was only aggravated by government action. He began to identify himself as a socialist revolutionary, true to the word of Marx. He had followed the familiar Russian path of imprisonment and exile, traveling around Europe, attending meetings with other revolutionaries, attempting to establish clandestine organizations that could escape police scrutiny, and editing a revolutionary paper (*Iskra*) while in Zurich.

If Lenin had a model it was Rakhmetov, the new man of Chernyshevsky's novel, *What Is to Be Done?* He shared the ascetic lifestyle, neither smoking nor drinking, and had a total devotion to the cause, for which he was prepared to sacrifice all. He also borrowed Chernyshevky's title for his first major statement of strategy, published in March 1902 when he was 33. The character he deliberately cultivated was hard, tough, disciplined, and uncompromising, prepared to break with old comrades over points of doctrine and tactics, blistering in his polemics. There was little attempt at empathy with those of different views; he could not admit to error. Into his own *What Is to Be Done?* Lenin poured all that he had studied in theory and learned in practice. He intended it as a landmark statement. It took broadly accepted positions in socialist circles to ruthlessly logical conclusions. Even those who deplored revisionism recoiled at the starkness of Lenin's message.

If moving quickly to a revolution meant accelerating the pace of historical development, in the case of Russia there was an awful lot of history to be passed through in short order. Russia was backward in its material development, straining to leave feudal times. At the same time, it was forever showing symptoms of mass discontent and militancy. Lenin's energies were geared to making revolution. His pamphlet explained why alternative approaches led to dead ends and why his own might succeed, but only if it was conducted relentlessly by a tightly controlled and disciplined party.

For much of *What Is to Be Done?* Lenin's main target was "economism." The economists in question derided doctrinaire Marxists for filling workers' heads with unrealizable demands. Better to concentrate on practical proposals that could show real and early results. In the context of the oppressive conditions prevailing in Russia, economic demands were less risky than political demands, which could be left to the bourgeoisie who were still waiting for their revolution. Lenin derided this approach as "tailism," following rather than leading the proletarian movement. He pointed to the German SPD as demonstrating how effective organizations could encourage workers to embrace socialism as the best explanation for their everyday struggles. Because socialism was the best explanation it must not be diluted. The "philosophy of Marxism" was "cast from a single block of steel." It was impossible to "eliminate a single substantial premise, a single essential part, without deviating from objective truth, without falling into the arms of bourgeois, reactionary falsehood."[15]

As his critics pointed out, this assumed that workers could not be trusted with their own struggle and so must be guided by those with the education to grasp socialist theory. "Social-Democratic consciousness," Lenin wrote, "had to be brought to the workers from without. The history of all countries shows that the working class, exclusively by its own effort, is able to develop only trade union consciousness." As there were only two forms of political consciousness—bourgeois and socialist—failure to adopt one inevitably meant being part of the other. Lenin did not seem, however, to have worried about this part of the equation. He was optimistic about the natural instincts of workers. So he was not suggesting that the efforts of a vanguard of professional revolutionaries could substitute for those of the working class. His main concern was with the defects of Russian socialism. With its limited political development and poor organization, it was unable to give the struggle the necessary coherence and purpose and steer it away from "bourgeois consciousness." This required professional revolutionaries. He was not against a democratic party in principle, but in practice revolutionaries were bound to act conspiratorially, otherwise they could not survive. One of Lenin's closest associates turned out to be a police agent.

None of this was particularly controversial among mainstream European Marxists, other than the sharpness of his bifurcation between bourgeois and socialist consciousness resulting in the odd conclusion that purely working-class movements were almost bound to be bourgeois unless they were led by professionals, versed in the theory, who were invariably from the bourgeoisie. Nor was Lenin expecting leadership from intellectuals, a group far too dreamy, individualistic, and impervious to party discipline for his taste. What mattered was the party, which needed proletarian roots and support, but which had to set the objectives and the associated strategy for the movement as a whole. The anarchists had warned how the party could become an end in itself, but the Marxists had insisted that any supreme role would be a momentary function of the exigencies of the revolutionary process rather than reflecting the self-interest of the leadership.

Lenin insisted that the party was no more than a means to an end, yet he lavished care and attention on matters of organization and leadership in a quite unique way. If the revolution was to succeed, then endless disputes about small points of theory and forms of internal democracy designed to give everyone their say—whether or not they were truly committed to the cause—were luxuries that could not be afforded. Essential political work required organization, and in the face of police agents and a dispersed leadership, often in exile, this was bound to take on conspiratorial aspects. In addition, many other energetic alternatives were competing in the same political space. The Russian Social Democratic Workers Party was in a fragile state. Lenin's ideas were therefore aspirational, looking forward to a party that could serve as the instrument of a decisive leadership, sure in theory and determined in practice.

Lenin's capacity for organization and drive was at first turned against critics within his party rather than the system he was trying to overthrow. The Second Party Congress met in Brussels in July 1903, with Lenin's group associated with *Iskra*, the party paper that he edited. The outcome was two parties rather than one, although it took another congress in 1905 for the split to be confirmed. The argument between Lenin's Bolsheviks (majority) and the Mensheviks (minority) came over control of the paper. This became linked to claims that Lenin was determined to create an all-powerful central committee, and was in turn connected to the question of whether membership should be confined to those wholly committed to the party program and prepared to work for it or opened up to those who were only prepared to give some support. One route turned the party into a focused elite group; the other created the basis for a mass party, with some expectation of democratic control of the leadership by the party. In addition there were wider differences over strategy. The Mensheviks were inclined to ally with the liberals and use parliamentary means. Lenin would place little reliance on parliament and saw peasants as more natural allies.

In all these radical groups there was tendency for disagreements to be naturally elevated to core issues of principle and theory. Lenin aggravated the situation even more. The Mensheviks (who bizarrely embraced a name that diminished their standing) were also not particularly good at compromises, largely as a result of inner disagreements. Their leadership was not united and their discipline was poor. Lenin was a polarizing influence, making no claim to an open mind and showing scant patience with trimmers and compromisers. He would rather control a small group than share power with a larger one. He recorded an argument with a party member who deplored "this fierce fighting, this agitation one against the other, these sharp polemics, this uncomradely attitude!" Lenin retorted that this was good:

> Opportunity for open fighting. Opinions expressed. Tendencies revealed. Groups defined. Hands raised. A decision taken. A stage passed through. Forward! That is what I like! It is something different from the endless wearying intellectual discussions, which finish, not because people have solved the problem, but simply because they have got tired of talking.[16]

Far from finding splits in the party depressing, he relished them even if they meant estrangement from old colleagues. His critics accused Lenin of being a Blanquist, aiming to achieve power through a coup d'état. Lenin denied this. The masses must be there but they would need direction. Revolution was bound to be an authoritarian event, needing a coercive dictatorship inspired by "a Jacobin mentality."

Rosa Luxemburg was appalled at these organizational proposals, undoubtedly with her own experience of the German SPD bureaucracy in mind. She saw them strengthening the forces of conservatism and undermining creativity, denying all sections of the party—and the wider movement—the ability to use their initiative. Lenin's "ultra-centralism" was "full of the sterile spirit of the overseer." It was all about control, binding the movement rather than unifying it. Yet social democracy in Russia stood "on the eve of decisive battles against Tsarism." Surrounding the party with a "network of barbed wire, is to render it incapable of accomplishing the tremendous task of the hour." The question of the moment, she argued, was "how to set in motion a large proletarian organization. No constitutional project can claim infallibility. It must prove itself in fire."

One Step Forward, Two Steps Back

The events of 1905 could be taken as a vindication for Luxemburg. Despite all the failures, she emerged with a vision for the future and a grand strategic project. For Lenin, by contrast, it was the start of a difficult period. Even as that year's revolution got underway, the infighting continued through into February 1905 at yet another congress. This time the Mensheviks got the upper hand, largely because the party's elder statesman, Plekhanov, swung away from Lenin. The title of Lenin's assessment of the congress, *One Step Forward, Two Steps Back*, conveyed his gloom at the setbacks. His opponents were accused of being opportunistic. Now in charge of *Iskra*, they countered by lambasting his intolerance and elitist centralism. Both factions claimed to be acting in the interests of the proletariat. For the Mensheviks this meant supporting the developing workers movement; for the Bolsheviks this meant ensuring the supremacy of a true proletarian ideology, whatever the current beliefs expressed by actual workers.

So as the divided party leadership squabbled and exchanged polemics in exile, a real revolutionary situation, which they were unable to lead, appeared to be developing at home. Their contribution to the events was tiny, part of a wide range of political tendencies—including those of liberals and disgruntled junior officers, who all sought the end of the monarchy. The focal points were the local workers' councils—the Soviets—that emerged in St. Petersburg and Moscow. The Bolsheviks viewed them with suspicion but they had to make some accommodation. Their evident limitations confirmed Lenin's misgivings about the consequences of a lack of organization. After the authorities broke up the Soviets, there was a desperate uprising in Moscow. In the face of the army, the inadequately armed revolutionaries were slaughtered.

It was November before a general amnesty made it safe for Lenin to return to Russia from Geneva. By this time the revolution had peaked. An all-Russian strike had begun in October and the Tsar had promised constitutional changes which helped diffuse the immediate crisis, and then the authorities persecuted the revolutionaries. All options seemed poor for socialists and they argued among themselves on where and how to position themselves in the narrow political space available.

The experience clearly left Lenin unsettled. So long as there was general sympathy for the broad political movement, there was no need to distract it through terrorism and random violence. Once it had been defeated, he became more militant, demanding more direct action. Like Engels after 1849, Lenin concluded after 1905 that he must study military strategy. "Great historical struggles can only be resolved by force and in modern struggles the organization of force means military organization."[17] He enthused about armed militants building barricades, with "a revolver, a knife, a rag soaked in kerosene for starting fires." He complained about his comrades having talked for six months about bombs without a single one being manufactured. This appears to have reflected frustration more than strategy. He toyed with the methods of the terrorists, including expropriation of funds from banks. This action for action's sake confirmed Lenin's reputation as a hard man, but it also made him appear reckless.

War and Revolution

On the eve of the Great War, the socialist parties of Europe had confidence in their future. In France and Germany in particular, they were becoming formidable electoral forces. They met together in the Second International, founded in 1889 to mark the centenary of the French Revolution, and with anarchists safely excluded to avoid the fate of the First International. The ideological arguments were strong, but the different factions were generally on speaking terms (which is why Lenin's behavior was considered so outlandish). Issues of revisionism and mass strikes were divisive but rarely caused comrades to fall out completely. There was one issue, however, that was potentially more divisive than the ideology and that was war. War involved nationalism, which was in principle threatening to class solidarity.

While Marxists were not pacifists they had been assumed to be antimilitarist and antiwar, for war would do nothing for the working classes. They were well aware of the great power tensions of the time and the risk that this could turn into a major conflict. There were earnest debates about what socialists could do to stop such a catastrophe, including use of strikes and demonstrations. None of this got very far, in part because there was a disbelief that anything so awful would ever come to pass, whatever the bellicosity evident in a number of countries, and a pacifist action could be easily presented as unpatriotic, providing an excuse for repression and the loss of public support. The only agreed position was that workers should hinder the outbreak of war; but if it occurred, they should bring it to a rapid conclusion. Here Luxemburg and Lenin came to a similar discordant view. If war came it should be used to hasten the revolution.

As the crisis developed during July 1914, the mainstream socialist parties lacked urgency. They did not appreciate how serious it was this time compared with previous crises. There was not necessarily much the Second International could do. Among socialists, views of war had been shaped by theories of imperialism and "a stock image of territorial acquisitiveness generated by economic competition." They were unprepared for popular wars justified as self-defense. A formal position had been adopted by the Second International designed to maintain unity. This stressed the danger of peacetime militarism but treated the threat of a European war as being sufficiently remote that it need not expose the "latent nationalist splits in its own body." Thus, they were caught out by the sudden rush to war.[18] The Second International collapsed. Each party went its separate way as patriotic fervor overcame their members.

Lenin saw the danger that war posed for the Tsar and argued from the start that it would be for the best if Russia was defeated. So it proved. The monarchy collapsed in February 1917 following bread riots, strikes, and street demonstrations. Tsar Nicholas II abdicated. At the time, with their leaders still in exile, the Bolsheviks were in no position to take advantage. Those that were in Russia initially gave their support to the liberal constitutionalists who were trying to run the government. When Lenin returned in April from his Swiss exile, he immediately called for a worldwide socialist revolution and made it clear that there should be no support for the new government. The risks were high: his party was isolated. But that meant it had no responsibility for the dire conditions. Meanwhile the government was struggling, divided, and postponing hard issues until a constitutional assembly could be put in place. The economy deteriorated while the war continued. Amid accusations of pro-German treachery, Lenin fled to Finland.

Despite Lenin's strictures on the need for an elite vanguard party, in the fevered atmosphere of the time Bolsheviks were becoming a mass party with a membership not fully indoctrinated into scientific socialism. Lenin was the party's leader; but he was on its extreme wing, while others were ready to compromise. Lenin's success was not the result of painstaking organization or ideological purity but of his unique grasp of the dynamics of the situation. He understood the desperation of the people and how they were ahead of all the parties in their complete frustration with the existing order. This was not a time for the propagandist, who gave many ideas to a few, but rather the agitator, who gave a few ideas to many. He led the Bolsheviks to campaign on the slogan "Peace, Bread, Land" and to distinguish themselves by their unrelenting opposition to the war. As fresh military offensives brought fresh disasters, the credibility of the Bolsheviks grew. A misjudged insurrectionary push in the summer almost cost everything. A crackdown by the authorities could have forced the Bolshevik leadership to scatter, but they survived. By August, popular support for the Provisional Government had collapsed.

Should the Bolsheviks go for a broad-based government or a revolution which risked civil war? By September, Lenin had concluded that the country was so polarized that there was going to be a dictatorship of either the Left or Right. In October, Lenin returned from Finland. The slogan was now "All Power to the Soviets!" This meant no power to the government. He gained the assent of the Bolshevik Central Committee for an armed uprising. With his former antagonist Leon Trotsky now a close ally, the two worked together to use the Military-Revolutionary Committee of the Petrograd Soviet as their instrument for seizing power. Troops loyal to the Soviets began to seize key buildings. Nobody was prepared to resist on behalf of the provisional government—not the liberals nor the military nor the Right.[19]

Lenin won in 1917 because he survived. A couple of times he could have been lynched or incarcerated, or he could have thrown in his lot with the Provisional Government and then been as culpable as everybody else. The isolation that had left him apparently irrelevant before now turned out to be his greatest advantage. He did not need a coalition from the top down when his numbers were growing from the bottom up.

The Bolshevik Revolution changed forever strategic discourse on the Left. This had always been lively and often vituperative, but until 1914 was also inclusive, fluid, and responsive to events. In the meetings of the Second International before the war, socialists of all persuasions rubbed shoulders and argued. With Lenin's success, a progressive rigidity was introduced. The center of the movement shifted from Berlin to Moscow. Lenin, who judged ideas and arguments in terms of their political effects, could now be the arbiter of Marxist interpretation. In *State and Revolution*, a pamphlet written in 1917 but only published in 1918, Lenin asserted an extreme and uncompromising view of Marx, calling him to aid when explaining why Russia should bypass a bourgeois revolution on a quick road to communism. Much of the pamphlet was devoted to denouncing Karl Kautsky, previously recognized—even by Lenin—as the most authoritative interpreter of Marx and Engels but now forever labeled as a "renegade."

If Lenin had fallen during his revolutionary exertions, this pamphlet would be long forgotten. But as the thoughts of a man on the verge of achieving a revolutionary victory, the first professional in his field to do so, it achieved a canonical status. Lenin and his successor, Josef Stalin, were to be the popes of a movement in which doctrinal orthodoxy was rigidly enforced, with excommunication or worse consequences facing dissenters. The official position was not merely the better view; it was the "correct" and scientifically based view. The incorrect were not just wrong but class traitors.

The new Third International, established by Lenin in 1919, insisted that communist parties should be centralized, prepared for violent revolution and then dictatorship. They split away from the established socialist parties, stressing their differences more than shared values and objectives. At the time, Lenin and Trotsky believed themselves to be the vanguard of a revolutionary surge and looked expectantly for others to follow their example. In the postwar tumult, the expectation was not unreasonable, and some of the attempted revolutions of 1919 made progress. In the end, except for the Soviet Union, this was a period of disappointment comparable to 1848. This was particularly so in Germany. With the sudden defeat in November

1918, the monarchy fell and a new government led by Social Democrats was formed. The radical Spartacist League, which had already broken with the Social Democrats over their support for the war, assumed the moment had come. Led by Karl Liebknecht and a wary Rosa Luxemburg, an uprising was called for New Year's Day 1919. It was a disaster and soon both were murdered by rightists. More progress was made in Bavaria where there was a brief Soviet Republic, but it was soon crushed. In Hungary, communists did seize power for a while, but the regime was inept and soon collapsed under worsening economic conditions and international isolation. There were stirrings in Italy, especially in the factories of Turin, but the authorities were able to cope.

While all this was going on, the Bolsheviks fought their own civil war, unable to help their European comrades. The nearest they got to exporting revolution was a skirmish with Poland which ended in failure as the Polish workers and peasants responded more to national than class solidarity. Later attempts from Moscow in 1921 and 1923 to reignite the revolutionary flame in Germany ended in farcical failures.

Alone and beleaguered, the Bolsheviks managed to cope with civil war, external intervention, and famine. All this confirmed their need to retain a firm grip on the levers of power. The grip was further tightened by Stalin, who maneuvered to become Lenin's successor. He achieved his position by mastering party organization and then excluded all potential opponents, using show trials and mass purges. Leon Trotsky, Lenin's close lieutenant, was forced into exile. As an eloquent intellectual who could trade insults with the best, Trotsky had credentials which were hard to dismiss and ensured, especially as Stalinist methods became more transparent and despised, a persistent challenge to the Moscow line, at least until he was assassinated by one of Stalin's agents in Mexico in 1940.

Although Trotsky denounced Stalin's methods, he was in no position to question an uncompromising dictatorship of the proletariat. Nor did he try. He had been complicit in the ruthless methods of the revolution's early days and would not accept that the original Soviet concept was in error. He insisted that the Soviet Union had been undermined by its leadership but was still a workers' state and could recover from the bureaucratic degeneracy under which it temporarily suffered. Stalin's paranoia, which attributed everything bad to Trotsky, fed Trotsky's own egomania. He retained a delusional view of himself as the leader of an effective "Left Opposition" in the Soviet Union and an international mission still destined to perform its historic mission. His writings undoubtedly were more stylish than those of the turgid Stalin, but he was as dogmatic and tended to fall out with his supporters over deviations.

He played his own role in ensuring that the discourse on the Left became arid and unreflective, focused entirely on the legacy of 1917.

Left-wing politics outside of the Soviet Union was marked by a bitter sectarianism, highlighting the gap between capacities and its resources, and between political forms and democratic ideals. Moscow demanded support against its external and internal enemies as the first priority for the mainstream communist parties. Responses to local conditions and issues were smothered by the need to fit in with the latest stage of Soviet foreign policy and to deny any succor to anti-party elements, even if in practice this made life easier for the capitalist classes. This stultifying atmosphere turned idealists into party hacks and forced intellectuals into agonizing choices between loyalty to the working-class movement and to their own integrity. European Marxism as a source of strategic innovation never recovered.

CHAPTER 21 | Bureaucrats, Democrats, and Elites

And having answered so I turn once more to those who
sneer at this my city, and I give them back the sneer
and say to them:

   Come and show me another city with lifted head singing
so proud to be alive and coarse and strong and cunning.

   Flinging magnetic curses amid the toil of piling job on
job, here is a tall bold slugger set vivid against the
little soft cities.

—Carl Sandburg, *Chicago*

ANY STUDENT OF SOCIETY, at least in Europe, during the last decades of
the nineteenth century was unavoidably engaged with Marx as the most
substantial as well as the most inflammatory figure in the field. However
doubtful one may have been of his conclusions, let alone the revolutionary
agitation undertaken in his name, the strength and range of his analysis commanded attention. Sociology developed as a discipline in response to Marx.
One of its founders, Émile Durkheim, planned a study of Marx, although it
was never undertaken. His motives were both intellectual and political. He
had begun to study pre-Marxian socialism, according to his colleague Marcel
Mauss, "from a purely scientific point of view, as a fact which the scholar
should look upon coldly, without prejudice, and without taking sides."[1]

While rebutting Marx, sociology also served as a source of the "general form of social consciousness of the bourgeois intelligentsia" and the "reformulation of liberal ideology."[2] Liberalism lacked a dominant doctrinal source and contained many different strands. There was nonetheless a clear political project which was to find a way to avoid divisive class wars, which meant providing a credible basis for a program of reform to be implemented by an enlightened state. To those, particularly in the United States, who despaired of unconstrained capitalists or corrupt and manipulative party bosses as a source of wise policy, scientific research offered the possibility of real progress.

In Marx's schema, questions of power and interest were central. A more positivist science suggested something apolitical, disinterested, and dispassionate—as if investigating natural phenomena. When so much was at stake politically, could they really follow the evidence wherever it took them and be indifferent to the implications for the powerful and those who challenged them? In practice, mainstream social science was not politically innocent. Some supported conservative arguments by demonstrating the resilience of established social structures and, in the face of democratic optimism, the persistence of hierarchy. On the whole, however, the practitioners placed themselves on the side of progressive forces, representing the assertion of reason in human affairs, challenging myth and superstition. A Marxist had no trouble recognizing in such claims the ideology of a ruling group, professing a truth that happened to suit the interests of the bourgeoisie. The test of this ideology was whether it could provide a compelling account of economic and social change, and in the process, a guide to purposive action.

Max Weber

Max Weber exemplified both the problems and potential of social science. Born in 1864, he was the son of a minor liberal politician with whom he had a distant relationship. Weber's reputation and influence grew after his death from pneumonia in 1920, not least because (like Clausewitz) his devoted widow ensured that his writings were properly organized for posthumous publication. Her biography, published after the Second World War, presented him as moderate liberal, representing the best of Germany that had been suppressed by the Nazis. His views (along with his personal life) are now acknowledged to have been much more complex, certainly liberal (always evident in his readiness to speak up for the right of individuals to voice their opinions) but also imperialist and committed to a strong German state.[3]

He would not naturally appear on a list of strategic theorists, yet his influence was considerable. First, he sought to make the case for a value-free social science. Second, in his most famous work, *The Protestant Ethic and the Spirit of Capitalism*, he offered an alternative to Marx, demonstrating the role of cultural factors in the development of capitalism. Third, he described the spread of the rationalism of science into all aspects of life, turning him into an unenthusiastic prophet of bureaucratization. Fourth, he offered a view of politics that accepted it as part of a constant drama. Lastly, from this came a way of describing strategic choices that demanded attention to consequences as much as a yearning for an ideal.

The *Protestant Ethic* was notable for its concluding note of despair at the progressive "rationalism of western culture," with its celebration of routines, the calculable, predictable and instrumental, so that nature was subordinate to science and society to bureaucracy. The progressive complexity of organization, the specialism of knowledge, and the need for professional staffs all ensured bureaucracy's ascent. His conclusion warned of a coming "iron cage" in which a rational civil service administration, whose true value was only technical, would be viewed as the "ultimate and single value in reference to which the organization of all affairs ought to be decided." Those who lived in this cage would be "specialists without spirit, sensualists without heart." Bureaucracy was soulless and insensitive, staffed by pliant men with a narrow vision, competent but lacking in creativity, without any sense of a deeper purpose.

Bureaucracy played the same sort of role in Weber's worldview as capitalism did in Marx's. He understood its growing strength and irresistibility, for in his own work he sought to be a professional and competent technician, but he was unable to cheer. And while Marx had confidence that history would overturn capitalism, Weber held no such hope with regard to bureaucracy. Science had encouraged disenchantment in the loss of an unquestioning religious belief but could not offer a new enchantment. Weber valued freedom and openness and could not object in principle to legal codes, sound administration, and responsible officials. Life might be drained of a deeper meaning and stuck with the mundane, but at least the system worked. Bureaucracy was "formally the most rational known means of carrying out imperative control over human beings. It is superior to any other form in precision, in stability, in the stringency of its discipline, and in its reliability."[4] Likewise, politics was a permanent condition, unavoidable yet vexing, for nothing of permanence could result, whether peace, justice, or redemption. The sphere of politics was one of power and constant struggle. Power was about the ability to impose one's will in the face of resistance, which pointed to matters governed by force or the potential use of force. Politics was therefore bound up with the state. Politicians had to persuade others to follow, but this could no longer be done on the basis of custom and religion, and the bureaucratic method could not in itself be a source of values. This created the challenge of legitimacy, a test Weber posed in terms of acceptability rather than inherent worth.[5] The nature of political belief was a central puzzle for Weber, although one he tended to address in terms of types of belief rather than their substantive content.

During and just after the Great War, Weber delivered two lectures in Munich at the invitation of the Free Student Youth. The first, in November 1917, considered "Science as a Vocation," and the second, in January 1919, "Politics as a Vocation." Both are now considered landmark events in the history of social science. Weber had personally followed each vocation (or calling), but science most successfully. Part of his challenge was to work out what one could do for the other. The objectivity of science and the partisanship of politics had to be kept separate. The professor, he insisted, should not demand the right "to carry the marshal's baton of the statesman or reformer in his knapsack." This had an important consequence: once values were excluded, social science could not generate a political theory on its own. Though his own views were strongly held, Weber avoiding claiming that they were founded on science.[6] By the end of the war, the strain of holding strong views while resisting the temptation to insist that they were scientifically based was evident. One of the audience at the 1919 lecture has described how "this gaunt, bearded man looked now like a prophet tormented by visions of disaster, now like a medieval warrior before leaving for battle."[7]

For different reasons he did not make either the scientific or political vocations particularly appealing. Social science came over as especially forbidding,[8] combining a highly disciplined work ethic with ascetic self-denial. As Weber stressed practical difficulties and the need for specialist expertise, he adopted conceptual formulations that were not always accessible. While the importance of science as a vocation came to be seen in Weber's emphasis on the fact/value distinction, he went beyond discussing the limits of scientific knowledge as a source of political values to how it might "be employed to clarify the existence of facts and value in the world, and to aid thereby the selection of the means through which values should be pursued."[9] In this way science could serve strategy, by identifying the means necessary to achieve goals. Then it might be discovered that when faced with the appropriate means they are "such that you believe you must reject them. Then you simply must choose between the end and the inevitable means. Does the end 'justify' the means? Or does it not?" Science could not be a source of strategy because ends had to be identified by means of values which were outside its purview, but it could be of great strategic value by explaining why certain means might work or why certain ends were out of reach. The choice could be between "the lesser evil or of the relatively best." The interaction between science and values, effectively between means and ends, pointed not to their essential harmony but to constant tension. In "numerous instances," Weber observed, "the attainment of 'good' ends is bound to the fact that one must be willing to pay the price of using morally dubious means or at least dangerous ones—and facing the possibility or even probability of evil ramifications."[10] These dilemmas may now seem commonplace, but none before and few since have expressed them with such clarity, such an underlying conviction that no political system could ever resolve them definitively.

This theme was picked up in the second lecture. The context was even darker. Now the war was over, but Germany was still reeling from the surrender to Allied armies of the previous November and subsequent revolutionary and counterrevolutionary activity. While there was no doubt about his personal vocation as a scientist, at this his period of most active engagement, he displayed no special aptitude for politics. During the war he had worried about over-ambitious and aggressive war aims and was unhappy that his country was fighting the United States. When the war historian Hans Delbrück organized a petition, to counter one organized by more extreme academic nationalists, Weber signed up. In 1918, he returned to Germany from Vienna, where he had a visiting professorship, and seemed ready to take on a leading political role. It did not happen. He was involved in the committee on the new constitution and played some part in the formation of the new centrist German Democratic Party, but he was given no senior role in its leadership. A biographer observed that his political understanding was not always the best and "his tiresome tendency to get bogged down in unnecessary and unproductive controversies is not exactly evidence of a born politician."[11] As an active campaigner for the party, his tendency to lambast Left and Right alike in his speeches did not make him a natural coalition maker just when a coalition was needed. After it became apparent in 1920 that he was not going to be a major player, he withdrew from the party leadership, observing: "The politician should and must make compromises. But I am a scholar by profession... The scholar does not need to make compromises or to cover folly."[12] The political vocation was not for him.

Sentimentally he remained attached to the notion of a strong German state, was hostile to pacifism, and was angered by the sudden surge of revolutionary activity despite the involvement of a number of his friends.[13] He feared the demilitarization of the country, which would leave it powerless, and was annoyed at the disorder fomented by the revolutionaries. When he spoke in Munich, it was not long after the murder of the Spartacist leaders Luxemburg and Liebknecht, an action that he deplored though he had also recently expressed his irritation with the two theorists ("Liebknecht belongs in the madhouse and Rosa Luxemburg in the zoo"). He had only agreed to give the lecture because he feared that if he did not the lectern would be taken instead by Karl Eisner, the radical head of what Weber considered to be an incompetent Bavarian government.

This was a time when the dilemmas of political life were thrown into sharp relief. Defeat in war and convulsive revolutions illuminated how imperfect could be the fit between ends and means. It led Weber to present an analysis that went to the heart of the tensions in strategic thinking, insisting on the pointlessness of lofty goals if there was no means of achieving them. He continued to stress the need to analyze means by reference to their consequences.

Weber opened his lecture with his customary refusal "to take a position on actual problems of the day." This was followed with compelling definitions of politics and the state. Politics was about "the leadership, or the influencing of the leadership, of a political association, hence today, of a state." As the state could not be defined by its ends, for there were many possibilities, it had to be defined by its means, "namely, the use of physical force." By this he was not saying that force was the normal or only means available to the state, just that it was specific to the state. The state was therefore defined as "a human community that (successfully) claims the monopoly of the legitimate use of physical force within a given territory." Only the state could legitimize violence. Once that monopoly was threatened (as it was both externally and internally at that time), then the state was in trouble.

The state's authority would come from one of three sources: tradition, bureaucracy, or charisma. As tradition was no longer available and bureaucracy was too narrow, Weber looked to charisma, by which he meant a certain quality of political leadership, the ability to gain authority through sanctity, heroism, or exemplary character. Charisma was a political quality defining a leader's separate role from a civil servant. The politician must be prepared to "take a stand, to be passionate," while the civil servant must "execute conscientiously the order of the superior authorities, exactly as if the order agreed with his own conviction." The issue was how would power best be exercised: "What kind of a man must one be if he is to be allowed to put his hand on the wheel of history?"

The choice was between an ethic based on convictions (ultimate ends) and one based on responsibility, between acting according to underlying principle—even if this was detrimental to the cause—and acting according to the likely outcome. The lecture challenged those who refused to compromise on principle, the "intellectuals in this carnival we decorate with the proud name of 'revolution,'" for their empty romanticism, "devoid of all feeling of objective responsibility." Refusing to think about outcomes gave evil its opportunities. He scorned the revolutionaries whose actions favored the forces of reaction and oppression yet blamed others. Pure motives were not enough if they led to bad consequences.

Those who at that time in Germany sought "to establish absolute justice on earth by force," a number of whom were presumably in his student audience, should think about what this would mean. Could they be sure that their followers shared the same agenda? Might not this really be about the emotions of hatred, revenge, resentment, "and the need for pseudo-ethical self-righteousness," or else about a desire for "adventure, victory, booty, power, and spoils"? Could such followers be kept sufficiently rewarded and motivated? Would doing so contradict the original motives and objectives of the leaders? Would not this "emotional revolutionism," therefore, eventually give way—probably quite soon—to "the traditionalist routine of everyday life"? If the revolutionaries really thought the problem was the stupidity and baseness of the world, how did they think they were going to eradicate it? He challenged the pacifism of the Sermon on the Mount. The politician, he insisted, must take the opposite view, for without resistance he was "responsible for the evil winning out."

So Weber was speaking up for an ethic of responsibility, which recognized from the start the deficiencies of others and evaluated actions in terms of likely consequences. Yet he also worried about a politics focused purely on immediate effects without an underlying cause to give it meaning. His ideal was one in which the ethic of ultimate ends and responsibility come together in "a genuine man—a man who can have the 'calling for politics.'" Here he was looking for the charismatic figure, a hero as well as a leader, who would not "crumble when the world from his point of view is too stupid or too base for what he wants to offer." He was not optimistic: "Not summer's bloom lies ahead of us, but rather a polar night of icy darkness and hardness, no matter which group may triumph externally now." He urged a politics based on "both passion and perspective," for "man would not have attained the possible unless time and again he had reached out for the impossible."[14]

Weber's distrust of actions based on purity of motive rather than assessment of consequences reflected confidence in the ability to assess consequences and the role of scientific research in facilitating such assessments. Social action might always remain something of a gamble, but the odds could be shortened by formulating a reasonable hypothesis on what might be expected from alternative courses of action. Without this confidence, how was one proposed course of action to be assessed against another?

Tolstoy

If Weber had one figure in mind as representative of the ethic of ultimate ends it was Count Leo Tolstoy. The author was addressing all the issues connected with science, bureaucracy, and modernism that bothered him, but from a completely different perspective. At one point, Weber even thought about writing a book on Tolstoy as the great idealist of his time. Tolstoy, Weber allowed, was at least consistent, if "nothing else," in opposing both war and revolution, but that left him irreconcilable not only with war but with the world and the benefits of culture.[15] The preoccupation with Tolstoy was evident when Weber took aim at Tolstoy's antirationalist and antiscientific views in "Science as a Vocation." In "Politics as a Vocation," Weber picked on Tolstoy's favorite text, the Sermon on the Mount, when mocking the ethic of love which said "Resist not him that is evil with force."

This was Tolstoy's creed. Through a series of spiritual crises he had come to reject the pomp and privilege of the Orthodox Church and devise his own unique form of Christianity. The Sermon on the Mount and the principle of turning the other cheek was at its core. This led to a set of rules revolving around living in peace, not hating, not resisting evil, renouncing violence in all circumstances, and avoiding lust and swearing. If only these rules could be embraced universally, there would be no more wars nor armies, nor indeed police and courts. He challenged established ecclesiastical and secular power but was also against violent revolution as immoral and futile. He rejected the urban for the rural, and the generation of wealth for communion with nature.

We have already met Tolstoy in his role as an antistrategist. The wellsprings are the same. He was deeply skeptical about the ease with which deliberate causes could be linked with specific effects and therefore disdained those who claimed this as their expertise. He despised most of all, noted Berlin, "experts, professionals, men who claim special authority over other men." In *War and Peace*, he had mocked the presumption of those who claimed that a great general's act of will, expressed through orders delivered down the chain of command, could affect the actions of large numbers of men and so turn history. Generals and revolutionary intellectuals could claim to be following a scientific strategy, but they were deluded because they had become separated from and did not understand the ordinary people upon whom their schemes depended. Change, for better or worse, was the result of countless decisions of individuals caught up in events. Unfortunately, ordinary people were ignorant and uneducated, connected perhaps through their common feelings and values but unable to make sufficient sense of their plight or come together to create a new world.

Tolstoy might be of the Enlightenment when it came to his search for truth and an intense, gnawing belief that with a determined enough search it could be found, but he was also of the counter-Enlightenment in so many key respects, horrified by modernization and an exaggerated confidence in science, by efforts at political reform that lost sight of what he saw to be the fundamentals of the good life. He could not be "fitted into the public movements of his own, or indeed any other, age. The only company to which he belongs is the subversive one of questioners to whom no answer has been, nor is likely to be given."[16] Gallie observed, with understatement, that organized action was not Tolstoy's "forte" and that he was "distressingly weak on the practical side."[17] Even his own family was far from convinced about his new way of life.[18] What he offered, and in his case this was not trivial, was the power of example and many books and articles.

His uncompromising pacifism, challenge to tsarism, and exposés of the sufferings of the poor meant that his core messages were received loud and clear, and his effectiveness as a propagandist for his own views was enhanced by not only the way he lived but his literary gifts. His polemics included vivid descriptions of the struggles for existence in the city slums, the routine cruelties of army life, and the aristocracy's capacity for self-deception. His analyses of the iniquities of militarism and myopic patriotism were laced with sardonic wit and at times prophetic insight. He described the war fever of the future, as priests "pray on behalf of murder" and newspaper editors "set to work to arouse hatred and murder," and described how thousands of "simple, kindly folk" will be "torn from peaceful toil" and trudge off to war, until these poor souls "without knowing why, will murder thousands of others whom they had never before seen, and who had done nor could do them any wrong."[19] In this respect, war for Tolstoy was an extreme version of a much more general malaise, of unnatural divisions within humanity, which it both reflected and aggravated. And to explain how men could allow this to happen to them he deployed his own version of false consciousness—men had been "hypnotized" not only by their governments but, most tragically of all, by each other. Only by exposing the myth of patriotism could the spell be broken. At the heart of his antistrategic vision was the belief that divisions within human society were unnatural, and so if they were healed there would be no need for struggle and conflict.

In 1882, Tolstoy participated in the census of Moscow. He wrote an article that year, asking the "What Is to Be Done?" question that Russians often seemed to ask themselves at this time.[20] Moscow had experienced a period of fast growth, swelled by immigration from the countryside, with all the associated problems of overcrowding, poverty, crime, disease, and exploitation. The census, he explained, was a "sociological investigation." He added that, uniquely for a science, sociology's object was the "happiness of the people."[21] Unfortunately, despite this objective, whatever "laws" might be elucidated by gathering information, and whatever long-term benefits came through following these laws, little would happen of immediate benefit to the poor people whose lives were being reported. A compelling description of a wretched state of affairs could be an essential first step to action: "All the wounds of society, the wounds of poverty, of vice, of ignorance—all will be laid bare." But it was not enough. When encountering someone hungry and in rags, insisted Tolstoy, it was "more moment to succor him than to make all possible investigations." Instead of scientific detachment and a hurried moving on from one sad case to another, he urged forming relations with the poor and needy.

The true aim should be to break down "the barriers which men have erected between themselves."[22] This meant rejecting charity, which did no more than assuage the guilty consciences of the elite while reinforcing divisions. All should work together to heal the wounds of society. His call was to community and fraternity, which required like-minded people to reach out to the poor and oppressed. The benefits would be both material and spiritual. The alternative he warned was class warfare: "It need not be thus, and it should not, for this is contrary to our reason and our heart, and it cannot be if we are living people."

Unfortunately, as he soon discovered, where he led few followed. Furthermore, as he explored the under-life of the city, the more he concluded that have-nots were as corrupted by city life as the haves. The issue was not just the scale of the problem but the sort of society Moscow had become. He still could find some nobility among the poor, but when it came to drinkers and prostitutes he could make as much sense of them as they could of him. This was an alien culture, resistant to his overtures, surviving in ways that he found disagreeable. The more he explored city life the more his previous hopes appeared naïve. Eventually one night he stopped researching. He felt foolish and impracticable, like a physician who has uncovered the sore of a sick man but must recognize that "his remedy is good for nothing." He stopped taking notes. "I asked no questions, knowing that nothing would come of this."[23] The answer to "What Is to Be Done?" appeared to be "Nothing."

While he still blamed the excesses of his class for social divisions, he now saw urban life as the problem. Cities were venal and corrupt places, beyond reform. The cause went even deeper—the fault lay in the whole path humankind had taken in pursuit of economic development. Money had been allowed to get in the way of proper human relations. They could only be restored on the land where money could be irrelevant and people need not be alienated from each other and the beauty of nature. He set an example, returning to his estate in Yasnaya Polyana where he sought to create his own rural utopia, with but one garment, no money, and fulfillment through manual labor. With this complete retreat from modernity, Tolstoy insisted that he was living the only life that could be true to his faith. His stance was passive and uncooperative, but there was no direct action, for that would have involved both a degree of organization and a presumption of human agency.

"The Anarchists are right in everything," he wrote in 1890, "in the negation of the existing order, and in the assertion that, without Authority, there could not be worse violence than that of Authority under existing conditions." Their one mistake, he continued, was to think that this could come about through a revolution. It would only come about by there being "more and more people who do not require the protection of governmental power...There can be only one permanent revolution—a moral one: the regeneration of the inner man."[24]

Jane Addams

In May 1896, Tolstoy received a visitor at Yasnaya Polyana: Miss Jane Addams of Chicago. The daughter of a wealthy Illinois farmer, Addams was then in her mid-30s, and on her way to becoming one of the most admired and influential women in America. Her fame rested on the Hull House Settlement, founded in Chicago in 1889. This was modeled on the Toynbee Settlement in the East End of London, which she had visited a few years earlier. The underlying concept was that the educated and privileged should settle among the poor and deprived to the benefit of both. At Hull House, which at its peak was composed of thirteen buildings, could be found shelter, facilities for bathing, and a playground. In addition to opportunities to learn about and enjoy the so-called high culture of art, literature, and music, there were guest speakers and opportunities for debate, research, and campaigning.

Addams had read many of Tolstoy's books. She described *What to Do?*, published in the United States in 1887, as the source of her view that "only he who literally shares his own shelter and food with the poor, can claim to have served them."[25] The influence was evident, to the point of the great man being depicted in a mural in the Hull House dining room. As a strong pacifist and Christian with doubts about organized religion, she also explicitly embraced Tolstoy's commitment not to resist evil. She declared herself "philosophically convinced of the futility of opposition, who believe that evil can only be overcome with good and cannot be opposed." Poverty, disease, and exploitation were a challenge for society as a whole and must be resolved through forms of reconciliation before they led to conflicts that could tear society apart. She described the Gospel as "an outward symbol of fellowship, some bond of peace, some blessed spot where the unity of the spirit might claim right of way over all differences."[26]

Nonetheless, her encounter with Tolstoy was disappointing. He paid little attention to her description of Hull House while "glancing distrustfully at the sleeves of my travelling gown." The amount of cloth this involved, he declared, was sufficient to clothe many young girls. Was this not a "barrier to the people"? And, when discovering that she had a farm in Illinois, was she not an "absentee landlord"? He suggested she would do more use "tilling her own soil" than by adding to the crowded city. The charges were unjust, but bothered her sufficiently to determine to spend two hours each day at the bakery on her return to Chicago. She tried but failed. This was not the best use of her time.[27] This small incident revealed why she could not be a true follower of Tolstoy.

Tolstoy found the division of labor a crime against nature; Addams accepted that it was unavoidable. Her whole project was about getting people to accept the logic of inter-dependence. Whereas Tolstoy gave up on the city because it forced divisions among humanity, Addams believed that the city could and must be made to work for all its inhabitants. The fundamental point of principle Addams, and other progressives, shared with Tolstoy was a belief that social divisions were unnatural and could and must be transcended. But whereas Tolstoy believed in a world in which men, the land, and the spirit joined in unity, Addams sought to create a world without struggle in one of the least likely cities of the world, Chicago.

Chicago was then the world's fifth largest—after London, New York, Paris, and Berlin. It had taken shape far more recently than the others. The combined effects of the railroads, the city's position as the commercial and business center of the Midwest, and massive immigration had resulted in the population doubling from five hundred thousand in 1880 to over a million in 1890, and to double again to well over two million by 1910. Some 60 percent of the population had been born abroad, and all but 20 percent were of recent immigrant stock. Germans, Poles, Russians, Italians, and Irish all formed distinctive and self-conscious communities, often in uneasy relationships with each other. After a great fire in 1871 destroyed the old wooden buildings, the city was largely rebuilt in stone and steel.[28] Chicago invented the skyscraper. Money went into the arts, parks, and a brand new university, paid for by John D. Rockefeller. Life in the city was tough and conditions were dire. The "first in violence," wrote radical journalist Lincoln Steffens in 1904, "deepest in dirt; loud, lawless, unlovely, ill-smelling, new; an overgrown gawk of a village, the teeming tough among cities. Criminally it was wide open; commercially it was brazen; and socially it was thoughtless and raw."[29] For his novel *The Jungle*, Upton Sinclair went undercover in the stockyards to expose the awful circumstances of immigrant workers in the meatpacking industry.

Max Weber visited Chicago in the fall of 1904 en route to a major scientific congress in St. Louis. He described it, in a striking metaphor, as being "like a human being with its skin peeled off and whose intestines are seen at work."[30] He toured the stockyards, watching the automated process whereby an "unsuspecting bovine" entered the slaughtering area, was hit by a hammer and collapsed, gripped by an iron clamp, hoisted up and started on a journey which saw workers "eviscerate and skin it." It was possible, he observed, to "follow a pig from the sty to the sausage and the can." At the time of his visit the Amalgamated Meat Cutters and Butcher Workman's Union were smarting after a defeat in a strike aimed at getting the stockyards unionized. Weber, apparently with a degree of exaggeration, described the aftermath: "Masses of Italians and Negroes as strike-breakers; daily shootings with dozens of dead on both sides; a streetcar was overturned and a dozen women were squashed because a non-union man had sat in it; dynamite threats against the Elevated Railway, and one of its cars was actually derailed and plunged into the river."[31] He also visited the Hull House Settlement, about which his wife Marianne wrote in glowing terms: "It includes a day nursery, accommodations for 30 women workers, a sports facility for young people, a large concert hall with a stage, an instructional kitchen, a kindergarten, rooms for all kinds of instruction in needlework and manual tasks, etc. During the winter 15,000 people of both sexes come here to receive instruction, inspiration, counsel, and enjoy themselves."[32]

Addams had inserted herself and Hull House into a maelstrom of urban divisions, a result of the persistent issue of race and the treatment of blacks, agrarian decline and urban rise, inter-ethnic tensions, and constant clashes between capital and labor. She attached herself to Progressivism, the major liberal project in the United States at the time. The Progressives saw the social problems of the time as the core challenge for government and feared that without urgent action they would lead to fractures that would be impossible to heal. Government must be a unifying force, above sectional interests, on behalf of society as a whole. In this Addams was a democratic optimist, convinced of the capacity of ordinary people to play constructive roles in civic affairs, with their own ideas on how to bring order and decency into their lives. She contrasted this to what she considered the naïve view, attributed to the English Fabians, "that somewhere in Church or State are a body of authoritative people who will put things to rights as soon as they really know what is wrong."[33] By making great art and big ideas available to ordinary people, she believed that they would be better able to develop themselves and make informed choices in their lives.

As a formidable social and political critic, she castigated the failure of the city government to clean the streets, educate the children, and regulate the workplace. She was a feminist, believed in racial equality, and backed labor unions. Yet her deepest conviction was that no conflict need be pursued to the point of violence and that ways could be found to reconcile the apparently irreconcilable. While she associated with socialists, she rejected economic determinism, class consciousness, and all preparations for a violent confrontation. While supporting unions, she wished they would make more of an effort to reach out to those they saw as their enemies. Hull House, she insisted, was "soberly opened on the theory that the dependence of classes on each other is reciprocal."[34] She understood why people were driven to extreme ends, but could not approve. She was at the same time appalled by a city apparently out of control, failing to ensure a decent way of life for its inhabitants, and desperate for an alternative to class warfare as a source of change. Somehow she wanted to get all the sections of the community, capitalist and worker, conservative and agitator, meeting under one roof. Then they would see through their differences to let the bemused immigrant, coping daily with the unscrupulous and exploitative, meet a "better type of American."[35]

Her philosophy was set out in an essay prompted by a bitter dispute in Chicago involving the Pullman Company. The origins of this dispute did not lie simply in crude business practices but Pullman's paternalism in providing their workers with their own township. A recession led to cuts in workers' wages but not the rents for their homes. The workers' reaction was intense, leading to a dispute that lasted for months, considerable violence (thirteen deaths), and martial law. In her essay, Addams likened the conflict to that between King Lear and his daughter Cordelia, a conflict that both lost because of their failure to appreciate the other's position.[36] "We are all practically agreed that the social passion of the age is directed toward the emancipation of the wage-worker," she wrote:

> But just as Cordelia failed to include her father in the scope of her salvation and selfishly took it for herself alone, so workingmen in the dawn of the vision are inclined to claim it for themselves, putting out of their thoughts the old relationships; and just as surely as Cordelia's conscience developed in the new life and later drove her back to her father, where she perished, drawn into the cruelty and wrath which had now become objective and tragic, so the emancipation of working people will have to be inclusive of the employer from the first or it will encounter many failures, cruelties and reactions.[37]

Addams recognized the existence of conflicts, acknowledged that they were not wholly artificial, and accepted that groups might frustrate and irritate each other. But she also believed that it must be possible to prevent these conflicts from descending into violence. The problem, as Elshtain observed, was that she was committed to a "best-case scenario of the cosmopolitan future," which played down the pugnacity of the various ethnic groups. Her own ability to navigate the complex ethnic politics of Chicago and identify shared interests turned this into her core mission. She saw sufficient examples of people putting aside their prejudices and traditional antagonisms as a result of the exigencies of the daily struggle for survival to make her optimistic about what could be achieved with any conflict, including one between states. Given the chance to express itself, the inherent goodness of people could overcome difference and even render war irrelevant. Presenting herself as "spokesperson for all peace loving women of the world," she risked her popularity by opposing the U.S. entry into war in 1917. After the war, she devoted her energies to promoting peace, to the point of winning the Nobel Prize in 1931. She assumed that "the reconciliations resulting from the imperatives of city life could be replicated at an international level" and was convinced that "any concern for defense and security was tantamount to accepting militarism and authoritarianism."[38]

John Dewey

Addams shared Tolstoy's wariness about detached academic research that did little for the subjects. Nonetheless, largely at the instigation of Florence

Kelley, who had a doctorate from Zurich and past dealings with Engels, Hull House was the center of a series of studies of the neighborhood, providing a compelling description of urban life at the turn of the century. It reflected progressive optimism that if the facts could be made known about social conditions, then measures might be taken to address them.[39]

At the University of Chicago, the idea that social research and action should go together was taken as almost a given. Albion Small was the founding head of the university's sociology department, the first in the United States, and until the start of the Second World War, the discipline's American "capital."[40] Small was an ordained minister who saw little incompatibility between his Christianity and social inquiry, and promoted sociology as charting a way forward between the forces of reaction and revolution. It was a tool for democratic change: "Conventionality is the thesis, Socialism the antithesis, Sociology is the synthesis."[41] In an article tellingly entitled "Scholarship and Social Agitation," he provided a robust defense of the progressive creed. American scholars, he wrote, should "advance from knowledge of facts to knowledge of forces, and from knowledge of forces to control of forces in the interest of more complete social and personal life." He lacked either sympathy with or confidence in any conception of sociology, "which is satisfied with abstractions, or which does not keep well in mind the relation of all research to the living interests of living men." For these purposes, Chicago provided an exceptional base. It was a "vast sociological laboratory."[42]

This experimental aspect excited John Dewey, who joined the University of Chicago in 1894 with an established reputation in psychology and philosophy. By the time he arrived he was moving into more radical political and intellectual positions, encouraged by his wife Alice. The university itself was not a comfortable place for radicals. Men had been fired for giving too vocal support for labor. But Dewey also saw Chicago as "filled with problems holding out their hands and asking somebody to please solve them." He found his outlet at Hull House, where he became a friend of Addams and lectured regularly. His arrival coincided with the Pullman strike. Although at first all his sympathies had been with the unions, Addams persuaded him of the need to promote reconciliation rather than struggle. This view was reinforced by the costs of the union's failure. His distinctive brand of liberalism reflected an interest in the health of the social organism, which could be damaged by unnecessary divisions, rather than in the more classical liberal concerns with individual rights. But he also felt a firm conviction that this could be achieved through democracy, which he later claimed to be the one constant in his long life.[43] He shared this particular form of democratic optimism with Addams. It was reflected in an educational philosophy focused on creating conditions in which all could realize their potential by learning how to think about the self as part of society, which in turn would encourage compromise and accommodation. His view was that all those affected by institutions, from schools to the workplace, should have a role in their decision-making. He advocated participatory democracy, a source of both better government and an improving and civilizing experience. Unlike Addams, he was not a pacifist and did support America's entry into the First World War, although he took an ardent antiwar stance thereafter.[44]

What he sought from philosophy was not a "device for dealing with the problems of philosophers" but instead "a method, cultivated, by philosophers, for dealing with the problems of men."[45] It was to offer a challenge to conservatism and an alternative to revolution. The radicals and conservatives needed to be brought together. The radicals would provide the "future vision and the stimulus to act," but "without the wisdom of past experience," they would be "wanton and disorganized," following only "the random and confused excitation of the hour."

This created a special role for the social reformer. As "psychologist, social worker, and educator," this person had to "interpret opposing sides to each other, simultaneously reconciling social antagonists and completing the incomplete personalities of individuals involved."[46] A view of society as an organic whole challenged laissez-faire economics based on assumptions of autonomous individuals. Lazy Darwinian talk about the survival of the fittest, which taken too literally was a recipe for violence, had to be replaced by the imperatives of social solidarity. If there was an evolutionary process at work it was the gradual acceptance that the rational way forward would be based on cooperation and reciprocity rather than individual gain.[47] This was a philosophy for the non-strategist, whose aim was to overcome conflicts rather than conduct them effectively. Yet he also adopted pragmatism, which as a philosophy has come to be associated with strategy.

The origins of the word *pragmatism* lie in the Latin *pragmaticus*, linked in Roman times to being active and businesslike. For a while it had a negative connotation as excessive activity, in the sense of meddling or interfering. By the nineteenth century, however, pragmatism had become more positive. It referred to treating facts or events systematically and practically, being realistic and factual, aiming at what was achievable rather than what was ideal. Its origins as a philosophical construct go back to the eighteenth-century German philosopher Immanuel Kant. As an example of a situation in which it was necessary to act in the face of uncertainty, Kant used a doctor treating a patient and making a diagnosis on the basis of observed symptoms. As he could not be sure that this was the right treatment, his belief was contingent.

Another physician might come to a different and better conclusion. "Such contingent belief, which yet forms the ground for the actual employment of means to certain actions, I entitle pragmatic belief." This describes exactly the sort of belief required for strategy, one acknowledged to be no more than a best guess in the face of uncertainty, but sufficient to permit action.

Charles Pierce took the view that Kant was not describing a particular type of belief but all belief, for all was contingent. All actions were bets because all depended on a degree of guesswork. A belief that worked was a winning bet. The psychologist and philosopher, William James, who died aged 68 in 1910, is widely considered to be the true father of pragmatism. He took Pierce's insight and developed it further. He defined the pragmatic method as "the attitude of looking away from first things, principles, 'categories,' supposed necessities; and of looking toward last things, fruits, consequences, fact."[48] For James, ideas did not start true but became true as a result of events. An idea's "verity is in fact an event, a process; the process namely of its verifying itself." What were described as beliefs were not about truth but about preparations for action. "Beliefs, in short, are really rules for action; and the whole function of thinking is but one step in the production of habits of action."[49] On this basis, the test was not how much a belief described reality but whether it was effectively prescriptive. As with banknotes, which had value so long as they were accepted as currency, so with ideas. They were true so long as this was acknowledged by others. This could stand as a shrewd observation about the fate of ideas in the public arena, though it had awkward implications for the reliability of claims about truth.

Pragmatism could be a prescription of how to think, a form of reasoning that encouraged a proper evaluation of the outcomes of actions, to be commended to strategists and contrasted with modes of thought that were crude and insensitive. Or it could be a description of how everybody thought, with the understanding that some were more effective thinkers than others. As a response to a growing awareness of the conditionality of knowledge, beliefs became working hypotheses and events experiments. Just as physical scientists could only confirm their hypotheses through experiment, so all social action was an attempt to validate through experiment a hypothesis about consequences.

It was on this basis that Dewey retained a commitment to the idea of a progressive, experimental science. This was captured in his preference for the term "instrumentalism" rather than "pragmatism," though this did not catch on.[50] Pragmatism worked for him as a means of making sense of the origins of beliefs and how they developed through experience. Unlike Weber, he did not consider facts to exist separately from values. The viewer's perspective was bound to shape how he saw the world. The worldview changed not because of shifting values but because of different forms of engagement. Dewey was sufficiently confident in the working hypothesis that thinking and acting were part of the same process to not only develop an educational theory on this basis but also apply it in what became known, tellingly, as the Laboratory School in Chicago.

Thoughts were therefore not so much revelations of reality as means of adapting to reality. Truth was what worked in practice. Views of reality were always partial and incomplete, our own constructions rather than objective representations. As critics observed, this line of argument led to relativism if pushed too far; one set of beliefs was as good as any other so long as it worked as a guide to action. But whether or not it "worked" depended on how effects were evaluated.[51] This is why social research was important, for if it were cumulative, then the risk of being surprised by the consequences of actions should be reduced. So when considering the standard ethics question of whether ends justified the means, Dewey had no doubt that means could only be justified by results. He accepted that confidence in particular means leading to a desirable end might need to be qualified by the same action having other, less-desired consequences. Before acting, therefore, it was necessary to consider the full range of possible consequences, intended as well as unintended, and on that basis make a choice.[52] That required considerable foresight. Without it, the value of pragmatism was undermined.

Dewey linked an intellectual process with a social process. He was in accord with Tolstoy in assuming that a good life was one developed as part of a community. Because of the potential for conflict—and here he differed from Tolstoy—Dewey saw democracy as a way of bringing individuals' needs in line with each other and the wider community, transcending apparent antagonisms, and integrating the private with the public. This meant accepting that individual goals might not be met in full while there was progress toward social goals, and that this could be achieved by an active state. Conflict was not a means of resolving problems; it was the problem to be resolved.

Dewey decided not to go to the 1904 Congress to which Weber had been invited and so the two did not meet (although he met James at Harvard). Weber would have been aware of Dewey's work because of the overlap, at least in some core themes, with his own. They were on similar tracks in their appreciation of the scientific method, their focus on the relationship of thought to action, and their stress on the need to judge actions by consequence as much as intent. There were also crucial differences between the two. While Dewey did not take seriously attempts to separate fact from value, Weber insisted upon it. While Dewey saw democracy as inclusive and participatory, for Weber the value of democracy was as a means of electing a proper leader from a wide pool and ensuring a degree of accountability.

It was as a strategist's philosophy that pragmatism prospered. It came to be taken to refer to a particularly political virtue, a talent for adapting ends and means to a changing environment; demonstrating flexibility; accepting a world of contingency, trial, error, policy reversals, and shifting positions. A pragmatist could be compared favorably with the dogmatist, who refused to compromise and was impervious to circumstances and negligent of evidence. But Dewey combined this strategist's philosophy, pragmatism, with an a-strategic worldview, which sought to deny deep conflicts and supplant politics with research-led reform. Menand observes that "a time when the chance of another civil war did not seem remote, a philosophy that warned against the idolatry of ideas was possibly the only philosophy on which a progressive politics could have been successfully mounted."[53] In this respect it provided a form of thinking that appeared both provocative and reassuring. But there was no inherent reason why this should be so. Consideration of consequences depended on confidence that they could be discerned, at least to a useful approximation. This might allow the best choice to be made, but that choice might still be between two evils.

In 1936, Robert Merton, an American sociologist influenced by Weber, wrote "The Unanticipated Consequences of Purposive Social Action."[54] The main explanation normally offered for why all consequences could not be anticipated, Merton noted, was ignorance, which led to the view that more and better knowledge would steadily improve the quality and effectiveness of action. But there were limits to what knowledge could be acquired and, anticipating a point that would be made many years later by behavioral economists, Merton questioned whether it was always worth the time and energy to acquire extra knowledge. Another factor was error, assuming for example, that just because a course of action had produced a desired result a previous time it would do so again, without paying regard to variations in circumstances. This could reflect carelessness or something more psychological, "a determined refusal or inability to consider certain elements of the problem."

Next came what Merton called the "imperious immediacy of interest," putting an emphasis on the short term to the exclusion of consideration of later consequences. An action might be rational in seeking to ensure a particular outcome, but "precisely because a particular action is not carried out in a psychological or social vacuum, its effects will ramify into other spheres of value and interest." Lastly, he made the point central to all strategy: "Public predictions of future social developments are frequently not sustained precisely because the prediction has become a new element in the concrete situation, thus tending to change the initial course of developments." He took the example of Marx's predictions. The "socialist preaching in the nineteenth century" led to labor organizations which took advantage of collective bargaining, "thus slowing up, if not eliminating, the developments which Marx had predicted."

At the heart of any debate on strategy was the question of cause and effect. Strategic action presumed that desired effects would follow from the choice of appropriate courses of action. In principle, social science should have made strategic choices easier, because causal relationships would be much better understood. This created its own ethical imperatives. For Weber, the possibility of appreciating the likely consequences of action or inaction meant that it was irresponsible not to take advantage of the greater insights that social science had to offer. For Dewey, it was also foolish, because it meant denying an opportunity to get the most from every action. For Tolstoy, the foolishness was only in the conceit that social processes—in all their complexity—could ever be properly grasped. There could be no true experts in these matters. No human mind could grasp the totality of factors that were at play in great and social and political processes. There could be no strategy because there could be no confidence in the difference any particular action could make.

In the early decades of the twentieth century, to deny the possibility of strategy was to abandon hope in the face of enormous and pressing social and political issues. Yet there were undoubtedly good reasons for caution. The more complex and novel the situation, the harder it would be to link actions with consequences. Unintended outcomes might be as significant as the intended. Even when short-term goals were reached the benefits might be overwhelmed by adverse longer-term consequences. Most challenging of all were those situations where there was an opponent seeking to refute one's working hypothesis. Even if cause-effect relationships were properly understood, there might still not be available measures sufficient to generate the required effects. It was one thing to change education policy and quite another to alter the course of capitalism or dispel a pernicious myth to which the masses were in thrall. The optimism that enlightened social policies informed by a progressive social science could heal the wounds of industrialization was a casualty of the mid-century's ideological, economic, and military calamities. The transformational social and political changes that were set in motion in the later decades of the century were barely influenced by the prescriptions of mainstream social science, but were the result of individuals and groups seeking to improve their lives through collective action.

CHAPTER 22 | Formulas, Myths, and Propaganda

Frankly to manufacture thought

Is like a masterpiece by a weaver wrought.

—Goethe, *Faust*

WHEREAS WEBER AND Dewey represented distinctive strands of the liberal critique of Marxism, there was a more conservative critique developed by the so-called Italian school of neo-Machiavellians. Notable among them were the Sicilian Gaetano Mosca, who held a number of academic and political positions within Italy during a long life; the German sociologist Robert Michels, who spent most of his career in Italy; and the Italian Vilfredo Pareto, who began his career in Italy but then decamped to Geneva. Their ideas developed as an explicit correction to expectations of a progressively more equal and democratic society, and were marked less by strategic considerations than by a keen sense of the limits of what strategy might achieve. They were part of a movement away from political economy and into sociology, as explanations were sought for the less rational aspects of social behavior. They were described as the heirs of Machiavelli,[1] not only because of the Italian link but also because they took him to be a model of an unsentimental approach to the study of politics, accepting the harsh realities of its practice and refusing to take at face value the comforting rhetoric of its practitioners.

The core proposition was that a minority would always rule over a majority. The key questions therefore revolved around the means by which the elite sustained its position and how it might be displaced. The most significant empirical work on the impact of organizational needs on democratic claims was undertaken by Robert Michels, a student of Weber's. As an active member of the German Social Democrat Party, Michels had come to recognize the importance of the party bureaucracy in shaping its goals and strategy. While nobody doubted that capitalist parties were non-democratic, whatever they might say about the "will of the people,"[2] socialist parties posed a sharper test for the democratic principle because of their proclaimed egalitarianism. Michels's analysis fitted in perfectly with Weber's theories of bureaucratization. Unlike his radical student, however, Weber was content with the consequential loss of revolutionary élan. Concepts such as the "genuine will of the people," he explained to Michels, "have long since ceased to exist for me; they are fictitious notions."[3]

Michels's study of the pre-war SPD demonstrated how growth and electoral success drained the party of militancy: "Organization becomes the vital essence of the party." So long as the party was growing the leadership was content, reluctant to put the organization at risk by taking any bold steps that might challenge the state. As they developed an interest in their own self-perpetuation, Michels noted, "from a means, organization becomes an end."[4] Organization was demanding and complicated, requiring specialist skills. Those who knew how to manage finances, look after members, produce literature, and direct campaigns acquired superior knowledge and controlled both the form and content of communications. So long as they stayed united, the relatively incompetent masses had no chance to impose their will. "Who says organization, says oligarchy." This was Michels's "iron law."

Beyond this law, and his consequential disillusionment with socialism, Michels did not offer much of a general theory. In this respect, Mosca was more important. His starting point was simple: in all political systems, at all times and places, there was a ruling class, a "minority of influential persons, to which management, willingly or unwillingly, the majority defer."[5] Mosca considered rule by a single individual to be as unlikely as by the majority. This was because of the necessity of organization. Majorities were inherently disorganized and individuals by definition lacked organization. So only minorities could stay organized, which meant that key political struggles must also take place within the elite. To become preeminent, hard work and ambition made a difference, more so than a sense of justice and altruism. Most important were "perspicacity, a ready intuition of individual and mass psychology, strength of will and, especially confidence in oneself."[6] Changing circumstances influenced the rise and fall of elites—priests would fare best in a religious society and warriors in one at war. If a particular social force declined in importance so would those who derived their power from it.

Pareto followed closely on Mosca (not always, Mosca suggested, with full attribution). Trained in engineering and after a spell in industry, Pareto first made his name in economics and then in sociology. As an economist at the University of Lausanne he worked in the neoclassical tradition. Here he followed Léon Walras, the father of general equilibrium theory, responsible for the proposition that if all other markets in an economy are in equilibrium, then any specific market must also be in equilibrium. In his 1885 book *Elements of Pure Economics*, Walras proved this mathematically, thereby setting a precedent for economic theory that would be picked up enthusiastically in the middle of the next century, particularly in the United States.

Pareto gave his name to two contributions. The Pareto principle suggested that 80 percent of effects came from 20 percent of the causes. This rough rule of thumb indicated that a minority of inputs could be responsible for a disproportionate share of outputs, in itself a challenge to notions of equality. Secondly, and more substantively, he gave his name to the concept of Pareto efficiency, which also influenced later economic thought. In 1902 he published a critique of Marxism, which marked his move away from economics toward sociology. Pareto appreciated Marx's idea of class conflict and his hard-edged approach to the analysis of human behavior, but parted company on the belief that class conflict would be transcended through proletarian victory. The people might well believe that they were fighting for a great cause, and maybe the leaders did too. In practice, however, the elite would look after itself. Even in a collectivist society there would still be conflict—for example between intellectuals and non-intellectuals. One of Pareto's most important and influential themes, derived from his background in engineering and economics, was that of social equilibrium. He argued that societies were inherently resistant to change. When disturbed by either internal or external forces, some counteracting movement developed and they tended to return to their original state. His elitism was reflected in his view of the masses as the body of humanity left over after the elite have been subtracted ("the incompetent, those lacking energy, character and intelligence"),[7] just as most conduct was in a residual nonlogical category once the logical had been subtracted.

An intriguing aspect of Pareto's work was his analysis of the role of strategy in political systems. This was not quite how he phrased the issue, but it is a reasonable decoding of the rather idiosyncratic language he adopted, notably in his most important work, the four-volume study published in English as *The Mind and Society*.[8] Rather than talk of strategy Pareto referred to "logical conduct." This was essentially procedural rationality: action should be oriented to an attainable goal using means appropriate to that goal. In his terminology, that would mean that the objective end (what was achieved) and the subjective purpose (what was intended) would be identical. This set a very high standard for logicality. With "nonlogical conduct," by contrast, objective ends and subjective purposes would diverge. Here, either action lacked purpose, or the claimed purpose was out of reach or could not be attained by the methods employed. Not surprisingly, he found this to be common. Examples of nonlogical conduct might be the practice of magic, reliance on superstition, dependence on routine, yearnings for utopias, and exaggerated confidence in the competence of individuals and organizations or in the effectiveness of particular tactics.

Pareto saw the roots of nonlogical action in "residues" (what is left over when the logical is taken away). These were constant, instinctive factors influencing behavior, while "derivations" changed over time and space. The analysis of residues began in the second of a four-volume work and soon became extraordinarily discursive and complicated. Well into volume four, the previous six residues were effectively reduced to two, and these were shown to match Machiavelli's distinction between lions and foxes, as representatives of force and guile. The residue associated with foxes, Pareto's Class I, reflected the "instinct of combinations"—the impulse to make connections between disparate elements and events, to think imaginatively, encourage attempts to outwit others, maneuver out of trouble, generate ideologies, and form expedient coalitions.

By contrast, Class II residues, those associated with lions, reflected the "persistence of aggregates," referred to tendencies to consolidate established positions, instincts for permanence, stability, and order. The lions would demonstrate an attachment to family, class, nation, and religion and make their appeals to solidarity, order, discipline, property, or family. Pareto associated lions with a greater readiness to use force. Although the lions seemed to be more conservative and foxes more radical, this was not necessarily the case. In Pareto's terminology, ideology was a derivation and thus a rationalization for something deeper. Force might be used to protect the status quo as well as to overthrow it. In this way Pareto represented as "residues" the two poles of classic strategy, force and guile, one solving problems with physical strength and the other with brainpower. Pareto did not present these characteristics as matters of degree but as distinctive and exclusive types.

The elite was more likely to be composed of intelligent foxes, maintaining their position through cunning and deceit, with the more stolid and unimaginative lions found among the masses, bound by a sense of group loyalty. Foxes would seek to govern through consent, and so would devise ideologies to keep the masses satisfied and seek short-term fixes to crises rather than use force. Here lay the vulnerability of the foxes. Their readiness to compromise and squeamishness when it came to using force would weaken the regime. At some point, their maneuvers would no longer work and they would face hard opponents who could no longer be outwitted. When the more tough-minded lions governed, they tended to rely on force and would be uninterested in compromise, claiming to be defending higher values. As neither group would endure on its own, the most stable regime would have a mixture of both types. In practice, each would tend to recruit their own kind. Fox regimes would degenerate over time and become vulnerable to a sudden show of force; lion regimes would more likely be infiltrated by foxes and would thus experience more gradual decline. Out of all of this Pareto postulated the "circulation of elites." There was always an elite, but it could change in composition. The advantage should be with the shrewd and the cunning, but not to the point where violence could never be advised.

The idea that political history can be viewed as a dialectic between practitioners of force and guile had a certain appeal. But Pareto was generalizing out of his own political context, reflecting his skepticism of democratic claims and distaste for the corrupt and cynical politics of his time, and then looking for historical parallels to bolster his theory, playing down the impact of material changes and the growing importance of bureaucratic organization.[9] This did not, as we shall see, prevent his ideas from influencing conservative circles as they looked for intellectually robust alternatives to socialism and Marx.

Crowds and Publics

Conservatives might assume that elites were always present; radicals might be convinced that they could be overthrown. Both had an interest in how they managed to hold on to power when force was used so rarely. Both looked to ideology as the explanation. Whether or not elites were vulnerable would depend on the strength of the ideological hold over the masses. Marx assumed that such a challenge would develop with the class struggle. A growing self-consciousness would lead the working class to acquire a political identity and become more than an analytical category. Unfortunately for the theory, not only had the class structure developed in more complex ways than Marx envisaged but workers had also persistently embraced incorrect thoughts.

The challenge for socialists was to demonstrate the scientific correctness as well as the political potential of a true class consciousness. They must battle with the purveyors of false consciousness, from the clergy filling workers' minds with religious nonsense to reformers—possibly even more pernicious—claiming that they could make the system responsive to the needs of workers without revolution. For the conservative elitists, political stability did not depend on whether beliefs were false or correct but whether they kept the masses satisfied, or else encouraged insurrectionary sentiments.

Mosca wrote of a "political formula" that would serve the ruling class by providing a persuasive link to broader concepts that were generally understood and appreciated. Examples might be racial superiority, divine right, or the "will of the people." The formula needed to be more than "tricks and quackeries," deliberate deceptions by cynical rulers. Instead, it should reflect a popular need. Mosca assumed a mass preference to be "governed not on the basis of mere material or intellectual force, but on the basis of a moral principle." A formula might not correspond to "truth" but it needed acceptance: should skepticism about its validity become widespread, then the effect would be to undermine the social order.

The fascination with consciousness was boosted by the developing field of social psychology. A particularly influential book was Gustave Le Bon's *The Crowd: A Study of the Popular Mind,* which we have already encountered as an influence on the military thinker "Boney" Fuller. Published in France in 1895 but soon widely translated, it was in many respects another deeply conservative, elitist lament about the unraveling of hierarchy, about how the "divine right of the masses" had displaced the "divine right of kings." Le Bon was hostile to socialism and labor unions as examples of how the masses could be exploited by malign demagogues. What caught attention was his exploration of the sources of irrationality in the psychology of crowds. Le Bon argued, in a theme that was to become ever more prominent in social thought, that a far more important influence on conscious acts than deliberate reason was "an unconscious substratum created in the mind in the main by hereditary influences." Such influences became strong as individuals turned into crowds, and irrationality was given full rein.

> Moreover, by the mere fact that he forms part of an organized crowd, a man descends several rungs in the ladder of civilization. Isolated, he may be a cultivated individual; in a crowd, he is a barbarian—that is, a creature acting by instinct. He possesses the spontaneity, the violence, the ferocity, and also the enthusiasm and heroism of primitive beings, whom he further tends to resemble by the facility with which

he allows himself to be impressed by words and images—which would be entirely without action on each of the isolated individuals composing the crowd—and to be induced to commit acts contrary to his most obvious interests and his best-known habits. An individual in a crowd is a grain of sand amid other grains of sand, which the wind stirs up at will.[10]

Le Bon's tone was pessimistic but he held out a possibility for getting a grip on the masses. Because their views did not reflect their interests, or indeed any serious thought, the same impressionable crowd that could fall prey to the nonsensical notions of socialist demagogues might be just as suggestible to contrary notions put forward by a shrewd elite that had studied group psychology. Making appeals to reason was pointless when illusion was the key. The requirement was for drama, for a compelling and startling image— "absolute, uncompromising and simple"—that "fills and bests the mind." Mastering the "art of impressing the imagination of crowds is to know at the same time the art of governing them." Le Bon became essential reading for governing elites.

A subversive version of a similar idea came from the Frenchman Georges Sorel, a provincial engineer who turned in middle age to study and writing. His politics veered wildly during his life, although his contempt for rationalism and moderation was a constant. Hughes described his mind as "a windy crossroads by which there blew nearly every new social doctrine of the early twentieth century."[11] His critical stance turned him into a perceptive social theorist who was taken seriously in his time.[12] He embraced Marx idiosyncratically, presenting him as less the prophet of capitalism's economic collapse and more the predictor of the bourgeoisie's moral collapse.[13] He took from Le Bon the conviction that the rationality of man was lost among the masses, which meant that he was unable to place a faith in mass political movements.

Disgusted with decadent elites, cowards, and humbugs who lacked the gumption to fight for their privileges and were eager to make accommodations with their adversaries, he imagined them being swept away in an act of decisive, cleansing violence. The model he had in mind was a Napoleonic battle, ending with the utter defeat of the enemy. He is largely remembered for one book, *Reflections on Violence*, written during his syndicalist phase, a movement which appealed to him partly because it did not involve political parties. Here he developed his most potent idea, that of the myth. In its content, a myth need be neither analytical nor programmatic. It could be beyond refutation, nonlogical and irrational, a composition of images as much as words, which "by intuition alone, before any considered analyses are made, is capable of evoking as an undivided whole the mass of sentiments which correspond to the different manifestations of the war undertaken by socialism against modern society."

The stress on the importance of intuition betrays the influence of the French philosopher Henri Bergson, whose lectures Sorel attended in Paris. The only real test of a myth was whether it could drive a political movement forward. It would be more about conviction and motivation than the expositions of systematic ideas. A successful myth would compel men to act in a great radical cause, convincing them of their ultimate triumph. Myths were negative in their inspiration—more about destruction than creation. Sorel had a particular aversion to utopianism and claims that men would act out of goodness. Examples were primitive Christianity or Mazzinian nationalism. At the time of *Reflections*, the myth that he had in mind was a syndicalist general strike. He had lost confidence in a Marxist revolution. Later he was prepared to accept either Lenin's Bolshevism or Benito Mussolini's Fascism. Arguably, the focus on finding a myth that worked and evaluating ideas by their ideological effects could be considered pragmatic, even if this was not quite what the pragmatists had in mind.

Gramsci

One of those influenced by Sorel was Antonio Gramsci. A childhood accident had left him short, hunchbacked, and sickly, but his formidable intellect and wide-ranging interests enabled him to get a scholarship to university and then establish himself as a radical journalist. He was active in the Factory Council movement in Turin, supported by Sorel, and then helped found the Italian Communist Party (PCI) after it split from the socialists in 1921. After spending eighteen months in Moscow as Italian delegate to the Communist International, Gramsci watched with dismay as disunity on the left allowed for the rise of Fascism in Italy. Though initially spared prison as a member of the Chamber of Deputies, and so almost by default becoming general secretary of the PCI, he was eventually arrested in November 1926. Aged 35, he was sentenced to twenty years imprisonment by the Fascists. By the time of his release, his health was shattered and he died in 1937.

While in prison he filled numerous notebooks with notes on a vast range of issues, stimulated by voracious reading. His thoughts were intended to be developed more systematically once he regained his freedom. They remained notes, however—sketchy, incomplete, and often deliberately lacking in clarity to confuse his jailors. As a body of work they are now considered to represent an important contribution to both Marxist and non-Marxist theory. Gramsci was not truly "discovered" until after the Second World War, long after his death, when he was acclaimed as a humane and non-dogmatic Marxist. He challenged the mechanistic formulations inherited from the days of the Second International, arguing against reliance on historic laws of progress to produce a happy socialist conclusion and taking account of culture as much as economics. Of particular note was his attempt to address the docility of the working classes in the face of their evident exploitation.

He was aware of the neo-Machiavellians and shared some of their conclusions. For example, he accepted that for the moment, while there were classes, there really were "rulers and ruled, leaders and led." Any politics that ignored this "primordial, irreducible" fact was doomed to failure.[14] For the rulers, consent was preferable to coercion. This could only be achieved by convincing the ruled that the established political order served their interests. The ability to dominate through the power of ideas rather than brute force Gramsci called "hegemony." He was not the first to use the word, derived from the Greek *hegeisthai* (to lead), and the underlying proposition was not new. The *Communist Manifesto* observed that "the ruling ideas of each age have ever been the ideas of the ruling class." Lenin had warned that trade unionism served bourgeois rather than proletarian ideology, and used "hegemony" in its original sense as leadership.[15] Gramsci's explorations into the sources of hegemonic rule, however, enriched the concept to the point where it became part of the mainstream political lexicon.

The problem for Marxism was the supposedly close relationship between economics and politics, so that a change in material conditions should lead inexorably to changes in political consciousness. Yet, noted Gramsci, "at certain moments the automatic drive produced by the economic factor is slowed down, obstructed or even broken up momentarily by traditional ideological elements."[16] To take the obvious example, bourgeois claims that democracy and equality could be achieved through parliamentary means had proved persuasive. So long as this continued, the ruling class could avoid force. Only when they lost hegemonic ground would more authoritarian measures be necessary. This would be tested at times of crisis, when governments seeking to deflect popular anger would need to find ways of manipulating thoughts and creating an acquiescent public.

Gramsci divided society into its political and civil components. Political society, the realm of force, included the instruments of the state: government, the judiciary, the military, and the police. Civil society, the realm of ideas, included all those other bodies, from religious, media, and educational institutions to clubs and political parties relevant to the development of political and social consciousness. Here the ruling class must market its ideas if it was to achieve the appearance of rule by consent. Successful hegemony was evident in shared patterns of thought, concepts of reality, and notions of what was commonsensical. This would be reflected in language, customs, and morality. The ruled were persuaded that their society could and should be integrated rather than divided by class conflict.

This did not happen by cynically implanting a big idea in the popular consciousness. The ruling class could naturally draw on tradition, patriotic symbols and rituals, linguistic forms, and the authority of the Church and schools. The elite's vulnerability was that there still had to be a relationship to actual experience. For this reason, the effort to sustain hegemonic consent might well involve concessions. Even so there was still a puzzle, for the working classes might be expected to have a conception of the world reflecting their condition. Gramsci believed that they did, but it might only be embryonic. It would manifest itself in action, but this would be "occasionally, by fits and starts," when "the group is acting as an organic totality." This conception could coexist, "for reasons of submission and intellectual subordination," with one derived from the ruling class.[17] Thus two theoretical consciousnesses almost competed with each other, one reflected in practical activity, binding workers together, the other inherited from the past and uncritically accepted, reinforced through language, education, politics, and the mass media. True consciousness was therefore obscured or deflected. Given the opportunity, however, it would assert itself.

It was not necessary for hegemonic thoughts to be truly believed; their presence could be sufficient to cause confusion and thereby paralysis. The challenge for communists was to engage in counter-hegemonic work, to provide the conceptual tools to enable the workers to appreciate the causes of their discontents. This would require activity in all the relevant arenas of civil society. Indeed, until this was complete, the party would not really be ready for power. It must first turn the tables on the ruling class and become itself hegemonic. Gramsci presented the party as a Machiavellian prince acting for a group: "The modern prince . . . cannot be a real person, a concrete individual. It can only be an organism, a complex element of society in which the cementing of a collective will, recognized and partially asserted in action, has already begun. This organism is already provided by historical development and it is the political party."[18] This would only work, however, if it remained closely in touch with those whose will it was seeking to forge and direct. Gramsci was no fan of democratic centralism, which was geared to seizing dictatorial power. He wrote doubtfully about how this would require of the masses a "generic loyalty, of a military kind, to a visible or invisible political center." This would be sustained, ready for the moment when direct action could be taken, by means of "moralizing sermons, emotional stimuli, and messianic myths of an awaited golden age in which all present contradictions and miseries will be automatically resolved and made well."[19]

To explain what he had in mind he used a military analogy. The ruling classes' intellectual domination of civil society could be understood as a series of trenches and fortresses that could only be undermined and subverted by a patient but relentless war of position. The alternative, a war of maneuver—actually a form of frontal attack on the state—had long been the revolutionaries' dream and had recently been successful in Russia. But Lenin was able to mount an opportunistic campaign to seize power by taking advantage of an organized party, a disorganized state, and a feeble civil society. These, Gramsci believed, were exceptional and peculiarly "eastern" conditions, quite different from the complex civil societies and structures of Western states, where the only course was first to fight the battle of ideas. "The war of position in politics," he insisted, "is the concept of hegemony." This was, according to one authority, "a capsule description of his entire strategic argument."[20]

Gramsci never got the chance to complete his analysis, let alone put it into practice. Nonetheless, there was a tension at its heart that flowed from his core Marxism. He would not abandon the idea that, ultimately, economics drove politics, that class struggle was real and could shape consciousness, and that there would come a time when a majority working class would be able to attain power and rule with genuine hegemonic consent. Yet his analysis suggested a much more fluid set of relationships and possibilities, and patterns of thought that were disjointed and incoherent. It was problematic for a Marxist to accept that politics was an arena autonomous from economics, with its own tendencies and passions, but allowing the possibility of a range of factors intervening between the two rendered their relationship tenuous. If ideas had consequences of their own and were more than reflections of shifts in the means of production and the composition of classes, how could it be assumed that the battle for ideas would remain linked with the underlying class struggle? Once it was admitted that individuals could hold notionally contradictory thoughts in their heads, why stop with the contest between the hegemonic ideas of the ruling class or the incipient counter-hegemony of the ruled? What about normal muddle and confusion, or ideas which cut across those linked to class struggle, or inaction resulting from calculations based on prudence, a fear of unemployment, recollections of past failures, or distrust of party leaders?[21]

The military analogy Gramsci adopted was essentially that first introduced by Delbrück, between strategies of annihilation and exhaustion. It had been employed by Kautsky in 1910, and then Lenin in his argument for preparatory work and building up strength. Gramsci may have been updating the metaphor to take account of the past war, comparing the failed maneuvers of the war's early stages with the hard slog that followed, including the trenches and fortifications, but the underlying point was the same. A strategy of annihilation or overthrow or—for Gramsci—maneuver promised a quick and decisive outcome but required surprise and an unprepared opponent. Given the advantages of the state in such a contest, it was only prudent to think in the long term. Gramsci argued therefore for an extended campaign for hegemonic influence. By the time state power came, socialism would already be on its way to being achieved.

As a prescription, this was barely different from Kautsky's, except that Gramsci envisaged a broader advance in the field of ideas and was more skeptical about the parliamentary route. His starting point was also weak. Notably, his ideas on how a war of position might be fought seemed designed to avoid early violence, with a focus on demonstrations, boycotts, propaganda, and political education. The problem of how successful counter-hegemonic work in the civil sphere would eventually translate into a transfer of power in the political sphere was left ambiguous, presuming a point at which the ruling class would be dominant but no longer hegemonic. It was hard to see how a war of maneuver could be avoided at this point. Nor did Gramsci deal with the even larger problem of how this new hegemony would develop in circumstances where economic and social structures were becoming more variegated.

Outside of prison, this strategy would have appeared moderate and patient, avoiding the charges of authoritarianism attracted by Leninists, but effectively putting off the revolution and leading inevitably to pacts and compromises with other parties. In practice, Gramsci was himself the intellectual prisoner of the party line just as he was a physical prisoner of the Fascists. He was fighting a hegemonic war within himself. Every time he acknowledged that the way men thought affected the way they acted and that thoughts would by no means necessarily follow the imperatives of class, he was subverting the intellectual and political tradition in which he had been reared but which, consciously or subconsciously, he was coming to challenge.

Gramsci's situation was poignant. Not only would he never get the chance to apply his ideas in practice, but also he would have been thwarted if he had tried. He would probably have been expelled from the party if he had propounded his ideas as an activist. When his work was eventually published posthumously, it initially included only those selections the PCI considered safe to release. Once confidence was lost in Marxism as a scientific revelation of the laws of history, Gramsci's project would unravel or at least go off in directions that had little to do with his original purpose (which is what happened after the war when it inspired academic cultural studies).

The Communist Party turned into a project to maintain hegemony. Party members were required to be faithful to the prevailing line and to explain it without hesitation or any hint of incredulity to followers, however inconsistent, contradictory, or at odds with the evidence it might seem. Official ideologists engaged in whatever intellectual contortions were necessary to support the leadership and knew they were in trouble if they showed signs of doubt or independent thought. As the ideologies moved from the streets to government, ideological discipline was extended to the population as a whole. As the party line was tested daily against everyday experience and divergences had to be explained away, the requisite shifts in the official position caused confusion. An ideology that claimed to explain everything had to have positions on everything and sometimes these could be risible. Even with core support among the population, doubts were bound to develop and hegemony was in the end maintained less by the credibility of the case than by threats of retribution against doubters, apostates, critics, and deviants. In this way, the extremism of the original propositions on class consciousness, political formulas, myths, and hegemony came to be matched by the extremism of their implementation by totalitarian states.

The Nazis in Germany, possibly with Le Bon and Sorel in mind, provided the most disturbing example of how a ruling elite, with ruthlessness and little intellectual shame, could work to shape the thoughts of the masses. They used modern forms of propaganda, from staged rallies to controlled radio broadcasts. Although neither Adolf Hitler nor his propaganda chief Joseph Goebbels ever admitted that they would stoop to what they called the "big lie," their descriptions of how their enemies could do so left little doubt about their views. In explaining the success of Jews in deflecting blame for Germany's defeat in the Great War away from themselves, Hitler drew attention to "the principle—which is quite true within itself—that in the big lie there is always a certain force of credibility; because the broad masses of a nation are always more easily corrupted in the deeper strata of their emotional nature than consciously or voluntarily." Because of "the primitive simplicity of their minds," they were more likely to fall victim to the big lie than the small lie as it "would never come into their heads to fabricate colossal untruths, and they would not believe that others could have the impudence to distort the truth so infamously."[22]

Burnham

The impact of Stalinism on leftist thought in open societies can be seen in the United States as questions were raised as to whether Western capitalist societies really were following the path set down by Marx or might instead be becoming more durable and less self-destructive. The Communist Party, following the Soviet line, dominated far-left politics during the 1930s. Trotsky, in exile in nearby Mexico, became a rallying point for those who remained attracted by Marxism, especially during the terrible economic conditions of the Great Depression, yet were appalled by Stalinism's vicious and devious nature. The Trotskyist group in the United States was the largest of any (although at about one thousand members, it was not enormous). Many of the key figures attracted to a Marxism independent of Moscow came together in New York, a redoubtable intellectual grouping in terms of its vitality, if not political influence. Eventually practically all abandoned their Marxism, and many became conservatives, driven by their anti-Stalinism. Out of this group came some of the most formidable intellectuals and writers of postwar America. This included the contemporary neoconservative movement, initially composed of leftist veterans, often deploying the polemical skills developed during the faction fights of the 1930s.

One of the key figures to emerge from this milieu was James Burnham, a professor at New York University. He was one of the sharpest Trotskyist brains until he broke away over Trotsky's support for Stalin's pact with Hitler, which Burnham saw as a complete betrayal. This was coupled with a more esoteric dispute over the philosophical validity of dialectical materialism. From that point anti-communism dominated his thoughts and he moved firmly to the right. In 1941, during the early stages of this journey, without changing his rigorous, quasi-scientific, predictive style, and still focusing on the means of production to see where power lay, Burnham published a highly influential book, entitled *The Managerial Revolution*. He identified a new class—not the proletariat—moving into a dominant position. As the title implied, the book's core thesis was that the managers, who provided the technical direction and coordination of production, were now in charge, replacing capitalists and communists alike. Within this trend he saw both Nazi Germany (at the time assuming a German victory in Europe) and President Roosevelt's New Deal.[23] After the war he was accused of plagiarism, possibly with some justice, by Bruno Rizzi, an eccentric leftist who earned his living as a traveling shoe salesman. Even if he had not read Rizzi's 1939 *The Bureaucratization of the World*,[24] he would have been aware of it. Trotsky felt the need to address it because it drew on his own critique of the Soviet Union and then took it further than any good Marxist could allow, in identifying a bureaucratic class controlling the state apparatus in diverse types of society.

Burnham's next book, *The Machiavellians*, attempted to give a more political dimension to the economic analysis of *The Managerial Revolution*. This drew explicitly on Mosca, Sorel, Michels, and Pareto. It sought to reassert Machiavelli's candor about the role of elemental interests and instincts in politics, with power exercised for its own sake, maintained if necessary by force and fraud. He asserted the possibility of an objective science of politics, neutral with respect to any political goal, undertaken independent of personal preferences, considering the struggle for social power "in its diverse open and concealed forms." This could not rely on taking what was said at face value; everything that was said and done needed to be related to a broader social context to appreciate its meaning. Much of the book was given over to an exposition of the theories associated with the neo-Machiavellians, stressing the core division between the rulers and the ruled. His summation was a mixture of Pareto and Sorel. He took from the former the minor role played by logical or rational action in political and social change. "For the most part it is a delusion to believe that in social life men take deliberate steps to achieve consciously held goals." More frequent was nonlogical action "spurred by environmental changes, instinct, impulse, interest." Sorel came in with the proposition that to maintain its own power and privilege, the elite depended on a political formula, "which is usually correlated with a generally accepted religion, ideology or myth."

Burnham identified the new elite as the men "able to control contemporary mass industry, the massed labor force, and a supra-national form of political organization." He assumed that this control could be exercised by means of a compelling political formula. So, rational behavior for the elite would be to get the masses to accept unscientific myths. If they failed to sustain beliefs in the myths, the fabric of society would crack and they would be overthrown. In short, the leaders—if they themselves were scientific—must lie.[25]

This was the nub of the problem with Burnham's analysis. Under a Nazi or Stalinist state, myths could be manufactured and sustained as a means of social control. In both these cases, the underlying ideology was rooted in the leadership but it could also be sustained by coercive means. Dissent could be punished. Certain ideas played an important role in Western societies, but this role required a much more subtle analysis than Burnham's because the marketplace of ideas was much larger. Critics objected to Burnham's cynical approach to American democracy as if it were comparable to totalitarianism, and to his muddled analysis of power and where it was located.[26] The proposition that a political formula could be developed by an elite and then just handed down to the masses was far too simplistic. Ideas were far more difficult to control than physical conditions. Not all of the original message would be picked up even by a willing recipient.

Experts and Propaganda

Up to the point when the Nazis moved the art of propaganda to a new and disturbing level, great strides had been made in developing the theory and practice in the United States. Because of the totalitarian experience, it became very difficult to read earlier claims about what might be achieved by propaganda without a painful sense of where it could all lead. Given the importance attached to influencing the way people thought about their condition, which continued into the twenty-first century, it is important to consider the earlier development of Western theories of public opinion.

Robert Park provides a starting point. He was a former student of Dewey's who went on to succeed Small as head of the Chicago Sociology Department. His doctoral dissertation was written in Germany in 1904 on "The Crowd and the Public."[27] He contrasted Le Bon's vivid descriptions of how individuals joining a crowd lost their personalities and instead acquired a collective mind with the views of Gabriel Tarde, another Frenchman who thought Le Bon outdated. Tarde was interested in how power could flow from some individuals as they were imitated by many others. In addition to imposed, coercive power, this imitation gave society its coherence. The developing print media had special significance because it made possible simultaneous and similar conversations without regard for geography. Views could be packaged like commodities and then transmitted to millions, a capability which he recognized to be a powerful weapon.

As he reflected on the Dreyfus affair in France during the 1890s (the controversy surrounding a Jewish officer's conviction of spying for Germany), Tarde observed a collective opinion developing without individuals gathering together. From this came his view of the public as a "spiritual collectivity, a dispersion of individuals who are physically separated and whose cohesion is entirely mental."[28] For this reason he could not agree "with that solid writer, Dr. Le Bon, that this was 'the age of the crowd.'" It was the "age of the public, or the publics—and that is quite different."[29] An individual could only join one crowd but could be part of many publics. A crowd might be excitable but a public would be less emotional with calmer opinions.

Park developed this idea of a dichotomy between crowds—homogenous, simple, and impulsive, responding emotionally to perceptions of events—and the much more admirable public—heterogeneous and critical, addressing facts, comfortable with complexity. The hope for an ordered and progressive society depended on the public, which "precisely because it is composed of individuals with different opinions—is guided by prudence and rational reflection."[30] Once the public ceased to be critical, it became tantamount to a crowd, with all feelings moving in the same direction.

Whether the crowd or the public would predominate depended on the role of the media. The so-called muckraking journalists saw the newspapers as an agent of enlightenment and democracy. "Publicity," wrote one in the 1880s, is "the great moral disinfectant."[31] But if the media lost its higher role and pandered to the crowd, the public could be pulled down with it. The possibility that the suggestibility of crowds could be magnified rather than countered was underlined by the experience of the First World War. The U.S. Government's Committee on Public Information (CPI), set up as the country entered the war in 1917, impressed all those involved with the apparent ease with which a bellicose opinion could be shaped by using every available means to put out the word about the danger of German militarism and the need for a robust response. Led by former progressive journalist George Creely, who famously observed that "people do not live by bread alone: they live mostly by catch phrases," the CPI used all media from townhall meetings to movies to get across core messages.

One of those who had urged the formation of the CPI, was involved in its activities, and was impressed by its performance was Walter Lippmann.[32] A precocious, high-minded, articulate, and influential journalist, Lippmann was alive to the intellectual currents of the time. Before the war, he had struck up a friendship with the elderly William James and was intrigued by the psychoanalytical movement's insights regarding the development of consciousness and the sources of irrationality. He had become uneasy about how the popular press was always pointing to conspiracies and searching for sensationalist revelations. He saw this as fomenting unrest and making rational debate impossible. In 1922 he published his landmark book *Public Opinion*. What people knew, he argued, was only through a "picture in their heads" of the "pseudo-environment" to be found between people and their real environment. Understanding the way these pictures were formed, sustained, and challenged was important because it affected behavior. "But because it *is* behavior," Lippmann observed, "the consequences, if they are acts, operate not in the pseudo-environment where the behavior is stimulated, but in the real environment where action eventuates." Or, as Chicago sociologist William Thomas put it a few years later in a theorem which came to bear his name: "If men define situations as real, they are real in their consequences."[33]

Lippmann also noted the extent to which individuals clung on to their "system of stereotypes" because it provided an "ordered, more or less consistent picture of the world, to which our habits, our tastes, our capacities, our comforts and our hopes have adjusted themselves." Because of this,

> any disturbance of the stereotypes seems like an attack upon the foundations of the universe. It is an attack upon the foundations of OUR universe, and, where big things are at stake, we do not readily admit that there is any distinction between our universe and the universe. A world which turns out to be one in which those we honor are unworthy, and those we despise are noble, is nerve-racking. There is anarchy if our order of precedence is not the only possible one.[34]

In addition to the familiar perceptual problems of prejudicial stereotypes, most people lacked the time and the inclination to engage in a more disciplined search for the truth. If they relied on newspapers, then what they got was selective and simplified.

Some form of picture was unavoidable but, picking up on a standard progressive theme, Lippmann feared that the pictures would be drawn by sectional interests or by a press which played to natural selfishness, supported by dubious advertising. All this meant that "public opinion" was suspect. Contrary to the notion of a "common will" emerging naturally from the people, public opinion in practice was a construct and democratic consent could therefore be manufactured. The test of good government was not the degree of public participation in the process but the quality of the output. Unlike Dewey, who was confident that people were the best judges of their own interests and participatory democracy the best means of creating a sense of shared community, Lippmann was firmly on the side of representative democracy. He was, however, with Dewey in his optimism about science, including the social sciences, as a motor of progress.

Lippmann regretted that the social scientist was not yet playing this role, whereas the engineer had been doing so for some time. He put this down to a lack of confidence. The social scientist was unable to "prove his theories before offering them to the public," yet "if his advice is followed, and he is wrong, the consequences may be incalculable. He is in the nature of things far more responsible, and far less certain." Social scientists were therefore explaining decisions already taken but not influencing those yet to be taken. "The real sequence," according to Lippmann, "should be one where the disinterested expert first finds and formulates the facts for the man of action, and later makes what wisdom he can out of comparison between the decision, which he understands, and the facts, which he organized." They could bring another dimension to government, representing "the unseen" with a "constituency of intangibles," covering "events that are out of sight, mute people, unborn people, relations between things and people." Contrary to later suggestions that he wanted experts to rule, Lippmann's prescription went no further than encouraging them to tutor governments in what would make for wise policy. Nor was he arguing that experts were superior to ordinary people. They were required not so much as a counter to the masses but to the standard progressive bugbears—the urban party machines, the big trusts, and a press that was driven more by advertising revenue than a mission to inform.[35]

One form of expertise that he saw coming to the fore was "persuasion" as "a self-conscious art and a regular organ of popular government." He continued with what turned out to be understatement: "None of us begins to understand the consequences, but it is no daring prophecy to say that the knowledge of how we create consent will alter every political premise." Like many others writing on this topic at this time, he was prepared to describe this as "propaganda" without necessarily implying a sinister meaning. The term's origins lay in the Catholic Church's methods of taking its teaching to those who were not yet converted. The standard definition of the time simply saw propaganda as any method "for the propagation of a particular doctrine or practice."

During the Great War, it had acquired its more sinister meaning as accusations were made of deliberate lying in order to bolster morale or to confuse or slander enemies. Harold Lasswell, who was to become a major figure in U.S. political science, made his name with a theory of propaganda. By his definition it involved "the management of collective attitudes by the manipulation of significant symbols" and was socially "indispensable" given the unavoidable gap between the public and the elite. He deplored the negative connotations the concept had acquired. It was no more moral or immoral than a "pump handle." It was necessary because individuals were poor judges of their own interests and so had to be helped by officially sanctioned communication. With experts on the mobilization of opinion, what could once "be done by violence and intimidation must now be done by argument and persuasion."[36] The strategic challenge for the propagandist was "to intensify the attitudes favorable to his purpose, to reverse the attitudes hostile to it, and to attract the indifferent, or, at the worst, to prevent them from assuming a hostile bent."

This sense of a struggle between reason and emotion, evident in the individual but now elevated to a feature of a whole society, was become increasingly influenced by Freudian theories. Freud challenged the distinction between individual and group psychology. After the war he moved on from his dialectic of the unconscious and the conscious to a more complex structure.[37] Now he identified the "Id," reflecting those unconscious, instinctual, passionate, amoral, disorganized aspects of the personality, seeking pleasure, "a cauldron full of seething excitations," which the organized, conscious, knowing ego seeks to manage by bringing in line with reality. It represented reason and common sense, acting on the Id like "a man on horseback, who has to hold in check the superior strength of the horse." Its task was complicated by the super-ego, which brought to bear considerations of conscience and morality—a legacy of the father figure and a reflection of external influences such as teachers—posing socially appropriate behavior against whatever instant gratification was sought by the Id.

An example of Freud's influence was William Trotter, a British surgeon who became an early follower. In 1916, Trotter published his book on the "herd instinct," based on articles written in 1908 and 1909 but reinforced by the experience of war. Trotter argued that human beings were naturally gregarious, and so were insecure and feared loneliness. This led to a fourth instinct—in addition to self-preservation, nutrition, and sex—which had the distinction of exercising "a controlling power upon the individual from without" so that it impelled people to do things they would not otherwise wish to do. Trotter saw this as a source of the tension between individuals and society, between commonsense and prevailing norms, the source of senses of sin and guilt. The idea of the "mass mind" and a fascination with the psychology of crowds was not new, but those who had written on it before were apt to see it as a negative force, the source of mob actions, whereas Trotter encouraged a more positive view. Freud respected Trotter's views, although he judged that they took too little account of the role of leadership and the need of members of a group to be "loved" by their leader.[38]

The practical possibilities of these various ideas were demonstrated by Edward Bernays, the best available example of the working propagandist at this time. He was a nephew of Sigmund Freud and he traded on this relationship when explaining his understanding of emotions and irrationality. After getting involved in the CPI, Bernays set himself up in 1919 as a public relations counsel (he was the first to use the descriptor). Though his methods were all his own, both Lippmann and Freud were major influences on his thinking. Politically he was a progressive and optimistic that the techniques he was describing could be used for the betterment of society, although this optimism was shaken when he discovered that Goebbels's library contained his books. His first book, *Crystallizing Public Opinion*, was published in 1923, a year after Lippmann's *Public Opinion*, from which Bernays quoted liberally. He sought to demonstrate that his was a respectable profession with serious credentials, rooted in social science and psychiatry. In a complex society, governments, corporations, parties, charities, and a number of other groups were constantly striving to gain favor and advantage. Even if they had wanted to ignore public opinion, the public had an interest in what they were up to. He noted that large corporations and labor unions were now seen as "semi-public services" and that the public, now enjoying the benefits of education and democracy, expected a voice in their conduct. Given this, there was a requirement for expert advice about how to do this effectively.[39]

This much in Bernay's argument was unexceptional. What was striking was the blunt language he used to describe what public relations professionals could offer, and the presumption of success. In *Crystallizing Public Opinion*, Bernays explained how "the natural inherent flexibility of individual human nature" made it possible for governments to "regiment the mind like the military regiments the body." He opened a 1928 book, entitled *Propaganda*, by asserting that: "The conscious and intelligent manipulation of the organized habits and opinions of the masses is an important element in democratic society." Those responsible constituted "an invisible government which is the true ruling power of our country." As a result, "we are governed, our minds molded, our tastes formed, our ideas suggested, largely by men we have never heard of." He argued for a strict ethical code for his profession, including that the needs of society as a whole come first. He insisted that the masses could not be made to act against their core interests and that political leaders were by far the most important influences when it came to creating "the established point of view." Nonetheless, his formulations aggravated the sense of an affront to democracy. If, as Lippmann also appeared to be saying, opinions were shaped from the top down, this undermined the view that in democracies, power should come from the bottom up. The conclusion that Bernays drew from this was that by understanding the "mechanism and motives of the group mind" it might be possible "to control and regiment the masses according to our will without their knowing about it." This he thought could be done "at least up to a certain point and within certain limits."[40]

Bernays as an advisor to governments, charities, and corporations was a natural strategist. He distinguished himself from advertising men, whom he portrayed as special pleaders seeking to get people to accept a particular commodity. His approach was more holistic (advising his clients on their complete relationship with their environment) and indirect (seeking to get people to view the world in different ways). In a later article with the provocative title "The Engineering of Consent,"[41] he explicitly discussed the strategy of public relations. He also adopted the military metaphor. Having urged careful preparation in terms of available budget, clarity of objectives, and a survey of current thinking, attention must be given to the major themes, which he described as "ever present but intangible," comparable to the "story line" in fiction, appealing to both the conscious and subconscious of the public. Then came the campaign: "The situation may call for a blitzkrieg or a continuing battle, a combination of both, or some other strategy." An election might be close and need something quick. It would take longer to get people to think differently about a health issue. When it came to tactics, he emphasized that the aim was not simply to get an article into a newspaper or get a radio slot but "to create news," by which he meant something that "juts out of the pattern of routine." Events which made news could be communicated to "infinitely more people than those actually participating, and such events vividly dramatize ideas for those who do not witness the events." His more famous campaigns were encouraging "bacon and eggs" for breakfast by getting leading physicians to endorse the need for a "hearty" breakfast, having famous figures from vaudeville meet with President Calvin Coolidge in an attempt to boost his image, and—notably—an imaginative stunt for the American Tobacco Company. He persuaded ten debutantes to light up with their cigarettes during the 1929 Easter Parade, thereby notionally striking a blow for feminism by undermining the taboo against women smoking in public. The cigarettes became "torches of freedom."[42]

Bernays invited obvious criticisms: usurping the role of democracy by taking upon himself to shape peoples' thoughts, encouraging mass effects rather than individual responsibility, and relying on cliché and emotional attitudes rather than intellectual challenge. Bernays argued that in an age of mass media, the techniques were unavoidable and propaganda was ubiquitous. People and groups had a right to promote their ideas and the competition in doing so was healthy for both democracy and capitalism. He also invited an exaggerated response, because of the exaggerated claims he made for his profession and his eager embrace of the mantle of propagandist.[43] While after the Second World War this was a mantle few would accept, the issue of how political consciousness developed and could be influenced was well established. Bernays's contribution was to demonstrate that the impulses need not only be to shape thinking about underlying political ideologies but also to frame more specific issues. During the course of the political struggles of the 1950s and 1960s over race and war, strategies came to focus increasingly on how to create the right impression.

The totalitarian ideologies of Communism and Nazism attempted to demonstrate in practice the suggestibility of the broad masses to political formulas devised by a privileged elite. They sought deliberately to insert coherent worldviews into the consciousness of whole populations and enforce their dictates, sliding over the evident anomalies and inconsistencies and gaps that developed with lived experience. Their success, moreover, owed much to the fearful consequences of any shows of dissent, doubt, or deviation from the party line. Once the coercive spell was broken, the underlying ideas struggled to survive on their own. Belief systems turned out to be more complex and varied and public opinion less malleable than the elite theorists had supposed. What Bernays was pointing to was something more subtle, at levels below grand ideological confrontations, where the attitudes involved were more specific and the behavioral consequences less demanding. Rather than words governing deeds, as anticipated by the ideologists, there was a close relationship between the two, and successful politicians and campaigners realized that this needed to be understood if even fleeting victories were to be achieved, never mind lasting change.

CHAPTER 23 | The Power of Nonviolence

When evil men plot, good men must plan.

—Martin Luther King, Jr.

A N IMPROVED UNDERSTANDING of how to influence public opinion offered new opportunities for political strategy. Those who for reasons of ethics or prudence did not wish to resort to force could consider strategies based on creating persuasive impressions, moving opinion in their direction without coercion. The strength of these strategies, however, depended on the extent to which they were moving elites along with the public. Even if there were shifts among the public, what would be the mechanisms by which this would affect the policies of governments? Was it just a question of repackaging good ideas to ensure that they attracted attention, or would they still need some pressure behind them to achieve the desired response?

Many of these issues were addressed by the suffragette movement. The advance of democracy in Western capitalist states might have blunted the revolutionary ardor of the labor movement by offering constitutional means to redress grievances, but it also added to the sense of injustice felt by those denied democratic rights. The British Empire, with a liberal ideology at its beating heart but institutionalized suppression around its periphery, was rocked most by demands for political equality. Among these, including anti-colonial campaigns and agitation for Irish Home Rule, was a determined and eventually successful campaign by women demanding the right to vote. This campaign was unique because it posed a challenge not only to the political system but also to orthodox views of gender and the most basic of human relationships. The tactics adopted by the suffragette movement had a lasting impact not only as a means of gaining attention in the face of male condescension but also as a direct challenge to stereotypes of femininity, such as a supposed inability to develop and sustain a political argument. At the same time, part of the case was that women not only deserved equality but would bring special qualities to public life.

The campaign in Britain stretched from proposals to include women's suffrage in the Reform Act of 1867 to the Equal Franchise Act of 1928. Female political rights extended slowly over this period, as women moved into philanthropic and civic affairs. There was dogged resistance to granting women the same rights as men, and it only broke under the weight of the First World War. The suffragette campaign had many strands: some were prepared to work with the established political parties while others found this futile; some framed the issue narrowly in terms of political rights while others sought to address economic issues and challenge orthodox male expectations of a woman's role. In terms of strategy, there was a constitutional wing—which worked through petitions, lobbying, and demonstrations—and a militant wing—the Women's Social and Political Union (WSPU), led by the redoubtable mother and daughter team of Emmeline and Christabel Pankhurst. As to which had the most effect, or whether they detracted from or reinforced each other, opinions are still divided. The militants are now best remembered for the direct action: slashing paintings, arson, breaking windows, chaining themselves to railings, and prison hunger strikes. But they were only one part of a movement that was extremely varied in its forms and preoccupations.

The militancy developed as a result of progressive disillusion, first with the Liberal Party reluctance to honor its ideals, then with the lack of priority given to women by the labor movement, and a growing conviction that legislative routes were being exhausted. The core themes, however, were derived from classic liberal ideals: opposition to forms of arbitrary power that resulted in individuals having obligations but no rights. The rhetoric could be traced back to the French Revolution and then the Chartists, except that gender now displaced class. The militant tactics were justified on the basis, as Christabel Pankhurst put it, that "those who are outside the Constitution have no ordinary means of securing admission; and therefore they must try extraordinary means." The techniques used by the WSPU helped them gain attention, although what might have worked most to their advantage was the opportunity as a result of being arrested to make their case in court and turn a defense against criminal charges into a political debate. In a jury trial in 1912, for example, Emmeline Pankhurst was able to present herself and her organization as smart, eloquent, capable, well organized, and not at all emotional or hysterical. In particular, she and other suffragettes were able to give their acts a compelling political rationale, which led in Emmeline's case to the jury calling for leniency.

After this, the rhetoric became more extreme. Christabel Pankhurst even invoked terrorism. The "politically disinherited ones, whether they are men or whether they are women," she insisted, "are obliged to challenge the physical force used by their tyrant to keep them in bondage." While passive resistance was dismissed as subservient, active resistance was claimed as "grander and more purifying." There were more attacks on property, though not on people. This led to concerns elsewhere in the movement that militancy rather than suffrage was becoming the issue. Supporters drifted away, and WSPU moved more underground. In the end, the war provided a useful pretext for ending the militancy without losing face. Indeed, while those on the nonviolent wing of the movement were antiwar, the Pankhursts became active in war work and were notable for strident anti-German, anti-pacifist, and later anti-Bolshevik rhetoric.[1]

The American suffragette movement, which achieved its goal in 1920, was far less militant. There was a close link with the progressive movement, which pushed to the fore the stresses of industrialization, such as poor women forced to work for meager wages while still caring for children. Although it did become more activist in the years before the First World War in response to the rather staid practice of the main association and contacts with the British movement, the preferred method in America was to show numerical strength through picketing, rallies, and parades. Quakerism, which had long allowed women a role—even as preachers—particularly influenced the movement. Quakers provided much of the early leadership and insistence on nonviolence. The American movement's eventual success reflected a grasp of the basics of political organizing, with conventions, speaking tours, and full-time activists keeping the issue to the fore.[2] One consequence of this was to open up the possibility of pacifism as the foundation for a successful political strategy and not just the assertion of a particular morality.

The term *pacifist* had come into use during the nineteenth century to refer to those who renounced all violence. They faced some standard challenges: how, defensively, would they cope with another's aggression and then how, offensively, could they achieve change without violence. The most difficult charge was that by stressing peace more than injustice pacifists were bound to the status quo. By ruling out force on behalf of the disadvantaged, they would be stuck with existing hierarchies of power and left either playing down grievances or claiming their susceptibility to improbable remedies, such as appeals to love and to reason. The pacifists' counter was that underdogs had most to lose when disputes became violent, and that once violence was used, even in the name of a good cause, it became less likely that something truly better would result from the struggle and that effective forms of nonviolent pressure could be devised.

The Impact of Gandhi

Pacifism was at its strongest after the First World War. This was largely because the slaughter on the Western Front had shaped popular attitudes on the futility and waste of war. It was also due to evidence of a pacifist effectively leading a movement for radical change as Mohandas Gandhi challenged British rule in India.

Gandhi's thought was shaped by his experiences in South Africa and India. One influence was Henry David Thoreau of Concord, Massachusetts, whose opposition to slavery led him to refuse to "pay a tax to, or recognize the authority of, the state which buys and sells men, women, and children." After six years of noncompliance, Thoreau was arrested and spent a night in jail, which resulted in his 1849 lecture on "The Relation of the Individual to the State." Although his strategy went no further than arguing that if everybody followed his example slavery would be doomed, and in his time he was considered an isolated, eccentric figure, his lecture (published as "Civil Disobedience") became the classic statement of the ethical case for refusing to accept unjust laws.[3] Gandhi had read Thoreau as a young activist and later reported that it helped shape his thinking and was a point of contact with like-minded Americans.[4]

The link with Tolstoy was closer. In his autobiography, Gandhi described Tolstoy's *The Kingdom of God Is Within You* as having "overwhelmed" him. In 1908, Gandhi translated and circulated *A Letter to a Hindu*, which Tolstoy had written in response to a request from the editor of an Indian journal. It contained one point that Gandhi deemed unassailable. It was astonishing, Tolstoy had written, that "more than two hundred million people, highly gifted both physically and mentally, find themselves in the power of a small group of people quite alien to them in thought, and immeasurably inferior to them in religious morality." From this he concluded that it was "clear that it is not the English who have enslaved the Indians, but the Indians who have enslaved themselves." Instead of violent resistance Tolstoy urged nonparticipation "in the violent deeds of the administration, in the law courts, the collection of taxes, or above all in soldiering," and love as "the only way to rescue humanity from all ills, and in it you too have the only method of saving your people from enslavement."[5]

There were obvious similarities between the two men. Both sought to lead lives based on self-purification, love, and nonviolence. Both, despite their privileged births, sought to bring themselves closer to the poor, toiling masses. Their conspicuously ascetic ways of life gained them moral authority and an international audience. Gandhi also embraced the idea of self-perfection, but unlike Tolstoy he saw it not as an alternative to political activism but as an essential part. He had a canny understanding that his private spirituality not only protected him against the temptations of public life but added luster to his political claims. His genius was in his ability to use the teachings that guided his personal life as the foundations for a mass movement.

His philosophy of *satyagraha*, a word of his own devising, involved a combination of truth, love, and firmness. Those who embraced this philosophy had an inner strength giving them the courage and discipline to endure and overwhelm those who relied on violent means. He argued the inseparability of ends and means: violent methods could not deliver a peaceful society.[6] Prison should be embraced piously, assault cheerfully, and death peacefully. When he spoke he did so quietly, almost professorially, and never as a demagogue. All this was combined with a shrewd political sensibility. Gandhi had a gift for putting his opponents on the defensive, not only by claiming the moral high ground but also by identifying issues which were particularly awkward for the British.

In March 1930, he began a 240-mile march to the coast in order to demonstrate the injustice of the Raj both monopolizing salt production and then taxing it. The protest was not initially taken seriously but it gathered momentum, leading to Gandhi being jailed and not released until the next year. Though the campaign was unsuccessful in its immediate objective, Gandhi's methods were now attracting notice and the authorities had to take note of the numbers prepared to align themselves with the protest. The extent and intensity of popular discontent impressed the British. They lacked a compelling response to Gandhi's theatricality and moral advantage. William Wedgewood Benn, the secretary of state for India, observed in 1931 the similarities to the suffragettes, as well as the Irish and South African campaigns against British rule. "They are all aimed at rallying public sympathy as an ally. They strive to present to the Government the alternative of giving way or appearing in the role of oppressor . . . they first deliberately provoked severity and then complained to the world of it." Earlier he had understood that the best way to deal with such a challenge was to deny the choice between concession and oppression, but denial was impossible. "They won't let us leave them alone." How preferable it would be to have "a straight fight with the revolver people, which is a much simpler and more satisfactory job to undertake."[7]

Gandhi's campaigns did not push the British out of India. They helped confirm, along with the strain resulting from the Second World War, that the subcontinent was just too large to be effectively controlled by a relatively small and distant state of declining authority and capacity. There was a nationalistic swell in Indian opinion that could not be contained indefinitely. But while Gandhi's efforts did not by themselves make British rule impossible, they did turn his Congress Party into a credible alternative government to the Raj. The fact that his methods worked with other deeper social and political factors was not a reason to dismiss them, although it did raise questions about their effectiveness in other contexts.

At a time of brutality and upheaval across the world, Gandhi stood out as a leader who personified dignity and goodness in the simplicity of his dress and diet, and in his spiritual message. At the same time, he managed to forge an authentic and successful mass movement. Gandhi took the familiar tactics of the underdogs—marches, strikes, and boycotts—and employed them as part of a grander and nobler narrative. His claim to be reaching out to the good in his opponents and the promise of reconciliation left open the possibility of compromise. Was this a strategic formula of wide application or one specially suited to the circumstances of India? It depended on a moral authority that rested on claims to be asserting universal and timeless values, but might its success be due to a very particular set of circumstances?

To argue that nonviolence would be invariably effective ducked the moral question, because it ignored the possibility of hard choices. The method acquired authority and dignity precisely because one possible outcome was extreme suffering and no political gain. Yet if there was no reasonable promise of success, then insisting on nonviolence meant tolerating a greater evil and putting followers at risk, leaving them without defenses and in danger. Even accepting that no good would ever come out of a resort to violence, it might still be that nonviolence could result in greater harm. The issue was posed in a particularly sharp form with the rise of Hitler and the Second World War. Nonviolence might work well with the British, who wished to avoid a violent struggle and could be embarrassed by displays of popular resistance, but Gandhi's conviction that his methods would work against the Nazis was barely credible. Nor did he cope well when his own people fought each other, as India gained independence. Despite his best efforts, he was unable to bridge the vicious sectarian divide between Hindus and Muslims and he suffered a violent death at the hands of an assassin in 1948.

The Potential of Nonviolence

Gandhi's influence was felt in the campaign for civil rights for blacks in the American South, where segregation and discrimination were rigidly enforced. Although the possible use of nonviolent tactics was mentioned during the interwar years, it was not until after the Second World War that such methods were embraced in what became a remarkably successful campaign.

There were obvious differences in the two settings. Gandhi was stirring up the whole Indian population against a distant imperialist power. Blacks were a minority facing an unforgiving local majority. Their predicament posed in a sharp form the underlying dilemmas facing a nonviolent strategy. The so-called Jim Crow laws (named after a caricature black from a minstrel show) had been passed by southern legislatures after the Civil War and were often backed by crude violence. They made it extremely difficult for blacks to vote; meant segregated facilities for eating, transportation, burial, medical, and school facilities; and banned cohabitation and marriage between whites and non-whites. A search for goodness among the segregationists appeared a short and futile journey, and defiance could be suicidal.

The barriers imposed on the ability of blacks to make their way economically as well as politically had undermined the Atlanta Compromise of 1895, proposed by Booker T. Washington. "The wisest of my race," he had observed, "understand that agitation of questions of social equality is the extremest folly." Instead, his people would work at thrift and industry, become model employees, and so gradually join American society as equals (for "no race that has anything to contribute to the markets of the world is long in any degree ostracized"). Citizenship would assuredly follow. Not surprisingly, the compromise was warmly embraced by black and white moderates. The premise that it would be hard to attain political power without economic power had some validity. In practice, however, with little progress on either the economic or political front, the compromise was increasingly seen as a recipe for prolonged servitude. A more radical but also analytical edge was provided by W. E. B. Du Bois, the first African-American to secure a Ph.D. from Harvard. He had studied with Weber in Germany and the two kept in touch. Weber considered him to be one of America's most gifted sociologists and cited him as a counter-example when challenging racial stereotypes. Du Bois undertook major research programs on the "Negro problem," demonstrating the impact of political choices rather than some primordial difference between the races. He campaigned for civil rights and founded the National Association for the Advancement of Colored People (NAACP) with the support of such white reformers as Jane Addams and John Dewey.

In 1924, Du Bois published a critique of nonviolence by Franklin Frazier, another black (and Chicago-trained) sociologist, in *The Crisis*, the NAACP's official organ. Frazier mocked the idea of turning the other cheek in the face of violence. This was just after an anti-lynching law had been filibustered out of the Senate, demonstrating that the southern white establishment condoned racist murders as a way of intimidating blacks. Responding to Frazier, the white Quaker Ellen Winsor pointed to Gandhi and wondered whether a similar figure could "arise in this country to lead the people out of their misery and ignorance, not by the old way of brute force which breeds sorrow and wrong, but by the new methods of education based on economic justice leading straight to Freedom." A rejoinder came from Frazier:

> Suppose there should arise a Gandhi to lead Negroes without hate in their hearts to stop tilling the fields of the South under the peonage system; to cease paying taxes to States that keep their children in ignorance; and to ignore the iniquitous disenfranchisement and Jim Crow laws, I fear we would witness an unprecedented massacre of defenseless black men and women in the name of Law and Order and there would scarcely be enough Christian sentiment in America to stay the flood of blood.

When, a few years later, Du Bois invited and received an article from Gandhi, he added his own observation: "Agitation, non-violence, refusal to cooperate with the oppressor, became Gandhi's watchword and with it he is leading all India to freedom. Here and today he stretches out his hand in fellowship to his colored friends of the West."[8] Du Bois focused more on Gandhi's readiness to engage in direct action and his refusal to yield to oppression than on his underlying philosophy. On that he remained skeptical. As other American black activists started to talk of Gandhian campaigns, Du Bois pointed out how tactics of fasting, public prayer, and self-sacrifice were alien to the United States but had been "bred into the very bone of India for more than three thousand years."[9]

Gandhi never visited the United States but understood its political importance to his own cause—gaining independence from the British—and also the potential relevance of his ideas to the divisions within American society.[10] The initial impetus of contact with Gandhi was not specifically related to the black cause. It reflected the traditional pacifist focus on war and a more recent interest in labor unrest. While Richard Gregg was working as a lawyer on labor disputes in the early 1920s, he developed sympathy with the unions and was appalled by the violence used by employers to suppress them. Worried about the dangers if workers responded in kind, he explored passive resistance. This led him to take up residence in India where he was in regular contact with Gandhi. On his return, he wrote a series of books encouraging a move away from traditional pacifism as a difficult moral choice, an expression of an inner conviction about the sanctity of human life preoccupied with the problem of war, to a more strategic appreciation of the special power conferred by a commitment to nonviolence when engaged in domestic conflicts. He sought to extricate pacifism "from the profitless atmosphere of emotional adjectives and of vague mysticism, futile protests and sentimentalism combined with confused thinking." Rather than stress the contrast with traditional military strategy, he urged his readers to see nonviolence as another type of weapon, an innovation in warfare that made it possible to struggle without killing.[11]

Gregg was particularly intrigued by the possibility of using suffering to dramatize issues. At issue was not personal belief but whether actions could shame opponents and gain sympathy from onlookers. He described how nonviolent resistance to violent attack would work as a "sort of moral jiu-jitsu," causing the attacker to "lose his moral balance." This depended on a change of heart, which in turn depended on the nervous system triggering an almost involuntary empathetic response to another's suffering. In the modern age the extent and impact of such responses would be far greater because of mass media. The unique drama of defenseless men and women accepting vicious assaults made for a fascinating "story" and "wonderful news." The likely bad publicity posed a threat to the attacker. He was alive to the potential relevance of this approach to the struggle for black rights and was in touch with his fellow Harvard alumnus, W. E. B. Du Bois. It is unclear what Du Bois thought of Gregg's characterization of Negroes as a "gentle race, accustomed to marvelous endurance of suffering" and thus ideally suited to a nonviolent campaign.

While Gregg was exploring whether nonviolence could be made to work as a strategy, Reinhold Niebuhr, a Protestant minister, was concluding that it could not. His starting point was similar in that he had also been radicalized by his experience of labor relations, in this case as a pastor in Detroit working with Ford workers. Gradually he came to see nonviolence as supporting the status quo. He could not object to the principle, but he warned about the consequences of its application in an imperfect world. He did not share the optimism in man's essential goodness. It was unwise to expect those who benefited from inequality and injustice to respond positively to reasonable requests for equality and justice. Instead of approaching the powerful with a perfect and somehow irresistible love they must be confronted with counter-power. His views were expressed in a remarkable and influential book, *Moral Man and Immoral Society*.[12]

Niebuhr's focus on power led him to become identified as a key realist thinker, unique because he framed the issues in theological terms. For our purposes we do not need to explore the theological issues too deeply. Niebuhr saw the urge to power as the way by which men sought to give themselves significance in the face of an infinite universe. This inherent self-regard was aggravated by the nature of human consciousness. Because human beings could imagine how their desires could be fulfilled well beyond immediate possibilities, there was an urge to self-aggrandizement which, unless checked, would see any possibility of compromise displaced by preparations for a fight. Though reason would dictate cooperation and nonviolence, unfortunately there was "no miracle by which men can achieve a rationality high enough to give them as vivid an understanding of general interests as of their own." Groups made matters worse, for crowds were poor at reasoning. As a result, attempts to deal with groups by the sort of loving morality that might work with individuals could well be disastrous.

Niebuhr was aware that this gloomy view of human nature and the role of power and interest in human affairs could lead to defeatism among the victims of injustice and inequality. But realism, he judged, was a better place to start than a naïve and sentimental idealism, overestimating the potential goodness and trustworthiness of others. Those who refused to recognize the reality of conflict and address issues of power tended to propose measures that were in practice timid and ineffectual. Their discomfort with forms of compulsion, including force, rendered them incapable of achieving justice. "Immediate consequences," he observed in terms of which Weber would have approved, "must be weighed against ultimate consequences." Contrary to the view that some means could never be justified, Niebuhr was prepared to argue that ends do provide a justification. Again, a society's morality was different from an individual's because there was so much more at stake. An individual's pursuit of the absolute may be futile. When a society pursues the absolute, it "risk[s] the welfare of millions." Better then to discourage a search for perfection in societies and accept compromise.

The next stage in his argument was to deny any rigid distinction between violent and nonviolent coercion. "As long as it enters the field of social and physical relations and places physical restraints upon the desires and activities of others, it is a form of physical coercion." Even apparently nonviolent action could lead to hurt. Gandhi's boycott of British textiles, for example, hurt British textile workers. Niebuhr gave the impression of being more irritated by the self-righteousness of the practitioners of nonviolence than the practice itself. He appreciated its potential advantage as protecting "the agent against the resentments which violent conflict always creates in both parties to a conflict." It could also demonstrate an interest in a peaceful resolution. Intriguingly, Niebuhr noted the potential strategic value of nonviolence "for an oppressed group which is hopelessly in the minority and has no possibility of developing sufficient power to set against its oppressors." He added that for that reason it would be appropriate for the "emancipation of the Negro race in America."

An American Gandhi?

In May 1942, "the first organized civil rights sit-in in American history" took place at the Jack Spratt Coffee House in Chicago when a group of twenty-eight people divided themselves up into small groups, each including at least one black man or woman, and sat down. The coffee house's small staff was caught in confusion, especially as attempts to avoid serving the blacks at all, or at most serve them out of sight, gained little sympathy from either other customers or the police when they were called.[13] This effort was successful. Taking place in Chicago, before the city's later deterioration in race relations, it was not as severe a test as would later be faced in southern states, but it demonstrated the possibility that firm but polite action might disorient racists and expose discrimination.

At the heart of the action was James Farmer, a young African-American from Texas who had graduated in theology. He was then the race relations secretary for the Fellowship of Reconciliation (FOR), a strongly pacifist group based in New York. It was formed in 1915 by a number of leading antiwar figures, including Jane Addams and A. J. Muste. A minister who later became an active trade unionist and socialist, Muste was FOR's executive director from 1940 to 1953.[14] Over this period, pacifists once again found themselves on the wrong side of a popular cause. This time the evil of the enemy was more than propagandistic bombast and the country had been caught by a surprise attack.

Farmer had been agitating to establish a distinct organization charged with promoting racial equality and was permitted to see if something could be achieved in Chicago before consideration was given to taking his idea further. There was already a FOR group at the University of Chicago, led by George Houser, who had been thinking along similar lines. Together they formed the Committee (later Congress) of Racial Equality (CORE). It eventually became more important than its parent. Distracted already by the war, FOR now had young activists wishing to employ tactics that were provocative and bound to raise tensions, moving beyond love and reason to coercion. When Farmer first presented to FOR his "Brotherhood Mobilization Plan," he faced objections on the grounds that not only would this divert effort and attention away from the antiwar effort but also that the protests would be warlike, not overtly violent but sufficient to disrupt peace and tranquility and fail to turn the racist's heart toward justice. Farmer saw these Tolstoy-like arguments as supporting passivity. Failure to act would perpetuate the everyday violence of segregation. He believed in the nonviolent creed, but his standard was effectiveness not purity of motive. For the same reason he did not wish CORE to be open only to true pacifists.[15] He told a disappointed Muste, who had mixed feelings about a new national and not overtly pacifist organization, the "masses of Negroes will not become pacifists. Being Negroes for them is tough enough without being pacifist, too. Neither will the masses of whites."[16]

Farmer's guide when taking on Jack Spratt's Coffee House was Krishnalal Shridharani, a journalist who had followed Gandhi in India to the point of being arrested. His *War Without Violence* was pragmatic, a practical manual alerting practitioners to focus on the evil rather than the evildoer and ensure that the action was directly relevant to the particular evil being addressed. His description of the effect of nonviolence on opponents was largely drawn from Gregg and stressed the psychological confusion caused by unexpected tactics. He was the guest speaker at CORE's founding conference in June 1943. Farmer recorded his surprise that instead of a Gandhi-like figure, ascetic and bony, he found a well-dressed and well-fed Brahman, with rings on his fingers and smoking a cigar. Perhaps it was therefore not surprising that Shridharani played down the moral aspects of Gandhism and stressed the strategic, dwelling on the opportunities provided by modern media to use dramatic actions to spread a political message. He suspected that American pacifists exaggerated the spiritual dimensions of an Indian movement that was largely secular. The religious aspects of satyagraha were of "propaganda and publicity reasons as well as for the personal satisfaction of deeply conscientious men like Gandhi" and his disciples. Nonviolence had been adopted for "earthly, tangible, and collective aims" and so could be "discarded if it does not work."[17] He grasped the impact of the refusal to engage with the fight with Hitler on the credibility of pacifism, which led to his own skepticism about FOR and its leadership.

The man who saw most clearly how nonviolence could be made to work for blacks was Bayard Rustin. Born in 1912, Rustin was raised in a Quaker family in Pennsylvania. He was gifted intellectually, athletically, and musically. Refined and cultured, he affected an upper-class British accent, but was also a consistent activist, moving between campaigns against war and for racial justice, ready to accept jail for either cause. Enthused by the febrile radical, intellectual atmosphere of late 1930s New York, he joined the Young Communist League until he realized that it had no special commitment to racial justice. In 1941 he became involved with Philip Randolph, a leading black campaigner close to the labor movement. Randolph had picked up on how the early mobilization for war increased the economic importance of black workers. He proposed a march of ten thousand people on Washington demanding desegregation of the armed forces and an end to racial discrimination in the war industries.[18]

The march was canceled when President Roosevelt signed the Fair Employment Act which banned discrimination in the war industry, though not the armed forces. Rustin thought Randolph should have held out for more concessions, and went off to work for Muste. In practice, Randolph—the wise elder statesman of the civil rights movement—became Rustin's most consistent and loyal patron. When two decades later Rustin eventually got his own organization to run, it would be the Philip Randolph Foundation. Randolph's support and admiration for Rustin's political and administrative skills were particularly important because Muste disapproved of Rustin's homosexuality, both morally and politically. At the time it was a crime, judged as a perverse sexual choice. A 1953 Californian conviction for immorality, combined with his past communism, obliged Rustin to keep a low profile. This prevented him being recognized as one of the key leaders of the civil rights movement. He was described as "an intellectual engineer behind the scenes—probably the most adroit tactical aide to almost all the frontline black leaders and organizations."[19]

In retrospect it is difficult to understand how the Jim Crow laws had survived so long. In the media age, and with a global struggle underway to win over allegiances to the United States at a time of growing anti-colonial sentiment, there was something jarring about a situation so at odds with the country's proclaimed values. But the entrenched power structures of the old confederacy were not so easy to dislodge, and while northern politicians deplored segregation, there were few political prizes to be gained doing anything about it. The landmark 1954 Supreme Court decision (*Brown v. Board of Education*) which declared segregated public schools unconstitutional was at one level a morale-booster to blacks, but at another it hardened southern white opinion against integration, undermining moderates. As new challenges arose, the segregationists were in a determined mood.

The main black organization—the NAACP—was based in the North, lacked a mass organization, and was barred from operating in some southern states on grounds of subversion. Nonetheless, in November 1955, it was the secretary of the local branch of the NAACP, Rosa Parks, who refused to give up her seat to a white man on a bus in Montgomery, Alabama, and was arrested. This was a moment for which local activists had prepared: soon Montgomery's buses were being boycotted. This was "no bolt from the blue,"[20] and the effects were as anticipated. A crisis was created for the bus company, which depended on blacks for up to three-quarters of its customers. There were already precedents. In some cases, notably Baton Rouge, action had led to concessions, although not full integration. The compromises still involved blacks sitting at the back of buses. In Montgomery, the white establishment refused to budge. As the blacks found ways of getting their people to work without the buses, their demands escalated into a challenge to the principle of segregation. The boycott ended in late 1956 when the Supreme Court declared bus segregation laws to be unconstitutional.

For those looking for lessons for direct action, three appeared salient. First, the economic effects were as important as the political. In that respect, the actions were coercive. Second, the political effects grew as the boycott endured and the national and international media became progressively more intrigued by the struggle. Third, on balance, the harsher the local response the more the campaign benefited. A subsequent bus boycott in Tallahassee, Florida, faced a more sophisticated local police chief, determined not to make martyrs, and authorities showing a degree of flexibility. This helped take the steam out of the protest and cause divisions in the campaign, although the Supreme Court case that confirmed the illegality of bus segregation in Alabama had the same effect in Florida.

The leaders of the Montgomery campaign, who became the key figures in a burgeoning civil rights movement, applied these lessons over the next decade. The young Baptist pastor, Dr. Martin Luther King, Jr., who reluctantly agreed to preside over the campaign's organization, the Montgomery Improvement Association (MIA), became its most familiar and eloquent face. Though a female group had provided the impetus for the boycott, the church provided leadership and organization. The churches were the only local institutions independent of white society, financed and run by blacks.

Their congregations had been swelling with the migration from rural to urban areas. They offered the movement both respectability and a religious theatricality.

King turned out to be a natural leader, a gifted orator who could reach out to an audience beyond his local congregation. He had an understanding of organization and tactics and a readiness to learn. He was aware of Gandhi and Thoreau, but he had not thought through nonviolence as a strategy.[21] As a theological student he had wrestled with the issues of morality and politics, was aware of Niebuhr's Christian realism, and remained unconvinced by those who spoke of the power of love to change hearts. He wrote in a college essay that "pacifists fail to recognize the sinfulness in man" and the need for a degree of "coercion to keep one man from injuring his fellows." Later he said he believed at this time that the "only way we could solve our problem of segregation was an armed revolt."[22]

As the Montgomery boycott began, neither he nor the other members of the MIA had much of an idea of strategy. They were nonviolent but that was not a deliberate choice. Violence was the segregationists' weapon. If it came to a fight, blacks would lose. As the pressure against them was stepped up during the first weeks of the boycott, they felt obliged to consider forms of self-defense, including their own weapons, especially after King's house was bombed at the end of January 1956. The shift in tactics and philosophy came as King acquired a number of advisers seeped in Gandhism. The first to reach him was Rustin. Not only had Rustin extraordinary practical experience, including the credibility derived from time in India and in jail, but also confidence in his own beliefs, acumen, and powers of persuasion. Because of his controversial past, Rustin had to withdraw from Montgomery almost as soon as he arrived. But he did not stop advising King, with whom he stayed close thereafter. Most accounts put him to the fore as an influence on the campaign.[23] His replacement was another FOR/CORE activist, Glenn Smiley. He brought King's attention to the works of Richard Gregg. In late 1956, King listed Gregg's *The Power of Non-Violence* with Thoreau and Gandhi as particular influences.[24] In addition to Rustin and Smiley, and later Gregg himself, another Gandhian influence was Harris Wofford, who later worked for President Kennedy and had also spent time in India studying nonviolence. Stanley Levison, a wealthy lawyer and former communist, introduced to King by Rustin, eventually became one of King's closest confidants.

The immediate effect of their arrival was to make nonviolence a guiding principle rather than a prudent tactic. Rustin argued that nonviolence had to be unconditional, so there could be no guns, even if only for self-defense, let alone armed bodyguards. He also demonstrated how this could be turned to tactical advantage, by persuading MIA leaders indicted by a grand jury for violating a state anti-boycott statute to dress smartly, smile broadly, and turn themselves in, thus depriving the arrests of gravity and intimidation. By the end of the Montgomery campaign, King was personally committed to a Gandhian philosophy. Within two years, he was making his own pilgrimage to India to meet with followers of the great teacher. "There is more power in socially organized masses on the march," he declared, "than there is in guns in the hands of a few desperate men. Our enemies would prefer to deal with a small armed group rather than with a huge, unarmed but resolute mass of people." He drew confidence from history which taught that "like a turbulent ocean beating great cliffs into fragments of rock, the determined movement of people incessantly demanding their rights always disintegrates the old order."[25] Unavoidably, King's nonviolence had to draw as much from the Sermon on the Mount as from Gandhi. Its spirituality and dignity fitted a pastor. How well it was appreciated by black opinion is another matter. They could understand that there was little to be gained by initiating violence, but suggestions that high-minded actions in the name of racial justice might touch a segregationist's heart could seem far-fetched. Moreover, the personal risks involved in inviting time in jail, especially for those who needed jobs and had to care for families, could be considerable.

For King, the strategy made perfect sense. For many of his supporters it was conditional, but then the same had been true for Gandhi. King's own theorizing was largely derivative. Indeed, as his biographers discovered when reviewing his doctoral thesis, King had an unfortunate tendency to plagiarism. At its most benign, this meant that he was relaxed when others willingly offered him drafts to which he could put his own name. Rustin drafted King's first political article and then published it in his own journal, *Liberation*.[26] The article described a "new Negro" who had "replaced self-pity with self-respect and self-depreciation with dignity." The bus boycott had undermined many of the stereotypes Negroes had about themselves and others had about them, that they lacked nerve and staying power. The boycott had "broken the spell." Six lessons were listed from the struggle: the community could stick together and their leaders did not have to sell out; they need not be intimidated by threats and violence; the church was becoming militant; there was a new self-belief; the importance of economics was understood, as white businessmen were anxious about the loss of business; a "new and powerful weapon" had been discovered in nonviolence, strengthening the movement by facing violence without returning it. King used more or less the same lessons when he spoke in December 1956 after the favorable Supreme Court ruling.[27]

He never really put the effort into developing a coherent philosophy. Without the direct engagement of Rustin and Levison, his first book, *Stride Toward Freedom*, would not have been published. Garrow described the chapter on nonviolence as an embarrassment. Here too King's contributions indicated a tendency to borrow liberally from others. The key chapter on "Pilgrimage to Nonviolence" was "in part a poorly organized and at times erroneous hodgepodge of contributions from a number of King's editorial advisers."[28] Despite the shortcomings of the book, King was on his way to becoming an iconic figure and Rustin understood better than most his value to the civil rights movement.

Any comparison with Gandhi was suggestive but potentially misleading. King was only in his mid-20s and had neither prepared for nor sought a political role. He was at times a muddled thinker and, it later transpired, somewhat reckless in his private life. And yet for all his flaws and inexperience, there was no denying his courage, commitment, and grasp of southern black culture. His eloquence was special, almost poetic, drawing on the familiar cadences and rhythms of black preachers but also the classical tropes of American democracy and Western philosophy. The evident risks he was running, in the face of regular death threats, real violence, and occasional spells in prison, demonstrated that he was a man who suffered for his cause. He soon became a media star and so came to personify the black movement as its most visible face and most compelling voice. He had the quality described by Weber as "charisma."

As he reflected on the Montgomery campaign, Rustin noted the strategic benefits of a bus boycott. It had a clear purpose, economic impact, and was susceptible to direct action. Unlike other targets, such as integrated education, there was no "administrative machinery and legal maneuvering" to get in the way. The action required a "daily rededication" to the struggle and so raised community solidarity and pride, making "humble folk noble" and turning "fear into courage." Notably it had depended upon "the most stable social institution in Negro culture—the Church."[29] In early 1957, Rustin masterminded the formation of the Southern Christian Leadership Conference (SCLC). Each word was significant. Southern meant "not national." "Christian" reflected the special role of the Church in the South (for whites as well as blacks) and incidentally undermined claims that the movement was communist. "Leadership Conference" eschewed a mass membership organization. The advantage of this formulation was to avoid a fight with the NAACP, a national organization, which considered itself best able to speak for blacks. The NAACP's director, Roy Wilkins, was wary of King as a young upstart. King made little secret of his concern that based in the

North, Wilkins was too preoccupied with mounting legal challenges to the Jim Crow laws and had done little to challenge them directly. Nonetheless, he did not want to foment disunity in the movement. The serious advantage of the SCLC was that it provided institutional support to King as the leader capable of giving meaning to the struggle and describing the strategy in terms that made sense to those who had to follow it. Wofford later recalled how "Rustin seemed ever-present with advice, and sometimes acted as if King were a precious puppet whose symbolic actions were to be planned by a Gandhian high command."[30]

Rustin understood that King was no puppet and had special leadership qualities. The real problem, as he acknowledged, was that the Church was a natural autocracy, without serious bureaucratic procedures. Ministers organized politically in the same way that they organized their congregations.[31] This suited King but it soon led to complaints. One of King's most severe critics was Ella Baker, an effective organizer who ran the SCLC. She became discouraged by the developing cult of personality, reflecting an urge to find a savior, which held back the emergence of a democratic mass movement.[32] Without a mass base, there was no secure financial stream and much of King's time was spent touring to raise funds. Fairclough argues that the "decision against creating a national mass-membership organization...turned out to be a serious and eventually crippling handicap."[33]

Even with a larger organization there would have been problems when it came to major campaigns of nonviolent direct action. There were a limited number of volunteers, perhaps no more than 5 percent of a given population. From those with jobs or responsibilities to their families it was unrealistic to expect major commitment. The real difference when it came to the surge of militancy that marked the early 1960s was that substantial numbers of students, black and white, developed a taste for direct action. The Student Nonviolent Coordinating Committee (SNCC) formed with SCLC's help in 1960 and began to make their mark by reviving the sort of action pioneered by James Farmer and his colleagues in 1942, starting with four students sitting-in at a Woolworth's lunch counter in Greensboro in 1961. At the time, this was presented as a spontaneous expression of anger that somehow sparked a movement, a representation that dried up "like a raisin in the sun" as it became apparent that the students had been activists in the youth wing of the NAACP, were drawing on experience of sit-ins over the previous two years, and had planned the activity carefully. The movement spread through a network of churches and campuses.[34] In May the first "freedom rides" intended to desegregate bus terminals across the South left Washington, DC. The tactic fit in naturally with the direct action philosophy of King and

Rustin, and they had little difficulty embracing it as a new stage in the campaign. By this time the white establishment was becoming more subtle in their tactics. Rustin may have been right that transport was a natural target, but following the Supreme Court ruling cities did not put up much resistance to desegregating buses. Voter registration, the other major push, was the best way to get real political power for blacks over the long term, but it was a slow process, especially when local officials felt able to interpret the law to keep out black voters.

In December 1961, the first "community-wide protest campaigns" began in Albany, Georgia. Now rather than focusing on a particular target, such as a lunch counter or bus terminal, the aim was to develop a concerted attack on all local forms of segregation in order to create a crisis that would test the segregationists' tolerance. This was not a great success, but lessons were learned and then "refined through a process of trial and error to the point where it was responsible for the most dramatic campaigns of the entire movement."[35] The new campaign was much more provocative, almost designed to incite violence, showing how far strategies of nonviolence had moved from when they had sought to inspire a reciprocal goodness in the hearts of segregationists. Now it was the contrast between official brutality and dignified demands for basic rights that provided the impact. As Rustin observed, "protest becomes an effective tactic to the degree that it elicits brutality and oppression from the power structure."[36] If so, the logic was to search for the more brutish police chiefs, a task that became more challenging as the more astute police forces were training their men to arrest without violence. In the spring of 1963 in Birmingham, Alabama, such a chief was found in Eugene "Bull" Connors. He exceeded expectations in arresting children and in his resort to fire hoses and dogs. This ensured that the demonstrators were clearly the victims.[37]

The strategy behind the Birmingham campaign was not so much to provoke violence as to generate a crisis of which violence could be a symptom. When he found himself in jail in Birmingham, facing criticism from local clergyman for "unwise and untimely" activities, King set out a clear statement of his philosophy. The demonstrations, he insisted, should not be deplored more than the conditions which stimulated them. The objective of nonviolent direct action was negotiation, but to achieve that it was necessary to "create such a crisis and foster such a tension that a community which has constantly refused to negotiate is forced to confront the issue. It seeks to so dramatize the issue that it can no longer be ignored."[38] This was a nonviolent version of "Propaganda of the Deed." In the case of Birmingham, this was achieved as much by sustained economic pressure on the city center as by the excesses of the local police. The two combined to produce a dramatic effect. Again to quote Rustin, "Businessmen and chambers of commerce across the South dreaded the cameras."[39] By causing protracted disorder, the hope was that business leaders in Birmingham would be persuaded to accept that desegregation and hiring more blacks was the price of economic survival. A further objective was to shift the political calculus of the Kennedy administration in favor of a civil rights bill.

The theater of conflict was the city center, a relatively compact space that could be flooded with protestors unless the authorities found a way to stop them. Unlike the Alabama campaign, Birmingham was well planned and drew on a strong local organization. It began at the start of April 1963, a couple of weeks before Easter, one of the busiest times of the year for city shops. It opened with the black community boycotting shops and holding demonstrations and sit-ins at lunch counters. All blacks (250,000 out of a city of 600,000) could participate in the boycott of downtown shops. The effect was immediate and damaging. To get the city under control, police chief Connor's first tactic was borrowed from Albany. He combined a court injunction to ban sit-ins and demonstrations with the imposition of high bail bonds. Instead of obeying the injunction, as in Albany, this time the leadership decided to disobey. King and his top lieutenant, Ralph Abernathy, were arrested on Good Friday. King thought the timing symbolic and propitious.

This was followed by mass defiance of the injunctions. On May 2, the numbers participating in the demonstrations increased with the introduction of thousands of high school students. Soon one thousand were in jail. The authorities now faced the problem of either filling the jails until they were overflowing or trying to stop the demonstrators from reaching their destination. This is when the violence began, as fire hoses, clubs, and dogs were used to stop the demonstrators from moving downtown. These measures failed to stem the tide. A report from the Birmingham sheriff spoke of "stuffed jailhouses with rebellious staffs and budgets already overspent for the year; street officers on the point of cracking from relentless stress, helpless to make further arrests but caught between taunting demonstrators, omnipresent news cameras, and the conflicting orders of an unstable and divided high command that included Bull Connor."[40] The culminating moment came on May 7, when the whole downtown area was flooded by demonstrators. The police cordons were outflanked by using decoy marches, starting the main marches earlier than normal (while the police were having their lunch), and then holding other marchers back until the police were preoccupied. With some three thousand people effectively occupying the city center, the police had to acknowledge a loss of control. King recalled how one of the businessmen returning from a lunch he had been unable to reach "cleared his throat and said: 'You know, I've been thinking this thing through, we ought to be able to work something out.'"[41] The next day the business community threw in the towel, although the political elite wanted to carry on the struggle.

On June 19, 1963, President Kennedy sent a national civil rights bill to Congress. This was followed by the dramatic march to Washington in late August 1963, organized by Rustin, involving a quarter of a million people and culminating in King's famous "I have a dream" speech. Civil rights were now assured a place at the top of the American political agenda.

Inevitably, at this point the movement came to face the fact that political rights did not guarantee improvement in economic or social conditions. The vote did not feed the children or pay the rent, although it did make possible further forms of political activity that might help over time. But King's campaign culminated not with black satisfaction but with frustration, as riots broke out in the inner cities. As King began to turn his attention to issues of poverty, the question was whether the methods that had brought political gains in the South and launched him to national prominence could work across the country on issues that were much more intractable.

King had led a focused campaign with a clear set of objectives, working with communities he understood and with tactics that—once refined—served both to coerce local white establishments through economic pain and turn the media spotlight on to the iniquities of segregation by provoking their police forces into violence. The whites saw their local businesses being hurt by bus boycotts and city center mayhem. If they tried to suppress the movement with the methods that had served them well in the past, they alienated northern politicians and the media. If they held back, they had few options other than to find a new modus vivendi with blacks. The movement's strategists could comfort themselves even as their people suffered harsh treatment that this played into their hands. So long as their people did not buckle under the pressure, the contrast between the dignity of the protestors and the brutality of the police created a stunning media spectacle.

The problem was never with the clarity of the cause. The segregationists' arguments were incredible and untenable, at odds with liberal values. The challenge was to convince blacks that to gain the same rights as other Americans they had to work together and to develop a considerable local organization. In meeting both these requirements, the Church played a central role. The strategy also required nonviolence. This was not because of any expectation that segregationist hearts could be turned by this form of witness but because it ensured that the movement kept the moral high ground. Those who learned their politics in the civil rights movements were convinced of the value of direct action and saw comparable causes to demand their attention, but these causes would not be so clear cut as civil rights. The radical politics of the sixties began with dignity and restraint but soon turned angrier, with riots in the urban ghettoes and sharp reactions against an illegitimate war.

CHAPTER 24 | Existential Strategy

There is a time when the operation of the machine becomes so odious,
makes you so sick at heart, that you can't take part; you can't even tacitly
take part, and you've got to put your bodies upon the levers, upon all the
apparatus and you've got to make it stop. And you've got to indicate to
the people who run it, to the people who own it, that unless you're free, the
machines will be prevented from working at all.

—Mario Savio, *Free Speech Movement, December 1964*

IT HAD BEEN young people who had sustained the later campaigns of the
civil rights movement. Their experiences in the South had radicalized
them, both in their critique of American society and their demand for a new
politics. In the early 1960s to the extent that they were organized it was as
part of the Student Nonviolent Coordinating Committee (SNCC), which was
largely made up of black activists (although initially not exclusively so), or
else the Students for a Democratic Society (SDS), which as the name suggests
was based in the universities and was largely white. Both initially reflected
anger at the gap between the ideals upon which their country was based and
the reality of racial divides and preparations for nuclear war. Both were set
up with firm commitments to nonviolence, but both by the end of the 1960s
had embraced violence and factionalism.

Of the two, SDS attracted the most comment: an active and radical political force emerging out of a disadvantaged minority was less surprising than one emerging out of the affluent majority. Moreover, SDS came to be seen as part of a broad cultural shift that went well beyond politics. There was a generational break between those whose formative experiences had been depression and the fight against Germany and Japan and those who had grown up in relative comfort but found the social constraints they had inherited frustrating. This was reflected in changing musical preferences, attitudes to sex, and the use of recreational drugs. A key word for the decade, borrowed from anti-colonial struggles, was "liberation." The word came to be applied to any group, including women and gays, that felt constrained by social conventions and outdated laws. In this respect, it challenged the role of the state in everyday life and was individualistic rather than collectivist in inspiration.

This helps explain why there was such an uneasy fit with the orthodox Left, which was collectivist and enthusiastic about the possibilities of the state and the role of labor unions. It had been marginalized by affluence, its rhetoric seen as an echo of old struggles long lost and won, with its internal politics still marked by in-fighting between communists, Trotskyites, and social democrats. The young activists fresh from the freedom rides in the South, where they had often been in jail or suffered beatings, had little time for those who had spent their time trading theoretical blueprints for socialism. Although SDS was intended initially to be the student branch of the League for Industrial Democracy, another of John Dewey's causes which now represented the pro-union, anti-communist strand in American socialism, it took off on its own trajectory. So the revolt was against not only the complacent liberalism and social conservatism of mainstream America but also the social democratic tradition. This tradition of mass parties organized to fight parliamentary elections on the basis of an agreed program reflecting a more or less coherent ideology had never really taken root in America. The new radicals were more in a libertarian, anarchist, anti-elitist tradition, desperate for authenticity even at the expense of lucidity, suspicious of all authorities and organizational discipline. Instead of decisions being taken by individuals who were detached, remote, and looking after their own interests, a way had to be found to engage ordinary people so that they could shape their own destinies.

When SDS was formed in 1962, meeting at the United Auto-Workers retreat at Port Huron, Michigan, there was a clash with the social democrats of the League for Industrial Democracy. Tom Hayden, a Michigan student journalist and the lead author of the Port Huron Statement that set SDS in motion, described his wonder that "seemingly serious people could get so enmeshed in such endlessly divisive hair-splitting debates." "As a formative experience," he noted, "we learned a distrust and hostility toward the very people we were closest to historically, the representatives of the liberal and labor organizations who had once been young radicals themselves."[1] The old leftists in turn were shocked by the indifference of the young activists to the working-class cause and the unions, and their reluctance to get drawn into denunciations of communism. Instead of the rigorous analysis of classic texts, the new radicals were suspicious of theory. Political acts had to be genuine expressions of values and sentiments. Convictions took priority over the calculation of consequences, reflecting a wariness of expediency and a refusal to compromise for the sake of political effects. At times it seemed as if deliberate and systematic thought was suspect and only a spontaneous stream of consciousness, however inarticulate and unintelligible, could be trusted. Todd Gitlin, an early activist and later analyst of the New Left, observed how actions were undertaken to "dramatize" convictions. They were "judged according to how they made the participants feel," as if they were drugs offering highs and lows. If it was the immediate experience which counted for most, then there was little scope for thinking about the long term.[2]

This left the new radicals caught by Weber's paradox. Though Weber was dispirited by the steady bureaucratization of society and politics, he considered it irresponsible to ignore the logic of functionality. The emerging political form of the new radicals embraced an ethic of irresponsibility. There could be no separation of means and ends. Every compromise, every denial of a core value meant that something precious had been lost, diminishing whatever might eventually be achieved. Their tactics, highlighted by the sit-in, instinctively challenged all rules. They were often strikingly lacking in both theory and organization, reveling in activism but without a clear direction. The underlying philosophy was existentialist rather than socialist.

This experiment in existential strategy failed because those features that made it so culturally liberating, and where the effects were actually long-lasting, also made it politically exasperating. When positions were articulated in terms of core values rather than alternative outcomes compromises were hard to arrange and coalitions became fragile. Without hierarchy, when every decision was subject to constant challenge and re-examination, organization became slow and ponderous, and implementation tentative. The activists, doubting rationality and trusting feelings, became increasingly angry. Their distaste for the politics of expedience and compromise led to isolation and irrelevance and vulnerability to the intervention of groups based on hard theory and disciplined organization against which they had initially rebelled.

Rebels

Instead of the polarized class struggle anticipated by Marx, postwar capitalist society was marked by an improved standard of living, apparently developing into a self-satisfied but undifferentiated mass society. The salaried middle classes were on the ascendant, largely to be found in large, impersonal organizations. The daily grind of life was hardly grueling. Yet there appeared to be something missing. The critique was not of growing misery and poverty but of dreariness, not so much physical deprivation but of a psychological void. William Whyte's *The Organization Man* suggested a degree of homogenization in the American middle class, reflected in standardized career paths, consumer tastes, and cultural sensibilities, with an accompanying degree of docility. The fault, he argued, was not in organization but its worship, "the soft-minded denial that there is a conflict between the individual and society."[3] Indeed, much of the writing about this group, including David Riesman's *The Lonely Crowd* and C. Wright Mills's *White Collar Workers*, suggested that the rise of this class was joyless.

Riesman argued that inner-directed personalities followed life goals established at an early age, had a strong sense of values, and were therefore apt to suffer from guilt when deviating from those values. They were giving way to other-directed personalities, who took cues from their environment and were dependent on their contemporaries or even the media for direction. The distinction was between following either an internal gyroscope or an external radar. *The Lonely Crowd* became one of the most popular books ever written by a sociologist. In contrast to the earlier progressives who looked to other-directedness as a means of binding society together and encouraging a democratic sensitivity, it encouraged the view, probably more than Riesman intended, that there was something pernicious about social conventions and political orthodoxy as uncritically transmitted through the mass media.[4] The idea that adapting to the social environment risked denying core values was also a theme of Erich Fromm's *Fear of Freedom*. Fromm, a refugee from Nazi Germany, warned of the dangers of rootless individuals seeking security in conformism or authoritarianism. Freedom had to be about more than lack of restrictions. It needed to be more positive, creative, authentic, expressive, and spontaneous, as well as less respectful of the received wisdom of experts or the dictates of common sense. Social structures were presented as suppressing the natural, positive side of human nature rather than as restraining the negative, coercive side.[5]

The enthusiasts for the cultural developments of the 1960s saw it as an affirmation of this positive side of human nature against the conformism of the corporate state. When in 1970 Theodore Roszak looked back approvingly over that decade, he described the many developments he applauded as responses to the "technocracy." This, echoing Weber, was described as corporate power combined with a state of mind according to which

> the requirements of our humanity yield wholly to some manner of formal analysis which can be carried out by specialists possessing certain impenetrable skills which can then be translated by them directly into a congeries of economic and social programs, personnel management procedures, merchandise, and mechanical gadgetry.

These experts, to be found at the corporate center, believed that most human needs had been filled; where there was a problem, it was the result of a misunderstanding.[6] In different ways, Roszak claimed, the poetry, literature, sociology, political tracts, and demonstrations of the time challenged this technocratic presumption. In this respect, the politics of the decade was but one part of a general revolt against rationality, whether in challenges to bureaucracy and scientific expertise, or in hedonistic life styles and the disparagement of conventional careers. Claims of objective knowledge were distrusted. Instead of worldviews being shaped by the accumulation of knowledge, "knowledge" always deserved quotation marks, reflecting an underlying worldview rather than actual reality.

What did this mean for strategy? At a general level it challenged an idea of strategy based on not only the presumption of choice but also the availability of methods for choosing well, which included the need to pay close attention to the operating environment and think ahead. In some respects, liberalism as it had developed through the twentieth century could pride itself on having created the optimal conditions for strategy-making: the right of free political expression, the ability to organize, and respect for the scientific method as a means of bringing clarity to choice and thinking through consequences. Now the New Left appeared to see this approach as problematic, a form of thinking that constrained the range of choice and excluded those affected by decisions from contributing to their resolution, and a stress on organization, which meant hierarchy.

It could also be the case that there was little point in worrying too much about relating ends and means because of the utter hopelessness of the strategic task in the face of a complacent majority culture. The aspirations of the young radicals were beyond the scope of rational planning. Not surprisingly, therefore, a strategy of absolute ends emerged, heroic and romantic, doomed to fail but magnificent in its ambition and noble in its honesty. The aim was to affirm existence rather than realize goals, and in this there was a nod across the Atlantic to the French existentialists with their deep musings about the human condition, full of absurdity, abandonment, and despair, but also stressing the unavoidability of choice. Jean-Paul Sartre might seem to dwell on the futility of action, but his point was that hopelessness was not in itself a reason for passivity. Indeed, choice was unavoidable for men were "condemned to be free." They did not choose the circumstances of their existence, but they were obliged to respond. The quality of their responses, whether heroic or cowardly, was their responsibility and would eventually define their lives.[7] More influential than Sartre, at least in the United States, was Albert Camus. Politically, Camus was closer to the anarchists than the communists, and his strong anti-Soviet views caused a break with Sartre. In 1940, he was a pacifist but the experience of occupation led him to join the resistance, eventually editing the underground journal, *Combat*. This was the inspiration for his allegorical 1947 novel, *The Plague*. As a plague almost overwhelmed the Algerian City of Oran, the citizens were in denial and then, instead of abandoning hope, the community found a way of defeating the disease and regained its solidarity in the process. The doctor, Bernard Rieux, summed up the philosophy: "All I maintain is that on this earth there are pestilences and there are victims, and it's up to us, so far as possible, not to join forces with the pestilences."[8] From Camus came the argument that rebellion made a life worth living, even when this meant acting in the face of overwhelming odds. So long as one was acting with integrity there was no need to worry about being an underdog, for integrity mattered more than consequences.

Mills and Power

C. Wright Mills died of a heart attack in his mid-40s in 1962. Mills was controversial at the time and has remained so since, not least because of his larger than life personality and his readiness to cast himself as a dissident.[9] He was the classic inner-directed man, true to his own values, describing himself as a loner who never worked with a political group. The early years of his career saw him subjected to three influences, two of which remained critical for his own ideas. The pragmatists were the first influence, and the subject of his doctorate. He shared their belief in the public role of intellectuals. There was an affinity with James's anti-militarism and Dewey's advocacy of participatory democracy. At the same time, Mills was skeptical of Dewey's quasi-scientific framework and over-mechanical view of politics, his reluctance to come to terms with the problem of power and to acknowledge its manipulative, emotional, and coercive elements.[10] Yet Mills also appreciated

Dewey's commitment to intelligence as a form of power. Both were opinionated, although by contrast with Dewey's ponderously functional prose, Mills's was laced with invective and value-laden categories.

Hans Gerth, an émigré from the Frankfurt School, helped move Mills from philosophy to sociology, and introduced him to the work of Max Weber. From Weber, Mills then derived his basic explanatory framework, the interweaving of class, status, power, and culture, and the alarm at the role of large bureaucracies in all areas of life. Marx was not read or taken seriously by Mills until well into his career, after which Mills became progressively more Marxist. He was also becoming more of an activist intellectual toward the end of his life, defending the Cuban Revolution and developing links with the British New Left (composed of Marxists, often scholarly, who had left the Communist Party). Part of his appeal to students was that he already identified them as potential agents of change, ready to challenge the forces of inertia and conservatism.[11]

His books combined subtle analysis and research with a searing social critique. The critique became more strident during the course of the 1950s as his own international reputation as a dissenting intellectual grew. He was preoccupied with the structures of power: how in modern corporate America the elite no longer needed brute force or coercion to sustain its position but could instead rely on manipulation. His target was what came to be described as the "pluralist" school, which argued that democracy could function with a relatively low level of citizen participation. Since everybody got something out of the political process and had no cause for either excessive distress or joy, somehow it was working effectively and fairly.

The debate on power was an important one and Mills's book, *The Power Elite*, was always cited on one side of the argument, often against Robert Dahl's *Who Governs: Democracy and Power in an American City*.[12] Part of the difficulty was that they reflected two different views of power and how to measure it, and both views were relevant to the developing debates about radical politics. Power was, and still is, regularly referred to as an attribute of a political entity, measured in terms of the more blatant indicators of military and economic strength. Yet it was evident that an ample stock of both did not guarantee favorable outcomes in all encounters. The powerful did not always get their way. Resources needed to be considered in the context of the problems they were supposed to solve. A card player might have great skill and a wonderful hand of cards for bridge but not for poker. There was therefore a difference between *putative* and *actual* power, between capabilities and effects, the potential and the act.[13] Dahl's definition stressed the ability to influence: "A has power over B to the extent that he can get B to do something that B would not otherwise do."[14] It was not enough that A had capacity: it was only really power as revealed in quite specific relationships through measurable effects, by B being made subject to A's will.

One of the most important and lasting challenges to this view came not from Mills but two political scientists, Peter Bachrach and Morton Baratz, in a 1962 article:

> Of course power is exercised when A participates in the making of decisions that affect B. But power is also exercised when A devotes his energies to creating or reinforcing social and political values and institutional practices that limit the scope of the political process to public consideration of only those issues which are comparatively innocuous to A. To the extent that A succeeds in doing this, B is prevented, for all practical purposes, from bringing to the fore any issues that might in their resolution be seriously detrimental to A's set of preferences.[15]

This second face of power had an almost insidious quality: it was about how A sustained a position in a power structure, of power over others, by keeping issues off the agenda and creating a background consensus that denied B the opportunity to begin to challenge A, never mind defeat A in a direct confrontation. It was this line of critique that by the end of the decade had been embraced by the radicals, although often in a far cruder, "false-consciousness" way than these authors intended. Mills avoided the simple Marxist analysis of government being the executive committee of the ruling class or of mass consciousness being shaped by bourgeois ideology. His description of the power elite was more about a bureaucratic convergence of interests, including corporate executives and the "warlords," than an organized conspiracy, but he insisted that the system of checks and balances was no longer working and so encouraged the view of a vital resource being monopolized by a privileged view, so that they could get what they wanted when they wanted it.[16]

Mills became as much of a pamphleteer as a scholar, "prepared to step forth and brazenly pin his indictment like a target to the enemy's chest."[17] His catchy rhetoric remained nonetheless an extension of his sociology. His impatience with mainstream sociology was reflected in his book *The Sociological Imagination*,[18] in which he derided what he saw to be the two false paths of mainstream sociology: self-important grand theory on the one hand and abstracted empiricism, full of microscopic studies that remained marginal to the big questions of the day, on the other. The true purpose, he insisted, should be to connect private troubles with social and political structures. If an individual was unemployed that was a private trouble: if 20 percent of the population was unemployed that was a structural issue and thus a task for sociology. In this role, he argued, sociology could be the master discipline of politics. The sociological imagination would feed the political imagination. "Before you are through with any piece of work, no matter how indirectly on occasion," he insisted, "orient it to the central and continuing task of understanding the structure and the drift, the shaping and the meanings, of your own period, the terrible and magnificent world of human society in the second half of the twentieth century."

The Port Huron Statement

Tom Hayden was a natural wordsmith and was the first to find fresh language to convey a new mood. The Port Huron Statement, for which he was the lead author, was discussed in June 1962 by a group of about sixty people, feeling—as he later remarked—that they "were giving voice to a new generation of rebels."[19] There were a number of influences. Arnold Kaufman, Hayden's philosophy professor at Michigan, had introduced him to John Dewey as an exponent of the democratization of all social institutions. From Camus came a way of thinking about rebellion as a way of life, and from C. Wright Mills a critique of the prevailing distribution of power, but also something more personal. It was partly that they were both lapsed Catholics. But it was also that what unsettled him about his own family could be explained. As he read Mills, Hayden saw a portrait of his father, an accountant for Chrysler: "proud in his starched white collar, occupying his accountant's niche above the union work force and below the real decision makers, penciling in numbers by day, drinking in front of the television at night, muttering about the world to no one in particular."[20]

Mills explained for Hayden "the factors that made people uninterested and apathetic in the face of Camus's plague." Bureaucratic elites welcomed passivity and had no incentive to encourage true democracy. Mills had written of the emergence of the "cheerful robot," a creature of mass society with an illusion of freedom but unable to influence the larger structures of power. "Between the little man's consciousness and the issues of our time, there seems to be a veil of indifference. His will seems numb; his spirit meager." In this spirit the Port Huron Statement opened, acknowledging the awkwardness of the position of students: "We are people of this generation, bred in at least modest comfort, housed now in universities, looking uncomfortably at the world we inherit." They did not claim to be speaking for the masses but were a self-declared minority observing that "the vast majority of our people regard the temporary equilibriums of our society and world as eternally-functional parts." Students "don't even give a damn about the apathy."[21]

A Millsian analysis was offered of why people felt so powerless and had succumbed to indifference: "People are fearful of the thought that at any moment things might be thrust out of control. They fear change, since change might smash whatever invisible framework seems to hold back chaos from them now." Yet here was optimism about humanity. "We regard men as infinitely precious and possessed of unfulfilled capacities for reason, freedom, and love." If core values could be rediscovered in a "moral realignment" then there was a possibility of a "political realignment."[22] Politics was not a means to an end. It was an end in itself, participation and engagement serving to heal the divide that had opened up between people and their society. The New Left, the statement insisted,

> must transform modern complexity into issues that can be understood and felt close-up by every human being. It must give form to the feelings of helplessness and indifference so that people may see the political, social and economic sources of their private troubles and organize to change society. In a time of supposed prosperity, moral complacency and political manipulation, a new left cannot rely on only aching stomachs to be the engine of social reform.[23]

The immediate cause for the students was civil rights in the South. This met their appetite for activism and provided experiences that were more instructive and meaningful than anything that could be gained through studying the political classics. But that could only take the movement so far. The aim was to move the demand for rights into all institutions rather than just the electoral process. The starting point for their demands to be heard was therefore their own institutions—the universities. Here they were expected to conform, accept what they were told in class without demur, and follow all rules at risk of expulsion. Gradually this new mood made itself felt. A clash over the rights of CORE to organize on the San Francisco Berkeley campus led to the first big student demonstrations.

Dick Flacks, a young academic closely involved with the Port Huron Statement, observed the tension between the developing movement as a way of life and as an agency of change. The way of life he called "existential humanism," which required no more than acting according to core beliefs, constantly striving "to approach an ethical existence," but he saw that this could be irresponsible, searching "for a personally satisfying mode of life while abandoning the possibility of helping others to change theirs; of placing tremendous hope in the movement of the immediate community for achieving personal salvation and gratification—then realizing that these possibilities are, after all, limited and, consequently suffering disillusionment." As did Weber, Flacks sought to reconcile convictions with responsibility. This meant acting "politically because our values cannot be realized in any durable sense without a reconstruction of the political and social system." Politics, however, apart from an existential ethic would be "increasingly manipulative, power-oriented, sacrificial of human lives and souls,"—in short, "corrupted." The answer, suggested Flacks, was "strategic analysis," though he acknowledged the prevailing suspicion of an "explicit and systematic preoccupation with strategy" as imposing artificial constraints, restricting spontaneity, and reducing responsiveness to what people really wanted. As it was the property of a few, "acting in terms of strategy is elitist." Unfortunately, without strategy there would be no sense of priorities, inarticulateness, and "almost random behavior among students who want to do effective social action."[24]

This described the problem rather than identified solutions. As with previous generations of radicals, the only way out of the dilemma appeared to be to get among the people, working with them to address their issues without claiming that they had all the answers. So it was that Hayden joined a community program, the Economic Research and Action Project, in Newark. The prohibition on elitism was limiting. There were other "liberal forces" in the area with whom it might be advisable to coalesce, but Hayden found them "extremely self-serving," with "wide community contact but no active and radical membership base" and programs that "would do very little to change the real lives of the poor." Entering into "political bartering" would violate "the basic trust we have with the neighborhood people. Our place is at the bottom."[25] Liberal strategies assumed that the "masses are apathetic and can only be roused because of simple material needs or during short periods of great enthusiasm." Because of this, "they need skilled and responsible leaders." The complaint then followed a familiar path: leaders presumed that only they could maintain the organization. Because people reacted with "disinterest or suspicion" to such elitism, the leadership was able to call the masses apathetic, although he also acknowledged a worrying tendency to "think subserviently."

Hayden was considering not the broad masses of Marxist mythology but a minority underclass.[26] He recoiled from the obvious answer, which was to form coalitions or at least make temporary arrangements with the powerful. This was rejected because no more than "welfare-state reforms" would be on offer, bound to fail because they were "not conceived by the poor people they are designed for" and allowed the middle class to relax "into the comfortable sense that everything is being managed well." His focus was so relentlessly about power, and avoiding appearing to want it, that the assumption had to be that if those at the bottom had power they would do well by themselves and others. But would they want the things that the activist believed they ought to want? If their minds had been turned by years of powerlessness and a consumerist culture, might their demands and the efforts they were prepared to put behind be disappointing?

Unsurprisingly, he was left with a "mystery" when looking for a "workable strategy." His aim was "a thoroughly democratic revolution," reversing the abdication of power to "top-down organizational units," out of which a "new kind of man" might emerge who could not be manipulated because it was "precisely against manipulation that he has defined his rebellion." The poor would transform decision-making by acting on their aspirations, working against the grain of "an affluent and coercive society." As he later accepted, the flaw in this analysis was assuming that the aspirations of the poor would be any different from the middle-class society whose values he personally derided. He already was aware of the difficulty of finding leaders who could forswear an interest in the organization for its own sake or a rank and file who understood and committed themselves to the movement's goals.[27]

While Hayden was struggling to sustain his commitment to participatory democracy, SNCC was in the process of abandoning it. James Forman, as executive secretary, had argued in 1964 for a proper mass organization rather than uncoordinated activists to compete with other civil rights organizations. To the centralizers, this simply required individuals to subordinate their own issues to the needs of the collective.

This was hard for many activists to take. They were afraid that a distant center would be insensitive to local concerns and indulge in empire-building. Moreover, it went against SNCC's founding ethos. Participatory democracy in practice, however, had been found frustrating and exhausting. There were the familiar problems of finding local people able to commit time and energy to the cause, and the tendency for the principle to paralyze decision-making with constant discussions which nobody dared bring to a conclusion, as every attempt to take an initiative was challenged as usurpation of democratic rights. In her book, *Freedom Is an Endless Meeting*, Francesca Polletta recounts how demands to "let the people decide" came up against the exasperating tendency of the people to be moderate and risk averse, seeking social services rather than revolution. This led to the conviction that people needed to have their real interests explained to them. There were also deeper factors at work. There was an issue with educated northerners who were often seen by the local southerners as being self-serving, with a patron-izing reverence for the untutored wisdom of the poor and ignorance of local culture. According to Polletta, this was more about class and education than race, though there were concerns about white liabilities as black community organizers. By 1966, however, black power had taken over and the new lead-ership of SNCC wanted to distinguish themselves from northern liberals by something tougher and more militant.[28]

The Heroic Organizer

It is worth comparing the experience of community organization as an exer-cise in participatory democracy with that of the man who did more than most to develop the idea of organizing local communities to take on local power structures. Saul Alinsky was born in Chicago in 1909 and joined the University of Chicago's sociology department as an undergraduate in 1926. The department was then under the leadership of Robert Park. Park, who had come to sociology later in his career after starting off as a reporter, was attuned to city life in all its forms and studied it with an almost voyeuristic curiosity. *Introduction to the Science of Sociology*, the book he published in 1921 with his close colleague Edwin Burgess, was for two decades a core text in the field. Burgess, a diffident man and in Parks's shadow, was more of a social reformer. He viewed "social research as the solutions to society's ills," but less in terms of elite prescriptions and more in democratic terms, as a means of "harnessing social change."[29]

Park and Burgess took students on field trips to explore Chicago, from the dance halls to the schools, the churches, and the families. The city was large and diverse, with distinctive immigrant communities. Organized criminal gangs, of which Al Capone's was the most famous, flourished during the Prohibition Era. The proximity to Canada meant that Chicago was a natural base for smuggling illicit liquor into the United States, and vicious com-petition developed over the control of the trade. The city should be a focus of study, Park argued, for it showed "the good and evil in human nature in excess. It is this fact, perhaps, more than any other which justifies the view that would make of the city a laboratory or clinic in which human nature and social processes may be most conveniently and profitably studied."[30] Critical to this school of thought was the conviction, bolstered by research, that social problems had social rather than personal causes. Burgess took this a step further than Park, arguing that the role of researchers was to "organize the community for self-investigation." The community should survey its own problems, educate themselves about social issues, and develop a core group of leaders prepared to organize for "social advance."

Burgess became a major influence on Alinsky, not least because he recognized in his student an ability that his academic record had obscured.[31] Alinsky was drawn to criminology and upon graduation, he got a fellowship with Burgess's support. He decided to make a study of the Capone gang, if possible from the inside. Eventually he made contact by hanging around the gangsters and listening to their stories.[32] For a while he worked as a criminologist in a state prison. Then, in 1936 he joined the Chicago Area Project designed to show how delinquency could be addressed socially. The cause of criminality was not individual feeble-mindedness but neighborhoods marked by multiple and reinforcing problems of poverty and unemployment. Burgess set the principles for the organizers. The program should be for the neighborhood as a whole, with local people autonomous in planning and operations. This required an emphasis on training and local leadership, strengthening established neighborhood institutions, and using activities as a device to create participation.[33] He argued that local organizers, preferably former delinquents, could help show their own people a way to more acceptable behavior. This approach was controversial. He was directly challenging paternalistic social work and was accused of tolerating criminality, encouraging populist agitators to stir up local people against those who were trying to help them and had their best interests at heart.

In 1938, Alinsky was assigned to the tough Back of the Yards neighborhood in Chicago, already notorious as the jungle of Upton Sinclair's 1906 novel. He was a natural in the organizer's role. Clever, street-wise, and brash, Alinsky had a knack of gaining the confidence of people who might otherwise feel neglected and marginalized. His approach was more political than the project allowed, however. Not only did he use the issue of delinquency to move into virtually all problems facing the neighborhood, but he also put together a community organization based on representatives of key groups who had clout because of who they represented and not just as individuals. Alinsky also drew organized labor into his campaign, well exceeding his brief by getting involved in a struggle against the meatpacking industry. By 1940 he had left the project and struck out on his own.

Over time he became more scathing in his critique of the social sciences as remote from the realities of everyday existence. Quoting a description of the University of Chicago's sociology department as "an institution that invests $100,000 on a research program to discover the location of brothels that any taxi driver could tell them about for nothing," he added his own observation that "asking a sociologist to solve a problem is like prescribing an enema for diarrhea."[34] Certainly tendencies in sociology had moved on since the Park/Burgess era at Chicago. Nonetheless, Alinsky's initial trajectory reflected the preoccupations of the discipline during the interwar years.

In an article published in the *American Journal of Sociology* in 1941, Alinsky provided a clear account of his approach. He described the wretched lives of those working in the slaughter houses and packing-houses of the Back of the Yards area. The neighborhood was a "byword for disease, delinquency, deterioration, dirt, and dependency." The traditional community organization would be of little value in such an area because it considered individual problems in isolation from each other and the community in isolation from the "general social scene." Instead, by placing each community within its broad context, its limited ability to "elevate itself by means of its own bootstraps" could be acknowledged. He identified "two basic social forces which might serve as the cornerstone of any effective community organization." These were the Catholic Church and organized labor: "The same people that comprise the membership of a parish also form the membership of a union local." He got local organizations to come together to form the Back of the Yards Neighborhood Council. Membership did not just involve the church and the unions, but also the local chamber of commerce, the American Legion post, as well as "the leading businessmen, the social, the nationality, the fraternal, and the athletic organizations."

Through the council, problems such as unemployment and disease were shown to be threats to all the people, both labor unions and businesses dependent upon local purchasing power. The various leaders "learned to know one another as human beings rather than as impersonal symbols of groups which, in many cases, appeared to be of a hostile nature." Behind this was a "people's philosophy" that emphasized rights rather than favors and the need to rely on an organization "built, owned, and operated by themselves" to get their rights.[35]

This was obviously a completely different philosophy to Hayden's. Alinsky went out of his way to draw in local organizations; Hayden was worried that this kept ordinary people excluded and reinforced local power structures. At the time, many on the Left would have queried working with the Catholic Church, which was deeply hostile to the atheistic Communist Party. Alinsky's self-definition as a radical was reflected, as his biographer notes, in his "inclinations, convictions and rhetoric, and wishes" but less so "in his actions, which took a more pragmatic form."[36] He was prepared to forge coalitions with whosoever appeared appropriate. His role model was not so much the communist agitator but the labor organizer.

This was the heroic age of the American labor movement, led by John Lewis of the United Mineworkers, which had broken away from the sleepy American Federation of Labor, dominated by elitist craft unions, and formed the Confederation of Industrial Organizations (CIO). Lewis combined a strident anti-communism with a belief in a centralized state stabilizing and planning the economy. He provided dynamic leadership to the burgeoning labor movement, with his tough and imaginative negotiating style demonstrated to the full in the sit-down strike at the General Motors Flint plant in 1937. After Flint, other industries were wary of head-on confrontations. He was able to do a deal with U.S. steel without making direct threats. He challenged the racial discrimination of southern mineworkers (who argued that black workers could make do with lower wages to support their more modest lifestyle). Within two years, the CIO had 3.4 million members. Alinsky met Lewis in July 1939 when he spoke on behalf of the Chicago packing workers. Lewis's daughter Kathryn was on the board of Alinsky's Industrial Areas Foundation.

Lewis was Alinsky's role model. He was egocentric, entered confrontations with relish, and led with nerve and panache. Later, Alinsky would write an admiring biography. From Lewis he learned how to provoke and goad opponents, promote conflict and then negotiate its resolution, using power to best advantage at all stages. Alinsky paid attention to the intellectual justifications for action and their rhetorical expression. He was impressed by the way Lewis managed to pursue a program which menaced the establishment by associating the CIO with American ideals of fairness and justice. "Similarly, Alinsky's own argumentation sought to place the objectives of his Industrial Areas Foundation firmly within familiar-sounding American political tradition."[37]

In 1946, Alinsky published his first book, *Reveille for Radicals*, which became a surprising bestseller. The basic idea behind this was that the sort of techniques that had been used so effectively by the labor unions in the factories could be used within urban communities—as he put it, "collective bargaining beyond the present confines of the factory gate." The radical was described as a militant idealist, someone who "believes what he says," has the common good as the "greatest personal value," "genuinely and completely believes in mankind," takes on every struggle as his own, avoids rationalization and superficiality, and deals in "fundamental causes rather than current manifestations." His goals were described in terms of a utopia—where every individual's worth was recognized and potentiality realized; all would be truly free politically, economically, and socially; and war, fear, misery, and demoralization would be eradicated. By contrast, liberals attracted Alinsky's scorn, for flaws in temperament and attitude rather than philosophy. They came over as feckless, hesitant, complacent, lacking the stomach for a fight, combining "radical minds and conservative hearts," paralyzed by their insistence on seeing both sides of an issue, and fearful of action and partisanship.

The fundamental difference revolved around the "issue of power." Radicals understood, according to Alinsky, that "only through the achievement and better use of power can people better themselves." Where liberals protested, radicals rebelled.[38] Given the heroic concept of community organization (a "program is limited only by the horizon of humanity itself"), it was not surprising that Alinsky also had a heroic concept of the organizer. "One could envision Alinsky's organizing flying high in a Superman cape," observed his biographer, "swooping into a forlorn industrial community, ready to fight for truth, justice and the American Way!" The organizer would lead the "war against the social menaces of mankind."[39]

Over the next couple of decades, before his sudden death in 1972, Alinsky's acolytes were involved in a number of organizational efforts across the United States. Alinsky himself was particularly associated with two: one in the Woodlawn District of Chicago and the other in Rochester, New York. Both involved largely black communities and had as their key demands improved employment and an end to the discriminatory practice of only hiring blacks for the most menial jobs. In Rochester, the target was the town's dominant corporation, Eastman Kodak. In both cases Alinsky enjoyed a degree of success, though this required negotiations rather than the capitulation of the employers.

Not long before he died, he published another book, *Rules for Radicals*, which set out his basic philosophy. We shall return later to this book, which is important in terms of how he positioned himself in relationship with the other radical social movements of the 1960s. For the moment, we can consider the "rules" themselves.

He set down eleven. A number were basic to any underdog strategy. The first was pure Sun Tzu: persuade the opponent that you were stronger than was really the case ("If your organization is small, hide your numbers in the dark and raise a din that will make everyone think you have many more people than you do"). The second and third were about staying close to the comfort zone of your own people and going outside that of the opponent in order to "cause confusion, fear, and retreat." Rule 4 was to use the opponent's own rulebook against them, and Rule 5 was to use ridicule ("man's most potent weapon") because it was hard to counterattack and infuriated the opposition. This led to Rule 6, which was that a good tactic was one your people enjoyed, while a bad tactic was not only not fun but also (Rule 7) dragged on and became hard to sustain. This was because (Rule 8) the essence of a good strategy was to keep the pressure on the opponent. "The major premise for tactics is the development of operations that will maintain a constant pressure upon the opposition. It is this that will cause the opposition to react to your advantage." Rule 9 was an observation about how threats could be more terrifying than the reality, and Rule 10 was about the need for a constructive alternative, an answer to the question, "Okay, what would you do?" Lastly, Rule 11 commanded: "Pick the target, freeze it, personalize it, polarize it. Don't try to attack abstract corporations or bureaucracies. Identify a responsible individual. Ignore attempts to shift or spread the blame."

These rules were those of a campaigner and in that respect were different from a form of strategic thinking that consisted largely of worrying about how to relate, if at all, to the local power structure and the principles that should govern any action. Alinsky was all about the campaign and the specific goals that had been set for it. The rules reflected Alinsky's appreciation of the elemental requirements of strategy in terms of endurance, coalitions, a capacity for surprise, and a need to keep an eye on public perceptions. The sense of community and confidence in the organization must grow with the campaign until it became strong enough to withstand setbacks and was able to move from one issue to another. One of Alinsky's admirers, Charles Silberman, compared his approach to guerrilla warfare. He explained the need "to avoid a fixed battle where the forces are arrayed and where the new army's weakness would become visible, and to concentrate instead on hit-and-run tactics designed to gain small but measurable victories. Hence the emphasis on such dramatic actions as parades and rent strikes whose main objective is to create a sense of solidarity and community."[40] The aim was not just to keep pressure on the targets but also to build up the community and its organization at the same time. Certainly Alinsky was clear that violence was a bad idea. This was not a moral issue. He was against actions that almost guaranteed defeat, and resort to arms came into that category.

Some of the tactics for which Alinsky became best known reflected a sense of mischief and provocation. One was to unnerve a Chicago department store that had discriminatory hiring policies by sending thousands of blacks on a normally busy Saturday for a shopping spree that would lead to very few purchases while deterring normal customers. Another tactic, intended to pressure Chicago's mayor, was to occupy all the toilets at O'Hare airport so that arriving passengers would be left desperate. The most notorious ploy, though possibly largely intended to amuse his audiences, was a proposed "fart-in" at the Rochester Philharmonic, sponsored by Eastman Kodak. The effect was to be achieved by feeding copious quantities of baked beans to young men prior to their joining the audience. What is notable about these tactics, apart from their dependence to some extent on white stereotypes of blacks, was that none of them were actually implemented, although Alinsky claimed that getting word to the targets had a coercive effect. One of his tactical innovations was the use of share proxies to gain a right to speak at shareholder meetings and put companies on the spot, first achieved with Kodak stock in April 1967. Reports of the meeting suggest little sympathy from other shareholders, but here was a way to embarrass company boards and put them on the spot in a way that might be picked up by the media.

Alinsky's distrust of liberals and tendency to romanticize the poor were traits he shared with the young radicals who moved into community organizing in the mid-1960s. But there were important differences. He was results oriented. He wanted victories, even if small, which meant that he would form coalitions and cut deals. He knew that his natural constituents were minorities, and this became even more so as a majority of the American people identified with the middle class. He therefore understood the need for support from those who might otherwise be spectators. He was prepared to get his funds from rich liberals, and was always looking to his targets' vulnerabilities on external support as a source of pressure (for example, customers or stockholders or some higher governmental authority). In terms of tactics, his basic need was to find new ways of sustaining campaigns and keeping them in the public eye (and here his own notoriety could be an advantage). He also understood that the degree of organization required, especially when undertaken by outsiders and professionals, was bound to be an issue in itself. The establishment was quick to point to the malign presence of outside "agitators" (a label Alinsky happily embraced) to delegitimize campaigns, just as the young radicals were wary of strong leaders who could easily set themselves up as an alternative establishment and leave the people as powerless as they had been at the start. Just as the young radicals now hoped, Alinsky had begun assuming that the organizer was drawing out a latent political consciousness, creating awareness not only of injustice but of the possibility of redress. Communities would be self-reliant and self-sustaining not only in their organization but in their consciousness, with a local leadership able to give voice to this consciousness and ensure its long-term authenticity. Alinsky made it a rule, which he only came to question toward the end of his life, that no more than three years' support should be provided to a community organization, after which they were on their own.[41]

Yet he was working with people with few resources and little self-confidence, who were almost completely absorbed by coping with the everyday problems of existence. Alinsky's colleague, Nicholas von Hoffman, who worked with him for a decade before leaving in 1962 to become a journalist, described how the "lumpen proletariat" faced a series of emergencies and a chain of bad news: "Gas is cut off, electrical service terminated, the landlord is evicting them, a cousin is in jail, the baby has to be rushed to the emergency room, one of the kids sassed a social worker and the family is getting cut off, the reigning male came home and beat the hell out of the mother, Wilson stole the food money, Janice is pregnant, Mother missed her appointment with the vocational counsellor because she was drunk." As a result, the poor were "unreliable, not the stuff of organizations which are bound together by keeping their commitments." In practice that meant (as the civil rights movement also discovered) that the pool of credible and capable local leaders was small; the activist base was narrow. Only a few percent of any community were involved in Alinsky's campaigns. His methods, therefore, came to rely on careful organization and strong leadership. While that did not fit with the later fashion for spontaneity and participatory democracy, he judged that he got better results. His pragmatism was also reflected in his choice of campaigns. Von Hoffman recalled that Alinsky "had no tolerance for a defeat that could have been avoided, no patience with moral victories." He picked fights that he could win on the grounds that not all injustices could be righted.[42]

Chávez

Although the younger Alinsky had been prepared to cast himself in the role of heroic organizer, the elder Alinsky was more wary of the notion. The people who grasped power and its uses were rarely pure in their motives, if only because they enjoyed the rough and tumble of politics. That could make them devious and cynical, relishing their notoriety, as he certainly did. An awareness of imperfection was to be preferred to a claim of perfection. In this regard, he worried about Cesar Chávez, a man whose work he supported. Chávez had been hired in the early 1950s by Fred Ross, who was running the Alinsky-sponsored Community Service Organization in California to promote voter registration and workers' rights among Mexican farm workers. A decade later, Chávez left to form what became the United Farm Workers Union (UFW). He was a follower of Gandhi, adopting methods such as fasting and pilgrimages and insisting on nonviolence. In the spring of 1966 he led farm workers in a march from Delano to Sacramento, the California state capital. This was combined with a campaign for a nationwide boycott of Californian grapes. Alinsky was skeptical, but the boycott gained widespread support. It lasted five years and ended in victory: higher wages and rights to organize unions enshrined in law.

Traditional unions were wary of migrant workers, who were presented as threats to white employment. An earlier attempt by the American Federation of Labor and Congress of Industrial Organizations (AFL-CIO)[43] to organize farm workers failed because the leadership did not understand local conditions or speak Spanish and instead relied on familiar models from old labor campaigns, despite having to work with a transitory workforce with a high turnover. Chávez saw the value of rooting the union in local communities, which offered educational possibilities, access to the church, and added to the tactical repertoire—for example, rent strikes. He could also use the example of the civil rights movement:

> How have negroes won their battles? When everyone expects them to run...they kneel and pray. When they appear beaten, they turn their defeat into victory. They use only what they have, their bodies and their courage...We farm workers have the same weapons—our bodies and our courage...The day we farm workers apply this lesson with the same courage as they have shown in Alabama and Mississippi—on that day, the misery of the farm workers will come to an end.[44]

Chávez's strategy put him at the center of his movement. An iconic moment came in 1968 when his people were wearying of a long strike that appeared to be going nowhere, and the value of nonviolence was being questioned. He embarked on a fast to reassert his authority, spiritual more than coercive, and to demonstrate the power of suffering. His penitence was presented as a response to those in the union who had spoken of violence. Mexican Catholics appreciated the symbolism and saw him to be suffering on their behalf. With ministers in attendance, the fast became a religious event. It had a galvanizing effect on the workers, many of whom made their own pilgrimages to the site of the fast.

The advantages gained in strengthening union support were further reinforced when the grape growers, who apparently believed that the fast was a fraud, decided to issue an injunction against the union's tactics at this point. This provided a frail Chávez with a perfect opportunity to turn up in the courtroom, attended by thousands of praying supporters. When he ended his fast after twenty-five days (one day more than Gandhi's longest fast) he did so after an ecumenical service with a piece of bread handed to him by Senator Robert Kennedy (about to declare his candidacy for the presidency). A minister read Chavez's speech:

I am convinced that the truest act of courage, the strongest act of manliness is to sacrifice ourselves for others in a totally non-violent struggle for justice. To be a man is to suffer for others. God help us to be men.[45]

Alinsky was wary of piety. He told Chávez that he found the fast "embarrassing." Nor was he impressed by Chávez's insistence on living on a low wage, ensuring an appropriate level of suffering, when he had a family to support. Eventually Chávez's insistence that UFW staff all work on a subsistence wage became a source of discontent.[46]

One of those who worked with Chávez, Marshall Ganz, observed the importance of the initial motivation as a source of strategic creativity. Strategy did not come first but followed the commitment to act, which inspired "concentration, enthusiasm, risk taking, persistence, and learning." The intense interest in the problem at hand encouraged critical thinking, challenging expectations and contexts.[47] Chávez provided the impetus, but he also had a view of organization that depended on strong leadership, and in which the people who did the work made the decisions. This was far removed from participatory democracy, or any sort of democracy, really. Building a movement and running an organization were two different activities. In the latter role Chávez became autocratic and eccentric, eventually leaving the UFW in disarray. Chávez remained an inspirational figure, and many of the alumni of the UFW went on to play important roles in other social movements. Nonetheless, he ended up destroying his own creation by purging insufficiently sycophantic staff.[48]

Imperfect Communities

The natural imperfections of human beings were reflected in the rank and file as well as the leaders. Perhaps Alinsky's most bitter lesson was that there was no natural coincidence of views between politically aware outside organizers and the communities they urged to seize power. After 1945, the collective efforts of the revitalized Back of the Yards community were devoted to keeping out blacks. As von Hoffman observed, once the area had been rebuilt and revitalized it became "a stable rock of racial exclusion." There was now something to defend. Even people who were not actively racist still believed that blacks coming into the community "were harbingers of slumification, crime, bad schools and punishing drops in real estate values."[49]

In his last interview (where he was described as one "who looks like an accountant and talks like a stevedore"), Alinsky recognized somewhat rue-fully the irony of this and a less-than-romantic view of "the people." When he arrived at the Back of the Yards in the late 1930s, it was already "a cesspool of hate; the Poles, Slovaks, Germans, Negroes, Mexicans and Lithuanians all hated each other and all of them hated the Irish, who returned the senti-ment in spades." As he diagnosed the problem, it was one of "dreams of a better world" being replaced by "nightmares of fear—fear of change, fear of losing their material goods, fear of blacks." He was thinking "of moving back into the area and organizing a new movement to overthrow the one I built 25 years ago." He still thought it was right to help people escape from "filth and poverty and despair," even if they now shared the "establishment's prejudices." Just because the "have-nots exist in despair, discrimination and deprivation" did "not automatically endow them with any special qualities of charity, justice, wisdom, mercy or moral purity." They were just ordinary people with all the normal weaknesses.

> History is like a relay race of revolutions; the torch of idealism is car-
> ried by one group of revolutionaries until it too becomes an establish-
> ment, and then the torch is snatched up and carried on the next leg of
> the race by a new generation of revolutionaries. The cycle goes on and
> on, and along the way the values of humanism and social justice the
> rebels champion take shape and change and are slowly implanted in
> the minds of all men even as their advocates falter and succumb to the
> materialistic decadence of the prevailing status quo.

During the 1960s, such sentiments ensured that Alinsky was a popular speaker on campuses. He argued for radical, though not revolutionary, change and the redistribution of power. And he did not pretend that it would be easy or straightforward: "Change means movement; movement means friction; friction means heat; heat means controversy." Yet he had little affinity with the leaders of the New Left. In the summer of 1964, a meeting was arranged between Alinsky and a few of the key figures in SDS, including Tom Hayden and Todd Gitlin. It did not go well. Alinsky was dismissive. Little would be achieved without leadership and hierarchy, and it was naïve to suppose that the poor wanted anything other than the lifestyles that these middle class youngsters were rejecting.[50] For Alinsky, being the underdog was a liability to be overcome rather than a badge of honor.

Alinsky's skepticism also extended to Martin Luther King, Jr., although he admired his achievements and copied some of his tactics. There was an attempt to get them to join forces when King came to Chicago in 1966, but they never met. Alinsky was resistant, wary of such a celebrity entering his home base, especially as he had made a deliberate decision not to try to campaign in the South, where he suspected he would be neither welcome nor effective. He was not one to take second place, even to a Nobel Peace Prize winner, and he also questioned whether a southern preacher could succeed in this setting. Alinsky appreciated that the civil rights movement's basic approach was similar to his own, in terms of using direct action to dramatize key issues. The key to its success, he thought, was the stupidity of the southern establishment and international pressure. "A Bull Connor with his police dogs and fire hoses down in Birmingham did more to advance civil rights than the civil rights fighters themselves."[51] Alinsky had always insisted on proper organization, and his people noticed the difference with King's entourage. Some were "very talented and some crazy as hoot owls," but too many spent time bickering with each other, seeking to get close to King. The leadership never fired anyone and exercised no control over spending.[52]

Bayard Rustin had argued vehemently with King about Chicago, warning him about the harsh, cynical culture of the northern ghettoes and the complexity of city politics, especially the formidable machine of Mayor Michael Daley. Life was often tough, but blacks were not excluded from the political process and local conditions were less simple than the morality play that had been played out in the South. In one row Rustin told King that he did not know what Chicago was like. "You're going to be wiped out." King ended the argument by saying that he was going to pray and consult with the Lord. Rustin was furious. "This business of King talking to God and God talking to King," he complained was no way to resolve serious strategic questions.[53] Rustin's misgivings were justified. King received a hostile reception and failed to gather any momentum behind his campaign. Rather than choosing a single issue around which to mobilize, nothing was precluded and any issue might be picked up. In other words, the campaign lacked focus. The aim was to draw a number of potential constituents, from slum dwellers to the unemployed to students, into activity and then escalate into a mass movement that could take dramatic action. Financial difficulties, poor local leadership, distractions in the South, and the complexities of which Rustin had warned all meant that King's campaign never acquired momentum.

Alinsky demonstrated what could be done with community organization but also the limits of a bottom-up approach. Battles could be won and lives improved, but the results were bound to be disillusioning if set against romantic notions about what the people might achieve collectively once mobilized. The people, especially those with tough lives, had their own priorities and ways of coping. Only on occasion did these coincide with those of activists. Moreover, few campaigns could have the moral clarity of the civil rights movement, which put the establishment on the spot from the start. It was impossible in a liberal society to argue against the principle of desegregation, so the only issues were about pace and method. Other issues were more complex, both analytically and ethically. In addition, as Rustin began to argue forcefully, the changes sought—whether in civil rights or addressing the causes of poverty—required support from central government. Merely raging against the system resulted in largely unproductive consequences for the people on whose behalf the activists claimed to be raging.

| Black Power and White Anger

We had fed the heart on fantasies,

The heart's grown brutal from the fare;

More Substance in our enmities

Than in our love.

—William Butler Yeats, *"The Stare's Nest by My Window"*

IN THE ABSENCE of perceptible progress, the consequences of the reluctance to accept compromise and forge coalitions lay either in disillusionment and apathy or else anger and more extreme policies. This could be seen in the swift evolution of the SNCC during the course of the 1960s. SNCC's founding statement affirmed "the philosophical ideal of nonviolence as the foundation of our purpose, the presumption of our belief, and the manner of our action." This affirmation became strained as the SNCC activists became impatient, uncertain about what they were achieving for their pains, frustrated at the limits of their open and inclusive political style and with the restraint required by a nonviolent philosophy. They were told to play safe to keep the support of white liberals, even as the Democrats refused to disown racist politicians. They became suspicious, not only of the segregationists and police, but also of the elitism of Martin Luther King.

In the North there was already a more radical aspect to black politics. For example, Malcolm X, who converted to the Nation of Islam while in jail and became its most prominent and charismatic figure, provided a striking contrast to King's Christian message of love and peace. Malcolm X proclaimed black separatism, denounced whites as devils, and refused to reject violence. Self-defense, he insisted, was not really violence but "intelligence." He spoke in ways that King could not to the disaffected and frustrated blacks of the inner cities. The civil rights leaders rebuked him for stirring up racial hatred and playing to white stereotypes of blacks. Eventually he did have a change of heart. He continued to push for a distinctively black consciousness but left the Nation of Islam in 1964 and moderated his rhetoric. He was murdered soon after, in February 1965.[1]

A more distant influence with a clearer message was Frantz Fanon. His views developed through his encounters with French colonialism and culminated in his time in Algeria, where he went as a psychiatrist before joining the National Liberation Front (FLN). His main testament, *Wretched of the Earth*, was written in 1961 as he was dying from leukemia. It was later argued that the English translation of this book, and Jean-Paul Sartre's introduction, sharpened the tone, more so than Fanon intended. His insights on colonial conditions were played down as a result of the stress on violence as the only strategic language that colonizers recognized.[2] The psychiatrist in him offered an existentialist take on violence, providing the book's intensity.

Fanon picked up on Sartre's claim that it was not the Jewish character that provoked anti-Semitism but instead "the anti-Semite creates the Jew," and so argued that "the settler" had "brought the native into existence and perpetuates his existence."[3] Violence was a means of escaping from this psychological as well as physical domination. "At the level of the individuals, violence is a cleansing force. It frees him from his inferiority complex and restores his self-respect . . . the colonized man finds his freedom in and through violence." Sartre added: "The native cures himself of colonial neurosis by thrusting out the settler through the force of arms. When his rage boils over, he rediscovers his lost innocence and comes to know himself in that he himself creates himself."[4] The philosopher Hannah Arendt suspected that most of Fanon's admirers had not gone beyond his first chapter—"Concerning Violence"—for later he showed awareness of how "unmixed and total brutality" would lead "to the defeat of the movement within a few weeks." She was most appalled by Sartre's claim to be a Marxist while espousing notions that owed more to Nechayev and Bakunin, and his excitement over what might be achieved by "mad fury" and "volcanic outbursts."[5]

Fanon's anger resonated with young black activists who were concluding that it was pointless trying to work with white power structures. Jacobs and Landau, who surveyed the New Left in 1965, observed how "the weary veterans of harassment, arrests, beatings, and the psychological torture of living in the South, have begun to re-examine their objectives at the very time they confront the full and often subtle power of the American economic and political system."[6] The idealism was being drained away from SNCC. The "generals," influenced by Malcolm X and ready to contemplate their own form of guerrilla warfare, replaced the "poets." The dire economic position of blacks in the urban ghettoes and the escalation of the Vietnam War, which disproportionately drafted blacks into the army, added to the grievances. "No Vietcong ever called me a nigger," observed the boxer Cassius Clay, now Mohammed Ali. The alarmed reaction of white society to the prospect of black violence and the rioting in the inner cities brought a satisfaction in itself.

One of the pioneering SNCC activists and chairman of the organization in 1965, Stokely Carmichael, became an advocate of black power. Raised in Harlem, he spoke the language of the streets more naturally than that of the Church. He began to toy with ideas for a new SNCC slogan in 1966. Then after yet another arrest (his twenty-seventh), this time in Greenwood, Mississippi, he exclaimed to a crowd:

> We want black power! That's right. That's what we want, black power. We don't have to be ashamed of it. We have stayed here. We have begged the president. We've begged the federal government—that's all we've been doing, begging and begging. It's time we stand up and take over.[7]

He claimed that any white person, even those in the movement, had "concepts in his mind about black people, if only subconsciously. He cannot escape them, because the whole society has geared his sub-conscious in that direction." With racism so ingrained it was meaningless for blacks to talk about coalition—"there is no one to align ourselves with." Only once it was shown that blacks could speak and act for themselves would it perhaps be possible to work with whites again, but then on equal terms. SNCC would henceforth be "black-staffed, black-controlled and black-financed."[8]

A book coauthored with the academic Charles Hamilton argued for "pride rather than shame, in blackness, and an attitude of brotherly, communal responsibility among all black people for one another." White Americans could afford to "speak softly, tread lightly, employ the soft-sell and put-off" because they "own the society." It would be ludicrous for black people to "adopt *their* methods of relieving *our* oppression." If they followed this path they would gain "crumbs of co-optation" in return for holding back on condemnation.

The problem was not with the underlying premise. There were many other examples in American politics of groups organizing politically on the basis of ethnicity, using a shared identity to create an effective bargaining position. "Before a group can enter the open society, it must first close ranks." Only when blacks spoke up, not asking for favors but seeking power, could they expect the system to respond. But Carmichael sought a shared "sense of people-hood" on the basis of an extremely radical posture. Blacks must not adopt the values of the middle class that had sanctioned and perpetuated black oppression, yet if the aim was economic advancement then this would lead naturally to a black bourgeoisie.

The big question was whether to continue with nonviolence, the stance which had sustained recent political advances. Carmichael and Stevenson answered that nonviolence had handicapped blacks by creating an image of passivity. "From our viewpoint," they argued, "rampaging white mobs and white night-riders must be made to understand that their days of free head-whipping are over. Black people should and must fight back." This was about self-defense: "Those of us who advocate Black Power are quite clear in our own minds that a 'non-violent' approach to civil rights is an approach black people cannot afford and a luxury white people do not deserve."[9]

Martin Luther King was appalled by the turn of events. Not only did he object to the resort to violence, but he found it frustrating that violence became the issue rather than those his movement was trying to highlight. He insisted that power should be a means to an end—the "creation of a truly brotherly society"—rather than an end in itself.[10] In a posthumously published book, he critiqued Black Power, pointing to its self-defeating character as blacks were a minority in the United States and defended alliances with whites. In the end, both races needed each other. They were "bound together in a single garment of destiny."[11]

In 1967, whites were expelled from SNCC and the commitment to non-violence was dropped. The new chairman, H. Rap Brown, described violence as "American as cherry pie." Carmichael, who later acknowledged that black power killed SNCC, joined up with the Black Panthers, a group that had been set up in Oakland, California, in 1966, and employed a tough, violent rhetoric from the start. In his autobiographical account of the origins of the Black Panthers, Bobby Seale described the early fixation with acquiring an arsenal, paid for by selling at a profit copies of the "Little Red Book" of Chinese leader Mao Zedong, compared with the casual way the party's manifesto was put together.[12] The striking imagery and rhetoric associated with the Panthers, and their militarist affectations, gave them an influence beyond their actual numbers, probably never more than five thousand.

Carmichael continued with his own advocacy of black separatism. "The major enemy," he said in a speech in 1967, "is not your brother, flesh of your flesh and blood of your blood. The major enemy is the honky and his institutions of racism, that's the major enemy, that is the major enemy. And whenever anyone prepares for revolutionary warfare, you concentrate on the major enemy. We're not strong enough to fight each other and also fight him."[13] He fell out even with the Panthers, who were more willing to work with whites than he was. He decided the only way to get close to the African people was to move to Africa and adopt an African name, Kwame Ture.

The trend in black politics alarmed Bayard Rustin. He became disenchanted as his former friends in SNCC turned to violence and black separatism. "The minute you had black anger, rage," he later observed, "you automatically had to have white fear, because we're always enumerator to their denominator...These two things have to move with each other." A focus on direct action added to the polarization, alienating whites and "breeding despair and impotence" among blacks.[14] He agreed with Martin Luther King that poverty and unemployment were significant triggers of race riots, but that led him to explore how blacks and whites could be united in struggle under the aegis of the labor unions. His conviction that the big issues were economic, requiring federal programs, meant that it was vital to support a government prepared to fund a "war on poverty." This led to another disagreement, which included most of his former colleagues, over whether protest against the Vietnam War should be a priority. The case for coalitions was made with particular force and provocation in a February 1965 article. Rustin observed the "strong moralistic strain in the civil rights movement which would remind us that power corrupts, forgetting that the absence of power also corrupts." Self-help was not enough. "We need allies" he insisted, and that meant compromises. In particular, he wanted to work with the labor unions and the Democratic Party. "The leader who shrinks from this task reveals not his purity but his lack of political sense."[15]

The compromises involved at this time were just too much, especially in the light of the escalation in Vietnam. Where Rustin now led few followed, and he became increasingly distant from his former colleagues, no longer a pacifist and unconvinced that the tactics of nonviolent direct action he had pioneered were of much relevance. He became, as a biographer put it, "a strategist without a movement." Rustin was accused of exaggerating the liberalism of the Johnson administration, and therefore its ability to solve fundamental problems, while encouraging blacks to abandon the direct action that could give them an independent voice.[16] Carmichael and Hamilton charged Rustin with promoting three myths: the interests of black people were identical with the interests of liberals and labor; a "viable coalition could be effected between the politically and economically secure and the politically and economically insecure"; and "political coalitions are or can be sustained on a moral, friendly, sentimental basis; by appeals to conscience." The proposed coalition was with groups with no interest in a "total revamping of society" but only peripheral reforms.[17] In line with their general argument they insisted that they were not against coalitions, only those that were paternalistic. Until blacks could stand on their own they would be too weak to make a coalition work.[18] The only acceptable coalition would be between poor blacks and poor whites.

Revolution in the Revolution

Vietnam was a nagging issue in 1965 but an overriding one two years later. This made it impossible for radicals to imagine having anything to do with an administration prosecuting such a terrible war. The troops sent to fight were inevitably young, largely draftees, and disproportionately black. Anger against the war, which reached a crescendo in 1968, changed the whole direction of the movement. The SDS activists, instead of settling down to the patient cultivation of poor communities, turned to antiwar agitation. From the micro preoccupation with the frustrations of ghetto life they moved to the macro issues of imperialism and war. Nonviolence, so natural and effective just a few years earlier, began to seem soft and unworldly. It was no longer good enough to campaign on particular issues. It was necessary to get to the source of the problem.

The SDS president in 1965 was Paul Potter, a thoughtful intellectual who had studied sociology and anthropology and had been developing the idea of the "system" rather than individuals working within it as the main problem. This was a radical idea, for if the "system" was at fault, then reform would achieve little. He saw Vietnam as one issue among many. A march on Washington, which had been organized for April 1965, and so took place at a time when the U.S. intervention in Vietnam was escalating, was far larger than anticipated and gave the occasion an edge. Potter used it to offer his radical critique of an American social order that could not help itself in its oppressiveness. "We must name that system," demanded Potter. "We must name it, describe it, analyze it, understand it and change it. For it is only when that system is changed and brought under control that there can be any hope for stopping the forces that create a war in Vietnam today or a murder in the south tomorrow."[19]

Thereafter "the system" appeared as the enemy. But its designation was vague, its make-up nebulous, and its workings unclear. Potter's academic background may well have led him to adopt a systemic approach, which considered societies as made up of interconnected parts, as a matter of course. In mainstream sociology this encouraged the view that political and social change would always find its own equilibrium. For radicals such as Potter, the system was not a neutral representation of how a complex social organization could be made to work for the general benefit but instead a distortion that had become ingrained and self-reinforcing. The United States had become systematically dysfunctional, turning people against themselves and their better nature. The result was a "cultural genocide," a sort of mass lobotomy, so that people could not appreciate what was being done or imagine alternative possibilities. If they could, then they might regain control of this system, "make it bend itself to their wills rather than bending them to its." Talk of the "system" could easily convey some grand but hidden conspiracy, the power elite pulling the economic, social, and political strings. Potter wanted to avoid the old labels of capitalism or imperialism, but in the end they were the easy labels to use. As essentially a radical pragmatist in the tradition of James and Dewey, Potter became concerned that the movement would become more violent and confrontational, and that the words he had used in his Washington speech would encourage it to be so. Potter's successor as SDS president, Carl Oglesby, challenged the notion that naming or analyzing this system would be enough, as if "statements will bring change, if only the rights statements can be written." Words were to be discarded in favor of action. Eloquent language could be disregarded; eloquent deeds would be harder to ignore.[20]

Hayden went to North Vietnam in December 1965, his first trip abroad, to witness the consequences of American bombardment. He moved from opposing America's war to supporting the National Liberation Front of South Vietnam as it fought the Americans. Questions about the extent to which this was a true insurgency or a creation of the communist regime in North Vietnam, or exactly the nature of the ideology and freedoms promoted by the North, tended to get neglected or played down in the face of the awfulness of the government in the South and the American tactics. A belief that some Americans should keep open lines of communication to the communists was another argument against being too critical. Hayden was aware of the danger. In a book he wrote with Staughton Lynd, *The Other Side*, he insisted that they were not pretending that their hosts were admirable in all respects ("We do not believe we are Sartres who require a Camus to remind us of the existence of the slave labor camps"). Yet the overall impression given was that these young middle-class activists were in awe of the tough revolutionary cadres who suffered for their beliefs and who were committed selflessly to a protracted struggle. There were similar results when pilgrimages were made to Cuba. In the background, there were hints of a local politics that was crude and cruel, but this got lost in the excitement of association with true revolutionary spirits.

If the aim was to develop a broad coalition against the Vietnam War, these visits made little sense. Public opinion was turning against the war and did so increasingly during 1968, because it was both costly and futile. That was not the same as embracing the nation's enemies, and many recoiled from the apparent lack of patriotism and naïveté of those who did so. Yet for the activists this did not matter. They were giving up on the United States, and its docile population, in the conviction that it was bound to be left behind as the tide of history worked through the anti-imperialist people of the third world. At best they could serve as the supporters and agents of these people, gaining their revolutionary credentials by acting from within against the imperialist behemoth.[21] Once Cuba and Vietnam were accepted as sources of radical inspiration, Marxism-Leninism had to be taken seriously. The old ideologies of the Left were able to stage a comeback. One radical later ruefully recalled how the Maoist faction in SDS became an "external, disciplined ingredient in our ultra democratic anarchist soup."[22]

The emerging analysis linked the American poor with the whole of the third world as victims of the same system of corporate power and liberal indifference. Instead of being a hopeless minority, American radicals started to see themselves as part of a global campaign. The term "third world" had been coined in France in the early 1950s to describe countries that were economically underdeveloped and politically unaligned, keeping their distance from the liberal capitalist first world and the state socialist second world. The long-forgotten inspirational model was the "third estate" of commoners, who eventually revolted in 1789 against the first and second estates of priests and nobles. The term therefore captured an idea of a coherent group, a coalition of the disadvantaged, which might one day overthrow the established order. It came to include many states who gained independence as a result of post–Second World War decolonization. The issue of imperialism moved beyond the baleful influence of the decadent old European powers to the pernicious domination of American neocolonialism, rationalized by a crude anti-communism and driven by corporate greed. Cuba was one example of this struggle; Vietnam was another. There were more confrontations to come, and at some point imperialism would be unable to cope. This was the point which the movement within the United States must work to bring about as soon as possible.

This line of thought was validated by Herbert Marcuse, who had taken over from C. Wright Mills as the vogue intellectual of the New Left in its uncompromising late 1960s form. He had been a member of the Frankfurt Institute for Social Research, a base for Marxists who kept their distance from the Communist Party, which moved to New York in the 1930s. His reputation was largely as an Hegelian with an interest in Freud until the publication of his book *One Dimensional Man* in 1964. This explained why despite all the apparent qualities of Western countries—political pluralism, affluence, welfare states, access to art—it was natural to feel intensely dissatisfied. All good things turned out to be instruments of social control, preventing people from realizing their true nature and achieving genuine happiness. Even worse, notional forms of opposition had been co-opted, creating a new liberal totalitarianism through what he later described as "repressive tolerance," which claimed to "reconcile the forces opposing the system and to defeat or refute all protest in the name of the historical prospects of freedom from toil and domination." Because people were not free, they could not pass judgment on their own lack of freedom.

With his newfound fame among student radicals, Marcuse returned the compliment in *An Essay on Liberation* by celebrating them as agents of change, not only in the West but also on behalf of the whole world. The Cuban and Vietnamese revolutions might not survive the weight of Western repression. The "preconditions for the liberation and development of the Third World must emerge in the advanced industrial countries." The system must be broken at its strongest link. This required resistance against both political and mental repression. This would be done without bureaucracy and organization, through small groups acting autonomously. The aim was explicitly utopian, the alternative to be developed through trial and error. "Understanding, tenderness towards each other, the instinctual consciousness of that which is evil, false, the heritage of oppression, would then testify to the authenticity of the rebellion."[23]

The inspirational figure symbolizing the direct challenge to "Yankee Imperialism" was Ernesto "Che" Guevara. Che, as he was known, had been born to a middle-class Argentinean family, trained as a doctor, and then became a lieutenant of Fidel Castro in his campaign to overthrow the Cuban dictator Fulgencio Batista. Although a minister in Castro's government when barely 30 years old, he returned to the field, determined to open up new fronts against imperialism, putting into practice his theories of guerrilla warfare first in the Congo and then in Bolivia. Both campaigns were unsuccessful. The second led to his capture in 1967 and summary execution.

The poster image of him—handsome, hirsute, and determined, sporting his revolutionary beret—became, and remains, iconic.

In January 1966, he sent a message to the founding conference of the Tricontinental, or the Organization of Solidarity with the People of Asia, Africa, and Latin America taking place in Havana. He warned against allowing Vietnam to be isolated in its struggle. There should be "a constant and a firm attack in all fronts where the confrontation is taking place." Imperialism was "a world system, the last stage of capitalism—and it must be defeated in a world confrontation." It was therefore necessary to create the "Second and Third Vietnams of the world." The Americans would gradually be drained by being forced to fight in diverse and unwelcoming regions. The road ahead would be hard, he warned, but the imperative was to carry out "armed propaganda" to galvanize the spirit, putting aside national differences so that all should be prepared to fight in any relevant arena of armed struggle.[24]

In subsequent years, his manual on guerrilla warfare and the diary of his doomed campaign in Bolivia were published (making clear his inability to win over peasants). The key concept was the "foco." This small group of dedicated men would stimulate the insurrection by both forcing the state to reveal its inner brutality while demonstrating the availability of an alternative, more sympathetic government. In practice, Guevara's ideas were more influential among "the generation of 1968" in Europe and the United States than in the third world. Outside Latin America, revolutionaries tended to look at the quite different, and generally more successful, Maoist model.

Che's romantic model was based on a misreading of the Cuban revolution. Castro had presented himself as a liberal and leader of a wide anti-Batista coalition, not as a Marxist-Leninist—an affiliation that was only announced after the seizure of power. Castro claimed that the major influence on his concept of irregular war was Ernest Hemingway's novel on the Spanish Civil War, *For Whom the Bell Tolls*. He was careful to work hard to gain sympathy from Americans. Just as Mao had used Edgar Snow to burnish his image in the 1930s as a moderate, "Lincolnesque" and with a "lively sense of humor," so Castro used *New York Times* reporter Herbert Matthews, who reported back on the idealism, probable anti-communism, and strength of Castro's force. At the time it was probably about forty men, but by talking of "groups of ten to forty" and having an aide deliver a message about a non-existent second-column, Castro conveyed an illusion of numbers.[25] This helped bring in external funding, notably from sympathetic Americans. Castro's importance had grown because his rural base allowed him to survive while the key figures in the urban leadership were killed. At first the urban aspects of the struggle and the support of key elements of the middle class were acknowledged, but postrevolutionary politics and Castro's own shift to the left led to the systematic distortion of the "lessons" of the revolution.[26] Castro and Che rewrote the history of the revolution in order to stress their own role and play down the importance of the urban working class and its leadership.

In 1961 Che presented the three key elements of his theory:

Popular forces can win against the army.
It is not necessary to wait until all the conditions for making revolution exist; the insurrection can create them.
In underdeveloped America the countryside is the basic area of armed struggle.[27]

The question of preconditions went to the heart of revolutionary theory. To be a revolutionary at a nonrevolutionary time could be intensely frustrating, but the risks involved in acting as if the conditions were latent and could be brought to the surface by dramatic action had led to many futile campaigns in the past. If discontent was present but inchoate, then it was possible that it could be turned by some spark into mass anger, but the professional revolutionaries tended not to be the source of the spark. Rather, they came in after the event. Mao, for example, understood the importance of political education and action to create mass support and never claimed that guerrillas could take on an army by themselves. Che claimed that it was possible for a revolution to be Marxist in character without this being recognized by the participants. This meant playing down the political context, and thus failing to take it properly into account. When Che wrote a prologue to Giap's *People's War, People's Army*, he reinterpreted the Vietnamese experience as fitting in with his theory, as if Giap had started in Vietnam with a "foco" and had paid no attention to the politics of the struggle.[28]

The foco substituted for the vanguard party, and the fighters generated support through their military courage and by provoking the regime into atrocities, turning opinion against it. Che at first acknowledged the importance of democratic institutions in giving legitimacy to a regime and so rendering it less vulnerable. By 1963, democracy was dismissed as representing the dictatorship of the ruling class. The doctrine was further transformed by its internationalization, exemplified by the Message to the Tri-Continental, according to which the revolutionary struggle could and should be conducted without regard to geographical boundaries. Che may have been an audacious and brave commander, but he lacked political nous and paid a high price for his simplified theory. He never forged effective political alliances and did not appreciate the need for a strong local leader to be the public face of a revolution. Rather, he believed in his own mystique, as if the presence of such a famous fighter would inspire courage and confidence.[29]

Nonetheless, Che had a significant influence on Western radicals. First, and not to be discounted, he looked the part. Second, he provided a theory for the defeat of U.S. imperialism that did not depend on the efforts of those living in its midst. Last, for impatient young radicals who could not face the hard grind of building a mass movement with such unpromising materials, here was a theory about the difference a small group of committed revolutionaries might make if only they could find a way of unleashing the revolutionary potential of the masses. Che's ideas were most effectively spread by a young French intellectual-cum-journalist Regis Debray, whose book title *Revolution in the Revolution* captured the erroneous idea that the Cubans had hit upon a way of modernizing the very idea of a revolution.[30] Debray's book was actually sponsored more by Castro than Guevara. Che only saw it when Debray visited him in Bolivia, a journey that accelerated his defeat, especially after the Frenchman was picked up by the Bolivian authorities and confirmed that Che was in the country. Che was critical of Debray for simplifying his theory, focusing on a "micro-level" of the foco and, most importantly, failing to give due note to the Tricontinental aspect of his "macro-strategy."[31]

Another Latin American, Carlos Marighela, picked up for a short time where Che had left off. He was a veteran communist politician in Brazil, into his fifties when Che was killed. He attended the Tricontinental in Havana in 1966. In 1968, he broke with the Communist Party, which he considered ossified, and announced his support for urban guerrilla warfare. The urban element was his main divergence from Che. Largely as a result of the Bolivian failure, Marighela believed the guerrilla should operate in familiar terrain. He was most familiar with the city. Until he was shot dead by police in late 1969, Marighela's group carried on a number of actions, including kidnappings and seizure of railway stations. Most notably he was famous for the *Mini-manual of the Urban Guerrilla*, circulated in Havana after his death.[32] Although Marighela looked forward to a popular army after a campaign designed "to distract, to wear out, to demoralize the militarists," his methods for getting the revolution underway were essentially terrorist. They relied on a version of "propaganda of the deed" to attract the mass media. Terrorism's "most conspicuous effect," he supposed, was to provoke a "violent counterattack that may be so offensive as to drive the populace into the arms of the insurgents." As was often the case, the effect was the opposite.

Mirages of Violence

In December 1967, the issue of the legitimacy of violence was addressed at a forum in New York. The panel on the topic included Hannah Arendt and Noam Chomsky. Arendt argued against the "mirages of violence," warning that this was a weapon of impotence and not power, a means that could overwhelm the ends it was supposed to serve. It was not hard for fellow panelists to provide examples where violence was justified and effective, but the most striking intervention came from the floor. Tom Hayden ("a thin, pale young man whose untied tie flapped loosely as he spoke," according to the *New York Times*) observed how in Cuba violence had been "amazingly successful" when used by a small group to create the "political foundations." He argued that people in the ghettoes "getting mattresses and clothes and a supply of liquor for the winter is a constructive and revealing form of violence" and then decried the failure of democratic procedures:

> It seems to me that until you can begin to show—not in language and not in theory, but in action—that you can put an end to the war in Vietnam, and an end to American racism, you can't condemn the violence of others who can't wait for you.

Arendt objected: "To oppose the government in the United States with violence is absolutely wrong."[33] Over the next year, she developed her arguments on violence further, insisting that it could destroy but not create power.[34]

Attempts by the American radicals to emulate Latin American guerrillas were disastrous. The Black Panthers went so far as to establish a training center in Cuba and had a plan to set up focos in the more mountainous areas of the United States. The plan, as Eldridge Cleaver (a Black Panther leader of the time) recalled, was "to have small mobile units that could shift easily in and out of rural areas, living off the land, and tying up thousands of troops in fruitless pursuit." He added that in retrospect it seemed "pretty ridiculous."[35] The most serious emulation came from the Weathermen, a faction of SDS.

This group can be traced to the April 1968 occupation of New York's Columbia University by students who complained about the university's encroachments into black neighborhoods and professors doing weapons research. This was not a unique event. Around the world there were upheavals on campuses and demonstrations against Vietnam. In May, the Fifth French Republic was almost brought down by rioting on the streets of Paris. Most depressingly for liberals, Martin Luther King was murdered that April as was Robert Kennedy in June, just when his presidential bid was gathering pace. These murders eliminated in turn the leaders of nonviolent direct action and those seeking change through electoral politics. After this, Hayden—who knew Kennedy[36]—saw no hope in democratic politics. He wrote an article headed "Two, Three, Many Columbias," picking up on a slogan written on a university wall, which in turn picked up on Che's call to the Tricontinental. He still clung to his own original vision:

> The student protest is not just an offshoot of the black protest—it is based on authentic opposition to the middle-class world of manipulation, channeling and careerism. The students are in opposition to the fundamental institutions of society.

But his analysis was now harsher. Universities were linked to imperialism. Hayden spoke of barricades, threats to destroy buildings in face of police attacks, and raids on offices of professors doing weapons research. "A crisis is foreseeable that would be too massive for police to handle."[37]

Even sharper was Mark Rudd, one of the leaders of the Columbia revolt. Unlike Hayden, whose radicalism had developed slowly and thoughtfully during the late 1950s, Rudd had radicalized abruptly. His political analysis was correspondingly less subtle and his politics more outraged. He later provided a candid description of himself as "a member of the cult of Che Guevara" who had "evolved a belief in the necessity for violence in order to end the war and to make revolution." He recalled a regular line in his speeches—"The ruling class will never give over power peacefully"—and Mao Zedong's famous aphorism: "Political power grows out of the barrel of a gun." With the Panthers already fighting a revolutionary war within the United States, a "heroic fantasy" developed by which "eventually the military would disintegrate internally, and the revolutionary army—led by us, of course—would be built from its defectors."[38]

Faced by Maoists who brought to the campus a developed revolutionary theory, Rudd's group believed that they had to counter with one of their own, based on a combination of Cuba and Columbia University. They would be urban guerrillas, "rejecting the go-slow approach of the rest of the Left, just as Che and Fidel had begun to reject the Cuban Communist Party's conservatism by beginning guerrilla warfare in Cuba. Our bible was Debray's *Revolution in the Revolution.*" It was out of this faction that the Weather Underground was formed with the aim of moving out of the universities to organize young people for a coming armed struggle. The name came from one of Bob Dylan's lyrics ("You don't need a weather man to know which way the wind blows"). In place of the sense of experimentation and openness of the early SDS, there was now an old-fashioned Marxist factional fight. The attempts at being urban guerrillas involved farce and tragedy, with their numbers never more than three hundred and with key figures soon killed by their own explosive devices, on the run, or imprisoned. The fate of the Black Panthers was similar, and even more violent. Rudd later lamented how with his friends he had chosen to "scuttle America's largest radical organization—with chapters in hundreds of campuses, a powerful national identity, and enormous growth potential—for a fantasy of revolutionary urban-guerrilla warfare."[39] Sociologist Daniel Bell, a professor at Columbia, saw it coming. He remarked that "desperado tactics are never the mark of a coherent social movement, but the guttering last gasps of a romanticism soured by rancor and impotence." The SDS, he predicted, would "be destroyed by its style. It lives on turbulence, but is incapable of transforming its chaotic impulses into a systematic, responsible behavior that is necessary to effect broad societal change."[40]

Back to Chicago

The 1960s had begun with innovative forms of protests that dramatized the gap between the American dream and the harsh reality of southern segregation. Its participants embodied American idealism—dignified, restrained, and articulate. During the course of the 1960s, the context for protest changed dramatically. Political advances in the South came up against the economic despair of the urban ghettoes and the fear of being sent to fight in a vicious war that was widely seen to be both pointless and illegitimate. As the hard political core of the movement began to turn into an approximation of a Leninist vanguard or a Guevarist foco, around the edges a much more individualistic, libertarian, permissive culture was taking root, posing a provocative and enduring challenge to the American way of life. Though they swam in the same demographic tides, there was no logical reason why the counterculture and radical politics had to move hand in hand, other than Vietnam. This pulled them together.

During 1967, gentle, hedonistic "hippies"—often high on drugs—made their appearance offering "love and peace" as a form of "flower power." They had nothing so formal as a leader, but as a prophet there was the beat poet Allen Ginsberg. Although his parents were communists, this had, if anything, turned Ginsberg against political activism. His primary focus, as his reputation grew during the 1950s, was not "rebellion or social protest" but the "exploration of modes of consciousness."[41] A visit to Saigon in 1963, however, had led him to be more political and he became a strong opponent of the Vietnam War.[42] There was playfulness about Ginsberg, as if he knew at times his claims were absurd, yet his belief in the ability of poetry and Buddhist chants to affect consciousness was sincere. His ideas, which were not always intelligible in conception or execution, depended on the power of language.

In 1966, after a poetry reading, he had screamed "I declare the end of the war" to the National Student Association convention. He later explained that the aim was to "make my language identical with the historical event," so when he declared "the end of the war" this would "set up a force field of language which is so solid and absolute as a statement and a realization of an assertion by my will, conscious will power, that it will contradict—counter-act and ultimately overwhelm the force field of language pronounced out of the State Department and out of Johnson's mouth." In almost postmodern terms he offered his language in a trial of strength with the "black mantras" of the war-makers. It was a political critique which traded "argument for incantation."[43] The theme was picked up by the folk singer Phil Ochs and led to a November 1967 demonstration in New York with three thousand young people running through the streets, proclaiming loudly "I declare the war is over." Out of this came the idea for the "Yippies" as the political wing of the hippies.

The founders of the Yippies were Abbie Hoffman and Jerry Rubin. Both had been involved in radical protests since the start of the decade. Rubin had been involved in the Berkeley free speech movement and had become a full-time activist, organizing "teach-ins" against the war. He had a reputation as an imaginative tactician but had also moved well to the left. Both had con-cluded that standard forms of protest were losing their bite and that new types of spectacle were needed to gain media attention and get the message across. Rubin had urged in 1966 that activists become "specialists in propaganda and communication" and saw in the counterculture a way to challenge the system he opposed on every possible front, from comic books to street theater. This is why Ginsberg's mantra had appealed to them. As they thought ahead to the protests planned for the August 1968 Democratic Party convention in Chicago, they wanted something more than a conventional demonstration. They hit upon the idea of a counterculture event, a "Festival of Life" that would help turn the convention into a circus, blending surreal humor and anarchism. When the Yippie manifesto was launched in January, it looked forward to the festival: "We are making love in the parks. We are reading, singing, laughing, printing newspapers, groping and making a mock conven-tion and celebrating the birth of FREE AMERICA in our own time."[44]

With the war going so badly, Lyndon Johnson had decided not to stand for reelection. His vice president and anointed successor, Hubert Humphrey, got the nomination after Robert Kennedy's assassination and antiwar senator Eugene McCarthy's effective withdrawal from campaigning. Johnson's withdrawal was no reason to abandon the protest. All the different factions of the movement converged on Chicago "like moths to the flame." There were the new hard men of the SDS, radical pacifists still committed to nonviolent direct action, and the Yippies taunting the authorities with talk of LSD in the water supply, smoke bombs in delegates' halls, and sexual shows of varying degrees of provocation. The gathering mood spoke more of violence than peace. The city's long-time mayor, Michael Daley, who ran one of the most formidable machines in American politics, had form when it came to turning the police onto demonstrators. He was determined to make life as difficult as possible for all those who opposed the careful orchestration of the convention. The police were under orders to show no restraint. Some were operating undercover. Both sides had their provocateurs and both had an interest in confrontation.

Tom Hayden was at the center of the preparations for Chicago, including seeking permits for demonstrations. His rhetoric when talking with other activists was becoming wilder. This was his existential moment. He could show he was not like the "good Germans" who were in denial about the Holocaust. In making his stand against a terrible war, he was prepared—as an existentialist—to pay his own personal price. This was reinforced by the persistent notion that underdogs benefited by appearing as innocent victims of police brutality. Heightened confrontation would push up the internal costs of the war. The establishment, he had concluded, would only abandon South Vietnam on the basis of a cost-benefit calculation, even if this involved arousing "the sleeping dogs on the right."[45] Rubin also bought into the theory that the movement required repression to grow. Repression, he enthused, would turn "demonstration protest into wars. Actors into heroes. Masses of individuals into a community." It would eliminate "the bystander, the neutral observer, the theorist. It forces everyone to pick a side."[46]

Such talk made Ginsberg wary. He had never, he explained later, been a poet of "revolt." That would have meant trying to "become wiser by becoming dumber, you want to become more peaceful by getting angry." His aim was to alter consciousness.[47] In Chicago, instead of the "academies of self-awareness" and "classes in spirituality" he favored, he saw "bloody visions of the apocalypse."[48] He flew there writing a poem ("Remember the Helpless order the/ Police armed to protect/the Helpless Freedom the Revolutionary/ Conspired to honor"). He later explained his presence at Chicago as a "religious experimenter," not only on behalf of the Yippies but "also in the context of our whole political life, too." In the face of police determination to close down the music festival, he urged caution. Presenting himself as a calming influence, he encouraged demonstrators to chant "Om" in the face of violence or hysteria. "Ten people humming Om can calm down one hundred. One hundred people humming Om can regulate the metabolism of a thousand. A thousand bodies vibrating Om can immobilize an entire downtown Chicago street full of scared humans, uniformed or naked." At one point during the demonstrations he led chanting for seven hours. The aim of this, and his other antiwar performances, was not to transmit a thought or assert a principle but to "bring about a state of being."

Once again we see the idea that getting the state to reveal its true nastiness would set people against it, without considering the circumstances in which ordinary people might support the state. The radicals, disappointed with their own numbers, sought to use police brutality as a means of expanding their constituency. Watching it all were the world's media, who were treated to a spectacle of baton charges and bloodied demonstrators.[49] Tactically, the hard-liners had won and the movement lost. The progressive radicalization of the decade had reflected the limits of a politics based on gaining attention through sacrifice, appeals to conscience, and assertions of shared values. The early concepts of dignified nonviolence, which "implied erect bearing, silent passage, and respectable dress," had given way to "shouting and threats, hissing, hoaxes, foul language, heckling, garbage-dumping, a sense of great anger vented, and a growing tendency to violence."[50]

One type of Marxist analysis of the clashes at Chicago would have observed that they were largely between working-class police and middle-class demonstrators. Working-class anger was directed at those who had enjoyed privileged lives and now turned on the system that had pampered them, mocking those who upheld traditional values, turning away from responsibilities and challenging the patriotic symbols (notably the flag) of which they should be proud. Fears of disorder and decadence began to influence working-class political attitudes. Alinsky feared that the rise of the right would be the inevitable response to violence and extremism on the left. He wrote *Rules for Radicals* to remind the new revolutionaries of the "central concepts of action in human politics that operate regardless of the scene or the time." He argued the need for a "pragmatic attack on the system." He warned, correctly, of the dangers of insulting and ignoring ordinary working people. "If we fail to communicate with them, if we don't encourage them to form alliances with us, they will move to the right." In urging an ethic of responsibility on a new generation of radicals, Alinsky and Rustin were aware that they must appear like old men jealous of the energy of youth and with evidence of their failures all around them in persistent poverty, inequality, and violence. At the same time they recognized that the people for whom they struggled were underdogs precisely because they lacked the capacity to become the majority, and that organizing them was a hard slog that would require compromises and certainly coalitions. They understood the futility of expecting people absorbed in a daily struggle for survival to sign up for an even larger and more dangerous struggle defined only by vague slogans.

The United States did not withdraw from Vietnam until 1973. But the American role became less toxic politically with the end of conscription. The young activists of the New Left moved on, some becoming milder versions of their former selves, others abandoning their commitments. What lasted was the critique of everyday life, reflected in music and fashion, and to a degree in the use of recreational drugs, but also in a distrust of elitism and hierarchy and a wariness of bureaucracy.[51] The focus on the worth of individuals led to the anticolonial language of self-determination and liberation coming to be applied to groups, such as gays and women, who had felt stigmatized and oppressed.

Women's Liberation

Feminism was not a new cause and important books were written prior to the growth of the student movement, but "women's liberation" flowed naturally out of a movement dedicated to the idea of humans controlling their own destinies and asserting their worth. The original groups from the suffragette era had disappeared. Demands for equal rights tended to be promoted through the labor movement, if at all. Women had been given a boost in 1961 when President Kennedy established a Commission on the Status of Women, chaired by Eleanor Roosevelt. It produced a report in 1963 detailing the restrictions on women's rights and opportunities. "Sex" was added to the 1964 Civil Rights Act, suggested at first by a segregationist congressman as something of a joke and then pushed through in a curious coalition with feminists. The Equal Employment Opportunities Commission treated it as a joke and did nothing. In 1966, the National Organization of Women (NOW) was founded in response to this rebuff. Its president was Betty Friedan, whose book *The Feminine Mystique* gave voice to a generation of women who felt marginalized by both workplace practices and the expectations of home-making.[52] Women were steadily becoming a vital part of the American workforce (40 percent by the start of the 1970s) and were increasingly disinclined to accept second-rate pay and conditions. Friedan was an effective publicist and used her role as the head of what was a relatively small organization to gain media attention for her views and those of her colleagues. From the start, the movement had an articulate leadership.

Quite apart from NOW, another strand of the movement was developing among numerous young women who had experienced their own rebuffs as they worked as New Left activists. They could not help but notice the contrast between the denunciations of oppression coming from a largely male leadership, coupled with expectations of women occupying subordinate roles and offering sexual favors. The "only position for women in SNCC," observed Stokely Carmichael in 1964, "is prone." In a landmark essay, Mary King and Casey Hayden (Tom Hayden's first wife) reported that women in the movement were not "happy and contented" with their status, and that their talent and experience was being wasted. In what now appears as a rather tentative document they judged that "objectively, the chances seem nil that we could start a movement based on anything as distant to general American thought as a sex-caste system." For that reason they expected to continue to work on the problems of war, poverty, and race. They nonetheless insisted that "the very fact that the country [couldn't] face, much less deal with" the questions they were raising meant that the "the problems of women functioning in society as equal human beings are among the most basic that people face."[53]

Soon, however, the dismissive attitude of male activists became too annoying to ignore. The more women were treated with condescension by their male colleagues, the greater their anger. In 1967, groups began to push a more distinctively feminist agenda and by 1968 they had their own national conference. Unlike NOW, this group of women had considerable experience of protest and grass-roots organization.[54] In 1969, Carol Hanisch wrote a paper reflecting on the position of women in the movement and complained that when they got together for mutual support it was a form of "therapy," as if they were seeking a cure for some sickness. The key was to understand that the personal was political. These were issues that could only be solved through collective action.[55] The reason this worked as an existential strategy was that it did not depend on leadership and organization, other than when seeking legislative changes, but on the routine assertion of core principles of equality and worth, often without agreement on where the movement should or could lead, and accommodating a range of lifestyle choices. The core feminist complaints, once they were out in the open, were easy to understand and hard to ignore. Some might recoil at more radical denunciations of patriarchy and the coercive quality of marriage and motherhood but they were free to ignore this and concentrate on issues that mattered to them, whether abortion, indifference to sexual assault or rights to equal pay.[56]

As women moved increasingly into the space opened up by the civil rights movement, so did gays. After blacks, they pointed out, they constituted the largest minority group in America. Many just craved respectability, so that they were not stigmatized for their sexual preferences. This was the time when homosexuality was considered aberrant, a psychiatric disorder that might benefit from treatment. During the 1960s there was a push to end this pariah status, insisting that whatever consenting adults did together in private was no business of government or employers. Under the influence of the counterculture, concerns about mainstream respectability came to be pushed to one side by demands for "gay liberation" and full sexual freedom. In July 1969, a police raid at the Stonewell Inn, a gay bar in New York's Greenwich Village, produced an outraged response that led to a riot. The more conservative homophile groups were anxious, but the event encouraged radical activists to embrace gay rights as a vital cause.[57]

In some respects, the activism against the Vietnam War was similar. The more dramatic acts of protest—burning draft cards, let alone the American flag—might not have been to everybody's taste, but the increasingly large demonstrations against the war demanded attention. The fact that SDSers had been to the fore of the original opposition did not endow it with a right to continue to set its terms. As opposition became broad-based, backed by opinion polls and mainstream commentators, it carried a political weight that the government could not ignore. These movements had a Tolstoyan quality in that out of the individual decisions of many people emerged new lifestyles, cultural forms, and political expressions.

The methods that could be used to dramatize issues that mattered to many individuals, helping the personal to become political, could not forge a broader political consciousness. The initial preoccupation with power, as a precious resource unequally distributed, led to wariness about anybody getting an unfair share. Power should not be sought; indeed, the appearance of an interest in power created suspicion. The preferred organizational forms were designed to hold back putative leaders and avoid a stifling bureaucracy. Such organizations could work, to a point, when populated by educated, articulate, committed, and energetic young people communicating in a common cause, but they soon faltered when energy levels dropped; the causes became routine; difficult choices had to be faced; the emerging strategies had to be implemented over extended periods; and when the feelings reflected boredom, fatigue, and confusion.

Alternatively, when the feelings were intense anger and deep frustration, actions could be impulsive, involving lashing out and grandiose gestures. The fate of SDS and SNCC could be taken as a warning of the consequences of a lack of deliberation and distrust of leadership. Even here, however, there was a legacy: the inclination to think about power from the bottom up and not solely from the top down, for making organizations and their decisions more transparent, had a lasting effect on governmental and corporate bureaucracies, reflected in demands for flatter hierarchies and more open structures. The futile terrorism of Far Left groups made more headlines in the 1970s and 1980s than nonviolent direct action. Yet events in Eastern Europe in 1989 and—at least initially—in the "Arab Spring" of early 2011 provided echoes of the techniques used by the civil rights movement in the early 1960s. The link between the two was provided by Gene Sharp, a long-standing pacifist who had worked with Muste and participated in some of the early sit-ins. He became the leading contemporary theorist of nonviolence, even gaining the patronage of Tom Schelling, who supplied the introduction to Sharp's major three-volume treatise, *The Politics of Nonviolent Action*.[58] This emphasized Gandhi's innovative role and employed Gregg's concept of jiu-jitsu, but was mainly notable for a view of power by which governments were assumed to be dependent upon the "people's good will, decisions and support" rather than the other way around. When this was the case, obedience was voluntary and consent could be withdrawn. He listed many ways by which this could be achieved, from demonstrations and petitions to boycotts, strikes, and even mutinies.[59] Authoritarian regimes in the 2000s, from Iran to Venezuela, identified Sharp as a dangerous agitator, and his ideas reached the Arab streets.[60] The experience underlined both the potential and limits of nonviolence. A regime so intolerant of disobedience that it was prepared to use uncompromising violence was likely to push its opponents to violence as well.

The inspirational and imaginative aspects of the movement during the 1960s provided its initial momentum. Those who thought about short-term consequences would probably have been deterred if they placed their hopes on what might be achieved in the early boycotts, sit-ins, and demonstrations. The weight of experience was against them. It was the cause which animated the movement and the sense of worth that came from doing what was right, even against the odds. Once mobilized, a movement that was about political rather than social change would be under pressure to become more organized and calculating, thinking about consequences. Todd Gitlin, one of Tom Hayden's early comrades in SDS, became an academic sociologist and also memoirist of the movement. He was aware of the impact of the counterproductive talk of violence, and how that had played into the Right's agenda, allowing the New Left to be portrayed as mindlessly disruptive rather than idealistic. This was a common theme of rueful SDS memoirs. At an age approaching Saul Alinsky's when he wrote *Rules for Radicals*,

Gitlin wrote *Letters to a Young Activist* in which he advised how to avoid the mistakes of his generation. He opened with Max Weber and later returned to him, acknowledging that he had found "Politics as a Vocation" irritating and "anti-inspirational" in his youth. Against Weber's assertion of an ethic of responsibility, Gitlin noted that then he would have responded with the claim that "radical action might just transform the circumstances, make the impossible somewhat more possible." Now he accepted: "Consequences: there's no getting away from them. How disconcerting that ideals and passions are compatible with gross miscalculations!" For activists considering a campaign of civil disobedience to address contemporary ills, he urged that it be "farsighted, strategic." Such a campaign should "not hope to reinvent the world at will" or "simply express itself." It must argue and "take place within history, not beat on its doors from outside," seizing opportunities and calling on "popular (even if latent) convictions and sentiments."[61]

CHAPTER 26 | Frames, Paradigms, Discourses, and Narratives

I'm no prophet. My job is making windows where there were once walls.

—Attributed to Michel Foucault

THE IDEAS OF the counterculture, carried forward by the educated middle classes, had profound influences not only on social choices but also on the conduct of politics and business, and on intellectual life in general. These ideas did not prompt a leftward shift in American politics—far from it, as we shall see in the next chapter—but they did have a major impact on the way that big ideas were discussed. The major insight, which was not at all new, was that as mental constructs are needed to make sense of the world, we can never have more than a particular take on reality. Nor was it new to argue that those who could shape the constructs of others could thereby influence their attitudes and behavior. This was the whole point of Lippmann's theory of public opinion and Bernay's approach to the "engineering of consent." Lippmann and Bernays claimed this could be benign, if undertaken by enlightened people in the name of sound public policy. The effects of the state manipulation of the media by Nazi and Communist totalitarianism, demonstrating just how insidious propaganda could be, undermined any optimism on this score.

The liberal response to totalitarianism was to argue that whatever the natural limits to human comprehension, the best course was to open up minds to a range of possibilities and share experiences and experiments. Rather than the imposition of a single view, however well intentioned and researched, the best hope for humankind lay in diversity and plurality, a marketplace of ideas. Liberal democracy could be guaranteed by a free, diverse, and argumentative media, combined with the highest standards in the search for truth. This put the onus on the media—and even more so, the academy—to seek to the extent possible objectivity in their reporting and analysis. The exemplary philosopher of the tolerant, open society was Karl Popper, who grew up in Austria but moved to London to escape the Nazis. He asserted the need for a rigorous empiricism in all scientific endeavors, putting every proposition to the test of falsifiability, gaining comfort from the wealth of accumulated and tested human knowledge upon which the flawed constructs of individuals were founded.[1]

The challenge posed by the New Left was to argue that the apparent plurality and diversity of Western liberal democracies was an illusion. Propositions that deserved challenge were taken for granted, while other perspectives and claims were marginalized. This was standard fare for Marxists and had been at the heart of Gramsci's concept of hegemony, which gained increasing attention during the 1950s. Debates on the left were also influenced by the legatees of the Frankfurt School, such as Herbert Marcuse. Émigré theorists, gathered at the New School of Social Research in New York, explained how knowledge was developed and maintained through social interactions, and introduced the concept of the "social construction of reality."[2] Of increasing importance were French theorists, this time not so much the existentialists but the poststructuralists and postmodernists.

The field research and experimental observations of mainstream social science might avoid the higher reaches of European theory but regularly confirmed the limits of cognition and the importance of interpretative constructs. The political issue was whether the interpretative constructs could be deliberately manipulated from outside. Research suggested that this was done regularly, not necessarily as part of some organized elite conspiracy but in the way that the issues were moved on and off the political agenda, and how these issues were posed in the first place, setting the terms for subsequent debate.

William James had addressed this question as early as 1869. Instead of asking whether what we know is real, James had asked, "Under what circumstances do we think things are real?" Building on James, the sociologist Erving Goffman explained, "We frame reality in order to negotiate it, manage it, comprehend it, and choose appropriate repertoires of cognition and action." Goffman considered how individuals struggled to make sense of the world around them and their experiences and so needed interpretative schemas or primary frameworks to classify the knowledge.[3] When there were a number of possible ways of viewing an issue, framing meant that one particular way appeared to be the most natural. This was achieved by highlighting certain features of a situation, stressing likely causes and possible effects, and suggesting the values and norms in play.

The Whole World Is Watching

The media was bound to play a major role in creating and sustaining the background consensus, especially now that TV had supplanted newspapers and the radio as the main source of information about political affairs. The possibility that media might play a less than benign role had been considered in the 1940s by Robert Merton, attuned to the question of the social influences on knowledge from the 1930s. Although he had been skeptical about Lasswell's claims about the effects of propaganda and concerned about how little was known about the "propagandee," he was also alarmed as a Jew by the rise of the Nazis. When he joined Columbia University in 1941, he began an intensive collaboration with Paul Lazarsfeld, who had some psychological training and now ran the Bureau of Applied Social Research at Columbia. Merton believed strongly that empirical research had to be combined with theory, and this is what he brought to the partnership.[4]

Their early research noted the limited effects of mass communications compared to friends and family. They tended to reinforce more than convert. In a joint piece published in 1948 they addressed the question of media impact on "social action," by which they meant progressive causes such as improved race relations or sympathy for the labor unions. They noted the concerns of high-minded critics that after all the efforts reformers had put into releasing people from wage slavery and constant toil, the masses now spent their extra leisure immersed in media products marked by triviality and superficiality.

They summed up the media's political impact in terms of enforcing social norms, by exposing deviations from these norms in private lives; by acting as a narcotic, encouraging public apathy and leaving people with only a secondary exposure to political reality; and lastly by encouraging conformism. Because they provided "little basis for a critical appraisal the commercially sponsored mass media indirectly but effectively restrain the cogent development of a genuinely critical output." Any minor tokens of progressive attitudes would be dropped from TV or radio shows if they went against the economic interests of the owners. "He who pays the piper generally calls the tune." Were there circumstances in which the media could shape public attitudes in a more progressive direction? This could happen, but it would require that the media itself was not divided and that preexisting views could be channeled in the preferred direction (instead of attempting to change basic values). Even then it would be necessary for any movement to be supplemented by face-to-face contact.[5]

By the early 1970s, it had become established that there was a relationship between the importance attributed to issues by a mass audience and the processes of agenda-setting, referring to how some issues gained prominence while others were barely noticed, resulting from the coverage given to an issue and where it was placed—on a page or in a news bulletin.[6] It was a truism in that if there was nothing in the media about a "topic or event, then in most cases it simply will not exist in our personal agenda or in our life space."[7] Some issues reflected the agenda of the media outlets; in many cases, it was the government that was best placed to set the agenda.

The media therefore could encourage people to think about certain issues to the exclusion of others, but could people be told what to think? In moving from radical activism to professional sociology, Todd Gitlin reflected on the divergence between what he considered to be the character and course of SDS and the way it had come to be portrayed. As we have seen, it had been a general assumption that one way to get sympathy for a cause was to be beaten by the police while demonstrating on behalf of that cause. In Chicago, as the police were wading into the activists, they chanted back, "The whole world is watching," as if this should serve as a warning that their attackers would be subjected to international condemnation. Yet, unlike the civil rights activists of earlier in the decade, the political effects were at best ambiguous. In many media outlets, it was the demonstrators rather than police who were condemned.

Gitlin sought to demonstrate that the media did not so much hold up a mirror to reality as shape what people assumed to be reality. "I was still in the grip of a noble, rationalist, post-Sixties prejudice," he later recalled, "that started with a distaste for bad ideas and proceeded to a sort of retrospective optimism to the effect that if the ideas and images had been different, a thoughtful population would have warmed to the movement instead of turning a cold shoulder, and the movement would therefore have created a healthier political climate for the years, even decades to come."[8] His book *The Whole World Is Watching* acknowledged the importance of the media in reporting the movement's demonstrations, for without a report they might as well not have happened, but that created a dependence on how they were interpreted.

Gitlin was aware of Gramscian analyses of hegemony, as shaping popular acceptance of the established order, by uniting persuasion from above with consent from below. By tracing the history of the movement and how it had been reported, he was in some respects updating Gramsci in the light of the modern mass media. He drew on Goffman's notions of frames in explaining how the media made choices about what to report and how. "Media frames are persistent patterns of cognition, interpretation, and presentation, of selection, emphasis, and exclusion." They were a way of organizing discourse, and there had to be some way. It was impossible completely to report the world that exists.

> Many things exist. At each moment the world is rife with events. Even within a given event there is infinity of noticeable details. Frames are principles of selection, emphasis, and presentation composed of little tacit theories about what exists, what happens, and what matters.[9]

What concerned him was how the media had undermined SDS by at times ignoring, trivializing, marginalizing, and disparaging it, as well as by highlighting differences among its members and focusing on its more disruptive behavior rather than addressing the issues being raised. This led him to ruminate on the circumstances in which radicals could make space to challenge hegemony. When elites were unsure of the situations, they could not define them to suit their interests. The key factor might not be the unity of the radicals but the unity of the establishment. Also relevant were the responses of ordinary people, with their own values and norms, which they saw being challenged by the protests. The issue went beyond establishment views or media methodology.

Thomas Kuhn

The idea that there were loose systems of ideas which could be politically influential despite their limited empirical basis was captured by Kenneth Galbraith's notion of the "conventional wisdom." This term had been around for some time to refer to commonplace ideas, but Galbraith used it in 1958 for "those ideas which are esteemed at any time for their acceptability." What was held to be truth, he suggested, was often a reflection of convenience, self-esteem, and familiarity as much as relevance. At the simplest level, the conventional wisdom could be seen in the rarity with which the businessman was denigrated as an economic force before the chamber of commerce. But it was found even at the "highest levels of social science scholarship." Minor heresies, he noted, may be much cherished, but the vigor of debate surrounding these heresies "makes it possible to exclude as irrelevant, and without seeming to be unscientific or parochial, any challenge to the framework itself." Galbraith accepted that the conventional wisdom had value as a check against a facile flow of intellectual novelties which could deny any possibility of stability and continuity. The danger lay in avoiding "accommodation to circumstances until change is dramatically forced upon it." The enemy of the conventional wisdom, according to Galbraith, was obsolescence, not "ideas but the march of events."[10]

Galbraith gave the conventional wisdom a negative connotation. A more neutral term, which also caught on more, was "paradigm." Thomas Kuhn described the dynamic that might be created by the combination of elite uncertainty and the march of events, while reinforcing the view that structures of power were dependent on embedded structures of thought, in one of the most influential books of the 1960s. *The Structure of Scientific Revolutions* addressed an area often held up as being separate from politics, propelled forward by the experimental method and the accumulation of evidence. Instead of scientific endeavor representing the progressive revelation of objective reality, Kuhn argued that it was actually a series of paradigm shifts. A "paradigm" was a set of ideas that could become so embedded within a scientific community that dislodging them became as much a political as an empirical challenge. When the scientific community worked within a prevailing paradigm this was "normal science." Its core precepts would be taught to students and research encouraged and celebrated which followed its framework and validated its conclusions. Eventually, challenges would appear as observations threw up apparently inexplicable anomalies. The cumulative impact of these anomalies would eventually become overwhelming. This Kuhn described as a "scientific revolution," when everything scientists thought they knew would be reassessed, all the prior assumptions and information reappraised, often against fierce resistance from the old guard. Eventually the new paradigm would usurp the old. The classic example of this was the Copernican Revolution, which overturned the prior assumption that planets revolved around the earth by showing how they were actually in orbit around the sun.

Kuhn's message was that beliefs, even in an area committed to reason and experimentation, could be influenced by factors that were at their root non-rational. This was an intensely political account, involving a confrontation between radicals and defenders of an old order that could no longer be accommodated within the established institutions of governance. Just as approved political strategies no longer sufficed at revolutionary times, so with approved scientific methods and reasoning. What made the difference at critical moments were factors extraneous to the scientific method, such as force of personality or the scientific equivalents of the revolutionary mob and coercive pressure. A new paradigm would acquire a form of collective consent, there would be a consequential circulation of elites, and normal science would continue until the process began again with the accumulation of more anomalies.[11] As revolutions went, this was more Pareto than Marx.

Kuhn himself stressed the underlying conservatism of his view when discovering to his horror during the student rebellions of the 1960s that he was being cast as a revolutionary for having identified paradigms as instruments of intellectual oppression. "Thank you for telling us about paradigms," the students were saying, "now that we know what they are we can get along without them." At this point he felt "badly misunderstood," disliking "what most people were getting out of the book."[12] He was not saying that paradigms were invariably harmful and misleading. They made sense of material that would otherwise appear inchoate and confusing. Scientific inquiry would be impossible without "at least some implicit body of intertwined theoretical and methodological belief that permits selection, evaluation, and criticism."[13] Nor was he arguing that it was only scientific politics that would allow a paradigm to become entrenched or supplanted. Crises in normal science would develop because of the continuing search for new discoveries and impatience with research designed to do no more than reaffirm what was already supposed. Kuhn did however insist that the "decision to reject one paradigm is always simultaneously the decision to accept another, and the judgment leading to that decision involves the comparison of both paradigms with nature *and* with each other."[14]

There were many criticisms of Kuhn, not least that his history represented an oversimplification. While there had clearly been occasions when the processes he described had been present, theories also changed significantly during periods of "normal science" and even adherents of old paradigms could get excited by new breakthroughs. It was also suggested that his focus was too internal to the scientific profession, with insufficient attention paid to the broader social context in which scientists operated and the developing impact of professionalism and bureaucratization. Kuhn polished and developed his ideas after the book's publication, notably in a 1970 revision. Thereafter, the radicalism of his message was diminished as his intellectual energies became focused on the more abstruse aspects of the philosophy of science.

By this time, however, whatever meaning he wished to assign to his ideas, his terminology was already well on its way to being co-opted by people working in a range of other disciplines. In 1987, Kuhn's work was reported to be the twentieth-century book most frequently cited from 1976 to 1983 in the arts and the humanities.[15] A "paradigm shift" became a cliché, used in circumstances far removed from a full-blown scientific revolution. His model, at least in a simplified version, appeared as a gift to relativists, suggesting that what mattered with any coherent set of views, including social philosophies, was not their relationship to any discernible reality but the political power behind them. An influential example of this was Sheldon Wolin's use of Kuhn to challenge the claimed objectivity of the "behaviorist" tendency in political sciences, which claimed to be following the same methodological path as the physical sciences. "Up to a certain point," Wolin observed, "what matters is not which the truer paradigm is but which is to be enforced."[16]

From a way of describing explicit, formal scientific theories that could be unsettled by contrary evidence, paradigms started to allow bundles of prejudices and preconceptions that were implicit, informal, and often confused, contradictory and in flux, to be treated as if they were embedded, internally coherent, tight and controlled, and in key respects impervious to facts. The tendency to categorize systems of belief as strong paradigms and then fit individuals and groups into them often failed to do justice to the extent to which individuals and groups were likely to deviate from a paradigm in particular aspects, interpret paradigms in culturally specific ways, tailor them to their political circumstances, or draw from them quite divergent inferences on how to act. If what counted for truth could be the result of political manipulation as much as scientific endeavor, then possibilities were opened up for a range of topics to become politicized.

Consider, for example, the curious case of intelligent design. In 1996, a Center for the Renewal of Science and Culture, based in California, set itself the objective of replacing "materialism and its destructive cultural legacies with a positive scientific alternative." By 1999 a strategy had been developed. This was known as The Wedge Project.[17] The metaphor was materialistic science as "a giant tree," the trunk of which could nonetheless be split by a small wedge applied at its weakest points. The "thin edge of the wedge" was represented by a number of books challenging evolutionary theory, beginning in 1991 with Phillip Johnson's *Darwinism On Trial*. The alternative to evolutionary theory was intelligent design. This challenged Darwinism by insisting that the world could not be explained by the randomness of evolution but must have required a coherent design, although it stopped short of saying that the God of the scriptures was *the* intelligent designer. The proponents used Kuhn's theory to argue that evolutionary biology was no more than a dominant paradigm upheld by a scientific elite willfully dismissive of contrary views, denying them publication in peer-reviewed journals. Social pressure discouraged inquisitive young scientists from exploring subversive notions.[18]

The wedge was to be broadened by promoting intelligent design as "a science consonant with Christian and theistic convictions." The next phase would involve "publicity and opinion-making." This work would be widely communicated into schools and the media, with a particular emphasis on mobilizing Christian opinion behind this cause. The big challenge would come with the third phase of "cultural confrontation and renewal," with direct challenges in academic conferences, a determined push—backed by law if possible—into the schools. The challenge would then be directed at the social sciences and humanities. The long-term aim was not only to make intelligent design "the dominant perspective in science" but to extend into "ethics, politics, theology, and philosophy in the humanities, and to see its influence in the fine arts."

The proponents were aware of the importance of framing. Johnson urged: "Get the Bible and the Book of Genesis out of the debate because you do not want to raise the so-called Bible–science dichotomy." The need was to get heard in the secular academy and unify religious dissenters. One practical reason to avoid creationism was that court rulings prohibited its teaching as science. The arena for the battle was school textbooks, and the key demand was that intelligent design be taught in schools. This involved getting proponents to sit on school boards. As the movement faced difficulty in getting their views accepted as suitable for textbooks, the demand had to be watered down to evolution being taught as a contested and contro-versial theory whose rightness should not be taken for granted, especially when other compelling theories were available as alternatives. In the end, the December 2005 *Kitzmiller v. Dover Area School District* court case decided against intelligent design on the grounds that it was insufficiently distinctive from creationism to deserve a place on the science curriculum.[19]

The case demonstrates the difficulty with the "paradigm" paradigm. Neither evolution nor intelligent design referred to fully coherent world-views. Among evolutionary biologists there were substantial differences but no sense of crisis: evolution was accepted as a powerful theory that kept on pointing researchers in fruitful directions. In Kuhn's terms, within the dominant matrix there were still a number of exemplary paradigms under challenge. Nor did intelligent design base its case on anomalous experimen-tal evidence. Its own paradigm did not stand up to scientific scrutiny. As a design the world is not always intelligent, with many obvious imperfec-tions and curiosities. There was not even a single creationist theory. Much depended on how literally the scriptures were followed. The Bible, for example, referred to the "four corners of the earth," so extreme literalists could claim that the earth really was flat. Others still argued with Galileo that the sun was at the center of the solar system. More common was Young Earth Creationism, following the Bible sufficiently literally to assert that the earth was six to ten thousand years old, was created in six days, that subsequent death and decay were the fault of Adam and Eve's original sin, and that Noah's Flood could provide a key to much of the world's geology. By contrast, Old Earth Creationists believed God created the earth but accepted that it was really ancient. Other versions suggested that the biblical sequence of creation worked so long as it was accepted that each biblical "day" really referred to extremely long periods. Others argued that the record of fossils could be accepted, but that the emergence of new organisms reflected deliberate acts of God rather than the accidents of evolution.[20] While creationists would be Christians (or Muslims), there were plenty of Christians (and Muslims) who had no problem with evolutionary theory. The material world might be explained by DNA as created by God, leading to a natural evolutionary course, which would still leave the spiritual world and the human soul to be addressed by religion.

So even within a self-conscious paradigm that had its own label there were a number of distinctive and contradictory viewpoints. The same was true among evolutionary biologists, although at least they had the scientific method to manage and even resolve disputes. While, as Kuhn observed, the scientific community had its gatekeepers and dogmatists, it could also be pluralistic and theories of evolution have, for want of a better term, evolved. Because intelligent design eschewed the methodology of "naturalist" science, there was no basis for it to cause a paradigm shift. Its only hope was to develop a sufficiently strong and vocal constituency to get its paradigm put onto the curriculum and if possible have evolution taken off. This was not at all the sort of struggle Kuhn had in mind, because it was between two very distinct communities rather than within one.

Michel Foucault

Another thinker whose ideas developed over the 1960s and thereafter shaped the way questions of ideology and power were addressed was the French social philosopher Michel Foucault. A thinker for whom the interplay between the personal and the philosophical was unusually intense, his engagement with the history of both psychiatry and sexuality reflected his difficulties with his homosexuality and depression. After an early dalliance with the French Communist Party, he appeared to distance himself from Marxism only to return as an enthusiastic proponent of the "spirit of '68," encouraging student occupations and leftist scholarship. In turn, he enthused about and then became disillusioned with Mao's Cultural Revolution and the Ayatollah Khomeini's revolution in Iran. He died from an AIDS-related illness in 1984, aged 57, halfway through writing a six-volume work on sexuality. As with many important thinkers, there were significant shifts in his work over the course of his life, and he refused to accept any label, although he came to be regularly identified as a leading postmodernist. Interpretations of what Foucault really meant can reach special levels of paradox as arguably, by his own account, he never "really meant" anything at all. His abstract writings, though not his histories, were dense and hard to follow, so any attempt to present his ideas in a simplified form (or indeed any form) posed a challenge. Yet his approach shaped much contemporary social thought, including the study of strategy and, in some respects, its practice.

There were obvious comparisons with Kuhn. Both men drew attention to the extent to which claims about truth were contingent and dependent upon structures of power. Where Kuhn had his paradigms, Foucault had "epistemes." He described these as the "apparatus" which made possible "the separation, not of the true from the false, but of what may from what may not be characterized as scientific."[21] At least in his earlier thought, epistemes were at any time unique, dominant, and exclusive, unable to coexist with others. There was "always only one *episteme* that defines the conditions of possibility of all knowledge."[22] Kuhn always assumed a greater plurality in the social sciences and broader culture in which distinctive schools challenged each others' foundations. Unlike the natural sciences they did not share the same problem-solving approach. In addition, his paradigms were quite conscious and deliberate frameworks for scientific research. Foucault's epistemes could be and often were unconscious, setting the terms for thought and action in ways that could be invisible to those affected. While Kuhn acknowledged the importance of empirical observation and that there might be more or less objective tests against which competing paradigms might be judged, Foucault admitted of no such possibility. There was a constant battle for truth, not in order to discover some absolute but to establish the boundaries on action.

This was because all forms of thought were inextricably linked to questions of power. He described a historical sequence of power systems. In feudal society, power was about sovereignty, with general mechanisms of domination but little attention to detail. The great invention of the next period with the coming of bourgeois society was the mechanisms that made possible "disciplinary domination" with forms of surveillance and incarceration that controlled the activity of individuals, whether in prisons, schools, mental hospitals, or factories. Thus what interested him about the development of the mass armies spawned by the French Revolution were the practices they employed for turning a multitude of individuals into employable armies. In this way Foucault could show that the conceptualization of bodies was a reflection of new forms of power.

> By the late eighteenth century, the soldier has become something that can be made: out of a formless clay, an inapt body, the machine required can be constructed; posture is gradually corrected; a calculated constraint runs slowly through each part of the body, mastering it, making it pliable, ready at all times, turning silently into the automatism of habit; in short, one has "got rid of the peasant" and given him "the air of the soldier."

This was the basis for the disciplinary power which migrated into civil society where comparable forms of control were instituted.

This control did not require violence, as it taught forms of behavior that constituted a form of self-discipline.[23] In this way, power and knowledge became one and the same, and Foucault referred to them together as "power/knowledge." Such power was not something owned or wielded, but an essential feature in all spheres of life, including the notionally most personal and intimate. It was diffuse rather than concentrated, discursive as much as coercive, unstable rather than fixed. There was no real "truth," so it could neither be repressed nor excluded. Considerations of truth were really about power, about who was served by what, and the forms of domination and resistance to which it gave rise.

His approach to power therefore underplayed physical constraint and queried the durability of apparent consent. It was through discourse that the thought of others was shaped so that actions followed a particular view of the world. "Regimes of truth" set standards for what was true and false and the procedures by which they might be discerned. These became embedded in everyday discourses, ensuring that certain matters were taken for granted while others were given prominence. In this way, views of reality could take hold, reinforcing structures of power without it being realized, resulting in accommodating forms of behavior being adopted without the necessity of enforcement. For Foucault, strategy was inextricably linked with power. While he discussed strategy in a mainstream sense, referring to "winning choices" in overt struggles, his concept was much broader. Strategy was "the totality of the means put into operation to implement power effectively or to maintain it."

Foucault's influence on the humanities came to be profound, its value still a matter for intense debate. His influence on thinking about strategy was also significant. First, his view of the ubiquity of power potentially turned all social relationships into arenas of struggle, touching the micro-level of social existence as well as the macro-level of the state. Second, he conveyed a sense of the continuity of struggle without end. There was confrontation, an apparent victory, and a stable period, but then it could all open up again. There was thus an ever-present possibility of resistance and so reversion. A victory might allow "stable mechanisms" to "replace the free play of antagonistic reactions," but it would only be truly embedded when the other was reduced to impotence. There could then be "domination," a "strategic situation more or less taken for granted and consolidated by means of a long-term confrontation between adversaries." But even periods of apparent stability, sustained by the dominance of a particular discourse, could turn to struggle, following the opening up of the discourse.

> In effect, between a relationship of power and a strategy of struggle there is a reciprocal appeal, a perpetual linking and a perpetual reversal. At every moment the relationship of power may become a confrontation between two adversaries. Equally, the relationship between adversaries in society may, at every moment, give place to the putting into operation of mechanisms of power.[24]

In an inversion of Clausewitz, he presented politics as a continuation of war.[25] War was a "permanent social relationship, the ineradicable basis of all relations and institutions of power." Social relations were thus orders of battle in which there was "no such thing as a neutral subject" and in which "we are all inevitably someone's adversary." Taking sides meant it was "possible to interpret the truth, to denounce the illusions and errors that are being used—by your adversaries—to make you believe we are living in a world in which order and peace have been restored." Therefore as much as the discourses of power were diffused throughout society, so too could be resistance, with forms of evasion, subversion, and contestation. In this respect, claims about knowledge were weapons in a struggle over truth. He wrote of "knowledges" (in the plural) in conflict "because they are in the possession of enemies, and because they have intrinsic power-effects."[26]

Analyses of discourses, by exploring what appeared settled and noncontentious, could reveal their contingency and relationship to structures of power. This could have a liberating effect, offering the subjugated a way out. This was not a particularly new thought and was one of the themes of the intellectual currents circulating around the New Left. There was the same notion of a form of unspoken warfare throughout society that had yet to manifest itself but might break out once the victims understood their situation. What was different with Foucault was that rather than focus on questions of class struggle and revolutionary politics, which he seemed to find passé, he focused instead on the "specific struggles against particularized power" of "women, prisoners, conscripted soldiers, hospital patients and homosexuals."[27] When lecturing in 1976, while the spirit of '68 was still fresh, he was impressed by the "dispersed and discontinuous offensives" within Western societies during the previous decade. The "increasingly autonomous, decentralized, and anarchistic character of contemporary forms of political struggle" suited his method. He referred to the "antipsychiatry movement" which had "helped in opening up the space of the asylum for social and political critique." At this time he was becoming involved in a movement giving voice to prisoners. His project was about the "desubjugation and liberation of disqualified peoples and their knowledges." One of Foucault's lasting impacts lay in the recognition that the plight of individuals at the margins of society, often in institutions where they had been placed for their own safety and that of society, were part of power relationships which could and should not be beyond challenge.

Foucault's theories made it possible to undermine established power structures without mounting physical challenges, but instead analyzing the "specificity of mechanisms of power...locate the connections and extensions...build little by little a strategic knowledge."[28] It could be argued, at least on the evidence of Foucaldian scholarship, that the language by which discourses were analyzed could obscure as much as illuminate, and be of little practical help to subjugated groups.[29] Moreover, while this was a way into understanding power relationships, it raised its own difficulties by bypassing questions of agency and structure, the intent of individuals, and the role of force. So much was loaded on his concept of power, and indeed of strategy, that these concepts risked losing any precise meaning. When everything, whether a written communication or a pattern of behavior, could be considered as strategy, then nothing was worth considering because the term was losing its meaning. Playing down coercive power might be sensible for subjugated groups. Seeking a liberating discourse should be safer. But in the end, force could still be an arbiter of struggles.

Narrative

The word which came to describe the essential instrument in the battles over ideas was not *discourse* but *narrative*. During the 1990s, this became a requirement for any political project: explaining why a political movement or party deserved to be taken seriously and conveying its core messages. This was based on another set of ideas that could be traced back to the radical intellectual ferment in France of the late 1960s that saw the concept move from being literary and elaborate to elemental and at the heart of all social interaction. It gained traction from reflecting evident aspects of human behavior as well as the better understanding of the workings of the brain.

Until the late 1960s, narrative was still largely to be found in literary theory, referring to works distinguished by a character telling of an event (rather than a stream of consciousness or some interaction between personalities).[30] It moved into wider theory under the influence of the French post-structuralists. They rejected the idea of meaning as a reflection of the intention of an author but instead insisted that texts could support a range of meanings, depending on the circumstances in which they were read. With every reading there could be a new meaning. A key figure in this group, with whom Foucault was linked, was the literary theorist Roland Barthes. He pushed the idea of the narrative to the fore, moving it away from purely literary texts into all forms of communication. There were, he wrote in 1968, "countless forms of narrative," including "articulated language, whether oral or written, pictures, still or moving, gestures, and an ordered mixture of all those substances; narrative is present in myth, legend, fables, tales, short stories, epics, history, tragedy, drama . . . comedy, pantomime, paintings . . . stained-glass windows, movies, local news, conversation." It was to be found "at all times, in all places, in all societies." There had "never been anywhere, any people without narrative; all classes, all human groups, have their stories, and very often those stories are enjoyed by men of different and even opposite cultural backgrounds: narrative remains largely unconcerned with good or bad literature. Like life itself, it is there, international, transhistorical, transcultural."

Not only were there an "infinite number of narratives," they could be considered from many vantage points, including history, psychology, sociology, ethnology, and aesthetics. Barthes believed it possible to identify common structures through deductive theory.[31] The next year another member of this group, Tzvetan Todorov, introduced "narratology," which involved distinguishing the component parts of a narrative and considering the relationships between them. What was narrated was the story, a sequence of events with characters, held together by a plot line that gave it structure and explained causation—why the events occurred when they did. Discourse described the presentation of the story, what determined its eventual appearance to an audience.

By the late 1970s, there was talk of a "narrative turn" in social theory. A recollection of a conference at the University of Chicago in 1979 spoke of an "aura of intellectual excitement and discovery, the common feeling that the study of narrative, like the study of other significant human creations, has taken a quantum leap in the modern era." It was "no longer the province of literary specialists or folklorists borrowing their terms from psychology and linguistics but has now become a positive source of insight for all the branches of human and natural science."[32] It was later reported how during the 1980s the social sciences became caught up in a "wave of theorizing about narratives," inspired by the belief that analyzing the stories people told would provide vital insights into how they lived their lives.[33]

Narratives were often described as being interchangeable with stories, and stories could be extremely simple. The argument that anything could count as a story reflected their importance in basic human communication. Mark Turner argued that life would be chaotic without simple stories turning pieces of information into a coherent pattern. Even babies developed links between containers, liquid flows, mouths, and taste in a story that eventually became entitled "drinking." With only partial information, these simple stories facilitated imagining the next step or what happened before. Narrative imagining, argued Turner, was fundamental both to our ability to explain and our ability to predict.[34] William Calvin suggested a close relationship between our ability to plan and our construction of narratives. "To some extent, we do this by talking silently to ourselves, making narratives out of what might happen next and then applying syntax-like rules of combination to rate a scenario as unlikely, possible or likely."[35]

Here was a concept that could explain how meaning was given to lives and relationships and how the world was understood. It fit in with theories of cognition and accounts of culture. The narrative turn therefore captured the uncertain confidence about what was actually known, the fascination with the variety of interpretations that could be attached to the same event, and the awareness of the choices made when constructing identity. It highlighted the importance of human imagination and empathy while challenging the idea of a perfect knowledge of an external reality.

Soon the academic interest in narrative found its way into the public domain. Psychologists used narratives as forms of therapy, lawyers employed them in their efforts to move juries, and claimants needed them when seeking redress. Over time, the self-conscious use of narratives extended to all types of political actors. Initially the major interest appears to have been among radical groups and others who were seeking to compensate for a lack of material resources. It was another way the weak could take on the strong: less muscle but better stories. A battle of narratives was to be preferred to a real battle. Eventually any political project, from whatever part of the spectrum, demanded its very own narrative.

The narratives could have a number of functions: means by which support could be mobilized and directed, solidarity sustained and dissidents kept in line, strategies formulated and disseminated. Their role, not always particularly deliberate, could be detected in the movements coming out of the counterculture, such as those demanding rights for women and gays and other marginalized groups. Their use gained credence from Foucauldian type analysis, using stories of victimhood, humiliation, and resistance to let people in similar situations gain strength from being part of a wider movement, linking their private frustrations with a public cause.

They would challenge stories firmly embedded in the culture, casting doubt on their veracity and fairness. As early as the 1950s, for example, Native Americans began to object to the classic westerns, which pitched brave cowboys against savage Indians. Italian Americans complained about their image being dominated by mobster movies. The civil rights movement depended on the contrast between the comfortable presentations of the American dream and the black experience. The black singer Paul Robeson deliberately changed the lyrics of "Ol' Man River" from "I gets weary and sick of trying, I'm tired of living and scared of dying" to "I keep trying instead of crying, I must keep fighting or else I'm dying."[36] In this case there was an established sense of oppression, and the question was whether much could be done about it. Many of the movements of the late 1960s began with far less clarity about whether personal feelings of frustration could be translated into political action. Here autobiographical stories could help otherwise disparate individuals find common cause through their shared experiences. In 1972 in the first issue of *Ms.*, a magazine for the women's movement, an article by Jane O'Reilly described the immediate understanding a group of women had to another's story. This was the "click," a moment of recognition, "that parenthesis of truth around a little thing that completes the puzzle of reality in women's minds—the moment that brings a gleam our eyes and means the revolution has begun." Soon "click" had become a "feminist term of art," a way of referring to a shared understanding of the deeper meaning of an apparently banal comment.[37]

Narratives describing social situations from the perspectives of those who in the past might have been belittled or marginalized found their way into more established literary forms, such as novels, movies, and even situation comedies. Black and gay characters were shown in positive lights, women were expected to be more assertive, and male assertiveness and insensitivity was often derided. Especially on TV, the story-telling might be controlled, with the progressive themes sanitized so as to render the new characters safe and unthreatening. There was no single, approved narrative of what it meant to be a "liberated" woman or a gay man operating among "straights." It was easier to confront white prejudice when the victims epitomized goodness, for example, a figure such as Sidney Poitier as the idealistic physician in the 1967 movie *Guess Who's Coming to Dinner*. It took some time before the full complexity of black experience and its encounters with white society could be portrayed. Change of this sort was only barely politically directed or controlled, although political leaders were obliged to give their views on where it all might be leading. So the process was nothing so simple as one paradigm or narrative being changed for another. The diversity of the contributions and their cumulative effects altered the terms of the debate, but this was not the result of any deliberate strategy.

According to David Ronfeldt and John Arquilla, who were at the fore in exploring the new forms of politics made possible in the information age, stories could express "a sense of identity and belonging" and communicate "a sense of cause, purpose, and mission." This would help a dispersed group cohere and guide their strategy. They knew the sort of action expected of them and the message to be conveyed.[38] Within a movement, inspirational stories might be told to enthuse activists, exemplary ones to reinforce approved norms, and cautionary tales to warn of the danger of rash moves or deviations from the agreed line. In developing support, stories could be told to illustrate the core message and to undermine the claims of opponents. This also meant that internal arguments about strategy could take the form of debates over narratives. Those nervous about strategic departures might offer warnings based on reminiscences about how campaigns were waged in the past and how well they fared.

The greatest challenges came with attempts to influence those who were not natural supporters. As the concept moved into the political mainstream, there was talk of grand narratives as setting the basic terms in which a political group would wish to be identified, its aims and values, and its relationship to the issues of the day. Once this narrative was set, then individual episodes might be "spun" by specialist communicators known as "spin doctors," who understood the media and made it their business to influence the daily news agenda and frame events.[39] Convincing the public that the economy was really doing well when the latest data suggested the opposite, or that the murky past of a candidate for high office was irrelevant, required a keen sense of media methods and schedules, including how to time news announcements and brief key journalists. Such narratives were not necessarily analytical and, when not grounded in evidence or experience, could rely on appeals to emotion or suspect metaphors and dubious historical analogies. A successful narrative would link certain events while disentangling others, distinguish good news from bid tidings, and explain who was winning and losing.

The impact of these ideas, whether framing paradigms or discourses—or propaganda, consciousness, hegemony, belief-systems, images, constructs, and mind-sets for that matter—was to encourage the view that a struggle for power was at root a struggle to shape widely accepted views of the world. In the past, a similar understanding had led socialists to prepare for long campaigns of political education, conducted by means of pamphlets and lectures. This was now a media age and the opportunities to shape and disseminate opinions and presentations of the truth were now many and various. The techniques pioneered by Bernays, with his intuitive grasp of the importance of framing, now promised an even greater impact. The struggle over images and ideas did not become one between radicals and resisters but between mainstream political activists, with the beneficiaries in the first instance turning out to be the Right rather than the Left.

CHAPTER 27 | Race, Religion, and Elections

Don't you see that the whole aim of newspeak is to narrow the range of
thought?

—George Orwell, *1984*

IN THE AFTERMATH of President Bush's victory over Senator John Kerry in November 2004, an election Democrats thought they could and should have won, early postmortems stressed the lack of a narrative. Kerry's pollster, Stanley Greenberg, observed that the Republicans had "a *narrative* that motivated their voters." Robert Shrum, another member of Kerry's team regretted: "We had a *narrative*, but in the end, I don't think it came through." Top Democrat consultant, James Carville, was harsher. "They say, 'I'm going to protect you from the terrorists in Tehran and the homos in Hollywood.' We say, 'We're for clean air, better schools, more health care.' And so there's a Republican *narrative*, a story, and there's a Democratic litany." William Safire, a columnist with a keen eye for shifts in political language, reported the views of Jim Phelan, editor of a journal on narrative studies, that all this sounded like the development of a new Democrat narrative. "That is, they are selecting events from the campaign and abstracting from them in order to supply a coherent *narrative* of why Kerry lost. Their coherent *narrative* is that he had no coherent *narrative*." He suggested that if Kerry had won he would be being congratulated for the coherence of his narrative.[1]

It was the case that Republicans had been paying attention for some time to the use of language to sharpen their political message. In this the key event had been the collaboration between Representative Newt Gingrich and consultant Frank Lutz to take Congress for the Republicans in the 1994 midterm elections. The centerpiece of the campaign was the "Contract with America." According to Lutz, the word *contract* was chosen because plan sounded insufficiently binding, promises were made to be broken, pledges went unfulfilled, platforms were too political, oaths too legal, and covenants too religious. The adjective "Republican" was left off to encourage independents to keep an open mind.[2] In the actual document, a lot of effort went into talking about personal responsibility, family reinforcement, and tax cuts ("American Dream Reinforcement"). In 1995, the two men combined on a memo for the new Republican Congressmen entitled "Language: A Key Mechanism of Control," which urged that they talk of themselves using such words as "opportunity, truth, moral, courage, reform, prosperity" and portray their opponents in term of such words as "crisis, destructive, sick, pathetic, lie, liberal, betray."[3]

Even before the 2004 presidential election, anxious Democrats who specialized in language, notably the linguist George Lakoff, had been urging that attention be paid to the clever way that issues were being framed to put Democrats on the defensive (for example, talking about the "inheritance tax" as the "death tax"). Once the conflict was being fought in the enemy's language, too much had been conceded. To Lakoff the great challenge was to turn these frames around so that Americans came to see the issues with new ideas. "Reframing is social change."[4] After the election, he pressed home his point, insisting that big philosophical debates were arguments over metaphors, and that impact of facts depended on the frames with which they were understood.[5] Drew Westen, a clinical psychologist and active Democrat, expressed his frustration by writing a book urging his party to learn to appeal to voters' emotions. It was enthusiastically endorsed by Bill Clinton and Westen appears to have been read carefully and consulted by the Democratic field during the 2008 campaign.

The problem, Westen suggested, was that Democrats wanted to believe that campaigns were about issues and that it would be possible to appeal to the rationality and better nature of voters. Unfortunately, human beings are barely rational creatures. Instead, they respond to messages which tug on their emotions and are prone to feel as much as see the world. "Most of the time, this battle for control of our minds occurs outside of awareness, leaving us as blind spectators to our own psychodrama, prisoners of the images cast on the wall of our skulls." Republicans understood this and developed a narrative of themselves as on the side of patriotism and God. Democrats were soft and fuzzy, inattentive on crime and limp in facing the nation's enemies, stuck with rhetoric about fighting for the working people of America as if the country was still facing the challenges of the 1930s. When persuading voters to back them, Republicans had no compunction about resorting to negativity, while Democrats continued to act as if they could rise above such aggression, dismissing the negativity as irrelevant and a turn-off for voters.

To remedy the situation, Democrats had to learn to frame issues to their advantage and go on the attack, finding ways of convincing voters that their candidate was in tune with voters' interests and values, defining the party and its principles in ways that were emotionally compelling. This involved developing a grand narrative that was coherent, using policy positions to illustrate principles and not the other way around. Such a narrative would be simple, coherent, and accessible, not depend on too many leaps of inference or imagination. It could be understood and then told and retold. "It should have a moral, be vivid and memorable, and be moving. Its central elements should be easy to visualize, to maximize its memorability and emotional impact." It was best to act first, before views had been fully formed, when there might be opportunities to "inoculate" against the opponent's negativity by acknowledging minor weaknesses. Westen's basic claim was that elections were "won and lost not primarily on the issues but on the values and emotions of the electorate including the gut feelings that summarize much of what voters think and feel about a candidate and a party."[6]

Westen's proposals, and those of Lakoff, indicated a considerable faith in the power of words and images, encouraging a belief that even the most liberal platform could be embraced by a majority of the electorate if only it was put together with sufficient emotional intelligence and professional media skills. It reflected in its own way a rather dismal view of public opinion as malleable and manipulable, tugged in one direction or another by the quality of rival narratives. The psychologist Stephen Pinker warned that this approach exaggerated the importance of metaphors, which were often used without much sense of the origins or implications, and of the role of frames. The idea that better metaphors and frames could be pounded into voters' brains risked turning into a retreat from reason, caricaturing opposing beliefs and underestimating opponents.[7] Lutz's own guide to the use of language acknowledged the importance of framing issues, but his stress was on more basic rules of communication. He aimed for simplicity and brevity; short words and short sentences; attention to consistency, imagery, sound, and texture; and language that was aspirational and offered novelty. Only toward the end of his list did he point to the need to "provide context and explain relevance." Credibility, he noted, was as important as philosophy. Explicitly addressing Lakoff, he observed that "language alone cannot achieve miracles. Actual policy counts at least as much as how something is framed."[8]

Studies of the influence of mass communications gave little encouragement to suggestions that it was easy to shift public opinion in a direction it was not prepared to go. Partisans might be engaged, but the bulk of the target audience tended to be inattentive and distracted, so key messages did not reach many people. People could remain indifferent to issues in which they had little interest and resistant to views which contradicted those already held. Either they deliberately avoided such views or saw them as weak and riddled with error when they did confront them. One account of the relevant research recorded as a core finding that personal influence was more important than mass communication: "Political persuasion is contingent on circumstance. Persuasion grows more likely when campaigns face little opposition, when resistance is diminished, when well-placed sources provide simple and decisive cues, and when history intrudes on attentive citizens."[9]

The New Politics

The issue of the political use of language emerged out of the "new politics" of the 1960s. The events of 1968 turned out to serve the American Right more than the Left. This was in part because the upheavals on the campuses and the inner cities created a strong negative reaction that Republicans were able to exploit thereafter, and they were still trying to do so four decades later. Norman Mailer observed that year, while waiting for a civil rights leader to turn up for a press conference for which he was already forty minutes late, of how he had experienced a "very unpleasant emotion: 'he was getting tired of Negroes and their rights.'"[10] This led him to reflect that if he felt "even a hint this way, then what immeasurable tides of rage must be loose in America?" The "backlash" was already underway, directed not only at blacks but also at unpatriotic radicals, drug-taking hippies, and protesting students. One beneficiary was Richard Nixon, who regained the White House for the Republicans. If a new politics was making an appearance, it depended less on the rejection of professional politicians as a barrier to the authentic expression of popular feelings and more on the cultivation of more professional political forms, as a way of maximizing voter turnout. The New Left's despairing attitude to electoral politics had left the field open to the New Right.

Successful politicians always had campaign managers. By and large these were close associates of the candidates with a feel for popular moods and the sort of ruthless streak that left them with little compunction when it came to blackening the names of their opponents. By the late 1960s, the role was becoming much more professional. A series of advances in polling, advertising methods, and tactical analysis were coming together. The possibilities for shaping opinion opened up by the mass media reached a new level when television was added to newspapers and radio. The ability to disseminate a message to extraordinary numbers of potential voters was coupled with possibilities for tailoring that message to the interests and views of particular constituencies. Sophisticated forms of polling based on demographic sampling, pioneered by George Gallup in the 1930s, made it possible to monitor developing trends in opinion and identify issues of high salience.

In 1933, the campaigning socialist journalist Upton Sinclair, author of *The Jungle*, wrote a short book entitled *I, Governor of California and How I Ended Poverty*. It was a bestseller, a history of the future. Sinclair claimed it was a unique attempt by a historian "to make his history true." California was then a one-party Republican state, but also had 29 percent unemployment. Sinclair decided to run as a Democrat on a promise to end poverty through cooperative factories and farms and higher taxes. The first part of his story became a reality. He did get the nomination for governor and generated great national excitement. Unfortunately for him, the possibility that the script set out in his book might be followed alarmed California Republicans. Clem Whitaker and Leone Baxter, publicists for the "California League against Sinclairism," adopted a simple method to head off this threat. They immersed themselves in everything he had written and found a stream of deadly quotes—for example, statements doubting the sanctity of marriage—without worrying about context or whether these were attributed to characters in his novels. They appeared on a regular basis in the *Los Angeles Times*. Sinclair's nonfiction sequel was "How I Got Licked."

Whitaker and Baxter ran Campaigns Inc., the first political consultancy to offer their services at a price. They took advantage of reforms which had been initiated by the Progressives in order to break the hold of local party bosses over state politics. These prevented parties from endorsing candidates who therefore had to engage more directly with the electorate. Whitaker and Baxter claimed that in their first two decades, they had won seventy out of the seventy-five contests in which they were involved. They only worked for Republicans, which was often the case for the first generation of consultants. They also ran campaigns against health care reforms, first in California and then nationally, helping create the bogey of socialized medicine. They pioneered techniques to influence public opinion that continue to be employed: sending rural newspapers press releases dressed up as ready-made editorials and features, focusing on personalities rather than issues, always attacking ("You can't wage a defensive campaign and win"), taking the opponent seriously and anticipating their moves, and keeping the campaign theme simple. Subtlety was bad; repetition was good. According to Baxter, "Words that lean on the mind are no good. They must dent it."[11] Their services did not come cheap, but their clients were big businesses and the Republicans, the party of business. Republican senator Mark Hanna of Ohio, an accomplished campaign manager, remarked early in the century that "the three most important things in American politics are money, money and I forget what the other one is." Over time, fundraising became so important that it became yet another task for which consultants were needed.[12]

The party bosses were undermined by the increased role of primary elections in the nominating process, which after 1968 involved the majority of the states. The complexity of the American political system, with regular timetabled elections for numerous positions at all levels of government, provided plenty of business for consultancies with credible track records of getting their people elected. One estimate in 2001 suggested that if all elected posts were included, some quite lowly, there were over five hundred thousand elected officials in the United States with about a million elections over a four-year cycle.[13] This was one reason why James Thurber described campaign consultants in 2000 as being at "the core of the electoral process in the United States and in many other states."[14] As early as 1970 it was claimed that campaigns were less between candidates than between "titans of the campaign industry working on behalf of those personalities."[15]

When the journalist James Perry wrote *The New Politics* in 1968, it was therefore not about how protests, demonstrations, civil disobedience, and community organizations might be shaking up the old elite, but about how polling and marketing were becoming more sophisticated. He even drew attention to the potential uses of computers.[16] Yet these techniques, no more than the efforts of the New Left, did not guarantee success. Much of Perry's book described how the moderate George Romney was taking advantage of these techniques in the race for the 1968 Republican presidential nomination. By the time the book was published, Romney's campaign had collapsed, having failed to connect with voters—a problem aggravated by Romney's disastrous claim that his past support for the Vietnam War was the result of "brainwashing" by the Pentagon.

The importance of television had been underlined in different ways in the previous two elections. John Kennedy had famously gained an advantage over Nixon in the televised presidential debate in 1960, and then the possibilities of negative advertising had been underlined by one used by the Democrats against the hawkish Barry Goldwater in 1964. This showed a small girl counting daisies as a missile countdown began leading toward a nuclear explosion, with President Johnson in the background urging peace. This became identified as a turning point in technique. It played on an established image of Goldwater's recklessness. The appeal of the ad was emotional. It contained no facts and Goldwater's name was not mentioned.[17]

On the basis of his 1960 experience, Nixon's attitude toward television was one of deep suspicion, but he was persuaded by television producer Roger Ailes that it could work to his advantage. His efforts in that regard were recorded by a journalist friend of Ailes, Joe McGinnis. The title of his book, *Selling of the President*, captured the idea that someone so unprepossessing could be turned into a marketable political product. In contrast to the later focus on negative advertising, the aim at this stage was positive. The intention was to create a Nixon image independent of his words. As McGinnis explained:

> Nixon would say his same old tiresome things but no one would have to listen. The words would become Muzak. Something pleasant and lulling in the background. The flashing pictures would be carefully selected to create the impression that somehow Nixon represented competence, respect for tradition, serenity, faith that the American people were better than people anywhere else, and that all these problems others shouted about meant nothing in a land blessed with the tallest buildings, strongest armies, biggest factories, cutest children and rosiest sunsets in the world. Even better: through association with the pictures Richard Nixon could become these very things.[18]

Ailes was probably happier with the book's message than Nixon.

The aim of the media campaign was to demonstrate that Nixon was more likable than supposed and could be found safely in the center ground of politics. In this respect it fit in with what was in practice a rather "old politics" campaign. This was the last Republican nomination in which the majority of delegates were chosen by the party organization rather than primaries, so Nixon was able to follow a traditional route through deals with party insiders rather than demonstrating broad appeal. His basic strategy was standard for a candidate whose core support did not command a majority: he moved to the center and sought to soften his own right-wing image. Positions were carefully formulated to draw in the maximum amount of support, even if few were left excited. His former speech writer described Nixon's "centrism" as based on the "pragmatic splitting of differences along a line drawn through the middle of the electorate." The aim was to find the "least assailable middle ground." Instead of the "grand theme," his interest was in the "small adjustment, which might provide an avenue of escape."[19] Moreover, however expertly Nixon was marketed, his cautious approach to the campaign meant that his early lead was whittled down and he became president on a surprisingly narrow margin.

The New Conservative Majority

To one commentator, who worked for Nixon in 1968, the candidate's failure was in not recognizing the true opportunities created by the turmoil of the 1960s. Kevin Phillips, a young lawyer with an interest in ethnography, wrote a book in 1967 entitled *The Emerging Republican Majority*. Because the publisher had held it back to see whether it was validated in the 1968 presidential election, it was not actually published until 1969. The book was long and analytical, with 143 charts and 47 maps, but the underlying message was straightforward. The country had been dominated by a liberal establishment that was now old and out of touch, "a privileged elite, blind to the needs and interests of the large national majority," a position of course also taken by the New Left. The elite had created "a gap between words and deeds which helped to drive racial and youthful minorities into open revolt."

Phillips saw in the developing racial politics an opportunity for Republicans, because they could mobilize whites even as the Democrats attracted new black voters. Against the New Left's idealism and the old progressive hope that ethnic differences could be transcended, Philips asserted that these identities were strong and enduring. While Jews and blacks might go with the Democrats, the minorities with a more Catholic background—Poles, Germans, Italians—were lining up against the liberals. Though immigrant communities once saw the Democrats as a defense against the Protestant Republican establishment in the North, now their children saw the Democrats as hostile. In New York, Phillips charted the movement of working-class Catholics to the right, mapping it by district and showing that it was safe for Republicans to oppose the urban liberal agenda of rent subsidies, equal opportunity, and community action. This agenda, he argued, was pushing whites away from the inner cities to suburbia, and this was part of a wider movement from the decaying North to the "sunbelt" of the South and West. Phillips was not arguing that the new configuration was inevitable.

It required Republicans to seize the opportunity. He argued that Richard Nixon's majority in 1968 was so thin precisely because Republicans did not follow his ideas and tried to pretend that the candidate was something milder than was actually the case.

One objection to Phillips's thesis was with his "grim satisfaction" in the "incorrigible meanness of the American voter" and his "undisguised scorn" for "sentimentalists" who resisted his findings.[20] The fact that politics could play on human difference was anathema to many. Against this it could be argued that he was only making explicit what had long been a feature of American politics. Roosevelt's New Deal coalition had worked precisely because he found a way of keeping in the same party racists and blacks, anti-labor and pro-labor groups, ardent reformers and corrupt party machines. The Depression made it possible to subsume ethnic identities under shared economic interests, but few working in city politics believed that they had gone away.[21]

A second objection was that it was poor political science because it required Republican Party politics to follow a path many Republicans would resist.[22] There were limits to the southern strategy Nixon could follow in 1968. Governor George Wallace of Alabama was running as a third-party candidate on a segregationist platform and eventually took five southern states. Nixon's main nod in the direction of the new political configuration was to snub the Republican Party's liberal wing in his choice of vice president. New York governor Nelson Rockefeller had fought a poor campaign, and so Nixon felt able to ignore him as a possible running mate and opt instead for the relatively unknown Maryland governor Spiro Agnew, who had a moderate past but was moving to the right. As vice president he made his name by attacking the liberal elite with some memorable alliteration ("pusillanimous pussyfooters," "nattering nabobs of negativism").

In 1970, Phillips's message was repeated in a more careful form by two moderate Democrat pollsters, Richard Scammon and Ben Wattenberg. The Republican majority was not yet in place but, they warned, it could be if the Democrats did not acknowledge anxiety among their natural constituents about crime and permissiveness.[23] Instead, the Democrats moved to the left, with young activists pushing those issues that alarmed centrist voters, thus marginalizing the party's former establishment. The Democratic nominee in 1972, the liberal and antiwar George McGovern, was trounced by Nixon. The administration was then rocked by scandal as first Agnew was forced to resign because of corruption and then Nixon because he was being impeached for dirty tricks during the 1972 campaign and an attempted cover-up. The accidental president Gerald Ford and his vice president Nelson Rockefeller, neither of whom had been on the ticket in 1972, lost in 1976. The conservative theme was then picked up with a vengeance by Ronald Reagan.

Ronald Reagan

After his Hollywood career came to an end, Ronald Reagan had made his political name as a right-wing speaker. In 1954, he was hired as official public spokesman for General Electric Corporation—which meant he spoke at GE plants around the country, lauding the virtues of free enterprise and warning of the dangers of big government and communism. Reagan was telegenic with an easy, affable style that helped him link with people who might otherwise recoil from his politics. Reagan also had an ability to drift in and out of the fictional and nonfictional worlds which he inhabited, which made his claims credible even when they were fanciful. His biographer described a mind occupied by "stories, a make-believe world in which heroic deeds had the capacity to transform reality." The make-believe and real worlds coalesced in his mind. He always sounded sincere because he said what he believed, even if it did not correspond to the facts. In any conflict between feelings and fact, feelings won. "He believed in the power of stories, sincerely told."[24]

When he ran for governor of California in 1966, he followed the traditional route by edging sufficiently to the center to ensure that voters were not put off by his reputation. He avoided replying to attacks that he was right wing and inexperienced, toned down his speeches, and put together supporting committees which included known moderates. One of his managers later explained that they dealt with the inexperience charge by agreeing that "Reagan was not a professional politician. He was citizen politician. There, we had an automatic defense. He didn't have to have the experience. A citizen's politician's not expected to know all the answers to all of the issues." It even put his opponent, long-time governor Pat Brown, on the defensive for being a professional. This became a theme in many American elections thereafter. Reagan's team relied on question and answer sessions to address the charge that he was no more than an actor who knew how to memorize and deliver a good speech. While the campaign managers had not intended to dwell on the unrest of the Berkeley campus, they also noted that it worked in their favor.[25]

Once elected as governor, Reagan was seen as a potential conservative candidate for the presidency. His hat was tentatively in the ring in 1968 but his real preparation did not begin until after he had finished his second term as governor in 1974. He used a nationally syndicated column and radio program to keep himself in the public eye and also as a means of refining his messages, identifying the words and themes that got the best response from his audiences. By this time, more than twice as many Americans (38%) described themselves as conservative rather than liberal (15%). This still left a majority describing themselves as middle of the road (43%).[26] In 1976, Reagan's bid for the Republican nomination against Ford made sufficient headway to set him up for a successful campaign in 1980. In this he was helped by Jimmy Carter's doleful presidency as he struggled to cope with the economic and international crises of the late 1970s. Reagan's message began by noting the distinction between the social conservatism associated with the Democratic Party and the economic conservatism, opposed to deficit spending and big government, associated with the Republican Party. He then insisted that "the old lines that once clearly divided these two kinds of conservatism are disappearing." He envisioned "not simply a melding together of the two branches of American conservatism into a temporary uneasy alliance, but the creation of a new lasting majority."[27] The second strand was to claim that not only could these two traditions be combined, but that this would lead to a bountiful future. In this respect he offered a traditional politician's promise of more of everything, an America both stronger and wealthier, a sunny optimism in sharp contrast to Carter's melancholy. When he debated Carter as the Republican nominee, Reagan sought to present himself as the mainstream and sealed his bid by asking the pointed question of whether people were better off than they were four years earlier.

In two areas Reagan demonstrated the importance of getting messages across that cemented his support among groups that were essential to his new Republican majority. One part of this was his appeal to Southern voters, who had to be weaned away from Jimmy Carter—one of their own. While carefully avoiding overt racism, Reagan began his campaign in Philadelphia, Mississippi, a town notorious for the murder of three civil rights workers in the 1960s. Standing beside a known segregationist, Reagan stressed his belief in "states' rights," an evident code for the obstruction of black advances. The second area in which Reagan made a definite appeal for a particular constituency was in his pitch to the religious right.

Reagan, who was not known to be a regular churchgoer, concluded his acceptance speech in 1980 with a moment that was apparently spontaneous although actually carefully prepared. He had been wondering, he said, whether to include some thoughts as an addition to the distributed version of his speech. "Can we doubt," he then asked, "that only a divine Providence placed this land, this island of freedom, here as a refuge for all those people in the world who yearn to breathe freely." Carefully he turned his presidential campaign into a religious crusade. He asked for a moment of silent prayer and concluded with what became his customary "God bless America." A new religious politics was born. This was in part because of the positive reaction Reagan's ploy elicited among two-thirds of Americans. More importantly, it was because he knew before he stood up that if he could send the right message he would get the support of an increasingly powerful evangelical bloc.

Although Carter was clearly deeply religious and regularly spoke of his faith, in no sense could he be said to be following a particularly religious agenda in his presidency. The landmark January 1973 Supreme Court vote on abortion, *Roe v. Wade*, galvanized evangelicals and Catholics. The radical claim that the personal was the political was now embraced by conservatives as they looked to politics to reverse what they saw as a deep moral decline, marked by drugs, crime, and sexual permissiveness. Jerry Falwell, a Southern Baptist with his own television show, published a sermon in 1979 entitled *America Can Be Saved*. The gravamen was that the secular and the sacred could not be separated. Therefore, men of God needed to be trained to "go on to be directors in the largest corporations, who can become the lawyers and the businessmen and those important people in tomorrow's United States. If we are going to turn this country around we must have God's people mobilized in the right direction and we must do it quickly." The aim was to establish a moral majority with an agenda that opposed abortion, supported prayer in school, and favored traditional notions of sexuality and gender. "If all the fundamentalists knew who to vote for and did it together, we could elect anybody." He formed the Moral Majority, and if Reagan offered an exciting platform that it could support he promised three to four million votes. Another leader of the Moral Majority, Paul Weyrich, described the organization as "radicals working to overturn the present power structures in this country."[28] Reagan's speech and the appearance of a proposal for a constitutional amendment to "protect the unborn child" did the trick for Reagan. He got the votes.

Lee Atwater

The man who came to be credited as ensuring that the new conservative majority survived the 1980s was Lee Atwater. He made his name as a Republican political activist in the South during the 1970s and then was a leading figure in Reagan's 1984 campaign before managing Vice President Bush's successful campaign of 1988. He was then promoted to chair the

Republican National Committee before being struck down suddenly by a brain tumor in 1991, at the age of 40.

Atwater was an intriguing figure. He was charming and charismatic, but also devious and manipulative, with people notionally on his side as well as obvious opponents. With his existentialism and casual lifestyle he appeared to be at one with other student radicals of his generation. He also had a musical affinity with black culture. In his case, being rebellious and anti-establishment led to Republicanism. "The young Democrats were all the guys running around in three-piece suits, smoking cigars and cutting deals," he later observed, "so I said 'Hell, I'm a Republican.'" He added that this was also "a response to what was going on in the early '70s. I resented the way the left wing claimed to have captured the hearts and minds of American youth. They certainly hadn't captured mine." Being a Republican in the South put him in the position of insurgent. Victory could not be based on the issues, so it had to be based on character. "You had to make the case that the other candidate was a bad guy." Atwater marketed himself as "a Machiavellian political warrior, skilful at using ad hominem strategies and tactics, characterized by personal attacks, dirty tricks, and accentuating the negative."[29]

Atwater's timing was significant in another respect, as he entered politics when opportunities were opening up for professional strategists. The structure of American politics, with its numerous elections and constant campaigning, created opportunities for those who combined an understanding of the mechanics of getting out the vote with the possibilities of modern communications and a flair for campaigning. His reputation was as a maestro of negative campaigning, manipulating the "wedge" issues connected with race and crime. This reputation was confirmed by the ruthlessness with which he disposed of the Democratic nominee in 1988, Michael Dukakis. A driven outsider, he understood that he was in a profession where a single slip could abruptly end a career, yet he enjoyed the limelight and was constantly telling a story about himself as well as his clients. He understood the needs of the media and played upon them. As a creature of the television age, he grasped how a carefully contrived stunt or a hard-hitting advertisement could become a talking point for days and reframe the voters' views of a candidate.

He was also an intense student of strategy, who was said to be a regular reader of Machiavelli and always liked to have at hand Clausewitz's *On War*. Sun Tzu was his favorite. He claimed to have read it at least twenty times. Quotes from *The Art of War* were included in the program for his memorial service. "There's a whole set of prescriptions for success," he observed in 1988, "that includes such notions as concentration, tactical flexibility, the difference between strategy and tactics, and the idea of command focus."[30]

He considered Lyndon Johnson to be a master of the political art and took Robert Caro's biography of the Texan politician's rise as a sort of bible.[31] He studied the battles of the Civil War, acknowledging that it was the Union's Sherman who best understood the merciless logic of total war.

The only sport that interested Atwater was wrestling. Here was a tussle between two tough men who were expected to use deception and tricks in their fights, in a setting that was knowingly phony. This helps explain the appeal of Sun Tzu. He was operating in a context where craftiness could reap dividends, especially if the opponent was playing a less imaginative game. Atwater insisted on thorough research of the opponent ("know the enemy"), so that he could target weakness. Likewise, awareness of his own candidate's vulnerabilities was important for defensive purposes. In helping Bush gain the Republican nomination, he exploited Senator Robert Dole's known temper and managed to get under his skin ("anger his general and confuse him"), and then confounded Dukakis by attacking him in his home state Massachusetts on one of his preferred issues, the environment. Dukakis was forced to devote resources to an area in which he had felt safe ("move swiftly where he does not expect you").[32]

As the traditional ideological element, and party discipline, waned in American campaigns, more depended on the qualities of individual candidates. Strategy for elections was like that of battles in being geared to one-off, climactic duels. Elections were zero-sum games, so that what one gained the other must lose. This gave the contest its intensity. Given the size of the electorates, personal contact with the voters was impossible and so campaigns had to be conducted through the mass media. They were competitions of character as much as policy. Atwater was considered the master of spin, providing each situation with its own logic, so that everything that happened could be explained in a way that served a larger narrative. Through spin, innocent candidates could be tarnished with an undeserved label, while guilty parties could escape untainted; the fake and the true could be muddled; and the accidental could become deliberate, while the planned became happenstance. Even though he spoke on his deathbed about the Bible and sent apologetic notes to some of his victims, there remained a question mark as to whether this was sincere or just the latest way of managing his own image. According to Mary Matalin, one of his protégés, he wanted to apologize to people to whom he had been personally rude, but there was "no deathbed recantation" of his political methods.[33]

Atwater worked hard on the media, playing to the desire of individual reporters to have their own stories. He developed his techniques from his early days as a campaigner, with press releases hand delivered—never mailed—to increase reporters' "feelings of importance and help them feel appreciated and taken into confidence." The delivery would be an hour before deadline so that reporters could work the "news" into their day's work without necessarily having time for checks. A release would rarely run longer than one page, with no more than twenty-five words at the head, so they could be read at a glance. "The average reporter is lazy, as the rest of us are," he observed, "and sufficiently harassed by deadlines that he will want to use material as filler without need for an extensive rewrite."[34] The media beats can "only be chewing on one ankle at the time." Matalin described his talent as having "the pulse of the press."[35]

Behind all of this was a shrewd analysis of American politics and society. In the early 1980s, Atwater came across the memo sent by Clark Clifford to Harry Truman in November 1947 on "The Politics of 1948," which accurately predicted the nominees for the next year's election and also that Truman would win. By looking at the Electoral College, he realized that Truman could lose some of the big eastern states, normally assumed to be essential to victory, so long as he held the "Solid South" and those western states carried by the Democrats in 1944. Atwater picked this up in a memo of March 1983 entitled the "South in 1984," which described how Reagan could get reelected on the same basis. "The South's gut instincts are still Democratic," he observed. Southerners would "only vote Republican when they feel they must." But he noted that Reagan had managed to persuade southerners to vote against one of their own (Jimmy Carter) in 1980. He identified as the key a swing constituency which he described as the "populists." This group could go either with the Republican "country clubbers" or else the Democratic blacks.[36] Another memo the next year emphasized the South as the key to victory and urged driving "a wedge between the liberal (national) Democrats and traditional southern Democrats."

What interested him about populism was that, unlike conservatism, it was not so much an ideology as a set of largely negative attitudes. "They are anti-Big Government, anti-Big Business, and anti-Big Labor. They are also hostile to the media, to the rich and to the poor." This negativity meant that it was difficult to mobilize them. "When they do get mobilized, it is just about as likely that they will support a liberal, or a Democratic, cause as a conservative or Republican cause."[37] To the populists he added the libertarians. This group he considered to be as important as liberals or conservatives. This philosophy he associated with the baby boomers (born from 1946 to 1964) who would come to represent about 60 percent of the electorate. They had been born into the television age and were into "self-actualization" and "inner-direction," with an interest in values and lifestyles.

They therefore opposed government intervention in their personal lives as well as in economic affairs. In all this, Atwater was exploring prevailing attitudes, which he saw as more deeply ingrained than opinions, emotional as much as intellectual. All this resulted in a more fluid political context than in the past and challenged campaigns to engage with voters' attitudes. The logic was "to find the specific example, the outrageous abuse, the easy-to-digest take that made listeners feel—usually repulsion—rather than think."

For Bush's presidential campaign of 1988, the election had to be about Dukakis rather than Bush, who was assumed to suffer from his privileged background and his association with some of the less savory moments of the Reagan presidency. Initially the polls went against him. Rescue came in the form of Willie Horton, a Massachusetts prison inmate, who committed armed robbery and rape after being let out on a weekend furlough program that Dukakis had supported as governor. While sparring for the Democratic nomination, Al Gore had mentioned that Dukakis had handed out "weekend passes for convicted criminals." Nothing more came of this, but Atwater's team took note, researched the issue, and saw how badly it could damage Dukakis. "Willie Horton has star quality," exclaimed Atwater, "Willie's going to be politically furloughed to terrorize again. It's a wonderful mix of liberalism and a big black rapist."[38] Ronald Reagan had established a similar plan in California, and the one in Massachusetts was set up by Dukakis's Republican predecessor. Although Dukakis did not want to abandon the policy, he had agreed to tighten it when it involved first-degree murderers. Yet this was turned into a story about Dukakis as a weak liberal making a habit of releasing rapists and murders to commit crimes. The main ad introducing Horton was not an official part of the Bush campaign, but Republicans followed it up remorselessly (Illinois Republicans: "All the murderers and rapists and drug pushers and child molesters in Massachusetts vote for Michael Dukakis." Maryland Republicans had a flier showing Dukakis with a fearsome-looking Horton: "Is This Your Pro-Family Team for 1988?"). Horton was used to address issues of crime and race, the latter more subliminally. Dukakis's image of being indifferent to crime was reinforced when he answered a question in a presidential debate about how he would respond to his wife being raped and murdered by restating his opposition to capital punishment. Although by the time the ad appeared, Bush was already ahead of Dukakis, the Democrat later said that the failure to respond was "the biggest mistake of my political career."[39]

The Bush team also played the religion card effectively. The movement of southern evangelicals toward the Republicans continued. They might support Carter but not Mondale, Reagan's opponent in 1984, or Dukakis. In the end, was complicit in his own downfall because he ran a lackluster campaign. The Clinton campaign in 1992 noted well the consequences of failing to respond to negative, personal attacks, as if it would be undignified to offer more than a disdainful silence.

The Permanent Campaign

The Democrats made their own contributions to political strategy. One of the more important, which pre-dated Atwater, was to recognize that elections were only one moment in a stream of activity. A period of intensive campaigning might culminate in an election, but that did not mean that the candidate could get on with the business of governing, the ostensible purpose of all this effort. It was Jimmy Carter who stretched the campaigning season at both ends. His campaign manager Hamilton Jordan advised him to start as early as possible to get name recognition, which required early fundraising so that he could get involved in the early state primaries. This was described by journalist Arthur Hadley as the "Invisible Primary," the period between the end of one election campaign and the formal start of the next with the first state primaries, during which time prospective candidates need to prepare themselves, in particular by raising funds. For the same reason the period has also been referred to as the "money primary."

It was a natural step from the invisible primary to the "permanent campaign," a concept introduced by Pat Caddell (Carter's pollster) in a memo written in December 1976, during the transition, when he observed that: "Too many good people have been defeated because they tried to substitute substance for style; they forgot to give the public the kind of visible signals that it needs to understand what is happening." According to Caddell, "governing with public approval requires a continuing political campaign." The concept was developed by Sidney Blumenthal, a journalist who later became an advisor to Bill Clinton.[40] One imperative behind the permanent campaign was the intensity of the daily news cycle and evidence of the costs of failure to deal with negative material as soon as it first appeared. The sense that the daily narrative mattered at least as much as and possibly more than the business of policy formation and government pushed short-termism to its limits.

In 1992, the lesson the Clinton campaign drew from the Willie Horton episode and the general ease with which the Democratic nominees Walter Mondale and Michael Dukakis had been blown aside in the previous two elections was that there must be an immediate and aggressive riposte to any negative campaigning from the opposition. As soon as stories of Clinton's infidelity surfaced during the primaries, the team was able to swing into action and deflect attention away from them. Campaign manager James Carville told Hillary Clinton that the campaign needed a "focal point...It's gotta look like a military campaign. I want some maps up there, some signs, anything to project a sense of urgency. I almost wish we could get some big electronic color-coded map." Clinton's response was that this was "a war room." There were similarities between electi ons and war as a battle between two opposing camps in which there could only be one winner. Carville admitted that while he began by trying to "look at things in an analytical, calculating way and not let my own emotions get in there," in practice "it never works. I end up hating the opposition, I hate the media, I hate everybody who is not completely swept up in getting my candidate elected. If you're not in a campaign, if you're not living it every day, if you're not working eighteen hours a day, you're not part of this." On the same basis, he added: "And, it almost never fails, I always fall in love with my candidate." Staying with the war metaphor, it was much more satisfying to be on the offensive. It was much more "psychically rewarding" to "slash the opposition than to cobble together another round of gushy, flag-waving, isn't-our-guy-great ads."[41] In 2012, Carville provided an enthusiastic commentary on a guide to electioneering in ancient Rome, noting the advice to go negative early ("smear these men at every opportunity with the crimes, sexual scandals, and corruption they have brought on themselves").[42]

In a book written with another veteran of the 1992 campaign, Carville explained his philosophy by linking it to the demands of the media. The starting point was an observation he attributed to Ailes. If a politician called the media to announce a cure for cancer and then fell into the orchestra pit, the headline would be "Politician Falls into Orchestra Pit." As the media were only interested in scandals, gaffes, polls, and attacks, the only hope of controlling the agenda was going on the attack.[43] Attacks could be prepared over time, waiting for the right moment to pounce, but timing was still essential, linked to both the progressive contraction of the news cycle, which created a media appetite for a new story even before the last one had fully worked its way through, and to the small chunks of time allowed by broadcasters for any story. In 1968, each candidate could be heard without interruption on network news for 42.3 seconds; by 2000, the length of a sound bite was 7.8 seconds.

This led to a stress on the importance of speed, which in turn put a premium on accuracy, agility, and flexibility. There was no time for the "paralysis of analysis" and no "second chance to make a first impression." The original media take was the one that would last, so it was important to be the first in the news cycle and not the follow-up. Once a judgment was made and acted upon, there could be no second thoughts; hesitation would be fatal. To frame the debate, the core message must be simple and repeated relentlessly. Communication required memorable stories: "Facts tell, but stories sell." Carville's team worked the media continually, making sure that the right messages were received after the debates and that nothing negative about the Bush campaign was missed. Having noted Dukakis's fate, a rapid-response team was set up to respond to any challenge to the candidate. Even as Bush was delivering his acceptance speech in 1992, point-by-point rebuttals were being sent out. By the time of the candidates' debates, knowledge of Bush's stances and his record in office was leading to "prebuttals," countering his claims before he actually made them.[44] Whether or not they were aware of each other, Carville was following Boyd's OODA loop by seeking to keep the opponent disoriented. At the final meeting of the aptly named war room, the slogan on his T-shirt read "Speed Killed...Bush."

The steady domination of negative campaigning at all levels of American politics reflected the conviction of candidates and campaign strategists that it worked, especially when races were tight and money was not a major constraint.[45] The reason why it could work was that people tended to be more attentive to negative than positive information, in part because it raised issues of risk (Can this person be trusted with my security and standard of living?). Positive messages extolling the virtues of the candidate were less likely to elicit a strong response. Negative messages would not work so well either, if they were too shrill, came into the crude "mud-slinging" category, or appeared irrelevant to current concerns. A riotous youth or past infidelities were likely to be seen as irrelevant, unless the candidate appeared incompetent or devious when allegations were made.[46] Rebuttal was therefore important not only to deny allegations but also to demonstrate that the targeted candidate posed no risk. In addition, as with all messages, there would be multiple audiences. A constant problem in national campaigns was that the claims that might inspire the base could turn off moderate opinion.

This was one of the important lessons of 1992. Aware of the danger, Clinton was well placed to neutralize attacks from Bush. He could focus on the tough economic conditions and the need for change by regular references to twelve Reagan/Bush years. As a southerner, he could also play the populist role identified by Atwater, skillfully adopting religious themes but giving them a more liberal twist, by speaking of a "new covenant" and "one nation under God." In this he was helped by Bush believing that he could continue to play to the religious right without alarming the more secular center.[47]

Bush, having so effectively used religion in 1988, found it did not work so well for him this time. Part of his problem was that the persistent push from the Moral Majority had led to the Republican Party taking minority positions on matters that might have been considered more social than political. The evangelicals, now joined by Catholics, compared themselves to the abolitionists by presenting abortion as the equivalent of slavery. They not only opposed same-sex marriage but condemned homosexuality. Paul Weyrich declared that "if you're for gay rights, you're violating a specifically articulated tenet of Holy Scripture."[48] The target then became the Supreme Court, for it had banned school prayer, permitted legal abortion, and tolerated same-sex relationships. Meanwhile, as they sought constitutional amendments and challenged judicial nominees on these issues, they were urging the Republican Party away from an equal-rights amendment. At the Republican Convention in 1992, the Christian Coalition hosted a "God and Country" rally, Jerry Falwell had a prominent seat in the hall, and the Republican platform—along with many of the convention speeches— was full of religious language. In his acceptance speech, Bush criticized the Democrats for leaving three letters out of their platform: "G-O-D."

The move backfired. There was no post-convention "bounce" for Bush in the polls. The pollsters recorded anxiety at divisive attempts to suggest that the opposition was irreligious, and the extremity of some of the positions being taken by Bush's Christian supporters. "The feminist agenda," observed Pat Robertson, "is not about equal rights for women. It is about a socialist, anti-family political movement that encourages women to leave their husbands, kill their children, practice witchcraft, destroy capitalism and become lesbians."[49] The associations damaged Bush; he was putting himself outside mainstream social values and ducking the main issue, the economy.

The problem was the social policy rather than the religious inspiration. After all in 2000, Bush's son, George W., could claim when asked in debate which thinker influenced him most, "Christ," he replied, "because he changed my heart." Evangelist Billy Graham described this as a "beautiful answer." The younger Bush continued to speak of an almost intimate relationship with God, and still got the votes.

In 1992, the Republican problem was that they were missing the significance of changes taking place in American society. Dan Quayle, Bush's running mate in both elections, had sought to identify the Republican Party with traditional values. "The gap between ourselves and our opponents," he had declared in 1988, "is a cultural divide." At the 1992 convention he wanted to demonstrate the importance of the family. To do so, he picked on Murphy Brown, a fictional character played by Candace Bergen in a television comedy series. The latest plotline had her deciding to become a single mother. Quayle complained this ignored "the importance of fathers by birthing a child alone." It illustrated the challenge being posed to the American family, connected with the rise in divorce, sexual permissiveness, crime, and a general moral decline. This was soon shown to be a muddled line of attack. Would she have been a better model if she had gotten an abortion instead? It was also unwise to attack single mothers, working women, and the divorced—a substantial segment of the American electorate. By 1990, only about a quarter of American families approximated the nuclear family ideal. The percentage of mothers in the workforce with children under 18 was 27 percent in 1955; by 1992, it was 76.2 percent. Women, who were also often uncomfortable with the Republican anti-abortion stance, were soon moving into Clinton's camp.[50]

Given Bill Clinton's success in the 1990s, it was a surprise that in 2008 his wife Hillary lost an intense battle for the presidential nomination of the Democratic Party to an outsider, Barack Obama, who had apparent disadvantages of being of mixed race and liberal. Both offered "firsts" if elected—either the first female president or the first black president. In other respects, the intensity of the struggle reflected the similarities of the candidates. Both were senators who had trained as lawyers. Clinton was more senior, could claim broader experience, and—as the former first lady—came out of the party establishment. Obama was the insurgent, who had only recently achieved a national profile and had been an early opponent of the unpopular Iraq War. Beyond that, their policy differences were not huge. Obama was a gifted orator, and it was tempting to attribute his success to his way with words. He also symbolized the American dream, for he had overcome many disadvantages to aspire to the country's top job.

It was not just in oratory (he was bested in many of the debates by Clinton) but in basic organization that Obama scored. His strategy was set out clearly enough in June 2007, when his campaign had yet to make much headway in the polls. It was going to be a "classic insurgent's campaign," relying on a "surge of momentum from early-state victories." He was already winning the fundraising race in terms of the number of contributors and the amount raised. David Axelrod, his chief strategist, explained that they were not running a national campaign but focusing hard on the early states with an aim of getting a "sequential series" of victories. There was, it was noted, nothing new in the script. Reform candidates would always try to combine grassroots energy with media momentum, and they normally failed.[51]

Looking back on the victory against Clinton, Obama's campaign manager, David Plouffe, observed that what made the difference was the combination of a clear message—which was an amalgam of "vision, issues and biography"—and identifying the "most accessible path to a winning vote margin." Part of the strategy was not to change the strategy. There would be no dithering or second-guessing. They stuck with a core slogan and allocated time and resources strictly by reference to the chosen approach through the many caucuses and primaries. Plouffe quoted Obama as saying he was not going "to cast about for a political identity," and one of George W. Bush's advisors who observed that he would "rather have one flawed strategy than seven different strategies." A key factor was using technology, in particular becoming the dominant Internet presence. Having started in early 2007 with ten thousand email addresses, the Obama campaign had over five million by June 2008. Of these, 40 percent had either volunteered or contributed. The people they needed to attract were already immersed in social networking and the Internet, and this made it easier for them to engage with the campaign. They did not rely solely on digital communications but also on traditional media, direct mail, and personal conversations.

> The principle underlying this was fairly simple: we live in a busy and fractured world in which people are bombarded with pleas for their attention. Given this, you have to try extra hard to reach them. You need to be everywhere. And for people you reach multiple times through different mediums, you need to be sure your message is consistent.[52]

Obama's campaign also benefited from wider demographic shifts. America was becoming a more diverse society, racially and culturally, and the Republicans risked being seen as the party of a white, male middle-class elite that had once been dominant but was now on the defensive. The underlying coalitions behind the American parties were shifting again. For three decades the Republicans had benefited from the reaction to the cultural shifts foreshadowed in the 1960s; now these shifts were starting to make themselves felt in turn.

In somewhat unfortunate timing, a book published in 2002 promised an emerging Democrat majority based on the fact that those sections of the population most inclined to vote for the Democrats were growing: upper-class professionals, working women, blacks, Asian-Americans, and Hispanics.[53] The problem was not with the trends but with the framing. From September 2001, the issue was national security and George W. Bush worked hard to use his status as commander in chief to forge a winning coalition. By 2006, as a result of events in Iraq, this was wearing thin. By 2008, it completely failed to work for a Republican candidate in the face of developing economic crisis, which reached crisis proportions during the closing stages of the campaign and for which the Republican Party was taking the blame.

There was therefore nothing automatic about a new political realignment in the United States. It required an ability to relate to the shifting demographic and socioeconomic trends with messages that were both appealing and credible. In this respect, the Republican Party did face a problem if its main appeal continued to be to white voters, particularly from rural areas and without higher education. The themes that worked in the 1970s and 1980s were increasingly turning off new voters while at the same time continuing to motivate Republican Party activists, especially those associated with the Tea Party movement, whose prime motivation was to defend a way of life and set of values they saw as threatened.

The two candidates who battled it out for the Democratic nomination in 2008 illustrated the shifts in attitudes that had taken place since the 1960s. They both had a Chicago link. It was Clinton's home town and it was where Obama settled and learned his political trade. Chicago provided another link: Saul Alinsky.[54] Clinton, the former student radical, had written her senior year thesis about Alinsky while a student at Wellesley College in 1969, in which she described him as "that rare specimen, the successful radical."[55] He had even offered her a job. Obama, who was castigated during the campaign for his connections to Bill Ayers, a former member of the Weathermen, worked in the mid-1980s in the community organization established by Alinsky in Chicago. Once Obama had secured the nomination in 2008, a number of his Republican opponents sought to use the Alinsky connection to discredit him, portraying him as a replica of this Marxist firebrand who preferred direct action to democratic politics. Obama's rise could be seen as a vindication of Rustin's belief that black political advancement would most likely come through working the system. Both represented the triumph of an ethic of responsibility over one of ultimate ends.

The ethic of responsibility was intended by Weber to undermine those prepared to risk calamity in the pursuit of utopian goals. Had he lived he would have found grim vindication in the onset of totalitarianism. This represented the victories of those revolutionary utopians of both left and right who formed vanguard parties to seize power. The few who were successful (Lenin, Hitler, Mao, and Castro) came to be idolized as heroic strategists. They were celebrated for their foresight, grasp of theory, resolve, and dedication as they saw and took opportunities for power missed by lesser mortals, playing down the extent to which they might have been helped by circumstances or the errors of their opponents. Western liberal democracies rejected this model. They came to define themselves in opposition to totalitarianism by asserting a commitment to the rule of law and rejection of cults of personality.

The corollary of limits to arbitrary power was limits to what political strategy could be expected to achieve. Constitutions must be respected, terms of office honored, spurious reasons to eliminate opponents or muzzle the media resisted. This reduced possibilities for one-party rule—domination of one group over another—but also the definitive resolution of disputes. The result was constant but inconclusive and restrained political struggle. Strategy was in regular demand, even as its scope was restricted. No sooner was one election over than preparations had to be made for the next. Legislative programs were subject to attempted influence, challenge, and potential repeal. Social movements generated divisions within their ranks as well as counter movements. All this could keep numerous amateur and professional strategists very busy but offered few definitive victories. Only on occasion, when political efforts combined with broad social and economic changes, could new ways of thinking be institutionalized, transformational policies implemented, or new constitutional provisions enacted to the point where it came to be forgotten that these were once contentious. This is what happened, for example, with the civil rights movement or the introduction of the welfare state. The normal political experience was of more modest advances and regular frustration. Not all campaigns were winnable, resources imposed constraints on what could be achieved, the most compelling narratives were temporary, coalitions were fragile, and overpromising created hostages to fortune. The best causes could be misunderstood, the best legislation could be misinterpreted, and the best candidates could make stupid mistakes. When the going got tough, there would always be temptations to focus on personalities, usually negatively, rather than issues. This was perhaps not what the progressive proponents of pragmatism had in mind, because they hoped that it would provide a means to transcend social divisions. Instead, political life could at times appear irresponsible and even outrageous in its practices. Yet, in another sense, this was the logic of eschewing an ethic of ultimate ends. This messy, infuriating, unceasing political activity reflected the limiting logic of an ethic of responsibility.

PART IV | Strategy from Above

CHAPTER 28 | The Rise of the Management Class

Imagine the consequences of that comprehensive bureaucratization and
rationalization which already today we see approaching. Already now,
throughout private enterprise in wholesale manufacture, as well as in all
other economic enterprises run on modern lines... rational calculation is
manifest at every stage. By it, the performance of each individual worker
is mathematically measured, each man becomes a little cog in the machine,
and, aware of this, his one preoccupation is to become a bigger cog.

—Max Weber, *1909*

THE PREVIOUS SECTION was concerned with strategy from below, that
is, how those who lacked power sought to acquire it for the people they
claimed to represent. This section is concerned with those who already had
power, in the sense of being in a position to take authoritative decisions,
but had to work out what to do with it. The focus is largely on business,
but much of the discussion is as relevant to those at the top of any large
organization, including in the public sector. This group, which we will call
the managers, has been the recipient of more strategic advice than any other
group, including generals. The provision of advice to the top of organizations and then to subunits explains why the idea of strategy became so
ubiquitous.

Strategy was necessary because relationships were complicated. Executives in a major corporation, for example, would have to deal at the same time, inter alia, with owners, unit heads, suppliers, competitors, governments, and customers. Each relationship was likely to involve a mixture of cooperation and conflict, often in ways that were not quite captured in the official rhetoric of partnership and collegiality internally and cutthroat competition externally. The challenges of managing down the vertical axis of the organizational hierarchy would be quite different to doing so across the horizontal axis of competitors and regulatory bodies, and thus generated different types of strategic literature. Because the advice in this literature was largely generic and often not geared to any particular scenario, it discussed relationships in broad terms, more about how to relate over time to the internal and external operating environments than how to mount specific campaigns. It was more about the impact of changes in administrative practice or available technology than how to address the power of others. The diversity of relationships, activities, and structures meant that management strategy struggled more with theory than did the military and political spheres. There developed a relationship with the social sciences as intense as it was unsatisfactory. The interactions with economics, largely in the form of game theory, and sociology, largely in the form of organization theory, demonstrated both the possibilities and the limitations of the social sciences.

In this section, therefore, we will take forward issues of contemporary social theory, which began in the last section with consideration of notions of paradigms and narratives. Just as the rise of the managers represented the logic of bureaucratization and rationalism, so too was the rise of the social sciences. They developed as reflections on and studies of modern industrial societies, with all their upheavals and conflicts, and then came to offer remedies to the troubles they described. Yet the processes of professionalization took them into forms of specialist analysis and presentation that left them detached from those who might have been expected to find their work the most valuable. Theory and action struggled to relate to each other.

The Managers

The derivation of the verb "to manage" is found in late thirteenth-century Italian. *Maneggiare* referred to the ability to handle a horse, drawn from *manus*, the Latin for "hand." It was used in the sixteenth century in this way and eventually moved over to the conduct of any affairs, from war to marriage, from the plot of a novel to personal finances. It suggested something more than administration but less than total control, requiring persuasive or manipulative as well as coercive skills, a flair for extracting more from a person, organization, or situation than might have otherwise been expected. The sense of less than total control remained important. Managing implied coping, dealing with a state of affairs that could never fully be controlled.

The profession of management referred to people employed for their administrative and supervisory skills in handling complex affairs, such as those of an estate or business. For this reason, the role of the manager could be expected to stop short of strategy. Ultimate control, and therefore strategy, would stay in the hands of the owner. This remained the case in standard forms of business governance. Managers reported to a board appointed by the shareholders, responsible for approving budgets and making big decisions. The more complex the organization to be managed, however, the greater the dependence on the managers, and so whatever the organizational charts might say, effective power began to rest with those who actually understood the issues. Full-time managers could soon learn how to frame an issue so that their preferred outcome was the obvious one for a board to take.

As business enterprises grew into massive corporations, the managers appeared to be effectively in charge, with their own preferred candidates appointed to the boards that were notionally supervising them. Nonetheless, management still involved less than control. Managers were employees who could be—and often were—fired when affairs were badly handled. Their success would depend on an ability to get the best out of those beneath them in the hierarchy, but unlike the military chain of command (with which comparisons were natural), there was likely to be a greater range of functions to be coordinated and less reliance on unquestioning obedience.

The notion that management was a new profession of increasing importance, essential to the performance of modern businesses, was recognized in the establishment of business schools. The first was the Wharton School at Pennsylvania, founded in 1881. The management in question, however, was of potentially unruly workforces as much as complex business processes. The "labor issue" was a major preoccupation. Joseph Wharton wished the school to teach "the nature and prevention of strikes" as well as "the necessity for modern industry of organizing under single leaders or employers great amounts of capital and great numbers of laborers, and of maintaining discipline among the latter."[1] A quarter of a century passed before the Harvard Business School opened in 1908. It followed an endowment to promote an "applied science," initially assumed to be engineering. Eventually the university opted for business, raising at once the tension between what many supposed to be vocational training and the university's true purpose of disinterested scholarship. As the first dean, Edwin Gay, searched for a way to resolve this tension he came across the ideas of Frederick Winslow Taylor. Taylor himself was skeptical, to say the least, about the value of a university education. He declined to join the faculty, but he did give regular lectures to the new school, and more importantly, his philosophy permeated the early curriculum.

Taylorism

Taylor had begun work as an engineer in the steel industry where he started to address the question of how the workforce could be used more efficiently. He claimed that he had hit upon a form of management that was "a true science, resting upon clearly defined laws." So the attraction of Taylor was that he offered a way to bring together a business culture, inclined to the practical and suspicious of unnecessary erudition, with an academic culture prone to disparage the merely technical. Dean Harlow Person of the Dartmouth Business School, which had been founded in 1900, described Taylorism as the "only system of management which was coherent and logical, and therefore was teachable." In 1911, Person organized the first international conference on scientific management.[2] For the new managers this was an important development: their expertise and professionalism could now be recognized with proper qualifications and cloaked in academic respectability.

The starting point for Taylor's method was the belief that for each elemental task of an organization there should be "one best way" found through careful analysis and measurement. Those who analyzed and measured, and acted upon the findings, would become a new profession. Here he posited an extremely sharp distinction between planning and doing. The first required very clever people; for the second it did not matter if people were stupid. A doer, he remarked, would not be able to "understand the principles of this science," because of either a "lack of education or insufficient mental capacity," and so would have to be guided at all times by the educated.[3] It required people to work smarter but not by being smart themselves.

The more a worker could be treated as an unthinking machine the better, because without the complication of independent thought it would be possible to calculate how best to extract optimal performance. Part of the pretence of science was the presence of quantification and mathematics in establishing the most efficient way to work with given tools when accomplishing defined tasks. Work tasks would be broken down into constituent elements and then standardized in a form that simple workers could follow. "Time-and-motion" studies used stopwatches to time each element so a rate could be set for its completion. Once the scientific basis of work could be demonstrated, there should be no argument about how it should be done. Thus this would also represent progress in solving the "labor problem." Taylor wrote about workers as natural "loafers," who failed to work as hard as they could. Their managers let them get away with this because they did not know any better. They evaluated performance by rules of thumb and looked to the workers to use their "initiative," which to Taylor meant only that they persisted with traditional, inefficient ways of working. Moreover, without greater efficiency, the management would have to reward the workers with means other than pay, and Taylor clearly thought that pay was the best motivation of all.

Taylor's claims about the efficiency improvements he had achieved in the steel industry were exaggerated. Those for which he took credit could often be attributed to other sources. The limits of his actual achievements were established long after his death, and after his path-breaking work had been described to generations of management students. His basic story was about a worker called Schmidt at Bethlehem Steel (one quarter of this company was owned by Joseph Wharton). Schmidt was presented as an exemplary worker, none too bright but ready to work harder for better pay, who met the target of quadrupling the amount of pig iron loaded. Charles Wrege and Amadeo Perroni, who discovered just how flawed Taylor's research had been, regretted that he had not been scrutinized early enough, before this idol with "feet of clay" had been "hoisted onto a pedestal."[4] Jill Hough and Margaret White later came to Taylor's defense, arguing that his purpose was to argue for a new approach, that the discrepancies between his account and the evidence were not that great, and that others successfully replicated his results. The original story must have been embellished, but this was still a compelling way to illustrate his arguments about industrial efficiency. The stories were part of Taylor's strategy: acts of communication rather than research reports. He should therefore be viewed "with an artistic appreciation for his story telling style" and recognition that his principles have served as a building block for later theorists addressing issues such as how to select and train workers, especially for standardized procedures. The basic lesson remained: "Even the most basic processes can be substantially improved while providing benefit to both employer and employee."[5]

Certainly Taylor packaged his ideas in a systematic and coherent manner. By this means he was able to turn himself into the first management "guru" providing seminars to business leaders and with a bestselling and influential book, *The Principles of Scientific Management*. After he died in 1915, described on his gravestone as "The Father of Scientific Management," his followers—such as Henry Gantt and Frank and Lillian Gilbreth—continued to develop and spread his ideas.[6] They promoted a form of "aggressive rationality," with science sweeping away custom and superstition for the benefit of all.[7] This involved, as Taylor put it, a "mental revolution," required of both the workers and the management. Instead of arguing about the division of the current profit they should work together to increase the size of the profit to mutual benefit. Here was the key to another part of Taylor's appeal. He was offering a great compromise between management and labor, made possible by a new caste of "efficiency engineers." Peter Drucker, who three decades later saw himself picking up where Taylor had left off, suggested that scientific management

> may well be the most powerful as well as the most lasting contribution America has made to Western thought since the Federalist Papers. As long as industrial society endures, we shall never lose again the insight that human work can be studied systematically, can be analyzed, can be improved by work on its elementary parts.[8]

This philosophy was in tune with the temper of the times. Taylor opened his book by urging efficiency as a great national goal rather than just one for companies. He hoped the principles could be applied to all social activities, from the management of homes to churches, universities, and government departments.

The idea that this was a "science," which raised the standing of Taylor's claims, came from progressive lawyer Louis Brandeis, who eventually became a member of the Supreme Court. During a court case in 1910, Brandeis challenged a rise in freight rates on the railroads and sought to show how the railroads could save money by introducing new techniques (described as "scientific management") rather than by charging more. Brandeis's advocacy went well beyond the courtroom. He linked scientific management with a wider social goal of "universal preparedness." Planning in the form of a predetermined schedule, clear instructions, and constant supervision would bring great rewards: "Errors are prevented instead of being corrected. The terrible waste of delays and accidents is avoided. Calculation is substituted for guess; demonstration for opinion."[9] Brandeis was by no means the only figure in the progressive movement to see Taylor as the answer to a rationalist's dream. The investigative journalist Ida Tarbell praised Taylor as one of the creative geniuses of the time, contributing to "genuine cooperation and juster human relations."[10] Science offered a way to circumvent the powerful conflicts that threatened to tear industrial society apart and a way to promote the general good out of the tangle of clashing sectional interests.

The progressives were particularly interested in Taylor because they were perplexed by the large organizations that were now essential to economic growth but challenged both liberal economic and democratic theory. Thus far they had gone for legal solutions, trying to cut the large corporations down to size. Scientific management suggested a possible administrative solution. "Efficiency" fit in with the progressive conviction that science rather than intuition could provide a neutral and objective basis for evaluating policies and reorganizing society to serve the needs of the majority rather than the self-interest of the few. Brandeis urged the labor unions to embrace it, taking the chance to become actively involved in running the enterprises which employed them. To the dismay, even bewilderment, of the progressives, the unions bitterly resisted Taylorism. They had no interest in blurring the line between capital and labor and understood that at root scientific management was not about partnership but centralized control based on strict hierarchy. Providing management with insights into core tasks undermined workers' control over the shop floor and treated them in a patronizing and dehumanizing manner. They saw Taylor's methods as means by which more could be extracted from workers without commensurate reward.

The hostility to Taylorism in the labor movement makes its adoption by the Soviet Union even more significant. Before the revolution, Lenin studied Taylor and pronounced his methods exploitative—at least so long as they were being applied within capitalism. A fourfold increase in productivity would not lead to a commensurate increase in wages. Yet the ideas continued to intrigue him and once in power, facing a desperate economic situation, he urged their careful study. In May 1918, he advised that this "last word in capitalism" be adapted for socialist purposes. "We must introduce in Russia the study and teaching of the new Taylor System and its systematic trial and adaptation." He recognized that this would mean drawing on bourgeois experts in a system that the unions had bitterly opposed. But this would be different, Lenin insisted, for now the "workers' commissars" could watch management's "every step."[11] It was Trotsky, charged as commissar of war, who followed this up with enthusiasm, against the objections of the so-called left-communists who saw this as another example of the new regime's move away from true socialism.

Lenin and Trotsky had little trouble with a system dependent on an enlightened elite and docile followers. For Trotsky, this was about the "wise expenditure of human strength participating in production." The work of Taylor and his acolytes was published and applied, and a number of theorists were invited to the Soviet Union as advisors. The urgency came because of the struggle to cope with a country whose infrastructure was in a mess and where a civil war was raging. Discipline and productivity were essential. For the same reasons, the Bolsheviks welcomed returning tsarist administrators, engineers, and officers with vital practical knowledge. Part of this package was piecework for workers and bonuses for specialists. Unions were abolished on the grounds that in a socialist society they were no longer necessary.

In the short term, all this effort did help raise productivity and sort out the infrastructure. In the longer term, it helped set the framework for the Soviet system of industrial organization, based on centralized planning and detailed instructions to workers who had little choice but to obey as well as they could, more out of fear of punishment than expectation of reward. The system as it evolved during the1920s, including the abolition of the unions and the militarization of industry, has been described as "Taylorism with teeth."[12] This is not to hold Taylorism responsible for everything that befell the Soviet Union. In the circumstances of the time, there were many reasons why Lenin and Trotsky—and then Stalin—would have been inclined to regiment the Soviet workforce. It fit in with their ideological predispositions and authoritarian leadership. Nor were they applying Taylor as his followers, who tended to be less bombastic in their claims, intended. But the grotesque version of scientific management that emerged in the Soviet Union, disconnecting planning from doing, relying on instructions from the center to a disciplined workforce, and persistent insistence on "one best way," in the end illustrated the limits of the approach when followed to its logical conclusion.

Mary Parker Follett

In some respects, it became far easier to push Taylorism in the Soviet Union, where resistance was crushed, than in the United States, where resistance remained active and labor unrest high. This led to a search for a business strategy that went beyond extracting greater efficiency out of the workforce but also addressed the broader "labor problem." The management theorists of this time claimed a way forward to harmony through better management.

Mary Parker Follett was as much a philosopher as a social scientist, with an impressive background in social work and education rather than business. She was following in the same line as Jane Addams, that of a "social feminist." This built on a traditional woman's role but broadened it to include "city housekeeping," which suffered—according to Addams—because women, who understood such things, had not been properly consulted. Follett followed Addams into community work and progressive politics. Like Addams she challenged the popular dichotomies of the time, whether elite/mass or capital/labor, as imposing divisions instead of creating an integrated community. The crude elitist view that some were better than others seemed to her to be a recipe for disharmony and discord. In particular, she objected to the word *masses* and she challenged Le Bon's corrupting "conception of people as a crowd," susceptible to "the spread of similarities by suggestion and imitation."

Her aim was to find means of bringing the community together as an integrated whole.[13] Follett objected to the idea of power ("the ability to make things happen") when it was a domineering "power over." Exercising power in this way left the dominated resentful and reluctant to change their prior positions, which would be reasserted as soon as an opportunity arose. Better to have "power with," because all energies—not just those of elites—would then be mobilized in the same direction toward shared goals. This faith in humanity led her to view democracy in terms of the evolving views of individuals coming together in groups. There was so much going on within any group, with ideas interweaving, modifying, and reinforcing each other; returning in new forms; and focusing on shared problems. Crude assertions of interest would be undermined and prejudices challenged. The outcome would represent integration, her key goal. There would neither be individuals nor society but "only the group and the group-unit—the social individual." In this context, consent should be positive and not grudging, a result of participation in decisions and a sense of shared responsibility and ownership. She was not after partnerships between previously antagonistic entities, such as negotiated agreements between management and unions, for these were inherently non-creative. The integrated outcomes she sought would be far more valuable. In this way (and following Dewey), democracy was a process as much as an attainment, informed by the interplay of individual interventions. Authority would come not from specific individuals but from "the law of the situation" which required all to accept and address the problem as framed. If anything, therefore, her approach was anti-strategic, creating situations which it would be difficult for individuals to manipulate.

Although her views developed as she addressed the larger issues of democratic theory, her stress on the importance of group processes, and her determination to turn conflict into a creative rather than a destructive factor, led her naturally into the study of organizations. From 1926, she began to challenge business groups about the need to view their enterprises within the wider social context. She urged them to reassess their reliance on delegation and take advantage of the social bonds forged within groups,[14] arguing the need for more bottom-up approaches to management and innovation. Follett now appears ahead of her time with her strictures against micromanagement ("bossiness"), in favor of flatter management structures and participatory approaches. She argued the importance of the more informal aspects of business organization, noting how social interactions contributed to overall performance. At the same time she did not challenge Taylorism directly, accepting the expanded role for management and the advantages of authority being vested in those with technical expertise and access to knowledge. This did not remove hierarchy, but at least it was not based on social position nor exercised arbitrarily. The problem went back to consent, and was reflected in her definition of management as "the art of getting things done through people."[15]

Follett was influential in her time more as a social philosopher than as a management theorist, although she did have practical experience in Boston on management-union relations and the development of personnel policies. Her mission can be discerned from the title of her 1918 book: *The New State: Group Organization—The Solution of Popular Government.* Here she observed, "Our political life is stagnating, capital and labor are virtually at war, the nations of Europe are at one another's throats because we have not yet learned how to live together."[16] Her remedy, however, only worked when the conditions were already in place, when there was a prior willingness to work together on shared problems. Beyond that, there was little more than an injunction to put differences aside and think about power relations differently. The method required that people did not think strategically for themselves but only on behalf of the group. This did not of course mean that the integrated outcome would be wise or appropriate, noted much later in reference to "groupthink" when individuals reinforced each others' wrong assumptions.[17] Furthermore, as representatives of groups met with each other in a higher group, were they supposed to disregard the views of the lower group in pursuit of a higher integration? If each group was responding to the laws of its own situation, then at some point the variations in group situations would matter, and there would still be conflict to be resolved by hard bargaining or else a tough fight. Follett's shrewd observations on group dynamics illustrated the organizational benefits of enlightened self-interest, but they provided no answer to the problems of conflict, the point at which strategy would be most needed.

The Human Relations School

Follett overlapped with another group of management theorists, with whom she is often associated and almost certainly influenced, the so-called human relations school. These other theorists had a harder edge to their philosophy and were more clearly part of the elitist school, although they also stressed the importance of social networks in making organizations work. A key figure here was Elton Mayo, an Australian who managed to get himself attached to Harvard Business School in 1926 and whose name has come to be linked to the first sociological studies of industrial practice at Western Electric's Hawthorne plant near Chicago. Before considering how he got to Harvard and the Hawthorne studies, it is worth noting his general views.

Mayo did not present himself as a fan of Western civilization, individualism, or democracy. In his view, democracy took advantage of voter emotions and irrationality, left little room for reason, encouraged class war, and favored "collective mediocrity" rather than the sovereignty of the "highest skill." The idea of workplace democracy, which appealed to Follett, was anathema to Mayo, for it would hand over control to people who had no real understanding of business issues. His knowledge of psychological theory encouraged him in his belief that economics could not grasp the human factor because it ignored the extent to which feeling and irrationality shaped motives. It also suggested how to deal with conflict without addressing what were claimed to be the underlying issues. Radical movements and industrial unrest were not responses to genuine grievances but more the expression of the "hidden fires of mental uncontrol." If agitators were essentially neurotic, "prone to conspiratorial delusions, with minds obsessed with rage and the savage lust of destruction," then democratic processes could do little to help. In fact they made matters worse, dividing society into two hostile camps and leading workers, unaware of the real sources of their discontent, to pursue "will-o-the-wisp phantasies with all the energy of his starving intellect and will." Mayo's remedy was to treat not the material conditions of the working class but the psychopathological tendencies of democracy, reflected in disoriented lives, disintegrated personalities, and disordered values.[18]

Mayo's views were well known when the dean of the Harvard Business School, Wallace Donham, approached him about joining the faculty. Donham was a banker who had trained at Harvard Law School. After being appointed in 1919, he stayed until the early 1940s. He saw his task as raising the academic standards of the school while also improving links with business. This was essential for fundraising, but Donham also had to contend with the university's reputation for harboring radicals and socialists. Funding for Mayo eventually came directly from industry rather than the university. The attraction of Mayo lay in his underlying views, which Donham shared, and in his claimed expertise in psychology. The gap to be filled was explained in a letter to the university's president in 1927: "I see no really promising hope of lessening the critical nature of the Labor Problem in Industry except through a scientific study of Industrial Physiology including Psychology." As O'Connor observed, "Mayo's research spoke directly to the core of executive concerns: it revolved around how to calm the worker's irrational, agitation-prone mind and how to develop a curriculum to train managers and executives to do so." In 1933, Mayo reinforced the point. The problem was not the lack of an "able administrative elite," but the elite's lack of understanding of the "biological and social facts involved in social organization and control." Donham saw training this elite as an essential task for the business school.[19]

Complementing the efficient physical engineering of the ordinary worker by Taylor, Mayo offered a psychological revival. Like Taylor, Mayo also had a story about how he realized this could be done, this time based on a flash of inspiration as he pondered the meaning of experiments with a small group of workers at Western Electric's Hawthorne plant. The research, which had begun well before Mayo joined, was designed to see whether changes in physical conditions, such as better illumination, made much difference to productivity. In this regard, the most important stage in the experiments involved a group of six women working on relay assembly. The aim was to ascertain the impact of rest periods and hours of work. Eventually it was decided to consider them on a group rather than an individual, so that there was a shared bonus for higher productivity. The researchers found a 30 percent increase of productivity over two and a half years, along with greater work satisfaction.

Explanations of exactly why this had happened were uncertain until, as Mayo reported, he had his "great éclaircissement" and realized what made the difference was that the researchers were actually showing interest in them. His large conclusion was that psychological conditions were more important than the physical and that workers responded to their own group dynamics and informal social networks. Motivations went beyond self-interest into seeking recognition and security. The recommendation was that management should seek a good working relationship with their staff, and that happy workers would be more productive. As with Taylor, the original story was embellished and interpreted within Mayo's own preconceived notions. Once again a simple explanation was offered to make sense of a complex set of facts. In retrospect, the best explanation for the improvements in productivity was a combination of pay incentives (in a non-unionized plant and against the background of the depression) and the attitudes of individual workers. The replacement of two women who had not joined in the spirit of the experiment by two who did was a turning point.[20] Mayo's conclusion was not in itself preposterous. It fit in with the theories of Follett in encouraging managers to view their workers in more rounded, softer, human terms and was widely considered to have encouraged a turn for the better in management practice.

In this way the so-called human relations school was founded, attending to the informal aspects of the organization and the social conditions of the workplace. Mayo's place was assured in the history of industrial sociology, though were it not for the Hawthorne experiments he would by now be forgotten. He had exaggerated his own qualifications, including his psychiatric training, and was considered by colleagues to be snobbish, lazy, and uninterested in teaching, with only the occasional publication to his name. As we have seen, Mayo's underlying philosophy was deeply conservative, seeing conflict as in effect a "social disease" to be remedied by healthy cooperation across the supposed divides.[21] By the same token, cooperation among workers for their own ends was unhealthy. Because he saw politics as aggravating the problem, and was generally reluctant to consider the problem of power, any solution was the responsibility of the administrative elite, who must be trained to develop social competence to match their technical competence.

In the Hawthorne Studies, the claimed positive response had been to inadvertently enlightened researchers rather than truly enlightened managers. In the mid-1930s, Mayo made acquaintance with Chester Barnard, president of New Jersey Bell, a cerebral man and a voracious reader with hard experience in industry and practical administration. By 1938 he was giving lectures at Harvard. With some rewriting, these were turned into what is now considered to be a seminal text on management thought, *The Functions of the Executive*. Barnard forged an extraordinary bond with the physiologist Lawrence Henderson, a leading figure in the university and a colleague of Mayo's. This was based on their shared interest in the Italian sociologist and notable elitist Vilfredo Pareto.

Having discovered Pareto in the mid-1920s, Henderson became something of an evangelist in the 1930s, establishing what became known as the "Pareto Circle" at Harvard. To Henderson's scientific mind, Pareto's notions of social equilibrium struck a chord as well as matched his own conservative inclinations. Although he dominated the circle, with a seminar technique that was said to be "only feebly imitated by a pile-driver," the group did include people such as Talcott Parsons and George Homans among the most influential of their generation of sociologists.[22] It was also a refuge for conservative academics seeking an alternative to Marx and attracted by the underlying treatment of society as an interdependent and largely self-correcting system. Henderson was impressed by Barnard as a man who not only had read Pareto originally in French but had sought to apply his ideas in the real world.

Pareto's influence can certainly be detected in Barnard. This was evident in his stress on nonlogical factors in human decision and action, on how choice was shaped by the logic of situations, and on the circulation of elites. Pareto is there in the idea of organizations as social systems analogous to human bodies seeking some sort of equilibrium. To achieve equilibrium, the organization needed to achieve both effectiveness and efficiency, and he emphasized how many declined because they failed both tests. By efficiency he meant the ability to satisfy the individuals who made up the organization; effectiveness involved the ability to meet goals. Management must formulate the organizational goals and decide how to meet them, but it must do so in a way that kept all members involved, not least through forms of direct and accessible communications. He emphasized the importance of respect and cooperation, suggesting—in line with Mayo—that the former was more important than material incentives and that the latter was put at risk by divisive ideologies and forms of political action. In both these aspects, the workforce was prone to mistaken notions about their interests and therein lay the special leadership role of management.[23]

In addition to their technical and social skills, managers should work actively to create a cooperative organization underpinned by appropriate values. Otherwise the organization would fail.[24] It was therefore important "to educate and to propagandize" people to "inculcate" appropriate motives and perceptions. The executive must not only conform to a moral code but also create moral codes for others which would be reflected in high morale. To this end, "points of view, fundamental attitudes, loyalties to the organization or cooperative system, and to the system of objective authority" must be inculcated to encourage the subordination of "individual interest and the minor dictates of personal codes to the good of the cooperative whole."[25]

Barnard also had a story to illustrate his point. In a popular lecture he referred to an episode involving a riotous situation at New Jersey in 1935 when he was director of the New Jersey Emergency Relief Administration. He claimed that he defused the situation by respecting the dignity of the rioters.[26] According to Barnard's account, a meeting with representatives of Trenton's unemployed in his office had to be adjourned when some two thousand unemployed demonstrators, who had been urged on by New York radicals, clashed with the police in the street outside, leading to a number being arrested and some taking a beating. Barnard saw that publicity such as this could harm the cause of the unemployed by increasing taxpayer animosity to the relief program. This was the point he made when the delegation returned, after he had first carefully listened to a litany of their grievances, and a degree of harmony was restored. According to Barnard's account, picked up enthusiastically by his friends at Harvard, the problem was solved through human relations rather than by economics. Dignity was important to the unemployed, even more than food for themselves or their families.

It may well be that Barnard's sensitivity and tact did make a difference, but once his account was checked against contemporary reports of the episode it became evident that this was only part of the story.[27] There was in fact a strong economic dimension: the unemployed were demanding a substantial increase in food allowances and Barnard had promised to help. Nonetheless, Barnard's argument that more mayhem would put the whole program at risk was a serious political point. This reflects the observation made earlier about Follett's promotion of group dynamics. There are groups within groups, and Barnard's strategy in this case was to make common cause with the unemployed in support of the relief program against those who resented the subsidies when their own economic circumstances were so tight. Talking about groups rather than classes or parties or states did not remove the problem of conflict. Unless society could be reshaped as one big amorphous group, individuals were going to identify with some groups against others, and the interests of these groups were going to clash. The more inter-group conciliation became necessary, the more intra-group harmony was likely to be put under strain.

The original role of managers was to manage the workforce. Their understanding of what this required was shaped by the social theories of the time, many of which encouraged unflattering views of ordinary people as essentially simple-minded, suggestible, and manipulable. At best, they could be encouraged to be efficient cogs in the machine by more pay, tempered by threats of dismissal. At worst they could be swayed by agitators, drawing on the psychology of crowds. As the century progressed, the possibilities of maintaining a docile, regimented workforce receded with the growing strength of labor unions and the increasingly demanding and specialist nature of much work. Moreover, while the original inspiration for the human relations school might have been to draw workers away from socialism and unions, it encouraged managers to recognize that their organizations were complex social structures rather than simple hierarchies and that their workers might respond positively to being treated as rounded human beings. The approach risked replacing autocracy with paternalism as it struggled to work out what these developing views of organizational life meant in terms of structures of power. The more these structures had to be addressed, and the more they had to be related to the wider social and economic changes underway, the more managers would need a strategy.

The business of business is business.

—Alfred P. Sloan

BEFORE WE CONSIDER how the next generation of management theorists discovered strategy, we need first to explore the issues of power being faced by business over this period. The important developments in theorizing about business strategy after the Second World War reflected the forms taken by large industrial corporations in the United States, at a point when the tensions between capital and labor were subdued if not eliminated. The origins of these corporations, however, were to be found in a much more turbulent period in the country's industrial development, marked by labor unrest and arguments over the excessive power of the large trusts.

Against the expectations of Marx, capitalism transformed itself as the nineteenth century turned into the twentieth. Capitalists found means of coping with the volatility of the system that produced cycles of growth followed by recession. One of the most important coping mechanisms appeared to be size. Very large companies were capable of surviving sudden changes in economic conditions. In this effort they were increasingly supported by layers of management. The process which led to those changes began at about the same time as Marx was arguing with Bakunin over how to prepare for revolution and then what to make of the Paris Commune.

John D. Rockefeller

The story of John D. Rockefeller and Standard Oil is well known.[1] In 1865 as an ambitious 26-year-old in Cleveland, Ohio, Rockefeller bought out his partner in the town's largest oil refinery. Taking advantage of the economic expansion that began with the end of the Civil War, he added to his refineries and the profits rolled in. Unfortunately, others had the same idea and soon refinery capacity far outstripped demand for kerosene and other oil products. To survive, Rockefeller determined to be the most efficient producer, improving quality while keeping costs down and then, more imaginatively, by integrating the business, controlling both supply and distribution. In addition, he made sure that he had enough cash so he would not be caught short by sudden market fluctuations. He then strengthened his position by controversial links with the railroads, gaining discounted rates in return for shipping a guaranteed number of carloads a day.

Rockefeller did not accept for one second that it was improper to tamper with market forces. He was convinced that it was too easy to open a refinery resulting in an overcrowded industry and a chaotic, chronically unstable market. Instead of living by the market's capricious disciplines, Rockefeller decided to exert control. "The oil business was in confusion and daily growing worse." As each refiner "struggled hard to get all of the business... he brought to himself and the competitors nothing but disasters."[2] Supply and demand might never reach equilibrium. Rockefeller's strategy was one which in other circumstances would have seemed wholly appropriate: he sought cooperation as a sensible alternative to a wasteful and disruptive competition.

Given the state of the oil industry, Rockefeller may well have been correct in his assumption.[3] This was nonetheless a challenge to the prevailing ideology of free markets. In the case of Rockefeller, the challenge was aggravated by his methods. He normally offered prospective partners reasonable terms and at times helped his erstwhile competitors out of a desperate position. Those who did not wish to combine, however, would often be harried into submission, their position worsened by means of aggressive price cuts by Standard Oil. In 1870, when it incorporated, Standard Oil controlled a tenth of America's refining capacity; by the end of the decade, the figure was 90 percent.

When independent companies made a last daring move by building a long-distance pipeline, even managing to catch Standard Oil by surprise, there was no real threat to the company's position. There was time and the financial muscle to respond. Standard Oil built its own pipelines and soon controlled the whole network connecting the Pennsylvanian oil regions with the rest of America. The only exception was the original line, and even here Standard Oil acquired a minority stake. When the remaining independent refiners demanded legal remedies to restrain Standard Oil, the court cases lifted the veil on the sort of techniques the company employed in its drive to a near monopoly. In 1882, Rockefeller found a way to bring the veil down again, using a legal device that was normally used for people who could not look after their own finances. The companies in which Rockefeller held stock came together by means of a secret agreement. The stockholders conveyed their shares "in trust" to nine trustees, including John and his brother, William. That meant that, strictly speaking and whatever the appearances, Standard Oil did not own other companies. It was only the trust, owned by the company's stockholders, which could appoint directors and officers and set up administrative offices in individual states.

Standard Oil had a virtual monopoly. All that was missing was any actual production of oil. Potentially that was a great vulnerability, especially if the oil ran out. But by the end of the 1880s, new oil fields were being found around the country and U.S. production was no longer dependent on the Pennsylvania fields. Rockefeller saw the opportunity for further integration and reduced dependency on suppliers. Energetic acquisition began. Soon Standard Oil was pumping a third of America's crude oil as well as marketing 84 percent of all petroleum products sold. As both producer and consumer, Standard Oil could set the prices. Without quite squeezing out all the competition, it was in effective control of the U.S. oil industry and was developing substantial interests overseas. Things also turned out well for Rockefeller on the demand side: kerosene was replaced by electricity as the major source of illumination, but the arrival of automobiles and gasoline-powered engines transformed the market again. Gasoline suddenly moved from a minor product to the major output of refineries.

By the turn of the century, Standard Oil had reached the peak of its influence. The size of the international market, which already included significant competitors, meant that its relative position was bound to decline. The process was accelerated, however, as a result of the trust's substantial political liabilities. Rockefeller was blamed for using dubious practices to gain vast wealth. Grudges were held by the small independent producers who had been gobbled up, broken, or marginalized during Rockefeller's inexorable rise. They could appeal to American values and the image of the virtuous little man struggling against concentrated, corrupt power and great wealth. Rockefeller was by no means the only "Robber Baron"—Andrew Carnegie, Cornelius Vanderbilt, and J. P. Morgan were similarly denounced. Nor was Standard Oil the only entity using the trust as a way of controlling markets and rebuffing competition. It was, however, the largest and most notorious. While Rockefeller believed combination to be a better way of guaranteeing efficiency and stability, the practice tended toward monopoly. The 1890 Sherman Antitrust Act gave the federal government power to investigate and pursue the trusts. Rockefeller acquired the best lawyers to take on the courts and develop elaborate arrangements to beat legislation. He used donations to buy political support and plant friendly stories in newspapers. New companies were established, proclaiming their independence, though they were in practice controlled by the trust. Meanwhile, with remarkable attention to detail, using superior intelligence and communications, and keeping track of markets and competitors on an increasingly global scale, Standard Oil kept its prices down and its hold on the market secure. Through all this it "treated the federal government as a meddlesome, inferior power."[4]

In the end, Rockefeller's nemesis proved to be a writer called Ida Tarbell, whom we met in the previous chapter as a champion of Frederick Taylor. As it happened, her father had struggled in the early oil business against Standard Oil and suffered as a result. This gave an edge to her reporting. The opportunity came because she was on the staff of *McClure's Magazine*, a progressive "muckraking" journal, which had decided to make the trusts its main target.[5] Tarbell got a break with an introduction to one of Rockefeller's lieutenants, who became a key source of information. In 1902, a monthly serial began which lasted for two years, telling the Standard Oil story in compelling detail, arousing great indignation as it exposed underhanded business methods. Tarbell insisted that she did not object to the company's size and wealth but rather its methods. "But they had never played fair, and that ruined their greatness for me."[6]

The exposure was timely. The antitrust cause had been taken up by the progressive president, Theodore Roosevelt. He argued that corporate power had to be brought under control, using legislation where the abuse was greatest. He launched investigations into Standard Oil, and in 1906 a suit was brought accusing it of restraint of trade under the Sherman Act. Standard Oil's legal defense was strong, but the evidence was damning. After an initial verdict ordering the trust's dissolution in 1909, it was confirmed by the Supreme Court in 1911. The "very genius for commercial development and organization," the chief justice concluded, "soon begat an intent and purpose to exclude others."[7] Standard Oil was dismantled, giving birth to thirty-four new entities, including what became Exxon.

At the time it seemed like a defeat, but Roosevelt had done Rockefeller a favor. It was increasingly beyond the capacity of a single company to control a developing market of such size and complexity. The ability of smaller units to respond flexibly to new conditions eventually made for a stronger and more profitable industry. Rockefeller, now retired, held stock in the new and largely successful companies. He lived until he was almost 100. A great philanthropic trust bore his name and soon came to affect the way that economics and management was studied in the United States. His descendents continued to have a major influence on business and politics. So this story hardly counts as a tragedy.

Rockefeller was undoubtedly a master strategist. He could take a view of the system as a whole and assess the position of the individual parts. Yergin describes Rockefeller as "both strategist and supreme commander, directing his lieutenants to move with stealth and speed and with expert execution." He was not averse to military metaphors, for example, justifying his secretive methods by wondering "what general of the Allies ever sends out a brass band in advance with orders to notify the enemy that on a certain day he will begin an attack."[8] Chernow describes him brooding over problems. Plans were "quietly matured plans over extended periods. Once he had made up his mind, however, he was no longer troubled by doubts and pursued his vision was undeviating faith."[9] But because his strategic success was the result of objectionable methods and in pursuit of retrograde aims, he could hardly be presented as the model for an aspiring businessman.

Henry Ford

By contrast, at least for a time, Henry Ford was presented as an exemplary and forward-looking businessman. Ford's vision for the automobile industry was developed while he tinkered with machinery as a young man on his father's farm in Michigan. He wondered about horseless carriages and how they could take some of the worst drudgery out of rural life. Steam engines were too big, heavy, and dangerous. Perhaps gas-powered internal combustion engines might be a way forward. In the mid-1880s, he got a chance to work with one of these engines, understand its principles, and then experiment on his own.

There was at the time no mass market for cars. They were considered expensive toys for racers, with speed more important than reliability. As good money could be made by selling individual cars to order at high prices, there was no incentive to go for a volume. Ford's genius was to see how to develop an affordable car for a mass market, anticipating both a public demand and a means of production that did not yet exist. He got no support from independent investors and banks. This left him with an enduring disdain for those who put money ahead of work, feared competition, and were uninterested in consumers. He sought to liberate himself from dependence on creditors and shareholders. Although when he founded the Ford Motor Company he did not at first have the controlling share, by 1906 he owned more than half the stock.

He also had to take on a cartel. The Association of Licensed Automobile Manufacturers (ALAM) used a dubious patent to control the entry into the industry of new manufacturers. In 1903, they refused entry to Ford. In the context of the antitrust campaigns of the time, Ford realized that ALAM could readily be castigated for its greed and the use of specious claims to exclude proper competition. He was in the opposite position to Rockefeller, on the side of the people versus the trusts, the underdog, "an industrial David standing alone against a powerful, monopolistic Goliath." He was, he claimed, infused with "that instinct of American freedom to cause us to rebel against oppression or unfair competition." It went against the grain to be "coerced, or bluffed, or sandbagged."[10] In 1909, after a long legal battle, Ford won—to general acclaim.

In the company's first advert, he explained the wish to "construct and market an automobile specially designed for everyday wear and tear," a machine to be admired for its "compactness, its simplicity, its safety, its all-around convenience, and—last but not least—its exceedingly reasonable price." To get the price down he needed the volume of a mass market, and that required new forms of assembly. The prevailing model was the bicycle industry, which offered customers a range of models, a new one coming out each year. To Ford this was the wrong philosophy, based on the "same idea that women submit to in their clothing and hats." He wanted to build to last, like the watches that had first kindled his fascination with machinery. His view was that price was the key. That meant fewer models and more focus on simplicity and reliability.

Out of this came the idea of the "universal car," built with high quality materials and simple to operate. He settled on a design that became famous as the Model T and then concentrated on manufacturing this one model in large numbers. When his salesmen worried about the lack of different models to appeal to distinctive customers, he remarked that: "Any customer can have a car painted any color that he wants so long as it is black." This car was not to be a luxury item for a few but one for "the great multitude." The assembly line, first introduced in 1913, had tools and men placed in sequence as each component moved along until the car was finished. This reduced "the necessity for thought on the part of the worker and...his movements to a minimum." When in 1914 Ford started to have difficulty maintaining a stable workforce because of the dreary and routine nature of assembly-line work, he announced that his workers would be paid five dollars a day. This he described as one of the "finest cost-cutting moves we ever made."

Ford understood better than any other manufacturer at the time what might happen if ordinary people were treated as consumers and how their growing aspirations might be met. He worked single-mindedly to realize his vision, exploring better materials and methods. At this stage he also had the advantage of no real competition, as the other manufacturers were tardy in appreciating that Ford represented the future. This was a new and rapidly expanding market without obvious bounds. Once Ford hit upon his successful formula he was made.

Ford claimed a breakthrough not only in car manufacturing but in the development of industrial society, offering an alternative course between socialism and crude capitalism. He had given a decisive impetus to two critical and related developments: the techniques of mass production which in turn fed the desires of mass consumption. The five-dollar pay offer bought stability in the workforce and turned the workers into consumers. He sought to show how his own ordinariness and simple tastes, his readiness to bridge the gap between rich and poor, and the civic action programs around his factory all made him close to ordinary people. This was part marketing, part genuine. It soon became wrapped up in populist rhetoric, turning Ford into a special sort of businessman. Not only had he not forgotten his roots but he understood that looking after people was good business, a source of loyalty, productivity, and customers.

This addressed a wider political agenda. His close associate James Couzens, as much responsible for the underlying philosophy as Ford, put it clearly: "The follies of socialism and the terrors of anarchy will fade away in an industrial system that guarantees to every man, rich or poor, a fair field and a square deal."[11] An answer had been found to the constant unrest that had marred the process of industrialization, as workers fought to improve their wages and conditions. The five-dollars-a-day move enthused many on the left as it appalled other industrialists who saw expectations created among their workforces that they could not afford to meet. Progressives saw a man of wealth who understood his debt to labor. Some socialists argued that it made more sense to look at the practice of Ford rather than the theories of Marx. A cult of personality developed around Ford as one who made good on his promises and guaranteed service, not only a master car builder but a mechanical genius and democratic hero.

Inevitably, the political implications of Fordism soon turned out to be more complex than a historic bringing together of the hitherto opposing demands of capital and labor. His approach was intensely paternalistic. Factories were organized to do everything possible to reduce the scope for individual initiative, as if a universal worker could be one of the universal parts in a universal machine to produce the universal car. In such an interconnected system, where if some went slow the whole line slowed down, there was need for discipline and no scope for initiative. "We expect the men," Ford insisted, "to do what they are told." He assumed an "unevenness in human mental equipments" that meant many men were content with tedious work. A "sociological department" was established at his main plant to ensure that newly enriched workers did not lose their sobriety or industriousness. Their private lives were monitored and regulated to an extraordinary extent.

Beyond industrial matters, he campaigned actively against war. He toyed with politics and was touted as presidential material in 1916, until he eventually threw his considerable weight behind Woodrow Wilson. In 1918, he ran to become a senator for Michigan. He refused to actually campaign but still only lost by a narrow margin. His loss was largely due to his past pacifism and anti-militarism now that the country was at war. Over time, his attitudes began to appear idiosyncratic and, in the case of his virulent anti-Semitism, downright dangerous.

Ford was an autocrat, encouraging sycophancy and unable to grasp the major changes in the social and political context in which he was operating. When he was riding high he used his dominance to prevent any interference in the development of company policy, whether from partners, stockholders, or independent-minded managers. He sought personal control and oversight over what had become a massive company, with hundreds of thousands of employees and sales in the millions, yet ran it "as if it were a mom and pop shop."[12]

The company reached its peak in 1923, when it produced two million cars as well as many tractors and trucks. But by then competition was developing from General Motors and Chrysler. While Ford stuck with the Model T, the others set the pace with a greater range of new cars. By 1926, Ford's production barely reached 1.5 million vehicles. The competitors also offered new forms of payment, accepting credit and installments. With his horror of debt, Ford was unwilling to offer similar terms. Convinced that price was all that mattered, he put pressure on his workforce to increase productivity and on his dealers to accept the risk of unsold cars. His reputation as an enlightened man of the people became tarnished. He did not even appreciate how consumers, whose aspirations he had championed, were becoming more demanding about products, fickle in their tastes, interested in style, and self-indulgent in their spending. He assumed that low prices would continue to persuade customers to forego the novelties and gadgets offered by his competitors. He even fought with his son Edsel, who argued the case for modernization of both products and practices. Henry considered Edsel to be weak and prone to panic. It was only as evidence of falling sales became impossible to ignore that he accepted the need for a replacement for the Model T. By the time the production run ended in 1927, some fifteen million had been sold. The price had come down from $825 in 1908 to $290.

By 1933, with the Great Depression taking hold, Ford was selling only 325,000 cars, less than Chrysler's 400,000 and half of the 650,000 produced by General Motors. Now an elderly man, Ford appeared distracted. Moreover, with the arrival of the Roosevelt administration and the New Deal, the days of a lax and benevolent attitude of government to big business were over. The accent was now on reform and regulation, including support for labor unions. Ford became a bitter opponent of the New Deal. He saw it as promoting collectivism, sapping energy and enterprise from the economy, and motivated by an urge to redistribute wealth rather than support its creation.

Ford had long been hostile to the unions, along with the notions of class antagonism they supposedly fostered. Their aim, he believed, was to claim for themselves the benefits of mass production rather than pass them on to the consumer. They were in the same parasitical category as financiers. Ford paid good wages in the early 1920s, but as the company struggled in the 1930s, the demands on workers had become excessive. In 1925, 160 men produced 3,000 units; by 1931, the same number were expected to produce 7,697 units. The productivity was maintained through worsening conditions policed by a security force, often likened to mafia enforcers. Workers could be dismissed for minor infractions.

Ford was prepared to use physical force to keep the unions out. This became apparent in March 1932 when there was a battle between some 2,500 unemployed workers, urged on by communist activists, and the police. The skirmish involved stones on one side and tear gas and water hoses—and eventually guns—on the other. It ended with four men dead. For a while the intimidation worked, helped also by the divisions within the union movement. By May 1937, unionism had received a political boost through President Franklin Roosevelt's New Deal and the 1935 Wagner Act, which tilted the law more in favor of the unions. After a wave of sit-down strikes, General Motors and Chrysler had both given in to demands to allow the United Auto Workers sole rights to represent their workers. When union leaders tried to do the same with Ford, they were set upon and beaten up by security men. The result was more dire publicity for the company. And although Ford continued to resist, his position became more isolated. When the state ordered a poll of workers it turned out that 70 percent favored unionization. Ford's subordinates wanted to accept the result. Ford appeared ready to resist whatever the consequences until his wife, fearing bloodshed, persuaded him to relent.

Though a great innovator, Ford was a terrible strategist. He was absolutely sure in his own views and put himself beyond challenge in the running of his company. So long as others agreed then all was fine, but he expected business to be undertaken on his terms and showed no flexibility when he faced resistance, whether from his own executives, workers, the government, or even consumers. He saw no need for advice from anybody else. "When you have to solve a problem that nobody has yet thought about, how can you learn the solution from a book?"[13] In his memoir, *My Life and Work*, he was contemptuous of "experts," associating them with a state of mind where everything was already known and therefore new methods were deemed impossible. "If ever I wanted to kill opposition by unfair means I would endow the opposition with experts." There was an obvious connection with Taylor, with whom Ford was often twinned. Ford's own ideas were infused with the same spirit of rationalizing the labor system, and the dangers of a thinking workforce. It is unlikely he had read Taylor. He reached his conclusions through his own experience, and much of his push for higher productivity came from innovations in techniques and materials. Nonetheless, many of those around Ford were well aware of Taylor's approach and considered that they were working in the same spirit. Certainly Ford's success could be taken as further validation of the approach. Both "Taylorism" and "Fordism" became bywords for advanced manufacturing methods.

His early paternalism might have been embraced by the human relations school, who would have endorsed his determination to transcend the capital-labor divide, but his treatment of his workforce became increasingly harsh and suspicious, and the result was the surge of industrial unrest which concluded when he had to give ground to the unions. The administration of Franklin Roosevelt gave no support to those who thought that labor unions represented outdated thinking based on conflict. By the 1930s, almost submerged by competition and defeated by the unions, Ford was also a poor model for the aspiring business strategist.

Alfred P. Sloan

The man who came to fit this bill was Alfred P. Sloan, the presiding genius of General Motors for some thirty-six years, first in charge of operations, then president, chief executive, and eventually chairman, until he retired in 1956. The company, also based in Michigan, was founded in 1908 by William C. Durant. While Ford was aiming for his universal car, General Motors grew through the acquisition of small companies until it got into so much debt that it was taken over by a bankers' trust and Durant lost control. Sloan, who had studied electrical engineering at MIT and then become president of a subordinate company, was put in charge of operations at General Motors in 1920. He became president in 1923, when the industry faced a slump. From the start he set about transforming the company's structures and products in ways that were widely copied in corporate America.

Sloan's position was different from Ford's in three key respects. First, and most obviously, Ford led the pack. Second, Sloan had a range of cars to sell, produced by the companies that had been brought together under the General Motors umbrella, rather than just one "universal car." Third, Sloan had to take account of his major stockholders, the DuPont family. It was the DuPonts, alarmed at the reckless way the company was being run, that bought Durant out. At first Sloan was reporting to Pierre DuPont, who was chairman and chief executive. This meant that, unlike Ford, Sloan had to have an internal strategy as well as one to deal with the competition. He had to debate company policy with colleagues and take care of a range of distinctive and possibly conflicting interests. For example, DuPont backed a bold scheme to challenge Ford by developing a new type of copper-cooled engine. If the scheme failed, as Sloan suspected it might, the result would be disastrous. Sloan was careful not to fight the project: he just made sure that there was a fallback position based on a safer, water-cooled engine, if it failed, which it did.

Over the 1920–1921 period, Sloan came up with two related sets of ideas that reshaped the modern corporation as well as the automobile industry. The first was a set of proposals about getting the best out of General Motors' complex structure while still providing a central lead. His plans were set out in a 1920 document known as the "organization study," later described as having a "canonic quality" and as a "touchstone for management theory and practice."[14] Sloan presented this study as a result of his scientific approach, as a man "who followed the factual approach to business judgment." He drew solely on his own business experience. He had not been in the military and was not a book reader. Had he been, he noted, "I would not have found much in that line in those days to help." The plan was adopted because it met the needs of a board that "desired a highly rational and objective mode of operation." It depended on two propositions that apparently contradicted each other. The first was that the company should be split up into divisions, each with its own chief executive with a responsibility for its operation that "shall in no way be limited." The second proposition was that certain "central organization functions are absolutely essential" to the Corporation's development and control. Sloan saw the contradiction between the two as "the crux of the matter."[15] One was about the ability to get on with the business without constant interference from the center; the second was about doing so within clear financial and policy guidelines. The intellectual breakthrough was to recognize that there was a tension and that this presented the core challenge for management. It introduced what Sloan's biographer described as "a new kind of corporate music, a symphony of controlled, decentralized production, operation, and administration in which there is a reward for the virtuoso performer and regard for the conductor."[16]

The key question of strategy was what to do about Ford, which at the start of the decade accounted for some 60 percent of all cars sold in the United States. Against the legendary Model T, General Motors had ten models produced by a number of divisions, some at the luxury end of the market and others more basic. In principle, the product range catered to all sections of the market, but in practice the company's cars were competing against each other in some areas. As things turned out, Ford was the ideal adversary, complacent and stubborn. But even if Sloan suspected this he could not rely upon Ford failing to respond to the challenge he intended to pose. His script for General Motors dared not assume complete stupidity on Ford's part. Sloan could, however, assume that he had some time. Ford was under no pressure in 1921 to abandon the Model T when it had served him so handsomely. Moreover, Ford's eventual likely response was also predictable, as he had the financial clout to push the price of the Model T lower to see off any direct competition.

Through the summer of 1921, Sloan headed a task force charged to address this conundrum. According to Sloan:

> We said first that the corporation should produce a line of cars in each price area, from the lowest price up to one for a strictly high grade, quantity production car, but we should not get into the fancy price field with small production; second that the price steps should not be such as to leave wide gaps in the line, and yet should be great enough to keep their number within reason, so that the greatest advantage of quantity production could be secured; and third that there should be no duplication by the corporation in the price field or steps.[17]

The genius of this formulation was that these classes did not reflect any existing market reality. They represented a new way of thinking about the market, about how customers might respond to variations in price and quality. If Sloan was right, then the market could be shaped to suit the company as it rationalized and marketed its range, under the slogan a car "for every purse and purpose." He was not so much relating to the external environment; he was completely reshaping it.

The test of the approach would be at the lower end of the market where a revamped Chevrolet, then with barely 4 percent of the market, would be pitched against the mighty Model T. Sloan saw this competition taking place within the price category of $450–$600. Ford took pride in the position of the Model T at the bottom end of this price range. Sloan judged it "suicidal" to compete with Ford head on. "The strategy we devised," he later explained, "was to take a bite from the top of his position, conceived as a price class, and in this way build up Chevrolet volume on a profitable basis."[18] This meant aiming for higher quality in order to justify a higher price. The intention was to get sales from those prepared to pay a bit more, but also to pick up sales from those looking at the next class up who might prefer to pay a bit less. Ford was left the low-class slot in the knowledge that he would be inclined to stick with his existing strategy and ignore the insurgency. Once Chevrolet was profitable it would have a secure basis from which to mount further and progressively more damaging inroads into Ford's space.

What were Ford's options? Essentially, he needed to prevent Chevrolet from reaching profitability. But in the short term all he could do was respond by further lowering the price of the Model T, perhaps hoping that the slump in car sales that marked the start of the decade would continue, and then counterattack with a new model designed to challenge the Chevrolet's superior design features directly. But as Ford relied on one model, it would take time to develop a new car (although he could have bought another manufacturer to provide a ready-made product). Any new car would also potentially take volume from the Model T. The market picked up, Ford's sales soared, and so he had no immediate incentive to deal with the Chevrolet threat. But while Ford had no price class below the one he was presently occupying from which to draw new consumers, Chevrolet could make the higher range its own and draw customers from the class above as well as from Ford. When its sales grew, there was no need for Chevrolet to match Ford's price cuts. As Sloan observed, "The old master had failed to master change." Ford had not understood "how completely his market had changed from the one in which had made his name and to which he was accustomed."[19] Within six years, General Motors led the market, selling 1.8 million vehicles in 1927.

In one respect Sloan was of the same mind as Ford. He deeply objected to the Roosevelt administration's readiness to interfere with business and campaigned vigorously against the president. This included sponsoring the virulently anti-New Deal Liberty League and campaigning for Roosevelt's defeat in the 1936 election. In the end, as a result of the backlash against Roosevelt followed by the war, the two came to terms. In the short term, it created extra challenges for the company. The most important was the relationship with the unions. Unlike Ford, Sloan never claimed to have answers to all the problems of industrial society and showed little interest in shop floor conditions. His attitude to unions was that they represented an alternative source of authority for the workers on matters of pay, rules, and conditions which the company could well do without. Instead of trying to create a larger and therefore more profitable cake from which all could benefit, the unions just wanted to carve the existing cake, whatever the damage to profitability.

To prevent the workforce being unionized, the company hired spies to inform on any subversive activities. Anybody attempting to organize on the shop floor could be fired and those taking an interest warned off. The knowledge that spies were around also served to create uncertainty and suspicion among the workers and made them harder to organize. This went on despite the passage of laws designed to protect organizers from harassment. By the summer of 1936, only about fifteen hundred of the company's forty-two thousand strong workforce belonged to the United Autoworkers Union. Once Roosevelt had been reelected in November 1936, and with Michigan's governor sympathetic, the situation changed abruptly and dramatically. Under the miners' leader, John Lewis, the newly formed umbrella organization, the Congress for Industrial Organization (CIO), decided to target the automobile industry. Local militants also decided that this was an opportune moment to attack the company. As General Motors struggled to get out of the recession, the workers complained that they were being asked to work harder for less. Jobs had been cut while productivity targets remained the same. Managers relied on the fear of unemployment to discipline workers and keep wages down. All this erupted in November 1936, resulting in one of the most consequential strikes of the decade, critical to the future course of unions in the United States and also to the automobile industry.

By December, sit-down strikes had spread to a number of plants including the crucial Fisher body plant at Flint. To Sloan, this represented a direct challenge. "The real issue," he told his workers, was "will a labor organization run the plants of General Motors Corporation or will the management continue to do so?"[20] This all confirmed his fears about the New Deal, as good economic order was being sacrificed to misguided, collectivist notions. Now workers were engaged in an illegal occupation of company property and should be removed. But how? Under the law, force could be used but what if there was resistance? Was the company prepared to sanction serious violence? Moreover, it was apparent that at the state and federal level, the pressure was to find a negotiated way out of the situation. Though Roosevelt could not condone the workers' actions, there was no doubt where his private sympathies lay. Sloan had not exactly gone out of his way to curry favor with the President.

For the unions, the vital thing was to maintain their position. So long as they stopped the plants operating properly General Motors was hurting. This required not only repelling anybody trying to expel them by force but also ensuring that they had heat and food. In practice, the plants were often occupied by very few men, because the union initially did not have many members to call on and also had to make supplies last. In one of the key plants which employed around seven thousand workers, there were at times no more than ninety in occupation, not all of which were General Motors employees. So in January, when the company first tried to turn the heat off and prevent food being delivered, the "sit-downers" took the offensive to capture the plant gates so they could ensure the supplies kept coming. The crisis escalated as the men fought back against the police's gas canisters with stones and fire hoses. The next round involved guns leading to injuries but not deaths. The union added to the pressure by going after Chevrolet production. A decoy sit-down was staged in a secondary plant diverting the attention of the company police, making it possible to seize a far more important plant where the engines were made.[21]

The company obtained an injunction confirming the illegality of the trespass, but the strikers refused to leave. Attempts were made to get negotiations going, but the company baulked at the union's key demand of sole collective bargaining rights for the United Auto Workers (UAW). Sloan claimed to be prepared to consider this but only after the sit-ins had ended. Lewis had no intention of losing his leverage or agreeing to a compromise. Before the strike, General Motors had been producing some 50,000 vehicles per month; by February, this was down to only 125. Politically, Sloan was becoming isolated, the Roosevelt administration was accusing him of going back on his word, and commentators were describing him as out of touch with the times.

The responsibility for the use of force to dislodge the strikers lay with new Michigan governor Richard Murphy. He took the lead in trying to broker a dispute. He was conscious that he had to uphold the law yet was horrified about the possibility of violence and major loss of life and then going down in history as "Bloody Murphy." If he needed to step up the pressure on the union he was more likely to tighten the cordon already ordered when the

Chevrolet engine plant was seized than to order in the National Guard to evacuate the buildings. Such a strategy would require patience, easier for him than for General Motors, which was losing serious money. Even the company was wary about possible violence. They could see how they would be blamed for substantial loss of life when a conciliatory move on union recognition might have brought the dispute to a close.

Toward the end of the confrontation, Murphy issued a formal warning to Lewis about how the law must be enforced. This was followed by some grandstanding by Lewis, who told the governor that he would go into the plants and prepare to be shot with the others. In language that captured exactly Engels's hopes for such a standoff, when there was no doubt about the superior physical force of the authorities but real doubt about whether it could be used, Lewis taunted Murphy. Without a settlement he was not going to withdraw the strikers. "What are you going to do?" he asked.

> You can get them out in just one way, by bayonets. You have the
> bayonets. What kind do you prefer to use—the broad double blade or
> the four-sided French style? I believe the square style makes a bigger
> hole and you can turn it around inside a man. What kind of bayonets,
> Governor Murphy, are you going to turn around inside our boys?

In fact, by this time a settlement was close. It was negotiated by one of Sloan's lieutenants who agreed to direct talks with Lewis, using the request of the president to sort out the conflict as an excuse for going back on the company's previous position. On February 11, 1937, General Motors signed an agreement ending the sit-down strikes. UAW got exclusive collective bargaining and had four hundred thousand members by October.

The administration was not yet finished with the company. In 1938, the Department of Justice secured an antitrust criminal indictment against General Motors, as well as against Ford and Chrysler. The charge, which did not stick, was that the manufacturers had illegally restrained trade by requiring their respective dealers to only use the company-associated finance company. Unlike Chrysler and Ford, Sloan decided to fight, not only because he considered this to be unwarranted interference in business matters, but because he sensed a larger vulnerability—the company was moving toward a 50 percent share in the car market. "Our bogie," he observed in late 1938, "is 45 per cent of each price class...We don't want any more than that." This meant that—against all corporate instincts—he had to keep market share down.

One of the New Deal figures with whom Sloan was tangling was Adolf Berle, who had been a professor at Columbia Law School but was also a key member of Roosevelt's Brain Trust before the 1932 election and a regular adviser to him in government. In 1932, he published a landmark book with Gardiner Means, entitled *The Modern Corporation and Private Property*, demonstrating the divergence between the ownership and control of large corporations, with the result that the management conducted affairs with little shareholder scrutiny. They also showed how the means of production in the United States had become concentrated in some two hundred large corporations, of which General Motors was a prominent example. Economic power was being concentrated in the hands of a few people who controlled these giant corporations. This was power that could "harm or benefit a multitude of individuals, affect whole districts, shift the currents of trade, bring ruin to one community and prosperity to another." With a social role far beyond anything implied by the term "private enterprise," this was an economic power that could compete on its own terms with the political power of the state. A new form of struggle was developing: "The state seeks in some aspects to regulate the corporation, while the corporation, steadily becoming more powerful, makes every effort to avoid such regulation."[22]

In the run-up to the Second World War, the sure touch which Sloan had showed in his handling of the competition with Ford and the internal structure of General Motors had deserted him when dealing with the government and the unions. In key respects, these were the big strategic issues facing large corporations during the 1930s and there was no reason to suppose that they would subside in the future. It was, however, the areas in which Sloan had been successful, rather than those in which he had failed, that led him and his company to provide the vital raw material for the next generation of management theorists.

CHAPTER 30 | Management Strategy

Most of what we call management consists of making it difficult for
people to get their work done.

—Peter Drucker

DISAFFECTED MARXISTS BECAME an important source of management
theory as they updated their concepts of class struggle to take account
both of their distress at Soviet totalitarianism and new developments in
industrial society. The previous section mentioned Burnham's *The Managerial*
Revolution, regularly cited because of its title rather than its content, as the
neatest description of how emerging structures of power were confound-
ing the expectations of communists and free-marketeers alike. A surprising
number of former Trotskyists, including Herbert Solow and John McDonald,
joined the business-oriented *Fortune Magazine*. McDonald retained a fascination with conflict and strategy. We have already met him as an important
writer on game theory.[1] Another member of the *Fortune* editorial team was
William Whyte, author of the *Organization Man*, reflecting the magazine's
critical edge at this time. Yet another was liberal economist John Kenneth
Galbraith, who observed that the magazine's right-wing owner, Henry Luce,
had discovered that "with rare exception, good writers on business were
either liberals or socialists."[2]

Galbraith also became associated with the thesis that power in society now rested with the management class. This challenged neoclassical economics (which assumed highly competitive markets) as much as socialism. Instead of individual firms being small in relation to the total market, and therefore limited in their individual influence, in the most important sectors a few firms enjoyed commanding positions. Instead of being caught between the conflicting interests of owners and customers, the managers had been able to restructure the relationships so that, if anything, owners and customers found themselves geared to managerial interests. They also had discovered ways of preventing potential competitors from mounting effective challenges and of bargaining on almost equal terms with the state. Business success and failure depended less on market conditions and more on the organizational capacity of the large corporations. Arthur Chandler captured the claim neatly when he wrote of the role of management as the "visible hand" as a contrast with Adam Smith's "invisible hand."[3] There was perhaps also another thought, which had been around since Plato, that there was something to be said for bright, educated people running things.

The most mature formulation of the thesis came in 1967 with Galbraith's *The New Industrial State*, at almost the last point when it could carry conviction. He had been influenced by Berle and Means and, as acknowledged in later editions of the book, Burnham. Galbraith reported on the declining influence of stockholders and the growing influence of the experts in development, production, and management—which he labeled the "technostructure." Power no longer resided with "anonymous shareholders or in a board of directors that is now largely subservient to senior management." It resided with "the association of men of diverse technical knowledge, experience or other talent which modern industrial technology and planning require. It extends from the leadership of the modern industrial enterprise down to just short of the labor force and embraces a large number of people and a large variety of talent." Yet only a small segment of this new class actually wielded power at the commanding heights of organizations. In doing so they might reflect broader interests and attitudes, but their basic responsibility was to the interests of the organization upon which they depended for their livelihood. The key texts were not always clear on this point. Galbraith's technostructure covered a large number of people. Burnham seemed to point to chief executives, but his analysis risked tautology as managers became defined essentially as those who wielded power.

In this scheme, planning played a decisive role. It was the means to overcome the laws of supply and demand. Despite suffering through association with Soviet economic organization, the necessity for a forward look and preparation for coming problems and opportunities was accepted by Western governments and companies. Only by planning could priorities be set and functions coordinated. Size and planning were now essential to ensure continual technological advances. "It is a feature of all planning that, unlike the market, it incorporates within itself no mechanism by which demand is accommodated to supply and vice versa. This must be deliberately accomplished by human agency."[4] This was a time of fear of unconstrained market forces and optimism about the rational exercise of control over human affairs, informed by the miserable experience of the 1930s.

One of the first academics to explore what it meant to manage a modern corporation was Peter Drucker. His background was cosmopolitan. Born in Austria, he arrived in the United States in 1937, via England, to get away from the Nazis. A 1942 book on *The Future of Industrial Man*, which inclined to managerialism, was noticed by General Motors, and Drucker was invited to undertake what was described as a "political audit" of the company. He was given full access, including to Alfred Sloan. For eighteen months he attended meetings, interviewed employees, and analyzed all the inner workings of the company. He viewed the company as a distinctive sort of power structure, not at all, as had been assumed, like a large army with the chief executive cast as the general, issuing commands. At least as far as Drucker was concerned, *The Concept of the Corporation* was the first book to consider business as an organization and "management" as "a specific organ doing a specific kind of work and having specific responsibilities."[5] He was later proud to be "credited with having established management as a discipline and as a field of study" and, even more important, "organization as a distinct entity, and its study as a discipline."[6]

In a 1954 book, *The Practice of Management*, he noted how the managers had become "a distinct and leading group in industrial society," displacing capital when it came to a relationship with labor. Nonetheless, it remained "the least known and least understood of our basic institutions." At the time (he later broadened the scope), he linked management specifically to business enterprises, which meant that it would be judged by economic performance—outputs rather than professional inputs. He was skeptical of scientific management, for good results might be achieved by intuition and hunch. Moreover, while he acknowledged Taylor's contribution, Drucker blamed Taylor for separating planning from doing. This reflected a "dubious and dangerous philosophical concept of an elite which has a monopoly on esoteric knowledge entitling it to manipulate the unwashed peasantry." This elitist philosophy led Drucker to class Taylor with "Sorel, Lenin and Pareto." It was wise to plan before doing, but that did not mean that different people need be involved, with some giving orders and others doing what they are told.[7] In strategic terms he recognized the limits of managers, unable to "master" the environment as they were "always held within a tight vice of possibilities." The job of management was "to make what is desirable first possible and then actual." The keystone of his philosophy was to seek to alter circumstances by "conscious directed action." To manage a business was to "manage by objectives." In this respect he understood that whatever the long-term vision, it had to be translated into proximate and credible goals when it came to implementation.[8] Drucker's philosophy was therefore rationalist—set ends, find means—but took due account of the complexities of both organizational structures and business environments. From the start he saw the dangers if companies paid insufficient attention to their staff. Later on he became more enthusiastic about the rhetoric of "empowerment," though he always recognized that management required someone to take decisions and be accountable, and so in that respect had to be top down.

These two books (followed by many more) set Drucker up as the first contemporary management theorist. He became a consultant to leading companies, such as Ford and General Electric. Yet General Motors gave *The Concept of the Corporation*, and thereafter Drucker himself, a frosty reception. In some respects this was surprising: he accepted the virtues of large corporations and the inefficiency of small businesses, and praised General Motors's decentralized structure to the point of urging it as a model for others to follow. The reason for the reaction, Drucker concluded, was that senior managers disliked even constructive criticism (for example, of their tendency to take short-term profits rather than make long-term investments). They were wedded to a set of successful and durable core principles that had served them well and had been elevated to much more than an expedient response to circumstances. "The GM executives, for all that they saw themselves as practical men, were actually ideologues and dogmatic, and they had for me the ideologue's contempt for the unprincipled opportunist." Their differences were also relevant to the two large and contentious issues that had shaped general management thinking during the first half of the century—antitrust and the "labor question."

It was because of the antitrust issue that General Motors was anxious about Drucker's notion that big businesses were "affected with the public interest." He also got embroiled in a critical strategic issue directly linked to antitrust. He shared the view of some managers that Sloan's decision to keep market share below 50 percent to avoid further antitrust suits had removed the incentive to grow and was draining the company of initiative. One proposal was to accept a split, following the Standard Oil example. A new company could be created around Chevrolet, the largest division, which could readily survive on its own. Senior management, however, strongly objected to this idea.

With regard to the labor problem, Drucker observed the dire legacy of the sit-down strikes of 1937, including years of "sniping and backbiting," and how this prevented the management and unions getting together to find common solutions in a spirit of understanding and sympathy. Too many in management were prepared to see workers as an almost subhuman race, while the workers saw management as fiends.[9] Drucker was unimpressed by the unions, but the company had failed to integrate workers by providing them with more status and opportunities. The dominant assembly-line methods did not make the most of their creativity. The shift to war work had shown how workers could take responsibility, learn, and improve methods and product quality. So he urged that they should be seen as a "resource rather than a cost." He encouraged the idea of the "responsible worker" with a "managerial aptitude" and a "self-governing plant community." When Charles Wilson became chief executive of General Motors, he was interested in exploring this idea, but the main union, the UAW, objected on the familiar grounds of blurring the necessary divisions between management and labor.

One result of the company's irritation with *The Concept of the Corporation*, according to Drucker, was that Alfred Sloan determined to write his own book "to set the record straight."[10] The actual origins of Sloan's book, *My Years with General Motors*, which appeared two decades after *Concept*, were actually quite different. Indeed Drucker's claim so incensed John McDonald, Sloan's cowriter, that he set down to correct this misrepresentation and to tell of the struggle to get the book published.[11] McDonald, a former Trotskyist writing for *Fortune Magazine* and an early publicist for game theory, was specializing in "strategic situations where individuals, institutions, and groups of various kinds interacted independently and thought in ways—both cooperatively and non-cooperatively—that escaped common classical economic and decision theory." As he worked with Sloan in the early 1950s on an article on these lines about General Motors, the two realized that there was sufficient material for a book.[12] They worked together on this project for the rest of the decade but on completion, publication was blocked by General Motors' corporate lawyers.[13] Their concern was that the U.S. Government might use the documents cited in the book as the basis for an antitrust action. It took five years and a civil lawsuit filed by McDonald before *My Years with General Motors* was finally published, to great acclaim in January 1964.

Their research assistant was Alfred D. Chandler, Jr., a young historian who came from a well-connected family, linked to the mighty DuPonts (who provided his middle name). He was also great-grandson of Henry Poor, of Standard & Poor, whose papers provided the basis of his Ph.D. and stimulated his interest in business organization. As did Drucker, who influenced his thinking, Chandler felt proper attention should be given to how businesses organized themselves. It was necessary to move beyond the opposing stereotypes of "robber barons" or "industrial statesmen" to more rounded and subtle depictions. In 1962, while Sloan's account was still blocked, Chandler described General Motors's corporate history in his book *Strategy and Structure*. *Strategy* was not a word used by Drucker, other than a single reference to the distinction between strategic and tactical decisions in *The Practice of Management*. Neither did the word appear in *My Years with General Motors*, despite McDonald being a great aficionado of strategy.

Chandler's use can be compared with that of Edith Penrose, who was thinking about organizations along very similar lines at the same time. She is now often credited with the creation of "resource-based" business strategy in her 1959 book *The Theory of the Firm*.[14] Yet she did not use the term *strategy* except in a more traditional sense when referring to "successful empire-building entrepreneurs" who were "aggressive and clever in the strategy needed to bargain with and successfully out-maneuver other businessmen." So it was Chandler who gave the concept of strategy prominence in a business setting. It was, however, a particular sort of strategy that he highlighted. He had picked up the concept when teaching the "basics of national strategy" at the U.S. Naval War College in Rhode Island in the early 1950s.[15] He defined strategy in terms of planning and implementation, as "the determination of the basic long-term goals and objectives of an enterprise and the adoption of courses of action and the allocation of resources necessary for carrying out these goals."[16]

Thus, from the start, strategy was established as a goal-oriented activity, geared to the long term and closely linked with planning. This approach flowed naturally from Chandler's particular focus on internal organizational response to market opportunities, and again this had a continuing influence on the way that strategy was understood in its early business incarnations. It was not linked to problem-solving or competitive situations in which a variety of outcomes was possible. This focus was expressed in Chandler's formula that strategy led to structure, the "design of organization through which the enterprise is administered." Chandler's innovation was to see strategy in how management addressed issues of diversification and decentralization. His big theme was the multidivisional structure, also lauded by Drucker and for which Sloan took credit.[17] Management consultants—including

McKinsey, which was advised by Chandler—encouraged other companies to follow this model.

The advantage of the multidivisional structure, the so-called M-form, in Chandler's view lay in the separation of strategic from tactical planning. It "removed the executives responsible for the destiny of the entire enterprise from the more routine operational activities and so gave them the time, information, and even psychological commitment for long-term planning and appraisal."[18] By avoiding the distractions of second-order issues, the corporate headquarters could formulate policy, evaluate performance, and allocate investment, while stopping heads of units from distorting general strategy for parochial reasons.

This was not, however, the whole story. Freeland points to Sloan's appreciation of the importance of retaining the consent of the units of General Motors to the strategy of the center. Crude hierarchies had their dangers. If middle managers were excluded from goal formation they would be less committed to goal implementation. In this way planning would be separated from doing. This had to be balanced against the desire of the DuPonts, who were the majority shareholders, to be closely involved in key decisions and their reluctance to accept any delegation of power to the heads of the divisions. Sloan had got around this tension by finding informal ways of engaging the division heads in long-term strategy and resource allocation. This structure worked well until the Depression, when divisions other than the low-price Chevrolet struggled to stay in the black. The company decided to consolidate the divisions, thereby destroying local autonomy, but without any obvious detriment to company performance. Two conclusions could be drawn from this experience. First, the relationship between structure and strategy was more complex than described by Chandler. Second, order within a company would reflect complex "social and political processes, involving bargaining and negotiation."[19]

Chandler paid scant attention to either of the contentious issues of antitrust and labor. Antitrust legislation was clearly on the corporate mind of General Motors (for good reason), which was why it wanted no provocations that might trigger the interest of the Department of Justice. The government opposition to individual firms dominating specific areas of production by expanding sales, reflected in the 1950 Celler-Kefauver Act, had created an incentive to expand instead into distinctive and new product lines. This explained the proliferation of "conglomerates."[20] Although Chandler had access to the General Motors archives, he was unable to "use this evidence in his own scholarship because of the overriding fear among executives of antitrust action."[21] Chandler generally considered business behavior in isolation from broader political developments, which is why he also played down the significance of labor issues. His was an "industrial universe in which labor's position was entirely that of the dependent variable."[22] Louis Galambos, who admired Chandler for his pioneering contributions to business history, complained that he also narrowed its scope, stepping too "daintily around questions of power" and assuming that "transformations of business take place without social friction or a problem of agency."[23]

On the eve of the boom in business strategy, the field was therefore given a narrow focus, shying away from questions of power within the corporation and between the corporation and its external environment. Instead the strategists focused on the many other issues facing senior executives: shaping organizational structures, deciding on products and investment priorities, controlling costs and dealing with outside suppliers, and so on. The focus was on big business, secure in its position, with the sort of hierarchy that seemed natural in all large organizations, including the military and government. The Sloan model also reflected the impact of strong leadership. Jack Welch, who made his name as the successful head of General Electric, later criticized this method for allowing managers to become lazy and for being driven by bureaucracy rather than customers. He described a Sloanist company as one with "its face toward the CEO and its ass toward the customer."[24]

Planners

In 1964, when Drucker sent a publisher his draft of a book which concentrated on executive decision-making, he entitled it *Business Strategies*. The publisher found that this elicited little enthusiasm among his potential corporate audience. The word *strategy* was associated with the military and possibly with politics, but not with business. The book was called instead *Managing for Results*.[25] "Almost the next day," Matthew Stewart reports, "strategy became the hottest word in management circles."[26] He explained the surge in interest to two events—the publication of Igor Ansoff's *Corporate Strategy* and the arrival of the Boston Consulting Group offering a specialist expertise in strategy.

Walter Kiechel III described the "corporate strategy revolution" as starting earlier, in 1960, and then argued that before this there had been no business strategy. The word was barely used and there was no systematic set of ideas that pulled together the key elements that determined corporate fates, in particular what he called the "three Cs": costs, customers, and competitors. Companies had plans, often no more than extrapolations of what had gone before and, at the top, an often intuitive "sense of how they wanted to make money." This was comparable to the claim that there was no military strategy before 1800, when the word began to be used. There was novelty in the specific forms that business strategy developed for the rest of the century, but in the more traditional sense of the word, figures such as Rockefeller and Sloan never lacked for strategy. Given the predilection among "captains of industry" for military metaphors, it would actually be surprising if a number had not reflected on military strategy as they prepared their campaigns. Moreover, even the new forms of strategy that were developing, as Kiechel acknowledged, were building on what had gone before. He used the term "Greater Taylorism," except that instead of seeking efficiencies in the performance of individual workers, the new strategic focus was on the totality of a firm's functions and processes.[27] The underlying theme was the continuation of the attempt to organize business affairs on a rationalist basis.

The change that did occur can be discerned by considering the key figure at Harvard through the 1950s and 1960s, running the course on "business policy," Kenneth Andrews. He was an English graduate who had written his Ph.D. on Mark Twain. His own writing could be stodgy, but he had a clear view about strategy. Like Chandler, he was concerned with "the long-term development of the enterprise."[28] It was the product of a leader's choices and therefore of all the issues that had to be confronted in the business environment and the wider society, including values and organizational structures. With so many variables to take into account, the single-minded pursuit of a single goal at the expense of everything else was impossible or at least usually unwise. The chief executive therefore had to be a generalist and accept that every situation was unique and multidimensional. There could be no sure templates, formulas, or frameworks. The nearest Andrews and his colleagues at Harvard got to a framework was the simple (but still widely used) SWOT analysis (Strengths and Weaknesses of organization in the light of the Opportunities and Threats in the environment). His approach fit the favored Harvard teaching method of the case study, asking students to examine individual examples of business success and failure. This reinforced the view that strategies had to be case specific, working for particular companies in a given environment rather than derived from general theories.

It also fit the established concept of rational action as internally consistent, feasible in the light of available resources, and consonant with the environment. It assumed a sequence of careful thought preceding action, so that once a strategy was formulated then implementation (or as Chandler put it, structure) must follow. Because it involved the production of a single, unique product, Henry Mintzberg has labeled this "the design school" and presented it as the foundation for much of what followed elsewhere. He criticized it for a command and control mentality, so that a decided and definitive strategy would be handed down. Implementation would be a quite separate process, reducing the possibilities for learning and feedback.[29]

As the environment in which businesses operated became increasingly complex, sustaining rationality in decision-making required processes to take in all the internal and external information and turn it into a guide for action. This is what Igor Ansoff sought to do in *Corporate Strategy*, a standard text first published in 1965, earning the author the accolade of "father of modern strategic thinking."[30] Ansoff had grown up in Russia, moved to the United States, studied engineering, and—after a spell at the RAND Corporation—gained practical management experience with the defense manufacturer Lockheed. He worked on identifying companies to buy for purposes of diversification before moving in the early 1960s to Carnegie Mellon University. His view of management strategy therefore came from the innards of a large corporation with a focus on getting a mix of products appropriate to the market. In a familiar theme, he sought to transform management strategy from an intuitive art into a science, by incorporating—in the most systematic and comprehensive way possible—every factor of possible relevance.

He brought a very particular view of strategy to this effort. Ansoff noted an "unfortunate coincidence" in definitions of strategy. He sought to distinguish between "strategic decisions, where 'strategic' means 'relating to the firm's match to its environment,' and of 'strategy,' where the word means 'rules for decision under partial ignorance.'"[31] No decisions could take place with perfect knowledge, though the planning model suggested that they might, and that all decisions of consequence had implications for the relationship to the environment. Yet there was certainly a difference between the conduct of a specific campaign, which could have the whiff of battle about it—a sense of urgency and crisis—as efforts had to be geared toward a pressing problem, and deliberations about current challenges and future possibilities that could take place in slower time, providing a general orientation to an environment. The planning model could never be about coping with crisis; it was about avoiding crisis, maintaining a strong position by paying attention to the total environment and ensuring that resources were used to maximum effect.

This holistic approach, with its exhaustive attention to detail and attachment to systematic process, reflected Ansoff's engineering background. The presentation was marked by lists, boxes, diagrams, matrices, charts, and timelines, with the environment typically appearing as an "irregular blob," organizational units in boxes, and concepts in circles or ellipses.[32] The result was, as Kiechel put it, "filigreed to an overwrought fault," with the finale a one-page diagram on which were to be found fifty-seven boxes of objectives and factors, with arrows ensuring that they were each considered in the proper order.[33] The process was so rigorous and demanding that it required that strategy moved from the chief executive to a specialized bureaucracy. It was the demands of planning that led Galbraith to see a shift in power to the technostructure.

This importance of planning, and a sense that this was an arena where the Soviet Union was stealing a march on its capitalist rivals, reinforced the cult of managerialism. Its exemplary figure in this mobilization of management to serve the nation was Robert McNamara. From early in his career he had illustrated how skills might be transferred from the spheres of business to military affairs and back again. McNamara was teaching accounting at the Harvard Business School when the Second World War came. He was recruited with a number of his faculty colleagues into the Army Air Corps to join the Office of Statistical Control, a group led by Charles Bates "Tex" Thornton. Combining a relentless pursuit of hard data with rigorous quantitative analysis, this group imposed order on the chaotic accounting systems in the Air Corps, so that personnel numbers were known and correct spare parts were connected to aircraft in their hangars. They also moved into operations research, showing how resources could be used more efficiently (for example, linking bombs dropped to petrol consumption and aircraft capacity). Their analyses not only saved money but also influenced deployments.[34]

After the war Thornton offered the services of his group to the Ford Motor Company. It was a perfect fit. When his son and anointed successor, Edsel, succumbed to stomach cancer in 1943, Henry Ford returned to lead the company, but he was ailing and unstable. He soon relinquished control to his grandson, Henry Ford II, who was still only in his late 20s. With considerable drive and energy, young Henry set about modernizing the company. As one of the key problems was a complete lack of financial discipline, he seized on Thornton's offer. The team's collective impact on the company was huge, probing systems and accounting methods, asking so many questions that they became known as the "Quiz Kids" (a popular radio program of the time featuring very clever children). As the group's methods bore fruit, this moniker changed to the "Whiz Kids." They epitomized rationalism in decision-making, deploring reliance on intuition and tradition, and were unbothered by their lack of industrial experience. For them, the company was about organizational charts and cash flows rather than industrial processes. Over time, the limitations of this approach became apparent: it was too dependent on the quality of the data; tended to ignore what could not be easily measured, such as customer loyalty; and gave insufficient credit to the long-term benefits of investment when there was no early gain. In the short term, however, the results were impressive. Ford was the first company to introduce a new car after the war. The Whiz Kids got the company on the road to recovery.

McNamara emerged as the leader of the group and on November 9, 1960, the day John F. Kennedy won the presidential election, he was made president of Ford Motor Company. Within two months, however, he resigned to become Kennedy's secretary of defense. We have already noted McNamara's impact on the Pentagon as he imposed forms of centralized, analytically based control. We can now see how this fit in with developments in management theory. It was telling that McNamara's predecessor at the Pentagon, Charles Wilson, who served President Eisenhower, had also come from the same industry. Wilson had been Sloan's successor as president of General Motors and had run the Pentagon on the M-form basis, seeing the individual services as separate divisions and the assistant secretaries in charge of each service as his vice presidents. As Eisenhower was determined to hold down defense expenditure, Wilson's tenure was marked by intensive inter-service rivalry, which he struggled to contain. The individual services worked independently from each other, with much animosity and little coordination, fortified by their friends in Congress and industry.[35] McNamara's approach was quite different, more Ansoff than Chandler and Drucker. His aim was to get a grip on the process by strengthening his office, challenging the services to justify their budgets and programs in the face of intensive questioning by his whiz kids, largely brought in from RAND and gathered in the Office of Systems Analysis. This aggressive, analytical approach had a major impact on the management of U.S. military programs and the conduct of operations, particularly Vietnam. Whereas at first McNamara was celebrated as the exemplar of the most modern management methods, by the time he left the Pentagon in 1968 his approach was derided for its relentless focus on what could be measured rather than what actually needed to be understood—criticisms that McNamara in later life accepted.

In corporations as in government, whole departments were established to develop the plans, working out in meticulous detail the steps to be taken and their appropriate sequence. Planning cycles came to dominate corporate life, with everybody waiting for a formal document that would tell them how to behave, setting out budgets and programs with warnings of the danger if they went off plan. Politically, the consequence was to strengthen the center at the expense of alienating those responsible for implementation, who were apt to become cynical in the face of meaningless targets. "The matrix picked the strategy," one executive exclaimed in frustration, "the matrix can implement it."[36] The long-range forecasts upon which they depended were inherently unreliable, and the organizational information was often dated, collected haphazardly into inappropriate categories and taking little account of cultural factors. Even Ansoff became concerned that the structures he had initially advocated risked paralyzing decision-making and came at the expense of flexibility.

One of the economist Friedrich Hayek's most famous papers put the central problem of planning for a rational economic order as "the knowledge of the circumstances of which we must make use never exists in concentrated or integrated form but solely as the dispersed bits of incomplete and frequently contradictory knowledge which all the separate individuals possess." The problem set by knowledge was not one that a single mind could solve in order to allocate resources but rather "how to secure the best use of resources known to any of the members of society, for ends whose relative importance only these individuals know. Or, to put it briefly, it is a problem of the utilization of knowledge which is not given to anyone in its totality."[37] Writing twenty-five years later, Aaron Wildavsky commented on the vogue for planning at both national and company levels. The intensely skeptical Wildavsky noted the lack of evidence that the process had any value. At one level, all decisions were forms of planning as attempts to improve on a future state of affairs. The success of planning depended on "the ability to control the future consequences of present actions." In a large corporation, let alone a whole nation, this meant "controlling the decisions of many people, with different interests and purposes, so as to secure a premeditated effect." Some causal theory must connect the planned actions with the desired future results, and then the ability to act on this theory. The more people and types of action involved, the greater the demands on the theory as it had to explain how to get all to act differently than would otherwise be the case.[38]

By the 1980s, strategic planning was losing its luster. The planning departments had become large and expensive, the next cycle began as soon as the previous one finished, and the outputs were ever more complicated. Evidence of past difficulties and failures were assessed not as symptoms of a flawed system but of too much independent thought in the course of implementation, requiring even more prescription and explicit budgets and targets. The break came when General Electric, a company famed for and apparently proud of its elaborate planning system, decided to abolish it completely. Complaints were reported about an isolated bureaucracy, relying on dubious data instead of market instincts, persisting with incorrect predictions because they lacked the flexibility to change course. The senior executives were at the mercy of the process, with no alternative to the grand plan. Meanwhile, as General

Electric's new chief executive, Jack Welch, observed: "The books got thicker, the printing got more sophisticated, the covers got harder, and the drawings got better."[39] Welch was said to have been impressed by a letter in *Fortune* in 1981 that criticized "the endless quest by managers for a paint-by-numbers approach, that would automatically give them answers." Drawing parallels with Clausewitz and von Moltke's senses of battle, he observed that: "Strategy was not a lengthy action plan. It was the evolution of a central idea through continually changing circumstances...Any cookbook approach is powerless to cope with the independent will, or with the unfolding situations of the real world." Welch embraced this approach at General Electric, using von Moltke's aphorism about plans not surviving the first contact with the enemy to explain why the company did not need a rigid plan but instead a central idea that could be adapted to circumstances.[40]

In 1984, citing General Electric, *Business Week* pronounced the end of the "reign of the strategic planner," with few achievements to its credit and many disappointments. The coup de grace was delivered by Henry Mintzberg in 1994 with his book *The Rise and Fall of Strategic Planning*.[41] In 1991, in response to an earlier article by Mintzberg, Ansoff complained that Mintzberg seemed to commit all prescriptive schools for strategy to the "garbage heap of history," adding sadly that if he was to accept this verdict he had spent "40 years contributing to solutions which are not useful to the practice of strategic management."[42]

In the business world, as in the military, the loss of confidence in models based on centralized control, quantification, and rational analysis left an opening for alternative approaches to strategy. These centralizing models had fewer shortcomings in theory than they turned out to have in practice. They set out an ideal of how a chief executive might operate, but this was based on heroic assumptions about how optimal decisions could be made and then implemented. In particular, it was a model for the powerful—a superpower country or even a superpower corporation. As the environments became less manageable, the cumbersome processes the model demanded became dysfunctional and unresponsive.

Alternative approaches required a better understanding of how to cope with conflict within and between organizations. By and large, economics helped answer the questions on the horizontal axis regarding developing strategies for competition, while sociology assisted with those on the vertical axis about how to get the best out of an organization. Before we come to these approaches, which developed as the flaws in the planning model became apparent, we shall first consider another type of approach, not least because it provides a further link with military thinking.

CHAPTER 31

Business as War

Managers have always fancied themselves in the officer class. Strategy is
what separates them from the sergeants.

—John Micklethwait and Adrian Wooldridge

A S HAD HAPPENED with the military, the reaction against the business
planning models of the 1950s and 1960s led to attempts to rediscover
the essence of strategy as practiced. Just as the experiences of Vietnam and
a sense of developing Soviet strength encouraged defense reformers in the
United States to return to the classics of military thought and insist on
addressing the harsh realities of war and battle, a harsher competitive environment also encouraged businesses to think more in terms of victory and
defeat, and the need to infuse their strategies with the mental toughness
and passion required in battle. Chief executives might imagine themselves
as generals, leading their troops into battle, with an appropriate blend of
cunning, charisma, and calculation. The resemblances between intense corporate tussles and war were a regular theme in management books, and the
language of campaigns, attacks, and maneuvers could seem quite natural.

At the popular end of this tendency were the regular suggestions that
lessons for the boardroom could be drawn from the battlefield exploits of
such figures as Alexander the Great or Napoleon. Military figures, even some
with mixed reputations, were turned into business models from which relevant leadership tips might be taken. In addition to the obvious candidates

(Alexander, Caesar, Napoleon), Albert Madansky has identified books drawing on the strategic wisdom of Attila the Hun, Sitting Bull, Robert E. Lee, Ulysses S. Grant, and George Patton.[1] The bestselling *Leadership Secrets of Attila the Hun* by Wess Roberts, for example, while not quite offering Attila as a role model hailed him as an exemplar of leadership, for he "accomplished difficult tasks and performed challenging feats against 'seemingly' insurmountable odds." This implied for Attila and his Huns "a slightly more positive image than can perhaps be found elsewhere." Great chieftains adapted rather than compromised, dealt with adversity, learned from mistakes, did not ask questions for which they did not want to hear answers, only engaged in wars they could win, preferred victory to stalemate, and they had tried their best even if they lost. And so on. There was only a vague hint of the sinister when reference was made to the importance of loyalty and how it might be enforced. In general, the chieftains emerged as enlightened and inspirational leaders—taking seriously their responsibility for the welfare of Huns, explaining to them what they were doing and why.[2]

When examples were picked selectively, and carefully extracted out of their context, historical events and figures could be used to illustrate a variety of business theories. In such books strategy became collections of aphorisms and analogies, often contradictory, trite, and at most pithy restatements of best practice—exactly what the social scientists with their careful methodologies sought to avoid. They were unlikely to lead to much behavioral change among their readership or affect corporate performance and plans. In the back of one such book, for example, there was a list of maxims and quotes. What was the business manager supposed to make of "War is cruelty and you cannot refine it" (General W. T. Sherman), or "Shoot them in the belly and cut out their living guts" (General George C. Patton), or "War, by definition, means a suspension of rules, laws and civilized behavior" (General Robert E. Lee)? This author dismissed "smiley-face, win-win, love-thine-enemy kinds of business thinking." Business, he insisted, "like war, is basically a zero-sum adversarial game with economic and professional stakes of the highest order."[3] Similarly Douglas Ramsey described modern business as a "brutal battlefield," sharing the goal of "victory." His aim was to show how some of the key principles of warfare, such as clarity of objective, unity of command, economy of force, and concentration of strength could be as relevant for chief executives as for generals. He did note that when it came to their strategic decisions, few business leaders drew on wartime analogies. There was, however, a clear inference that they might be better off if they did so.[4]

The influence of most books in this genre was limited, more of an enjoyable read than a manual to be kept at hand. There were occasions when business rivalry took on the appearance of a fight to the finish, but as often as not the competition was continuous, ebbing and flowing, with many participants. Moments of decisive victory would be few and far between. In fact, the elements of military experience, captured by the concept of "friction" or by examples of stunning incompetence, warned about how campaign plans could go very wrong. In a declining or stagnant market, where the spoils would go to the last firm left standing, a fight to the finish employing ruthless strategies might be encouraged. But in growing markets competition might be less intense, and in those marked by complexity there were opportunities for cooperation and even collusion as well as conflict. The military metaphor, if taken too seriously, could lead to inappropriate and unethical behavior. An enthusiasm for a fight and a reputational fear of losing might lead to "price wars" or "takeover battles" being pursued well beyond the point of possible gain and possibly into substantial losses. As with all metaphors, warfare could be illuminating for business so long as it was not mistaken for the real thing.[5]

Yet some of the standard tropes of military strategy could appear pertinent. As early as the 1960s, in his more conceptual musings about strategy, Bruce Henderson of the Boston Consulting Group[6] drew explicitly on Liddell Hart, emphasizing concentrating strength against a competitor's weaknesses. He sensed the drama of competition, which was lost when it was presented as "some kind of impersonal, objective, colorless affair," and discussed the trickery that might be employed to divert competitors. Strategy would be about exploiting differences in management style, as well as matters such as "overhead rate, distribution channels, market image, or flexibility." He noted how competitors might become friends when a system needed stabilizing. The fundamental strategic rule was: "Induce your competitors not to invest in those products, markets, and services where you expect to invest the most."[7]

In a seminal 1981 article, Kotler and Singh argued that the need of businesses "to develop competitor-centered strategies to win market share will lead managers to turn increasingly to the subject of military science."[8] *Marketing Warfare*, published by Al Ries and Jack Trout in 1986,[9] used Clausewitz for inspiration. Marketing strategy was distinct from military strategy because at stake was the mind of the consumer rather than territory (although few military strategists doubted the importance of psychology). Just like the strongest armies, the strongest companies should be able to use their power to stay on top. A company dominating the market had more resources to devote to keep prices down and develop products. Therefore, to have a chance, small companies, like weaker armies, must employ guile and not brute force. Better people, products, or even productivity would not be enough. A well-entrenched defensive position could only be overwhelmed by a much larger force. Nor, following Clausewitz, was surprise likely to compensate for weaker numbers.

Ries and Trout offered four strategies for a marketing war—defensive, offensive, flanking, and guerrilla—with market share determining which was appropriate. Those with the greatest share were interested in market domination, while those with the smallest could concentrate on survival. In the face of a serious challenge the strongest had to respond: if they failed to do so they would progressively lose market share until their dominant position was threatened. The second in the market could mount an offensive to gain some market share from number one, but this would best be done on a narrow front against a critical weakness in the leader's position. The weakness must be chosen carefully: if it was simply high prices, for example, a firm with sufficient resources would be able to respond by cutting prices. If an offense was too risky, a flanking attack could be mounted with a clearly differentiated product. The risks here involved unfamiliar territory and insufficient signaling to competitors. Small firms were best advised to adopt a guerrilla strategy, in a market segment all of their own, avoiding any serious competition with larger firms and staying nimble, ready to move in and out of an area as circumstances changed. Approaching the enemy indirectly à la Liddell Hart, and then attacking in strength at the enemy's weakest point, à la Clausewitz, were the key principles imported from military theory. The core advice was to avoid a frontal assault against well-established positions.

During the 1980s, there was a shift toward Sun Tzu.[10] Sun Tzu's influence was attested to by two references in popular culture. In the movie *Wall Street*, the villainous Gordon Gekko advises Bud Fox: "I don't throw darts at a board. I bet on sure things. Read Sun Tzu, THE ART OF WAR. Every battle is won before it is ever fought." Fox later used Sun Tzu to prevail over Gekko: "If your enemy is superior, evade him. If angry, irritate him. If equally matched, fight, and if not, split and re-evaluate." *Wall Street* was a morality tale involving junior stockbroker Bud Fox caught between his blue-collar father, a foreman and trade unionist who represented the virtues of hard and honest labor, and the ruthless, cynical Gordon Gekko, a corporate raider whose motto was "greed is good." Bud became wealthy by following Gekko's methods until he realized that a plan to buy the airline where his father worked was all about asset-stripping. The movie appeared in 1987, the year of a Wall Street crash, and seemed to capture the financial mindset that had created both financial mayhem and a loss of moral bearings.

Another villain, Tony Soprano, the eponymous mob boss in *The Sopranos*, was told, somewhat sarcastically, by his psychiatrist Dr. Malfi: "You want to be a better mob boss, read *The Art of War*."[11] Later Soprano reported back to her: "Been reading that—that book you told me about. You know, The Art of War by Sun Tzu. I mean here's this guy, a Chinese general, wrote this thing 2400 years ago, and most of it still applies today! Balk the enemy's power. Force him to reveal himself." Soprano clearly felt that his introduction to Sun Tzu had given him a competitive advantage; "Most of the guys that I know, they read Prince Machiavelli." Soprano claims to have found Machiavelli, whom he read in a study guide, no more than "okay." Sun Tzu, however, "is much better about strategy."[12] As a result of Tony Soprano's endorsement, Sun Tzu became Amazon's bestseller in New Jersey.

Sun Tzu's discovery by business strategists generated a whole library offering insights from the master. Mark McNeilly in *Sun Tzu and the Art of Business* promised explanations of "how to gain market share without inciting competitive retaliation, how to attack a competitor's weak points, and how to maximize the power of market information for competitive advantage."[13] The value of Sun Tzu was seen to spread wider. One book suggested that careful study of *The Art of War* would help "preserve your marriage vows, and attain the marital bliss that you and your partner deserve to help with marriage."[14] Following *The Art of War* elevated the strategist. Instead of encouraging managers to be mini-Napoleons, it urged them to use their wit and outthink their opponents. It was also far less dependent on the Clausewitzian "business-is-battle" metaphor.

Sun Tzu and Liddell Hart appealed to business strategists for the same reason they appealed to military strategists. They required intelligence, imagination, and nerve. There was no skill in outspending a weak opponent, other than possibly getting round anticompetitive regulation. The real skill was in creating new products and developing new services—even new markets that the most likely competitors had missed. Sun Tzu added a degree of moral complexity, illustrated by his supposed attraction to the fictional rogue trader who used insider information to get rich, and the gangster who got rich through extortion and intimidation. As with the tricksters of classical times, this could prompt admiration about their cunning but a deep unease about how this was used to better those who led more virtuous lives. The ability to deceive and outwit an external foe might be celebrated, but there was still something inappropriate about using these tactics at home to gain an unfair advantage.

Another reason for the fascination with Sun Tzu was that it might provide a clue to Asian thinking. Japan, the country defeated so decisively in the Pacific War, had gained a remorseless competitive advantage by adopting business methods that Americans might once have known but appeared to have forgotten. *The Art of War* suggested a distinctive philosophical outlook, a reliance on patience and intelligence, gaining advantage through a superior grasp of dynamic situations and an ability to conceal one's own capabilities and intentions while seeing through those of the opponent. By comparison, American managers had become myopic, fixated on finance and the short term, while their opponents thought long term and focused on products. Miyamoto Musashi, a swordsman of the seventeenth century, was a key Japanese figure. When close to death he set down his philosophy for his disciples in *The Book of Five Rings* (*Go Rin No Sho*). Although he did participate in a variety of battles, his main skill was in dueling, an art he practiced constantly after opening his account at the age of 13. Musashi's approach to dueling allowed for a degree of trickery (for example, arriving late to unnerve his opponent or early to catch him by surprise), but there was no doubting his strength and skill. He could fight with a sword in each hand and was still able to throw his short sword. During his life he is said to have fought at least sixty duels without defeat. Although Musashi claimed that his philosophy was relevant to all forms of combat, the duel provided a distinctive perspective, especially when it came to its objective, which was simply to cut down the opponent.

In terms of an overall approach, there was a lot in common with *The Art of War*, which Musashi almost certainly had read.[15] Musashi described strategy as "the craft of the warrior," to be enacted by commanders. He explained the importance of his insights by noting that "there is no warrior in the world today who really understands the Way of Strategy." He urged the development of the sort of intuitive wisdom that comes from hard study of everything that could possibly be relevant ("Know the smallest things and the biggest things, the shallowest things and the deepest things"), stressed staying calm in all circumstances, urged flexibility and a change in tactics (as an evident pattern would enable the opponent to identify vulnerabilities), and was wary of head-on clashes. In order to strike when the enemy was not properly focused, he urged getting to the high ground, checking whether the opponent was left- or right-handed, and trying to push him into difficult terrain. Timing was important, which meant varying pace and staying alert. His preference was to attack first, but attention had to be paid to whether the enemy's strength was waxing or waning.

Whether, as some claimed, a winning Japanese business strategy could be adduced from all of this was less clear. *The Book of Five Rings* was not intended for a general reader but for those being trained in a particular martial arts style and attuned to its distinctive spiritual foundations. One authority described it as being "terse to the point of incomprehensibility" and suggested that its "unintelligibility" allowed "the text to function as Rorschach inkblots within which modern readers (businessmen, perhaps) can discover many possible meanings."[16] To the extent that Musashi was taken seriously in Japan it was as likely to be less as a source of strategic insight and more as something of a role model, as a Samurai hero celebrated for his humility, inner peace, courage, strength, and ruthlessness.

George Stalk, who was sent by the Boston Consulting Group (BCG) to work in Japan in the late 1970s, was less interested in the softer side of Japanese strategy than in its harder, tougher side. He developed his ideas in a 1988 *Harvard Business Review* article and then a book.[17] This focused on the importance of time as a source of competitive advantage. He picked up on the similarity between his views, which stressed making decisions and implementing them faster than competitors, and those of John Boyd and his OODA loop, encouraging getting inside the decision cycle.[18] This led to a line of argument (and language) familiar to anyone who had been following the military reform debate in the United States. In a competitive situation, he noted, strategic choice was limited to three options: seek peaceful coexistence with competitors, which was unlikely to lead to stability; retreat, which meant getting out of markets or limiting exposure through consolidation and focus; or attack, which was the only option that offered growth. But a direct attack through cutting prices and expanding capacity carried high risk, so the best option would be "indirect attack," involving surprise, leaving competitors caught by the speed of the attack or by their inability to respond. He described how the Japanese did this by tightening up their "planning loops," from the start of the development of a new product to getting it to the customer. This not only saved money but also left competitors struggling to catch up.[19]

The serious question underlying the "business-as-war" literature was whether the two activities were sufficiently similar for military strategy to work in a business context. In some areas, where companies were competing hard for market share, trying to protect themselves from acquisitive predators, repulsing sneaky insurgents, or going on the offensive against a vulnerable establishment, the similarities could appear compelling. By and large, the case studies in this literature involved companies competing head-on (Coca-Cola versus Pepsi-Cola was a classic). Once companies could be represented as armies in battle they could be subjected to the same principles. American military strategists in the 1970s and 1980s began to explore the relevance of Sun Tzu and Liddell Hart, and contrast the virtues of maneuver warfare with unimaginative and costly attrition. Encouraged by John Boyd, they considered how to get inside the decision cycles of opponents to leave them disoriented and confused. With a certain lag, these themes were also picked up by business strategists. A number were certainly well aware of Boyd's work.

Military strategies were tested only occasionally in one-off encounters that might not always be as decisive as hoped but could be expected to change the terms of any future encounters. Business strategies were tested daily but did include opportunities that could be quite unique to one company and once exploited could create a durable advantage. It was not true that military strategy only involved states as fixed and unchanging entities. Though rare, states could disappear through takeovers and new ones come into existence through fragmentation. With business this was, however, far more normal and possibly its most important distinguishing feature. Companies could break up, be taken over, or simply go out of existence as new ones formed. This made the interaction of internal organization and external environment much more complex. The strategic literature, however, paid surprisingly little attention to this interaction. Arguably, the disciplinary divisions in the social sciences did not help. By and large, economics addressed questions of the relationship of firms to their markets. Its eventual forays into organizational structures were influential but generally disastrous. To understand organizations, sociology was much more helpful but provided few tools (and a disciplinary lack of interest) for analyzing relationships to operating environments. The division in the literature means that our account must follow the first of these strands, led by economics, before it can return to the second, led by sociology.

CHAPTER 32 | The Rise of Economics

The ideas of economists and political philosophers, both when they are right and when they are wrong, are more powerful than is commonly understood. Indeed the world is ruled by little else. Practical men, who believe themselves to be quite exempt from any intellectual influence, are usually the slaves of some defunct economist.

—John Maynard Keynes

ECONOMICS CAME TO acquire an almost hegemonic position in strategic management. This was not because it was uniquely fitted for this intellectual purpose but because of deliberate decisions to adopt it as the foundation of a new science of decision-making and the active promotion of this new science by bodies such as the RAND Corporation and the Ford Foundation, both of which encouraged its embrace by business schools. As with Plato's philosophy, a new discipline that offered eternal truths was created in part by disparaging and caricaturing what had gone before for its lack of rigor.

The best place to start this story is with the RAND Corporation, which we identified in the last section as the home of game theory and the belief that a formal science of decision could be developed. This effort gained credibility because of the very special issues posed by nuclear weapons. The effort transformed thinking about not only strategy but also economics because it demonstrated the possibilities opened up by powerful computing capabilities for modeling all forms of human activity. Philip Mirowski has written of the "Cyborg sciences," which developed along with computing, reflecting novel interactions between men and machines. They broke down the distinctions between nature and society, as models of one began to resemble the other, and between "reality" and simulacra. The Monte Carlo simulations adopted during the wartime atomic bomb project for dealing with uncertainty in data, for example, opened up a range of possible experiments to explore the logic of complex systems, discerning ways through uncertainty and forms of order in chaos.[1] RAND analysts saw them as supplanting rather than supplementing traditional patterns of thought. Simple forms of cause and effect could be left behind as it became possible to explore the character of dynamic systems, with the constantly changing interaction between components parts. The models of systems, more or less orderly and stable, that had started to become fashionable before the war could take on new meanings. And even in areas where intense computation was not required there was a growing comfort in scientific circles, both natural and social, with models that were formal and abstract, not based just on direct observations of a narrow segment of accessible reality but also on explorations of something that approximated to a much larger and otherwise inaccessible reality. They could be analyzed in ways which the human mind, left on its own, could not begin to manage. As one of the first textbooks on operations research noted, this work required an "impersonal curiosity concerning new subjects," rejection of "unsupported statements," and a desire to rest "decisions on some quantitative basis, even if the basis is only a rough estimate."

In their landmark book of 1957, which gave the field renewed vigor, Duncan Luce and Howard Raiffa noted prematurely the decline of the "naive bandwagon-feeling that game theory solved innumerable problems of sociology and economics, or at the least, that it made their solution a practical matter of a few years' work."[2] They urged social scientists to recognize that game theory was not descriptive. Instead it was "rather (conditionally) normative. It states neither how people do behave nor how they should behave in an absolute sense, but how they should behave if they wish to achieve certain ends."[3] Their injunction was ignored and game theory came to be adopted as more of a descriptive than normative tool.

One reason for this was the development of the Nash equilibrium, named after the mathematician John Nash (whose struggle with mental illness became the subject of a book and a movie).[4] This was an approach to non-zero-sum games. The idea was to find a point of equilibrium, comparable to those in physics when forces balance one another. In this case, players sought the optimum way to reach their goals. The equilibrium point was reached when the players adopted a set of strategies that created no incentive for any individual player to change strategy so long as the others stayed unchanged.[5] Nash's contribution came to be celebrated within economics as "one of the outstanding intellectual advances of the twentieth century."[6] But its value to strategy was limited. On the one hand, a lack of points of equilibrium led to chaos; on the other, too many points resulted in an indeterminate situation. As a contrast, Tom Schelling demonstrated the possibilities of using abstract forms of reasoning to illuminate real issues faced by states, organizations, and individuals. He encouraged people to think of strategy as an aid to bargaining, and he explored with great insight the awful paradoxes of the nuclear age. But he explicitly eschewed mathematical solutions and drew on a range of disciplines, thus abandoning any attempt to develop a pure, general theory. Mirowski found Nash's non-cooperative rationalism wanting but also found Schelling's more playful, allusive mode of analysis exasperating because of its lack of rigor. Schelling avoided the restrictive forms of game theory and the challenging mathematics of Nash in order to make paradoxical points about communication without communication and rationality without rationality.[7] Mirowski understated Schelling's importance as a conceptualizer and his recognition of the limits of formal theories when it came to modeling behavior and expectations. "One cannot, without empirical evidence," Schelling observed, "deduce whatever understandings can be perceived in a non-zero-sum game of maneuver any more than one can prove, by purely formal deduction, that a particular joke is bound to be funny."[8] Schelling, however, had many more admirers than imitators. In economics Nash became part of the mainstream.

The extraordinary boost from RAND's budget and advances in computing put social science on a new footing. The effect was particularly striking with economics. Orthodox economics had faced a crisis during the great depression of the 1930s. This led to greater empirical rigor backed by improved statistical analysis. Many key figures had learned the analytical techniques in wartime operational research. Even where there were important differences in emphasis and approach, as for example between the Chicago School and the Cowles Commission (which had been set up in 1932 to improve the collection and statistical analysis of economic data), they had much in common. Notably, they were rooted in the neoclassical tradition, going back to Walras and Pareto, and assumed that the safest assumption was of individual rationality. As Milton Friedman, the most prominent Chicago economist, put it: "We shall suppose that the individual in making these decisions acts as if he were pursuing and attempting to maximize a single end."[9] Friedman considered the debate about whether people really acted so rationally, following complex statistical rules, irrelevant. It was an approximation that was productive for theory, leading to propositions that could then be tested against the evidence.

Friedman and his colleagues were methodologically pragmatic, although dogmatic in their conviction that the market worked best when left alone by government. In this they were influenced by Friedrich Hayek, an Austrian who had acquired British citizenship in 1938 and had been teaching at the London School of Economics until he was recruited to Chicago, though not by the economics department, in 1950. His most famous book, *The Road to Serfdom*, was published during the war and warned against the inclination to central planning that was gathering momentum under the combined influence of socialism and the wartime experience. Meanwhile, the Cowles Commission, influenced by John von Neumann and sponsored by RAND, was up for new methodological challenges and was more inclined to believe that robust models could support enlightened policy. Either way the assumptions and methods associated with game theory became part of a wider project to develop new forms of social science.

Economics into Business

The Ford Foundation was at the fore in exploring how management within big government and big business could become vital instruments of efficiency and progress. In the late 1940s, the Foundation moved from addressing the needs of the Ford Company's own operations around Detroit to meeting a broader agenda. The deaths of both Henry and Edsel Ford led to a surge of money into the Foundation. The man chosen to head a study committee to set the objectives for the future was H. Rowan Gaither, then chairman of RAND and later to become the Foundation's president. He was convinced that social science could and should be mobilized to serve the nation, and that this required managers who understood this science and could appreciate the possibilities for its application. He spoke to the Stanford Business School in 1958 about how "the Soviet challenge requires that we seek out and utilize the best intelligence of American management—and in turn put on management a national responsibility of unparalleled dimensions."[10]

A report for the Foundation in 1959 deplored an "embarrassingly low" standard of acceptability among business schools, one which many schools did not actually meet. The point was illustrated by citing multiple study options on the "principles of baking" at one southern school. At the same time there was optimism that the situation could be rectified by a "management science" being transmitted to students as a methodology for decision-making. Instead of being taught to rely on judgment (which had been the basis of the Harvard curriculum), students could develop a more analytical competence by being immersed in quantitative methods and decision theory. Under Gaither's influence, Ford directed vast sums into the top business schools to create centers of excellence, raising the intellectual caliber and professionalism of the coming generations of managers and their teachers. Over two decades, the numbers of business schools in the United States tripled and the production of MBAs went up accordingly. By 1980, fifty-seven thousand MBAs were graduating from six hundred programs, accounting for 20 percent of the total number of master's degrees granted. At the same time, there was an equivalent expansion in the number of scholarly academic business journals, from about twenty at the end of the 1950s to two hundred two decades later.[11]

Harvard was the major beneficiary and the Hawthorne studies held as exemplars of the benefits of serious research, though it was the new Carnegie Institute of Technology's Graduate School of Industrial Organization that led the way in drawing upon the social sciences as a source of intellectual energy. Lee Bach, who led the Carnegie effort, was convinced that the best decisions must emerge out of the best reasoning process. He predicted a change that would involve clarifying and bringing to the surface "the variables and logical models our minds must be using now in decision-making and of persistently improving the logic of these models."[12] One of those he recruited, political-scientist-cum-economist Herbert Simon, recalled a determination to transform business education from a "wasteland of vocationalism" into a "science-based professionalism." By 1965, Ford was reporting "an increased use of quantitative analysis and model building" and more publications in disciplinary journals in economics, psychology, and statistics.

Its original concept had been to integrate the case study method as taught at Harvard with economics, sharpening the case studies while tempering economic theory with a dose of realism. The balance was to be shifted to more research with less description, more theory and less practice. Little balance was found. In what was later admitted to be a "tactical error," Ford's push for academic excellence in the business schools came to be dominated by economists who showed little interest either in adapting to other disciplines or even worrying unduly about real-world applications. In the early 1960s, however, they seemed like a breath of fresh air. The determination to stress the practical and avoid the theoretical had led to an absence of any sort of theory, which left everything to common sense and judgment. In remedying this deficiency, economics had clear advantages over the other, softer social sciences. It encouraged parsimonious models, simplifying the complex issues of management by focusing on core principles and assuming rational actors (which is just how managers liked to imagine themselves). The clarity of the assumptions would be reflected in the sharpness and testability of the hypotheses. The challenge for management was to achieve the best for their organization. It made sense to look at a theory that assumed that to be the aim of all individuals and organizations.

The change was reflected in Harvard. The business policy course, which treated corporate strategy in the "genteel tradition of those days, not as a set of formulas but as the mission of the company, its distinctive competence, reflecting the values of its managers," and was not particularly popular, was replaced by one entitled "Competition and Strategy," from which the material on the general manager and the values of society had been removed.[13]

Competition

It was not just the push on the supply side that created the interest in economic theories of decision-making but also changes in the demands posed by the business environment. The emphasis on planning processes had reflected the supposed interests of a limited number of very large corporations with huge financial and political clout, offering a range of product lines in a steadily growing economy. While for these behemoths internal organization was a major issue, precisely because of their size and strength and the restraint of antitrust legislation, competition was not so important. The word does not even appear in the index of Chandler's *Strategy and Structure* or Drucker's *The Practice of Management*.

For smaller firms in new or dying markets with much simpler structures, the challenges were always quite different, and new challenges began to develop even for the big corporations. The large as well as the small became subject to increasing foreign competition, notably from insurgent Japanese corporations with a better eye for new consumer technologies and lower costs. Basic structural shifts were occurring: the move from manufacturing to services, new technologies that were creating new forms of enterprise as well as new types of goods, plus the development of increasingly esoteric financial instruments. Then there were temporary factors with severe effects, such as the hike in oil prices in 1974 and the subsequent combination of stagnation and inflation.

In this first instance, this challenge was picked up not by the business schools but by consultants, who by necessity were tuned to the stresses and strains of changes in the business environment. The Boston Consulting Group (BCG), founded by Bruce Henderson in 1964, saw strategy as being about making direct comparisons with competitors, especially in relation to cost structures. While the business schools still encouraged the analysis of specific and unique situations, Henderson sought strong theories that would guide the consultant when considering the circumstances of new clients. His approach was more deductive than inductive. The aim was to find a "meaningful, quantitative relationship" between a company and its chosen markets.[14]

Like so many figures in business strategy, Henderson's background was in engineering. He was therefore attracted by the idea of systems tending to equilibrium, with the aim of strategy in a system including competitors to be one of first upsetting the equilibrium and then reestablishing it on a more favorable basis. The challenge was to develop the necessary thinking in terms sufficiently explicit to be "executed in a coordinated fashion in complex organizations."

His approach, in stark contrast to the complexity of Ansoff, was to apply micro-economic methodology, to develop what he called "powerful oversimplifications," which BCG then sold to companies.[15] The oversimplification that established his reputation was the "experience curve." Based on early studies of the aircraft industry, the core idea was that the more units produced, the lower the costs and the higher the profits. When plotted on a curve this could show the state of a competitive relationship. The presumption was that for companies making the same product, variations in costs were largely related to market share. Thus the effects of an increased share were calculable. Businesses should expect costs to decline systematically and predictably as a result of their superior productive experience. While the methodology encouraged companies to look at their total costs and recognize economies of scale, it could also be seriously misleading. In a mature industry the experience curve would flatten out. It could also encourage a race to the bottom, as prices were cut in the expectation of higher volumes which might not materialize, and then leave little scope for investment. As Ford's Model T experience demonstrated, even the master of a product with costs kept down to a minimum can still be caught out by a better product.

BCG's second powerful oversimplification was the growth-share matrix. A matrix was drawn with the growth in the market on one axis and share of the market on the other. Companies could then locate their various activities on the matrix. It was best to have a high share of a growing market (the stars) and worst to have a low share of a static or declining market (the dogs). The other two categories were "cash cows" and "question marks." The images were powerful and the logic compelling. The cows had to be looked after and the stars backed, while the dogs were candidates for divestment. Once that was sorted, only the question marks required serious thoughts. Again the imagery had a capacity to mislead. As one critic, John Seeger, noted, "The dogs may be friendly, the cows may need a bull now and then to remain productive, and the stars may have burned themselves out." Seeger warned of the dangers of allowing management models to "substitute for analysis and common sense." Just because a theory had elegance and simplicity did not "guarantee sanity in its use."[16]

It took until 1980 before a major breakthrough in business strategy came out of a business school. Michael Porter, who had the requisite engineering background and an enthusiasm for competitive sports, entered the Harvard MBA program, where he was taught the holistic, multidimensional "business policy" philosophy. Unusually, he then enrolled for a Ph.D. in business economics. One of the courses he took was on industrial organization. This was the area of economics most conducive to business strategy because it studied situations of imperfect competition. In perfect competition, the postulate through which economic theory largely developed, the choices available to buyers and sellers created the potential for equilibrium around a specific price. By definition, perfect competition allowed no scope for an individual unit to have a special and successful strategy. The most imperfect competition would be a complete monopoly where a single supplier could set the price, also leaving little scope for strategy. The oligopolist had options, neither fully constrained by the market but affected by the moves of its competitors. The oligopolist had to be strategic, because he must anticipate these moves. There was no law to govern this situation, which is why Simon declared oligopoly to be "the permanent and ineradicable scandal of economic theory."[17]

For economists, the question raised was why certain markets deviated from standard models of perfect competition. Profits should be more than sufficient to animate the company, but certain industries were extremely profitable. That was because of a lack of competitive pressure, which was the result of the "barriers to entry"—the difficulty faced when trying to establish a new position in a market. The thrust of the economics approach to industrial organization was to find ways to reduce these barriers to make the markets more competitive. With his business school background, Porter saw an opportunity to turn the theory on its head. This was a natural stance for a student of strategy, taking the point of view of the company within the industry rather than the industry as a whole. Instead of asking how the system could be made more competitive, he asked how the unit within the system could exploit and even intensify uncompetitive elements to gain strategic advantage.

Following Ansoff in defining strategy in terms of "relating a company to its environment," Porter devised a framework to help companies examine their competitive situation. The focus was still on providing a guide to a deliberative process for a large business, but he was more ambitious than Andrews, more focused than Ansoff, and less formulaic than Henderson.[18] Porter identified two key issues. The first was seller concentration (what percentage of the market was controlled by the top four firms) and barriers to entry. Out of this came the "five forces framework" for analyzing an industry. The forces were competitive rivalry between firms, bargaining power of suppliers and of buyers, threats of new entrants and of substitute offerings. A number of factors were connected with each. The presentation was methodical and rigorous, offering basic principles and some specific tactics about how to maintain and improve a competitive position. To the critics who claimed that his analysis was too static, Porter replied that the five forces all needed to be watched precisely because they changed.

For Porter, strategy was all about positioning. The menu of strategies was small and the choice would depend on the nature of the competitive environment, with the aim of finding a position that could be defended against existing competitors and those trying to enter the market. Porter offered three generic strategies: staying market leader by keeping costs down, having a product that was sufficiently different that it could not be challenged by other competitors (differentiation), and identifying a particular part of the market where there were few challengers (market specialization). He argued that it was important to pick one of these strategies, stick to it, and never get "stuck in the middle," because that would almost "guarantee low profitability." Since the best position would be extremely profitable, there would then be sufficient resources to improve the position. The key thing was to find and exploit the imperfections in the market. In terms of the SWOT framework, this was about addressing opportunities and threats rather than strengths and weaknesses. There was very little interest in internal organization and the actual implementation of a strategy.

Porter's method could be criticized for being deductive. He had plenty of examples of tactics used by companies seeking product differentiation or raising barriers, but these were illustrations of propositions derived from his theory. Some of his central claims about the generic strategies and the greater value to be gained by concentrating on market position as against operational efficiency did not seem to fit the evidence. As with all structural theorists the tendency was to assume that structure had "a strong influence in determining the competitive rules of the game as well as the strategies potentially available to the firm."[19] In practice the system was less rigid and certain than the theory assumed, and more susceptible to being transformed by truly imaginative strategies.

One striking feature of Porter's approach lay in its political implications. This was not something he dealt with explicitly, but as Mitzberg noted: "If profit really does lie in market power, then there are clearly more than economic ways to generate it."[20] The closest Porter came to making the link between competitive position and government assistance was in noting how governments "can limit or even foreclose entry into industries with such controls as licensing requirements and limits on access to raw materials." The key arena here was that affected by antitrust legislation. Porter was well aware of the issue, noting that companies under antitrust restraints might not feel able to respond to competitors attempting to take a small market share, or how large companies may use a private antitrust suit to harass small competitors.[21] He warmed to the theme in his second book, *Competitive Advantage*, noting how these suits could put financial pressure on competitors. Here he also discussed how barriers to entry could be raised higher than would naturally occur, by such methods as forming exclusive agreements with outlets to freeze out competitors, tying up suppliers, and even working in coalition with other established firms.[22] A number of the activities, he noted, were frowned upon by antitrust law and were the subject of successful suits. Porter insisted that he supported antitrust legislation,[23] and it was also the case that there was a degree of uncertainty surrounding this legislation in terms of the vigor with which it was applied at any time, often depending on economic circumstances. This uncertainty was a major problem for the strategist, as what might seem acceptable behavior at one moment became unacceptable the next.

In the mid-1980s, Porter advised the National Football League (NFL) in its dispute with the United States Football League (USFL). He characterized the dispute as "guerrilla warfare" and suggested aggressive strategies, such as persuading broadcasters to break their contract with the USFL, poaching the USFL's best players while encouraging the NFL's worst to go the other way, and co-opting the most powerful USFL owners while bankrupting the weakest USFL teams. This was cited in evidence when the USFL sought damages from the NFL for its anticompetitive practices. Ultimately, it was agreed that the NFL had violated the law, although only derisory damages were awarded. Porter's assistant acknowledged that legal issues had not been considered in offering advice; the NFL's defense was that it had ignored the advice.[24]

A similar problem emerged with Barry Nalebuff and Adam Brandenburger's *Co-Opetition*, an attempt to capture the insights of game theory for a popular audience. The title neatly captured the mixture of cooperation and competition that game theory addressed,[25] although the neologism was not actually new.[26] Their idea was that it would make sense to cooperate with other players in the industry to expand the business pie while competing over how it was divided up. They noted the complexity of relationships, not only with customers, suppliers, and competitors, but also complements—that is, other players with whom there was a natural cooperative and mutually dependent relationship (for example, hardware and software firms in computing). They discussed the advantages that could be gained by changing the rules of the game or by using tactics to shift perceptions of a position within the game. The influence of game theory was evident, but this was hardly a theoretical work. As with other practical work in the field it took some basic factors and reworked them in a variety of cases, offering readers some insight on how they might approach similar types of problems.

The more explicit recognition of the potential of cooperation, which would be natural in any other area of strategy, always risked appearing anti-competitive and falling foul of antitrust law. Nalebuff and Brandenburger thus celebrated Nintendo's achievements in gaining a competitive advantage in the computer games market, which allowed them to overcharge their customers (eventually requiring them to settle in the face of a suit from the Federal Trade Commission). The way the analysis was structured led the authors to naturally favor the company over the consumer. Stewart sharply commented that they "praise one company after another for cornering markets and duping customers" before acknowledging antitrust concerns. He accused them of developing an approach to strategy which was about "how to arrange a cartel without having to enter a smoke-filled backroom, how to organize a monopoly without going to the trouble of bribing government officials, and, in general, how to make extraordinary profits without having to make extraordinary products." As he noted, while they praised General Motors for its credit card strategy, which offered discounts to those who used it, Toyota, which did not bother with a credit card, was building better cars and eating into the market share of General Motors.[27]

John Rockefeller did not appear in the index to Porter's *Competitive Strategy*. He might have found the language and concepts unfamiliar but as one ready to try every trick in the book to position Standard Oil, the broad thrust of the argument would have been well understood. The management strategists of the late twentieth century were operating in an environment shaped significantly by the great trusts of the nineteenth century and the progressive movement's attempts to deal with them. The logic of any attempt to tame markets was to make life difficult for at least some competitors. While the first wave of management strategists ignored this issue, because they were dealing with firms that were in secure positions or close to the limits of their legal growth, this was not the case with the second wave, which—as exemplified by Porter—did not so much embrace competition as seek ways to subdue and circumvent it. The third wave embraced competition with enthusiasm.

CHAPTER 33 | Red Queens and Blue Oceans

Here, you see, it takes all the running you can do, to keep in the same place. If you want to get somewhere else, you must run at least twice as fast.

—The Red Queen in Alice Through the Looking Glass

AGAINST THE BACKDROP of intense competitive pressures, the role of the manager was increasingly thrown into relief. The rewards they could make at the top of major companies grew, but so did the risks of being fired. Their performance was being judged against ever more demanding standards, but short-term profitability of the sort that would impress investors increasingly became the most important objective by far. Investing for the long term appeared less attractive than selling off weaker units or taking aggressive action against all perceived inefficiencies.

The challenge to the role of the managers was posed by agency theory, derived from transaction cost economics. It directly addressed the issue of cooperating parties that still had distinctive interests. In particular, it considered situations in which one party, the principal, delegated work to another, the agent. The principal could be in a quandary by not knowing exactly what the agent was up to, and whether their views of risk were truly aligned. This issue went to the heart of relationships between owners and managers. The rise of managerialism reflected the view that the agents were the key people. In business and politics, the notional principals—the stockholders/ board members and the electorate/politicians—were transitory and amateurish compared with the fixed, professional elite. The progressive separation of ownership and control had been charted by Berle and Means in the 1930s. The question posed now was whether and how the principals could reassert control over their agents.[1] If the agents did not wish to be so controlled, they had to take the initiative in demonstrating their value to shareholders or else find ways of releasing themselves from this constraint by becoming the owners as well as the managers.

Agency Theory

Michael Jensen, a Chicago-trained economist at Rochester, was impressed by a 1970 article in the *New York Times* by Milton Friedman that announced his arrival as an outspoken advocate of free-market economics. Friedman's target was activist Ralph Nader's campaign to get three representatives of the "public interest" on the board of General Motors. Friedman countered that the only responsibility of the corporation was to make profits so long as it engaged in "open and free competition without deception or fraud." His arguments challenged the managerialism of the past two decades directly: the leaders of the big corporations should neither expect to act as agents of the state nor expect the state to shield them from competition. This led Jensen and a colleague, William Meckling, to try to turn Friedman's plain speaking into economic theory. They found little to work with. They then made a big leap, taking what had become a contentious hypothesis when applied to finance—that markets were sufficiently efficient to provide a better guide to value than individuals, notably fund managers—and applying it to management. In this way, Justin Fox remarked, "the rational market idea" moved from "theoretical economics into the empirical subdivision of finance." There it "lost in nuance and gained in intensity." It was now seeking to use the "stock market's collective judgment to resolve conflicts of interest that had plagued scholars, executives, and shareholders for generations."[2] By assuming perfect labor markets, so that employees cost no more than what they were worth to the company and if necessary could move without cost to an alternative job, their analysis concluded that the most important risks were those carried by shareholders.[3]

By 1983, because of the growing interest shown by economists, Jensen felt able to claim that a "revolution would take place" over the coming decades "in our knowledge about organizations." Though organization science was in its infancy, the foundation for a powerful theory was in place. This involved departing from the economists' view of the firm as "little more than a black box that behaves in a value- or profit-maximizing way" in an environment in which "all contracts are perfectly and costlessly enforced." Instead he argued that firms could be understood in terms of systems geared to performance evaluation, rewards, and the assignment of decision rights. Relationships within an organization, including those between suppliers and customers, could be understood as contracts. Taken together they formed a complex system made up of maximizing agents with diverse objectives. This system would reach its own equilibrium. "In this sense, the behavior of the organization is like the equilibrium behavior of a market." This insight, he argued, was relevant to all types of organizations. It led to cooperative behavior being viewed "as a contracting problem among self-interested individuals with divergent interests."[4]

The prescriptive implication of this approach was that the owners had every reason to worry that their managers were getting distracted. Getting the interests of owners and managers back into alignment through monitoring and incentives required challenging the claims of managerialism. Deregulated markets were favored because they put at risk the positions of managers who were not delivering value for shareholders. Contrary to the pejorative connotations of hostile takeovers, the argument of Jensen and his colleagues was that these could increase the efficiency of the market. Managers dare not get sidetracked by loose and fashionable talk of multiple "stakeholders" but must keep their focus on the needs of the "shareholders" for profit maximization. While managers might complain about takeovers, they were a way of increasing value, redeploying assets, and protecting companies from mismanagement. "Scientific evidence indicates that the market for corporate control almost uniformly increases efficiency and shareholders' wealth."[5] Companies were viewed as a bundle of assets, formed and reformed according to the demands of the market. The market was all-knowing, while managers were inclined to myopia. By 1993 *Fortune* could declare: "The Imperial CEO has had his day—long live the shareholders."[6]

Adopting this view reduced the need for strategy and management. Once free-market determinism was adopted, then it was possible to "assume a management" as all other factors might also be assumed. It became just another "substitutable" commodity or, even worse, an opportunistic actor "in need of market discipline."[7] The manager's obligations were not inward-looking but only outward-looking, toward the shareholders. This was despite the fact that shareholders might be transitory and incoherent as a group and short term in perspective, or that efficient organizations had to be formed and nurtured if the moves the market demanded were to be implemented. The implications for the standing and vocations of managers were profound. The theory suggested that an organization's history and culture were irrelevant, staffed by people who might as well be strangers to each other. Managers being trained in this theory would offer no loyalty and expect none in return. Their task was to interpret the markets and respond to incentives. Little scope was left for the exercise of judgment and responsibility.

Management: A Dangerous Profession

In the early 1980s, warnings were first heard about the potential consequences of such logic for the running of businesses. The malaise was identified in 1980 by Robert Hayes and William Abernathy, both professors at the Harvard Business School. American managers, they complained, had "abdicated their strategic responsibilities." Increasingly from marketing, finance, and law rather than production, they sought short-term gains rather than long-term innovation. Particularly pointed, especially in the leading business school journal, was the assertion that the problem lay in an increasing managerial reliance on "principles that prize analytical detachment and methodological elegance over insight, based on experience, into the subtleties and complexities of strategic decisions." Within both the business community and academia, a "false and shallow concept of the professional manager" had developed. Such people were "pseudoprofessionals" who had no special expertise in any particular industry or technology but were believed to be able to "step into an unfamiliar company and run it successfully through strict application of financial controls, portfolio concepts, and a market-driven strategy." It had become a form of corporate religion, with its core doctrine that "neither industry experience nor hands-on technological expertise counts for very much," which helped to salve the conscience of those that lacked these qualities but also led to decisions about technological matters being taken as if they were "adjuncts to finance or marketing decisions" and could therefore be expressed in simplified, quantified forms.[8]

At the end of the decade, an unimpressed Franklin Fisher observed, "Bright young theorists tend to think of every problem in game-theoretic terms, including problems that are easier to think of in other forms."[9] Even in oligopoly theory, to which game theory seemed most suited, Fisher argued that it had not made a fundamental difference. It remained the case, after game theory as before, that a "great many outcomes were known to be possible. The context in which the theory was set was important, with outcomes dependent on what variables the oligopolists used and how they formed conjectures about each other." The effects of market structure on conduct and performance, he argued, had to take account of context. It was true that game theory could model these contexts, but this would not be in a convenient language. In response, Carl Shapiro argued that game theory had much to show for its efforts. But the prospect he offered was explicitly close to Schelling, suggesting not so much a unified theory but tools to identify a range of situations, ideas of what to look for in particular cases, but still dependent on detailed information to work out the best strategy. He also suspected "diminishing returns in the use of game theory to develop simple models of business strategy."[10] The subtle and complex reasoning described in the models was rarely replicated by actual decision-makers, who were "far less analytic and perform far less comprehensive analyses than these models posit."[11] Saloner acknowledged the challenge, especially if the models were taken literally and supposed to mirror an actual managerial situation with the aim of coming up with a prescription for action. He argued that "the appropriate role for microeconomic-style modeling in strategic management generally, and for game-theoretical modeling in particular, is not literal but rather is metaphorical."[12] It was not a distinction that was regularly recognized. It was all very well producing elegant solutions, but they were of little value if they were to problems that practitioners did not recognize and expressed in forms that they could not comprehend, let alone implement.

Although there were available academic theories that might assist in the design of organizations fit for particular purposes or at least explain why apparently rational designs produced dysfunctional results, nobody in business or government seemed to be taking much notice. Despite this growing divergence, the framework for research was difficult to change. Journals put a premium on established theories and methods. The apparently harder, quantitative work inspired by the economists assuming rational actors was dominant. Because modern software made large-scale number crunching possible, there was also a large database mentality. Research students were advised to avoid qualitative studies.[13] The effects could be seen not only in the research but in the norms for behavior the standard models were suggesting. In 2005, Sumantra Ghoshal observed:

> Combine agency theory with transaction costs economics, add in standard versions of game theory and negotiations analysis, and the picture of the manager that emerges is one that is now very familiar in practice: the ruthlessly hard-driving, strictly top-down, command-and

control focused, shareholder-value-obsessed, win-at-any-cost business leader.[14]

During the 1990s, theories were developed for this new breed of manager, promising success that could be measured in profit margins, market share, and stock prices. They reinforced the challenge to the idea of manager as the secure and steady, but essentially gray, bureaucrat who knew his place in the large corporation, which in turn knew its place in the larger economy. They offered "a conception of management itself in virtuous, heroic, high status terms."[15] As James Champy, who was at the heart of the neo-Taylorist push in the 1990s, observed, "Management has joined the ranks of the dangerous professions."[16] The sense of danger reflected the greater demands being placed on managers, as they had to fear not only absolute but even relative failure. In the world as celebrated by Jensen, stockholders were demanding faster and larger returns, and predators had their eyes open for potential acquisitions. Survival and success required not only attention to customers and products but a readiness to be ruthless, to hack away at the least efficient parts of the business, to push away and overwhelm competitors, and to lobby hard for changes in government policy—especially deregulation—that would open up new markets.

Attitudes toward finance had been transformed. The oil shocks and inflation of the 1970s extended a period of modest returns on equities, combined with a traditional reluctance to carry excessive debt. By the end of that decade, new and imaginative ways of raising capital were found. Companies could grow ambitiously and quickly by issuing bonds. Those investors prepared to take a greater risk could anticipate higher yields. With capital plentiful, many companies grew through mergers and acquisitions rather than by developing new products and processes. Attitudes became increasingly aggressive, with the focus on extracting value from corporate assets that had been missed by others or which current owners were unable to exploit. The logical next step was for the senior executives of companies to challenge the ownership model which saw others get the greatest benefit from their achievements. Management buyouts liberated them from their boards, providing greater scope for initiatives while incidentally generating a lot of money. This surge of activity eventually ran its course as the deals became more expensive and the returns disappointed. The debt still had to be serviced, and if it was too large, bankruptcy followed.

Businesses were now judged by their market value. This should reflect their intrinsic quality and the longer-term prospects for their goods and services, but that was not always easy to assess and all the incentives were for those who held the stock, including managers, to talk up its current value. This made success tangible and measurable compared with the longer-term development of a business which might require patience and low returns before the rewards became evident. But assessments of market value were vulnerable to sentiment and hype, as well as downright fraud. The energy company Enron was the prize exhibit of the latter possibility. This risk was greatest in areas that were hard to grasp, whether because of the sophistication of the financial instruments or the potential of the new technologies. Within companies, any activities that might be holding down the price, not providing the value that was being extracted elsewhere, came to be targeted. Thus they encouraged remorseless cost cutting.

Business Process Re-engineering

The Japanese success over the postwar decades could be taken as a triumph of a focused, patient, coherent, and consensual culture, a reflection of dedicated operational efficiency or else a combination of the two. Either way, the pace-setter was the car manufacturer, Toyota. Having spent the Second World War building military vehicles, the company struggled after the war to get back into the commercial market. Hampered by a lack of capital and technical capacity and by a strike-prone, radicalized work force, Toyota would probably have gone bankrupt were it not for the Korean War and large orders to supply the American military with vehicles. It then began to put together what became known as the Toyota Production System. The starting point was a solution to labor unrest by a unique deal which promised employees lifetime employment in return for loyalty and commitment. Together they would work to establish a system which would reduce waste. Ideas for improving productivity could be raised and explored in "quality circles." As this was a country where everything was still in short supply, a visit to a Ford plant in Michigan in 1950 left an abiding impression of the wastefulness of American production methods. Toyota aimed to keep down inventories and avoid idle equipment and workers. With excess inventory identified as both a cause of waste and a symptom of waste elsewhere in the system, methods were developed to process material and then move it on "just in time" for the next operation. Within Japan, Toyota's methods were emulated and further developed by other companies. In one industry after another, including motorcycles, shipping, steel, cameras, and electronic goods, Western companies found themselves losing market share to the Japanese. Government policy, the need to start from scratch after the war, and a cheap currency all helped.

In comparison with Japanese super-managers, their American counterparts appeared as a feeble bunch. During the course of the 1970s, the management literature became more introspective as mighty American firms were humbled by the Japanese insurgency, not only losing markets to more nimble opponents but also being caught out by a business culture that was far more innovative. Although the momentum behind the Japanese advance came to a juddering halt after the hubris and boom years of the late 1980s, Western companies were determined to mimic the Japanese by radical approaches to their own operational effectiveness. These came first under the heading of total quality management (TQM) and the second as business process re-engineering (BPR). Of the two, BPR was more significant in its impact and implications. The basic idea behind BPR was to bring together a set of techniques designed to make companies more competitive by enabling them to cut costs and improve products at the same time. The challenge was posed in terms of a fundamental rethink of how the organization set about its business rather than a determined effort to make the established systems run more efficiently. Information technologies were presented as the way to make this happen, by flattening hierarchies and developing networks. A close examination of what the organization was trying to achieve would lead to questions about whether goals were appropriate and whether structures could meet the goals. The idea seemed so attractive that Al Gore sought to re-engineer government while he served as vice president.

The underlying assumption of BPR, as with agency theory, was that an organization could be disaggregated as if it was a piece of machinery into a series of component parts, to be evaluated both individually and in relation to each other. It could then be put back together in an altered and hopefully improved form, with some elements discarded altogether and new ones added where necessary, to produce a new organization that would work far more effectively. Once an organization was viewed in these terms, there was no need for incrementalism. It should be possible to start from scratch and rethink the whole organization.

> Re-engineering is about beginning again with a clean sheet of paper. It is about rejecting the conventional wisdom and received assumptions of the past. Re-engineering is about inventing new approaches to process structure that bear little or no resemblance to those of previous eras.[17]

Thus, the history of an organization could be ignored and its old culture replaced with a brand new one. Workers would be indifferent and docile, or possibly even enthused by this process.[18]

At one level, BPR appeared strategic because it was demanding a fundamental reappraisal of businesses. But the main driver was not an assessment of competitive risks and possibilities or even internal barriers to progress but rather the potential impact of new technologies on efficiency. In this respect there were parallels with the coincident "revolution in military affairs." There was the same claim that this was the start of a new historical epoch, the same expectation that affairs would be shaped by the available methodologies rather than the competitive challenge, the same presumption that technology would drive and everything else would follow, and the same tendency to take the underlying strategy for granted, assuming that opponents/competitors would accept the same path rather than starting with the strategy and working out what processes were required.

Michael Hammer, one of the figures most associated with BPR, provided the transformational tone when he explained the idea in the *Harvard Business Review*: "Rather than embedding outdated processes in silicon and software, we should obliterate them and start over. We should…use the power of modern information technology to radically redesign our business processes in order to achieve dramatic improvements in their performance."[19] Hammer teamed up with James Champy, chairman of CSC Index, Inc., a consulting firm that specialized in implementing re-engineering projects.[20] Their 1993 book, *Reengineering the Corporation*, sold nearly two million copies. The rise of the concept was startling. Prior to 1992, the term "re-engineering" was barely mentioned in the business press; after that it was hard to escape it.[21] A survey in 1994 found that 78 percent of the *Fortune* 500 Companies and 60 percent of a broader sample of 2,200 U.S. companies were engaged in some form of re-engineering, with several projects apiece on average.[22] Initial reports were also positive about success rates. Consulting revenues from re-engineering were an estimated $2.5 billion by 1995. While Champy expanded CSC Index's revenues from $30 million in 1988 to $150 million in 1993, Hammer gave seminars and speeches for high fees. *Fortune* magazine described him as "re-engineering's John the Baptist, a tub-thumping preacher who doesn't perform miracles himself but, through speeches and writings, prepares the way for consultants and companies that do."[23]

There were both practical and rhetorical reasons for the success of the concept. At a time of tumult and uncertainty for industry, Champy and Hammer were able to play on the fear of being left behind, captured by Peter Drucker's endorsement on the cover of their book: "Reengineering is new, and it must be done." Hammer, in particular, pushed forward the message that however tough and brutal it all might be, the alternative was so much worse: "The choice is survival: it's between redundancies of 50 per cent or 100 per cent." Senior managers must hold their nerve: "Companies that unfurl the banner and march into battle without collapsing job titles, changing the compensation policy and instilling new attitudes and values get lost in the swamp." The anxiety generated by such language could be used to press forward: "You must play on the two basic emotions: fear and greed. You must frighten them by demonstrating the serious shortcomings of the current processes, spelling out how drastically these defective processes are hurting the organization."[24]

BPR began as a set of techniques. It was soon elevated into the foundation of a transformational moment. So while Hammer claimed that "just as the Industrial Revolution drew peasants into the urban factories and created the new social classes of workers and managers, so will the Reengineering Revolution profoundly rearrange the way people conceive of themselves, their work, their place in society."[25] Champy took this revolutionary theme a step further by arguing: "We are in the grip of the second managerial revolution, one that's very different from the first. The first was about a transfer of power. This one is about an access of freedom. Slowly, or suddenly, corporate managers all over the world are learning that free enterprise these days really is free."[26] Speaking of the virtues of "radical change," Champy described to managers the "secret satisfaction" of learning to do "what other managers in your industry thought to be impossible." They would not only "thrive" but would also "literally redefine the industry."[27]

Thomas Davenport, who had been director of research at the Boston-based Index Group, which was eventually turned into the CSC Index, was one of those closely associated with the development of the original concept. He later described how a "modest idea had become a monster" as it created a "Reengineering Industrial Complex." This was an "iron triangle of powerful interest groups: top managers at big companies, big-time management consultants, and big-league information technology vendors." It suited them all to make BPR appear not only essential in theory but successful in practice. The result was that specific projects were "repackaged as reengineering success stories." Managers found that they could get projects approved if they used the BPR label, while consultants repackaged what they had to offer as BPR specialists, discarding the previous set of buzzwords.

> Continuous improvement, systems analysis, industrial engineering, cycle time reduction—they all became versions of reengineering. A feeding frenzy was under way. Major consulting firms could

routinely bill clients at $1 million per month, and keep their strategists, operations experts, and system developers busy for years.

As companies made layoffs, these too were rebranded as "reengineering." Whatever the actual relationship, staff reductions "gave reengineering a strategic rationale and a financial justification." Meanwhile the computing industry also had a stake in BPR as it encouraged large expenditure on hardware, software, and communications products.

It did not take too long for the bubble to burst. Too many claims had been made, too much money had been spent, and too much resistance was growing—largely because of the association of re-engineering with layoffs—and it had all been accompanied, according to Davenport, by too much "hype." "The Reengineering Revolution" took potentially valuable innovation and experimentation but added exaggerated promise and heightened expectation leading to "faddishness and failure." The "time to trumpet change programs is after results are safely in the can." Most seriously, the fad treated people as if they were "just so many bits and bytes, interchangable parts to be reengineered." Dictums such as "Carry the wounded but shoot the stragglers" were hardly motivating, while young consultants with inflated salaries and even higher billing charges treated veteran employees with disdain. Whether or not this was a moment of historic change, employees were naturally inclined to think about protecting their own positions rather than enthuse about broad and expansive visions for the future of the company that could leave them without a job.

By 1994, the CSC Index "State of Reengineering Report" indicated that half the participating companies were reporting fear and anxiety, which was not surprising as almost three quarters of the companies were seeking to eliminate about a fifth of their jobs, on average. Of the re-engineering initiatives completed, "67% were judged as producing mediocre, marginal, or failed results." As was often the fate of the examples cited in the bestselling management books, companies hailed as champions of BPR were discovered to have either gotten into serious trouble or abandoned the idea. The CSC Index itself was in jeopardy. Its credibility was not helped by revelations in *Business Week* describing an intricate scheme to promote what Michael Treacy and Fred Wiersema, two of the CSC Index's consultants, hoped to be the next big book in the field, *The Discipline of Market Leaders*. The aim was to get it on the *New York Times* bestseller list. It was alleged (though denied) that employees of CSC Index had spent at least $250,000 purchasing more than ten thousand copies of the book, with yet more copies being bought by the company. The basis of the investment lay in the fees that were expected to come back to the company and consultants through their association with the "next big thing." Treacy was giving some eighty speeches a year, and his fee had jumped up to $30,000 per talk from $25,000. The importance of these books was further illustrated by reports that they were ghostwritten to ensure maximum effect. The allegations backfired on CSC Index. The *New York Times* re-jigged its bestseller list and also took a contract away from CSC Index. The next year Champy, whose book *Re-Engineering Management* was also implicated in the scandal, left the company. The firm, which had six hundred consultants at its peak, was liquidated in 1999. Its rise and fall was a symptom of a business that had become dependent upon staying ahead of the latest fashion.[28]

Escaping Competition

Was it the case that the road to success meant emulating the methods of those who were already successful? Precisely because their techniques were well known it was likely that following them would result in diminishing returns. Like the military concern with the operational art, it offered little by itself if put in the service of a flawed strategy. This was why Michael Porter questioned whether Japanese firms had any strategy at all—at least as he understood the term, that is, as a means to a unique competitive position. The Japanese advance during the 1970s and 1980s, he argued, was not the result of superior strategy but of superior operations. The Japanese managed to combine lower cost and superior quality and then imitated each other. But that approach, he noted, was bound to be subject to diminishing marginal returns as it became harder to squeeze more productivity out of existing factories and others caught up by improving the efficiency of their operations. Cutting costs and product improvements could be easily emulated and so left the relative competitive position unchanged. In fact, "hypercompetition" left everyone worse off (except perhaps the consumers). For Porter, a sustainable position required relating the company to its competitive environment. Outperformance required a difference that could be preserved.[29]

The problems facing companies trying to maintain a competitive advantage when everyone was trying to improve along the same metric was described as the "Red Queen effect." It was named after the line in *Alice Through the Looking Glass* with which this chapter opened. This was originally the name of a hypothesis used by evolutionary biologists to describe an arms race between predators and prey, a zero-sum game between species, none of which could ever win.[30] In the business context, it tended to be used as more of a race between similar entities. So, for example, early and striking gains might be made by saving time on standard processes, but soon others would catch up and gains would become increasingly marginal. The comparison was with a war of attrition. By focusing solely on operational effectiveness the result would be mutual destruction, until somehow the competition was stopped, often by means of consolidation through mergers.[31]

If the main arena was full of increasingly worn and wan warriors desperately trying to land blows on equally exhausted competitors as they dismissed the walking wounded and tripped over company corpses, then the logic was to find a less crowded, less competitive, and much more profitable place. The history of business after all was one of the rise and fall of whole sectors and of companies within them. It was an arena marked by instability. Of the original S&P 500 companies in 1957, for example, only seventy-four were still on the list thirty years later. Much management strategy literature was addressed to those in charge of existing companies, whereas in practice the most important innovations often came with new companies, which grew with new products. As noted by W. Chan Kim and Renee Mauborgne, there were "no permanently excellent companies, just like there are no permanently excellent industries." For this reason they argued that the hopeless firms were likely to be those competing without end in the "red oceans" instead of moving out to the blue oceans where they might "create new market space that is uncontested." Those who failed to do so would go the way of many past companies and simply disappear or be swallowed up. They argued that the "strategic move" should be the unit of analysis rather than the company although they did not suggest that blue oceans were only found by new companies.

Kim and Mauborgne contrasted business with military strategy. The military was bound to focus in a fight "over a given piece of land that is both limited and constant," while in the case of industry the "market universe" was never constant. Confusing their metaphors somewhat, they therefore argued that accepting red oceans meant accepting "the key constraining factors of war," which were "limited terrain and the need to beat an enemy to succeed," while failing to capitalize on the special advantage the business world offered of being able to "create new market space that is uncontested."[32] If their theory really depended on this idea of military strategy as being solely about battle, then it was off to a poor start. We have charted in this book how the desire to avoid battle except on the most favorable terms animated much military strategy. There was also a similar impulse at work here, the belief that the unimaginative plodders would stick with the most simplistic formulas, creating opportunities for the bold and the visionary to gain the advantage. Though Kim and Mauborgne acknowledged that red oceans were sometimes unavoidable, and that even blue oceans might eventually turn red, they made it clear that they found red ocean strategy fundamentally uninteresting. And here they fell exactly in line with the tradition in military strategy that sought to escape the brutal logic of battle and urged the application of superior intelligence to achieve political objectives while avoiding slaughter. There was the same infatuation with dichotomy, as if the choice was always to go one way or the other—direct/indirect, annihilation/exhaustion, attrition/maneuver, red ocean/blue ocean.

It was rarely denied that the orthodox route might at times have to be followed, but there was normally a clear implication that this could never satisfy the truly creative. As with so much writing on military strategy, the best way was illustrated by examples of success from companies that had transformed themselves and their industries, whether through meticulous plan, an empowered workforce, lateral thinking, bold re-engineering, or innovative design. The failures tended to be those who had stuck with orthodoxy, drifted in complacency, or moved from one crisis to another without ever getting a grip.

In an appendix to their book, Kim and Mauborgne developed a more analytical distinction between the red and blue oceans, now described as structuralist and the reconstructionist strategies. The structuralist approach derived from industrial organization theory, with Porter its most famous proponent. It was "environmentally determinist" because it took the market structure as given and thus posed the strategic challenge of competing for a known customer base. To succeed meant addressing the supply side. This meant doing whatever competitors did but better, relying on either differentiation or low cost. Sufficient resources might result in a form of victory, but the competition was essentially redistributive in that the share gained by one would be lost by another, which led to an attritional logic. The theory assumed exogenous limits. By contrast, the reconstructionist approach was derived from endogenous growth theory, which claimed that the ideas and actions of individual players could change the economic and industrial landscape. Such a strategy would suit an organization with an innovative bent and sensitivity to the risks of missing future opportunities. This addressed the demand side by using innovative techniques to create new markets. Those following a reconstructionist strategy would not be bound by the existing boundaries of the market. Such boundaries existed "only in managers' minds," so with an imaginative leap new markets might be identified. A new market space could be created through a deliberate effort. The wealth was new, and need not be taken from a competitor.[33]

In a later article, Kim and Mauborgne developed the distinction further, identifying the importance of not only a value proposition that would attract buyers but also a profit proposition so that money could be made, and lastly a people proposition to motivate those within the organization to work for or with the company. From this they defined strategy as "the development and alignment of the three propositions to either exploit or reconstruct the industrial and economic environment in which an organization operates." If these propositions were out of alignment—a great value proposition but no way of making a profit or a demotivated staff—then the result would be failure. Only at the top of the organization, with a senior executive able to take a holistic view, could the propositions be developed. On this basis they argued that "strategy can shape structure." The title marked the shift from Chandler, whose formulation was about the effect of strategy on internal organization, to the new quest to use strategy to change the external environment.[34]

This takes us back to Ansoff's distinction between strategy as a relationship to the environment and strategy as decision-making with imperfect information. The broad thrust of business strategy came under the first heading. The second more campaigning form of strategy, which dominated the military literature, was put in a more subordinate position, a challenge of implementation. Porter argued that the environment shaped and limited a business's strategic options; Kim and Mauborgne claimed that these limits could be transcended through imagination and innovation. Porter claimed that the competition could be beaten by either differentiation or price; Kim and Mauborgne claimed that it was better still to develop products in areas where there was no competition, but they then had to develop a business case and have the staff to make it work.

This view of strategy as a general orientation toward the environment offered a framework for evaluating all other endeavors within the organization. Strategy of this sort had to be long term, and it might have the elements of a plan, with an anticipated sequence of events geared to an ultimate goal. The strategy could be much looser than that, however, setting out a number of goals with some sense of priorities, available resources, and preferred means, maintaining considerable flexibility to allow for changing circumstances. How well either approach would work would depend on the nature of the environment. The more stable the less the freedom to maneuver and so less scope for a strategy of any sort other than one of internal adaption. Even a reconstructionist strategy would still be affected by responses from potential competitors who might appreciate what was going on or other actors who might be able to influence the demand for new products.

Such theories still lacked a formulation as compelling as Clausewitz's portrayal of the dynamic interaction of politics, violence, and chance. There was not even a concept comparable to Clausewitz's friction, although executives were always likely to experience their own versions of the fog of war. There were few incentives to dwell on such matters in a literature increasingly infused with promotions of particular strategic nostrums as the author's unique product. The promise was of success following a true interpretation of these nostrums according to circumstances, and the will to see it through. The tendency therefore was to play down the unforeseeable factors that could frustrate the best laid plans, whether a rogue calculation in product design, a misjudged advertisement, sudden fluctuations in exchange rates, or a terrible accident. Moments could arise in business as in politics when long-term aspirations had to be put to one side in a desperate struggle for survival, as a reliable market evaporated or development process failed to deliver or debts were called in. At such moments, priorities would need to be clarified, help sought wherever it could be found, and exceptional demands made of the organization. Other types of events might require no more than mid-course corrections or a reappraisal of one element of the overall approach. Knowledge of a coming event—such as a presentation to investors, a product launch, or a meeting with customers—could raise issues that had hitherto been neglected or illuminate aspects of the changing environment that had been missed before.

The influence of equilibrium models from classical economics on business strategy remained strong, while alternative concepts of non-linearity, chaos, and complex adaptive systems, though picked up by military strategists, were less in evidence. An article by Eric Beinhocker pointed to the challenge. An open system constantly in flux, shaped and reshaped by many agents acting independently, could seem more relevant to companies than a closed system tending to equilibrium. For example, a characteristic of complex adaptive systems was described as "punctuated equilibrium," referring to when times of relative calm and stability are interrupted by stormy restructuring periods. At such time, those whose strategies and skills were geared to the stable periods risked sudden obsolescence. Those who survived were likely to have prepared to adapt even if they could not be sure what adaptations would be required. Strategy, therefore, could not be based on a "focused line of attack—a clear statement of where, how and when to compete," but instead on preparations to perform well in a variety of future environments. Small organizations with relatively few parts were unlikely to adapt as well as those with more parts and a larger repertoire of responses to new situations, but after a certain point the capacity to adapt would fall off as response times shortened. There was a new balance to be struck, between complete resistance to change on the one hand and oversensitivity to shifts in the environment on the other, between stasis and chaos.[35]

A strategy could never really be considered a settled product, a fixed reference point for all decision-making, but rather a continuing activity, with important moments of decision. Such moments could not settle matters once and for all but provided the basis for moving on until the next decision. In this respect, strategy was the basis for getting from one state of affairs to another, hopefully better, state of affairs. Economic models might find ways of describing this dynamic but were less helpful when it came to guidance on how to cope.

CHAPTER 34 | The Sociological Challenge

I learned a great deal about military history and Confucian metaphors.
But the only practical advice that we were given was that every company
should send teams of people from different disciplines to country hotels
every year to think about the future.

—Participant in a fifteen-part course on business strategy given
by a leading name in the field, quoted by John Micklethwait
and Adrian Wooldridge.

WE NOW NEED to follow the second strand in management scholarship, drawn more from sociology than economics, which was
inclined from the start to consider human beings as social actors and organizations as bundles of social relationships. Although this strand had a separate course, there were overlaps with the economic strand in the challenge
to managerialism and in the propensity to follow fashion. It was influenced
by the counterculture of the 1960s in two respects. The first was distaste for
bureaucratic rigidity and hierarchy. This challenged the processes of rationalization and bureaucratization, arguing that a new and more enriching
form of organization needed to be devised. The second was the influence of
postmodernism, not only in the critique of the modernist forms of rationalist bureaucracy but also in offering a completely new way of considering
human affairs.

The critical anti-managerialist literature of the 1950s presented a mono-lithic, homogenized dystopian vision, only one step short of George Orwell's *1984*. The elites of large corporations were described as presiding over armies of white-collar workers, formed in their own bland—and obedient—image. During the 1960s and 1970s, however, demographic trends and lifestyle choices worked against conformity. The new businesses based on information and communication technologies often seemed to celebrate relaxed workplace practices and freethinking rather than crude hierarchy. Moreover there was a better anthropological understanding of organizations, the complex social for-mations that developed within and between individual units, and the incen-tives for individuals to develop practices that satisfied their needs as much as those of the organization for which they were supposed to be working.

The human relations school provided the foundations for this work, but it moved on after the war and turned into a rich field of organizational studies. Once organizations began to be viewed as social systems in their own right rather than as means to some management goal, questions arose not only about how this insight could lead to greater efficiency—which had been the concern of Elton Mayo and Chester Barnard—but how organizations could be arranged to make for a more fulfilling life for the workforce. This also fit in with a trend for individual pathologies to be explained by reference to their social set-tings. Structures that encouraged harmony, solidarity, and support should also therefore promote general well-being. An example of this was the book by the influential British social psychologist, James Brown, who after his experiences in the army and industry had concluded that mental illness was more of a social than a biological problem. He argued that organizations should be judged by their social as much as their technical and economic efficiency.[1]

Douglas McGregor's *The Human Side of Enterprise* opened with the ques-tion, "What are your assumptions (implicit as well explicit) about the most effective way to manage people?"[2] He offered two alternative theories. Under Theory X, which had developed with the factory shop floor, the presump-tion was that people disliked work and preferred direction rather than initia-tive, and so they must be controlled by means of threats and rewards. Under Theory Y, individuals wished for fulfillment and responsibility, and if offered the chance, they would commit themselves more thoroughly to the organi-zation. He developed these ideas while on the staff at MIT and then had a chance to put them into practice as president of Antioch College. While he found support for his theory, the experience of coping with fractious students and faculty convinced him of the need for active leadership. He had believed, he later recalled, "that a leader could operate successfully as a kind of adviser to his organization. I thought I could avoid being a 'boss'...I hoped to duck the unpleasant necessity of making difficult decisions...I finally began to realize that a leader cannot avoid the exercise of authority any more than he can avoid responsibility for what happens to his organization."[3] He did not, however, reject his more humanistic approach to management or embrace authoritarianism. While critics might have worried that the dichotomy between Theory X and Theory Y was too sharp, and that actual practice would be contingent on circumstances, McGregor appeared as a champion of consent against coercion, the democratic against the autocratic, the active against the passive.

Herbert Simon's ideas of bounded rationality encouraged a realistic assessment of how managers actually went about their business.[4] Another organizational psychologist, Karl Weick, challenged standard models in his book *The Social Psychology of Organizing* by demonstrating how uncoordinated and apparently chaotic systems could nonetheless prove adaptable when faced with the unexpected—more so than systems geared to assumptions of linearity. Weick drew on a range of disciplines, and introduced into the lexicon concepts such as "loose-coupling" (a distance and lack of responsiveness between individual parts of an organization created a form of adaptability), "enactment" (how structures and events are brought into existence by individual actions), and "sensemaking" (the processes by which people give meaning to experiences). Sensemaking was necessary because individuals must operate in inherently uncertain and unpredictable environments ("equivocality"). There were a variety of ways individuals could make sense of things, and his work focused on the different forms communication could take within an organization, notably in the face of external shocks. Weick's theories were, however, complex and did not offer the easiest read. His definition of an organization, for example, was "the resolving of equivocality in an enacted environment by means of interlocked behaviors in conditionally related processes."[5]

Business Revolutionaries

The idea that management should focus on the softer side of organizational life came to be developed and promoted by two McKinsey analysts, Tom Peters and Robert Waterman. The starting point was the pressure felt by McKinsey's in the late 1970s to come up with a credible response to Henderson's Boston Consulting Group. Peters, who had recently returned from completing a Ph.D. at Stanford in organization theory, was asked to work on a project out of the San Francisco office that addressed "organization effectiveness" and "implementation issues." At the time McKinsey's was still working largely with Chandler's concept of structure following strategy. At Stanford, Peters had been influenced by the work of Simon and Weick, both of whom challenged simple models of rational strategy formation and decision-making. He was joined by Waterman, who was also heavily influenced by Weick ("mesmerized," according to Peters), and wanted to reshape the way McKinsey's thought about organizations. One weekend with Tony Athos of the Harvard Business School and another McKinsey's consultant, Richard Pascale, who had been working on the success of Japanese firms, they developed what came to be known as the "7-S framework." Athos insisted— correctly, as it turned out—that any model had to be alliterative. A memorable shape was also required, in this case demonstrating, in contrast to the idea that strategy drives structure, that no a priori assumption could be made about which of the seven would make the difference at a particular time. The seven S's were structure, strategy, systems, style, skills, staff, and the somewhat awkward "superordinate goals."

The model was launched in a 1980 article. "At its most powerful and complex," the authors suggested, "the framework forces us to concentrate on interactions and fit. The real energy required to re-direct an institution comes when all the variables in the model are aligned."[6]

Athos and Pascale used the model specifically in a Japanese context. They argued that the Japanese scored on the softer side of management, by developing a sense of common purpose and culture in ways that American management had forgotten, if it had ever known.[7] A translated book, originally published in 1975, by Kenichi Ohmae, who had been head of McKinsey's Tokyo office, explained how strategy in Japan would not come from a large analytical department, fully formed in terms of rational, structured steps, but as something more ambiguous and intuitive, relying on a key figure with a grasp of the market whose ideas could be grasped in terms of the organization's culture.[8]

The most important book to emerge using the model was Peters and Waterman's *In Search of Excellence*.[9] Their book was presented as an answer to a straightforward question: what makes an excellent company? Possible candidates were identified by what appeared to be a sophisticated methodology. Sixty-two companies that appeared fairly successful were evaluated according to six performance criteria. The forty-three truly successful companies were those that were above the fiftieth percentile in four of the six performance metrics for twenty consecutive years. These were then studied in more detail, with key executives being interviewed. Out of this they distilled eight shared keys to excellence: a bias for action, customer focus, entrepreneurship, productivity through people, value-oriented CEOs, sticking to the knitting (that is, do what you know well), keeping things simple and lean, and simultaneously centralized and decentralized (that is, tight centralized control combined with maximum individual autonomy).[10]

Twenty years after publication, Peters acknowledged that the research that had gone into the book had been unsystematic though he remained convinced by the message.[11] The book was, he claimed, "an inflection point—a punctuation mark—that signaled the end of one era and the beginning of another." The target was not so much the Japanese as the American management model. Peters described his motivation at the time and since as being "genuinely, deeply, sincerely, and passionately pissed off!" His targets included Peter Drucker, because he encouraged "hierarchy and command-and-control, top-down business operation" and organizations in which everyone knew their place, and Robert McNamara, besotted by systems at the Pentagon which had led to people being "driven out of the equation." A third target was Xerox Corporation, where he had worked as a consultant, which to Peters demonstrated all that was wrong with the modern corporation: "the bureaucracy, the great strategy that never got implemented, the slavish attention to numbers rather than to people, the reverence for MBAs." He therefore saw the book as challenging "Management 101" based on Taylorism, reinforced by Drucker, and implemented by McNamara. He objected in particular to the bean-counting mentality focused entirely on numbers and finance. "The numerative, rationalist approach to management is right enough to be dangerously wrong, and it has arguably already led us astray."[12]

Waterman provided a slightly different, although not contradictory, account. In an article he coauthored, published in 1999, claims were made about the role of the book in translating the key themes in organizational studies, to the point of describing it as an accessible version of Weick.[13] They addressed the issue of whether it was possible to simplify without being simplistic. Even if the situation demanded complex theories, managers would not find them interesting and so good theory would not affect practice. The article claimed immodestly that *In Search of Excellence* succeeded by saying "pretty much everything there was to say about behavior in organizations and got it right, by virtue of the experts cited." Ideas of learning organizations, bounded rationality, narratives, and agenda-setting could all be found, with key theorists getting mentioned. Yet a description of the key messages suggested a set of values as much as scholarly findings, for example that "it's OK for guys to have feelings"; "don't take yourself too seriously"; it's "not your fault" if the world does not look neat and tidy; and "people who espouse rational models of decision-making want you to feel responsible for the disorder in the world, but don't for a moment let them get away with that silliness."

Whether or not this was truly an act of translating academic theory for practitioner consumption, the account of the book's gestation did reveal the effort that went into ensuring its appeal. There were some two hundred briefings to managerial audiences before publication. "During this process it became apparent that if the examples were retold in the form of a story then they compelled attention and promoted retention." Their audiences were averse to "numbers, charts and graphs," and also to "mid-level abstraction." Feedback also suggested that the original twenty-two attributes seemed too many, so they were whittled down to eight. The original number was seen as "too confusing not to mention also antithetical to the basic premise that it isn't as complex as you think if you pay attention to people!"

The book's positive message (America did have excellent companies) and uplifting prescription for success (work closely with your staff and customers and do not get bogged down with committees and reports) was a runaway success. It was the first business book to become a national bestseller, and eventually sold well over six million copies. Neither author stayed long at McKinsey's. Peters, resenting the patronizing attitude of the New York headquarters toward the marginal endeavors at the San Francisco office, had left before the book was published and was soon in demand as an inspirational, though expensive, speaker. His style, in speaking and writing, was dramatic and extravagant. The message and its ebullient communication were more important than the method. Whatever the original sources, *In Search of Excellence* relied on anecdote and secondary material rather than hard research.[14] It had failed to identify a reliable basis for sustainable growth or even survival. The excellent companies often struggled: soon after the book was published, a third were reported to be in financial difficulties.[15]

Instead of numbers, bureaucracy, control, and hard metrics, Peters and Waterman argued for people, customers, and relationships, which were much softer but could explain how things actually got done and what was accomplished. Business should be about heart, beauty, and art—not some "disembodied bloodless enterprise" but "the selfless pursuit of an ideal." As with most revolutionaries, the creative and destructive were never too far apart. In *Liberation Management*, an explicitly countercultural title, Peters wrote: "R-I-P. Rip, shred, tear, mutilate, destroy that hierarchy."[16] In 2003 he asserted that "a cool idea is by definition a Direct Frontal Attack on the Holy Authority of Today's Bosses."[17] Peters was undoubtedly a Theory Y man. A constant theme in his many books was to emphasize the positive side of work and argue that companies that cherished and encouraged this side would do better than those who suppressed their employee's creativity by trapping them in doleful hierarchies and assessing them against soulless metrics. Beyond that there was not a lot of consistency. He made the point himself when opening his 1987 book *Thriving on Chaos* by observing that there were "no excellent companies."

He was hardly alone in pointing to the need for flatter structures; units with more autonomy; and attention to quality, service, and innovation—not just to cost. Nor did he even claim much influence for himself. He opened a 2003 book proclaiming himself "madder than hell." He had "been screaming and yelling and shouting about bankrupt business practices for 25 or 30 years...mostly to no avail." Notably this book began with the army (about to go into Iraq but not yet experiencing real difficulties) as an innovative organization. He had already shown an interest in John Boyd and now he embraced the revolution in military affairs with its combination of "greater battlefield flexibility and greater information intensity," the decentralization and networking, the pursuit of indirection in strategy. He did not note the additional need for an operational environment that would allow the army to play to its strengths, rather than have the irritating "asymmetry" of an opponent playing to different rules.

Peters could express the frustrations of the functionary stuck in a cubicle, as he had been the neglected bright spark in a secondary regional office, too far down the management food chain to be able to exercise influence and put right all those things self-evidently going wrong. Much of his success was in expounding on the need for more humane and "cool" enterprises in countless speeches and seminars "with the exuberance and evangelistic zeal," according to the *Economist*, "of a 19th-century cough-syrup salesman."[18] Others spoke with both awe and alarm at how he turned management theory into something "so personal, so spiritual, so impractical."[19] This quasi-religious theme was the reason why Peters, and other leading management thinkers, came to be known as "gurus" (from the Sanskrit word for a teacher who could introduce light where there was darkness). Drucker, who came to be retrospectively described as the first of this class, disliked the term, observing sniffily that "guru" was used "because 'charlatan' is too long to fit into a headline."[20]

Gary Hamel had similar targets to Peters and a similar commanding presence at high-priced seminars. He worked in business schools and as a strategic consultant, and was regularly named as one of the top—if not the top—gurus. His focus, at least initially, was much more explicitly on strategy. His starting point was the transformation of the business environment as a result of deregulation, the decline of protectionist pressures, and the impact of information technologies. These opened up markets and introduced a new fluidity, requiring companies to be very clear about what they were good at but also agile enough to see opportunities for new types of markets and different sorts of business relationships. Those who stuck to the old models were doomed to fail; those who embraced the new had a chance.

Hamel originally gained attention with a series of articles with C. K. Prahalad, a professor at the University of Michigan, where Hamel had been a doctoral student. Together they attacked past strategic constructs, mocking the various qualities adumbrated by the consultancies and the business schools and suggesting that companies were trying to cope with the Japanese challenge by looking at surface features rather than the underlying concepts from which their competitors derived their "resolution, stamina, or inventiveness." They cited Sun Tzu: "All men can see the tactics whereby I conquer, but what none can see is the strategy out of which great victory is evolved." From strategic intent, once identified, could be derived a sense of direction, discovery, and destiny.[21] Their notion of "core competence," which suggested something more straightforward than turned out to be the case, was described as the "collective learning" in the organization. This was not so much about doing one thing well but about coordinating diverse skills and integrating streams of technology.[22] In a 1994 article, they claimed that the discontinuity in business practice was now so great that the various strategic concepts developed during the previous couple of decades—by Porter, for example—were no longer valid. They had assumed stable industrial structures, focused on business units, relied on economic analysis, and separated strategic analysis from its execution, which was presented as an organizational matter. Instead, Hamel and Prahalad argued for an approach that recognized the major transitions in industrial structure then underway, acknowledged the interplay of economics with politics and public policy, and involved those charged with executing strategies in their original design.[23]

Hamel's explicitly revolutionary turn came two years later. Although the medium was the *Harvard Business Review*, Hamel invoked Martin Luther King, Nelson Mandela, Gandhi, and even Saul Alinsky. Corporations, he argued, were reaching the limits of incrementalism. Everything now was at the margins, so there might only be a bit extra market share and a bit less cost, a bit faster response to customers and a bit more quality.[24] Hamel assumed his audience would not be satisfied with just getting by. They were unlikely to be the rule makers, the big companies who were the creators and protectors of industrial orthodoxy, but they would not be satisfied with being mere rule takers, those following behind for whom life was bound to be hard. Better to be among the rule breakers, the "malcontents, the radicals, the industry revolutionaries." They could overturn the industrial order because they were shackled "neither by convention nor by respect for precedent." The various trends that had opened up the international economy, coming under the heading of "globalization," meant that this was the time for the revolutionary. To those managers clinging to the status quo he raised the specter of being left behind in the revolutionary tide. In this vision, the only role for strategy was to create the revolution. "Strategy is revolution. Everything else is tactics."

To be revolutionary, it was necessary to rethink the business. In this respect he echoed Mintzberg's castigation of strategic planning, which took the boundaries for granted and failed to look for the opportunities in new, uncontested space. With an elitism that hampered any capacity for discovery, the planners harnessed "only a small proportion of an organization's creative potential." By not engaging the lower reaches of the organization, senior management encouraged reaction, as change became a "synonym for something nasty," something to be feared, imposed from above. So strategy-making had to be democratic. This was where Hamel quoted Alinsky, who had decried elitist planning as anti-democratic, as "a monumental testament to lack of faith in the ability and intelligence of the masses of people to think their way through to the successful solution of their problems."[25]

Hamel did not deviate from his core theme, that the old strategic model was as outdated as the business model it sought to help. His 2000 book, *Leading the Revolution*,[26] developed what had become familiar themes but with the motivational, inspirational style expected of a business guru, suggesting that the only limits to what they could accomplish lay in their imaginations. This was not a book, he insisted, about "doing better" or for "people who want to tinker at the margins." Instead, it was an "impassioned plea to reinvent management as we know it—to rethink the fundamental assumptions we have about capitalism, organizational life, and the meaning of work."

Unfortunately, he adopted Enron as his company of choice. Enron had transformed itself over the 1990s from a pipeline company to an energy trader, using its expertise and muscle to buy and sell contracts. Hamel celebrated Enron as a company that had "institutionalized a capacity for perpetual innovation" and as "an organization where thousands of people see themselves as potential revolutionaries." He became chair of the Enron Advisor Council. Enron's management had a suitably populist rhetoric ("power to the people") and claimed to have empowered its employees, describing them all as fellow revolutionaries.[27] It adopted Hamel-type themes, including likening its quest for free markets with the civil rights campaign of the 1960s, and challenged all conventional assumptions about how businesses should operate. Enron was celebrated as having found a way to extraordinary profits through forms of integration and agility that had eluded others. But the company collapsed at the end of 2001, taking auditor Arthur Anderson down with it. The source of its major profits was exposed as fraud, helped by deals of such complexity that nobody quite understood what was going on. It had made a political push for deregulation of energy markets, ready to accuse any external analyst who expressed doubts about its claims as being ideologically antagonistic. Hamel expunged Enron from the second edition of his book and could argue that he was by no means alone in being caught out by the elaborate efforts undertaken by Enron's senior management to hide its debt and its vulnerability to a deteriorating trading position.[28]

In a 2003 book, Hamel complained that companies were being driven by "the theorists and practitioners" who had invented the rules of "modern" management a century earlier. Contemporary managers were still beholden to the ideas of Frederick Taylor and Max Weber (whose ambivalent attitude toward bureaucracy Hamel was apparently unaware of). The old management model had become dysfunctional in a world where the need was for flexibility and creativity. Instead of the "stultifying" focus on the bureaucratic values of "control, precision, stability, discipline and reliability,"[29] he sought innovation, adaptability, passion, and ideology. Reflecting the traditional romantic reaction against rationalism he urged organizations to be more like communities, dependent "on norms, values, and the gentle prodding of one's peers," offering emotional rather than financial rewards.[30] Martin Luther King's most famous speech was invoked, as Hamel described his own dream in which "the drama of change is not accompanied by the wrenching trauma of a turnaround . . . An electric current of innovation pulses through every activity . . . where the renegades always trump the reactionaries." What he was careful not to do was predict the future of management. His aim, he insisted, was "to help you invent it." A later book, which addressed directly questions of norms and values in business, captured the underlying complaint: "There's nothing wrong with utilitarian values like profit, advantage and efficiency, but they lack nobility." Organizations needed an uplifting sense of purpose and individuals an allegiance to the "sublime and the majestic" and a cause greater than oneself.[31] Although Hamel began writing about strategy, he had veered into broad social theory. The analysis had become almost a parody of Theory X and Theory Y, pushing dichotomies to their limits, community versus bureaucracy, renegades versus reactionaries, innovation and change versus stability and order, emotional rewards versus financial rewards.

The underlying propositions could be rephrased in terms of classic radical thought, demanding the upending of obsolescent hierarchies so that shackles could be removed, productive energy and imagination could be released, and all could realize their potential. But this was always a strange revolution, certainly more bourgeois than proletarian. As it was never a real movement, it lacked institutional expression. It reflected the counterculture's revolt against rationalism and bureaucracy, a yearning for passion and the play of imagination, and the urge to trust in feelings and experience, assuming that the best things happened spontaneously. But, as with the counterculture, this was a false prospectus. It exaggerated the democratic possibilities of a business organization. There was also the same presumption that participatory democracy would not lead to reactionary and myopic policies but instead to the most progressive, in this case the sort that a sagacious strategic consultant might advise.

Work could be fun and exciting; full of challenge and innovation; with congenial, stimulating, and supportive colleagues; it could also include essential but boring tasks, pressing deadlines and tight budgets, angry customers and slipshod suppliers, irritating co-workers and myopic bosses. It was one thing to recognize the value of a workforce and regret that too much of it was left untapped; it was quite another to suggest that the inspired subordinate, with drive and imagination, could subvert power structures, recast cultures, and reshape institutional systems. Common sense argued for engaging employees earlier in company decisions and drawing upon the expertise of those actually running the key processes before overhauling them. Only at the top, however, was it possible to take an overview of all aspects of a company's activities, make authoritative decisions, allocate resources, and accept responsibility.

This is why corporate claims of higher purpose were often treated cynically. Occasional transformational change might be exciting, but too much could also be exhausting. Some calm and stability might be welcomed. Structure, discipline, and accountability were necessary for the innovative to make changes and then sustain them. Many employees would assume their senior management should work out the strategy and would prefer not to be badgered for new ideas that were then ignored. The need for an antidote to the soaring rhetoric of the gurus and the exaggerated claims of the consultants was reflected in the popularity of Scott Adams's subversive cartoon strip "Dilbert" with its world of persecuted engineers, fantasizing marketeers, stupid bosses, and greedy consultants. Consultants, Adams observed, "will ultimately recommend that you do whatever you're *not* doing now. Centralize whatever is decentralized. Flatten whatever is vertical. Diversify whatever is concentrated and divest everything that is not 'core' to the business." In Dilbert's world, companies needed strategies "so the employees will know what they don't do." Dilbert explained how he put together a strategy: "I collected optimistic data, put it in the context of bad analogies, seasoned it with saliency bias...added herd instinct, a pinch of confirmation bias." When his company announced that it would abandon a strategy of making good products in favor of a "desperate strategy of mergers, business spin-offs, fruit-less partnerships, and random reorganizations" and an accelerated "program of paying the good employees to leave," the stock price went up by three points.[32]

| Deliberate or Emergent

If many remedies are prescribed for an illness, you may be certain that the illness has no cure.

—Anton Chekhov, *The Cherry Orchard*

THE QUESTION OF whether senior management really could give a business strategic direction was turned into one of the more influential dichotomies in the field, that between deliberate or emergent strategies. Henry Mintzberg, who was responsible for the most sustained challenge to the so-called design model of strategy, stressed the possibility of a continuing, intelligent learning response to a changing environment. In a seminal article with James Waters, Mintzberg urged that instead of considering strategy as a single product, handed over to others for implementation, it should be understood as a "pattern in a stream of decisions." On this basis they distinguished between "intended" and "realized" strategy. If what was realized was intended then this was "deliberate"; patterns that were realized despite of or in the absence of intentions were "emergent."

A deliberate strategy depended on the intentions disseminated in an organization being precise, so there could be no doubt about what was desired, and realizable. There could be no interference from any external force, whether the market, politics, or technology. Such a totally benign environment, or at least one where the problems could be anticipated and controlled, would be a "tall order." By contrast, a perfectly emergent strategy would demonstrate consistency in action in the absence of intention. While a total absence of intention was hard to imagine, the reference was to the idea of the environment imposing a pattern of decision, as if notional decision-takers could not help themselves in the face of the structural constraints and imperatives they faced. Innumerable small decisions taken throughout the organization could move it to an unanticipated place, to the surprise and possible consternation of senior management. In practice, the sharp distinction was between a strategy that involved central direction and control based on an original plan, a model which Mintzberg considered extremely unwise, and one that was about learning and adaption.[1]

The idea of organizations being able to stick to an original plan in the face of uncertainty was easy enough to challenge. In some respect, all strategies were bound to be emergent. There was always a previous history, which had shaped the original plan, and even a strategy that had emerged and seemed to be working would at some point have to be addressed, if only because a particular goal had been reached. Mintzberg's main point therefore was about the need for the organization and its leadership to keep on learning. Just like the mētis of ancient Greece, this learning, flexibility, and responsiveness would be particularly important when an environment was "too unstable or complex to comprehend, or too imposing to defy." It was likely to require a degree of experimentation, or surrendering some control to those closest to situations who had the best information to develop realistic strategies. This was not to deny the importance of managers at times imposing their intentions and providing a sense of direction.

Mintzberg's careful conclusion was that "strategy formation walks on two feet, one deliberate, the other emergent." His heart, however, was clearly with the emergent, perhaps because it required more of the organization and was a surer test of its structures. An organization capable of benefiting from the experiences and insights of all its members should be in better shape than one where all the running had to be made by senior management. After the 2008 financial crisis, he bemoaned the consequences of "the depreciation in companies of community—people's sense of belonging to and caring for something larger than themselves." Human beings were social animals who could not "function effectively without a social system that is larger than ourselves." Communities were "the social glue that binds us together for the greater good." Admired companies managed to create this sense of community, and to this end he cited an article by the president of Pixar (an animated film production company) who attributed his studio's success to its "vibrant community where talented people are loyal to one another and their collective work, everyone feels that they are part of something extraordinary, and their passion and accomplishments make the community a magnet for talented people coming out of schools or working at other places."[2] Instead of the celebrated form of heroic egocentric leadership, an alternative sort was needed that was "personally engaged in order to engage others, so that anyone and everyone can exercise initiative." This required shedding "individualist behavior and many of its short-term measures in favor of practices that promote trust, engagement, and spontaneous collaboration aimed at sustainability."[3]

Learning Organizations

Mintzberg was by no means unique in celebrating "learning organizations." One justification was organizational efficiency: those with a commitment to knowledge, mechanisms for renewal, and openness to the outside world should perform more effectively. Another was that organizational life should be an uplifting social and collective experience, "a group of people working together to collectively enhance their capacities to create results that they truly care about."[4] As individuals did the learning, a firm which aspired to be a learning organization "must teach its employees how to learn, and it must reward them for success in learning."[5] These twin objectives reflected the ambition of the human relations school. If work became a positive experience, a source of personal fulfillment, it could serve the organization by also serving the individual, marrying humanism with bureaucratic efficiency. This was reflected in the rhetoric of Peters and Hamel. Charles Handy, a British management consultant and another enthusiast for this approach, described a learning organization as being about "curiosity, forgiveness, trust, togetherness."[6]

One book took these ideas to the extreme, advocating *Strategy without Design*. Rational, deliberate, strategy-making directed at specific goals was naïve, failing to grasp how actions reflected "invisible historical and cultural forces," unaware of the impossibility of comprehending the whole or the foolishness of attempts to move entities around like chessboard pieces (the favorite image from the master strategist). In practice there were "too many contingencies, too many alternative limits, too many system influences, and the pursuit is too debilitating, for such an intellectualized picture ever to emerge fully."[7] By contrast Chia and Holt, acknowledging Liddell Hart, pointed to the "surprising efficacy of indirect action." Action that is "oblique or deemed peripheral in relation to specific ends can often produce more dramatic and lasting effects than direct, focused action."[8] This alternative strategy was not only unintelligible but also discussed without reference to power, deal-making, coercion, or coalition construction. The result was a postmodern version of Tolstoy, with barely perceptible everyday gestures moving big organizations in ways that nobody intended but could still come out right at the end. Rather than success being attributed to "the pre-existence of a deliberately planned strategy," it could be "traced indirectly as the cumulative effect of a whole plethora of coping actions initiated by a multitude of individuals, all seeking merely to respond constructively to the predicaments they find themselves in." The wise strategist was advised to avoid the temptation to control and to go with the organizational flow. Chia and Holt called this "strategic blandness," involving a "will-o'-the-wisp endurance that invites no opposition and assumes no domination; it exists only in the plenitude of as yet unrealized possibilities." The aim should be "to shy away from once fervid ambition and stringently held commitments and, instead, nurture a curiosity whose meandering enquiry moves through infatuation, temperance and indifference with equal passion."[9] As "sensemaking," this left a lot to be desired. It was also some distance away from the more prosaic reality of organizational life for most people most of the time.

Management as Domination

Theories of strategy that lacked a theory of power were bound to mislead. With enthusiasm for organizations as learning and mutually supportive communities could come reluctance to address issues of power. If anything, organizational politics was deplored for its disruptive effects. Power plays by individuals promoting their own careers or just their pet projects generated bad feeling. This could be detrimental to overall efficiency as well as to morale. Power certainly could become an end in itself, a source of status and opportunities to boss others around. Nonetheless, it was also the case that without power it was hard to move organizations toward particular goals and little of value might be accomplished. With a grasp of power, bad decisions might be implemented too rigorously, but without such a grasp potentially good decisions might not be quite taken or followed through. Power structures within organizations, even more so than in states, would depend on personalities and culture, on social contacts as well as personnel contracts, on the reputation of particular units, and on the way budgets were put together and expenditures monitored. Addressing issues of power was not a strategy in itself but an unavoidable part of strategy. It meant considering how decisions might best be formed and implemented.

Jeffrey Pfeffer, one of the rare writers on organizations to make power his main focus, largely advised on the sources and exercise of power, emphasizing the importance of understanding the main players who need to be brought on board, acquiring positions on key committees, exercising a role over budgets and promotions, gaining allies and supporters, and learning how to frame issues to best advantage.[10] A later book provided guidance on how to succeed with power in organizations, including advice to beware of the leadership literature, with its "prescriptions about following an inner compass, being truthful, letting inner feelings show, being modest and self-effacing, not behaving in a bullying or abusive way," which explained how people wished the world to be rather than how it was.[11]

Critics of the more optimistic views of management picked up on their naïveté about power. Helen Armstrong described the "learning organization" as a "Machiavellian subterfuge" to encourage workers in their own exploitation. The "prevalence of insecure job markets, contract and part-time work, outsourcing and downsizing is hardly conducive to feelings of empowerment for most workers."[12] Even when there was evidence of shared meanings and values these were most likely to reflect the perspectives of senior management. What might be thought of as a benign culture could appear in a different light as a hegemonic project. Issues of power and ideology could not be avoided.[13]

This view formed part of a critical theory, influenced by postmodernism, that considered corporate strategy a natural target because it presented itself as a very modernist project, seeking to manipulate causes to achieve defined effects in a rational way. On this basis, strategy was an example of thinking that concealed more than it revealed in order to support established power structures. Individuals and what they said and did could not be understood outside of their social context, which was in turn reshaped by what they said and did. In one Foucault-inspired critique, reflecting a postmodern insurgency in British management schools, David Knights and Glenn Morgan challenged the idea of strategy as a set of rational techniques for managing complex businesses in a changing environment and instead proposed "focusing upon corporate strategy as a set of discourses and practices which transform managers and employees alike into subjects who secure their sense of purpose and reality by formulating, evaluating and conducting strategy."[14]

In this strategy was not a general approach to the problems of management but a specific corporate ideology. Thus they asked: "If strategy is so important, how did business manage to survive so long without 'consciously' having a concept of strategy?" Somewhat oddly, given Foucault's own extensive references to strategy, they criticized early writers, such as Chandler, for imputing "strategic intent to the business world as if it existed prior to practitioners having subscribed explicitly to the discipline of strategy." The crime, apparently, was for the academic to act as legislator, telling people what they really meant in a way which might be quite different from the actors' "own discursive understanding of their actions." This meant neglecting the interesting question of what people actually meant when they talked about strategy or whatever other descriptor they used for activity that an observer might consider to be strategic. Knights and Morgan argued that strategy only became important as the corporation had to explain what it was doing and why to internal and external audiences. It was about legitimizing the elite as much as deciding upon a course of action. The "discourse of corporate strategy" constituted "a field of knowledge and power which defines what the 'real problems' are within organizations and the parameters of the 'real solutions' to them." It was a "technology of power," enabling some actors while disabling others, and a source of "the problems it professes to resolve." As such it might have been challenged by alternative discourses, for example, reflecting more instinctive and or less hierarchical approaches or else the indifference and cynicism prompted by top-down pronouncements. For the discourse of strategic management to have become so embedded was a "triumph." It sustained and enhanced the prerogatives of management and gave them a sense of security, legitimized their exercise of power, identified those able to contribute to their discourse, and rationalized success and failure.

Stewart Clegg, Chris Carter, and Martin Kornberger, also representing the critical strand in British management theory, took this theme further. They argued that strategy of this type, especially in its manifestation as a corporate strategic plan, could be represented in Cartesian terms as an intelligent mind attempting to lead a dumb and submissive body or as a Nietzschean "will to power," an attempt to control, predict, and dominate the future.[15] This effort was, however, doomed. Strategic plans were often management fantasies, far exceeding organizational capabilities, with goals defined as if the future could be predicted. The effort was bound to fail because of the inevitable gaps between planning and implementation, means and ends, management and organization, order and disorder. Instead of managing these gaps, strategic planning actively generated and sustained them. The practice of strategic planning created "a system of divisions that constantly undermines and subverts the order that the strategic plan proposes." It created an illusion of "an ordered and cosy realm, as a controllable inside, confronting a more or less chaotic outside, an exterior that constantly threatens its survival.

Strategic planning reinforces and deepens this gap: it ignores the complexities and potentialities of 'disorganization.'"

This critique was directed at something of a straw man. Possibly in earlier decades senior managers had really believed in such an orderly and controllable interior world, and had been sustained in this belief by this comforting and ambitious ideology, manifested in a detailed plan, based on ultra-rationalist assumptions, passed down through the hierarchy, and prescribing behavior on almost Taylorist lines. In terms of the grip of economic theory on business schools, the idea that real businesses might try to work this way was not wholly preposterous. It lingered on, in a mild form, with "the balanced scorecard." Actual management practice, however, suggested a much greater sense of insecurity and uncertainty. Management strategy had become a much more capacious umbrella, including a range of approaches. Some managers might approximate to this caricature but others would be seeking to draw staff into decision-making and were well aware of the distorting effects of attempts at detailed plans with fixed targets.

Fads and Fashions

Mintzberg et al's influential *Strategy Safari* identified ten different approaches to the challenge of strategy. Elsewhere the concern was that the disagreements had become so numerous and "fractious" that "scholars despaired that [they] could not even come up with a logically coherent definition of the field."[16] Another described strategy as being in a "pre-paradigmatic state."[17] Yet another saw the source of confusion as a multiplicity of strategies rather than a single paradigm. The word *strategy* was being attached to every new initiative:

> Strategy has become a catchall term used to mean whatever one wants it to mean. Business magazines now have regular sections devoted to strategy, typically discussing how featured firms are dealing with distinct issues, such as customer service, joint ventures, branding or e-commerce. In turn, executives talk about their "service strategy," their "joint venture strategy," their "branding strategy" or whatever kind of strategy is on their minds at a particular moment.[18]

John Kay observed in a skeptical overview that: "Probably the commonest sense in which the word strategy is employed today is as a synonym for expensive."[19]

The proliferation of strategies had been both vertical, in the range of subsidiary activities given the label, and horizontal, in the range of both procedural and substantive prescriptions for relating to the environment. The 1980s and 1990s involved a dizzying sequence of grand ideas, the appearance of gurus such as Peters and Hamel, and the rise and fall of BPR. As a result, a new field of research developed around the proliferation of management fashions and fads. Their frequency and variety, the surrounding hype, and their short half-life prompted a degree of wonder at why they were taken at all seriously.[20] The management consumer was not confronted with a dominant paradigm but instead with cacophony and inconsistency, hints of unique keys to success that could be accessed by buying the book, attending the seminar, or—best of all—signing the consultancy contract. The ideas came thick and fast, tumbling over each other, the banal with the counterintuitive, genuine insights with implausible propositions, telling insights with dubious generalizations.

There were a variety of explanations for the phenomenon. Gurus helped the managers make sense of an uncertain world and provided a degree of predictability. They also offered an external authority to help legitimize what they were up to. Even the skeptics were anxious that they might be missing out on something, or that they might be perceived to be ignoring important developments. The succession of fads and fashions might have suggested something cynical and even random, but there was always the possibility of actual progress, as if some higher stage of management was really at hand. If so, the conscientious manager at least had to pay attention.[21] Nor was it the case that all products were useless.[22] Since Drucker first introduced management by objectives, certain techniques had been introduced that might once have been considered fads but were now considered generally helpful, such as SWOT analysis, the Boston matrix, or quality circles. Even with BPR the problem was in excessive radicalism, demanding too much at once and overstating the benefits. After the 1980s, it was the rare company that would not claim to be aspiring to excellence and quality, looking to encourage local initiative. One legacy was the regular insistence that senior managers were "passionate" about such matters.

The innovations most likely to endure were those that helped senior executives exert influence over the organization. Consider the example of the "balanced scorecard," first introduced in a 1992 *Harvard Business Review* article by Robert Kaplan and David Norton. Financial returns, they argued, were an inadequate guide to how well a company was doing. A much broader and also realistic view of performance was required. They understood strategy as being a "set of hypotheses about cause and effect" and proposed that by measuring key effects it should be possible to demonstrate whether or not a strategy was being properly implemented. Goals and appropriate measures should be developed, covering finance, the views of customers, internal organization, and the ability to innovate. This assumed that "people will adopt whatever behaviors and take whatever actions are necessary to arrive at those goals." The advantages of the balanced scorecard were that it was easy to understand, staff could be involved in its construction, and it improved the information available to management. The key performance indicators (KPIs) would reflect, however, what could be measured—not necessarily what was important—and then become ends in themselves. Staff would meet the goals as measured even if there was no obvious benefit to the organization. Managers who relied solely on monitoring the indicators could be swamped by data that was hard to interpret, fail to understand the complex interactions between the different measures, and still miss vital signs of dysfunction.[23] Without being clear on what needs to be done and why, Stephen Bungay pointed out, "the fetishization of the metrics is a near certainty." Though the scorecard could be a way of communicating intent, it was still fundamentally a control system.[24]

A study of sixteen management fashions from over five decades suggested that over time they had become "broader-based but shorter-lived and more difficult for upper management to implement."[25] When a particular management technique was adopted, few effects on organizational performance could be discerned. Nonetheless, adoption did influence corporate reputation and even executive pay. The research strengthened "previous arguments that firms do not necessarily choose the technologically best or most efficient techniques but, instead, seek external legitimacy by adopting widely accepted and approved practices."[26] Other research suggested that the new ideas that seemed to catch on were considered to be capturing "the zeitgeist or 'spirit of the times.'"[27] An analysis of the conceptual development of the word *strategy* gathered ninety-one definitions for the period from 1962 to 2008. Looking at the way nouns were used, the authors observed an abrupt drop in *planning*, a rise and then steady decline in *environment*, with *competition* showing a steady increase. While the verb *achieve* was a constant, over time *formulate* gave way to *relate*.[28]

This interest in the role of fads and fashions in enterprises reflected awareness that strategy could not be considered as a product, something that in the form of an input might give direction to an organization or as an output that might order relations with the external environment, but as a continuing practice, the everyday work of many people (not just those at the top) within an organization. Strategy was not the property of organizations but something that people did. This led to the idea of "strategy as practice." This was a natural continuation of the work of organizational sociologists and psychologists, such as Weick, with their interest in the disparate experiences and aspirations of individuals bound together by the demands of employment and developing social forms that were more or less creative or destructive, both for them and the broader purpose the organization was supposed to serve. It could bring together the macro-level of the institution with the micro-level of the individual with guidelines for observational research.[29]

One unfortunate consequence of the focus on strategy as practice was to encourage the use of the verb *strategizing*, meaning "to do strategy." It also encouraged the idea that this was a ubiquitous activity, "to the extent that it is consequential for the strategic outcomes, directions, survival and competitive advantage of the firm." This therefore involved multiple actors at all levels.[30] Strategy "practitioners," including managers and consultants, would draw on the established strategic "practices" particular to their organizations, turning these into a specific strategic "praxis" as they engaged with others to generate something called strategy, which in turn reshaped the organizational practices.[31] This challenged the idea of strategy as a deliberate, top-down process that was the purview of senior management. As soon as questions of implementation came in, it was evident that micro-level decisions could influence the macro-level performance. This was at the heart of the familiar critique of the strategic planning model. That was not the same, however, as organizations effectively being managed from the bottom up. The decisions of senior managers, for better or worse, more or less influenced by what they understood to be the character of organizational practices, were still normally much more significant than those further down the hierarchy thanks to their reach and the resources at their disposal. Strategy as practice was important when it came to understanding organizations, but so too was strategy as power.

Back to the Narrative

What about strategy as "sensemaking"? If there was one persistent theme it was the attraction of a good story to help convey the most important points. This was evident in Taylor's story of the hard-working Schmidt, Mayo's of the Hawthorne experiment, or Barnard's unemployed in New Jersey. It was behind the whole reliance on the case study method, underscoring the view that the best way to understand the challenges of management was to try to tell a tale around a specific set of circumstances. In much of the organizational literature, as a methodological contrast to rational actor theory, stories were elevated to a vital source of organizational communication and effectiveness.[32] This could draw on psychological research which confirmed their importance as ways of explaining the past but also convincing people about future courses of action. With businesses no longer run on military lines and employees expecting to be persuaded rather than just instructed, managers were urged to use stories to help make their case. "Gone are the command-and-control days of executives managing by decree," observed Jay Conger in 1998, for now businesses were run "largely by cross-functional teams of peers and populated by baby boomers and their Generation Y offspring, who show little tolerance for unquestioned authority."[33] "Stories are the latest fad to have hit the corporate communications industry," observed columnist Lucy Kellaway. "Experts everywhere are waking up to the something that any child could tell them: that a story is easier to listen to and much easier to remember than a dry string of facts and propositions."[34]

Stories made it possible to avoid abstractions, reduce complexity, and make vital points indirectly, stressing the importance of being alert to serendipitous opportunities, discontented staff, or the one small point that might ruin an otherwise brilliant campaign. Stories were to the fore in Weick's account of sensemaking, allowing "the clarity achieved in one small area to be extended to and imposed on an adjacent area that is less orderly."[35] Peters and Waterman came to appreciate through successive briefings that their ideas worked with business audiences as stories but not as charts and diagrams. They described how their excellent companies were "unashamed collectors and tellers of stories...rich tapestries of anecdote, myth, and fairy tale." Many business strategy books were essentially collections of stories, each intended to underline some general point.

Stories could come in all shapes and sizes: innocent and unstructured, as well as deliberate and purposeful; about technical specifications or perhaps the antics of a senior manager; elaborate or barely an anecdote; designed for regular re-telling or heard once and then forgotten; intended for a privileged few, and thus sharp and to the point, or knowingly prepared for multiple audiences, and so carefully ambiguous. Narratives could be found in minutes of meetings, presentations to clients, business plans, and even formulaic forms of analysis: in SWOT, analysis "opportunities" represented the "call," whereas "threats" became antagonists. "As strengths are employed and weaknesses transformed, the protagonist becomes a hero."

Eventually academics took notice, influenced by the "narrative turn," so that stories and storytelling came to be identified not only as essential to effective leadership when formulating and implementing its strategy, but at the heart of all communication in an organization, from low-level grumbles and mid-level pep talks up to the high-level visions. Stories were told about senior managers to show how reasonable or out of touch they might be, of past events to show how the organization was once great or had an enduring culture, of the chance insight that led to an exciting new product or the poor calculation that led to a flop. By studying stories, the development and reinforcement of institutional cultures could be explored as well as the beliefs and assumptions that underpinned them. In the constant conversations that made up any organization, this culture could be changed and even subverted, as individuals on the basis of their own experiences told their own stories that qualified or challenged those of senior management, while senior management picked up cues that led them to reappraise key assumptions.[36]

The narrative field became a battleground. The political practices that we discussed in the last section, as parties sought to present themselves in the best possible light and their opponents in the worst, were evident in the business world as well. Rockefeller's control of Standard Oil began to unravel as the trust's dubious claims were undermined by a muckraking journalist. Not surprisingly, one of the greatest storytelling organizations of recent times, Walt Disney Studios, was adept at fabricating stories about its own history, "as artfully constructed and as carefully edited as their legendary characters." Disney was acclaimed for the cartoon characters, such as Mickey Mouse, and the animation techniques. But this required denying others the credit they deserved. Disney's creativity was played up and his authoritarianism played down. His studios were organized, not at all uniquely, on Taylorist, paternalistic lines, yet employees were referred to as part of a family, an image that was put under strain as union disputes broke out in the 1940s.[37] This opened up the basic paradox of stories: they might have great explanatory power and be the most natural form of communication, but that could be at the expense of reinforcing explanations that suited those best able to control the means of communication while making it difficult to mount a challenge. Even the best and most liberating stories could be wide of the mark or else so ambiguous that the intended message was lost. The accomplished storyteller might derive an inspirational message from the mundane, but the inspiration could soon fade should the reality turn out to be more tedious.

The more academic business strategists tended to use their stories largely for illustration, selecting cases which made their points without always asking whether there were comparable cases where the outcomes had been quite different, or whether the same players would always get the same results by employing the approved strategic practices in slightly different circumstances. Sometimes the stories were not only selected carefully, but their telling was also highly contrived. We have seen how those of Taylor, Mayo, and Barnard were embellished. Weick's favorite story involved an incident during military maneuvers in Switzerland, when a small unit had got lost in bitterly cold weather and was feared lost. The unit eventually returned and the young lieutenant in charge was asked how they had made their way back. Though they had assumed they would die, they had gotten back by means of a map one of the men had in his pocket by which they were able to get their bearings. When the map was examined, however, it turned out not to be a map of the Alps but of the Pyrenees.[38] The strategic lesson was that with a map the unit calmed down and took action, which led to the conclusion that "when you are lost, any map will do!"[39] But luck would also have been required, as there are not many routes out of the Alps. Unfortunately, there was also no way of knowing whether the story was true or not. Weick received it via the Czech poet Miroslav Holub based on an anecdote told to him from the Second World War.[40]

Consider another of Mintzberg's favorite stories, as narrated by Richard Pascale, who we last met working for McKinsey's researching Japanese industrial success. Between 1958 and 1974, the American motorcycle market doubled but the British share shrank from 11 percent to 1 percent. Japan gained 87 percent of the new market, with Honda alone accounting for 43 percent. Pascale challenged the established explanation for Honda's successful entry into the American market in 1959, which stressed issues of price and volume. A much more intriguing story that highlighted "miscalculation, serendipity, and organizational learning" had been missed. When Honda sent its marketing team to the United States, the intention had been to compete with midsized bikes, but Honda struggled to find dealers and was plagued by technical problems. Then they received inquiries about the small 50cc SuperCubs they were using for their own transport. So they sold them instead. The moral of the story, according to Pascale, was that over-rational explanations, assuming that what happened was intended, could result in missing the most important reasons for a marketing success. Rather than a determined, long-term perspective, he pointed to the ability of an organization to learn from experience and show agility in the face of unexpected opportunities.[41] This lesson was picked up enthusiastically by Mintzberg, who referred to it regularly as he emphasized the importance of emergent strategies. He used it to show that the managers made every mistake in this case, except to learn when the market told them they were going wrong.[42] He described Pascale's article as the most influential in the management literature. Other writers have developed this "lesson" further to turn it into a story about how lowly employees can transform a strategy. Out of this single case study, a series of general propositions were developed about learning organizations.

This was not the only use made of the Honda story. This was one of the great Japanese success stories, from the company's formation in 1948 to becoming the world's largest manufacturer of motorcycles and an effective manufacturer of cars by 1964. It fascinated business strategists as a source of lessons for American companies. Andrew Mair warned, however, of the perils of extracting one episode, often imperfectly understood, and drawing large conclusions. For example, Honda had always intended to sell the SuperCub in the United States. This bike made up a quarter of those sent with the American team. The company had, however, supposed that it would first have to prove the worth of its bikes against larger models (which is why they put an emphasis on racing). The error was in not realizing that the American market was actually going to be similar to the Japanese. At any rate, sales collapsed in the late 1960s, and then Honda did have to rely on the larger bikes it had always expected would be the key to its American success. In practice, Honda's strategy followed the experience already successfully followed in Japan—it was not a leap in the dark.[43]

Its experience up to this point had demonstrated the importance of ruthless management and robust organization. The postwar Japanese market for motorcycles was huge because public transport could barely cope and gasoline supplies were limited. Unlike other industrial sectors, this one was barely regulated, resulting in something of a Darwinian struggle for survival. During the 1950s there were some two hundred companies competing for this market in what was known as the "motorcycle wars." This was a time when "doing business was a turbulent and hazardous pursuit involving all manner of lucrative opportunities and nasty surprises."[44] When the wars were over, four companies were left (Yamaha, Suzuki, Kawasaki, and Honda). Of these, Honda (formed in 1948) was the most prominent. Its success was due to a number of factors. It began with Soichiro Honda's own engineering genius, combined with the financial acumen of his business manager, Takio Fujisawa. They had some wartime experience of mass production techniques and they understood the Toyota production model and the importance of supply chains. Their internal organization was very strong, with careful financial control and—particularly important—great effort put into developing their dealer network.

In the late 1950s, Honda overtook the previous domestic leader Tohatsu (which soon went bankrupt). As Honda then went on to car production, Yamaha caught up in market share and, believing its rival to be distracted, decided to build a brand new factory with the aim of becoming the market leader. Instead, Honda mounted a strong defense leading to a fierce battle between the two (known as the "H-Y war") in 1981. Honda's response was neither subtle nor indirect. According to Stalk, who made this clash a centerpiece of his analysis of Japanese competitiveness, this was launched with a war cry, "Yamaha wo tsubusu!" which he roughly translated as "We will crush, squash, butcher, slaughter, etc., Yamaha!" Honda cut prices and boosted advertising expenditures, and introduced a number of new products, so that having the most up-to-date motorcycle became a fashion necessity. Yamaha's bikes were left looking "old, out-of-date, and unattractive" and demand for them dried up, leaving dealers stuck with old stock. Eventually Yamaha surrendered. Honda's victory had come at a price but had deterred other competitors besides Yamaha. Stalk was most impressed by the way that Honda had accelerated its production cycles to head off the competition and made this the central lesson he drew for Americans. Although this was undoubtedly impressive, this focus played down the extent to which Honda's strategy had been brutally attritional, with its price cuts and promotions.

Hamel and Prahalad also used Honda in 1994 as an example of exploiting core competence, mocking the experience curve, demonstrating great ambition and creativity in extracting maximum benefit from the mastery of the internal combustion engine (which allowed them to move successfully into a number of related production lines, from lawnmowers to tractors and marine engines), and enabling a challenge to Ferrari and Porsche in the high-end sports car market with the new NSX. They understood the needs of customers without following them slavishly. Yet as Mair reports, the NSX was a costly failure for Honda. This was not the result of only bad luck due to an appreciating currency undermining its competitiveness, but also the choice of market. The interest in sports cars was more a reflection of Honda's culture than of its core competence and meant that it missed the developing American market in the 1990s for recreational vehicles and minivans. In other areas, a determination to make a technological breakthrough meant that they lacked a follow-on car when it was needed. More generally, the only serious diversity made possible by Honda's engine technology was from motorcycles to cars. Other products remained a minor part of its portfolio. In fact, its strategy from the mid-1980s to the mid-1990s revealed a "narrow self-definition and a technological stubbornness" and so a lack of responsiveness to consumers.

Mair raised a number of basic methodological problems with these stories. They were often based on patchy research and focused on a particular period. All the way through Honda was treated as a great success, yet during the course of its history it had made a number of major errors and at times faced financial ruin. The failures were never deemed to be of interest. The business theorists who wanted to draw lessons might have asked why it never managed to dent Toyota's dominance of the Japanese car market or explain why companies that followed similar strategies did not do as well. Insufficient attention was paid to the less glamorous but vital aspects of Honda's approach, such as its operations and dealer management, perhaps equivalent to the disinterest in logistics often displayed by military strategists. There was always going to be more interest in sparks of genius than the tedious slog of administration. Mair criticized analysts seeing "only what they want to see" and of "acute one-sided reductionism."[45] He noted the tendencies toward polarization, as in deliberate/emergent and competence/capabilities, as if it had to be one or the other. The data was aligned to fit the theory, while inconvenient material was ignored or fudged.

Back to Basics

Military strategy had been launched at a time when it was believed that there were basic principles which, if applied properly, could at least increase the probability of success, even if success could not be guaranteed. It then struggled as it became apparent that the application of military force was a more complicated and frustrating business than envisaged by Jomini in the first glow of Napoleon's advances, especially as it proved hard to escape from the norm of decisive battle. Business strategy was the product of a similar bout of optimism of the mid-twentieth century, picking up on a general confidence in the possibilities of long-term planning, not only for nations but also for large companies, including the large American conglomerates. It also struggled as the limitations of the planning model became apparent, but unlike the military the managers did not have an agreed framework to provide coherence. As a result, business strategy lost its way, following many diverse paths and falling prey to temporary enthusiasms. There was a resulting tendency to prescriptive hyperbole. In a cautionary analysis, Phil Rosenzweig dismissed purveyors of business success stories for misleading their readers, sustaining the myth that there were reliable rules for success that once discovered could ensure the success of a business. He offered examples of sloppy thinking, by and large involving the standard muddle between correlation and causation, the tendency to explore explanations of success without worrying whether the same factors might be present in failures, and paying inadequate attention to the competition. The basic muddle he identified was the "halo effect," the tendency to assign factors such as culture, leadership, and values, responsibility for a strong performance when they are really attributions that resulted from a strong performance.[46]

Skeptical figures, who had seen fads and fashions come and go, urged a return to the basics. John Kay warned that strategies could not be generic because they had to be based on distinctive capabilities. The aim therefore should not be to come up with grand designs that even the most totalitarian institution would struggle to realize. Companies lacked the knowledge to construct the plans and the power to implement them. Instead of the "illusion of control" and the belief that success would result from superior vision and will, he urged a resource-based approach based on the work of Edith Penrose in the 1950s. The task was to find the best fit between the internal capabilities of the firm and its external environment. The place to start was with an understanding of a company's actual and possible position in the marketplace, as well as the distinctive capabilities it already had rather than those it would like to have.[47]

Positioning documents might describe desirable end points—places to be in five years' time—but the starting point would have to be the current situation. While there might be a temperamental preference for strategies that outsmarted competitors rather than relied on superior capacity, much would depend on the problem that was to be solved. Thus Stephen Bungay urged avoiding the pathologies of central control, with constant demands for extra information and reduced opportunities for individual initiative. His advice was to concentrate on what mattered, not to attempt to "plan beyond the circumstances you can foresee," and formulate strategy as intent and with a simple message, encouraging people to adapt their actions to circumstances.[48] A book based on the successful experience of Alan Laffley in charge of Proctor & Gamble (P&G), written with his chief consultant Roger Martin, considered strategy in terms of "making specific choices to win in the marketplace." The questions behind a winning strategy, they advised, were about describing a winning aspiration, where to play, how to win, the capabilities and management systems that needed to be in place. The book explained how this was done at P&G, but also commented on the need to avoid "strategic traps." The basic source of error was failing to set real priorities, traps described as "do-it-all," "something-for-everyone," or as Waterloo (starting with multiple competitors on multiple fronts). Other errors were described as Don Quixote, attacking the strongest competitor first; "program of the month," which meant going for the latest fashion; and last, "dreams that never come true."[49]

Similarly, Richard Rumelt described good strategy as starting with a diagnosis that defined or explained the nature of the challenge, thus simplifying the complexity of reality—which could be overwhelming—by identifying the most critical aspects of the current situation. This would facilitate a guiding policy for dealing with the challenge and a set of coherent actions designed to carry out the guiding policy. Rumelt recognized that the problem could be internal as well as external, found in both its routines and bureaucratic interests, and that rather than reaching for the sky the best course at times was to set proximate objectives, close enough at hand to be feasible.

> Many writers on strategy seem to suggest that the more dynamic the situation, the farther ahead a leader must look. This is illogical. The more dynamic the situation, the poorer your foresight will be. Therefore, the more uncertain and dynamic the situation, the more proximate a strategic objective must be.[50]

Rumelt also warned of the dangers of bad strategy, especially the quality he described simply as "fluff" or a "form of gibberish masquerading as strategic concepts or arguments," but also for failing to define the challenge to be addressed, mistaking goals for strategy, stating a desire without a means for achieving it, and setting objectives without considering their practicability.[51] He warned against senior management setting impossible targets and explaining how anything can be achieved with sufficient drive and will (though in practice they were unlikely to be able to manage more than a few challenges at any one time), seeking consensus between incompatible visions instead of making a definitive choice, and attempting to inspire by buzzwords ("charisma in a can") instead of natural, personal language. "Bad strategy flourishes," Rumelt suggested, "because it floats above analysis, logic, and choice, held aloft by the hope that one can avoid dealing with these tricky fundamentals and the difficulties of mastering them."[52]

Business strategy, like military and revolutionary strategy, could suffer from its own heroic myths. It acquired an unrealistically elevated status as the ingredient that could make all the difference between success and failure. Master strategists with master strategies were regularly identified to be admired and emulated: "captains of industry" keeping their organizations stable and set on a steady course; financial wizards taking aggressive action against all inefficiencies and so extracting the last ounce of shareholder value from a business; hard competitors scouring the marketplace for the most advantageous position; soft revolutionaries recognizing the creative potential of a committed workforce; innovative designers transforming a market with a truly unique product. Management theorists and gurus promoted their own preferred heroes. There were inevitably some managers who matched at least one of these types, but what worked in one situation could go wrong in another. Too often, the individuals and companies who soared one moment seemed to come crashing down the next. The hype that accompanied the promotion of successive strategic fashions exaggerated the importance of the enlightened manager and played down the importance of chance and circumstances in explaining success.

PART V | Theories of Strategy

CHAPTER 36 | The Limits of Rational Choice

In theory there is no difference between theory and practice. In practice there is.

—Yogi Berra (also attributed to Albert Einstein)

T HIS SECTION IS concerned with the possibility of strategic theory based on the insights of contemporary social sciences. We have already seen how apparently detached intellectual activity was the product of wider social forces, whether the effort put in by the RAND Corporation to develop new sciences of decision-making, the foundation grants that encouraged business schools to adopt these—and which the more sociologically inclined organizational theorists sought to resist—or else the impact of the radical thinking of the 1960s on the relationship between discourse and power.

A particularly influential theory was one that stressed the benefits of treating all choices as if they were rational. Adherents were confident that they, almost uniquely, could offer a theory deserving of the accolade "social science" in which all propositions could both be deduced from a strong theory and then validated empirically. Though rational choice theory consistently delivered far less than promised, and its underlying assumptions became vulnerable to a fundamental challenge from cognitive psychology, it was promoted effectively and in a highly strategic manner. In a remarkably short space of time, supporters of the theory became embedded in political science departments. They were not deterred by the widespread apprehension that the theory depended on an untenable view of human rationality. The claim, they insisted, was no more than that the premise of rationality helped generate good theory.

The Rochester School

As Kuhn observed, the promotion of new schools of thought in academia has rarely depended on reason alone. Successful promotion has also relied on access to the sources of academic power through dispensing grants, editing journals, or appointing acolytes to faculty positions. So it was that economics was given a singular boost after the Second World War with a substantial investment which made it possible to exploit the opportunities for the sophisticated quantitative methods opened up by computers. As it grew in confidence and assertiveness, economics offered itself as the master discipline of the social sciences. There were no obvious boundaries to its imperialism. The "economic approach provides a framework applicable to all human behavior," observed Gary Becker, "to all types of decisions and to persons from all walks of life."[1]

Before the Ford Foundation began to invest in business schools in the late 1950s, it had already undertaken a major investment in the so-called behavioral sciences. This investment did not create the field, which could be traced back to the 1920s and the work of Charles Merriam and Harold Lasswell at the University of Chicago. There was already a developing interest in analyzing large data sets, such as censuses, election results, and polling data. Ford, followed by other foundations, undoubtedly made a difference, encouraging universities to establish centers for behavioral studies by providing large grants—often unsolicited (so that some universities were unsure what was expected of them)—to the tune of some $24 million between 1951 and 1957. The RAND Corporation's influence was evident, with Gaither in charge of the Foundation and Hans Speier, the head of RAND's social science division, advising. The aim therefore was to move away from earlier forms of social and political theory and encourage an interest in phenomena that could be measured. This new approach was described as "behavioralism" to emphasize the positivist, empirical, and value-free quality of the research. Against the anti-communist backdrop of the time, there was also concern that "social science" smacked too much of a "socialist science" or social reform.[2] The individualistic assumptions behind this approach fit naturally with theories of markets and democracy and challenged Marxist notions of class struggle. This encouraged the view that liberal individualism was rational and collectivism irrational.[3] The core attraction of the theory, however, was not ideological but that it was elegant, parsimonious, and genuinely innovative. Some of those attracted by its virtues even gamefully sought to demonstrate that it was not incompatible with Marxism. Unfortunately it was often asserted dogmatically and embraced as a project of ambitious model-building.

There was ambiguity about whether this theory was descriptive or prescriptive. Did it explain how actors did behave or how they should behave? If prescriptive, then actors would need to make a deliberate decision to follow the advice. That would be the rational thing to do. "To identify a rational choice is to say that an agent would, in some sense and circumstances, do well to make it. If actual agents do not, they rather than the theory may be at fault."[4] So if actors chose not to follow rational advice, they therefore were capable of behaving irrationally. If that was generally the case, the theory was going to be limited in any descriptive, let alone predictive, capacity. If, on the other hand, the theory was reliably descriptive, the prescription would be both obvious and irrelevant. Why should actors bother with strategy when the solution was evident in advance?[5]

The starting point for the theory was that individuals made their own choices in order to maximize their utilities, which could be subjectively defined, although there was a tendency to assume that these were quite basic and could be measured in terms of economic rewards or the acquisition of power. The next stage was for actors with their preferences to play a structured game, presuming a certain amount of knowledge about their own position and those of the other players. The following, crucial step would be to identify the equilibrium point. Assuming that all players followed strategies to maximize their utilities, this point would be one from which individual actors had no incentive to deviate. In principle, it would represent the most logical outcome to the strategic game and would set the terms for future empirical work.

A key figure in the development of rational choice theory at RAND was Kenneth Arrow, who developed the "impossibility theorem" that explained why democratic systems do not always produce outcomes that conform to the wishes of the majority. His student Anthony Downs, in his *Economic Theory of Democracy* used the idea of individuals maximizing their self-interest to challenge notions of public interest. The person who turned all this into what he saw as a paradigm shift in political science was William Riker. Riker had followed a relatively mainstream path since graduating from Harvard in the late 1940s, yet was looking for a means to elevate political science to a new level. He found it in game theory.

When he first became aware of game theory in the mid-1950s, Riker was attracted by the presumption of amoral rationality. He was reacting against what he saw as the then dominant paradigm of normative political theory, written as a set of imperatives, about how politics should be conducted rather than as an analysis of how it was actually conducted. Yet he also wanted to move beyond a Machiavelli-like focus on the realities of power. He aspired to something truly scientific, offering testable models that could guide empirical work. This was why he was excited by game theory, with its "uncompromising rationalism." Asking what sensible people trying to achieve straightforward goals would choose to do was in line with traditional political science. This tradition he judged to have been lost during the first half of the century under the influence of biological, psychological, and metaphysical theories. Game theory left "no role for instinct, for thoughtless habit, for unconscious self-defeating desire, or for some metaphysical and exogenous will."

The second appeal lay in the emphasis on free choice. Here Riker was reacting to the historical determinism associated with Marxism. Game theory assumed that people consider their own preferences and how alternative strategies might satisfy them in the face of similar calculations by opponents. The outcomes therefore depended on free human choices rather than on "some exogenous plan for the world" or "built-in human irrationality." There was an obvious tension here, which Riker acknowledged. As a prescriptive theory this was fine. It was all about helping people make better choices. But as a descriptive theory, variations in choices caused all sorts of problems. The value of deterministic assumptions about rational choice was that they should help identify regularity of behavior and so make possible generalizations. Yet truly free choices allowed for quirky and random behavior that defied generalization.[6] Riker saw game theory as offering a way out of the dilemma by combining the possibilities of generalization with free choice. On the one hand, it could be presumed that all persons with the same goals in the same circumstances would rationally choose the same alternative, so regularities could be observed. That did not, however, remove the role of choice, especially in situations characterized by uncertainty. In the end it was the choices that fascinated Riker most, and this meant that by the time he died he was moving into areas where science was of little help. But by that time he had spawned a whole school determined to prove that politics could be a science and was resolutely disinterested in it as an art.

In 1959, Riker applied for a fellowship at the Center for Advanced Study in the Behavioral Sciences at Palo Alto with the aim of working in a field he described as "formal, positive, political theory." "Formal" referred to "the expression of the theory in algebraic rather than verbal symbols" and "positive" to the "expression of descriptive rather than normative prop-ositions." He sought the "growth in political science of a body of theory somewhat similar to . . . the neo-classical theory of value in economics." In particular he mentioned the potential role of the "mathematical theory of games" for "the construction of political theory."[7] The result of his fellowship was *The Theory of Political Coalitions*, which served as his manifesto. What made the difference in terms of the spread of his ideas, however, was his appointment to run the political science department at the well-endowed University of Rochester, already committed to forms of social science based on rigorous quantitative analysis. Here he insisted on students capable of sta-tistical analysis and faculty who were signed on to his own vision. Under his leadership, Rochester moved up the rankings, producing graduate students who went forth into other departments to spread the word of rational actor theory. Two of his acolytes have written of "consistent, thorough preparation of students who recognized themselves to be part of a distinct movement to alter political science, the camaraderie and tightknit sense of community among those students, and their impressive scholarly productivity." These students were "unyielding in their efforts to research and advance the theo-retical paradigm of rational choice" and determined to "displace other forms of political science."

In 1982, Riker became president of the American Political Science Association. He could observe the dominance of "the rational choice para-digm." Its success was "driving out all others."[8] He was now arguing against the need to add such modifiers as "positive" or "formal" as this was the only "political theory" deserving of the name because it met scientific standards.[9] By the 1990s, mathematics was an essential attribute for a political science program, and rational choice articles accounted for some 40 percent of all contributions to the *American Political Science Review*. There were complaints that the growing influence of the paradigm was due to a strong-arm mental-ity as much as clarity of thought. Rather than criticism being taken seri-ously, it was dismissed because the critics lacked the training to master the methods and so failed to understand what was going on. Because they sup-ported their own, it was alleged that rational choice scholars would prefer a second-rate member of their own fraternity to anyone else when it came to appointments.[10]

Their theory was not a simple imposition of an economics model. The development of economics as a discipline had been served by the assump-tions of self-interest, narrowly conceived, so that individuals facing the same constraints and with the same preferences would make the same choices each time. Both goals and the resources used to obtain them could be expressed in monetary terms and numerous comparable transactions could be observed in everyday economic life: the larger the sample the less important anomalous behavior and the more distinct the observable patterns and relationships. Riker was impressed by the robust market economics of the Chicago School, and this was present in his original Rochester curriculum. But he embraced game theory well before mainstream economists, and he was always careful to distinguish economics—which attributed a mechanical rationality to agents—from politics—in which rationality was deliberate and conscious, often in direct opposition to other actors. This was the basis of game theory, and on its use Riker's school followed rather than led.

As the theorists became more ambitious, they moved from the areas where it might be assumed to be most valuable, with large samples but few variables, into areas of small samples and many variables. This included international relations. When the available options were not naturally constrained, the approach struggled because the identification of both a clear interest and an optimum strategy were hard to discern. Even in areas where findings were expressed with high confidence—for example, election studies—quite subtle variations in underlying conditions might render these findings unreliable. The more stable the environment the more behavior within it should show regularity. The more uncertain the environment the harder for actors to discern a rational way forward. In the textbook he wrote with Peter Ordeshook, Riker observed that when the "range of alternatives is infinite and when the consequences of choosing each alternative are uncertain, it is likely that most choices involve error."[11]

If only certain sorts of solutions could be recognized, then only certain sorts of problems could be addressed. The most susceptible were likely to be the most narrow, with the model incorporating as few factors as possible. If any attempt was to be made at empirical validation, data sets were needed which involved a sufficiency of comparable instances that would occur in a measurable form. While the findings might confirm what had been deduced from the model, despite the mathematical trappings, this could rarely be considered a proof. Causation might have something to do with those factors that did not fit easily into the model or could not be readily measured. Even when goals were achieved it was not always possible to be sure whether this was the result of the actions chosen rather than chance, coincidence, or the critical intervention of an extraneous factor.

In the natural sciences, laws could be established. As particles did not have free will, cause and effect would be predictable. This was impossible when dealing with voluntary agents. Threats or inducements that normally produced one response could on occasion produce something quite different.

This might not matter when the aim was to affect numerous small and comparable transactions, as was often the case in economics. By insisting that research into politics must meet standards of formal rigor and mathematical elegance, priority could not be given to the quality of the questions asked or the value of the answers. One critic observed, "Rigor is subject to a conservation law, and the more rigor along mathematical dimensions, the less of it along other, perhaps more important, dimensions."[12] As game theorists addressed these limitations, they either had to move away from the strict confines of the theory or take it to levels of complexity that only the cognoscenti could savor or follow.

In one of the most serious challenges to rational actor theory in political science, Donald Green and Ian Shapiro observed that despite all the effort, what had been learned about politics was "exceedingly little."[13] They addressed one standard problem for rational choice theory which suggested that it would be irrational for anyone to vote since the time invested in the process would have to be set against the minimal impact that one person could expect to have on the final result. Yet people did vote in large numbers. How could the finding be reconciled without challenging a core precept of the theory? They mocked one response which explained the outcomes by "psychic gratification," which might be an interest, but then why that rather than other interests? And what was the source of this gratification? Was it a concern for a cause, or belief that democracy depends on voting, or the quality of the candidates? The theory offered no good answer. When an interesting finding was obtained, explanations had to be found outside the theory. Stephen Walt concluded after surveying the application of the rational actor model to international relations theory that its "growing technical complexity" had not been matched by any "corresponding increase in insight." The complexity allowed key assumptions to be buried and made the theories difficult to evaluate.[14]

One Kuhnian answer to this challenge was that "a theory cannot be rejected because of disconfirming facts." It could "only be supplanted by a superior theory."[15] But this exaggerated the status of what were often no more than speculative hypotheses deduced from suspect models. The fact that they might be discussed mathematically did not put these theories on the same level as those in the natural sciences.

Forming Coalitions

The book announcing Riker's new approach was on coalition formation. The nature of communication between players, and whether this could be incorporated within the game or involved working outside the confines of the game, was one of the most challenging issues for game theory. If the starting presumption of autonomous, rational individuals devoid of social ties and cultural references meant that there could be no presumption of empathy, cooperation would depend solely on the logic of situations rather than any natural inclinations. Von Neumann and Morgenstern had promised, without quite delivering, advice on how to form coalitions when more than one player came into the game. With three or more players (n-person games), it became harder to make simplifying assumptions. The conflicts of interest were less straightforward. With three players, two acting in concert should win. When such a coalition was formed the calculation was as simple as it would be for a two-person game with a minimax solution. The challenge was on working out whether the rational course for weak players was to gang up against a strong player (balancing) or ally themselves with a strong player (bandwagoning). As many alternative coalitions might be stable, it would be necessary to go methodically through all potential coalitions to work out an optimum strategy.

Just before Riker published his book, William Gamson had sought to develop a formal theory of coalitions. He agreed that the problem had to be reduced to a two-person game. He defined coalitions as "temporary, means oriented, alliances among individuals or groups which differ in goals." They were likely to come together for the pursuit of power itself, by which he meant the ability to control future decisions. This they would be able to do because their joint resources would be greater than those of other units or coalitions. Some of the goals of the component parts would remain incompatible, but they could concentrate on those that were distinctively their own. But when it came to predicting who would join with whom, which required understanding the resources most relevant for a given decision, their distribution, and what alternative coalitions offered the parties in terms of payoffs, Gamson found that game theory produced too many solutions. His general hypothesis was that participants would expect from a coalition a proportional share of the payoff according to the resources they contributed. This, he suggested, depended on reciprocity and a step-by-step process of pairing until a decision point was reached.[16]

Riker took this further and developed a strong proposition, based on a study of coalition formation in legislatures, that complete and winning coalitions were "minimal" in the sense that they were just large enough to win and no larger, with the rider that the less perfect and less complete the participants' information the larger the winning coalition would be. He found this "sparse model" worked quite well, though it deliberately excluded ideology and tradition.[17] He also concluded, however, by the end of the 1960s that "much more energy has been expended on the elaboration of the theory of coalitions than on the verification of it."[18] Once again, the limits of game theory became evident when there were too many potential inputs and many possible outcomes.

In his book on coalitions, Riker asserted, "What the rational political man wants, I believe, is to win, a much more specific and specifiable motive than the desire for power." This posed the issue in zero-sum terms, which for most political men might be true only in a narrow sense and suggested that attitudes toward coalition formation would at best be grudging. It also allowed him to define rationality without reference to power, giving his rational political man a definite personality: "The man who wants to win also wants to make people do things they would not otherwise do. He wants to exploit each situation to his advantage. And he wants to succeed in a given situation."[19] This reflected Riker's own personal interest not so much in the occasional political acts of ordinary voters, to which his reflections on democracy assigned only a limited significance, but on the key players among the political elite. Arguably, just as game theory worked best in economics when looking at oligopoly, where there were few players, this form of political science worked best when looking at oligarchy.

An important attempt to demonstrate how the theory might be applied to a wider range of situations came from Mancur Olson, who was intrigued by the implications of the logic of self-interested rationality when it came to cooperation. Whereas Marx had sought class consciousness as a way of turning a shared interest into a political force, Olson pointed to the difficulties of a large and dispersed group ever acting as a political force. This was because each individual would assess that the marginal benefit from making contributions to a public good (that is one that is shared collectively rather than held by a few alone) was normally below the marginal cost, and also that their own contributions would barely make a difference. It was therefore irrational to cooperate with others, even in great numbers, to achieve collective goals: "Unless there is coercion or some other special device to make individuals act in their common interest, rational, self-interested individuals will not act to achieve their common or group interests." An individual's rational self-interest was to shirk on his contributions while continuing to receive benefit from the work of others.[20]

This problem of the "free rider" was one that could be recognized, for example, in a member of a military alliance who gained protection but put few resources into the pool. This point was made forcefully by Olson while working as a consultant to RAND in the 1960s. He showed how NATO's smaller members found that they had "little or no incentive to provide additional amounts of the collective good," and so burdens were shared in a dispropor-tionate way.[21] Even though there was a shared interest, there was no point in acting on that interest if it was likely to be achieved whether or not you acted and without you paying any price. By contrast, however, if an indi-vidual's actions really would make a difference and the benefits would exceed the cost, then it was rational to act to secure the shared interest. In some respects, therefore, Olson offered a form of elite theory because he explained how small concentrated groups with resources could retain influence. The majority might hold a contrary interest, but so long as it was diffuse and dispersed its impact was muted.

Part of the explanation lay in a consideration of the social costs and ben-efits. An individual who did not bother to vote or join a union might escape notice, whereas in a small group engaged in an active campaign this would not be the case. On this basis Olson could explain, for example, why motor manufacturers might be able to lobby together for government measures that would keep car prices up, but the more numerous consumers would not be able to act equivalently to bring prices down. Collective goods affected every-one, but they were more likely to serve the interests of those best placed to lobby for them.

Once social pressures were admitted then the questions of where interests lay became more problematic. Questions of honor and reputation had to be socially validated. They were meaningless outside of a social context, but that also meant that they could vary with context. A theory in which inter-ests were narrowly conceived and pursued, in the form of money and power, might remain elegant and parsimonious but not necessarily very realistic. A variety of types of interests did not in itself damage the theory, which required only that they be pursued efficiently, but it made it less elegant and parsimonious.

The Development of Cooperation

It was not necessarily the case that game theory could not cope with behavior other than the most egotistical. The authors of a popular account of game the-ory as a strategic tool noted that one difference from the first edition (1991) to the second (2008) was the "full realization of the important part that cooperation plays in strategic situations."[22] One way of providing a game-theoretic understanding of the development of social behavior was through iterated games, a point made most strongly by Robert Axelrod's *The Evolution of Cooperation.* The origins of this book are intriguing. It can be traced to Anatol Rapoport, who combined intense interest in game theory with an equally intense anti-militarism. Discovering von Neumann's support for a preemptive war with the Soviet Union while the two were discussing support for mathematical biology was said to have been a turning point in his life. In 1964, he published a polemic against what he considered to be the misuse of game theory by strategists such as Schelling.[23] While at the University of Michigan (before he moved to Toronto in protest at the Vietnam War), he actively promoted experimental games as a means of exploring the validity of theoretical "solutions" to theories of rational cooperation. Among a group who continued this work at Michigan was Robert Axelrod, also with a background as an antiwar activist.

Axelrod saw the possibilities of using computers to experiment with game theory by setting up a tournament. He invited experts to send programs for a game of prisoner's dilemma that could be repeated up to two hundred times to see if it was possible to learn or signal in ways that produced a cooperative outcome. Not surprisingly, perhaps, the winner was a simple program submitted by Rapoport. The requirement was to play continuing games of tit-for-tat, which required that one side replicate what the other did in the previous round. The first command was "cooperate," and a continuing cooperative outcome flowed naturally. The message was that cooperative behavior could "thrive with rules that are nice, provocable, and somewhat forgiving."[24] This made a point about the possibilities of cooperation at a time of Cold War tension, and it had the great advantage of not depending on claims about how human goodness could trump amoral rationality. Other than the somewhat critical starting assumptions, the process was then computer dependent and untouched by human hand. Compared to the egotistical presumption of the theory, Axelrod demonstrated that cooperation could be rational.

Did this have any value for strategists? The presumption was that cooperation was a good thing except when it obviously was not (such as cartels). The book was a hymn to the virtues of altruism and reciprocity. Axelrod came up with four rules to establish cooperation. First, do not be envious. Be satisfied with absolute rather than relative gains, so that if you are doing nicely, do not worry is someone is doing even better. Second, do not be the first to defect, because you need to establish the logic of cooperation. Third, if another player defects, reciprocate in order to establish confidence in your retaliation. Last, do not be too clever, as others will not be sure what you are up to. Axelrod also pointed to the importance of a long-term perspective. If you were in a relationship for a long time then it made sense to continue cooperation, even when there were occasional wobbles, but in short-term encounters there were fewer incentives to do so. Little might then be lost by defecting.

Axelrod's analysis was not irrelevant to the conflicts with which strategy was largely concerned, especially those where there were significant areas of cooperation even against the backdrop of a general antagonism or competition. But the specific form of the tit-for-tat approach, even in situations which approximated to the form of prisoner's dilemma, would be hard to replicate. A symmetry in position between two parties was rare so that the impact of moves, whether cooperation or defection, would not be the same. Cooperation was as likely to be based on exchange of benefits of different types as on things of equivalent value. This was why there were many ways in which cooperation could develop, for example by means of barter, rather than through iterated games of prisoner's dilemma. One important point was reinforced by Axelrod's tournament. Strategies have to be judged over time, in a series of engagements rather than in a single encounter. This is why it was unwise to try to be too clever. Players who used "complex methods of making inferences about the other player" were often wrong. It was difficult to interpret the behavior of another without accounting for the impact of one's own. Otherwise, what might have been assumed to be complex signaling just appeared as random messages.

Using iterated games (though of assurance rather than prisoner's dilemma), Dennis Chong looked hard at the civil rights movement to address the issue raised by Olson of rational participation in what he called "public-spirited collective action." He saw the initial unwillingness to indulge in futile gestures and the later nervousness about taking personal risks when others were carrying the weight of the protest. This form of collective action offered no tangible incentives. Yet there were "social and psychological" benefits. It became a "long-term interest to cooperate in collective endeavors if noncooperation results in damage to one's reputation, ostracism, or repudiation from the community."

Chong noted the difficulty with looking at strategy in terms of the one-off encounters to which game theory seemed to lend itself. The ability to think long term required taking into account the "repeated exchanges and encounters that one will have with other members of the community." The difficulty collective movements faced was getting started. Chong's model could not explain where the leaders came from. They acted "autonomously" and got engaged without being sure of success or followers. Once a start had been made with the acquisition of the first followers but prior to any tangible results, momentum developed as a result of a form of social contagion. This led to the conclusion, which might have been reached by more straightforward historical observation, that "strong organizations and effective leadership" combined with "symbolic and substantive concessions" from the authorities. In addition, it was wise to be cautious about being able to identify any "combination of objective factors in a society that will predictably set off a chain of events leading up to a collective movement."[25]

The problem was not that the methods used in rational choice could not lead to intriguing and significant insights but that so many really interesting questions were begged. Unless preferences were attributed (such as profit or power maximization) because they would work well for most actors in most circumstances, then only the actors themselves could explain what they were trying to achieve and what their expectations were with regard to their own options and the reactions of others. This meant that before the theory could get to work it had to be told a great deal. As Robert Jervis observed, the "actor's values, preferences, beliefs, and definition of self all are exogenous to the model and must be provided before analysis can begin."[26] Rather than just take utility functions as givens, it was important to understand where they came from and how they might change with different contexts. "We need to understand not only how people reason about alternatives," observed Herbert Simon, "but where the alternatives come from in the first place. The processes whereby alternatives are generated has been somewhat ignored as an object of research."[27]

The point could be illustrated by the intellectual trajectory of William Riker. It was always an important feature of his approach that he did not assume that individuals were motivated by simple measures of self-interest, such as money or prestige, but allowed for other more emotional or ethical considerations. That is, utilities could be subjective, which reinforced the point about the prior determination of the preferences that were brought to the game.[28] He also stressed that the structure of the game made a big difference. If the issue at stake was framed one way rather than another, alternative possibilities were opened up even with the same set of players.

In his outgoing address as president of the American Political Science Association in 1983, Riker identified three analytical steps. The first was to identify the constraints imposed "by institutions, culture, ideology and prior events," that is, the context. Rational choice models came with the next step, which was to identify "partial equilibria from utility maximization within the constraints." The third step was "the explication of participants' acts of creative adjustments to improve their opportunities." Unfortunately, he noted, not very much effort had been devoted to this third step. This was the arena of what he dubbed "heresthetics, the art of political strategy."

This came from Greek roots for choosing or electing. As areas of comparative ignorance, he listed "the way alternatives are modified in political conflicts" and the "rhetorical content of campaigns which is their principal feature."[29] These means were important because that is how politicians structured the environment and required others to respond to their agenda. They could prevail by creating a situation with its own inexorable logic. It was through these devices that they could persuade others to join them in coalitions and alliances. This led the field away from the position where Riker had previously placed his flag. Simon commented, "I could wish he had not invented the word 'heresthetics' to conceal the heresies he is propagating."[30]

Heresthetics was about structuring the way the world was viewed so as to create political advantage. Riker identified a number of heresthetic strategies: setting the agenda, strategic voting (supporting a less favored outcome to avoid something even worse), trading votes, altering the sequence of decisions, and redefining a situation. Initially he saw these forms of manipulation as separate from rhetoric, although it was hard to see how many of these strategies could work without persuasive skills. In an unfinished book, published posthumously, he was focusing much more on rhetoric. His disciples claimed that he was returning the discipline to "the science behind persuasion and campaigning,"[31] but he acknowledged he was moving into terrain where the science would struggle. The point was made in the title of his book on heresthetics, *The Art of Manipulation*. He was clear that this was "not a science. There is no set of scientific laws that can be more or less mechanically applied to generate successful strategies."[32] In his posthumous book he expressed concern that "our knowledge of rhetoric and persuasion is itself minuscule."[33] Riker certainly did not abandon his conviction that statistical analysis could sharpen his propositions, and he was determinedly avoiding a large body of work that directly addressed exactly the issues of agenda setting, framing, and persuasion that were interesting him, because it was too "belle-lettres" and insufficiently rigorous. However, he still ended up where so many students of strategists found themselves, fascinated by why some players in the political game were smarter and more persuasive than their opponents.

CHAPTER 37 | Beyond Rational Choice

Reason is and ought only to be the slave of the passions, and can never
pretend to any other office than to serve and obey them.

—David Hume, A Treatise of Human Nature, 1740

THE PRESUMPTION OF rationality was the most contentious feature of
formal theories. The presumption was that individuals were rational if
they behaved in such a way that their goals, which could be obnoxious as well
as noble, would be most likely to be achieved. This was the point made by
the eighteenth-century philosopher David Hume. He was as convinced of the
importance of reason as he was that it could not provide its own motivation.
This would come from a great range of possible human desires: "Ambition,
avarice, self-love, vanity, friendship, generosity, public spirit," which would
be "mixed in various degrees and distributed through society."[1] As Downs
put it, the rational man "moves towards his goals in a way which to the best
of his knowledge uses the least possible input of scarce resources per unit of
valued output." This also required focusing on one aspect of an individual
and not his "whole personality." The theory "did not allow for the rich diversity of ends served by each of his acts, the complexity of his motives, the way
in which every part of his life is intimately related to his emotional needs.[2]
Riker wrote that he was not asserting that all behavior was rational, but only
that some behavior was "and that this possibly small amount is crucial for the

construction and operation of economic and political institutions."[3] In addition, the settings in which actors were operating—whether a congressional election, legislative committee, or revolutionary council—were also taken as givens, unless the issues being studied concerned establishing new institutions. The challenge then was to show that collective political outcomes could be explained by individuals ranking "their preferences consistently over a set of possible outcomes, taking risk and uncertainty into consideration and acting to maximize their expected payoffs." This could easily become tautological because the only way that preferences and priorities could be discerned was by examining the choices made in actual situations.

The main challenge to the presumption that intended egotistical choices was the best basis from which to understand human behavior, was that it was consistently hard to square with reality. To take a rather obvious example, researchers tried to replicate the prisoner's dilemma in the circumstances in which it was first described.[4] Could prosecutors gain leverage in cases involving codefendants by exchanging a prospect of a reduced sentence in return for information or testimony against other codefendants? The evidence suggested that it made no difference to the rates of pleas, convictions, and incarcerations in robbery cases with or without codefendants. The surmised reason for this was the threat of extralegal sanctions that offenders could impose on each other. The codefendants might be kept separate during the negotiations, but they could still expect to meet again.[5] To the proponents of rational choice, such observations were irrelevant. The claim was not that rational choice replicated reality but that as an assumption it was productive for the development of theory.

By the 1990s, the debate on rationality appeared to have reached a stalemate, with all conceivable arguments exhausted on both sides. It was, however, starting to be reshaped by new research, bringing insights from psychology and neuroscience into economics. The standard critique of rational choice theory was that people were just not rational in the way that the theory assumed. Instead, they were subject to mental quirks, ignorance, insensitivity, internal contradictions, incompetence, errors in judgment, overactive or blinkered imaginations, and so on. One response to this criticism was to say that there was no need for absurdly exacting standards of rationality. The theory worked well enough if it assumed people were generally reasonable and sensible, attentive to information, open-minded, and thoughtful about consequences.[6]

As a formal theory, however, rationality was assessed in terms of the ideal of defined utilities, ordered preferences, consistency, and a statistical grasp of probabilities when relating specific moves to desired outcomes. This sort of hyper-rationality was required in the world of abstract modeling. The modelers knew that human beings were rarely rational in such an extreme form, but their models required simplifying assumptions. The method was deductive rather than inductive, less concerned with observed patterns of behavior than developing hypotheses which could then be subjected to empirical tests. If what was observed deviated from what was predicted, that set a research task that could lead to either a more sophisticated model or specific explanations about why a surprising result occurred in a particular case. Predicted outcomes might well be counterintuitive but then turn out to be more accurate than those suggested by intuition.

One of the clearest expositions of what a truly rational action required was set out in 1986 by Jon Elster. The action should be *optimal*, that is, the best way to satisfy desire, given belief. The belief itself would be the best that could be formed, given the evidence, and the amount of evidence collected would be optimal, given the original desire. Next the action should be *consistent* so that both the belief and the desire were free of internal contradictions. The agent must not act on a desire that, in her own opinion, was less weighty than other desires which might be reasons for not acting. Lastly, there was the test of *causality*. Not only must the action be rationalized by the desire and the belief, but it must also be caused by them. This must also be true for the relation between belief and evidence.[7]

Except in the simplest of situations, meeting such demanding criteria for rational action required a grasp of statistical methods and a capacity for interpretation that could only be acquired through specialist study. In practice, faced with complex data sets, most people were apt to make elementary mistakes.[8] Even individuals capable of following the logical demands of such an approach were unlikely to be prepared to accept the considerable investment it would involve. Some decisions were simply not worth the time and effort to get them absolutely right. The time might not even be available in some instances. Gathering all the relevant information and evaluating it carefully would use up more resources than the potential gains from getting the correct answer.

If rational choices required individuals to absorb and evaluate all available information and analyze probabilities with mathematical precision, it could never capture actual human behavior. As we have seen, the urge to scientific rigor that animated rational choice theory only really got going once actors sorted out their preferences and core beliefs. The actors came to the point where their calculations might be translated into equations and matrices as formed individuals, with built-in values and beliefs. They were then ready to play out their contrived dramas. The formal theorists remained unimpressed by claims that they should seek out more accurate descriptions of human behavior, for example, by drawing on the rapid advances in understanding the human brain. One economist patiently explained that this had nothing to do with his subject. It was not possible to "refute economic models" by this means because these models make "no assumptions and draw no conclusions about the physiology of the brain." Rationality was not an assumption but a methodological stance, reflecting a decision to view the individual as the unit of agency.[9]

If rational choice theory was to be challenged on its own terms, the alternative methodological stance had to demonstrate that it not only approximated better to perceived reality but also that it would produce better theories. The challenge was first set out in the early 1950s by Herbert Simon. He had a background in political science and a grasp of how institutions worked. After entering economics through the Cowles Commission, he became something of an iconoclast at RAND. He developed a fascination with artificial intelligence and how computers might replicate and exceed human capacity. This led him to ponder the nature of human consciousness. He concluded that a reliable behavioral theory must acknowledge elements of irrationality and not just view them as sources of awkward anomalies. While at the Carnegie Graduate School of Industrial Administration, he complained that his economist colleagues "made almost a positive virtue of avoiding direct, systematic observations of individual human beings while valuing the casual empiricism of the economist's armchair introspections." At Carnegie he went to war against neoclassical economics and lost. The economists grew in numbers and power in the institution and had no interest in his ideas of "bounded rationality."[10] He gave up on economics and moved into psychology and computer science. This idea of "bounded rationality," however, came to be recognized as offering a compelling description of how people actually made decisions in the absence of perfect information and computational capacity. It accepted human fallibility without losing the predictability that might still result from a modicum of rationality. Simon showed how people might reasonably accept suboptimal outcomes because of the excessive effort required to get to the optimal. Rather than perform exhaustive searches to get the best solution, they searched until they found one that was satisfactory, a process he described as "satisficing."[11] Social norms were adopted, even when inconvenient, to avoid unwanted conflicts. When the empirical work demonstrated strong and consistent patterns of behavior this might reflect the rational pursuit of egotistical goals, but alternatively these patterns might reflect the influence of powerful conventions that inclined people to follow the pack.

Building upon Simon's work, Amos Tversky and Daniel Kahneman introduced further insights from psychology into economics. To gain credibility, they used sufficient mathematics to demonstrate the seriousness of their methodology and so were able to create a new field of behavioral economics. They demonstrated how individuals used shortcuts to cope with complex situations, relying on processes that were "good enough" and interpreted information superficially using "rules of thumb." As Kahneman put it, "people rely on a limited number of heuristic principles which reduce the complex tasks of assessing probabilities and predicting values to simpler judgmental operations. In general, these heuristics are quite useful, but sometimes they lead to severe and systematic errors."[12] *The Economist* summed up what behavioral research suggested about actual decision-making:

> [People] fear failure and are prone to cognitive dissonance, sticking with a belief plainly at odds with the evidence, usually because the belief has been held and cherished for a long time. People like to anchor their beliefs so they can claim that they have external support, and are more likely to take risks to support the status quo than to get to a better place. Issues are compartmentalized so that decisions are taken on one matter with little thought about the implications for elsewhere. They see patterns in data where none exist, represent events as an example of a familiar type rather than acknowledge distinctive features and zoom in on fresh facts rather than big pictures. Probabilities are routinely miscalculated, so...people...assume that outcomes which are very probable are less likely than they really are, that outcomes which are quite unlikely are more likely than they are, and that extremely improbable, but still possible, outcomes have no chance at all of happening. They also tend to view decisions in isolation, rather than as part of a bigger picture.[13]

Of particular importance were "framing effects." These were mentioned earlier as having been identified by Goffman and used in explanations of how the media helped shape public opinion. Framing helped explain how choices came to be viewed differently by altering the relative salience of certain features. Individuals compared alternative courses of action by focusing on one aspect, often randomly chosen, rather than keep in the frame all key aspects.[14] Another important finding concerned loss aversion. The value of a good to an individual appeared to be higher when viewed as something that could be lost or given up than when evaluated as a potential gain. Richard Thaler, one of the first to incorporate the insights from behavioral economics into mainstream economics, described the "endowment effect," whereby the selling price for consumption goods was much higher than the buying price.[15]

Experiments

Another challenge to the rational choice model came from experiments that tested propositions derived from game theory. These were not the same as experiments in the natural sciences which should not be context dependent. Claims that some universal truths about human cognition and behavior were being illuminated needed qualification. The results could only really be considered at all valid for Western, educated, industrialized, rich, and democratic (WEIRD) societies in which the bulk of the experiments were conducted. Nonetheless, while WEIRD societies were admittedly an unrepresentative subset of the world's population, they were also an important subset.[16]

One of the most famous experiments was the ultimatum game. It was first used in an experimental setting during the early 1960s in order to explore bargaining behavior. From the start, and to the frustration of the experimenters, the games showed individuals making apparently suboptimal choices. A person (the proposer) was given a sum of money and then chose what proportion another (the responder) should get. The responder could accept or refuse the offer. If the offer was refused, both got nothing. A Nash equilibrium based on rational self-interest would suggest that the proposer should make a small offer, which the responder should accept. In practice, notions of fairness intervened. Responders regularly refused to accept anything less than a third, while most proposers were inclined to offer something close to half, anticipating that the other party would expect fairness.[17] Faced with this unexpected finding, researchers at first wondered if there was something wrong with the experiments, such as whether there had been insufficient time to think through the options. But giving people more time or raising the stakes to turn the game into something more serious made little difference. In a variation known as the dictator game, the responder was bound to accept whatever the proposer granted. As might be expected, lower offers were made—perhaps about half the average sum offered in the ultimatum game.[18] Yet, at about 20 percent of the total, they were not tiny.

It became clear that the key factor was not faulty calculation but the nature of the social interaction. In the ultimatum game, the responders accepted far less if they were told that the amount had been determined by a computer or the spin of a roulette wheel. If the human interaction was less direct, with complete anonymity, then proposers made smaller grants.[19] A further finding was that there were variations according to ethnicity. The amounts distributed reflected culturally accepted notions of fairness. In some cultures, the proposers would make a point of offering more than half; in others, the responders were reluctant to accept anything. It also made a difference if the transaction was within a family, especially in the dictator game. Playing these games with children also demonstrated that altruism was something to be learned during childhood.[20] As they grew older, most individuals turned away from the self-regarding decisions anticipated by classical economic theory and become more other-regarding. The exceptions were those suffering from neural disorders such as autism. In this way, as Angela Stanton caustically noted, the canonical model of rational decision-making treated the decision-making ability of children and those with emotional disorders as the norm.[21]

The research confirmed the importance of reputation in social interactions.[22] The concern with influencing another's beliefs about oneself was evident when there was a need for trust, for example, when there were to be regular exchanges. This sense of fairness and concern about reputation, though it appeared instinctive and impulsive, was hardly irrational. It was important for an individual to have a good reputation to consolidate her social networks, while a social norm that sustained group cohesion was worth upholding. There was further experimental evidence suggesting that when a proposer had been insufficiently altruistic, the responders would not accept their reward in order to ensure that the miserly proposer was punished.[23]

Another experiment involved a group of investors. When each made an investment everyone else gained, though they made a small loss. These losses should not have mattered, for they were covered by the gains resulting from the investments of others. Those motivated by a narrow self-interest would see an incentive to become a free rider. They could avoid losses by making no personal investments while benefiting from the investments of others. They would then gain at the expense of the group. Such behavior would soon lead to a breakdown in cooperation. To prevent this would require the imposition of sanctions by the rest of the group, even though this would cost them as individuals. When given a choice which group to join, individuals at first often recoiled from joining one with known sanctions against free riders but eventually would migrate to that group, as they appreciated the importance of ensuring cooperation.

Free riders, or unfair proposers in the ultimatum game, were also stigmatized. In another experiment, individuals who expected to play by the rules were told in advance of the game the identities of other players who would be free riders. Once these individuals had been described as less trustworthy, they were generally seen as less likable and attractive. When the games were underway, this prior profiling influenced behavior. There was a reluctance to take risks with those designated untrustworthy, even when these individuals were acting no differently from others. Little effort was made to check their reputations against actual behavior during the game. In experiments which showed individuals described as either free-riders or cooperators experiencing pain, far less empathy was shown for the free riders than for the cooperators.[24]

One response from those committed to the rational actor model was that it was interesting but irrelevant. The experiments involved small groups, often graduate students. It was entirely possible that as these types of situations became better understood, behavior would tend to become more rational as understood by the theory. Indeed, there was evidence that when these games were played with subjects who were either professors or students in economics and business, players acted in a far more selfish way, were more likely to free ride, were half as likely to contribute to a public good, kept more resources for themselves in an ultimatum game, and were more likely to defect in a prisoner's dilemma game. This fit in with studies that showed economists to be more corruptible and less likely to donate to charity.[25] One researcher suggested that the "experience of taking a course in microeconomics actually altered students' conceptions of the appropriateness of acting in a self-interested manner, not merely their definition of self-interest."[26] In studies of traders in financial markets, it transpired that while the inexperienced might be influenced by Thaler's "endowment effect," for example, the experienced were not.[27] This might not be flattering to economists, but it did show that egotistical behavior could also be quite natural. This argument, however, could be played back to the formal theorists. To be sure, it showed the possibility of self-interested and calculating behavior but it also required a degree of socialization. If it could not be shown to occur naturally and if it had to be learned, then that demonstrated the importance of social networks as a source of guidance on how to behave.

When individuals were acting as consumers in a marketplace or in other circumstances that encouraged them to act as egotistical and self-regarding, their behavior could get close to what might be expected from models that assumed such conduct. The experiments employed to explore the degree of actual rationality reflected the preoccupations with a particular sort of choice, a type "with clearly defined probabilities and outcomes, such as choosing between monetary gambles."[28] It was almost by accident that as researchers sought to prove the rational actor models through experiments they came to appreciate the importance of social pressures and the value attached to cooperation. Within the complex social networks of everyday life, truly egotistical and self-regarding behavior was, in a basic sense, irrational.

Attempts were made to recast formal theories to reflect the insights of behavioral psychology, in the guise of behavioral economics, but they made limited progress. The most important insight from the new research was that rather than studying individuals as more complex and rounded than the old models assumed, it was even more important to study them in their social context.

Only a very particular view of rationality considered cooperation irrational and failed to understand why it made sense to make sacrifices to punish the uncooperative and free riders in order to uphold norms and sustain cooperative relationships. Many social and economic transactions would become impossible if at every stage there was suspicion and reason to doubt another's motives. The essence of trust was to knowingly and willingly accept a degree of vulnerability, aware that trustees might intend harm but finding it more profitable to assume that they did not. The evidence suggested that by and large people would prefer to trust others than not to trust. There were formidable normative pressures to honor commitments once made, and a reputation for untrustworthiness could prove to be a hindrance. Life became a lot easier if the people with whom one was dealing trusted and could be trusted in turn, saving the bother of complicated contracts and enforcement issues. Trusting another did not necessarily assume good faith. The calculus could be quite balanced. On occasion there might be no choice but to trust someone, even though there were indicators to prompt suspicion, because the alternative of not trusting was even more likely to lead to a bad result. In other circumstances, with little information one way or another, accepting another's trustworthiness would involve a leap of faith. This was why deception was deplored. It meant taking advantage of another's trust, hiding malicious intent behind a mask of good faith. Trust involved accepting evidence of another's intentions; deception involved faking this evidence.[29]

So important was trust that even when clues were arriving thick and fast that they were being deceived, individuals could stay in denial for a surprising time. A confidence trickster might be vulnerable to intensive probing and so would rely on those who were inclined to accept his story: the woman yearning for love or the greedy looking for a get-rich-quick proposition. Research showed that people were "poor deception-detectors and yet are overconfident of their ability to detect deception."[30] "Cognitive laziness" led to shortcuts that resulted in misapprehending people and situations, failing to explore context, ignoring contradictions, and sticking with an early judgment of another's trustworthiness.[31]

Mentalization

The ability to recognize different traits in people, to distinguish them according to their personalities, is essential to all social interaction. It might be difficult to predict the responses of people to particular situations, but to the extent that it is possible to anticipate the responses of specific individuals, their behavior might be anticipated or even manipulated.

The process of developing theories about how other minds work has been described as "mentalization." Instead of assuming that other minds resembled one's own, by observing the behavior of others it became evident that others had distinctive mental and emotional states. The quality of empathy, of being able to feel as another feels, was drawn from the German *Einfühlung*, which was about the process of feeling one's way into an art object or another person. Empathy might be a precursor to sympathy, but it was not the same. With empathy one could feel another's pain; with sympathy one would also pity another for his pain. It could be no more than sharing another's emotional state in a vicarious way, but also something more deliberative and evaluative, a form of role-playing.

Mentalization involved three distinct sets of activity, working in combination. The first set was an individual's own mental state and those of others represented in terms of perceptions and feelings, rather than the true features of the stimuli that prompted the perceptions and feelings in the first place. They were beliefs about the state of the world rather than the actual state of the world. When simulating the mental states of others, people would be influenced by what was known of their past behavior and also of those aspects of the wider world relevant to the current situation. The second set of activities introduced information about observed behavior. When combined with what could be recalled from the past, this allowed for inferences about mental states and predictions about the next stage in a sequence of behavior. The third set was activated by language and narrative. Frith and Frith concluded that this drew on past experience to generate "a wider semantic and emotional context for the material currently being processed."[32]

This wider context could be interpreted using a "script." The concept comes from Robert Abelson, who developed an interest during the 1950s in the factors shaping attitudes and behavior. His work was stimulated by a 1958 RAND workshop with Herbert Simon on computer simulations of human cognition. Out of this came a distinction between "cold" cognition, where new information was incorporated without trouble into general problem-solving, and "hot" cognition, where it posed a challenge to accepted beliefs. Abelson became perplexed by the challenges posed by cognition for rational thinking and in 1972 wrote of a "theoretical despond," as he "severely questioned whether information has any effect upon attitudes and whether attitudes have any effects upon behaviour." It was at this point that he hit upon the idea of scripts. His first thoughts were that they would be comparable to a "role" in psychological theory and a "plan" in computer programming, "except that it would be more occasional, more flexible, and more impulsive in its execution than a role or plan, and more potentially exposed in its formation to affective and 'ideological' influences."[33] This led to his work with Roger Schank. Together they developed the idea of a script as a problem in artificial intelligence to refer to frequently recurring social situations involving strongly stereotyped conduct. When such a situation arose, people resorted to the plans which underlay these scripts.[34] Thus, a script involved a coherent sequence of events that an individual could reasonably expect in these circumstances, whether as a participant or as an observer.[35]

Scripts referred to the particular goals and activities taking place in a particular setting at a particular time. A common example was a visit to a restaurant: the script helped anticipate the likely sequence of events, starting with the menu and its perusal, ordering the food, tasting the wine, and so on. In situations where it became necessary to make sense of the behavior of others, the appropriate script created expectations about possible next steps, a framework for interpretation. As few scripts were followed exactly, the other mentalizing processes allowed them to be adapted to the distinctive features of the new situation. We will explore the potential role of scripts in strategy in the next section.

Individuals varied in their ability to mentalize. Those who were more cooperative, had a higher degree of emotional intelligence, and enjoyed larger social networks tended to be better mentalizers. It might be thought that this would also be an attribute of those of a Machiavellian disposition, who were inclined to deceive and manipulate. This might be expected to depend on an ability to understand another's mind and its vulnerabilities. While such people might lack empathy or hot cognition, the expectation would be of a degree of cold cognition, an insight into what another knows and believes. Yet studies of individuals described as "Machiavellian"—used in psychological studies to refer to somewhat callous and selfish personalities largely influenced by rewards and punishments—suggested that both their hot and cold cognition were limited. This led to the proposition that these individuals' limited ability to mentalize meant that they found it easier to exploit and manipulate others because there was little to prompt guilt and remorse.[36] There could therefore be individuals who were so naturally manipulative that they were apparently incapable of dealing with other people on any other basis.

Such findings arguably provided more support for the view that the rational actor celebrated in economic theory tended to the psychopathic and socially maladroit. As Mirowski notes, in an awkward soliloquy, it was striking how many of the theorists who insisted on an egotistical rationality, who claimed to "theorize the very pith and moment of human rationality"—of which Nash was but one example—were not naturally empathetic and lived very close to the mental edge, at times tipping over into depression and even suicide.[37]

The issue, however, was relevant for two other reasons. First it highlighted an important distinction between traits such as deception or Machiavellianism as affecting instinctive behavior, and strategies involving deception emerging out of a deliberate process of reasoning. Second, it recalled attitudes toward those who relied on tricks and cunning, which was to deplore this when directed inward into one's own society while often applauding when applied outward against enemies. This pointed to a different sort of challenge, for mentalization should be relatively straightforward and reasonably reliable with the in-group with whom interaction was regular and a culture and background was shared. With an out-group, about whom less was known and suspicions were harbored, mentalization would be much more difficult. It was hard to empathize with those perceived to be remote, unattractive, and bad. So there could be an easy grasp of the likely thinking of fellow members of the in-group, facilitating cooperation. And where there were difficulties, they could be addressed through direct communication. The minds that were most important to fathom and penetrate, however—especially during a conflict—would be those of the out-group. Not only would it be a challenge to address preconceptions and prejudices in order to produce a rounded picture, but there would also be fewer opportunities to communicate to clarify areas of difference.

Systems 1 and 2

From all of this a complex picture of decision-making emerged. It was at all times influenced by the social dimension and emphasized the importance of familiarity; the effort required to understand the distant and menacing; the inclination to frame issues in terms of past experiences, often quite narrowly and with a short-term perspective; and the use of shortcuts (heuristics) to make sense of what was going on. None of this fit easily with descriptions in terms of the systematic evaluation of all options, a readiness to follow an algorithmic process to the correct answer, employing the best evidence and analysis, keeping long-term goals clearly in mind. Yet at the same time, and despite the regular derision directed at decision-making that relied on hunch and intuition, apparently instinctive decisions were often more than adequate and at times even better than might be managed by intensive deliberation.[38] It was even relevant to academics in their choice of theories. As Walt observed, the time spent learning the complex mathematics demanded by some formal theories was time spent not "learning a foreign language, mastering the relevant details of a foreign policy issue, immersing oneself in a new body of theoretical literature, or compiling an accurate body of historical data."[39]

As a combination of neuroimaging and experimental games illuminated the areas of the brain activated by different forms of cognition and decision, the sources of the tension between the bottom-up, instinctive processes and the top-down, deliberative processes could be detected. The parts of the brain associated with earlier evolutionary stages, the brain stem and the amygdale, were associated with choices defined by feelings and marked by instincts and mental shortcuts. Dopamine neurons automatically detected patterns in the stimuli coming in from the environment and matched them with stored information derived from experience and learning. These were connected by the orbitofrontal cortex (OFC) to conscious thought. It was the expansion of the frontal cortex during evolution that gave humans their comparative advantage in intelligence. Here could be detected the influence of explicit goals (such as holding on to a good reputation or making money). When trying to understand other people and what they might do, the medial prefrontal cortex and anterior paracingulate cortex became activated. These were not activated when playing a computer game because there was no point in trying to assess a computer's intentions. Yet compared with the notionally more primitive brain, the prefrontal cortex appeared limited in its computational capacity, barely able to handle seven things at once.

Jonah Lehrer summed up the implications of the research:

> The conventional wisdom about decision-making has got it exactly backward. It is the easy problems—the mundane math problems of daily life—that are best suited to the conscious brain. These simple decisions won't overwhelm the prefrontal cortex. In fact they are so simple that they tend to trip up the emotions, which don't know how to compare prices or compute the odds of a poker hand. (When people rely on their feelings in such situations, they make avoidable mistakes, like those due to loss aversion and arithmetical errors.) Complex problems, on the other hand, require the processing powers of the emotional brain, the supercomputer of the mind. This doesn't just mean

you can just blink and know what to do—even the unconscious takes a little time to process information—but it does suggest that there's a better way to make difficult decisions.[40]

When the actual processes of decision-making were considered, there was therefore very little relationship to the formal model of decision-making. Emotion could no longer be seen as something separate from reason and apt to lead reason astray, so that only a dispassionate intellectual discipline, the sort displayed by Plato's philosopher-kings, could ensure rational control. Instead emotion appeared as bound up with all thought processes.[41] Neuroimaging of the brain confirmed the extraordinary activity involved in evaluating situations and options before the conclusions reach human consciousness. The revelation lay in just how much computation and analysis humans were capable of before they were really aware of any serious thought underway at all. Here in the subconscious could be found the various heuristics and biases explored by the behavioral economists, or the repressed feelings that fascinated Freud and the psychoanalysts. It was here that decisions took form, and where people and propositions acquired positive or negative connotations.

Human beings did what felt right, but that did not mean their behavior was uninformed or irrational. Only when the circumstances were unusual did they have to ponder and wonder what to do next. Then thought processes became more conscious and deliberate. The conclusions might be more rational or they might be more rationalized. If the instinctive feelings were trusted, the natural course was to look for arguments to explain why they were correct rather than subject them to truly critical scrutiny. Two distinct processes were therefore identified, both capable of processing information and formulating decisions. Their combined effect was described as a "dual-process model of reasoning." Their least loaded labels were System 1 and System 2.[42] The distinction between the two may be drawn too sharply, as they clearly feed off each other and interact. The value for our purposes is to allow us to identify two distinctive forms of strategic reasoning which at least have some basis in cognitive psychology.

The intuitive System 1 processes were largely unconscious and implicit. They operated quickly and automatically when needed, managing cognitive tasks of great complexity and evaluating situations and options before they reached consciousness. This referred to not one but a number of processes, perhaps with different evolutionary roots, ranging from simple forms of information retrieval to complex mental representations.[43] They all involved the extraordinary computational and storage power of the brain, drawing on past learning and experiences, picking up on and interpreting cues and signals from the environment, suggesting appropriate and effective behavior, and enabling individuals to cope with the circumstances in which they might find themselves without having to deliberate on every move. Here could be found a grasp of how society worked and individuals operated, what had been internalized about societies and a variety of situations, bringing it together in ways faster and more focused than possible by more explicit and deliberate means. The outcomes were feelings—including strong senses of like and dislike, signals and patterns—with scripts for action that might be difficult to articulate but were followed without always understanding where they came from. What emerged out of System 1 did not need to be contrary to reason and could involve calculations and evaluations far exceeding those that could be accomplished with the more cumbersome and limited processes associated with System 2. In some ways, the modeling associated with game theory captured both the potential and limitations of System 2 thinking. If there was no System 1, that was probably how individuals might think, though without the prompts of System 1 they might find it difficult ever actually to reach a conclusion.

The intuitive System 1 thinking would still at times need to be supplemented by System 2 processes. These were conscious, explicit, analytical, deliberative, more intellectual, and inherently sequential—just what was expected of strategic reasoning. Unfortunately, System 2 processes were also slower and struggled with excessive complexity. They were also more demanding, for exerting self-control could be "depleting and unpleasant," leading to a loss of motivation.[44] The features of System 2 involved attributes that were uniquely human. Although the process may have started with chimps, they were assumed to reflect more recent evolutionary development, associated with language and the ability to address hypothetical situations, without immediate context, beyond immediate experience. The move from System 1 did not mean that feelings no longer played a part. For example, when deciding whether to cooperate or defect in the ultimatum game, players' positive or negative feelings about the options influenced their decisions. When another player was perceived to have acted unfairly, this could arouse strong feelings affecting the severity of the response.[45]

Whether the decisions emerging out of System 1 were good would depend on the quality and relevance of internalized information. As in other areas, instincts could often be reliable guides but a desire to believe could sometimes override best interests. Instinctive choices had features that potentially limited their effectiveness. First, shortcuts were used, turning new situations into something familiar in order to draw on apparently relevant experience or knowledge. This was the case even when the stakes were high.[46] Second, though more effort might be invested in high-stakes decisions, this could be to find evidence to support choices that seemed intuitively correct from the start.[47] Third, thinking was often short term, shaped by immediate challenges. Kahneman observed that "an exclusive concern with the long term may be prescriptively sterile, because the long term is not where life is lived." During the course of a conflict there would be responses to the "pain of losses and the regret of mistakes."[48] In this respect, the first encounters were bound to be more important, as these tested the accuracy of the initial framing and showed how issues were likely to be framed in the future. The next chapter notes the importance of considering strategy as starting from an existing situation rather than a distant goal.

Learning and training could make a difference, as was evident in those who had to work out what to do during the course of a competitive game, an intense battle, or any stressful situation without time for much deliberation. Intuitive decisions could therefore reflect strong biases, limited prior knowledge, narrow framing, and short time scales. With more deliberation decisions did not necessarily improve, especially if the extra deliberation was devoted to rationalizing intuitive conclusions. But deliberation did allow for correcting biases, more abstract conceptualizations, reconstructing the frame, and pushing out the time horizons. The evidence suggested that the more conscious reasoning kicked in when the circumstances had unique features, the information was poor, inconsistencies and anomalies were evident compared with expectations, or there was an awareness of the danger of bias. Individuals with a lack of empathy (psychopathy) were less inclined to cooperate and more likely to defect in games involving trust. When they were asked to act against type, so that the empathetic defected and the psychopathic cooperated, extra activity was observed in the prefrontal cortex because of the effort needed to exert control.[49] Deliberate System 2 thinking interacted with intuitive System 1 thinking, a potential source of control that was not always controlling.

The tension was evident when evidence challenged strongly held beliefs. Experts who had a considerable stake in a particular proposition could put considerable intellectual effort into discrediting the evidence and those who supported alternative propositions. A study of pundits by Philip Tetlock in the 1980s demonstrated that their predictions were no better than might have been achieved through random choice, and that the most famous and regarded were often the worst. Because of their self-image as being uniquely expert they would convey more certainty than was often justified by the evidence. The best pundits, he noted, were those who were ready to monitor how well their predictions were going and were not too quick to disregard dissonant findings.[50]

The two processes provided a compelling metaphor for a struggle that was central to the production of strategies. Simply put, strategy as commonly represented was System 2 thinking par excellence, capable of controlling the illogical forms of reasoning—often described as emotional—that emerged out of System 1. The reality turned out to be much more complicated and intriguing, for in many respects System 1 was more powerful and could overwhelm System 2 unless a determined effort was made to counter its impact. A strategy could involve following System 1 as it was posted into consciousness and appeared as the right thing to do, so that conscious effort was directed at finding reasons why it should be done—strategy as rationalization. One way to think of strategy, therefore, was as a System 2 process engaged in a tussle with System 1 thinking, seeking to correct for feelings, prejudices, and stereotypes; recognizing what was unique and unusual about the situation; and seeking to plot a sensible and effective way forward.

A key finding from experiments was that individuals were not naturally strategic. When they understood that they were taking part in a competitive strategic game and were told the rules, the criteria, and the rewards for success, then they acted strategically. They could appreciate, for example, that sticking to an established pattern of behavior just because it worked in the past would probably not work in the future because a clever opponent would know what to expect. They also realized that their opponent's future actions were likely to vary from those observed in the past. This was the essence of strategic reasoning: making choices on the basis of the likely choices of opponents and, in so doing, recognizing that opponents' choices would depend in turn on expectations about what they might choose.[51]

Yet when the need for strategy was left unexplained and implicit, individuals often missed cues and opportunities. Nor were they always enthusiastic and competitive when told they were playing a strategic game. Strategies were often inconsistent, clumsy, and unsophisticated; reflected shifting or uncertain preferences; responded to the wrong stimuli; and focused on the wrong factors, misunderstanding partners as well as antagonists. Players often had to be urged to make the effort to get into the minds of their opponents. This is why the next chapter argues that many everyday and routine encounters should not be really considered as "strategic."

David Sally compared what could be learned from experimental games with what might be predicted by game theory. The "explosion of experimental work in the past 20 years," he wrote in 2003, revealed that human beings, "despite their advantages in the areas of reasoning, rationality and mentalizing, can be the most befuddling and the least consistent game-players." At various times they came over as "cooperative, altruistic, competitive, selfish, generous, equitable, spiteful, communicative, distant, similar, mindreading or mindblind as small elements in the game structure or social setting are altered."[52] A lot of responses to events were intuitive, undertaken without much hard thought or analysis of alternatives, and produced judgments that were quick and plausible. Individuals were not natural strategists. It required a conscious effort.

| Stories and Scripts

There are no endings. If you think so you are deceived as to their nature.
They are all beginnings. Here is one.

—Hilary Mantel

C HAPTER 1 CONCLUDED, after a discussion of primates and the more primitive human societies, by identifying some elemental features of strategic
behavior. Such behavior emerged out of social structures that invited conflict, recognized the distinctive attributes of potential opponents or allies, displayed sufficient empathy to find ways to influence their actions, and were able
to prevail through deception or coalition as well as brute force. These features
have regularly come to the fore as we have considered strategy in both theory
and practice. We have also come across a number of definitions of strategy,
many of which are perfectly serviceable, although none quite capture all these
elements. Some have been quite specific to particular spheres, notably the
military, referring to engagements, maps, and deployments. Others have been
more general, referring to the interaction of ends, ways and means, combinations of long-term goals and courses of action, systems of expediencies and
forms of domination, dialectics of opposing wills and interdependent decision-making, relationships to environments, advanced problem-solving, and
a means of coping with uncertainty. The preface offered "the art of creating
power" as my short definition. This has the advantage of allowing the impact

of strategy to be measured as the difference between the outcome anticipated by reference to the prevailing balance of power and the actual outcome after the application of strategy. It helps explain why underdogs find strategy most challenging. It does not, however, provide guidance for practitioners. To this end this chapter explores the value of considering strategy as a story about power told in the future tense from the perspective of a leading character.

Those who want to be sure that their strategy is well done can draw on many forms of advice, from professional manuals to self-help books to specialist consultancies to academic journals. Some prescriptions are exhortatory while others are more analytical; some struggle to rise above banalities while others are couched in terms barely intelligible to lay readers lacking higher mathematics or the ability to penetrate postmodernist codes. Some insist on a paradigm shift. Others suggest nurturing an inspirational personality or urge close attention to detail. Faced with such diverse and often contradictory advice it is hard to avoid the conclusion that while strategy is undoubtedly a good thing to have, it is also a hard thing to get right. The world of strategy is full of disappointment and frustration, of means not working and ends not reached.

The various strands of literature examined in this book all began confidently with a belief that given the right measures demanding objectives could be achieved on a regular basis. The Napoleonic phenomenon led Jomini and Clausewitz to explain to aspiring generals how they might win decisive battles and so decide the fate of nations. The recollection of the French Revolution and gathering social and political unrest encouraged the first professional revolutionaries to imagine equally decisive insurrections from which new forms of social order would emerge. Over a century later, large American corporations—apparently unassailable and enjoying benign market conditions—were encouraged by Chandler, Drucker, and Sloan to look to strategy as a guide to the organizational structures and long-term plans that could sustain this happy state of affairs.

In all three cases, experience undermined the foundations of this confidence. Victory in battle did not necessarily lead to victory in war. The ruling classes found ways to meet popular demands for political and economic rights that diverted revolutionary pressures. The comfortable position of American manufacturers was rocked by international competition, notably—but not solely—from Japan. Yet these setbacks did not lead to the initial frameworks being abandoned. Military strategists continued to yearn for a route to decisive victories even as they were frustrated by grinding campaigns of attrition or popular resistance and guerrilla ambushes. Revolutionaries continued to seek ways to mobilize the broad masses to overthrow governments even as the Western democracies legitimated expressions of discontent and paths to reform, and as these encouraged quite different and generally more productive types of political strategy. It was only in the business sphere that the flaws in the early strategic models were so evident that they were soon left behind by a frenetic search for alternatives which came to involve a range of competing, often contradictory, and confusing propositions.

The problems experienced with strategy were a natural consequence of its Enlightenment origins. Progressive rationalism, later identified by Weber as an unstoppable secular trend manifest in the rise of bureaucracies, was expected to squeeze out emotions and romance, thereby removing intrusive sources of error and uncertainty. The prospect was one of human affairs ordered on the basis of accumulated knowledge. But relevant knowledge was hard to accumulate or present with sufficient precision to guide practitioners, who were faced with a series of competing demands and uncertainties and often had little real choice but to "muddle through."[1] The assumption of rationalism, influencing not only the theorizing but expectations of how it would be received and acted upon, turned out to be inadequate.

Strategies were neither designed nor implemented in controlled environments. The longer the sequence of planned moves, the greater the number of human agents who must act in particular ways, the more extensive the ambition of the project, the more likely that something would go wrong. Should the first moves in the planned sequence of events fail to produce the intended effects matters could soon go awry. Situations would become more complex and the actors more numerous and contrary. The chains of causation would become attenuated and then broken altogether. Without going as far as Tolstoy, who dismissed the idea of strategy as presumptuous and naïve, it was evident that successful outcomes would depend on trying to affect a range of institutions, processes, personalities, and perceptions that would often be quite impervious to influence. Warning against the belief that history was full of lessons, Gordon Wood argued that there was but one big one: "Nothing ever works out quite the way its managers intended or expected." History taught "skepticism about people's ability to manipulate and control purposely their own destinies."[2] Strategies were not so much means of asserting control over situations but ways of coping with situations in which nobody was in total control.

The Limits of Strategy

Did this leave strategy with any value? "Plans are worthless," observed President Eisenhower, drawing on his military experience, "but planning is everything."[3] The same could be said about strategy. Without some prior deliberation it might be even harder to cope with the unexpected, pick up the cues of a changing situation, challenge set assumptions, or consider the implications of uncharacteristic behavior. If strategy is a fixed plan that set out a reliable path to an eventual goal, then it is likely to be not only disappointing but also counterproductive, conceding the advantage to others with greater flexibility and imagination. Adding flexibility and imagination, however, offers a better chance of keeping pace with a developing situation, regularly re-evaluating risks and opportunities.

A productive approach to strategy requires recognizing its limits. This applies not only to the benefits of strategy but also to its domain. Boundaries are required. As strategy has become so ubiquitous, so that every forward-looking decision might be worthy of the term, it now risks meaninglessness, lacking any truly distinguishing feature. One obvious boundary is to insist on its irrelevance in situations involving inanimate objects or simple tasks. It only really comes into play when elements of conflict are present. Situations in which this conflict is only latent are rarely approached in a truly strategic frame of mind. Rather than assume trouble people prefer instead to trust others with the expectation of being trusted in turn. Within a familiar environment, working with an "in-group," overtly strategic behavior can lead to resentment and resistance without commensurate gain. People can be at the wrong end of power relationships without either realizing or caring, because of the way they have been encouraged to think about their life circumstances or because of their habitual reluctance to challenge established hierarchies and conventions. What makes the difference, so that strategy comes to the fore, is the recognition of conflict. Some event, or shift in social attitudes or patterns of behavior, can challenge what had previously been taken for granted. Familiar situations may be seen with fresh eyes and those previously part of the "in-group" come to be viewed with suspicion as defectors to the "out-group."

If emerging situations of conflict bring strategy into the picture, a desire to play down conflict can take it out. This can even be the case with official documents with strategy in the title which are largely designed to demonstrate a capacity for long-term thought. In these documents strategy is packaged as an authoritative forward look, reflecting the approved views of a government or company. Hew Strachan has complained of how strategy has come to be abused in this way, at the expense of its original role as a link between ends and means. By extending strategy into all governmental endeavors the word is "robbed" of its meaning leaving only "banalities" behind.[4] Certainly many "strategy" documents deliberately avoid the topic, lack focus, cover too many dissimilar or only loosely connected issues and themes, address multiple audiences to the satisfaction of none, and reflect nuanced bureaucratic compromises. They are often about issues that might have to be addressed rather than ways of dealing with specific problems. Consequently, their half-lives are often short. To the extent that such documents have any strategic content they are about a broad orientation to the environment, what became known in business strategy as "positioning." It may well be that in a broadly stable and satisfactory environment, in which goals are being realized with relative ease, there may be little need for anything sharper and bolder. Only at moments of environmental instability, as latent conflict becomes actual, when real choices have to be made does something resembling a true strategy become necessary.

So what turns something that is not quite strategy into strategy is a sense of actual or imminent instability, a changing context that induces a sense of conflict. Strategy therefore starts with an existing state of affairs and only gains meaning by an awareness of how, for better or worse, it could be different. This view is quite different from those that assume strategy must be about reaching some prior objective. It may well be more concerned with coping with some dire crisis or preventing further deterioration in an already stressful situation. So the first requirement might be one of survival. This is why as a practical matter strategy is best understood modestly, as moving to the "next stage" rather than to a definitive and permanent conclusion. The next stage is a place that can be realistically reached from the current stage. That place may not necessarily be better, but it will still be an improvement upon what could have been achieved with a lesser strategy or no strategy at all. It will also be sufficiently stable to be a base from which to prepare to move to the stage after that. This does not mean that it is easy to manage without a view of a desired end state. Without some sense of where the journey should be leading it will be difficult to evaluate alternative outcomes. Like a grandmaster at chess, a gifted strategist will be able to see the future possibilities inherent in the next moves, and think through successive stages. The ability to think ahead is therefore a valuable attribute in a strategist, but the starting point will still be the challenges of the present rather than the promise of the future. With each move from one state of affairs to another, the combination of ends and means will be reappraised. Some means will be discarded and new ones found, while some ends will turn out to be beyond reach even as unexpected opportunities come into view. Even when what had been assumed to be the ultimate goal is reached, strategy will not stop. Victory in a climactic event such as a battle, an insurrection, an election, a sporting final, or a business acquisition will mean a move to a new and more satisfactory state but not the end of struggle. What has gone before will set the terms for the next set of encounters. The effort required to achieve victory may have left resources depleted. A crushed rebellion may add to the resentment of the oppressed; bruising election campaigns can hamper coalition formation; hostile takeovers make merging two companies more difficult.

One reason why it is so difficult to anticipate how situations might develop over many stages results from the need to address many relationships. Strategy is often presented as being solely about opponents and rivals. In the first instance, however, colleagues and subordinates must agree on the strategy and how it should be implemented. Achieving an internal consensus often requires great strategic skill and must be a priority because of the weaknesses caused by divisions, but the accommodation of different interests and perspectives can result in a compromised product—suboptimal when dealing with a capable opponent. The larger the circle of cooperation required, including third parties who might become allies, the harder it can become to reach agreement. While there can be tensions among supposed friends, there can also be areas of shared interest that provide the basis for a negotiation. Rival states might prefer to avoid all-out war, political parties to maintain standards of civility, and businesses to avoid pushing prices down to unprofitable levels. This interaction between cooperation and conflict is at the heart of all strategy. There is a spectrum marked by complete consensus (absence of any disputes) at one end and complete control (disputes smothered by one party's domination) at the other. Both extremes are rare and almost certainly unstable as circumstances change and new types of interest emerge. In practice, the choice may well be between degrees of conciliation or coercion. As the best way of coping with superior strength is often to put together a coalition or break up that of the opponent, strategy is apt to involve compromises and negotiations. "The pursuit of relative power," Timothy Crawford has observed, "is as much about subtracting and dividing as about adding and multiplying." This can require difficult forms of accommodation to keep a party neutral and away from the enemy camp.[5] All this explains why strategy is an art and not a science. It comes into play when situations are uncertain, unstable, and thus unpredictable.

System 1 Strategy and System 2 Strategy

Developments in cognitive psychology mean that we now know much more than before about how human beings cope with uncertain situations. They encourage the view that strategic thinking can and often does start in the subconscious before it breaks into conscious thought. It can originate as apparently intuitive judgments, reflecting what can now be labeled System 1 thinking. System 1 strategies draw on an ability to read situations and see possibilities that less-strategic intelligences would miss. This form of strategic reasoning has been appreciated since classical times. It was manifested as mētis, exemplified by Odysseus, who was resourceful, coped with ambiguity, and used artful language to lead the in-group and disorient the out-group. Napoleon spoke of the *coup d'œil* as the "gift of being able to see at a glance the possibilities offered by the terrain." It was at the heart of Clausewitz's belief in military genius, a "highly developed mental aptitude" that allowed the great general to pick the right moment and place for attack. Jon Sumida described Clausewitz's concept of genius as involving "a combination of rational intelligence and subrational intellectual and emotional faculties that make up intuition." It was the only basis of decision in the "face of difficult circumstances such as inadequate information, great complexity, high levels of contingency, and severe negative consequences in the event of failure."[6] Napoleon described this as an inborn talent, but Clausewitz saw that it could also be developed through experience and education.

In one of his last published articles, the philosopher Isaiah Berlin spoke up for instinct and flair, challenging the idea that good judgment in politics could be scientific and founded on "indubitable knowledge".[7] "In the realm of political action," Berlin concluded, "laws are far and few indeed: skills are everything." The key skill was the ability to grasp what made a situation unique. Great political figures were able to "understand the character of a particular movement, of a particular individual, of a unique state of affairs, of a unique atmosphere, of some particular combination of economic, political, personal factors." This grasp of the interplay of human beings and impersonal forces, sense of the specific over the general, and capacity to anticipate the consequential "tremors" of actions involved a special sort of judgment. This was, he averred, "semi-instinctive." He described a form of political intelligence, closely resembling mētis and capturing the best of System 1 thinking:

> ...a capacity for integrating a vast amalgam of constantly changing, multicolored, evanescent, perpetually overlapping data, too many, too swift, too intermingled to be caught and pinned down and labeled like so many individual butterflies. To integrate in this sense is to see the data (those identified by scientific knowledge as well as by direct perception) as elements in a single pattern, with their implications,

to see them as symptoms of past and future possibilities, to see them pragmatically—that is, in terms of what you or others can or will do to them, and what they can or will do to others or to you.

It was a capacity that could be lost by a focus on formal methodologies and a determination to squeeze out the intuition and stress the analytical. "Many of the strategists I have examined," observed Bruce Kuklick of contributors to postwar American security policy, "were essentially apolitical, in that they lacked what I must call for want of a better phrase *elementary political sense*. It is almost as if they sought to learn in a seminar room or from cogitation what only instinct, experience and savvy could teach."[8]

The quality that often comes with political judgment is the ability to persuade others to follow a particular course. Indeed, for those who are not Napoleons, who cannot expect orders to be accepted without question, shrewd judgment is of little value unless it is coupled with an ability to express its meaning to those who must follow its imperatives. It is at this point that strategy moves from intuition to deliberation, from knowing that a particular course is the right one to finding the arguments to explain why this must be so. So system 2 thinking is needed for those situations that are too complex and unique for System 1. Such circumstances require that alternative arguments be weighed and measured against each other to identify a credible course of action. Thus, for the most part, strategy must be in the realm of System 2, but that may only be in terms of turning what are essentially System 1 judgments into persuasive arguments.

The reason this book has returned so often to questions of language and communication is because strategy is meaningless without them. Not only does strategy need to be put into words so that others can follow, but it works through affecting the behavior of others. Thus it is always about persuasion, whether convincing others to work with you or explaining to adversaries the consequences if they do not. Pericles gained authority for his ability to make a reasoned case in a democratic setting; Machiavelli urged princes to develop compelling arguments; Churchill's speeches gave the British people a sense of purpose in war. Brute force or economic inducements may play their part, but their impact may be lost without clarity about what must be done to avoid punishment or gain reward. "Power is actualized only where word and deed have not parted company," observed Hannah Arendt, "where words are not empty and deeds not brutal, where words are not used to veil intentions but to disclose realities, and deeds are not used to violate and destroy but to establish relations and create new realities."[9]

The greatest power is that which achieves its effects without notice. This comes about when established structures appear settled and uncontentious, part of the natural and generally benign order of things, even to those who might be supposed to be disadvantaged.[10] The ability of elites to render essentially sectional interests as a general good so that their satisfaction is taken for granted and put beyond challenge has been a source of intense frustration to radicals. The limited revolutionary zeal of the masses has been explained by grand stories—labeled as formulas, myths, ideologies, paradigms, and eventually narratives—which assumed that since people could not grasp objective reality they must depend on interpretative constructs, and those best placed to influence those constructs could acquire enormous power. The radicals sought to develop strategies promoting alternative, healthier forms of consciousness, contradicting any suggestion that the existing scheme of things must be accepted without question as natural and enduring rather than constructed and contingent. This question of how best to affect the attitudes of others has come to be seen to be relevant to all aspects of strategy and not just efforts to turn the existing order upside down. Partisan politicians have worked to set agendas and frame issues, offering damaging stories about opponents while portraying a party's own candidates in the best possible light. This "narrative turn" has also been evident in the military and business arenas, reflected in calls for sensitivity to "hearts and minds" in counterinsurgency, corporate lobbyists challenging regulatory restraints, or managers trying to convince employees that they will benefit from drastic organizational changes. Not only are stories instruments of strategy, they also give form to strategy. Reinforced by cognitive theories and the role of interpretative constructs and scripts in organizing attitudes and behavior, narratives have moved to the fore in the contemporary strategic literature in military, politics, and business. In order to come to terms with recent trends in thinking about strategy we need to come to terms with stories.

The Trouble with Stories

In his essay "The Trouble with Stories," Charles Tilly considered the persistent human tendency to seek explanations in terms of stories about individuals, along with collectives such as churches or states and even abstractions such as classes or regions. These stories would tell of deliberate, conscious, and often successful acts to achieve definite goals. They satisfied their audience, including social scientists, far too easily. All that seemed to be required was a degree of plausibility, recognition of the constraints of time and circumstance, and a match with cultural expectations. Yet, Tilly warned, stories had limited explanatory power. The most significant cause-effect relations tended to be "indirect, incremental, interactive, unintended, collective, or mediated by the nonhuman environment rather than being direct, willed consequences of individual action." The demand for stories encouraged analysis in terms of actors making deliberate choices among well-defined alternatives, when actual decision-making was likely to be far less calculating and deliberate, more improvised, often quite wobbly. Social scientists had a responsibility to seek something better. Tilly was not optimistic. Brains, he noted, would "store, retrieve and manipulate information about social processes" in terms of standard stories, thereby encouraging accounts of complex events in terms of the "interactions of self-motivated objects." If this was the case, Tilly at least hoped for superior stories, doing justice to the impersonal and collective forces at work as well as the human, and making the appropriate connections with time, places, actors, and actions outside their purview. Better still, we should tell stories about stories, giving stories context and considering how they were generated.[11]

Business historians have come to warn of accepting at face value narratives, such as Sloan's *My Life with General Motors*, that suggest that challenging decisions were matters of purely rational choice. Whether or not such narratives exaggerate the role of senior managers they leave the impression of inevitability, understating the possibility of different decisions leading to alternative outcomes.[12] Daniel Raff advocates recreating the choices of the past, looking at historical events as "sequences of challenges to be addressed rather than as initiatives which have already happened." This would mean recognizing the alternatives that were available in the past and how actors made sense of them.[13] Kahneman has also observed that although good stories "provide a simple and coherent account of people's actions and intentions," this encourages a readiness to "interpret behavior as a manifestation of general propensities and personality traits—causes that you can readily match to effects." As an example he cites analyses of corporate success. The numerous management books full of these stories "consistently exaggerate the impact of leadership style and management practices." He suggests that luck is as important a factor if not more so. The result of these biases is that when it comes to "explaining the past and in predicting the future, we focus on the causal role of skill and neglect the role of luck. We are therefore prone to an illusion of control." He further notes the paradox that it "is easier to construct a coherent story when you know little, when there are fewer pieces to fit into the puzzle." This reinforces the tendency to neglect factors about which little is known, thereby encouraging overconfidence.[14]

These flawed stories of the past shape our predictions of the future. In this he draws attention to the work of Nassim Taleb, who stresses the importance of unexpected and random events (which he calls "black swans") for which inadequate provision has been made because they are so out of line with past experience. Yet Taleb also acknowledges a contradiction in his method, for although he points to forms of narrative fallacy he also uses stories "to illustrate our gullibility about stories and our preference for the dangerous compression of narratives." This is because metaphors and stories are "far more potent (alas) than ideas; they are also easier to remember and more fun to read." As a result: "You need a story to displace a story."[15]

We have seen in this book how familiar stories with a strong message turn out on closer examination to be either fabricated or subject to alternative interpretations offering different lessons. David and Goliath is now understood to be about what an underdog might achieve, but it was originally about the importance of belief in God. Odysseus began as a celebration of a shrewd and crafty intelligence, but as he morphed into the Roman Ulysses he came to exemplify treachery and trickery. Plato outdid the sophists at their own game, making his claim for a pure discipline of philosophy by recasting those who came before him as caring more for money than truth. Milton sought to make sense of the Creation by constructing a Machiavellian Satan who many came to find a more compelling character than his worthy God. Clausewitz looked at Napoleon's ill-fated Russian campaign as flawed strategy; Tolstoy saw it as proof that there could be no such thing as strategy. Liddell Hart collected stories of battle and then gave them his own twist to validate his indirect approach. John Boyd and his acolytes took the idea of the blitzkrieg—as exemplified by the German success in Europe in 1940—stripped it of context by ignoring its failure in the East, and turned it into a model for future warfare. Marx complained about the persistent influence of the French Revolution but could not quite escape from it himself. As his predictions about the development of capitalism turned out to be flawed, his followers contorted themselves to prove that this was still scientific history and so bound to be vindicated. The traditional teaching of business strategy depended on stories known as case histories. The management gurus, from Frederick Taylor to Tom Peters, knew that they could make their points with a good tale that could illustrate their essential points. The very human temptation to seize on some specific incident to make a general point—demonstrated by the uses of anecdotes about Honda—led invariably to overstated conclusions that were far more contingent than their tellers would allow.

"Research suggests that power comes less from knowing the right stories than from knowing how and [how] well to tell them: what to leave out, what to fill in, when to revise and when to challenge, and whom to tell or not to tell."[16] In terms of everyday human interaction, persuasion through story-telling can be an important skill, especially when engaging those with simi-lar backgrounds and interests. When engaging those who might be skeptical or suspicious, with separate frames of reference, they may be of less value. Moreover, narratives deliberately manufactured to achieve some desired effect risk appearing forced and contrived. They suffer from all the problems once associated with propaganda, which lost credibility precisely because of its blatant attempt to influence how others thought and behaved.

Indeed, the current enthusiasm for "strategic narratives" might fade with greater appreciation of their roots in what was once unashamedly and posi-tively called propaganda, before it acquired totalitarian connotations. These narratives have to work within all the previously described constraints. With sufficient ambiguity, the same strategic story might hold a group together or advance a political project but then fall apart as soon as clarity is required, empirical tests present themselves, or contradictory messages emerge. When it comes to "battles of narratives," what matters is not only their inherent quality but the resources behind them, reflected in the capacity for an orga-nization to propagate its own myths and censor or counter contrary claims. Narratives are neither "fundamentally subversive nor hegemonic." They can be told effectively—and ineffectually—by authorities and their opponents. They are not precise strategic instruments because they can convey a range of messages, not all of which may be understood, and narrative devices such as metaphors and irony can cause confusion. The meaning of stories can be ambiguous and some interpretations may undercut the storyteller. Audiences may focus on minor features or impose their own experiences on the narra-tive. Familiar stories which apparently convey one message can be given a mischievous twist by groups promoting an apparently contrary cause.[17] We can recall the classicist Francis Cornford's definition of propaganda: "That branch of the art of lying which consists in very nearly deceiving your friends without quite deceiving your enemies."[18]

Scripts

These ambiguous aspects of narratives explain their limitations as strategic instruments. Are there ways of thinking about them that might help give them more value? We can assume that it is much easier to control for prob-lems of meaning and interpretation when the audience is quite small and already sharing much by way of culture and purposes. Reference was made in the last chapter to the concept of an internalized script as a source of orientation to a new situation. This concept has been influential in the psychology and artificial intelligence communities but less so in the strategic. Strictly speaking, the concept refers to stereotypical situations which set expectations for appropriate behavior. Scripts can be either weak, for example, deciding that somebody fits a certain personality type, or strong, in anticipating a whole sequence of events. In the original concept, scripts were about drawing on stored knowledge that led to almost automatic responses—which might turn out to be wholly inappropriate. Scripts can, however, be taken as starting points for deliberate action and even be developed and internalized by groups as they consider together a developing situation. Studies of scripts have therefore considered how individuals respond to organizational routines, such as appraisals, or to events which they are unlikely to have experienced ever before, such as fires in a public place. This work has demonstrated the hold scripts can have and the difficulty of persuading people who have committed to a particular script to abandon it. Scripts may be a natural way of responding to new situations, but they can also be seriously misleading. Thus, if people need to behave abnormally, they need to know that they are in an abnormal situation.[19]

The advantages of scripts for our purposes are twofold. First, the concept provides a way of addressing the problem about how individuals enter into new situations, give them meaning, and decide how to behave. Second, it has a natural link with performance and narrative. Indeed, Abelson discussed scripts in terms of being composed of a series of scenes made up of linked vignettes that are as likely to originate in reading, including fiction, as experience.[20]

One use of the idea in a wider context comes from Avner Offer's account of the origins of the Great War, in which he describes the importance of "honor" as a motivation and asks why it took precedence over survival. It was not as if the German High Command was confident of victory. They knew that the planned offensive was something of a gamble, even though they could think of no other way to wage the war. In the war counsels of Berlin in 1914, the view was that Germany dared not hold back. It had done so with the last crisis, and if it did so again its reputation would be lost. The only prospect would be an ignominious and decadent decline. The consequences were uncertain, but a fine intention would provide its own vindication. The German decision to go to war—and those equally belligerent decisions it provoked—was, Offer asserts, an "expressive rather than instrumental act." In this respect war was the outcome of a sequence of insults, a "chain of honorable reactions" which none felt able to ignore. Offer explains the emphasis on honor in deciding on war and then the military mobilization of whole societies on the basis of scripts. The honor script was not "overt" but was influential, sanctioning a "reckless attitude" and creating "a powerful social pressure to subordinate prudential considerations and to conform." This script, he suggests, was derivative of an even more implicit dueling script, which had its own sequence. When honor was challenged or questioned in some episode, the remedy was violence "in the case of nation-states, preceded by the polite maneuvers and language of diplomacy." If "satisfaction" was denied, there would be a "loss of reputation, status, [and] honor," which would lead to "humiliation and shame." This script proved to be powerful. It "provided a narrative in which decisions could be communicated, a justification and legitimation for sacrifice that everyone could understand and accept." So what started as an emotion among the few at the top could be transmitted through the culture. So powerful was this script that those in its grip were blinded to alternative scripts based on "other forms of courage and risk taking; to those of timely concession, of conciliation, cooperation, and trust."[21]

In this respect, a strategic script in a System 1 sense can be considered a largely internalized foundation for attempts to give situations meaning and suggest appropriate responses. These scripts may be implicit or just taken for granted, as in the assumptions that the logic of war is a battle of annihilation leading to enemy capitulation, that sea power must be about command of the sea, that the best form of counterinsurgency addresses hearts and minds, that appeasement always leads to an impression of weakness, or that an arms race always escalates into war. These are stereotypes that can often serve as substitutes for original thought or consideration of the particularities of situations. While they may be validated if acted upon, they may turn out to be wrong. At a less elevated level, scripts may be about the correct sequence of operations in a military campaign, the effect of state violence on popular movements, forming community organizations, securing a presidential nomination, managing organizational change, identifying the optimum time and place for a new product launch, or making the first move in a hostile takeover.

The point about these scripts is that if not challenged they may result in predictable behavior and miss variations in the context that should demand original responses. As I argued earlier, strategy really kicks in when there is something different and unfamiliar about the situation. System 1 scripts may be a natural starting point, but they may benefit from a System 2 appraisal that considers why the normal script might not work this time. In this respect, following established scripts risks strategic failure.

System 2 scripts should be more deserving of the adjective "strategic." For dramatists, a compelling narrative is something to be worked on and refined rather than merely a way of dignifying the inchoate mutterings of ordinary folk. Instead of being a subconscious set of internalized scripts, these scripts may be seen as acts of conscious communication. They do not need to take the form of screenplays in which each actor speaks in turn, but they should have a composed quality indicating the expected interaction between the main actors. They may be rooted in the past or draw on well-known events, but they have to take the present as a starting point and project forward. These strategies are stories about the future, starting with imaginative fiction but with an aspiration to nonfiction.

Jerome Bruner's discussion of narratives also illustrates the possibilities and limitations of strategic scripts. He suggested the following requirements. First, though they may not present reality accurately, they must meet the standard of verisimilitude, that is, the appearance of being true. Second, they will predispose an audience to a particular interpretation of events and an anticipation of what is to come. They do not involve empirical verification or steps in a logical sequence, but they create their own imperatives. "Narrative necessity" is the counterpart of "logical necessity." They can use devices such as suspense, foreshadowing, and flashbacks, and be allowed more ambiguity and uncertainty than formal analyses. Third, while they cannot be constituted as a formal proof of any general theory, they can be used to demonstrate a principle, uphold a norm, or offer guidance for the future. These, however, must arise naturally out of the narrative and not necessarily be stated explicitly in conclusion. It is often impossible to know where a good story is leading until the destination is reached. The audience must be taken to the required point by the "narrative imperative." According to Bruner, an "innovative story teller goes beyond the obvious." To get the audience's attention, the story must breach the expectations created by an "implicit canonical script" to contain an element of the unusual and unexpected.[22]

The purpose of such a strategic story is not solely to predict events but to convince others to act in such a way that the story will follow its proposed course. If it fails to convince, the inherent prediction will certainly be wrong. As with other stories, these must relate to the audience's culture, experience, beliefs, and aspirations. To engage, they must ring true and survive examination in terms of their internal coherence and consistency ("narrative probability"). They must also resonate with the historical and cultural understandings of their intended audience ("narrative fidelity").[23] The main challenges for strategic narratives lie in their potentially brutal encounter with reality, which may require early adjustment, and the need to address multiple audiences, which risks incoherence.[24] It might be possible to reconcile apparently incompatible demands through a rhetorical trick or to combine optimistic assumptions on top of each other, but such devices can soon be exposed. There needs to be candor and little make-believe.

What about the criticisms of Tilly and Kahneman that our dependence on stories leads us to exaggerate the importance of human agency, to assume that effects flow from the deliberate acts of the central characters in our stories (often ourselves) rather than large impersonal forces or chance events or questions of timing and happenstance that could never be part of the starting narrative? The answer is that ignoring these factors certainly makes for bad history but not necessarily bad strategy. When we seek to understand the present it is unwise to assume that things are the way they are solely because strong actors wished them to be thus, but when we look forward to the future we have little choice but to identify a way forward dependent upon human agency which might lead to a good outcome. It is as well to avoid illusions of control, but in the end all we can do is act as if we can influence events. To do otherwise is to succumb to fatalism.

Moreover, the unexpected and the accidental can be managed if provision is made from the start to accommodate them. A strategic plan, relating available means to desired ends through a series of steps which if followed carefully and in sequence produces the desired outcome, suggests a predictable world, with cause and effect known in advance. One large conclusion of this book is that such plans struggle to survive their encounters with an awkward reality. A script may share with a plan an anticipated sequence of events, but as it moves from System 1 to System 2, from a subconscious assumption to a deliberate composition, it can incorporate the possibility of chance events and anticipate the interaction of a number of players over an extended period of time. This requires an unfinished quality. The script must leave considerable scope for improvisation. There is only one action that can be anticipated with any degree of certainty, and that is the first move of the central player for whom the strategy has been devised. Whether the plot will unfold as intended will then depend on not only the acuity of the starting assumptions but also whether other players follow the script or deviate significantly from it.

Scripts: Strategic and Dramatic

Once strategies are considered as narratives a close relationship with drama becomes evident. David Barry and Michael Elmes consider strategy, "one of the most prominent, influential and costly stories told in organizations." It carries elements of "theatrical drama, the historical novel, futurist fantasy, and autobiography," with "parts" prescribed for different characters. "Its traditional emphasis on forecasting aligns it with visionary novels having a prospective, forward-looking focus."[25] If this is the case then there might be guidance for strategists in the methods by which dramatists work out their plots and write their scripts.

A good place to begin is Robert McKee's guide to the art of storytelling for movies.[26] The starting point is exactly the same as with strategy. The story, like the strategy, moves forward with conflict. Scripts fail, he warns, when they are marked by "either a glut of meaningless and absurdly violent conflict, or a vacancy of meaningful and honestly expressed conflict." This means recognizing that even within an apparently harmonious organization there is always some conflict. There is never enough space, time, or resources to go round, leaving aside the forms of conflict that result from discordant personalities and a clash of egos (which a successful organizational politician will also need to understand). Conflict does not necessarily lead to violence and mayhem. The conflict may be within the main character, which is reflected in the strategist's need to choose. As McKee observes, the interesting and challenging choices are not those between good and evil but those between irreconcilable goods or two evils. The challenge of choice, however, is to know what can be done to achieve the preferred outcome, so that aiming for one does not lead to the other. This is the role of the plot, so that when "confronted by a dozen branching possibilities" the correct path is chosen. The plot will contain its own internal laws of probability. The choices faced by the protagonists must emerge naturally out of the world as described. The plot represents the dramatist's "choice of events and their design in time." The strategist must also stick closely to what McKee calls the "archplot," in which "motivated actions cause effects that in turn become the causes of yet other effects, thereby interlinking the various levels of conflict in a chain reaction of episodes to the story climax, expressing the interconnectedness of reality."

In drama, plots provide the structure that holds stories together and gives meaning to particular events. Aristotle in his *Poetics* described a plot as an "arrangement of incidents" that should have an inner unity. The story should not contain anything of irrelevance and it must maintain its credibility throughout. This required that the key players stay in character. Aristotle insisted that cause and effect should be explicable within the terms of the story rather than as the result of some artificial, external intervention. The "function of the poet" was in relating not what had happened but what could happen, to show what was possible "according to the law of probability or necessity."[27]

The features of a good plot are therefore shared between drama and strategy: conflict, convincing characters and credible interactions, sensitivity to the impact of chance, and a whole set of factors that no plan can anticipate or accommodate in advance. In both, the line between fiction and nonfiction can be blurred. A dramatist may attempt to reconstruct real events by showing what might have happened, while the strategist opens with a current reality but must then imagine how it could be changed. In neither case is there value in a wonderful and compelling narrative that falls flat and fails to engage its intended audience. A story that is too clever, convoluted, experimental, or shocking may fail to connect, produce an appalled counterreaction, or convey the wrong set of messages. In strategy as in drama, a poor plot can result from incredible characters, too much disparate activity, too many discordant points of view, events moving too slowly or too fast, confusing links, or obvious gaps.

There are, however, important differences between the dramatist and strategist. These can be illustrated by an example. In 1921, secretary of the interior Albert Fall took bribes from oil executives to hand over leases to drill for oil under the Teapot Dome rock formation in Wyoming. The press picked up the story because of rumblings from those within the oil industry denied the opportunity to bid for the reserves, although one newspaper used evidence to blackmail rather than reveal. Fall refused to answer any questions, and the government tried to prevent progress. Ultimately, a Congressional panel concluded that the leases "were executed under circumstances indicating fraud and corruption." This was determined through tedious investigations, depending on a keen understanding of institutional processes.[28] One anti-corruption fighter in the Senate was Burton Wheeler of Montana, a lawyer who had made his name fighting for workers' rights and against corruption and had acted as prosecutor for another Congressional investigation into corruption at the Department of Justice. An unsuccessful attempt was made to discredit him through allegations that he had accepted a fee from a client to help secure government oil concessions.[29]

Wheeler was said to be the model for Jefferson Smith, the hero of Frank Capra's movie, *Mr. Smith Goes to Washington*. In the movie, Smith, the head of the state's Boy Rangers, is naïve and idealistic. He is sent by the boss of the local political machine (James Taylor), to go to Washington as a replacement for a recently deceased Senator in the mistaken belief that he will be easy to manipulate. The state's other Senator, Joseph Paine—once a good friend of Smith's father and a fellow idealist—has been corrupted by power. Smith proposes a bill to create a boys' camp in his home state, but the chosen site is one Taylor has found for a corrupt dam-building scheme. Taylor, therefore, forces a reluctant Paine to denounce Smith as planning to profit from the bill at the expense of the boys he claims to champion. The plan almost works. A disconsolate Smith almost gives up until his previously skeptical aide, Clarissa Saunders, persuades him to take a stand. As Paine is about to call for a vote to expel Smith from the Senate, Smith begins to filibuster, hoping to get the message about corruption to the people of his state. Though Smith stays on his feet, Taylor is able to use strong-arm tactics to prevent the message getting out. Paine prepares the final blow by bringing in to the Senate hundreds of letters and telegrams demanding Smith's expulsion. Before collapsing exhausted, Smith insists that he will continue fighting "even if this room gets filled with lies like these, and the Taylors and all their armies come marching into this place. Somebody'll listen to me." Paine is shocked. He tries to shoot himself and then exclaims that he is the one who should be expelled. He confesses all. Smith is now a hero and his Senate career is assured.

The movie contrasted the manipulative business trusts who put themselves beyond democratic accountability, through their control of party machines and a supine media, with the decent aspirations of ordinary folk. It conveyed distaste for Machiavellian political methods, wiles and ruses, pretense and deception, while applauding those who were straightforward, principled, and brave. It demonstrated how a good man could defeat evil lurking in the body politic. Although Capra was a Republican, the script was written by a communist, Sidney Buchman. Capra had found it expedient to play down Buchman's role, and he appears to have been happy with the movie as a simple morality tale, with the good rewarded and the bad punished. Buchman believed that his script was a challenge to dictatorship and emphasized "the spirit of vigilance which is necessary if one believes in democracy the refusal to surrender even before small things."[30]

Joseph Breen, the enforcer of the movie industry's Production Code Administration,[31] was at first hostile to the Senate's portrayal as "if not deliberately crooked . . . completely controlled by lobbyists with special interests." Aware that he needed to avoid the impression of political censorship, Breen accepted it as a "grand yarn" so long as most Senators were shown to be "fine, upstanding, citizens who labor long and tirelessly for the best interests of the nation."[32] Nonetheless, when first screened, senators (including Wheeler) and journalists were outraged. State Department officials feared that U.S. institutions were made to look ridiculous. The public—abroad as well as in the United States— was caught up in the brilliance of Capra's storytelling and accepted his claim that the movie idealized American democracy.[33] Ronald

Reagan almost modeled himself on Jefferson Smith, even as president quoting the line about fighting for lost causes.[34]

For Capra's purposes, Smith appeared as idealistic and a-strategic. His strategic advice came from Saunders, first mischievously and then lovingly. In a key scene, she finds Smith alone at the Lincoln Memorial, bemoaning the discrepancy between the "fancy words...carved in stone" and the lies he faced. She urges him not to quit. All the "good in the world" comes from "fools with faith." In the original screenplay she appeals to "a little fellow called David [who] walked out with only a sling-shot—but he had the *truth* on his side."[35] In the final version she has a strategy: "A forty foot dive into a tub of water, but I think you can do it." This strategy works for an underdog who must survive the stronger side's push for a quick victory. Paine, a master of the rulebook, is surprised by the filibuster. Smith knows enough not to yield the floor and so was not caught by Paine's request for him to do just that. The second part of Saunders's plan fails. As Smith speaks to encourage people in his state to "kick Mister Taylor's machine to kingdom come," Taylor observes: "He won't get started! I'll make public opinion out there in five hours. I've done it all my life!" He is even able to suppress the brave effort by the Boy Rangers to distribute their own paper. What actually makes the difference is the comparative fragility of the coalitions. That between Taylor and Paine breaks as the senator is reminded of his lost idealism. For his part, Smith is helped by a kindly vice president, who lets Smith get started on his filibuster and offers friendly smiles as he becomes weary.[36] The features of a strategy are therefore all present, even if not always explicit. They have to be to give the plot some credibility and to show that Smith was able, to a degree, to shape his own success. Where the drama takes over is in the compression of events, the lack of boring processes (such as the painstaking investigations of the Teapot Dome scandal), and a satisfactory conclusion dependent upon a sudden change of heart coming at the very last moment when it might have made a difference.

The dramatist controls the plot, manipulating the behavior of all parties and introducing elements of chance and coincidence to move the story to a predetermined conclusion. She sets boundaries to reduce the numbers of tangents and loose ends. All the main characters are under her control. She can decide how they meet and their interactions, which can be complicated through misunderstanding at crucial moments and then transformed by freak accidents or serendipitous encounters. She knows when there is going to be a surprising twist, a shocking revelation that presents a character in a completely new light, an accident that interferes with an apparently perfect plan, or an extraordinary opportunity that allows the hero to escape a terrible fate in the nick of time. She can introduce minor characters to make a point with complete confidence that they need never be seen again. She can hint at things to come, knowing that an attentive reader will pick up the clues or appreciate their relevance. By sustaining suspense to the end, she can ensure a thrilling denouement. Audiences expect a proper conclusion, which pulls together the distinct strands of the story, explains puzzles, and brings the suspense to an end. There may be a moral lesson, as evil characters get their comeuppance while the good are rewarded, or else deliberate moral ambiguity, confirming a sense of disappointment and injustice.

The strategist faces quite different challenges. The most important is that the stakes are for real. The dramatist may allow the "baddies" to win as a statement about the human condition; the strategist knows this will have real and possibly dire consequences. The dramatist can ensure that the plot unfolds as intended; the strategist has to cope with the choices of others while remaining relatively ignorant of what they might be. The dramatist can use these choices to reveal the true character of key players; the strategist must make a starting assumption about character when anticipating what choices may be made under intense forms of pressure. The strategist must avoid the standard plot lines of literature shaping expectations. It is unlikely that everything will come together in some sudden, thrilling climax. In drama, the most satisfactory foes appear as truly monstrous, malign, and egocentric. It might be tempting to denounce actual opponents in these terms but it is also dangerous if taken too seriously. An otherwise resolvable conflict might turn into a confrontation between the forces of light and darkness. Caricature depictions of opponents, along with glowing portrayals of friends, add to the risks of being caught by surprise by actual behavior. It must be understood that strategies that depend on others to act out of character, beyond their competence, or against their declared interests and preferences, are gambles. Rather than play out assigned roles that will leave them frustrated, contained, ambushed, or suppressed, they will write their own scripts. The challenge for the strategist—indeed, the essence of strategy—is to force or persuade those who are hostile or unsympathetic to act differently than their current intentions. The risk is always that the conclusions will be messier and less satisfactory than anticipated. There may not even be a proper conclusion. The plot may just peter out. The original story line may lead nowhere and be overtaken by a different story.

Both the dramatist and strategist must think about their audiences, but the problem of multiple audiences is more challenging for the strategist. If those who need to follow the plot are confused, they will be unable to play their parts. At the same time there may be others who are best kept in the dark, following false trails and deliberately ambiguous signals. The dramatist can reduce the demands on her audience. There is no need to show results being eked out through hard grind and close attention to detail over an expanded period. She also has the option of a thrilling climax. Here there can be complete closure, with absolute and irreversible change achieved. The strategist may face similar temptations: anxiety to bring matters to a swift conclusion, impatience at the thought of wearing opponents down over time or engaging potential allies in extended negotiations. A determination to seek a quick and decisive result is a frequent cause of failure. Unlike the dramatist, the strategist cannot rely on last-minute escapes from certain doom, in which chance, a sharp eye, a sudden revelation, or a uniquely cool head makes all the difference. The challenge is to identify moves that will require other players to follow the script out of the logic of the developing situation. The opening bid in negotiations, a feint on a battlefield, and a bellicose statement at a time of crisis may all assume a likely response by the other side. If that is not forthcoming, the improvisation will start early.

The strategist has to accept that even when there is an obvious climax (a battle or an election), the story line will still be open-ended—what McKee calls a "miniplot"—leaving a number of issues to be resolved later. Even when the desired endpoint is reached, it is not really the end. The enemy may have surrendered, the election won, the target company taken over, the revolutionary opportunity seized, but that just means that there is now an occupied country to run, a new government to be formed, a whole new revolutionary order to be established, or distinctive sets of corporate activity to be merged. Here the dramatist can leave the next stage to the reader's imagination or pick up the story again after the passage of time, perhaps even with many new characters. Strategists have no such luxury. The transition is immediate and may well be conditional on how the original endpoint was reached. This takes us back to the observation that much strategy is about getting to the next stage rather than some ultimate destination. Rather than think of strategy as a three-act play, it is better to think of it as a soap opera with a continuing cast of characters and plot lines that unfold over a series of episodes. Each of these episodes will be self-contained and set up the subsequent episode. Unlike a play with a definite ending, there is no need for a soap opera to ever reach a conclusion, even though the central characters and their circumstances change.

The dramatist can use coincidences to move the plot along, to ensure that the main protagonist faces the hard choices at the right time. The strategist knows that there will be events which were never part of the plot and which disrupt its logic but cannot be sure when, where, and how. Boundaries will be hard to maintain, and apparently irrelevant issues will intrude and complicate matters. The plot must therefore build in a certain freedom of action. The earlier definitive choices must be made, the greater the commitment to a particular course and the harder the adjustment when the actions of others or chance events deflect the protagonist from this course. The strategist cannot rely on the device of the *deus ex machina*, by which classical plays used divine intervention to sort out desperate situations at the last moment. Writers can allow a coincidence to turn an ending, acknowledges McKee, but this is the "writer's greatest sin" for it negates the value of the plot and allows the central characters to duck responsibility for their own actions. Aristotle also deplored the regular recourse to this device.

In ancient Greece, the most important distinction in plots was between comedy and tragedy. This was not a distinction between happy/sad or funny/miserable but between alternative ways of resolving conflicts.[37] It may be that the conflict is not between opposing characters but between individuals and society. Comedy ends with a satisfactory resolution and the main characters looking forward positively to the future; tragedy ends with a negative prospect—especially for the main character, who is probably largely responsible for his own misfortune—even if society as a whole is restored to some sort of equilibrium. When a new and positive relationship has been forged between society and the main character that is comedy; when the main character's attempt to change the status quo has been defeated that is tragedy. The dramatist knows from the start whether she is writing comedy or a tragedy: the strategist aims for comedy but risks tragedy.

ACKNOWLEDGMENTS

THE CONTRACT FOR this book is dated 1994. The original commission came from Tim Barton, and I appreciate his extraordinary patience as I busied myself with other projects and made a number of false starts on this one. Once it did get underway, he guided me to the capable hands of David McBride, who has been an extraordinarily supportive editor. It is thanks to him, Cammy Richelli, and the rest of the team at Oxford University Press that this book is making an appearance.

The project, however, would not have even been re-started had it not been for James Gow's encouragement and seminar opportunities to develop my ideas. James, with Brad Robinson, pushed me into applying to the Research Councils UK under their Global Uncertainties program and helped me put together a successful submission. This joint ESRC/AHRC Fellowship provided me with space to research and write that would otherwise have been impossible. I was particularly fortunate in my coworkers on the grant. I have benefited from Jeff Michaels's own work on strategic ideas, as well as his sharp critiques of my own. While I was supposedly supervising Ben Wilkinson's thesis, he was in practice supervising me—especially when it came to the Classics.

The department of War Studies at King's College London has been a stimulating home to me for over three decades. Conversations with staff and students inform many parts of this book. I have been grateful for the support of successive department heads: Brian Holden Reid, Christopher Dandeker, and Mervyn Frost. Other colleagues have also given me advice on the manuscript, notably Theo Farrell, Jan Willem Honig, and John Stone, who was a regular source of interesting references. Limor Simhony helped check my references, and Sarah Chukwudebe put in many corrections.

I have also benefited greatly from the advice of colleagues outside the department. Special mention must be made of two outstanding students of strategy, Beatrice Heuser and Bob Jervis, who provided detailed and meticulous annotations, far beyond the call of duty. Thanks for many useful comments are also due to Rob Ayson, Dick Betts, Stuart Croft, Pete Feaver, Azar Gat, Carl Levy, Albert Weale, and Nick Wheeler. Lastly, my son Sam was a source of good advice on structure and the title, and I was able to discuss the counterculture with my daughter-in-law Linda. I could mention many people with whom I have discussed the issues raised in this book—and a number of them appear in its pages—but two deserve special mention. The first is my teacher and mentor, Sir Michael Howard, who set me on this course and still inspires me to continue. The second is Colin Gray. Our careers have run in parallel, with many shared themes. Though our views have often diverged, the encounters have always been rewarding.

In all my books I have thanked my wife Judith for her forbearance. Once again she has had to cope with my "book daze," during which I am oblivious to everything around me other than the manuscript. It struck me, as we approach our ruby wedding, that it is about time I dedicated one of these books to her.

NOTES

Preface

1. *Matthew Parris,* "What if the Turkeys Don't Vote for Christmas?", *The Times*, May 12, 2012.
2. The concept of strategy as being "concerned with ways to employ means to achieve ends" is comparatively recent but is now well established in military circles, although not in such a way as always to capture the dynamic interaction between these elements. Arthur F. Lykke, Jr., "Toward an Understanding of Military Strategy," *Military Strategy: Theory and Application* (Carlisle, PA: U.S. Army War College, 1989), 3–8.
3. Ecclesiastes 9:11.
4. This can be tracked using Google's Ngram facility: http://books.google.com/ngrams/.
5. Raymond Aron, "The Evolution of Modern Strategic Thought," in Alastair Buchan, ed., *Problems of Modern Strategy* (London: Chatto & Windus, 1970), 25.
6. George Orwell, "Perfide Albion" (review, Liddell Hart's *British Way of Warfare*), *New Statesman and Nation*, November 21, 1942, 342–343.

1 Origins 1: Evolution

1. Frans B. M. de Waal, "A Century of Getting to Know the Chimpanzee," *Nature* 437, September 1, 2005, 56–59.
2. De Waal, *Chimpanzee Politics* (Baltimore: Johns Hopkins Press, 1998). First edition was in 1982.
3. De Waal, "Putting the Altruism Back into Altruism: The Evolution of Empathy," *Annual Review Psychology* 59 (2008): 279–300. See also Dario

Maestripieri, *Macachiavellian Intelligence: How Rhesus Macaques and Humans Have Conquered the World* (Chicago: University of Chicago Press, 2007).

4. Richard Byrne and Nadia Corp, "Neocortex Size Predicts Deception Rate in Primates," *Proceedings of the Royal Society of London* 271, no. 1549 (August 2004): 1693–1699.

5. Richard Byrne and A. Whiten, eds., *Machiavellian Intelligence: Social Expertise and the Evolution of Intellect in Monkeys, Apes and Humans* (Oxford: Clarendon Press, 1988); *Machiavellian Intelligence II: Extensions and Evaluations* (Cambridge: Cambridge University Press, 1997). The idea is often traced back to Nicholas Humphrey, "The Social Function of Intellect," in P. P. G. Bateson and R. A. Hinde, eds. *Growing Points in Ethology*, 303–317 (Cambridge: Cambridge University Press, 1976).

6. Bert Höllbroder and Edward O. Wilson, *Journey to the Ants: A Story of Scientific Exploration* (Cambridge, MA: Harvard University Press, 1994), 59. Cited in Bradley Thayer, *Darwin and International Relations: On the Evolutionary Origins of War and Ethnic Conflict* (Lexington: University Press of Kentucky, 2004), 163.

7. Jane Goodall, *The Chimpanzees of Gombe: Patterns of Behavior* (Cambridge, MA: Harvard University Press, 1986).

8. Richard Wrangham, "Evolution of Coalitionary Killing," *Yearbook of Physical Anthropology* 42, 1999, 12, 14, 2, 3.

9. Goodall, *The Chimpanzees of Gombe*, p. 176, fn 101.

10. Robert Bigelow, *Dawn Warriors* (New York: Little Brown, 1969).

11. Lawerence H. Keeley, *War Before Civilization: The Myth of the Peaceful Savage* (New York: Oxford University Press, 1996), 48.

12. Azar Gat, *War in Human Civilization* (Oxford: Oxford University Press, 2006), 115–117.

13. Keeping in mind that these societies were relatively simple and social moves within them, including deception, would be less demanding than those in more complex human societies. Kim Sterelny, "Social Intelligence, Human Intelligence and Niche Construction," *Philosophical Transactions of The Royal Society* 362, no. 1480 (2007): 719–730.

2 Origins 2: The Bible

1. Steven Brams, *Biblical Games: Game Theory and the Hebrew Bible* (Cambridge, MA: The MIT Press, 2003).

2. Ibid., 12.

3. Genesis 2:22, 23. All biblical references use the King James Version.

4. Genesis 2:16, 17; 3:16, 17.

5. Diana Lipton, *Longing for Egypt and Other Unexpected Biblical Tales*, Hebrew Bible Monographs 15 (Sheffield: Sheffield Phoenix Press, 2008).

6. Exodus 9:13–17.

7. Exodus 7:3–5.
8. Exodus 10:1–2.
9. Chaim Herzog and Mordechai Gichon, *Battles of the Bible*, revised ed. (London: Greenhill Books, 1997), 45.
10. Joshua 9:1–26.
11. Judges 6–8.
12. 1 Samuel 17.
13. Susan Niditch, *War in the Hebrew Bible: A Study in the Ethics of Violence* (New York: Oxford University Press, 1993), 110–111.

3 Origins 3: The Greeks

1. Homer, *The Odyssey,* translated by M. Hammond (London: Duckworth, 2000), Book 9.19–20, Book 13.297–9.
2. Virgil, *The Aeneid* (London: Penguin Classics, 2003).
3. Homer, *The Iliad,* translated by Stephen Mitchell (London: Weidenfeld & Nicolson, 2011), Chapter IX.310–311, Chapter IX.346–352, Chapter XVIII.243–314, Chapter XXII.226–240.
4. Jenny Strauss Clay, *The Wrath of Athena: Gods and Men in the Odyssey* (New York: Rowman & Littlefield, 1983), 96.
5. As "ou" is interchangeable with "me," this was linguistically equivalent to mētis.
6. *The Odyssey*, Book 9.405–14.
7. http://en.wikisource.org/wiki/Philoctetes.txt.
8. W. B. Stanford, *The Ulysses Theme: A Study in the Adaptability of the Traditional Hero* (Oxford: Basil Blackwell, 1954), 24.
9. Jeffrey Barnouw, *Odysseus, Hero of Practical Intelligence: Deliberation and Signs in Homer's Odyssey* (New York: University Press of America, 2004), 2–3, 33.
10. Marcel Detienne and Jean-Pierre Vernant, *Cunning Intelligence in Greek Culture and Society*, translated from French by Janet Lloyd (Sussex: The Harvester Press, 1978), 13–14, 44–45.
11. Barbara Tuchman, *The March of Folly: From Troy to Vietnam* (London: Michael Joseph, 1984), 46–49.
12. The word *stratēgos* was a compound of *stratos*, for an encamped army spread out over ground, and *agein* (to lead).
13. Thucydides, *The History of the Peloponnesian War,* translated by Rex Warner (London: Penguin Classics, 1972), 5.26.
14. The extent to which contemporary realist theories claim Thucydides as one of their own is discussed critically in Jonathan Monten, "Thucydides and Modern Realism," *International Studies Quarterly* (2006) 50, 3–25, and David Welch, "Why International Relations Theorists Should Stop Reading Thucydides," *Review of International Studies* 29 (2003), 301–319.
15. Thucydides, 1.75–76.

16. Ibid., 5.89.

17. Ibid., 1.23.5–6.

18. Arthur M. Eckstein, "Thucydides, the Outbreak of the Peloponnesian War, and the Foundation of International Systems Theory," *The International History Review* 25 (December 4, 2003), 757–774.

19. Thucydides, I.139–45: 80–6.

20. Donald Kagan, *Thucydides: The Reinvention of History* (New York: Viking, 2009), 56–57.

21. Thucydides, 1.71.

22. Ibid., 1.39.

23. Ibid., 1.40.

24. Richard Ned Lebow, "Play It Again Pericles: Agents, Structures and the Peloponnesian War," *European Journal of International Relations* 2 (1996), 242.

25. Thucydides, 1.33.

26. Donald Kagan, *Pericles of Athens and the Birth of Democracy* (New York: Free Press, 1991).

27. Sam Leith, *You Talkin' To Me? Rhetoric from Aristotle to Obama* (London: Profile Books, 2011), 18.

28. Michael Gagarin and Paul Woodruff, "The Sophists," in Patricia Curd and Daniel W. Graham, eds., *The Oxford Handbook of Presocratic Philosophy* (Oxford: Oxford University Press, 2008), 365–382; W. K. C. Guthrie, *The Sophists* (Cambridge, UK: Cambridge University Press, 1971); G. B. Kerferd, *The Sophistic Movement* (Cambridge, UK: Cambridge University Press, 1981); Thomas J. Johnson, "The Idea of Power Politics: The Sophistic Foundations of Realism," *Security Studies* 5:2, 1995, 194–247.

29. Adam Milman Parry, *Logos and Ergon in Thucydides* (Salem: New Hampshire: The Ayer Company, 1981), 121–122, 182–183.

30. Thucydides, 3.43.

31. Gerald Mara, "Thucydides and Political Thought," *The Cambridge Companion to Ancient Greek Political Thought,* edited by Stephen Salkever (Cambridge, UK: Cambridge University Press, 2009), 116–118. Thucydides, 3.35–50.

32. Thucydides, 3.82.

33. Michael Gagarin, "Did the Sophists Aim to Persuade?" *Rhetorica* 19 (2001), 289.

34. Andrea Wilson Nightingale, *Genres in Dialogue: Plato and the Construct of Philosophy* (Cambridge: Cambridge University Press, 1995), 14. See also Håkan Tell, *Plato's Counterfeit Sophists* (Harvard University: Center for Hellenic Studies, 2011); Nathan Crick, "The Sophistical Attitude and the Invention of Rhetoric," *Quarterly Journal of Speech* 96:1 (2010), 25–45; Robert Wallace, "Plato's Sophists, Intellectual History after 450, and Sokrates," in *The Cambridge Companion to the Age of Pericles,* edited by

Loren J. Samons II (Cambridge, UK: Cambridge University Press, 2007), 215–237.

35. Karl Popper, The Open Society and Its Enemies: The Spell of Plato, vol. 1 (London, 1945).

36. Book 3 of *The Republic*, 141b–c. Malcolm Schofield, "The Noble Lie," in *The Cambridge Companion to Plato's Republic*, edited by G. R. Ferrari (Cambridge, UK: Cambridge University Press, 2007), 138–164.

4 Sun Tzu and Machiavelli

1. Cited in Everett L. Wheeler, *Stratagem and the Vocabulary of Military Trickery. Mnemoseyne supplement 108* (New York: Brill, 1988), 24.

2. Ibid., 14–15.

3. http://penelope.uchicago.edu/Thayer/E/Roman/Texts/Frontinus/Strategemata/home.html.

4. Lisa Raphals, *Knowing Words: Wisdom and Cunning in the Classical Tradition of China and Greece* (Ithaca, NY: Cornell University Press, 1992), 20.

5. The first translation of Sun Tzu into English by Lionel Giles in 1910 remains a standard work. The translation by Samuel Griffiths in 1963 helped to popularize the book, as it drew the link with contemporary Asian approaches to warfare (New York: Oxford University Press, 1963). During the 1970s, new materials made possible a more complete version. Giles's text can be found at http://www.gutenberg.org/etext/132. For a more up-to-date translation and discussion of Sun Tzu, see http://www.sonshi.com.

6. Jan Willem Honig, Introduction to *Sun Tzu, The Art of War*, translation and commentary by Frank Giles (New York: Barnes & Noble, 2012), xxi.

7. François Jullien, *Detour and Access: Strategies of Meaning in China and Greece*, translated by Sophie Hawkes (New York: Zone Books, 2004), 35, 49–50.

8. Victor Davis Hanson, *The Western Way of War: Infantry Battle in Classical Greece* (New York: Alfred Knopf, 1989).

9. Pulling these criticisms together, Jeremy Black quotes John Lynn with approval: "Claims that a Western Way of Warfare extended with integrity for 2500 years speak more of fantasy than fact. No overarching theory can encompass the totality of Western combat and culture." J. A. Lynn, *Battle* (Boulder, CO: Westview Press, 2003), 25, cited in Jeremy Black, "Determinisms and Other Issues," *The Journal of Military History* 68, no. 1 (October 2004): 217–232.

10. Beatrice Heuser, *The Evolution of Strategy* (Cambridge, UK: Cambridge University Press, 2010), 89–90.

11. Michael D. Reeve, ed., *Epitoma rei militaris,* Oxford Medieval Texts (Oxford: Oxford University Press, 2004). An earlier translation is found in *Roots of Strategy: The Five Greatest Military Classics of All Time* (Harrisburg, PA: Stackpole Books, 1985).

12. Clifford J. Rogers, "The Vegetian 'Science of Warfare' in the Middle Ages," *Journal of Medieval Military History* 1 (2003): 1–19; Stephen Morillo, "Battle Seeking: The Contexts and Limits of Vegetian Strategy," *Journal of Medieval Military History* 1 (2003): 21–41; John Gillingham, "Up with Orthodoxy: In Defense of Vegetian Warfare," *Journal of Medieval Military History* 2 (2004): 149–158.

13. Heuser, *Evolution of Srategy*, 90.

14. Anne Curry, "The Hundred Years War, 1337–1453," in John Andreas Olsen and Colin Gray, eds., *The Practice of Strategy: From Alexander the Great to the Present* (Oxford: Oxford University Press, 2011), 100.

15. Jan Willem Honig, "Reappraising Late Medieval Strategy: The Example of the 1415 Agincourt Campaign," *War in History* 19, no. 2 (2012): 123–151.

16. James Q. Whitman, *The Verdict of Battle: The Law of Victory and the Making of Modern War* (Cambridge, MA: Harvard University Press, 2012).

17. William Shakespeare, *Henry VI, Part 3*, 3.2.

18. Victoria Kahn, *Machiavellian Rhetoric: From the Counterreformation to Milton* (Princeton, NJ: Princeton University Press, 1994), 40.

19. Niccolo Machiavelli, *Art of War*, edited by Christopher Lynch (Chicago: University of Chicago Press, 2003), 97–98. See also Lynch's interpretative essay in this volume and Felix Gilbert, "Machiavelli: The Renaissance of the Art of War," in Peter Paret, ed., *Makers of Modern Strategy* (Princeton, NJ: Princeton University Press, 1986).

20. Niccolo Machiavelli, *The Prince,* translated and with an introduction by George Bull (London: Penguin Books, 1961), 96.

21. Ibid., 99–101.

22. Ibid., 66.

5 Satan's Strategy

1. Dennis Danielson, "Milton's Arminianism and Paradise Lost," in J. Martin Evans, ed., *John Milton: Twentieth-Century Perspectives* (London: Routledge, 2002), 127.

2. John Milton, *Paradise Lost*, edited by Gordon Tesket (New York: W. W. Norton & Company, 2005), III, 98–99.

3. Job 1:7.

4. John Carey, "Milton's Satan," in Dennis Danielson, ed., *The Cambridge Companion to Milton* (Cambridge, UK: Cambridge University Press, 1999), 160–174.

5. Revelation 12:7–9.

6. William Blake, *The Marriage of Heaven and Hell* (1790–1793).

7. Milton, *Paradise Lost*, I, 645–647.

8. Gary D. Hamilton, "Milton's Defensive God: A Reappraisal," *Studies in Philosophy* 69, no. 1 (January 1972): 87–100.

9. Victoria Ann Kahn, *Machiavellian Rhetoric: From Counter Reformation to Milton* (Princeton, NJ: Princeton University Press, 1994), 209.

10. Milton, *Paradise Lost*, V, 787–788, 794–802.

11. Amy Boesky, "Milton's Heaven and the Model of the English Utopia," *Studies in English Literature, 1500–1900* 36, no. 1 (Winter 1996): 91–110.

12. Milton, *Paradise Lost*, VI, 701–703, 741, 787, 813.

13. Ibid., I, 124, 258–259, 263, 159–160.

14. Antony Jay, *Management and Machiavelli* (London: Penguin Books, 1967), 27.

15. Milton, *Paradise Lost*, II, 60–62, 129–130, 190–91, 208–211, 239–244, 269–273, 296–298, 284–286, 379–380, 345–348, 354–358.

16. Ibid., IX, 465–475, 375–378, 1149–1152.

17. Ibid., XII, 537–551, 569–570.

18. Barbara Kiefer Lewalski, "Paradise Lost and Milton's Politics," in Evans, ed., *John Milton,* 150.

19. Barbara Riebling, "Milton on Machiavelli: Representations of the State in Paradise Lost," *Renaissance Quarterly* 49, no. 3 (Autumn, 1996): 573–597.

20. Carey, "Milton's Satan," 165.

21. Hobbes, *Leviathan*, I. xiii.

22. Charles Edelman, *Shakespeare's Military Language: A Dictionary* (London: Athlone Press, 2000), 343.

23. *A Dictionary of the English Language: A Digital Edition of the 1755 Classic by Samuel Johnson*, edited by Brandi Besalke, http://johnsonsdictionaryonline.com/.

6 The New Science of Strategy

1. Martin van Creveld, *Command in War* (Harvard, MA: Harvard University Press, 1985), 18.

2. R. R. Palmer, "Frederick the Great, Guibert, Bulow: From Dynastic to National War," in Peter Paret, Gordon A. Craig, and Felix Gilbert, eds., *Makers of Modern Strategy: From Machiavelli to the Nuclear Age* (Princeton, NJ: Princeton University Press, 1986), 91.

3. Edward Luttwak, *Strategy* (Harvard: Harvard University Press, 1987), 239–240.

4. Beatrice Heuser, *The Strategy Makers: Thoughts on War and Society from Machiavelli to Clausewitz* (Santa Barbara, CA: Praeger, 2009), 1–2; Beatrice Heuser, *The Evolution of Strategy* (Cambridge, UK: Cambridge University Press, 2010), 4–5.

5. Azar Gat, *The Origins of Military Thought: From the Enlightenment to Clausewitz* (Oxford: Oxford University Press, 1989), Chapter 2. See R. R. Palmer, "Frederick the Great, Guibert, Bülow: From Dynastic to National War," in Paret et al., *Makers of Modern Strategy.*

6. Palmer, "Frederick the Great," 107.

7. Heuser, *The Strategy Makers*, 3; Hew Strachan, "The Lost Meaning of Strategy," *Survival* 47, no. 3 (August 2005): 35; J-P. Charnay in André Corvisier, ed., *A Dictionary of Military History and the Art of War*, English edition edited by John Childs (Oxford: Blackwell, 1994), 769.

8. All the definitions come from the Oxford English Dictionary.

9. From "The History of the Late War in Germany" (1766) cited by Michael Howard, *Studies in War & Peace* (London: Temple Smith, 1970), 21.

10. Peter Paret, *Clausewitz and the State: The Man, His Theories and His Times* (Princeton, NJ: Princeton University Press, 1983), 91.

11. Whitman, *The Verdict of Battle*, 155. "The Instruction of Fredrick the Great for His Generals, 1747," is found in *Roots of Strategy: The Five Greatest Military Classics of All Time* (Harrisburg, PA: Stackpole Books, 1985).

12. *Napoleon's Military Maxims*, edited and annotated by William E. Cairnes (New York: Dover Publications, 2004).

13. Major-General Petr Chuikevich, quoted in Dominic Lieven, *Russia Against Napoleon: The Battle for Europe 1807–1814* (London: Allen Lane, 2009), 131.

14. Lieven, *Russia Against Napoleon*, 198.

15. Alexander Mikaberidze, *The Battle of Borodino: Napoleon Against Kutuzov* (London: Pen & Sword, 2007), 161, 162.

7 *Clausewitz*

1. Carl von Clausewitz, *The Campaign of 1812 in Russia* (London: Greenhill Books, 1992), 184.

2. Carl von Clausewitz, *On War*, edited and translated by Michael Howard and Peter Paret (Princeton, NJ: Princeton University Press, 1976), Book IV, Chapter 12, p. 267.

3. Gat, *The Origins of Military Thought* (see chap. 6, n. 5).

4. John Shy, "Jomini," in Paret et al., *Makers of Modern Strategy*, 143–185 (see chap. 6, n. 2).

5. Antoine Henri de Jomini, *The Art of War* (London: Greenhill Books, 1992).

6. "Jomini and the Classical Tradition in Military Thought," in Howard, *Studies in War & Peace* (see chap. 6, n. 9), 31.

7. Jomini, *The Art of War*, 69.

8. Shy, "Jomini," 152, 157, 160, 146.

9. Gat, *The Origins of Military Thought*, 114, 122.

10. For a useful discussion on the relationship between the two, see Christopher Bassford, "Jomini and Clausewitz: Their Interaction," February 1993, http://www.clausewitz.com/readings/Bassford/Jomini/JOMINIX.htm.

11. Clausewitz, *On War*, 136.

12. Hew Strachan, "Strategy and Contingency," *International Affairs* 87, no. 6 (2011): 1289.

13. Martin Kitchen, "The Political History of Clausewitz," *Journal of Strategic Studies* 11, vol. 1 (March 1988): 27–30.

14. B. H. Liddell Hart, *Strategy: The Indirect Approach* (London: Faber and Faber, 1968); Martin Van Creveld, *The Transformation of War* (New York: The Free Press, 1991); John Keegan, *A History of Warfare* (London: Hutchinson, 1993).

15. Jan Willem Honig, "Clausewitz's *On War*: Problems of Text and Translation," in Hew Strachan and Andrews Herberg-Rothe, eds., *Clausewitz in the Twenty-First Century* (Oxford: Oxford University Press, 2007), 57–73. For biography, see Paret, *Clausewitz and the State* (see chap. 6, n. 10); Michael Howard, *Clausewitz* (Oxford: Oxford University Press, 1983); Hew Strachan, *Clausewitz's On War: A Biography* (New York: Grove/Atlantic Press, 2008). On historical context, see Azar Gat, *A History of Military Thought* (see chap. 6, n. 5). On influence, see Beatrice Heuser, *Reading Clausewitz* (London: Pimlico, 2002).

16. Christopher Bassford, "The Primacy of Policy and the 'Trinity' in Clausewitz's Mature Thought," in Hew Strachan and Andreas Herberg-Rothe, eds., *Clausewitz in the Twenty-First Century* (Oxford: Oxford University Press, 2007), 74–90; Christopher Bassford, "The Strange Persistence of Trinitarian Warfare," in Ralph Rotte and Christoph Schwarz, eds., *War and Strategy* (New York: Nova Science, 2011), 45–54.

17. Clausewitz, *On War*, Book 1, Chapter 1, 89.

18. Antulio Echevarria, *Clausewitz and Contemporary War* (Oxford: Oxford University Press, 2007), 96.

19. *On War*, Book 1, Chapter 7, 119–120.

20. Ibid., Book 3, Chapter 7, 177.

21. Terence Holmes uses this stress on planning to challenge the view that Clausewitz was preoccupied only with the chaotic and unpredictable. The point is that the potential chaos and unpredictability set the challenge for the general. This is why Clausewitz argued for cautious strategies. Holmes notes the reasons why plans may go awry, of which the most important would be a failure to anticipate the enemy's moves correctly, and that when the original plans do not work new ones will be needed. It is setting up a straw man to counter a claim that Clausewitz opposed all planning, because clearly the logistical and command issues posed by the great armies of the time demanded planning. Better to view the strategic challenge as drawing up plans that took account of the problems of friction and unpredictable enemies but would not necessarily solve them. Terence Holmes, "Planning versus Chaos in Clausewitz's *On War*," *The Journal of Strategic Studies* 30, no. 1 (2007): 129–151.

22. *On War*, Book 2, Chapter 1, 128, Book 3, Chapter 1, 177.

23. Ibid., Book 1, Chapter 6, 117–118.

24. Paret, "Clausewitz," in *Makers of Modern Strategy*, 203.

25. *On War*, Book 1, Chapter 7, 120.

26. Ibid., Book 5, Chapter 3, 282; Book 3, Chapter 8, 195; Chapter 10, 202–203; Book 7, Chapter 22, 566, 572.

27. Ibid., Book 6, Chapter 1, 357; Chapter 2, 360; Chapter 5, 370.

28. Clausewitz, *On War*, 596, 485. Antulio J. Echevarria II, "Clausewitz's Center of Gravity: It's Not What We Thought," *Naval War College Review* LVI, no. 1 (Winter 2003): 108–123.

29. Clausewitz, *On War*, Book 8, Chapter 6, 603. See Hugh Smith, "The Womb of War."

30. Clausewitz, *On War*, Book 8, Chapter 8, 617–637.

31. Strachan, *Clausewitz's On War*, 163.

32. "Clausewitz, unfinished note, presumably written in 1830," in *On War*, 31. Note this date is now put at 1827. See also Clifford J. Rogers, "Clausewitz, Genius, and the Rules," *The Journal of Military History* 66 (October 2002): 1167–1176.

33. Clausewitz, *On War*, Book 1, Chapter 1, 87.

34. Ibid., Book 1, Chapter 1, 81.

35. Strachan, *Clausewitz's On War*, 179.

36. Brian Bond, *The Pursuit of Victory: From Napoleon to Saddam Hussein* (Oxford: Oxford University Press, 1996), 47.

8 The False Science

1. Michael Howard, *War and the Liberal Conscience* (London: Maurice Temple Smith, 1978), 37–42.

2. Cited in Ibid., 48–49.

3. Clausewitz, *On War*, Book 1, Chapter 2, 90. See Thomas Waldman, *War, Clausewitz and the Trinity* (London: Ashgate, 2012), Chapter 6.

4. Leo Tolstoy, *War and Peace,* translated by Louise and Aylmer Maude (Oxford: Oxford University Press, 1983), 829.

5. Isaiah Berlin, *The Hedgehog and the Fox* (Chicago: Ivan Dee, 1978). The title, which is now the best remembered aspect of the book, comes from a quote from the Greek poet Archilocus: "The fox knows many things, but the hedgehog knows one big thing."

6. W. Gallie, *Philosophers of Peace and War: Kant, Clausewitz, Marx, Engels and Tolstoy* (Cambridge, UK: Cambridge University Press, 1978), 114.

7. Tolstoy, *War and Peace*, 1285.

8. Ibid., 688.

9. Lieven, *Russia Against Napoleon*, 527.

10. Berlin, *The Hedgehog and the Fox*, 20.

11. Gary Saul Morson, "War and Peace," in Donna Tussing Orwin, ed., *The Cambridge Companion to Tolstoy* (Cambridge, UK: Cambridge University Press, 2002), 65–79.

12. Michael D. Krause, "Moltke and the Origins of the Operational Level of War," in Michael D. Krause and R. Cody Phillip, eds., *Historical Perspectives of the Operational Art* (Center of Military History, United States Army, Washington, DC, 2005), 118, 130.

13. Gunther E. Rothenberg, "Moltke, Schlieffen, and the Doctrine of Strategic Envelopment," in Paret, ed., *Makers of Modern Strategy*, 298 (see chap. 6, n. 2).

14. See Helmuth von Moltke, "Doctrines of War," in Lawrence Freedman, ed., *War* (Oxford: Oxford University Press, 1994), 220–221.

15. Echevarria, *Clausewitz and Contemporary War*, p.142 (see chap. 7, n. 18).

16. Hajo Holborn, "The Prusso-German School: Moltke and the Rise of the General Staff," in Paret, ed., *Makers of Modern Strategy*, 288.

17. Rothenberg, "Moltke, Schlieffen, and the Doctrine of Strategic Envelopment," 305.

18. John Stone, *Military Strategy: The Politics and Technique of War* (London: Continuum, 2011), 43–47.

19. Krause, "Moltke and the Origins of the Operational Level of War," 142.

20. Walter Goerlitz, *The German General Staff* (New York: Praeger, 1953), 92. Cited by Justin Kelly and Mike Brennan, *Alien: How Operational Art Devoured Strategy* (Carlisle, PA: US Army War College, 2009), 24.

9 Annihilation or Exhaustion

1. Gordon Craig, "Delbrück: The Military Historian," in Paret, ed., *Makers of Modern Strategy*, 326–353 (see chap. 6, n. 2).

2. Azar Gat, *The Development of Military Thought: The Nineteenth Century* (Oxford: Clarendon Press, 1992), 106–107.

3. Quote from Mahan in Russell F. Weigley, "American Strategy from Its Beginnings through the First World War," in Paret, ed., *Makers of Modern Strategy*, 415.

4. Donald Stoker, *The Grand Design: Strategy and the U.S. Civil War* (New York: Oxford University Press, 2010), 78–79.

5. David Herbert Donald, *Lincoln* (New York: Simon and Schuster, 1995), 389, 499; Stoker, *The Grand Design*, 229–230.

6. Stoker, *The Grand Design*, 405.

7. Weigley, "American Strategy," 432–433.

8. Stoker, *The Grand Design*, 232.

9. Azar Gat, *The Development of Military Thought*, 144–145.

10. Ardant du Picq, "Battle Studies," in Curtis Brown, ed., *Roots of Strategy, Book 2* (Harrisburg, PA: Stackpole Books, 1987), 153; Robert A. Nye, *The Origins*

of *Crowd Psychology: Gustave Le Bon and the Crisis of Mass Democracy in the Third Republic* (London: Sage, 1974).

11. Craig, "Delbrück: The Military Historian," 312.

12. The debate has largely been conducted in the pages of the journal *War in History*. Terence Zuber has been conducting a lonely but vigorous campaign, against the deep skepticism of other historians, to assert that there was no Schlieffen Plan. Terence Zuber, "The Schlieffen Plan Reconsidered," *War in History* VI (1999): 262–305. The argument is developed fully in his *Inventing the Schlieffen Plan* (Oxford: Oxford University Press, 2003). For some responses, see Terence Holmes, "The Reluctant March on Paris: A Reply to Terence Zuber's 'The Schlieffen Plan Reconsidered,'" *War in History* VIII (2001): 208–232. A. Mombauer, "Of War Plan and War Guilt: The Debate Surrounding the Schlieffen Plan," *Journal of Strategic Studies* XXVIII (2005): 857–858; R. T. Foley, "The Real Schlieffen Plan," *War in History* XIII (2006): 91–115; Gerhard P. Groß, "There Was a Schlieffen Plan: New Sources on the History of German Military Planning," *War in History* XV (2008): 389–431.

13. Cited by Foley, "The Real Schlieffen Plan," 109.

14. Hew Strachan, "Strategy and Contingency," *International Affairs* 87, no. 6 (2011): 1290.

15. He did not start seriously publishing until he was 50, after which he published almost twenty books and numerous essays. The most important works are *The Influence of Sea Power Upon History, 1660–1783* (Boston: Little, Brown, and Company, 1890) and *The Influence of Sea Power Upon the French Revolution and Empire, 1793–1812* (Boston: Little, Brown, and Company, 1892).

16. Mahan, *The Influence of Sea Power Upon the French Revolution and Empire*, 400–402.

17. Jon Tetsuro Sumida, *Inventing Grand Strategy and Teaching Command: The Classic Works of Alfred Thayer Mahan Reconsidered* (Washington, DC: Woodrow Wilson Center Press, 1999).

18. Robert Seager, *Alfred Thayer Mahan: The Man and His Letters* (Annapolis: U.S. Naval Institute Press, 1977). See also Dirk Böker, *Militarism in a Global Age: Naval Ambitions in Germany and the United States Before World War I* (Ithaca, NY: Cornell University Press, 2012), 103–104.

19. Alfred Mahan, *Naval Strategy Compared and Contrasted with the Principles and Practice of Military Operations on Land: Lectures Delivered at U.S. Naval War College, Newport, R.I., Between the Years 1887 and 1911* (Boston: Little, Brown, and Company, 1911), 6–8.

20. Mahan, *The Influence of Sea Power Upon the French Revolution*, v–vi.

21. Seager, *Alfred Thayer Mahan*, 546. This was referring to *Naval Strategy Compared and Contrasted*.

22. Böker, *Militarism in a Global Age*, 104–107.

23. Cited in Liam Cleaver, "The Pen Behind the Fleet: The Influence of Sir Julian Stafford Corbett on British Naval Development, 1898–1918," *Comparative Strategy* 14 (January 1995), 52–53.

24. Barry M. Gough, "Maritime Strategy: The Legacies of Mahan and Corbett as Philosophers of Sea Power," *The RUSI Journal* 133, no. 4 (December 1988): 55–62.

25. Donald M. Schurman, *Julian S. Corbett, 1854–1922* (London: Royal Historical Society, 1981), 54. See also Eric Grove, "Introduction," in Julian Corbett, *Some Principles of Maritime Strategy* (Annapolis: U.S. Naval Institute Press, 1988). This book was first published in 1911. The annotated 1988 publication also contains "The Green Pamphlet" of 1909. See also Azar Gat, *The Development of Military Thought: The Nineteenth Century*.

26. On the relationship between Corbett and Clausewitz, see Chapter 18 of Michael Handel, *Masters of War: Classical Strategic Thought* (London: Frank Cass, 2001).

27. Corbett, *Some Principles*, 62–63.

28. Ibid., 16, 91, 25, 152, 160.

29. H. J. Mackinder, "The Geographical Pivot of History," *The Geographical Journal* 23 (1904): 421–444.

30. H. J. Mackinder, "Manpower as a Measure of National and Imperial Strength," *National and English Review* 45 (1905): 136–143, cited in Lucian Ashworth, "Realism and the Spirit of 1919: Halford Mackinder, Geopolitics and the Reality of the League of Nations," *European Journal of International Relations* 17, no. 2 (June 2011): 279–301. Also on Mackinder, see B. W. Blouet, *Halford Mackinder: A Biography* (College Station: Texas A&M University Press, 1987).

31. H. J. Mackinder, *Democratic Ideals and Reality: A Study in the Politics of Reconstruction* (Suffolk: Penguin Books, 1919), 86; Geoffrey Sloan, "Sir Halford J. Mackinder: The Heartland Theory Then and Now," *Journal of Strategic Studies* 22, 2–3 (1999): 15–38.

32. Ibid., 194.

33. Mackinder, "The Geographical Pivot," 437.

34. Ola Tunander, "Swedish-German Geopolitics for a New Century—Rudolf Kjellén's 'The State as a Living Organism,'" *Review of International Studies* 27, 3 (2001): 451–463.

35. The consequential discrediting of an approach that encouraged consideration of the strategic implications of the physical environment has been regretted by, among others, Colin Gray, *The Geopolitics of Super Power* (Lexington: University Press of Kentucky, 1988). See also Colin Gray, "In Defence of the Heartland: Sir Halford Mackinder and His Critics a Hundred Years On," *Comparative Strategy* 23, no. 1 (2004): 9–25.

10 Brain and Brawn

1. Isabel Hull argues that this behavior was the result of a reckless and insensitive military culture that had developed during the course of colonial wars. Isabel V. Hull, *Absolute Destruction: Military Culture and the Practices of War in Imperial Germany* (Ithaca, NY: Cornell University Press, 2005).

2. Craig, "Delbrück: The Military Historian," 348 (see chap. 9, n. 1).

3. See Mark Clodfelter, *Beneficial Bombing: The Progressive Foundations of American Air Power 1917–1945* (Lincoln: University of Nebraska Press, 2010).

4. Curiously, given his later role as an enthusiastic proponent of mass bombing, his first thoughts were to deplore even thinking about attacks on defenseless cities and to argue for an international convention to ban such a thing. See Thomas Hippler, "Democracy and War in the Strategic Thought of Guilio Douhet," in Hew Strachan and Sibylle Scheipers, eds., *The Changing Character of War* (Oxford: Oxford University Press, 2011), 170.

5. Giulio Douhet, *The Command of the Air*, translated by Dino Ferrari (Washington, DC: Office of Air Force History, 1983). Reprint of 1942 original. This was published by the War Department in Italy. Though judged a troublemaker during the war, he was now celebrated as something of a seer and became briefly commissioner of aviation under the Fascists. Mitchell's major statement is found in William Mitchell, *Winged Defense: The Development and Possibilities of Modern Air Power—Economic and Military* (New York: G. P. Putnam's Sons, 1925). Caproni's views were captured by a journalist Nino Salvaneschi who wrote a pamphlet in 1917 entitled *Let Us Kill the War, Let Us Aim at the Heart of the Enemy*, which advocated attacking manufacturing capacity. David MacIsaac, "Voices from the Central Blue: The Airpower Theorists," in Peter Paret, ed., *Makers of Modern Strategy*, 624–647 (see chap. 6, n. 2).

6. Azar Gat, *Fascist and Liberal Visions of War: Fuller, Liddell Hart, Douhet, and Other Modernists* (Oxford: Clarendon Press, 1998).

7. Sir Charles Webster and Noble Frankland, *The Strategic Air Offensive Against Germany*, 4 vols. (London: Her Majesty's Stationery Office, 1961), Vol. 4, pp. 2, 74.

8. Sir Hugh Dowding, "Employment of the Fighter Command in Home Defence," *Naval War College Review* 45 (Spring 1992): 36. Reprint of 1937 lecture to the RAF Staff College.

9. David S. Fadok, "John Boyd and John Warden: Airpower's Quest for Strategic Paralysis," in Col. Phillip S. Meilinger, ed., *Paths of Heaven* (Maxwell Air Force Base, AL: Air University Press, 1997), 382.

10. Douhet, *Command of the Air*.

11. Phillip S. Meilinger, "Giulio Douhet and the Origins of Airpower Theory," in Phillip S. Meilinger, ed., *Paths of Heaven*, 27; Bernard Brodie, "The

Heritage of Douhet," *Air University Quarterly Review* 6 (Summer 1963): 120–126.

12. Wells's scenario involved a preemptive German attack on the United States using dirigibles before the Americans had a chance to take full advantage of the Wright Brothers' new invention.

13. Brian Holden Reid, *J. F. C. Fuller: Military Thinker* (London: Macmillan, 1987), 55, 51, 73.

14. Ibid.; Anthony Trythell, *'Boney' Fuller: The Intellectual General* (London: Cassell, 1977); Gat, *Fascist and Liberal Visions of War*.

15. Gat, *Fascist and Liberal Visions of War*, 40–41.

16. J. F. C. Fuller, *The Foundations of the Science of War* (London: Hutchinson, 1925), 47.

17. Ibid., 35.

18. Ibid., 141.

11 The Indirect Approach

1. On the influence of the Somme on Liddell Hart, see Hew Strachan, " 'The Real War': Liddell Hart, Crutwell, and Falls," in Brian Bond, ed., *The First World War and British Military History* (Oxford: Clarendon Press, 1991).

2. John Mearsheimer, *Liddell Hart and the Weight of History* (London: Brassey's, 1988). Gat, without denying Liddell Hart's vanity and self-aggrandizement, has challenged Mearsheimer's critique. Azar Gat, "Liddell Hart's Theory of Armoured Warfare: Revising the Revisionists," *Journal of Strategic Studies* 19 (1996): 1–30.

3. Gat, *Fascist and Liberal Visions of War*, 146–160 (see chap. 7, n. 5).

4. Basil Liddell Hart, *The Ghost of Napoleon* (London: Faber and Faber, 1933), 125–126.

5. Christopher Bassford, *Clausewitz in English: The Reception of Clausewitz in Britain and America, 1815–1945* (New York: Oxford University Press, 1994), Chapter 15.

6. Griffiths, *Sun Tzu*, vii (see chap. 4, n. 5).

7. Alex Danchev, *Alchemist of War: The Life of Basil Liddell Hart* (London: Weidenfeld & Nicolson, 1998).

8. Reid, *J. F. C. Fuller*, 159 (see chap. 10, n. 13).

9. Basil Liddell Hart, *Strategy: The Indirect Approach* (London: Faber and Faber, 1954), 335, 339, 341, 344.

10. Brian Bond, *Liddell Hart: A Study of his Military Thought*. (London: Cassell, 1977), 56.

11. Basil Liddell Hart, *Paris, or the Future of War* (London: Kegan Paul, 1925), 12. Liddell Hart, like Fuller, was impressed by the impact of German bombing attacks on Britain in World War I: "Witnesses of the

earlier air attacks before our defence was organized, will not be disposed to underestimate the panic and disturbance that would result from a concentrated blow dealt by a superior air fleet. Who that saw it will ever forget the nightly sight of the population of a great industrial and shipping town, such as Hull, streaming out into the fields on the first sound of the alarm signals? Women, children, babies in arms, spending night after night huddled in sodden fields, shivering under a bitter winter sky." Basil Liddell Hart, *Paris, or the Future of War* (New York: Dutton, 1925), 39.

12. Richard K. Betts, "Is Strategy an Illusion?" *International Security* 25, 2 (Autumn 2000): 11.

13. Ian Kershaw, *Fateful Choices: Ten Decisions That Changed the World: 1940–1941* (New York: Penguin Press, 2007), 47.

14. Churchill's memoir of the war, written in its aftermath, denied that there was any consideration of whether or not to fight on. Resistance was "taken for granted and as a matter of course." It would have been a waste of time to worry about "such unreal, academic issues" as a negotiated settlement. Winston S. Churchill, *The Second World War, Their Finest Hour, vol. 2* (London: Penguin, 1949), 157. Reynolds explains the cover-up by a desire to protect Halifax, who was still a colleague in the higher ranks of the Conservative Party when the book was written in 1948, yet who later acquired the mantle of a would-be appeaser held back by Churchill's bellicosity. The record, however, shows that Churchill was aware that negotiations with Germany might at some point be necessary. He knew that the next stage might turn out very badly, and that a settlement that compromised British independence might have to be accepted, but his task was to make invasion as hard as possible for the Germans, and his vivid language and steely demeanor ("We shall fight on the beaches... We shall never surrender") were in that respect vital parts of his weaponry. The story he told in 1940 was of inevitable victory and he had no desire to correct it when he got the chance to rewrite it in 1948. David Reynolds, *In Command of History: Churchill Fighting and Writing the Second World War* (New York: Random House, 2005), 172–173.

15. Eliot Cohen, "Churchill and Coalition Strategy," in Paul Kennedy, ed., *Grand Strategies in War and Peace* (New Haven, CT: Yale University Press, 1991), 66.

16. Max Hastings, *Finest Years: Churchill as Warlord 1940–45* (London: Harper-Collins, 2010), Chapter 1.

17. The estimated 35,000 purged represented half the officer corps, 90 percent of all generals, and 80 percent of all colonels.

18. Winston Churchill, *The Second World War, The Grand Alliance*, vol. 3 (London: Penguin, 1949), 607–608.

12 Nuclear Games

1. Walter Lippmann, *The Cold War* (Boston: Little Brown, 1947).

2. Ronald Steel, *Walter Lippmann and the American Century* (London: Bodley Head, 1980), 445. In a subsequent correspondence, another journalist, Herbert Swope, claimed paternity in a speech he wrote for Bernard Baruch, a high-profile financier. He also claimed to have been thinking back to the late 1930s when he had been asked whether America would get involved in a "shooting war" in Europe. He was struck by the oddity of the phrase: "It was like saying a death murder—rather tautological, verbose, and redundant." He thought the opposite of a "hot war" was a "cold war" and he began to use the phrase. William Safire, *Safire's New Political Dictionary* (New York: Oxford University Press, 2008), 134–135.

3. Lippmann's analysis came in response to an article in *Foreign Affairs* written from Moscow by the American diplomat George Kennan, under the pseudonym "X," warning of Soviet ambitions and urging the new doctrine of containment. X, "The Sources of Soviet Conduct," *Foreign Affairs* 7 (1947): 566–582.

4. George Orwell, "You and the Atomic Bomb," *Tribune*, October 19, 1945. Reprinted in Sonia Orwell and Ian Angus, eds., *The Collected Essays; Journalism and Letters of George Orwell*, vol. 4 (New York: Harcourt Brace Jovanovich, 1968), 8–10.

5. Barry Scott Zellen, *State of Doom: Bernard Brodie, the Bomb and the Birth of the Bipolar World* (New York: Continuum, 2012), 27.

6. Bernard Brodie, ed., *The Absolute Weapon* (New York: Harcourt, 1946), 52.

7. Bernard Brodie, "Strategy as a Science," *World Politics* 1, no. 4 (July 1949): 476.

8. Patrick Blackett, *Studies of War, Nuclear and Conventional* (New York: Hill & Wang, 1962), 177.

9. Paul Kennedy, *Engineers of Victory: The Problem Solvers Who Turned the Tide in the Second World War* (London: Allen Lane, 2013).

10. Sharon Ghamari-Tabrizi, "Simulating the Unthinkable: Gaming Future War in the 1950s and 1960s," *Social Studies of Science* 30, no. 2 (April 2000): 169, 170.

11. Philip Mirowski, *Machine Dreams: Economics Becomes Cyborg Science* (Cambridge: Cambridge University Press, 2002), 12–17.

12. Hedley Bull, *The Control of the Arms Race* (London: Weidenfeld & Nicolson, 1961), 48.

13. Hedley Bull, "Strategic Studies and Its Critics," *World Politics* 20, no. 4 (July 1968): 593–605.

14. Charles Hitch and Roland N. McKean, *The Economics of Defense in the Nuclear Age* (Cambridge, MA: Harvard University Press, 1960).

15. Deborah Shapley, *Promise and Power: The Life and Times of Robert McNamara* (Boston: Little, Brown & Co., 1993), 102–103.

16. Thomas D. White, "Strategy and the Defense Intellectuals," *The Saturday Evening Post*, May 4, 1963, cited by Alain Enthoven and Wayne Smith, *How Much Is Enough?* (New York; London: Harper & Row, 1971), 78. For a critique of the role of systems analysis, see Stephen Rosen, "Systems Analysis and the Quest for Rational Defense," *The Public Interest* 76 (Summer 1984): 121–159.

17. Bernard Brodie, *War and Politics* (London: Cassell, 1974), 474–475.

18. Cited in William Poundstone, *Prisoner's Dilemma* (New York: Doubleday, 1992), 6.

19. Oskar Morgenstern, "The Collaboration between Oskar Morgenstern and John von Neumann," *Journal of Economic Literature* 14, no. 3 (September 1976): 805–816. E. Roy Weintraub, *Toward a History of Game Theory* (London: Duke University Press, 1992); R. Duncan Luce and Howard Raiffa, *Games and Decisions; Introduction and Critical Survey* (New York: John Wiley & Sons, 1957).

20. Poundstone, *Prisoner's Dilemma*, 8.

21. Philip Mirowski, "Mid-Century Cyborg Agonistes: Economics Meets Operations Research," *Social Studies of Science* 29 (1999): 694.

22. John McDonald, *Strategy in Poker, Business & War* (New York: W. W. Norton, 1950), 14, 69, 126.

23. Jessie Bernard, "The Theory of Games of Strategy as a Modern Sociology of Conflict," *American Journal of Sociology* 59 (1954): 411–424.

13 The Rationality of Irrationality

1. This is discussed in Lawrence Freedman, *The Evolution of Nuclear Strategy*, 3rd ed. (London: Palgrave, 2005).

2. Colin Gray, *Strategic Studies: A Critical Assessment* (New York: The Greenwood Press, 1982).

3. R. J. Overy, "Air Power and the Origins of Deterrence Theory Before 1939," *Journal of Strategic Studies* 15, no. 1 (March 1992): 73–101. See also George Quester, *Deterrence Before Hiroshima* (New York: Wiley, 1966).

4. Stanley Hoffmann, "The Acceptability of Military Force," in Francois Duchene, ed., *Force in Modern Societies: Its Place in International Politics* (London: International Institute for Strategic Studies, 1973), 6.

5. Glenn Snyder, *Deterrence and Defense: Toward a Theory of National Security* (Princeton, NJ: Princeton University Press, 1961).

6. Herman Kahn, *On Thermonuclear War* (Princeton, NJ: Princeton University Press, 1961), 126 ff. and 282 ff. It was originally going to be known as "Three Lectures on Thermonuclear War."

7. Barry Bruce-Briggs, *Supergenius: The Megaworlds of Herman Kahn* (North American Policy Press, 2000), 97.

8. Ibid., 98. Noting the appalling style, Bruce-Briggs concludes that: "The artlessness imparts authenticity; were the author a hustler, he would have been slicker and ingratiating."

9. Jonathan Stevenson, *Thinking Beyond the Unthinkable* (New York: Viking, 2008), 76.

10. http://www.nobelprize.org/nobel_prizes/economics/laureates/2005/#.

11. Schelling's major books were *The Strategy of Conflict* (Cambridge, MA: Harvard University Press, 1960); *Arms and Influence* (New York: Yale University Press, 1966); *Choice and Consequence* (Cambridge, MA: Harvard University Press, 1984); and, with Morton Halperin, *Strategy and Arms Control* (New York: Twentieth Century Fund, 1961).

12. Robin Rider, "Operations Research and Game Theory," in Roy Weintraub, ed., *Toward a History of Game Theory* (see chap. 12, n. 19).

13. Schelling, *The Strategy of Conflict*, 10.

14. Jean-Paul Carvalho, "An Interview with Thomas Schelling," *Oxonomics* 2 (2007): 1–8.

15. Brodie, "Strategy as a Science," 479 (see chap. 12, n. 7). One possible reason was the skepticism of Jacob Viner, professor of economics at Chicago and Brodie's mentor. Viner's 1946 essay on the implications of nuclear weapons was one of the foundation texts of the theory of deterrence and clearly influenced Brodie.

16. Bernard Brodie, "The American Scientific Strategists," *The Defense Technical Information Center* (October 1964): 294.

17. Oskar Morgenstern, *The Question of National Defense* (New York: Random House, 1959).

18. Bruce-Briggs, *Supergenius*, 120–122; Irving Louis Horowitz, *The War Game: Studies of the New Civilian Militarists* (New York: Ballantine Books, 1963).

19. Cited in Bruce-Biggs, *Supergenius*, 120.

20. Schelling, in the *Journal of Conflict Resolution*, then edited by Kenneth Boulding, in 1957.

21. Carvalho, "An Interview with Thomas Schelling."

22. Robert Ayson, *Thomas Schelling and the Nuclear Age: Strategy as a Social Science* (London: Frank Cass, 2004); Phil Williams, "Thomas Schelling," in J. Baylis and J. Garnett, eds., *Makers of Nuclear Strategy* (London: Pinter, 1991), 120–135; A. Dixit, "Thomas Schelling's Contributions to Game Theory," *Scandinavian Journal of Economics* 108, no. 2 (2006): 213–229; Esther-Mirjam Sent, "Some Like It Cold: Thomas Schelling as a Cold Warrior," *Journal of Economic Methodology* 14, no. 4 (2007): 455–471.

23. Schelling, *The Strategy of Conflict*, 15.

24. Schelling, *Arms and Influence*, 1.

25. Ibid., 2–3, 79–80, 82, 80.

26. Ibid., 194.

27. Schelling, *Strategy of Conflict*, 188 (emphasis in the original).

28. Schelling, *Arms and Influence*, 93.

29. Schelling, *Strategy of Conflict*, 193.
30. Dixit, "Thomas Schelling's Contributions to Game Theory," argues that many of Schelling's formulations anticipate later developments in more formal game theory.
31. Schelling, *Strategy of Conflict*, 57, 77.
32. Schelling, *Arms and Influence*, 137.
33. Schelling, *Strategy of Conflict*, 100–101.
34. Cited by Robert Ayson, *Hedley Bull and the Accommodation of Power* (London: Palgrave, 2012).
35. Wohlstetter was one of the most influential RAND analysts. See Robert Zarate and Henry Sokolski, eds., *Nuclear Heuristics: Selected Writings of Albert and Roberta Wohlstetter* (Carlisle, PA: Strategic Studies Institute, U.S. Army War College, 2009).
36. Wohlstetter letter to Michael Howard, 1968, quoted in Stevenson, *Thinking Beyond the Unthinkable*, 71.
37. Bernard Brodie, *The Reporter*, November 18, 1954.
38. Schelling, *The Strategy of Conflict*, 233. This essay on "Surprise Attack and Disarmament" first appeared in Klaus Knorr, ed., *NATO and American Security* (Princeton, NJ: Princeton University Press, 1959).
39. Schelling, *Strategy and Conflict*, 236.
40. Donald Brennan, ed., *Arms Control, Disarmament and National Security* (New York: George Braziller, 1961); Hedley Bull, *The Control of the Arms Race* (London: Weidenfeld & Nicolson, 1961).
41. Schelling and Halperin, *Strategy and Arms Control*, 1–2.
42. Ibid., 5.
43. Schelling, *Strategy of Conflict*, 239–240.
44. Henry Kissinger, *The Necessity for Choice* (New York: Harper & Row, 1961). This particular essay first appeared in *Daedalus* 89, no. 4 (1960). The first reference that I (and the OED) can find is an article by the English writer Wayland Young, an active proponent of disarmament, who referred to "the danger of what strategists call escalation, the danger that the size of the weapons used would mount up and up in retaliation until civilization is destroyed as surely as it would have been by an initial exchange of thermonuclear weapons." In his glossary, we find the following: "Escalation-Escalator: The uncontrolled exchange of ever larger weapons in war, leading to the destruction of civilization." Wayland Young, *Strategy for Survival: First Steps in Nuclear Disarmament* (London: Penguin Books, 1959).
45. Schelling, *Strategy of Conflict*.
46. Schelling, *Arms and Influence*, 182.
47. Schelling, "Nuclear Strategy in the Berlin Crisis," *Foreign Relations of the United States* XIV, 170–172; Marc Trachtenberg, *History and Strategy* (Princeton, NJ: Princeton University Press, 1991), 224.

48. I deal with this in my *Kennedy's Wars* (New York: Oxford University Press, 2000).

49. Fred Kaplan, *Wizards of Armageddon* (Stanford: Stanford University Press, 1991), 302.

50. Kaysen to Kennedy, September 22, 1961, *Foreign Relations in the United States* XIV-VI, supplement, Document 182.

51. Robert Kennedy, *Thirteen Days: The Cuban Missile Crisis of October 1962* (London: Macmillan, 1969), 69–71, 80, 89, 182.

52. Ernest May and Philip Zelikow, *The Kennedy Tapes: Inside the White House During the Cuban Missile Crisis* (New York: W. W. Norton, 2002).

53. Albert and Roberta Wohlstetter, *Controlling the Risks in Cuba*, Adelphi Paper No. 17 (London ISS, February 1965).

54. Kahn, *On Thermonuclear War*, 226, 139.

55. Herman Kahn, *On Escalation* (London: Pall Mall Press, 1965).

56. Cited in Fred Iklé, "When the Fighting Has to Stop: The Arguments About Escalation," *World Politics* 19, no. 4 (July 1967): 693.

57. McGeorge Bundy, "To Cap the Volcano," *Foreign Affairs* 1 (October 1969): 1–20. See also McGeorge Bundy, *Danger and Survival: Choices About the Bomb in the First Fifty Years* (New York: Random House, 1988).

58. McGeorge Bundy, "The Bishops and the Bomb," *The New York Review*, June 16, 1983. For a discussion of "existentialist" literature, see Lawrence Freedman, "I Exist; Therefore I Deter," *International Security* 13, no. 1 (Summer 1988): 177–195.

14 Guerrilla Warfare

1. Werner Hahlweg, "Clausewitz and Guerrilla Warfare," *Journal of Strategic Studies* 9, nos. 2–3 (1986): 127–133; Sebastian Kaempf, "Lost Through Non-Translation: Bringing Clausewitz's Writings on 'New Wars' Back In," *Small Wars & Insurgencies* 22, no. 4 (October 2011): 548–573.

2. Jomini, *The Art of War*, 34–35 (see chap. 7, n. 5).

3. Karl Marx, "Revolutionary Spain," 1854, available at http://www.marxists.org/archive/marx/works/1854/revolutionary-spain/ch05.htm.

4. Vladimir Lenin, "Guerrilla Warfare," originally published in PROLETARY, No. 5, September 30, 1906, *Lenin Collected Works* (Moscow: Progress Publishers, 1965), Vol. II, 213–223, available at http://www.marxists.org/archive/lenin/works/1906/gw/index.htm.

5. Leon Trotsky, "Guerrila-ism and the Regular Army," *The Military Writings of Leon Trotsky*, Vol. 2, 1919, available at http://www.marxists.org/archive/trotsky/1919/military/ch08.htm.

6. Leon Trotsky, "Do We Need Guerrillas?" *The Military Writings of Leon Trotsky*, Vol. 2, 1919, available at http://www.marxists.org/archive/trotsky/1919/military/ch95.htm.

7. C. E. Callwell, *Small Wars: Their Theory and Practice*, reprint of the 1906 3rd edition (Lincoln: University of Nebraska Press, 1996).

8. T. E. Lawrence, "The Evolution of a Revolt," in Malcolm Brown, ed., *T. E. Lawrence in War & Peace: An Anthology of the Military Writings of Lawrence of Arabia* (London: Greenhill Books, 2005), 260–273. It was first published in the *Army Quarterly*, October 1920. It forms the basis of Chapter 35 of *The Seven Pillars of Wisdom* (London: Castle Hill Press, 1997).

9. Basil Liddell Hart, *Colonel Lawrence: The Man Behind the Legend* (New York: Dodd, Mead & Co., 1934).

10. "T. E. Lawrence and Liddell Hart," in Brian Holden Reid, *Studies in British Military Thought: Debates with Fuller & Liddell Hart* (Lincoln: University of Nebraska Press, 1998), 150–167.

11. Brantly Womack, "From Urban Radical to Rural Revolutionary: Mao from the 1920s to 1937," in Timothy Cheek, ed., *A Critical Introduction to Mao* (Cambridge, UK: Cambridge University Press, 2010), 61–86.

12. Jung Chang and Jon Halliday, *Mao: The Unknown Story* (New York: Alfred A. Knopf, 2005).

13. Andrew Bingham Kennedy, "Can the Weak Defeat the Strong? Mao's Evolving Approach to Asymmetric Warfare in Yan'an," *China Quarterly* 196 (December 2008): 884–899.

14. Most of the key texts—"Problems of Strategy in China's Revolutionary War" (December 1936), "Problems of Strategy in Guerrilla War Against Japan" (May 1938), and "On Protracted War" (May 1938)—are found in *Selected Works of Mao Tse-Tung*, Vol. II. "On Guerrilla War" is in Vol. VI. They can be found at http://www.marxists.org/reference/archive/mao/selected-works/index.htm.

15. Mao Tse-Tung, "On Protracted War."

16. Beatrice Heuser, *Reading Clausewitz* (London: Pimlico, 2002), 138–139.

17. John Shy and Thomas W. Collier, "Revolutionary War," in Paret, ed., *Makers of Modern Strategy*, p. 844 (see chap. 6, n. 2). On Maoist strategy, see also Edward L. Katzenback, Jr., and Gene Z. Hanrahan, "The Revolutionary Strategy of Mao Tse-Tung," *Political Science Quarterly* 70, no. 3 (September 1955): 321–340. In "On Protracted War" he made the classic distinction between strategies of attrition and annihilation, which began with Delbrück, but Mao probably got it through Lenin (see below pp. 289).

18. Mao Tse-Tung, "Problems of Strategy in Guerrilla War Against Japan."

19. Mao Tse-Tung, "On Protracted War."

20. Mao Tse-Tung, "On Guerrilla War."

21. "People's War, People's Army" (1961), in Russell Stetler, ed., *The Military Art of People's War: Selected Writings of General Vo Nguyen Giap* (New York: Monthly Review Press, 1970), 104–106.

22. Graham Greene, *The Quiet American* (London: Penguin, 1969), 61. The contemporary importance of Greene's critique of American naïveté in

Vietnam and the debates this prompted comes over in Frederik Logevall, *Embers of War: The Fall of an Empire and the Making of America's Vietnam* (New York: Random House, 2012). William J. Lederer and Eugene Burdick, *The Ugly American* (New York: Fawcett House, 1958), 233. Hillendale was not the "Ugly American" of the title. Cecil B. Currey, *Edward Lansdale: The Unquiet American* (Boston: Houghton Mifflin, 1988). Edward G. Lansdale, "Viet Nam: Do We Understand Revolution?" *Foreign Affairs* (October 1964), 75–86. For an appreciation of Lansdale, see Max Boot, *Invisible Armies: An Epic History of Guerrilla Warfare from Ancient Times to the Present* (New York: W. W. Norton & Co., 2012), 409–414.

23. On counterinsurgency thinking and its development during the Kennedy administration, see Douglas Blaufarb, *The Counterinsurgency Era: US Doctrine and Performance* (New York: The Free Press, 1977); D. Michael Shafer, *Deadly Paradigms: The Failure of US Counterinsurgency Policy* (Princeton, NJ: Princeton University Press, 1988); and Larry Cable, *Conflict of Myths: The Development of American Counterinsurgency Doctrine and the Vietnam War* (New York: New York University Press, 1986). Apart from some work undertaken on the stresses and strains in newly independent states in the third world, there was very little academic work on the requirements of a counterinsurgency strategy prior to President Kennedy's embrace of the concept at the start of his administration. The early development of the doctrine within the administration is normally credited to Walt Rostow and Roger Hilsman. For the flavor of the doctrine, see W. W. Rostow, "Guerrilla Warfare in Underdeveloped Areas," address to the graduating class at the U.S. Army Special Warfare School, Fort Bragg, June 1961. Reprinted in Marcus Raskin and Bernard Fall, *The Viet-Nam Reader* (New York: Vintage Books, 1965). See also Roger Hilsman, *To Move a Nation: The Politics of Foreign Policy in the Administration of John F. Kennedy* (New York: Dell, 1967).

24. Robert Thompson, *Defeating Communist Insurgency: Experiences in Malaya and Vietnam* (London: Chatto & Windus, 1966).

25. Boot, *Invisible Armies*, 386–387.

26. David Galula, *Counterinsurgency Warfare: Theory and Practice* (Wesport, CT: Praeger, 1964).

27. Gregor Mathias, *Galula in Algeria: Counterinsurgency Practice versus Theory* (Santa Barbara, CA: Praeger Security International, 2011).

28. M. L. R. Smith, "Guerrillas in the Mist: Reassessing Strategy and Low Intensity Warfare," *Review of International Studies* 29, no. 1 (2003): 19–37; Alistair Horne, *A Savage War of Peace: Algeria, 1954–1962* (London: Macmillan, 1977), 480–504.

29. Charles Maechling, Jr., "Insurgency and Counterinsurgency: The Role of Strategic Theory," *Parameters* 14, no. 3 (Autumn 1984): 34. Shafer, *Deadly Paradigms*, 113.

30. Paul Kattenburg, *The Vietnam Trauma in American Foreign Policy, 1945–75* (New Brunswick, NJ: Transaction Books, 1980), 111–112.

31. Blaufarb, *The Counterinsurgency Era*, 62–66.

32. Jeffery H. Michaels, "Managing Global Counterinsuregency: The Special Group (CI) 1962–1966," *Journal of Strategic Studies* 35, no. 1 (2012): 33–61.

33. See, for example, Alexander George et al., *The Limits of Coercive Diplomacy*, 1st edition (Boston: Little Brown, 1971). John Gaddis, *Strategies of Containment: A Critical Appraisal of PostWar American Security Policy* (New York: Oxford University Press, 1982), 243.

34. See in particular an address at University of Michigan, Ann Arbor, December 19, 1962, discussed at length in William Kaufmann, *The McNamara Strategy* (New York: Harper & Row, 1964), 138–147.

35. Schelling reported that the response was that "Schelling's games demonstrate how unrealistic this Cuban crisis is." Ghamari-Tabrizi, 213 (see chap. 12, n. 10).

36. William Bundy, cited in William Conrad Gibbons, *The U.S. Government and the Vietnam War* (Princeton, NJ: Princeton University Press, 1986), Vol. II, p. 349.

37. *The Pentagon Papers, Senator Gravel Edition: The Defense Department History of the U.S. Decision-Making on Vietnam*, Vol. 3 (Boston: Beacon Press, 1971), 212.

38. Gibbons, *The U.S. Government and the Vietnam War: 1961–1964*, 254.

39. Ibid., 256–259. See Chapter 4 of *Arms and Influence*.

40. See Freedman, *Kennedy's Wars* (see chap. 13, n. 48).

41. Fred Kaplan, *The Wizards of Armageddon* (New York: Simon and Schuster, 1983), 332–336.

42. *Arms and Influence*, vii, 84, 85, 166, 171–172. Given this analysis, Pape "Coercive Air Power in the Vietnam War," is unfair to Schelling in assuming that he would have advocated only attacks on civilian targets as part of Rolling Thunder.

43. Richard Betts, "Should Strategic Studies Survive?" *World Politics* 50, no. 1 (October 1997): 16.

44. Colin Gray, "What RAND Hath Wrought," *Foreign Policy* 4 (Autumn 1971): 111–129; see also Stephen Peter Rosen, "Vietnam and the American Theory of Limited War," *International Security* 7, no. 2 (Autumn 1982): 83–113.

45. Zellen, *State of Doom*, 196–197 (see chap. 12, n. 5); Bernard Brodie, "Why Were We So (Strategically) Wrong?" *Foreign Policy* 4 (Autumn 1971): 151–162.

15 Observation and Orientation

1. Beaufre's two key works were published in French as *Introduction à la Stratégie* (1963) and *Dissuasion et Stratégie* (1964). Both were published

with English translations by Major-General R. H. Barry in 1965 as *Introduction to Strategy* and *Dissuasion and Strategy*, respectively, by Faber & Faber in London. This quote comes from *Introduction*, p. 22. Beaufre is discussed in Beatrice Heuser, *The Evolution of Strategy*, 460–463. See Chapter 6, n. 4.

2. Bernard Brodie, "General André Beaufre on Strategy," *Survival* 7 (August 1965): 208–210. For a more sympathetic review, at least of Beaufre's thought if not his policy advocacy in France, see Edward A. Kolodziej, "French Strategy Emergent: General André Beaufre: A Critique," *World Politics* 19, no. 3 (April 1967): 417–442. While he was unimpressed with Brodie's complaint about "majestic concepts" that got in the way, he acknowledged that Beaufre ideas were often expressed too vaguely to be convincing.

3. There is no evidence of this, although he had been influenced by Clausewitz (there are regular references to "centers of gravity") and Liddell Hart.

4. J. C. Wylie, *Military Strategy: A General Theory of Power Control* (Annapolis, MD: Naval Institute Press, 1989), first published in 1967. A biography is provided by John Hattendorf's introduction.

5. Henry Eccles, *Military Concepts and Philosophy* (New Brunswick, NJ: Rutgers University Press, 1965). On Eccles see Scott A. Boorman, "Fundamentals of Strategy: The Legacy of Henry Eccles," *Naval War College Review* 62, no. 2 (Spring 2009): 91–115.

6. Wylie, *Military Strategy*, 22.

7. On the importance of the distinction, see Lukas Milevski, "Revisiting J. C. Wylie's Dichotomy of Strategy: The Effects of Sequential and Cumulative Patterns of Operations," *Journal of Strategic Studies* 35, no. 2 (April 2012): 223–242. Twenty years after the first publication, Wylie believed that cumulative strategies were more important. *Military Strategy*, 1989 edition, p. 101.

8. His collected works can be found at http://www.ausairpower.net/APA-Boyd-Papers.html. The key books on Boyd are Frans P. B. Osinga, *Science, Strategy and War: The Strategic Theory of John Boyd* (London: Routledge, 2007); Grant Hammond, *The Mind of War, John Boyd and American Security* (Washington, DC: Smithsonian Institution Press, 2001); and Robert Coram, *Boyd, The Fighter Pilot Who Changed the Art of War* (Boston: Little, Brown & Company, 2002).

9. John R. Boyd, "Destruction and Creation," September 3, 1976, available at http://goalsys.com/books/documents/DESTRUCTION_AND_CREATION.pdf.

10. John Boyd, *Organic Design for Command and Control*, May 1987, p.16, available at http://www.ausairpower.net/JRB/organic_design.pdf.

11. The theory was popularized by Edward Lorenz, a diligent meteorologist who discovered the "butterfly effect" while searching for a way to produce more accurate weather predictions. Minuscule changes in his initial input to mathematical calculations for weather predictions could have extraordinary and unpredictable effects on the outcomes. The butterfly effect comes from a 1972 paper by Lorenz to the American Association for the Advancement of Science entitled, "Predictability: Does the Flap of a Butterfly's Wings in Brazil Set Off a Tornado in Texas?" For a history of chaos theory, see James Gleick, *Chaos: Making a New Science* (London: Cardinal, 1987). On complexity theory, see Murray Gell-Man, *The Quark and the Jaguar: Adventures in the Simple and the Complex* (London: Little, Brown & Co., 1994); Mitchell Waldrop, *Complexity: The Emerging Science at the Edge of Order and Chaos* (New York: Simon & Schuster, 1993). On the relationship between scientific theories and military thought, see Antoine Bousquet, *The Scientific Way of Warfare: Order and Chaos on the Battlefields of Modernity* (New York: Columbia University Press, 2009); Robert Pellegrini, *The Links Between Science, Philosophy, and Military Theory: Understanding the Past, Implications for the Future* (Maxwell Air Force Base, AL: Air University Press, August 1997), http://www.au.af.mil/au/awc/awcgate/saas/pellegrp.pdf.

12. Alan Beyerchen, "Clausewitz, Nonlinearity, and the Unpredictability of War," *International Security* (Winter 1992/93); Barry D. Watts, *Clausewitzian Friction and Future War*, McNair Paper 52 (Washington, DC: National Defense University, Institute for Strategic Studies, October 1996).

13. John Boyd, *Patterns of Conflict: A Discourse on Winning and Losing*, unpublished, August 1987, 44, 128, available at http://www.ausairpower.net/JRB/poc.pdf.

14. *Patterns of Conflict*, 79.

15. U.S. Department of Defense, *Field Manual 100-5: Operations* (Washington, DC: HQ Department of Army, 1976).

16. William S. Lind, "Some Doctrinal Questions for the United States Army," *Military Review* 58 (March 1977).

17. U.S. Department of Defense, *Field Manual 100-5: Operations* (Washington, DC: Department of the Army, 1982), vol. 2-1; Huba Wass de Czege and L. D. Holder, "The New FM 100-5," *Military Review* (July 1982).

18. Wass de Czege and Holder, "The New FM 100-5."

19. Ibid.

20. Cited in Larry Cable, "Reinventing the Round Wheel: Insurgency, Counter-Insurgency, and Peacekeeping Post Cold War," *Small Wars and Insurgencies* 4 (Autumn 1993): 228–262.

21. U.S. Marine Corps, *FMFM-1: Warfighting* (Washington, DC: Department of the Navy, 1989), 37.

22. Edward Luttwak, *Pentagon and the Art of War* (New York: Simon & Schuster, 1985).

23. Edward Luttwak, *Strategy: The Logic of War and Peace* (Cambridge, MA: Harvard University Press, 1987), 5. For a flavor, see Harry Kreisler's conversation with Edward Luttwak in *Conversations with History* series, March 1987, available at http://globetrotter.berkeley.edu/conversations/Luttwak/luttwak-con0.html.

24. Luttwak, *Strategy*, 50.

25. Gregory Johnson, "Luttwak Takes a Bath," *Reason Papers* 20 (1995): 121–124.

26. Edward Luttwak, "The Operational Level of War," *International Security*, Vol. 5 (Winter 1980–81): 61–79; Bruce W. Menning, "Operational Art's Origins," *Military Review* 77, no. 5 (September–October 1997): 32–47.

27. Jacob W. Kipp, "The Origins of Soviet Operational Art, 1917–1936" and David M. Glantz, "Soviet Operational Art Since 1936, The Triumph of Maneuver War," in Michael D. Krause and R. Cody Phillips, eds., *Historical Perspectives of the Operational Art* (Washington, DC: United States Army Center of Military History, 2005); Condoleeza Rice, "The Making of Soviet Strategy," in Peter Paret, ed., *Makers of Modern Strategy*, 648–676; William E. Odom, "Soviet Military Doctrine," *Foreign Affairs* (Winter 1988/89): 114–134.

28. See also Eliot Cohen, "Strategic Paralysis: Social Scientists Make Bad Generals," *The American Spectator*, November 1980.

29. He had also been given a prominent place in an essay by Gordon Craig in the remarkable 1943 collection, *Makers of Modern Strategy*. It was retained for the 1986 edition. Gordon A. Craig, "Delbrück: The Military Historian," in Paret, ed., *Makers of Modern Strategy*. Delbrück's *Geschichte der Kriegskunst im Rahmen der Politischen Geschichte*, 4 vols., 1900–1920 (a further three volumes in the series were completed by other writers by 1936), did not begin to appear in English until 1975: Hans Delbrück, trans. Walter J. Renfroe, Jr., *History of the Art of War Within the Framework of Political History*, 4 vols. (Westport, CT: Greenwood Press, 1975–1985).

30. J. Boone Bartholomees, Jr., "The Issue of Attrition," *Parameters* (Spring 2010): 6–9.

31. U.S. Marine Corps, *FMFM-1: Warfighting*, 28–29. See Craig A. Tucker, *False Prophets: The Myth of Maneuver Warfare and the Inadequacies of FMFM-1 Warfighting* (Fort Leavenworth, KS: School of Advanced Military Studies, U.S. Army Command and General Staff College, 1995), 11–12.

32. Charles C. Krulak, "The Strategic Corporal: Leadership in the Three Block War," *Marines Magazine*, January 1999.

33. Michael Howard, "The Forgotten Dimensions of Strategy," *Foreign Affairs* (Summer 1979), reprinted in Michael Howard, *The Causes of Wars* (London: Temple Smith, 1983). Gregory D. Foster, "A Conceptual Foundation for a Theory of Strategy," *The Washington Quarterly* (Winter

1990): 43–59. David Jablonsky, *Why Is Strategy Difficult?* (Carlisle Barracks, PA: Strategic Studies Institute, U.S. Army War College, 1992).

34. Stuart Kinross, *Clausewitz and America: Strategic Thought and Practice from Vietnam to Iraq* (London: Routledge, 2008), 124.
35. U.S. Department of Defense, *Field Manual (FM) 100-5: Operations* (Washington, DC: Headquarters Department of the Army, 1986), 179–180.
36. U.S. Marine Corps, *FMFM-1: Warfighting*, 85.
37. Joseph L. Strange, "Centers of Gravity & Critical Vulnerabilities: Building on the Clausewitizan Foundation so that We Can All Speak the Same Language," *Perspectives on Warfighting* 4, no. 2 (1996): 3; J. Strange and R. Iron, "Understanding Centres of Gravity and Critical Vulnerabilities," research paper, 2001, available at http://www.au.af.mil/au/awc/awcgate/usmc/cog2.pdf.
38. John A. Warden III, *The Air Campaign: Planning for Combat* (Washington, DC: National Defense University Press, 1988), 9; idem, "The Enemy as a System," *Airpower Journal* 9, no. 1 (Spring 1995): 40–55; Howard D. Belote, "Paralyze or Pulverize? Liddell Hart, Clausewitz, and Their Influence on Air Power Theory," *Strategic Review* 27 (Winter 1999): 40–45.
39. Jan L. Rueschhoff and Jonathan P. Dunne, "Centers of Gravity from the 'Inside Out,'" *Joint Forces Quarterly* 60 (2011): 120–125. See also Antulio J. Echevarria II, "'Reining in' the Center of Gravity Concept," *Air & Space Power Journal* (Summer 2003): 87–96.
40. Carter Malkasian, *A History of Modern Wars of Attrition* (Westport, CT: Praeger, 2002), 5–6.
41. Ibid., 17.
42. Hew Strachan, "The Lost Meaning of Strategy," *Survival* 47, no. 3 (Autumn 2005): 47.
43. Rolf Hobson, "Blitzkrieg, the Revolution in Military Affairs and Defense Intellectuals," *The Journal of Strategic Studies* 33, no. 4 (2010): 625–643.
44. John Mearsheimer, "Maneuver, Mobile Defense, and the NATO Central Front," *International Security* 6, no. 3 (Winter 1981–1982): 104–122.
45. Luttwak, *Strategy*, 8.
46. Boyd, *Patterns of Conflict*, 122.

16 The Revolution in Military Affairs

1. See Lawrence Freedman and Efraim Karsh, *The Gulf Conflict* (London: Faber, 1992).
2. Reflected in title of a book by editors of U.S. News & World Report, *Triumph Without Victory: The Unreported History of the Persian Gulf War* (New York: Times Books, 1992).
3. See Andrew F. Krepinevich, Jr., "The Military-Technical Revolution: A Preliminary Assessment," Center for Strategic and Budgetary Assessments,

2002, 1, 3. In the introduction to this edition, Krepinevich provides more detail on Marshall's role. See also Stephen Peter Rosen, "The Impact of the Office of Net Assessment on the American Military in the Matter of the Revolution in Military Affairs," *The Journal of Strategic Studies* 33, no. 4 (2010): 469–482. See also Fred Kaplan, *The Insurgents: David Petraeus and the Plot to Change the American Way of War* (New York: Simon & Schuster, 2013), 47–51.

4. Andrew W. Marshall, "Some Thoughts on Military Revolutions—Second Version," ONA memorandum for record, August 23, 1993, 3–4. Cited in Barry D. Watts, *The Maturing Revolution in Military Affairs* (Washington, DC: Center for Strategic and Budgetary Assessments, 2011).

5. A. W. Marshall, "Some Thoughts on Military Revolutions," ONA memorandum for record, July 27, 1993, 1.

6. Andrew F. Krepinevich, Jr., "Cavalry to Computer: The Pattern of Military Revolutions," *The National Interest* 37 (Fall 1994): 30.

7. Admiral William Owens, "The Emerging System of Systems," *US Naval Institute Proceedings*, May 1995, 35–39.

8. For an analysis of the various theories, see Colin Gray, *Strategy for Chaos: Revolutions in Military Affairs and the Evidence of History* (London: Frank Cass, 2002). Lawrence Freedman, *The Revolution in Strategic Affairs*, Adelphi Paper 318 (London: OUP for IISS, 1998).

9. Barry D. Watts, *Clausewitzian Friction and Future War*, McNair Paper 52 (Washington DC: NDU, 1996).

10. A. C. Bacevich, "Preserving the Well-Bred Horse," *The National Interest* 37 (Fall 1994): 48.

11. Harlan Ullman and James Wade, Jr., *Shock & Awe: Achieving Rapid Dominance* (Washington, DC: National Defense University, 1996).

12. U.S. Joint Chiefs of Staff, Joint Publication 3–13, *Joint Doctrine for Information Operations* (Washington, DC: GPO, October 9, 1998), GL-7.

13. Arthur K. Cebrowski and John J. Garstka, "Network-Centric Warfare: Its Origin and Future," *US Naval Institute Proceedings*, January 1998.

14. Department of Defense, Report to Congress, *Network Centric Warfare*, July 27, 2001, iv.

15. Andrew Mack, "Why Big Countries Lose Small Wars: The Politics of Asymmetric Conflict," *World Politics* 26, no. 1 (1975): 175–200.

16. Steven Metz and Douglas V. Johnson, *Asymmetry and U.S. Military Strategy: Definition, Background, and Strategic Concepts* (Carlisle, PA: Strategic Studies Institute, 2001).

17. Harry Summers, *On Strategy: A Critical Analysis of the Vietnam War* (Novato, CA: Presidio Press, 1982). The review was by Robert Komer, *Survival* 27 (March/April 1985): 94–95. See also Frank Leith Jones, *Blowtorch: Robert Komer, Vietnam and American Cold War Strategy* (Annapolis, MD: Naval Institute Press, 2013).

18. The distinction was developed in Department of Defense, *Joint Pub 3–0, Doctrine for Joint Operations* (Washington, DC: Joint Chiefs of Staff, 1993). See Jonathan Stevenson, *Thinking Beyond the Unthinkable,* 517 (see chap. 13, n. 9).

19. Douglas Lovelace, Jr., *The Evolution of Military Affairs: Shaping the Future U.S. Armed Forces* (Carlisle, PA: Strategic Studies Institute, 1997); Jennifer M. Taw and Alan Vick, "From Sideshow to Center Stage: The Role of the Army and Air Force in Military Operations Other Than War," in Zalmay M. Khalilzad and David A. Ochmanek, eds., *Strategy and Defense Planning for the 21st Century* (Santa Monica, CA: RAND & U.S. Air Force, 1997), 208–209.

20. Remarks by the President at the Citadel, Charleston, South Carolina, December 11, 2001. See also Donald Rumsfeld, "Transforming the Military," *Foreign Affairs*, May/June 2002, 20–32.

21. Stephen Biddle, "Speed Kills? Reassessing the Role of Speed, Precision, and Situation Awareness in the Fall of Saddam," *Journal of Strategic Studies*, 30, no. 1 (February 2007): 3–46.

22. Nigel Aylwin-Foster, "Changing the Army for Counterinsurgency Operations," *Military Review,* November/December 2005, 5.

23. For example, Kalev Sepp's critique of the American focus on killing insurgents rather than engaging the population and training local forces to be like the Americans in "Best Practices in Counterinsurgency," *Military Review*, May–June 2005, 8–12. See Kaplan, *The Insurgents*, 104–107. Kaplan provides a thorough account of the shift in American military thinking over this period.

24. John A. Nagl, *Counterinsurgency Lessons from Malaya and Vietnam: Learning to Eat Soup with a Knife* (Westport, CT: Praeger, 2002). The title picked up on T. E. Lawrence's aphorism.

25. David Kilcullen, *The Accidental Guerrilla: Fighting Small Wars in the Midst of a Big One* (London: Hurst & Co., 2009).

26. David H. Petraeus, "Learning Counterinsurgency: Observations from Soldiering in Iraq," *Military Review,* January/February 2006, 2–12.

27. On the "surge," see Bob Woodward, *The War Within: A Secret White House History* (New York: Simon & Schuster, 2008); Bing West, *The Strongest Tribe: War, Politics, and the Endgame in Iraq* (New York: Random House, 2008); Linda Robinson, *Tell Me How This Ends: General David Petraeus and the Search for a Way Out of Iraq* (New York: Public Affairs, 2008).

28. On the links with Boyd, see Frans Osinga, "On Boyd, Bin Laden, and Fourth Generation Warfare as String Theory," in John Andreas Olson, ed., *On New Wars* (Oslo: Norwegian Institute for Defence Studies, 2007), 168–197, available at http://ifs.forsvaret.no/publikasjoner/oslo_files/OF_2007/Documents/OF_4_2007.pdf.

29. William S. Lind, Keith Nightengale, John F. Schmitt, Joseph W. Sutton, and Gary I. Wilson, "The Changing Face of War: Into the Fourth

Generation," *Marine Corps Gazette*, October 1989, 22–26; William Lind, "Understanding Fourth Generation War," *Military Review*, September/October 2004, 12–16. This reports the findings of a study group which he convened at his house.

30. Keegan, *A History of Warfare* and van Creveld, *The Transformation of War*, for both see Chapter 7, n. 14; Rupert Smith, *The Utility of Force: The Art of War in the Modern World* (London: Allen Lane, 2005); Mary Kaldor, *New & Old Wars, Organized Violence in a Global Era* (Cambridge: Polity Press, 1999).

31. "The Evolution of War: The Fourth Generation of Warfare," *Marine Corps Gazette*, September 1994. See also Thomas X. Hammes, "War Evolves into the Fourth Generation," *Contemporary Security Policy* 26, no. 2 (August 2005): 212–218. This issue contains a number of critiques of the idea of fourth-generation warfare, including one by the author. This was republished as Aaron Karp, Regina Karp, and Terry Terriff, eds., *Global Insurgency and the Future of Armed Conflict: Debating Fourth-Generation Warfare* (London: Routledge, 2007). For a full account of Hammes's ideas see his *The Sling and the Stone: On War in the 21st Century* (St. Paul, MN: Zenith Press, 2004); Tim Benbow, "Talking 'Bout Our Generation? Assessing the Concept of 'Fourth Generation Warfare'" *Comparative Strategy*, March 2008, 148–163 and Antulio J. Echevarria, *Fourth Generation Warfare and Other Myths* (Carlisle, PA: U.S. Army War College Strategic Studies Institute, 2005).

32. Cited in Jason Vest, "Fourth-Generation Warfare," *Atlantic Magazine*, December 2001.

33. William Lind et al., "The Changing Face of War," *The Marine Corps Gazette*, October 1989, 22–26, available at http://zinelibrary.info/files/TheChangingFaceofWar-onscreen.pdf.

34. Ralph Peters, "The New Warrior Class," *Parameters* 24, no. 2 (Summer 1994): 20.

35. Joint Publication 3–13, *Information Operations*, March 13, 2006.

36. Nik Gowing, '*Skyful of Lies' and Black Swans: The New Tyranny of Shifting Information Power in Crises* (Oxford, UK: Reuters Institute for the Study of Journalism, 2009).

37. John Arquilla and David Ronfeldt, "Cyberwar is Coming!" *Comparative Strategy* 12, no. 2 (Spring 1993): 141–165.

38. Steve Metz, *Armed Conflict in the 21st Century: The Information Revolution and Post-Modern Warfare* (April 2000): "Future war may see attacks via computer viruses, worms, logic bombs, and trojan horses rather than bullets, bombs, and missiles."

39. Thomas Rid, *Cyberwar Will Not Take Place* (London: Hurst & Co., 2013). David Betz argues for the complexity of effect in "Cyberpower in Strategic Affairs: Neither Unthinkable nor Blessed," *The Journal of Strategic Studies* 35, no. 5 (October 2012): 689–711.

40. John Arquilla and David Ronfeldt, eds., *Networks and Netwars: The Future of Terror, Crime, and Militancy* (Santa Monica, CA: RAND, 2001). The full text is available at www.rand.org/publications/MR/MR1382/. For a summary of their arguments, see David Ronfeldt and John Arquilla, "Networks, Netwars, and the Fight for the Future," *First Monday* 6, no. 10 (October 2001), available at http://firstmonday.org/issues/issue6_10/ronfeldt/index.html.

41. Jerrold M. Post, Keven G. Ruby, and Eric D. Shaw, "From Car Bombs to Logic Bombs: The Growing Threat from Information Terrorism," *Terrorism and Political Violence* 12, no. 2 (Summer 2000): 102–103.

42. Norman Emery, Jason Werchan, and Donald G. Mowles, "Fighting Terrorism and Insurgency: Shaping the Information Environment," *Military Review*, January/Febuary 2005, 32–38.

43. Robert H. Scales, Jr., "Culture-Centric Warfare," *The Naval Institute Proceedings*, October 2004.

44. Montgonery McFate, "The Military Utility of Understanding Adversary Culture," *Joint Forces Quarterly* 38 (July 2005): 42–48.

45. Max Boot, *Invisible Armies*, 386 (see chap. 14, n. 22).

46. A useful guide to the academic debates on this issue is Alan Bloomfield, "Strategic Culture: Time to Move On," *Contemporary Security Policy* 33, no. 3 (December 2012): 437–461.

47. Patrick Porter, *Military Orientalism: Eastern War Through Western Eyes* (London: Hurst & Co., 2009), 193.

48. David Kilcullen, "Twenty-Eight Articles: Fundamentals of Company-Level Counterinsurgency," *Military Review*, May–June 2006, 105–107. This began as an e-mail that was widely distributed around the army.

49. Emile Simpson, *War from the Ground Up: Twenty-First-Century Combat as Politics* (London: Hurst & Co., 2012), 233.

50. G. J. David and T. R. McKeldin III, *Ideas as Weapons: Influence and Perception in Modern Warfare* (Washington, DC: Potomac Books, 2009), 3. See in particular Timothy J. Doorey, "Waging an Effective Strategic Communications Campaign in the War on Terror," and Frank Hoffman, "Maneuvering Against the Mind."

51. Jeff Michaels, *The Discourse Trap and the US Military: From the War on Terror to the Surge* (London: Palgrave Macmillan, 2013). See also Frank J. Barrett and Theodore R. Sarbin, "The Rhetoric of Terror: 'War' as Misplaced Metaphor," in John Arquilla and Douglas A. Borer, eds., *Information Strategy and Warfare: A Guide to Theory and Practice* (New York: Routledge, 2007): 16–33.

52. Hy S. Rothstein, "Strategy and Psychological Operations," in Arquilla and Borer, 167.

53. Neville Bolt, *The Violent Image: Insurgent Propaganda and the New Revolutionaries* (New York: Columbia University Press, 2012).

54. Al-Qaeda leader Ayman al-Zawahiri wrote in July 2005: "We are in the midst of war, and more than half of that struggle takes place on an information battlefield; we are in an information war for the hearts and minds of all Muslims." The text of the letter is available in English from the Office of the Director of National Intelligence, at http://www.dni.gov/press_releases/20051011_release.htm.

55. Benedict Wilkinson, *The Narrative Delusion: Strategic Scripts and Violent Islamism in Egypt, Saudi Arabia and Yemen,* unpublished doctoral thesis, King's College London, 2013.

17 The Myth of the Master Strategist

1. Colin S. Gray, *Modern Strategy* (Oxford: Oxford University Press, 1999), 23–43.

2. Harry Yarger, *Strategic Theory for the 21st Century: The Little Book on Big Strategy* (Carlisle, PA: U.S. Army War College, Strategic Studies Institute, 2006), 36, 66, 73–75.

3. Colin S. Gray, *The Strategy Bridge: Theory for Practice* (Oxford: Oxford University Press, 2010), 23.

4. Ibid., 49, 52. This was a reference to Albert Wohlstetter.

5. Yarger, *Strategic Theory for the 21st Century*, 75.

6. Robert Jervis, *Systems Effects: Complexity in Political and Social Life* (Princeton, NJ: Princeton University Press, 1997).

7. Hugh Smith, "The Womb of War: Clausewitz and International Politics," *Review of International Studies* 16 (1990): 39–58.

8. Eliot Cohen, *Supreme Command: Soldiers, Statesmen, and Leadership in Wartime* (New York: The Free Press, 2002).

18 Marx and a Strategy for the Working Class

1. Mike Rapport, *1848: Year of Revolution* (London: Little, Brown & Co. 2008), 17–18.

2. Sigmund Neumann and Mark von Hagen, "Engels and Marx on Revolution, War, and the Army in Society," in Paret, ed., *Makers of Modern Strategy*, 262–280 (see chap. 6, n. 2); Bernard Semmell, *Marxism and the Science of War* (New York: Oxford University Press, 1981), 266.

3. This section comes from Part I, Feuerbach. "Opposition of the Materialist and Idealist Outlook," *The German Ideology*, available at http://www.marxists.org/archive/marx/works/1845/german-ideology/ch01a.htm.

4. Azar Gat, "Clausewitz and the Marxists: Yet Another Look," *Journal of Contemporary History* 27, no. 2 (April 1992): 363–382.

5. Rapport, *1848: Year of Revolution*, 108.

6. Alan Gilbert, *Marx's Politics: Communists and Citizens* (New York: Rutgers University Press, 1981), 134–135.

7. Engels, "Revolution in Paris," February 27, 1848, available at http://www.marxists.org/archive/marx/works/1848/02/27.htm.

8. News from Paris, June 23, 1848, emphasis in original. Available at http://www.marxists.org/archive/marx/works/1848/06/27.htm.

9. Gilbert, *Marx's Politics*, 140–142, 148–149.

10. Rapport, *1848: Year of Revolution*, 212.

11. Engels, "Marx and the Neue Rheinische Zeitung," March 13, 1884, available at http://www.marxists.org/archive/marx/works/1884/03/13.htm.

12. Rapport, *1848: Year of Revolution*, 217.

13. Karl Marx, *Class Struggles in France, 1848–1850, Part II*, available at http://www.marxists.org/archive/marx/works/1850/class-struggles-france/ch02.htm.

14. Engels to Marx, December 3, 1851, available at http://www.marxists.org/archive/marx/works/1851/letters/51_12_03.htm#cite.

15. John Maguire, *Marx's Theory of Politics* (Cambridge, UK: Cambridge University Press, 1978), 31.

16. Ibid., 197–198.

17. *Manifesto of the Communist Party*, February 1848, 75, available at http://www.marxists.org/archive/marx/works/1848/communist-manifesto/.

18. Engels, "The Campaign for the German Imperial Constitution," 1850, available at http://www.marxists.org/archive/marx/works/1850/german-imperial/intro.htm.

19. David McLellan, *Karl Marx: His Life and Thought* (New York: Harper & Row, 1973), 217.

20. Frederick Engels, "Conditions and Prospects of a War of the Holy Alliance Against France in 1852," April 1851, available at http://www.marxists.org/archive/marx/works/1851/04/holy-alliance.htm.

21. Gerald Runkle, "Karl Marx and the American Civil War," *Comparative Studies in Society and History* 6, no. 2 (January 1964): 117–141.

22. Engels to Joseph Weydemeyer, June 19, 1851, available at http://www.marxists.org/archive/marx/works/1851/letters/51_06_19.htm.

23. Engels to Joseph Weydemeyer, April 12, 1853, available at http://www.marxists.org/archive/marx/works/1853/letters/53_04_12.htm.

24. Sigmund Neumann and Mark von Hagen, "Engels and Marx on Revolution, War, and the Army in Society," in Paret, ed., *Makers of Modern Strategy*; Semmell, *Marxism and the Science of War*, 266.

25. Engels had fought beside him in Baden. The story of Engels's military adventures is found in Tristram Hunt, *The Frock-Coated Communist: The Revolutionary Life of Friedrich Engels* (London: Allan Lane, 2009), 174–181.

26. Gilbert, *Marx's Politics*, 192.

27. Christine Lattek, *Revolutionary Refugees: German Socialism in Britain, 1840–1860* (London: Routledge, 2006).

28. Marx to Engels, September 23, 1851, available at http://www.marxists.org/archive/marx/works/1851/letters/51_09_23.htm.

29. Engels to Marx, September 26, 1851, available at http://www.marxists.org/archive/marx/works/1851/letters/51_09_26.htm.

30. This was originally published as articles under Marx's name in the *New York Tribune* and then brought together as a book under his own name, *Revolution and Counter-Revolution in Germany*. The quote is from p. 90. Available at http://www.marxists.org/archive/marx/works/1852/germany/index.htm.

19 Herzen and Bakunin

1. Isaiah Berlin's influential assertion that Herzen had been neglected in the West first appeared in the *New York Review of Books* in 1968 and appeared as an introduction to Herzen's diaries, *My Past & Thoughts* (Berkeley: University of California Press, 1973). For a long time, the most substantial biography was E. H. Carr's *Romantic Exiles* (Cambridge, UK: Penguin, 1949), from which Stoppard drew extensively. See also Edward Acton, *Alexander Herzen and the Role of the Intellectual Revolutionary* (Cambridge, UK: Cambridge University Press, 1979).

2. Tom Stoppard, "The Forgotten Revolutionary," *The Observer*, June 2, 2002.

3. Tom Stoppard, *The Coast of Utopia, Part II, Shipwreck* (London: Faber & Faber, 2002), 18.

4. Anna Vanninskaya, "Tom Stoppard, the Coast of Utopia, and the Strange Death of the Liberal Intelligentsia," *Modern Intellectual History* 4, no. 2 (2007): 353–365.

5. Tom Stoppard, *The Coast of Utopia, Part III, Salvage* (London: Faber & Faber, 2002), 74–75.

6. Cited in Acton, *Alexander Herzen and the Role of the Intellectual Revolutionary*, 159.

7. Ibid., 171, 176; Herzen, *My Past & Thoughts*, 1309–1310.

8. Stoppard, *Salvage*, 7–8.

9. Engels, "The Program of the Blanquist Fugitives from the Paris Commune," June 26, 1874, available at http://www.marxists.org/archive/marx/works/1874/06/26.htm.

10. Henry Eaton, "Marx and the Russians," *Journal of the History of Ideas* 41, no. 1 (January/ March 1980): 89–112.

11. Cited in Mark Leier, *Bakunin: A Biography* (New York: St. Martin's Press, 2006), 119.

12. Herzen, *My Past & Thoughts*, 573.

13. Ibid., 571.

14. Aileen Kelly, *Mikhail Bakunin: A Study in the Psychology and Politics of Utopianism* (Oxford: Clarendon Press, 1982). For a critique, see Robert M. Cutler, "Bakunin and the Psychobiographers: The Anarchist as Mythical

and Historical Object," KLIO (St. Petersburg), [Abstract of English original of article] in press [in Russian translation], available at http://www.robertcutler.org/bakunin/ar09klio.htm.

15. In his later confessions, cited by Peter Marshall, *Demanding the Impossible: A History of Anarchism* (London: Harper Perennial, 2008), 269.

16. Paul Thomas, *Karl Marx and the Anarchists* (London: Routledge, 1990), 261–262.

17. Marshall, *Demanding the Impossible*, 244–245, 258–259.

18. Proudhon, quoted in K. Steven Vincent, *Pierre-Joseph Proudhon and the Rise of French Republican Socialism* (Oxford: Oxford University Press, 1984), 148.

19. Thomas, *Marx and the Anarchists*, 250.

20. Alvin W. Gouldner, "Marx's Last Battle: Bakunin and the First International," *Theory and Society* 11, no. 6 (November 1982): 861. Special issue in memory of Alvin W. Gouldner.

21. Cited in Hunt, *The Frock-Coated Communist*, 259 (see chap. 18, n. 25).

22. Leier, *Bakunin: A Biography*, 191; Paul McClaughlin, *Bakunin: The Philosophical Basis of his Anarchism* (New York: Algora Publishing, 2002).

23. Mikhail A. Bakunin, *Statism and Anarchy* (Cambridge, UK: Cambridge University Press, 1990), 159.

24. Saul Newman, *From Bakunin to Lacan: Anti-authoritarianism and the Dislocation of Power* (Lanham, MD: Lexington Books, 2001), 37.

25. Leier, *Bakunin: A Biography*, 194–195.

26. Ibid., 184, 210, 241–242.

27. Proudhon's own *War and Peace* is extremely muddled, not least in its apparent glorification of war. A more literary inspiration for Tolstoy was Victor Hugo, whose *Les Misérables* demonstrated a way of writing about historical events.

28. Leier, *Bakunin: A Biography*, 196.

29. Carr, *The Romantic Exiles*.

30. Available at www.marxists.org/subject/anarchism/nechayev/catechism.htm.

31. Cited by Marshall, *Demanding the Impossible*, 346.

32. Carl Levy, "Errico Malatesta and Charismatic Leadership," in Jan Willem Stutje, ed., *Charismatic Leadership and Social Movements* (New York: Berghan Books, 2012), 89–90. Levy suggests that Malatesta's barnstorming around Italy from December 1919 to October 1920 meant that opportunities were missed to organize the workers.

33. Ibid., 94.

34. Joseph Conrad, *Under Western Eyes* (London: Everyman's Library, 1991).

35. Joseph Conrad, *The Secret Agent* (London: Penguin, 2007).

36. Stanley G. Payne, *The Spanish Civil War, the Soviet Union and Communism* (New Haven, CT: Yale University Press, 2004).

37. Levy, "Errico Malatesta," 94.

1. Engels, *Introduction to Karl Marx's* THE CLASS STRUGGLES IN FRANCE 1848 TO 1850, March 6, 1895, available at http://www.marxists.org/archive/marx/works/1895/03/06.htm.
2. Engels to Kautsky, April 1, 1895, available at http://www.marxists.org/archive/marx/works/1895/letters/95_04_01.htm.
3. Engels, Reply to the Honorable Giovanni Bovio, *Critica Sociale* No. 4, February 16, 1892, available at http://www.marxists.org/archive/marx/works/1892/02/critica-sociale.htm.
4. Marx, *Critique of the Gotha Programme*, May 1875, available at https://www.marxists.org/archive/marx/works/1875/gotha/index.htm. McLellan, *Karl Marx* see Chapter 20, n. 19, 437.
5. Leszek Kolakowski, *Main Currents of Marxism: The Founders, the Golden Age, the Breakdown* (New York: Norton, 2005), 391.
6. Stephen Eric Bronner, "Karl Kautsky and the Twilight of Orthodoxy," *Political Theory* 10, no. 4 (November 1982): 580–605.
7. Elzbieta Ettinger, *Rosa Luxemburg: A Life* (Boston, MA: Beacon Press, 1986), xii, 87.
8. Rosa Luxemburg, *Reform or Revolution* (London: Bookmarks Publications, 1989).
9. Rosa Luxembourg, *The Mass Strike, the Political Party, and the Trade Unions*, 1906, available at http://www.marxists.org/archive/luxemburg/1906/mass-strike/index.htm.
10. Engels, "The Bakuninists at Work: An Account of the Spanish Revolt in the Summer of 1873," September/October 1873, available at http://www.marxists.org/archive/marx/works/1873/bakunin/index.htm.
11. Rosa Luxemburg, *The Mass Strike.*
12. Leon Trotsky, *My Life: The Rise and Fall of a Dictator* (London: T. Butterworth, 1930).
13. Karl Kautsky, "The Mass Strike," 1910, cited in Stephen D'Arcy, "Strategy, Meta-strategy and Anti-capitalist Activism: Rethinking Leninism by Re-reading Lenin," *Socialist Studies: The Journal of the Society for Socialist Studies* 5, no. 2 (2009): 64–89.
14. Lenin, "The Historical Meaning of the Inner-Party Struggle," 1910, available at http://www.marxists.org/archive/lenin/works/1910/hmipsir/index.htm.
15. Vladimir Lenin, *What Is to Be Done?*, 35, available at http://www.marxists.org/archive/lenin/works/1901/witbd/index.htm.
16. Nadezhda Krupskaya, *Memories of Lenin* (London: Lawrence, 1930), 1: 102–103, citing *One Step Forward, Two Steps Back.*
17. Beryl Williams, *Lenin* (Harlow, Essex: Pearson Education, 2000), 46.
18. Hew Strachan, *The First World War, Volume One: To Arms* (Oxford: Oxford University Press, 2003), 113.

19. Robert Service, *Comrades: A World History of Communism* (London: Macmillan, 2007), 1427, 1448.

21 *Bureaucrats, Democrats, and Elites*

1. At the same time, Mauss also records Durkheim's concern that his students' interest in Marxism was leading them away from liberalism, his distrust of the "shallow philosophy of the radicals," and his "reluctance to submit himself to party discipline." Marcel Mauss's preface to Emile Durkheim, *Socialism* (New York: Collier Books, 1958).

2. David Beetham, "Mosca, Pareto, and Weber: A Historical Comparison," in Wolfgang Mommsen and Jurgen Osterhammel, eds., *Max Weber and His Contemporaries* (London: Allen & Unwin, 1987), 140–141.

3. See Joachim Radkau, *Max Weber: A Biography* (Cambridge, UK: Polity Press, 2009).

4. Max Weber, *The Theory of Social and Economic Organization*, translated by Henderson and Parsons (New York: The Free Press, 1947), 337.

5. Peter Lassman, "The Rule of Man over Man: Politics, Power and Legitimacy," in Stephen Turner, ed., *The Cambridge Companion to Weber* (Cambridge, UK: Cambridge University Press, 2000), 84–88.

6. Sheldon Wolin, "Legitimation, Method, and the Politics of Theory," *Political Theory* 9, no. 3 (August 1981): 405.

7. Radkau, *Max Weber*, 487.

8. Ibid., 488.

9. Nicholas Gane, *Max Weber and Postmodern Theory: Rationalisation versus Re-enchantment* (London: Palgrave Macmillan, 2002), 60.

10. Max Weber, "Science as a Vocation," available at http://mail.www. anthropos-lab.net/wp/wp-content/uploads/2011/12/Weber-Science-as-a-Vocation.pdf.

11. Radkau, *Max Weber*, 463.

12. Wolfgang Mommsen, *Max Weber and German Politics, 1890–1920,* translated by Michael Steinberg (Chicago: University of Chicago Press, 1984), 310.

13. Ibid., 296.

14. Max Weber, "Politics as Vocation," available at http://anthropos-lab.net/wp/wp-content/uploads/2011/12/Weber-Politics-as-a-Vocation.pdf.

15. Reinhard Bendix and Guenther Roth, *Scholarship and Partisanship: Essays on Max Weber* (Berkeley: University of California Press, 1971), 28–29.

16. Isaiah Berlin, "Tolstoy and Enlightenment," in Harold Bloom, ed., *Leo Tolstoy* (New York: Chelsea Books, 2003), 30–31.

17. *Philosophers of Peace and War*, see Chapter 8, n. 6, 129.

18. Rosamund Bartlett, *Tolstoy: A Russian Life* (London: Profile Books, 2010), 309.

19. Leo Tolstoy, *The Kingdom of God and Peace Essays* (The World's Classics), 347–348. Cited by Gallie, *Philosophers of Peace*, 122.

20. The essay appears as the introduction to Lyof N. Tolstoi, *What to Do? Thoughts Evoked by the Census of Moscow*, translated by Isabel F. Hapgood (New York: Thomas Y. Cromwell, 1887).

21. Ibid., 1.

22. Ibid., 4–5, 10.

23. Ibid., 77–78.

24. Mikhail A. Bakunin, *Bakunin on Anarchy* (New York: Knopf, 1972).

25. Jane Addams, *Twenty Years at Hull House* (New York: Macmillan, 1910).

26. Ibid., 56.

27. Jan C. Behrends, "Visions of Civility: Lev Tolstoy and Jane Addams on the Urban Condition in *Fin de Siècle* Moscow and Chicago," *European Review of History: Revue Européenne d'Histoire* 18, no. 3 (June 2011): 335–357.

28. Martin, *The Chicago School of Sociology: Institutionalization, Diversity and the Rise of Sociological Research* (Chicago: University of Chicago Press, 1984), 13–14.

29. Lincoln Steffens, *The Shame of the Cities* (New York: Peter Smith, 1948, first published 1904), 234.

30. Lawrence A. Schaff, *Max Weber in America* (Princeton, NJ: Princeton University Press, 2011), 41–43.

31. Ibid., 45. Schaff suggests that the descriptions of violence may have been overdrawn.

32. Ibid., 43–44.

33. James Weber Linn, *Jane Addams: A Biography* (Chicago: University of Illinois Press, 2000), 196.

34. Addams, *Twenty Years at Hull House*, 171–172. Her approach is set out in Jane Addams, "A Function of the Social Settlement" in Louis Menand, ed., *Pragmatism: A Reader* (New York: Vintage Books, 1997), 273–286.

35. Ibid., 98–99.

36. Lear was also Tolstoy's favorite Shakespeare play. The king's character at the end of the play was "English literature's nearest equivalent to the holy fool (yurodivy)—that peculiarly Russian form of sainthood to which Tolstoy aspired, and which is not encountered in any other religious culture." Bartlett, *Tolstoy*, 332.

37. Jane Addams, "A Modern Lear." This 1896 speech was not published until 1912. Available at http://womenshistory.about.com/cs/addamsjane/a/mod_lear_10003b.htm.

38. Jean Bethke Elshtain, *Jane Addams and the Dream of American Democracy* (New York: Basic Books, 2002), 202, 218–219.

39. The quality of the Hull House research has led to suggestions that were it not for the misogynist male sociologists at the University of Chicago, Addams and her colleagues would be properly appreciated as important figures in the history of American sociology. Mary Jo Deegan, *Jane Addams and the Men of the Chicago School* (New Brunswick: Transaction Books, 1988).

40. Don Martindale, "American Sociology Before World War II," *Annual Review of Sociology* 2 (1976): 121; Anthony J. Cortese, "The Rise, Hegemony, and Decline of the Chicago School of Sociology, 1892–1945," *The Social Science Journal*, July 1995, 235; Fred H. Matthews, *Quest for an American Sociology: Robert E. Park and the Chicago School* (Montreal: McGill Queens University Press, 1977), 10; Martin Bulmer, *The Chicago School of Sociology*.

41. Small, cited by Lawrence J. Engel, "Saul D. Alinsky and the Chicago School," *The Journal of Speculative Philosophy* 16, no. 1 (2002): 50–66. In addition to a mass of case studies in its neighborhood, the university had the added advantage of John D. Rockefeller's generous endowment, a free intellectual atmosphere, and a lack of the social elitism and discrimination associated with the Ivy League universities.

42. Albion Small, "Scholarship and Social Agitation," *American Journal of Sociology* 1 (1895–1896): 581–582, 605.

43. Robert Westbrook, "The Making of a Democratic Philosopher: The Intellectual Development of John Dewey," in Molly Cochran, ed., *The Cambridge Companion to Dewey* (Cambridge, UK: Cambridge University Press, 2010), 13–33.

44. Among the most important titles are *Democracy and Education* (New York: Macmillan, 1916); *Human Nature and Conduct* (New York: Henry Holt, 1922); *Experience and Nature* (New York: Norton, 1929); *The Quest for Certainty* (New York: Minton, 1929); *Logic: The Theory of Inquiry* (New York: Henry Holt, 1938).

45. Small, "Scholarship and Social Agitation," 362, 237.

46. Andrew Feffer, *The Chicago Pragmatists and American Progressivism* (Ithaca, NY: Cornell University Press, 1993), 168.

47. Ibid., 237.

48. William James, "Pragmatism," in Louis Menand, ed., *Pragmatism*, 98.

49. Louis Menand, *The Metaphysical Club* (London: HarperCollins, 2001), 353–354.

50. Ibid., 350.

51. Dewey came "perilously close to reconciling desire with deed." John Patrick Duggan, *The Promise of Pragmatism: Modernism and the Crisis of Knowledge and Authority* (Chicago: University of Chicago Press, 1994), 48.

52. Dewey, *Human Nature and Conflict*, 230.

53. Menand, *The Metaphysical Club*, 374.

54. Robert K. Merton, "The Unanticipated Consequences of Purposive Social Action," *American Sociological Review* 1, no. 6 (December 1936): 894–904.

22 Formulas, Myths, and Propaganda

1. H. Stuart Hughes, *Consciousness and Society: The Reorientation of European Social Thought* (Cambridge, MA: Harvard University Press, 1958).
2. Robert Michels, *Political Parties: A Sociological Study of the Oligarchical Tendencies of Modern Democracy* (New York: The Free Press, 1962), 46. First published in 1900.
3. Wolfgang Mommsen, "Robert Michels and Max Weber: Moral Conviction versus the Politics of Responsibility," in Wolfgang and Jurgen Osterhammel, 126.
4. Michels, *Political Parties*, 338.
5. Gaetano Mosca, *The Ruling Class* (New York: McGraw Hill, 1939), 50. First published in 1900.
6. Ibid., 451.
7. David Beetham, "Mosca, Pareto, and Weber: A Historical Comparison," in Wolfgang Mommsen and Jurgen Osterhammel, eds., *Max Weber and His Contemporaries* (London: Allen & Unwin, 1987), 139–158.
8. Vilfredo Pareto, *The Mind and Society*, edited by Arthur Livingston, 4 volumes (New York: Harcourt Brace, 1935).
9. Geraint Parry, *Political Elites* (London: George Allen & Unwin, 1969).
10. Gustave Le Bon, *The Crowd: A Study of the Popular Mind* (New York: The Macmillan Co., 1896), 13, available at http://etext.virginia.edu/toc/modeng/public/BonCrow.html.
11. Hughes, *Consciousness and Society*, 161.
12. Irving Louis Horowitz, *Radicalism and the Revolt Against Reason: The Social Theories of George Sorel* (Abingdon: Routledge & Kegan Paul, 2009). He notes, however, Sorel's "poverty of formal organization…indiscriminate shifting of the basis of an argument from fact to hypothesis to free speculation…tendentious style" (p. 9).
13. Jeremy Jennings, ed., *Sorel: Reflections on Violence* (Cambridge, UK: Cambridge University Press, 1999), viii. First published 1906 in *Le Mouvement Sociale*.
14. Antonio Gramsci, *The Modern Prince & Other Writings* (New York: International Publishers, 1957), 143.
15. Thomas R. Bates, "Gramsci and the Theory of Hegemony," *Journal of the History of Ideas* 36, no. 2 (April–June 1975): 352.
16. Joseph Femia, "Hegemony and Consciousness in the Thought of Antonio Gramsci," *Political Studies* 23, no. 1 (1975): 37.
17. Ibid., 33.
18. Gramsci, *The Modern Prince*, 137.

19. Walter L. Adamson, *Hegemony and Revolution: A Study of Antonio Gramsci's Political and Cultural Thought* (Berkeley: University of California Press, 1980), 223, 209.

20. Ibid., 223.

21. T. K. Jackson Lears, "The Concept of Cultural Hegemony: Problems and Possibilities," *The American Historical Review* 90, no. 1 (June 1985): 578.

22. Adolf Hitler, *Mein Kampf*, vol. I, ch. X. First published in 1925.

23. James Burnham, *The Managerial Revolution* (London: Putnam, 1941). See also Kevin J. Smant, *How Great the Triumph: James Burnham, Anti-Communism, and the Conservative Movement* (New York: University Press of America, 1991).

24. Bruno Rizzi, *The Bureaucratization of the World*, translated by Adam Westoby (New York: The Free Press, 1985).

25. Ibid., 223–225, 269.

26. See, for example, C. Wright Mills, "A Marx for the Managers," in Irving Horowitz, ed., *Power, Politics and People: The Collected Essays of C. Wright Mills* (New York: Oxford University Press, 1963), 53–71. George Orwell voiced many misgivings, noting Burnham's earlier presumption of German victory in the war, yet he nonetheless used Burnham's geopolitical analysis, predicting a world divided into three strategic centers for world control, each similar to the other yet engaged in a constant struggle, as the basis for his dystopian novel, *1984*. As always, Orwell's analysis makes for fascinating reading. See his "James Burnham and the Managerial Revolution," *New English Weekly*, May 1946, available at http://www.k-1.com/Orwell/site/work/essays/burnham.html.

27. This was not fully published in English until 1972, although it was reflected in other writings of Park.

28. Stuart Ewen, *PR! A Social History of Spin* (New York: Basic Books, 1996), 69.

29. Ibid., 68.

30. Robert Park, *the Mass and the Public, and Other Essays* (Chicago: University of Chicago Press, 1972), 80. First published in 1904.

31. Cited by Ewen, *PR!*, 48.

32. Ronald Steel, *Walter Lippmann and the American Century* (New Brunswick, NJ: Transaction Publishers, 1999).

33. W. I. Thomas and Dorothy Swaine Thomas, *The Child in America: Behavior Problems and Programs* (New York: Knopf, 1928). Robert Merton, who turned Thomas's aphorism into a theorem, described it as "probably the single most consequential sentence ever put in print by an American sociologist." "Social Knowledge and Public Policy," in *Sociological Ambivalence* (New York: Free Press, 1976), 174. See also Robert Merton, "The Thomas Theorem and the Matthew Effect," *Social Forces* 74, no. 2 (December 1995): 379–424.

34. Walter Lippmann, *Public Opinion* (New York: Harcourt Brace & Co, 1922), 59, available at http://xroads.virginia.edu/~Hyper2/CDFinal/Lippman/cover.html.

35. Michael Schudson, "The 'Lippmann-Dewey Debate' and the Invention of Walter Lippmann as an Anti-Democrat 1986–1996," *International Journal of Communication* 2 (2008): 140.

36. Harold D. Lasswell, "The Theory of Political Propaganda," *The American Political Science Review* 21, no. 3 (August 1927): 627–631.

37. Sigmund Freud, *Group Psychology and the Analysis of the Ego* (London: The Hogarth Press, 1949). First published 1922, available at http://archive.org/stream/grouppsychologya00freu/grouppsychologya00freu_djvu.txt.

38. Wilfred Trotter, *Instincts of the Herd in Peace and War* (New York: Macmillan, 1916); Harvey C. Greisman, "Herd Instinct and the Foundations of Biosociology," *Journal of the History of the Behavioral Sciences* 15 (1979): 357–369.

39. Edward Bernays, *Crystallizing Public Opinion* (New York: Liveright, 1923), 35.

40. Edward Bernays, *Propaganda* (New York: H. Liveright, 1936), 71.

41. The title of a 1947 article, Edward L. Bernays, "The Engineering of Consent," *The Annals of the American Academy of Political and Social Science* 250 (1947): 113.

42. There remains debate about whether or not this really made a difference to women's smoking habits. See Larry Tye, *The Father of Spin: Edward L. Bernays and the Birth of Public Relations* (New York: Holt, 1998), 27–35.

43. "Are We Victims of Propaganda? A Debate. Everett Dean Martin and Edward L. Bernays," *Forum Magazine*, March 1929.

23 *The Power of Nonviolence*

1. Laura E. Nym Mayhall, *The Militant Suffrage Movement: Citizenship and Resistance in Britain, 1860–1930* (Oxford: Oxford University Press, 2003), 45, 79, 107, 115.

2. Donna M. Kowal, "One Cause, Two Paths: Militant vs. Adjustive Strategies in the British and American Women's Suffrage Movements," *Communication Quarterly* 48, no. 3 (2000): 240–255.

3. Henry David Thoreau, *Civil Disobedience*, originally published as *Resistance to Civil Government* (1849). Available at http://thoreau.eserver.org/civil.html.

4. Writing in 1942 "To American Friends," he wrote how, "You have given me a teacher in Thoreau, who furnished me through his essay on the 'Duty of Civil Disobedience' scientific confirmation of what I was doing in South Africa." For evidence on Thoreau's influence, see George Hendrick, "The Influence of Thoreau's 'Civil Disobedience' on Gandhi's Satyagraha," *The New England Quarterly* 29, no. 4 (December 1956): 462–471.

5. Leo Tolstoy, *A Letter to a Hindu*, introduction by M. K. Gandhi (1909), available at http://www.online-literature.com/tolstoy/2733.

6. These paragraphs draw on Judith M. Brown, "Gandhi and Civil Resistance in India, 1917–47: Key Issues," in Adam Roberts and Timothy Garton Ash, eds., *Civil Resistance & Power Politics: The Experience of Non-Violent Action from Gandhi to the Present* (Oxford: Oxford University Press, 2009), 43–57.

7. Sean Scalmer, *Gandhi in the West: The Mahatma and the Rise of Radical Protest* (Cambridge, UK: Cambridge University Press, 2011), 54, 57.

8. "To the American Negro: A Message from Mahatma Gandhi," *The Crisis*, July 1929, 225.

9. Vijay Prashad, "Black Gandhi," *Social Scientist* 37, no. 1/2 (January/February 2009): 4–7, 45.

10. Leonard A. Gordon, "Mahatma Gandhi's Dialogues with Americans," *Economic and Political Weekly* 37, no. 4 (January–February 2002): 337–352.

11. Joseph Kip Kosek, "Richard Gregg, Mohandas Gandhi, and the Strategy of Nonviolence," *The Journal of American History* 91, no. 4 (March 2005): 1318–1348. Gregg published a number of books on nonviolence. The most influential was *The Power of Non-Violence* (London: James Clarke & Co., 1960). First published in 1934.

12. Reinhold Neibuhr, *Moral Man and Immoral Society* (New York: Scribner, 1934).

13. Described in James Farmer, *Lay Bare the Arms: An Autobiography of the Civil Rights Movement* (New York: Arbor House, 1985), 106–107.

14. On Muste's conversion from Marxism to Christian Pacifism, see Chapter 9 of Ira Chernus, *American Nonviolence: The History of an Idea* (New York: Orbis, 2004). Both Gregg and Niebuhr were members of FOR, although the latter's intellectual journey led him to leave.

15. August Meierand and Elliott Rudwick, *CORE: A Study in the Civil Rights Movement, 1942–1968* (New York: Oxford University Press, 1973), 102–103.

16. Ibid., 111.

17. Krishnalal Shridharani, *War Without Violence: A Study of Gandhi's Method and Its Accomplishments* (New York: Harcourt Brace & Co., 1939). See James Farmer, *Lay Bare the Heart: An Autobiography of the Civil Rights Movement* (New York: Arbor Books, 1985), 93–95, 112–113.

18. Paula F. Pfeffer, *A. Philip Randolph. Pioneer of the Civil Rights Movement* (Baton Rouge: Louisiana State University Press, 1990).

19. Jervis Anderson, *Bayard Rustin: Troubles I've Seen* (New York: HarperCollins, 1997), 17.

20. Adam Fairclough, "The Preachers and the People: The Origins and Early Years of the Southern Christian Leadership Conference, 1955–1959," *The Journal of Southern History* 52, no. 3 (August 1986), 403–440.

21. In his history of the movement, Garrow notes the comparison to Gandhi being made by a sympathetic white lady in a letter to a newspaper. David

Garrow, *Bearing the Cross: Martin Luther King Jr. and the Southern Christian Leadership Conference, 1955–1968* (New York: W. Morrow, 1986), 28.

22. Ibid., 43. Bo Wirmark, "Nonviolent Methods and the American Civil Rights Movement 1955–1965," *Journal of Peace Research* 11, no. 2 (1974): 115–132; Akinyele Umoja, "1964: The Beginning of the End of Nonviolence in the Mississippi Freedom Movement," *Radical History Review* 85 (Winter 2003): 201–226.

23. Scalmer, *Gandhi in the West*, 180.

24. The books referred to by King were: M. K. Gandhi, *An Autobiography; or, The Story of My Experiments with Truth, translated by Mahadev Desai* (Ahmedabad: Navajivan Publishing House, 1927); Louis Fischer, *The Life of Mahatma Gandhi* (London: Jonathan Cape, 1951); Henry David Thoreau, "Civil Disobedience," 1849; Walter Rauschenbusch, *Christianity and the Social Crisis* (New York: Macmillan Press, 1908); Richard B. Gregg, *The Power of Non-Violence*; Ira Chernus, *American Nonviolence: The History of an Idea* (Maryknoll, NY: Orbis Books, 2004), 169–171. See James P. Hanigan, *Martin Luther King, Jr. and the Foundations of Nonviolence* (Lanham, MD: University Press of America, 1984), 1–18.

25. Taylor Branch, *Parting the Waters. America in the King Years, 1954–63* (New York: Touchstone, 1988), 55.

26. Martin Luther King, "Our Struggle," *Liberation*, April 1956, available at http://mlk-kpp01.stanford.edu/primarydocuments/Vol3/Apr-1956_OurStruggle.pdf.

27. Branch, *Parting the Waters*, 195.

28. Garrow, *Bearing the Cross: Martin Luther King Jr. and the Southern Christian Leadership Conference, 1955–1968*, 111. One example: Gregg had written of the nonviolent resister: "Toward his opponent he is not aggressive physically, but his mind and emotions are active, wrestling constantly with the problem of persuading the latter that he is mistaken." King wrote: "For while the nonviolent resister is passive in the sense that he is not physically aggressive toward his opponent, his mind and emotions are always active, constantly seeking to persuade his opponent that he is wrong." Martin Luther King, Jr., "Pilgrimage to Nonviolence," in *Stride Toward Freedom: The Montgomery Story* (New York: Harper & Bros., 1958), 102; Gregg, *The Power of Non-Violence*, 93.

29. Daniel Levine, *Bayard Rustin and the Civil Rights Movement* (New Brunswick: Rutgers University Press, 2000), 95.

30. Cited by Anderson, *Bayard Rustin*, 192.

31. Aldon Morris, "Black Southern Student Sit-in Movement: An Analysis of Internal Organization," *American Sociological Review* 46, no. 6 (December 1981): 744–767.

32. For a balanced assessment of the relationship between Baker and King, see Barbara Ransby, *Ella Baker and the Black Freedom Movement: A Radical*

Democratic Vision (Chapel Hill: University of North Carolina Press, 2003), 189–192.

33. Alan Fairclough, "The Preachers and the People," 424.

34. Morris, "Black Southern Student Sit-In Movement," 755.

35. Doug McAdam, "Tactical Innovation and the Pace of Insurgency," *American Sociological Review* 48, no. 6 (December 1983): 748.

36. Bayard Rustin, *Strategies for Freedom: The Changing Patterns of Black Protest* (New York: Columbia University Press, 1976), 24.

37. Aldon D. Morris, "Birmingham Confrontation Reconsidered: An Analysis of the Dynamics and Tactics of Mobilization," *American Sociological Review* 58, no. 5 (October 1993): 621–636.

38. *Letter from Birmingham Jail*, April 16, 1963, available at http://mlk-kpp01.stanford.edu/index.php/resources/article/annotated_letter_from_birmingham/

39. Rustin, *Strategies for Freedom*, 45.

40. Quoted in Branch, *Parting the Waters*, 775.

41. Martin Luther King, Jr., *Why We Can't Wait* (New York: New American Library, 1963), 104–105; Douglas McAdam, *Political Process and the Development of Black Insurgency 1930–1970* (Chicago: University of Chicago Press, 1983); David J. Garrow, *Protest at Selma: Martin Luther King, Jr. and the Voting Rights Act of 1965* (New Haven, CT: Yale University Press, 1978); Branch, *Parting the Waters*; Thomas Brooks, *Walls Come Tumbling Down: A History of the Civil Rights Movement* (Englewood Cliffs: Prentice-Hall, 1974).

24 Existential Strategy

1. Tom Hayden, *Reunion: A Memoir* (New York: Collier, 1989), 87. For a history of SDS, see Kirkpatrick Sale, *The Rise and Development of the Students for a Democratic Society* (New York: Vintage Books, 1973).

2. Todd Gitlin, *The Sixties: Years of Hope, Days of Rage* (New York: Bantam Books, 1993), 286.

3. William H. Whyte, *The Organization Man* (Pennsylvania: University of Pennsylvania Press, 2002). First published 1956.

4. David Riesman, *The Lonely Crowd* (New York: Anchor Books, 1950).

5. Erich Fromm, *The Fear of Freedom* (London: Routledge, 1942).

6. Theodore Roszak, *The Making of a Counter-Culture* (London: Faber & Faber, 1970), 10–11.

7. See Jean-Paul Sartre, *Being and Nothingness: An Essay in Phenomenological Ontology* (New York: Citadel Press, 2001), first published in 1943; *Existentialism and Humanism* (London: Methuen, 2007), first published in 1946.

8. Albert Camus, *The Plague* (New York: Vintage Books, 1961). First published in 1949.

9. The ambiguity toward Mills is evident in Irving Horowitz, *C. Wright Mills: An American Utopian* (New York: The Free Press, 1983). This is explored in John H. Summers, "The Epigone's Embrace: Irving Louis Horowitz on C. Wright Mills," *Minnesota Review* 68 (Spring 2007): 107–124.

10. C. Wright Mills, *Sociology and Pragmatism* (New York: Oxford University Press, 1969), 423. Published posthumously.

11. In *Listen Yankee* (New York: Ballantine, 1960), he defended the Cuban Revolution in the imagined words of a Cuban revolutionary.

12. Robert Dahl, *Who Governs: Democracy and Power in an American City* (New Haven, CT: Yale University Press, 1962).

13. David Baldwin, "Power Analysis and World Politics: New Trends versus Old Tendencies," *World Politics* 31, no. 2 (January 1979): 161–194. He is drawing here on Klaus Knorr, *The Power of Nations: The Political Economy of International Relations* (New York: Basic Books, 1975).

14. Robert Dahl, "The Concept of Power," *Behavioral Science* 2 (1957): 201–215.

15. Peter Bachrach and Morton S. Baratz, "Two Faces of Power," *The American Political Science Review* 56, no. 4 (December 1962): 947–952. Also see Peter Bachrach and Morton S. Baratz, "Decisions and Non-Decisions: An Analytical Framework," *The American Political Science Review* 57, no. 3 (September 1963): 632–642.

16. C. Wright Mills, *The Power Elite* (Oxford: Oxford University Press, 1956).

17. Theodore Roszak, *The Making of Counter-Culture*, 25.

18. C. Wright Mills, *The Sociological Imagination* (New York: Oxford University Press, 1959).

19. Tom Hayden and Dick Flacks, "The Port Huron Statement at 40," *The Nation*, July 18, 2002. The statement was produced as a mimeographed pamphlet in 20,000 copies and sold for 35 cents. Note the use of the word *rebels*.

20. Hayden, *Reunion: A Memoir*, 80. On the impact of Mills, see John Summers, "The Epigone's Embrace: Part II, C. Wright Mills and the New Left," *Left History* 13.2 (Fall/Winter 2008).

21. The Port Huron Manifesto can be found at http://coursesa.matrix.msu.edu/~hst306/documents/huron.html.

22. Hayden, *Reunion: A Memoir*, 75.

23. Port Huron Manifesto.

24. Richard Flacks, "Some Problems, Issues, Proposals," July 1965, reprinted in Paul Jacobs and Saul Landau, *The New Radicals* (New York: Vintage Books, 1966), 167–169.

25. Tom Hayden and Carl Wittman, "Summer Report, Newark Community Union, 1964," in Massimio Teodori, *The New Left: A Documentary History* (London: Jonathan Cape, 1970), 133.
26. Tom Hayden, "The Politics of the Movement," *Dissent*, Jan/Feb 1966, 208
27. Tom Hayden, "Up from Irrelevance," *Studies on the Left,* Spring 1965.
28. Francesca Polletta, *"Freedom Is an Endless Meeting": Democracy in American Social Movements* (Chicago: University of Chicago Press, 2002).
29. Lawrence J. Engel, "Saul D. Alinsky and the Chicago School," *The Journal of Speculative Philosophy* 16, no. 1 (2002).
30. Robert Park, "The City: Suggestions for the Investigation of Human Behavior in the City Environment," *The American Journal of Sociology* 20, no. 5 (March 1915): 577–612.
31. Engel, "Saul D. Alinsky and the Chicago School," 54–57. One of Burgess's courses taken by Alinsky was on the "pathological conditions and processes in modern society," which included "alcoholism, prostitution, poverty, vagrancy, juvenile and adult delinquency." This would be done through "inspection trips, survey assignments, and attendance at clinics."
32. He got to know Capone's number two, Frank Nitti, and through him the mob's operations, from "gin mills and whorehouses and bookie joints to the legitimate businesses they were beginning to take over." Given that they had much of the local political class and police force in their pockets, he argued that there was not much he could do with the information he gathered. As he later noted, "the only real opposition to the mob came from other gangsters, like Bugs Moran or Roger Touhy." He claimed to have learned "a hell of a lot about the uses and abuses of power from the mob, lessons that stood me in good stead later on, when I was organizing." "Empowering People, Not Elites," interview with Saul Alinsky, *Playboy Magazine*, March 1972.
33. Engel, "Saul D. Alinsky and the Chicago School," 60.
34. "Empowering People, Not Elites," interview with Saul Alinsky.
35. Saul D. Alinsky, "Community Analysis and Organization," *The American Journal of Sociology* 46, no. 6 (May 1941): 797–808.
36. Sanford D. Horwitt, *"Let Them Call Me Rebel": Saul Alinsky, His Life and Legacy* (New York: Alfred A. Knopf, 1989), 39.
37. Saul D. Alinsky, *John Lewis: An Unauthorized Biography* (New York: Vintage Books, 1970), 104, 219.
38. Saul D. Alinsky, *Reveille for Radicals* (Chicago: University of Chicago Press, 1946), 22.
39. Horwitt, *"Let Them Call Me Rebel,"* 174.
40. Charles Silberman, *Crisis in Black and White* (New York: Random House, 1964), 335.
41. "This did not work out," he recorded in a notebook. See Horwitt, *"Let Them Call Me Rebel,"* 530.

42. Nicholas von Hoffman, *Radical: A Portrait of Saul Alinsky* (New York: Nation Books, 2010), 75, 36.

43. The two rival organizations had reunited in 1955.

44. El Malcriado, no. 14, July 9, 1965, cited by Marshall Ganz, *Why David Sometimes Wins: Leadership, Organization and Strategy in the California Farm Worker Movement* (New York: Oxford University Press, 2009), 93.

45. Randy Shaw, *Beyond the Fields: Cesar Chávez, the UFW, and the Struggle for Justice in the 21st Century* (Berkeley and Los Angeles: University of California Press, 2009), 87–91.

46. Von Hoffman, *Radical*, 163.

47. Ganz, *Why David Sometimes Wins*.

48. Miriam Pawel, *The Union of Their Dreams: Power, Hope, and Struggle in Cesar Chávez's Farm Worker Movement* (New York: Bloomsbury Press, 2009).

49. Von Hoffman, *Radical*, 51–52.

50. Horwitt, *"Let Them Call Me Rebel,"* 524–526.

51. "Empowering People, Not Elites," interview with Saul Alinsky.

52. Von Hoffman, *Radical*, 69.

53. David J. Garrow, *Bearing the Cross: Martin Luther King Jr. and the Southern Christian Leadership Conference* (New York: Quill, 1999), 455.

25 Black Power and White Anger

1. Malcolm X made no strategic statement. The key themes come over in his autobiography, written with Arthur Haley, *The Autobiography of Malcolm X* (New York: Ballantine Books, 1992).

2. David Macey, *Frantz Fanon: A Biography* (New York: Picador Press, 2000).

3. Frantz Fanon, *The Wretched of the Earth* (London: Macgibbon and Kee, 1965), 28; Jean-Paul Sartre, *Anti-Semite and Jew* (New York: Schocken Books, 1995), 152, first published 1948. See Sebastian Kaempf, "Violence and Victory: Guerrilla Warfare, 'Authentic Self-Affirmation' and the Overthrow of the Colonial State," *Third World Quarterly* 30, no. 1 (2009): 129–146.

4. Preface to Fanon, *Wretched of the Earth*, 18.

5. Hannah Arendt, "Reflections on Violence," *The New York Review of Books*, February 27, 1969. An extended version appeared in *Crises of the Republic* (New York: Harcourt, 1972).

6. Paul Jacobs and Saul Landau, *The New Radicals: A Report with Documents* (New York: Random House, 1966), 25.

7. Taylor Branch, *At Canaan's Edge: America in the King Years 1965–68* (New York: Simon & Schuster, 2006), 486.

8. SNCC, "The Basis of Black Power," *New York Times*, August 5, 1966.

9. Stokely Carmichael and Charles V. Hamilton, *Black Power: The Politics of Liberation in America* (New York: Vintage Books, 1967), 12–13, 58, 66–67.

10. Garrow, *Bearing the Cross*, 488 (see chap. 23, n. 21).

11. Martin Luther King, Jr., *Chaos or Community* (London: Hodder & Stoughton, 1968), 56.

12. Bobby Seale, *Seize the Time: The Story of the Black Panther Party and Huey P. Newton* (New York: Random House, 1970), 79–81.

13. Stokely Carmichael, "A Declaration of War, February 1968," in Teodori, ed., *The New Left*, 258.

14. John D'Emilio, *Lost Prophet: The Life and Times of Bayard Rustin* (New York: The Free Press, 2003), 450–451.

15. Bayard Rustin, "From Protest to Politics," *Commentary* (February 1965).

16. Staughton Lynd, "Coalition Politics or Nonviolent Revolution?" *Liberation*, June/July 1965, 197–198.

17. Carmichael and Hamilton, *Black Power*, 72.

18. Ibid., 92–93.

19. Paul Potter, in a speech on April 17, 1965, available at http://www.sdsrebels.com/potter.htm.

20. Jeffrey Drury, "Paul Potter, 'The Incredible War,' " *Voices of Democracy* 4 (2009): 23–40. Also Sean McCann and Michael Szalay, "Introduction: Paul Potter and the Cultural Turn," *The Yale Journal of Criticism* 18, no. 2 (Fall 2005): 209–220.

21. Gitlin, *The Sixties*, 265–267 (see chap. 24, n. 2).

22. Mark Rudd, *Underground, My Life with SDS and the Weathermen* (New York: Harper Collins, 2009), 65–66.

23. Herbert Marcuse, *One-Dimensional Man* (London: Sphere Books, 1964); "Repressive Tolerance" in Robert Paul Wolff, Barrington Moore, Jr., and Herbert Marcuse, eds., *A Critique of Pure Tolerance* (Boston: Beacon Press, 1969), 95–137; *An Essay on Liberation* (London: Penguin, 1969).

24. Che Guevara, "Message to the Tricontinental," first published: Havana, April 16, 1967, available at http://www.marxists.org/archive/guevara/1967/04/16.htm.

25. Boot, *Invisible Armies*, 438 (see chap. 14, n. 22). On Snow, see 341.

26. Matt D. Childs, "An Historical Critique of the Emergence and Evolution of Ernesto Che Guevara's Foco Theory," *Journal of Latin American Studies* 27, no. 3 (October 1995): 593–624.

27. Che Guevara, *Guerrilla Warfare* (London: Penguin, 1967). See also Che Guevara, *The Bolivian Diaries* (London: Penguin, 1968).

28. Childs, "An Historical Critique," 617.

29. Paul Dosal, *Commandante Che: Guerrilla Soldier, Commander, and Strategist, 1956–1967* (University Park: Pennsylvania University Press, 2003), 313.

30. Regis Debray, *Revolution in the Revolution* (London: Pelican, 1967).

31. Ibid., 51. Jon Lee Anderson, *Che Guevara: A Revolutionary Life* (New York: Bantam Books, 1997), suggests a more positive view of the book

by Che but not of Debray. Debray eventually decided that Castro and Che were not so admirable.

32. It was originally circulated in the *Tricontinental Bimonthly* (January–February 1970). It is available at http://www.marxists.org/archive/marighella-carlos/1969/06/minimanual-urban-guerrilla/index.htm. On Marighella and his influence, see John W. Williams, "Carlos Marighella: The Father of Urban Guerrilla Warfare," *Terrorism* 12, no. 1 (1989): 1–20.

33. The episode is covered in Branch, *At Canaan's Edge*, 662–664. Henry Raymont, "Violence as a Weapon of Dissent Is Debated at Forum in 'Village,'" *New York Times*, December 17, 1967. The proceedings are found in Alexander Klein, ed., *Dissent, Power, and Confrontation* (New York: McGraw Hill, 1971).

34. Arendt, *Reflections on Violence*.

35. Eldridge Cleaver, *Soul on Fire* (New York: Dell, 1968), 108. Cited by Childs, "An Historical Critique," 198.

36. Hayden, despite his denunciations of liberal corporatism, had maintained a conversation with Kennedy, and was pictured weeping by his coffin.

37. Tom Hayden, "Two, Three, Many Columbias," *Ramparts*, June 15, 1968, 346.

38. Rudd, *Underground*, 132.

39. Ibid., 144.

40. Daniel Bell, "Columbia and the New Left," *National Affairs* 13 (1968): 100.

41. Letter of December 3, 1966. Bill Morgan, ed., *The Letters of Allen Ginsberg* (Philadelphia: Da Capo Press, 2008), 324.

42. Interview with Ginsberg, August 11, 1996, available at http://www.english.illinois.edu/maps/poets/g_l/ginsberg/interviews.htm.

43. Amy Hungerford, "Postmodern Supernaturalism: Ginsberg and the Search for a Supernatural Language," *The Yale Journal of Criticism* 18, no. 2 (2005): 269–298.

44. On the origins of the Yippies, see David Farber, *Chicago '68* (Chicago: University of Chicago Press, 1988). The name had the advantage of fitting in with hippie (which came from being "hip") and sounding like a happy cry. To give it some jokey credibility, it was turned into an acronym through reference to a youth international party.

45. Gitlin, *The Sixties*, 289.

46. Farber, *Chicago '68,* 20–21.

47. Harry Oldmeadow, "To a Buddhist Beat: Allen Ginsberg on Politics, Poetics and Spirituality," *Beyond the Divide* 2, no. 1 (Winter 1999): 6.

48. Ibid., 27. By the mid-1970s, he was looking back with a rather conventional observation: "All of our activity in the late sixties may have prolonged the Vietnam war." Because the Left refused to vote for

Humphrey, they got Nixon. He had actually voted for Humphrey. Peter Barry Chowka, "Interview with Allen Ginsberg," *New Age Journal*, April 1976, available at http://www.english.illinois.edu/maps/poets/g_l/ ginsberg/interviews.htm.

49. After it was all over, Hayden, along with seven of the more notorious leaders of the New Left, including Bobby Seale of the Black Panthers, were arrested for inciting the mayhem. Their trial rapidly turned into farce.

50. Scalmer, *Gandhi in the West*, 218 (see chap. 23, n. 7).

51. Michael Kazin, *American Dreamers: How the Left Changed a Nation* (New York: Vintage Books, 2011), 213.

52. Betty Friedan, *The Feminist Mystique* (New York: Dell, 1963).

53. Casey Hayden and Mary King, "Feminism and the Civil Rights Movement," 1965, available at http://www.wwnorton.com/college/history/archive/ resources/documents/ch34_02.htm. On Casey Hayden, see Davis W. Houck and David E. Dixon, eds., *Women and the Civil Rights Movement, 1954–1965* (Jackson: University Press of Mississippi, 2009), 135–137.

54. Jo Freeman, "The Origins of the Women's Liberation Movement," *American Journal of Sociology* 78, no. 4 (1973): 792–811; Ruth Rosen, *The World Split Open: How the Modern Women's Movement Changed America* (New York: Penguin, 2000).

55. Carol Hanish, "The Personal Is Political," in Shulamith Firestone and Anne Koedt, eds., *Notes from the Second Year: Women's Liberation*, 1970, available at http://web.archive.org/web/20080515014413/http://scholar.alexanderstreet. com/pages/viewpage.action?pageId=2259.

56. Ruth Rosen, *The World Split Open*.

57. Robert O. Self, *All in the Family: The Realignment of American Democracy since the 1960s* (New York: Hill and Wang, 2012), Chapter 3.

58. Gene Sharp, *The Politics of Nonviolent Action*, 3 vols. (Manchester, NH: Extending Horizons Books, Porter Sargent Publishers, 1973).

59. A list of 198 tactics appears in vol. 2 of Sharp, *The Politics of Nonviolent Action*. The list can be found at http://www.aeinstein.org/organizations103a. html.

60. Sheryl Gay Stolberg, "Shy U.S. Intellectual Created Playbook Used in a Revolution," *New York Times*, February 16, 2011.

61. Todd Gitlin, *Letters to a Young Activist* (New York: Basic Books, 2003), 84, 53.

26 Frames, Paradigms, Discourses, and Narratives

1. Karl Popper, *The Open Society and Its Enemies* (London: Routledge, 1947).

2. Peter L. Berger and Thomas Luckmann, *The Social Construction of Reality: A Treatise in the Sociology of Knowledge* (Garden City, NY: Anchor Books, 1966).

3. Erving Goffman, *Frame Analysis* (New York: Harper & Row, 1974), 10–11, 2–3. William James, *Principles of Psychology*, vol. 2 (New York: Cosimo, 2007). The relevant chapter first appeared in the journal *Mind*. James observed the importance of selective attention, intimate involvement, and non-contradiction by what is otherwise known, and how there can be a variety of sub-worlds, each "real after its own fashion" before, according to Goffman, copping out.

4. Peter Simonson, "The Serendipity of Merton's Communications Research," *International Journal of Public Opinion Research* 17, no. 1 (January 2005): 277–297. One side effect of this collaboration was that Merton brought C. Wright Mills (the "outstanding sociologist of his age") to join the research, but Mills struggled with the statistical analyses of his project and was eventually fired by Lazarsfeld, which helps explain his appearance in *The Sociological Imagination* under the heading of "Abstracted Empiricism," that produce details that "no matter how numerous, do not convince us having anything worth having convictions about." The viciousness of the attacks led to Mills being virtually excommunicated by mainstream sociologists. John H. Summers, "Perpetual Revelations: C. Wright Mills and Paul Lazarsfeld," *The Annals of the American Academy of Political and Social Science* 608, no. 25 (November 2006): 25–40.

5. Paul F. Lazarsfeld and Robert K. Merton, "Mass Communication, Popular Taste, and Organized Social Action," in L. Bryson, ed., *The Communication of Ideas* (New York: Harper, 1948), 95–188.

6. M. E. McCombs and D. L. Shaw, "The Agenda-setting Function of Mass Media," *Public Opinion Quarterly* 36 (1972): 176–187; Dietram A. Scheufele and David Tewksbury, "Framing, Agenda Setting, and Priming: The Evolution of the Media Effects Models," *Journal of Communication* 57 (2007): 9–20.

7. McCabe, "Agenda-setting Research: A Bibliographic Essay," *Political Communication Review* 1 (1976): 3; E. M. Rogers and J. W. Dearing, "Agenda-setting Research: Where Has It Been? Where Is It Going?" in J. A. Anderson, ed., *Communication Yearbook 11* (Newbury Park, CA: Sage, 1988), 555–594.

8. Todd Gitlin, *The Whole World Is Watching: Mass Media in the Making and Unmaking of the New Left* (Berkeley and Los Angeles, CA: University of California Press, 2003), xvi.

9. Ibid., 6.

10. J. K. Galbraith, *The Affluent Society* (London: Pelican, 1962), 16–27.

11. Sal Restivo, "The Myth of the Kuhnian Revolution," in Randall Collins, ed., *Sociological Theory* (San Francisco: Jossey-Bass, 1983), 293–305.

12. Aristides Baltas, Kostas Gavroglu, and Vassiliki Kindi, "A Discussion with Thomas S. Kuhn," in James Conant and John Haugeland, eds., *The Road Since Structure* (Chicago: University of Chicago Press, 2000), 308.

13. Thomas Kuhn, *The Structure of Scientific Revolutions*, 2nd edn. (Chicago: University of Chicago Press, 1970), 5, 16–17. For an accessible intellectual biography see Alexander Bird, "Thomas S. Kuhn (18 July 1922–17 June 1996)," *Social Studies of Science* 27, no. 3 (1997): 483–502. See also Alexander Bird, *Thomas Kuhn* (Chesham, UK: Acumen and Princeton, NJ: Princeton University Press, 2000).

14. Kuhn, *Scientific Revolutions*, 77.

15. E. Garfield, "A Different Sort of Great Books List: The 50 Twentieth-century Works Most Cited in the *Arts & Humanities Citation Index*, 1976–1983," *Current Contents* 16 (April 20, 1987): 3–7.

16. Sheldon Wolin, "Paradigms and Political Theory," in Preston King and B. C. Parekh, eds., *Politics and Experience* (Cambridge, UK: Cambridge University Press, 1968), 134–135.

17. The Wedge Project, The Center for the Renewal of Science and Culture, http://www.antievolution.org/features/wedge.pdf.

18. Intelligent Design and Evolution Awareness Center, http://www.ideacenter.org/contentmgr/showdetails.php/id/1160. To add to the mix, some of Kuhn's critics were also critical of evolutionary theory, notably Steven Fuller, the author of both *Thomas Kuhn: A Philosophical History for Our Times* (Chicago: University of Chicago Press, 2000) and *Dissent Over Descent: Intelligent Design's Challenge to Darwinism* (London: Icon Books, 2008). See also Jerry Fodor with Massimo Piattelli-Palmarini, *What Darwin Got Wrong* (New York: Farrar, Straus, and Giroux, 2010).

19. A survey of high school teachers of biology showed about one in eight U.S. high school biology teachers did present creationism or intelligent design in a positive light in the classroom, and about the same number raised it at some point for discussion, http://www.foxnews.com/story/0,2933,357181,00.html. While it might be surprising that so many biology teachers are out of tune with the dominant scientific paradigm of the time, the important point is that they are still far more in tune with this paradigm than with the general public support for creationism and/or intelligent design. A 2008 Gallup poll suggests 44 percent of Americans believe that "God created man in present form" and another 36 percent believe that God guided man's development. Only 14 percent did not think that God played any part in the process. Gallup, Evolution, Creationism, Intelligent Design, http://www.gallup.com/poll/21814/evolution-creationism-intelligent-design.aspx polling for id (2008).

20. A useful guide to these various positions, and the controversies surrounding evolution, is found on the TalkOrigins Archive (www.talkorigins.org).

21. Michel Foucault, *Power/Knowledge: Selected Interviews and Other Writings, 1972–1977*, edited by C. Gordon (Brighton: Harvester Press, 1980), 197.

22. Michel Foucault, *The Order of Things: An Archeology of the Human Science* (London: Tavistock Publications, 1970).

23. Michel Foucault, *Discipline and Punish: The Birth of the Prison* (London: Penguin, 1991).

24. Michel Foucault, "The Subject and Power," *Critical Inquiry* 8, no. 4 (Summer 1982): 777–795.

25. Julian Reid, "Life Struggles: War, Discipline, and Biopolitics in the Thought of Michel Foucault," *Social Text* 86, 24:1, Spring 2006.

26. Michel Foucault, *Society Must Be Defended*, translated by David Macey (London: Allen Lane, 2003), 49–53, 179.

27. Michel Foucault, *Language, Counter-Memory, Practice: Selected Essays and Interviews* (Oxford: Blackwell, 1977), 27.

28. Foucault, Power/Knowledge, 145.

29. In J. G. Merquior's critique, *Foucault* (London: Fontana Press, 1985), he is described as being in a French tradition of philosophical glamour, combining brilliant literary gifts with a "theorizing wantonly free of academic discipline."

30. Robert Scholes and Robert Kellogg, *The Nature of Narrative* (London: Oxford University Press, 1968).

31. Roland Barthes and Lionel Duisit, "An Introduction to the Structural Analysis of Narrative," *New Literary History* 6, no. 2 (Winter 1975): 237–272. Originally published in *Communications* 8, 1966, as "Introduction à l'analyse structurale des récits." This journal set in motion the structuralist study of narrative in 1966 with a special issue on the topic.

32. Editor's Note, *Critical Inquiry*, Autumn 1980. The volume was published as W. T. J. Mitchell, *On Narrative* (Chicago: University of Chicago Press, 1981).

33. Francesca Polletta, Pang Ching, Bobby Chen, Beth Gharrity Gardner, and Alice Motes, "The Sociology of Storytelling," *Annual Review of Sociology* 37 (2011): 109–130.

34. Mark Turner, *The Literary Mind* (New York; Oxford: Oxford University Press, 1998), 14–20.

35. William Colvin, "The Emergence of Intelligence," *Scientific American* 9, no. 4 (November 1998): 44–51.

36. Molly Patterson and Kristen Renwick Monroe, "Narrative in Political Science," *Annual Review of Political Science* 1 (June 1998): 320.

37. Jane O'Reilly, "The Housewife's Moment of Truth," *Ms.*, Spring 1972, 54. Cited by Francesca Polletta, *It Was Like a Fever: Storytelling in Protest and Politics* (Chicago: University of Chicago Press, 2006), 48–50.

38. John Arquilla and David Ronfeldt, eds., *Networks and Netwars: The Future of Terror, Crime and Militancy* (Santa Monica, CA: RAND, 2001).

39. See, for example Jay Rosen, "Press Think Basics: The Master Narrative in Journalism," September 8, 2003, available at http://journalism.nyu.edu/pubzone/weblogs/pressthink/2003/09/08/basics_master.html.

1. William Safire, "On Language: Narrative," *New York Times*, December 5, 2004. By the same token, Al Gore had been criticized during the 2000 presidential debates for telling "tall tales." The problem, as Francesca Polletta noted, was Gore lacked a gift for "persuasive storytelling," and that intellectual policy wonks were less able to make appeals to emotions. Francesca Polletta, *It Was Like a Fever: Storytelling in Protest and Politics* (see chap. 26, n. 37).

2. Frank Lutz, *Words that Work: It's Not What You Say, It's What People Hear* (New York: Hyperion, 1997), 149–157.

3. http://www.informationclearinghouse.info/article4443.htm.

4. George Lakoff, *Don't Think of an Elephant!: Know Your Values and Frame the Debate* (White River Junction, VT: Chelsea Green Publishing Company, 2004).

5. George Lakoff, *Whose Freedom? The Battle Over America's Most Important Idea* (New York: Farrar, Straus & Giroux, 2006).

6. Drew Westen, *The Political Brain* (New York: Public Affairs, 2007), 99–100, 138, 147, 346.

7. Steven Pinker, "Block That Metaphor!," *The New Republic*, October 9, 2006.

8. Lutz, *Words that Work*, 3. As with many other effective political communicators, he went back to Orwell's famous 1946 essay on "Politics and the English Language," which stressed the importance of plain English; brevity; avoiding pretentious, meaningless, and foreign words; and jargon. See http://www.orwell.ru/library/essays/politics/english/e_polit/.

9. Donald R. Kinder, "Communication and Politics in the Age of Information," in David O. Sears, Leonie Huddy, and Robert Jervis, eds., *Oxford Handbook of Political Psychology* (Oxford: Oxford University Press, 2003), 372, 374–375.

10. Norman Mailer, *Miami and the Siege of Chicago: An Informal History of the Republican and Democratic Conventions of 1968* (New York: World Publishing Company, 1968), 51.

11. Jill Lepore, "The Lie Factory: How Politics Became a Business," *The New Yorker*, September 24, 2012.

12. Joseph Napolitan, *The Election Game and How to Win It* (New York: Doubleday, 1972); Larry Sabato, *The Rise of Political Consultants: New Ways of Winning Elections* (New York: Basic Books, 1981).

13. Dennis Johnson, *No Place for Amateurs: How Political Consultants Are Reshaping American Democracy* (New York: Routledge, 2011), xiii.

14. James Thurber, "Introduction to the Study of Campaign Consultants," in James Thurber, ed., *Campaign Warriors: The Role of Political Consultants in Elections* (Washington, DC: Brookings Institution, 2000), 2.

15. Dan Nimmo, *The Political Persuaders: The Techniques of Modern Election Campaigns* (New York: Prentice Hall, 1970), 41.

16. James Perry, *The New Politics: The Expanding Technology of Political Manipulation* (London: Weidenfeld and Nicolson, 1968).

17. The origins of the ad and its impact are discussed in Robert Mann, *Daisy Petals and Mushroom Clouds: LBJ, Barry Goldwater, and the Ad That Changed American Politics* (Baton Rouge: Louisiana State University Press, 2011).

18. Joe McGinniss, *Selling of the President* (London: Penguin, 1970), 76; Kerwin Swint, *Dark Genius: The Influential Career of Legendary Political Operative and Fox News Founder Roger Ailes* (New York: Union Square Press, 2008).

19. Richard Whalen, *Catch the Falling Flag* (New York: Houghton Mifflin, 1972), 135.

20. James Boyd, "Nixon's Southern Strategy: It's All in the Charts," *New York Times*, May 17, 1970.

21. Phillips eventually came to object to the conservative politics he had helped to promote and wrote of an "Erring Republican Majority." He moved to the left, for example, Kevin Phillips, *American Theocracy: The Peril and Politics of Radical Religion, Oil, and Borrowed Money in the 21st Century* (New York: Viking, 2006).

22. Nelson Polsby, "An Emerging Republican Majority?" *National Affairs*, Fall 1969.

23. Richard M. Scammon and Ben J. Wattenberg, *The Real Majority* (New York: Coward McCann, 1970).

24. Lou Cannon, *President Reagan: The Role of a Lifetime* (New York: PublicAffairs, 2000), 21; Ewen, *PR! A Social History of Spin* (see chap. 2, n. 28), 396.

25. Perry, *The New Politics*, 16, 21–31. He employed Spencer and Roberts, who had worked for Nelson Rockefeller against Barry Goldwater in 1966, and said afterwards that he would always in the future use "professional managers."

26. William Rusher, *Making of the New Majority Party* (Lanham, MD: Sheed and Ward, 1975). Rusher was making a case for a new conservative party, but his argument worked for an insurgency within the Republican Party.

27. Kiron K. Skinner, Serhiy Kudelia, Bruce Bueno de Mesquita, and Condoleezza Rice, *The Strategy of Campaigning: Lessons from Ronald Reagan and Boris Yeltsin* (Ann Arbor: University of Michigan Press, 2007), 132–133.

28. David Domke and Kevin Coe, *The God Strategy: How Religion Became a Political Weapon in America* (Oxford: Oxford University Press, 2008), 16–17, 101.

29. John Brady, *Bad Boy: The Life and Politics of Lee Atwater* (New York: Addison-Wesley, 1996), 34–35, 70.

30. Richard Fly, "The Guerrilla Fighter in Bush's War Room," *Business Week*, June 6, 1988.

31. By the time of Atwater's death, only the first volume, *The Years of Lyndon Johnson: The Path to Power* (New York: Alfred Knopf, 1982), had been

published. Caro is now up to volume 4. In his admiration for Caro, Atwater was by no means unique among political strategists.

32. John Pitney, Jr., *The Art of Political Warfare* (Norman: University of Oklahoma Press, 2000), 12–15.

33. Mary Matalin, James Carville, and Peter Knobler, *All's Fair: Love, War and Running for President* (New York: Random House, 1995), 54.

34. Brady, *Bad Boy*, 56.

35. Matalin, Carville, and Knobler, *All's Fair*, 48.

36. Brady, *Bad Boy*, 117–118.

37. Ibid., 136.

38. Sidney Blumenthal, *Pledging Allegiance: The Last Campaign of the Cold War* (New York: Harper Collins, 1990), 307–308.

39. Eric Benson, "Dukakis's Regret," *New York Times*, June 17, 2012.

40. Sidney Blumenthal, *The Permanent Campaign: Inside the World of Elite Political Operatives* (New York: Beacon Press, 1980).

41. Matalin, Carville, and Knobler, *All's Fair*, 186, 263, 242, 208, 225.

42. The document was from Quintus Tullius Cicero to his brother Marcus, running for Consul in 64 BCE. "Campaign Tips from Cicero: The Art of Politics from the Tiber to the Potomac," commentary by James Carville, *Foreign Affairs*, May/June 2012.

43. James Carville and Paul Begala, *Buck Up, Suck Up . . . And Come Back When You Foul Up* (New York: Simon & Schuster, 2002), 50.

44. Ibid., 108, 65.

45. For a defense of negative campaigning, see Frank Rich, "Nuke 'Em," *New York Times*, June 17, 2012.

46. Kim Leslie Fridkin and Patrick J. Kenney, "Do Negative Messages Work?: The Impact of Negativity on Citizens' Evaluations of Candidates," *American Politics Research* 32 (2004): 570.

47. A complicating factor in 1992 was the independent candidacy of Ross Perot. Although his campaign was somewhat chaotic, he managed to gain almost 20 percent of the popular vote. Although he seems to have taken equally from both Bush and Clinton, on balance he hurt Bush more.

48. Domke and Coe, *The God Strategy*, 117.

49. Leading to headline: "Pat Robertson Says Feminists Want to Kill Kids, Be Witches," Ibid., 133.

50. Domke and Coe, *The God Strategy,* 29.

51. James McLeod, "The Sociodrama of Presidential Politics: Rhetoric, Ritual, and Power in the Era of Teledemocracy," *American Anthropologist*, New Series 10, no. 2 (June 1999): 359–373. Quayle was not helped by an incident in June 1992 when he erroneously corrected an elementary school student's spelling of "potato" to "potatoe."

52. David Paul Kuhn, "Obama Models Campaign on Reagan Revolt," *Politico*, July 24, 2007.

53. David Plouffe, *The Audacity to Win: The Inside Story and Lessons of Barack Obama's Historic Victory* (New York: Viking, 2009), 236–238, 378–379. For a full account of the campaign, see John Heilemann and Mark Halperin, *Game Change* (New York: Harper Collins, 2010).

54. John B. Judis and Ruy Teixeira, *The Emerging Democratic Majority* (New York: Lisa Drew, 2002).

55. Peter Slevin, "For Clinton and Obama, a Common Ideological Touchstone," *Washington Post*, March 25, 2007.

56. She was quoting *The Economist*: "Plato on the Barricades," *The Economist*, May 13–19, 1967, 14. The thesis, entitled "THERE IS ONLY THE FIGHT... An Analysis of the Alinsky Model," was circulated by largely right-wing bloggers during 2008. See http://www.gopublius.com/HCT/HillaryClintonThesis.pdf.

28 The Rise of the Management Class

1. Paul Uselding, "Management Thought and Education in America: A Centenary Appraisal," in Jeremy Atack, ed., *Business and Economic History*, Second Series 10 (Urbana: University of Illinois, 1981), 16.

2. Matthew Stewart, *The Management Myth: Why the Experts Keep Getting It Wrong* (New York: W. W. Norton, 2009), 41. See also Jill Lepore, "Not So Fast: Scientific Management Started as a Way to Work. How Did It Become a Way of Life?" *The New Yorker*, October 12, 2009.

3. Frederick W Taylor, *Principles of Scientific Management* (Digireads.com: 2008), 14. First published 1911.

4. Charles D. Wrege and Amadeo G. Perroni, "Taylor's Pig-Tale: A Historical Analysis of Frederick W. Taylor's Pig-Iron Experiments," *Academy of Management Journal* 17, no. 1 (1974): 26.

5. Jill R. Hough and Margaret A. White, "Using Stories to Create Change: The Object Lesson of Frederick Taylor's 'Pig-Tale,'" *Journal of Management* 27 (2001): 585–601.

6. Robert Kanigel, *The One Best Way: Frederick Winslow Taylor and the Enigma of Efficiency* (New York: Viking Penguin, 1999); Daniel Nelson, "Scientific Management, Systematic Management, and Labor, 1880–1915," *The Business History Review* 48, no. 4 (Winter 1974): 479–500. See chapter on Taylor in A. Tillett, T. Kempner, and G. Wills, eds., *Management Thinkers* (London: Penguin, 1970).

7. Judith A. Merkle, *Management and Ideology: The Legacy of the International Scientific Movement* (Berkeley: University of California Press, 1980), 44–45.

8. Peter Drucker, *The Concept of the Corporation*, 3rd edn. (New York: Transaction Books, 1993), 242.

9. Oscar Kraines, " Brandeis' Philosophy of Scientific Management," *The Western Political Quarterly* 13, no. 1 (March 1960): 201.

10. Kanigel, *The One Best Way*, 505.

11. V. I. Lenin, "The Immediate Tasks of the Soviet Government," *Pravda*, April 28, 1918. Available at http://www.marxists.org/archive/lenin/works/1918/mar/x03.htm.

12. Merkle, *Management and Ideology,* 132. See also Daniel A. Wren and Arthur G. Bedeian, "The Taylorization of Lenin: Rhetoric or Reality?" *International Journal of Social Economics* 31, no. 3 (2004): 287–299.

13. Mary Parker Follett, *The New State* (New York: Longmans, 1918), cited by Ellen S. O'Connor, "Integrating Follett: History, Philosophy and Management," *Journal of Management History* 6, no. 4 (2000): 181.

14. Peter Miller and Ted O'Leary, "Hierarchies and American Ideals, 1900–1940," *Academy of Management Review* 14, no. 2 (April 1989): 250–265.

15. Pauline Graham, ed., *Mary Parker Follett: Prophet of Management* (Washington, DC: Beard Books, 2003).

16. Mary Parker Follett, *The New State: Group Organization—The Solution of Popular Government* (New York: Longmans Green, 1918), 3.

17. Irving L. Janis, *Groupthink: Psychological Studies of Policy Decisions and Fiascos* (Andover, UK: Cengage Learning, 1982)

18. This is drawn from Ellen S. O'Connor, "The Politics of Management Thought: A Case Study of the Harvard Business School and the Human Relations School," *Academy of Management Review* 24, no. 1 (1999): 125–128.

19. O'Connor, "The Politics of Management Thought," 124–125.

20. Elton Mayo, *The Human Problems of an Industrial Civilization* (New York: MacMillan, 1933) and Roethlisberger and Dickson, *Management and the Worker* (Cambridge, MA: Harvard University Press, 1939); Richard Gillespie, *Manufacturing Knowledge: A History of the Hawthorne Eexperiments* (Cambridge, UK: Cambridge University Press, 1991); R. H. Franke and J. D. Kaul, "The Hawthorne Experiments: First Statistical Interpretation," *American Sociological Review* 43 (1978): 623–643; Stephen R. G. Jones, "Was There a Hawthorne Effect?" *The American Journal of Sociology* 98, no. 3 (November 1992): 451–468.

21. On Mayo's life, see Richard C. S. Trahair, *Elton Mayo: The Humanist Temper* (New York: Transaction Publishers, 1984). Of particular interest is the damning foreword by Abraham Zaleznik, who joined the human relations team at Harvard as Mayo was leaving.

22. Barbara Heyl, "The Harvard 'Pareto Circle,' " *Journal of the History of the Behavioral Sciences* 4 (1968): 316–334; Robert T. Keller, "The Harvard 'Pareto

Circle' and the Historical Development of Organization Theory," *Journal of Management* 10 (1984): 193.

23. Chester Irving Barnard, *The Functions of the Executive* (Cambridge, MA: Harvard University Press, 1938), 294–295.

24. Peter Miller and Ted O'Leary, "Hierarchies and American Ideals, 1900–1940," *Academy of Management Review* 14, no. 2 (April 1989): 250–265; William G. Scott, "Barnard on the Nature of Elitist Responsibility," *Public Administration Review* 42, no. 3 (May–June 1982): 197–201.

25. Scott, "Barnard on the Nature of Elitist Responsibility," 279.

26. Barnard, *The Functions of the Executive*, 71.

27. James Hoopes, "Managing a Riot: Chester Barnard and Social Unrest," *Management Decision* 40 (2002): 10.

29 The Business of Business

1. I have drawn particularly on Ron Chernow, *Titan: The Life of John D. Rockefeller, Sr.* (New York: Little, Brown & Co., 1998) and Daniel Yergin, *The Prize: The Epic Quest for Oil, Money & Power* (New York: The Free Press, 1992).

2. Chernow, *Titan*, 148–150.

3. Allan Nevins, *John D. Rockefeller: The Heroic Age of American Enterprise*, 2 vols. (New York: Charles Scribner's Sons, 1940).

4. Ibid., 433.

5. Richard Hofstadter, *The Age of Reform* (New York: Vintage, 1955), 216–217.

6. The book made up of her articles is still in print: Ida Tarbell, *The History of the Standard Oil Company* (New York: Buccaneer Books, 1987); Steven Weinberg, *Taking on the Trust: The Epic Battle of Ida Tarbell and John D. Rockefeller* (New York: W. W. Norton, 2008).

7. Yergin, *The Prize*, 93.

8. Ibid., 26.

9. Chernow, *Titan*, 230.

10. Steve Watts, *The People's Tycoon: Henry Ford and the American Century* (New York: Vintage Books, 2006), 16; Henry Ford, *My Life and Work* (New York: Classic Books, 2009; first published 1922).

11. Cited in Watts, *The People's Tycoon*, 190.

12. Richard Tedlow, "The Struggle for Dominance in the Automobile Market: The Early Years of Ford and General Motors," *Business and Economic History* Second Series, 17 (1988): 49–62.

13. Watts, *The People's Tycoon*, 456, 480.

14. David Farber, *Alfred P. Sloan and the Triumph of General Motors* (Chicago: University of Chicago Press, 2002), 41.

15. Alfred Sloan, *My Years with General Motors* (New York: Crown Publishing, 1990), 47, 52, 53–54.

16. Farber, *Alfred P. Sloan*, 50.
17. Sloan, *My Years with General Motors*, 71.
18. Ibid., 76. See also John MacDonald, *The Game of Business* (New York: Doubleday: 1975), Chapter 3.
19. Sloan, *My Years with General Motors*, 186–187.
20. Ibid., 195–196.
21. Sidney Fine, "The General Motors Sit-Down Strike: A Re-examination," *The American Historical Review* 70, no. 3, April 1965, 691–713.
22. Adolf Berle and Gardiner Means, *The Modern Corporation and Private Property* (New York : Harcourt, Brace and World, 1967), 46, 313.

30 Management Strategy

1. Solow had the distinction of inspiring two novels, *The Unpossessed*, by his ex-wife Tess Slesinger, and James T. Farrell's posthumously published *Sam Holman*, which has a theme of intellectual brilliance transformed into mediocrity through the political journey of the 1930s. McDonald appears as Holman's (Solow's) closest friend, a source of skepticism and conscience.
2. Amitabh Pal, interview with John Kenneth Galbraith, *The Progressive*, October 2000, available at http://www.progressive.org/mag_amitpalgalbraith.
3. Alfred Chandler, *The Visible Hand* (Harvard, MA: Belknap Press, 1977), 1
4. Galbraith, *The New Industrial State*, 2nd edn. (Princeton, NJ: Princeton University Press, 2007), 59, 42.
5. Drucker, *The Concept of the Corporation*, see Chapter 28, n. 8.
6. Ibid., Introduction.
7. Peter Drucker, *The Practice of Management* (Amsterdam: Elsevier, 1954), 3, 245–247.
8. Ibid., 11.
9. Ibid., 177. See his observations in his autobiography, Peter Drucker, *Adventures of a Bystander* (New York: Transaction Publishers, 1994).
10. This account appeared in an appendix to the book's 1983 edition, and was repeated in an introduction he wrote to a 1990 edition of Sloan's *My Years with General Motors*. It also appears in his autobiography.
11. Christopher D. McKenna, "Writing the Ghost-Writer Back In: Alfred Sloan, Alfred Chandler, John McDonald and the Intellectual Origins of Corporate Strategy," *Management & Organizational History* 1, no. 2 (May 2006): 107–126.
12. Jon McDonald and Dan Seligman, *A Ghost's Memoir: The Making of Alfred P. Sloan's My Years with General Motors* (Boston: MIT Press, 2003), 16.

13. The lawyers were worried about references to Sloan's early plan to take on Ford. A phrase in the original plan, stating that the company was not after a monopoly, might concede the point that a monopoly was an option.

14. Edith Penrose, *The Theory of the Growth of the Firm* (New York: Oxford University Press, 1959). In 1995, she described Chandler's "analytical structure congruent with my own" (Foreword to the third edition). John Kay, *Foundations of Corporate Success: How Business Strategies Add Value* (Oxford: Oxford University Press, 1993) stresses Penrose's foundational role, 335.

15. Alfed Chandler, "Introduction," in 1990 edition of *Strategy and Structure* (Cambridge, MA: MIT Press, 1990), v. In 1956, when he had first published on the topic, Chandler had described as long-range policy what he now called strategy.

16. Chandler, "Introduction," *Strategy and Structure*, 13.

17. Chandler saw other examples of the same theme, for example with DuPont. Alfred D. Chandler and Stephen Salsbury, *Pierre S. du Pont and the Making of the Modern Corporation* (New York: Harper & Row, 1971).

18. Chandler, *Strategy and Structure*, 309. Robert F. Freeland, "The Myth of the M-Form? Governance, Consent, and Organizational Change," *The American Journal of Sociology* 102 (1996): 483–526; Robert F. Freeland, "When Organizational Messiness Works," *Harvard Business Review* 80 (May 2002): 24–25.

19. Freeland, "The Myth of the M-Form," 516.

20. Neil Fligstein, "The Spread of the Multidivisional Form Among Large Firms, 1919–1979," *American Sociological Review* 50 (1985): 380.

21. McKenna, "Writing the Ghost-Writer Back In." Other large firms studied by Chandler, such as IBM and AT&T, would also have discouraged too much exploration of the impact of antitrust legislation on corporate structure.

22. Edward D. Berkowitz and Kim McQuaid, *Creating the Welfare State: The Political Economy of Twentieth Century Reform* (Lawrence, KS: Praeger, 1992), 233–234. Cited by Richard R. John, "Elaborations, Revisions, Dissents: Alfred D. Chandler, Jr.'s, 'The Visible Hand' after Twenty Years," *The Business History Review* 71, no. 2 (Summer 1997): 190. Sanford M. Jacoby, *Employing Bureaucracy: Managers, Unions, and the Transformation of Work in American Industry, 1900–1945* (New York: Columbia University Press, 1985), 8. John, "Elaborations, Revisions, Dissents," 190.

23. Louis Galambos, "What Makes Us Think We Can Put Business Back into American History?" *Business and Economic History* 21 (1992): 1–11.

24. John Micklethwait and Adrian Wooldridge, *The Witch Doctors: Making Sense of the Management Gurus* (New York: Random House, 1968), 106.

25. See foreword to the 1986 edition of *Managing for Results*.

26. Stewart, *The Management Myth*, see Chapter 28, n. 2, 153.

27. Walter Kiechel III, *The Lords of Strategy: The Secret Intellectual History of the New Corporate World* (Boston: The Harvard Business Press, 2010), xi–xii, 4.

28. Kenneth Andrews, *The Concept of Corporate Strategy* (Homewood, IL: R. D. Irwin, 1971), 29.

29. Henry Mitzberg, Bruce Ahlstrand, and Joseph Lampel, *Strategy Safari: The Complete Guide Through the Wilds of Strategic Management* (New York: The Free Press, 1998). See also the companion volume of readings, *Strategy Bites Back: It Is Far More, and Less, Than You Ever Imagined* (New York: Prentice Hall, 2005).

30. "The Guru: Igor Ansoff," *The Economist*, July 18, 2008; Igor Ansoff, *Corporate Strategy: An Analytic Approach to Business Policy for Growth and Expansion* (New York: McGraw-Hill, 1965).

31. Igor Ansoff, *Corporate Strategy* (London: McGraw-Hill, 1965), 120.

32. Stewart, *The Management Myth*, 157–158.

33. Kiechel, *The Lords of Strategy*, 26–27.

34. John A. Byrne, *The Whiz Kids: Ten Founding Fathers of American Business— And the Legacy They Left Us* (New York: Doubleday, 1993).

35. Samuel Huntington, *The Common Defense: Strategic Programs in National Politics* (New York: Columbia University Press, 1961).

36. Mintzberg et al., *Strategy Safari*, 65.

37. Friedrich Hayek, "The Use of Knowledge in Society," *American Economic Review* 35, no. 4 (1945): 519–530.

38. Aaron Wildavsky, "Does Planning Work?" *The National Interest*, Summer 1971, No. 24, 101. See also his "If Planning Is Everything Maybe It's Nothing," *Policy Sciences* 4 (1973): 127–153.

39. Cited in Mitzberg et al., *Strategy Safari*, 65.

40. Jack Welch, with John Byrne, *Jack: Straight from the Gut* (New York: Grand Central Publishing, 2003), 448. The letter was by Kevin Peppard. It appeared in *Fortune Magazine*, November 30, 1981, p. 17. See also Chapter 3 of Thomas O'Boyle, *At Any Cost: Jack Welch, General Electric, and the Pursuit of Profit* (New York: Vintage, 1999).

41. Henry Mintzberg, *The Rise and Fall of Strategic Planning* (London: Prentice-Hall, 1994).

42. Igor Ansoff, "Critique of Henry Mintzberg's 'The Design School: Reconsidering the Basic Premises of Strategic Management,'" *Strategic Management Journal* 12, no. 6 (September 1991): 449–461.

31 Business as War

1. Albert Madansky, "Is War a Business Paradigm? A Literature Review," *The Journal of Private Equity* 8 (Summer 2005): 7–12.

2. Wess Roberts, *Leadership Secrets of Attila the Hun* (New York: Grand Central Publishing, 1989).

3. Dennis Laurie, *From Battlefield to Boardroom: Winning Management Strategies in Today's Global Business* (New York: Palgrave, 2001), 235.

4. Douglas Ramsey, *Corporate Warriors* (New York: Houghton Mifflin, 1987).

5. Aric Rindfleisch, "Marketing as Warfare: Reassessing a Dominant Metaphor—Questioning Military Metaphors' Centrality in Marketing Parlance," *Business Horizons*, September–October, 1996. For a skeptical look, although with a concluding endorsement of Sun Tzu, see John Kay, "Managers from Mars," *Financial Times*, August 4, 1999.

6. On BCG see pp. 519.

7. Bruce Henderson, *Henderson on Corporate Strategy* (New York: HarperCollins, 1979), 9–10, 27.

8. Philip Kotler and Ravi Singh, "Marketing Warfare in the 1980s," *Journal of Business Strategy* (Winter 1981): 30–41.The start of this line of work has been attributed to Alfred R. Oxenfeldt and William L. Moore, "Customer or Competitor: Which Guideline for Marketing?" *Management Review* (August 1978): 43–38.

9. Al Ries and Jack Trout, *Marketing Warfare* (New York: Plume, 1986); Robert Duro and Bjorn Sandstrom, *The Basic Principles of Marketing Warfare* (Chichester, UK: John Wiley & Sons, Inc., 1987); Gerald A. Michaelson, *Winning the Marketing War* (Lanham, MD: Abt Books, 1987).

10. In addition to editions of *The Art of War* and other Chinese masters, see, for example, the titles collected by Madansky, including Foo Check Teck and Peter Hugh Grinyer, *Organizing Strategy: Sun Tzu Business Warcraft* (Butterworth: Heinemann Asia, 1994); Donald Krause, *The Art of War for Executives* (New York: Berkley Publishing Group, 1995); Gary Gagliardi, *The Art of War Plus The Art of Sales* (Shoreline, WA: Clearbridge Publishing, 1999); Gerald A Michaelson, *Sun Tzu: The Art of War for Managers: 50 Strategic Rules* (Avon, MA: Adams Media Corporation, 2001).

11. Episodes: "Big Girls Don't Cry"; "He Is Risen." See http://www.hbo.com/the-sopranos/episodes/index.html.

12. Richard Greene and Peter Vernezze, eds., *The Sopranos and Philosophy: I Kill Therefore I Am* (Chicago: Open Court, 2004). In one episode, one of Soprano's lieutenants, Paulie 'Walnuts' Gualtieri, reports that "Sun-Tuh-Zoo" says: "A good leader is benevolent and unconcerned with fame." He explains that "Sun-Tuh-Zoo" is the "Chinese Prince Machiavelli," at which point his colleague Silvio Dante corrects him: "Tzu, Tzu! Sun Tzu, you fucking ass-kiss!" In the next episode, Paulie, trying to reestablish himself after a spell in prison, is listening to a tape of Sun Tzu while driving to his aunt's neighborhood. At an appropriate moment, as the tape refers to catching an enemy by surprise, he comes across two brothers pruning trees in an area which they have just taken from one of Gualtieri's friends. His tactics are similar to those used by the brothers: intimidation based on brute force. When they refuse to give the area back, Gualtieri hits one brother

over the head with a shovel causing him to let go of the rope holding the other brother in the tree, who then plunges down. Not really Sun Tzu! (Series 5).

13. Marc R. McNeilly, *Sun Tzu and the Art of Business* (New York: Oxford University Press, 2000).

14. Khoo Kheng-Ho, *Applying Sun Tzu's Art of War in Managing Your Marriage* (Malaysia: Pelanduk, 2002).

15. William Scott Wilson, *The Lone Samurai: The Life of Miyamoto Musashi* (New York: Kodansha International, 2004), 220; Miyamoto Musashi, *The Book of Five Rings: A Classic Text on the Japanese Way of the Sword, translated by Thomas Cleary* (Boston: Shambhala Publications, 2005).

16. Thomas A. Green, ed., *Martial Arts of the World: An Encyclopedia* (Santa Barbara, CA: ABC-CLIO, 2001).

17. George Stalk, Jr., "Time—The Next Source of Competitive Advantage," *Harvard Business Review* 1 (August 1988): 41–51; George Stalk and Tom Hout, *Competing Against Time: How Time-Based Competition Is Reshaping Global Markets* (New York: The Free Press, 1990).

18. The two are also brought together in Chet Richards, *Certain to Win: The Strategy of John Boyd as Applied to Business* (Philadelphia: Xlibris, 2004).

19. A later book spoke about crushing more than outsmarting competitors, by such means as unleashing "massive and overwhelming force," threatening their "profit sanctuaries," and enticing them into retreat. This was not for the soft-hearted. "The common theme" in his ideas, he later observed, was that they were "about taking advantage to the point where competitors are left astounded by what's happened." George Stalk and Rob Lachenauer Hardball, *Are You Playing to Play or Playing to Win?* (Cambridge, MA: Harvard Business School Press, 2004); Jennifer Reingold, "The 10 Lives of George Stalk," Fast Company.com, December 19, 2007, http://www.fastcompany.com/magazine/91/open_stalk.html.

32 The Rise of Economics

1. Mirowski, *Machine Dreams*, 12–17 (see chap. 12, n. 11). The term *Cyborg* only came into use in the 1960s to refer to humans with artificial, technological enhancements.

2. Duncan Luce and Howard Raiffa, *Games and Decisions: Introduction and Critical Survey* (New York: John Wiley & Sons, 1957), 10.

3. Ibid., 18.

4. Sylvia Nasar, *A Beautiful Mind* (New York: Simon & Schuster, 1988).

5. John F. Nash, Jr., *Essays on Game Theory*, with an introduction by K. Binmore (Cheltenham, UK: Edward Elgar, 1996).

6. Roger B. Myerson, "Nash Equilibrium and the History of Economic Theory," *Journal of Economic Literature* 37 (1999): 1067.

7. Mirowski, *Machine Dreams*, 369.

8. Richard Zeckhauser, "Distinguished Fellow: Reflections on Thomas Schelling," *The Journal of Economic Perspectives* 3, no. 2 (Spring 1989): 159.

9. Milton Friedman, *Price Theory: A Provisional Text*, revised edn. (Chicago: Aldine, 1966), 37. (cited by Mirowski)

10. Cited in Rakesh Khurana, *From Higher Aims to Higher Hands: The Social Transformation of American Business Schools and the Unfulfilled Promise of Management as a Profession* (Princeton, NJ: Princeton University Press, 2007), 239–240.

11. Ibid., 292, 307.

12. Cited by Ibid., 272.

13. Ibid., 253–254. 275, 268–269, 331.

14. Pankat Ghemawat, "Competition and Business Strategy in Historical Perspective," *The Business History Review* 76, no. 1 (Spring 2002): 37–74, 44–45.

15. Interview with Seymour Tilles, October 24, 1996.

16. John A. Seeger, "Reversing the Images of BCG's Growth/Share Matrix," *Strategic Management Journal* 5 (1984): 93–97.

17. Herbert A. Simon. "From Substantive to Procedural Rationality," in Spiro J. Latsis, ed., *Method and Appraisal in Economics* (Cambridge, UK: Cambridge University Press, 1976), 140.

18. Michael Porter, *Competitive Strategy Techniques for Analyzing Industries and Competitors* (New York: The Free Press, 1980).

19. Porter, *Competitive Strategy*, 3.

20. Mitzberg et al., *Strategy Safari*, 113 (see chap. 30, n. 29).

21. Porter, *Competitive Strategy*, 53, 86.

22. Porter, *Competitive Advantage*.

23. Michael Porter, Nicholas Argyres, and Anita M. McGahan, "An Interview with Michael Porter," *The Academy of Management Executive (1993–2005)* 16, no. 2 (May 2002): 43–52.

24. Vance H. Fried and Benjamin M. Oviatt, "Michael Porter's Missing Chapter: The Risk of Antitrust Violations," *Academy of Management Executive* 3, no. 1 (1989): 49–56.

25. Adam J. Brandenburger and Barry J. Nalebuff, *Co-Opetition* (New York: Doubleday, 1996).

26. As demonstrated by Wikipedia: http://en.wikipedia.org/wiki/Coopetition.

27. Stewart, *The Management Myth*, 214–215.

33 Red Queens and Blue Oceans

1. Kathleen Eisenhardt, "Agency Theory: An Assessment and Review," *Academy of Management Review* 14, no. 1 (1989): 57–74.

2. Justin Fox, *The Myth of the Rational Market: A History of Risk, Reward, and Delusion on Wall Street* (New York: Harper, 2009), 159–162.

3. Michael C. Jensen and William H. Meckling, "Theory of the Firm: Managerial Behavior, Agency Costs and Ownership Structure," *Journal of Financial Economics* 3 (1976): 302–360.

4. Michael C. Jensen, "Organization Theory and Methodology," *The Accounting Review* 58, no. 2 (April 1983): 319–339.

5. Jensen, "Takeovers: Folklore and Science," *Harvard Business Review* (November–December 1984), 109–121.

6. Cited by Fox, *The Myth of the Rational Market*, 274.

7. Paul M. Hirsch, Ray Friedman, and Mitchell P. Koza, "Collaboration or Paradigm Shift?: Caveat Emptor and the Risk of Romance with Economic Models for Strategy and Policy Research," *Organization Science* 1, no. 1 (1990): 87–97.

8. Robert Hayes and William J. Abernathy, "Managing Our Way to Economic Decline," *Harvard Business Review* (July 1980), 67–77.

9. Franklin Fisher, "Games Economists Play: A Noncooperative View," *RAND Journal of Economics* 20, no. 1 (Spring 1989): 113.

10. Carl Shapiro, "The Theory of Business Strategy," *RAND Journal of Economics* 20, no. 1 (Spring 1989): 125–137.

11. Richard P. Rumelt, Dan Schendel, and David J. Teece, "Strategic Management and Economics," *Strategic Management Journal* 12 (Winter 1991): 5–29.

12. Garth Saloner, "Modeling, Game Theory, and Strategic Management," *Strategic Management Journal* 12 (Winter 1991): 119–136. See also Colin F. Camerer, "Does Strategy Research Need Game Theory?" *Strategic Management Journal* 12 (Winter 1991): 137–152.

13. Richard L. Daft and Arie Y. Lewin, "Can Organization Studies Begin to Break Out of the Normal Science Straitjacket? An Editorial Essay," *Organization Science* 1, no. 1 (1990): 1–9; Richard A. Bettis, "Strategic Management and the Straightjacket: An Editorial Essay," *Organization Science* 2, no. 3 (August 1991): 315–319.

14. Sumantra Ghoshal, "Bad Management Theories Are Destroying Good Management Practices," *Academy of Management Learning and Education* 4, no. 1 (2005): 85.

15. Timothy Clark and Graeme Salaman, "Telling Tales: Management Gurus' Narratives and the Construction of Managerial Identity," *Journal of Management Studies* 3, no. 2 (1998): 157. See also T. Clark and G. Salaman, "The Management Guru as Organizational Witchdoctor," *Organization* 3, no. 1 (1996): 85–107.

16. James Champy, *Reengineering Management: The Mandate for New Leadership* (London: HarperBusiness, 1995), 7.

17. Michael Hammer and James Champy, *Reengineering the Corporation: A Manifesto for Business Revolution* (London: HarperBusiness, 1993), 49.

18. Peter Case, "Remember Re-Engineering? The Rhetorical Appeal of a Managerial Salvation Device," *Journal of Management Studies* 35, no. 4 (July 1991): 419–441.
19. Michael Hammer, "Reengineering Work: Don't Automate, Obliterate," *Harvard Business Review*, July/August 1990, 104.
20. Thomas Davenport and James Short, "The New Industrial Engineering: Information Technology and Business Process Redesign," *Sloan Management Review,* Summer 1990; Keith Grint, "Reengineering History: Social Resonances and Business Process Reengineering," *Organization* 1, no. 1 (1994): 179–201; Keith Grint and P. Case, "The Violent Rhetoric of Re-Engineering: Management Consultancy on the Offensive," *Journal of Management Studies* 6, no. 5 (1998): 557–577.
21. Bradley G. Jackson, "Re-Engineering the Sense of Self: The Manager and the Management Guru," *Journal of Management Studies* 33, no. 5 (September 1996): 571–590.
22. Hammer and Champy, *Reengineering the Corporation: A Manifesto for Business Revolution.* See also John Micklethwait and Adrian Wooldridge, *The Witch Doctors: Making Sense of the Management Gurus.*
23. Iain L. Mangham, "Managing as a Performing Art," *British Journal of Management* 1 (1990): 105–115.
24. Michael Hammer and Steven Stanton, *The Reengineering Revolution: The Handbook* (London: HarperCollins, 1995), 30, 52.
25. Michael Hammer, *Beyond Reengineering: How the Process-Centered Organization Is Changing Our Work and Our Lives* (London: HarperCollins, 1996), 321.
26. Champy, *Reengineering Management*, 204.
27. Ibid., 122.
28. Willy Stern, "Did Dirty Tricks Create a Best-Seller?" *Business Week*, August 7, 1995; Micklethwait and Wooldridge, *The Witch Doctors*, 23–25; Kiechel, *The Lords of Strategy*, 24 (see chap. 30, n. 27). Timothy Clark and David Greatbatch, "Management Fashion as Image-Spectacle: The Production of Best-Selling Management Books," *Management Communication Quarterly* 17, no. 3 (February 2004): 396–424.
29. Michael Porter, "What Is Strategy?" *Harvard Business Review*, November–December 1996, 60–78.
30. Leigh Van Valen, "A New Evolutionary Law," *Evolutionary Theory* I (1973): 20.
31. Ghemawat, "Competition and Business Strategy in Historical Perspective," 64.
32. Chan W. Kim and Renee Mauborgne, *Blue Ocean Strategy: How to Create Uncontested Market Space* (Boston: Harvard Business School Press, 2005), 6–7.
33. Ibid., 209–221.
34. Chan W. Kim and Renee Mauborgne, "How Strategy Shapes Structure," *Harvard Business Review* (September 2009), 73–80.

35. Eric D. Beinhocker, "Strategy at the Edge of Chaos," *McKinsey Quarterly* (Winter 1997), 25–39.

34 The Sociological Challenge

1. James A. C. Brown, *The Social Psychology of Industry* (London: Penguin Books, 1954).

2. Douglas McGregor. *The Human Side of Enterprise* (New York: McGraw-Hill, 1960). See also Gary Heil, Warren Bennis, and Deborah C. Stephens, *Douglas McGregor Revisited: Managing the Human Side of the Enterprise* (New York: Wiley, 2000).

3. Cited in David Jacobs, "Book Review Essay: Douglas McGregor? The Human Side of Enterprise in Peril," *Academy of Management Review* 29, no. 2 (2004): 293–311.

4. These are discussed below, p. 592.

5. Karl Weick, *The Social Psychology of Organizing* (New York: McGraw Hill, 1979), 91.

6. Tom Peters, Bob Waterman, and Julian Phillips, "Structure Is Not Organization," *Business Horizons,* June 1980. Peters's account comes from Tom Peters, "A Brief History of the 7-S ('McKinsey 7-S') Model," January 2011, available at http://www.tompeters.com/dispatches/012016.php.

7. Richard T. Pascale and Anthony Athos, *The Art of Japanese Management: Applications for American Executives* (New York: Simon & Schuster, 1981).

8. Kenichi Ohmae, *The Mind of the Strategist: The Art of Japanese Business* (New York: McGraw-Hill, 1982).

9. It was originally going to be called *The Secrets of Excellence*, but McKinsey's were worried that would sound like they were giving away the secrets of clients.

10. Tom Peters and Robert Waterman, *In Search of Excellence: Lessons from America's Best Run Companies* (New York: HarperCollins, 1982).

11. Tom Peters, "Tom Peters's True Confessions," *Fast Company.com*, November 30, 2001,http://www.fastcompany.com/magazine/53/peters.html. On Tom Peters, see Stuart Crainer, *The Tom Peters Phenomenon: Corporate Man to Corporate Skink* (Oxford: Capstone, 1997).

12. Peters and Waterman, *In Search of Excellence*, 29.

13. D. Colville, Robert H. Waterman, and Karl E. Weick, "Organization and the Search for Excellence: Making Sense of the Times in Theory and Practice," *Organization* 6, no. 1 (February 1999): 129–148.

14. Daniel Carroll, "A Disappointing Search for Excellence," *Harvard Business Review*, November–December 1983, 78–88.

15. "Oops. Who's Excellent Now?" *Business Week,* November 5, 1984. The book did note that of its "excellent companies most probably will not stay

buoyant forever" (pp. 109–10), and a number did actually show considerable endurance.

16. Tom Peters, *Liberation Management: Necessary Disorganization for the Nanosecond Nineties* (New York: A. A. Knopf, 1992).

17. Tom Peters, *Re-Imagine! Business Excellence in a Disruptive Age* (New York: DK Publishing, 2003), 203.

18. "Guru: Tom Peters," *The Economist*, March 5, 2009. Tom Peters with N. Austin, *A Passion for Excellence: The Leadership Difference* (London: Collins, 1985); *Thriving on Chaos: Handbook for a Management Revolution* (New York: Alfred A. Knopf, 1987).

19. Stewart, *The Management Myth*, 234.

20. "Peter Drucker, the Man Who Changed the World," *Business Review Weekly*, September 15, 1997, 49.

21. C. K. Prahalad and G. Hamel, "Strategic Intent," *Harvard Business Review* (May–June 1989), 63–76.

22. C. K. Prahalad and G. Hamel, "The Core Competence of the Corporation," *Harvard Business Review* (May–June 1990), 79–91.

23. C. K. Prahalad and G. Hamel, "Strategy as a Field of Study: Why Search for a New Paradigm?" *Strategic Management Journal* 15, issue supplement S2 (Summer 1994): 5–16.

24. Gary Hamel, "Strategy as Revolution," *Harvard Business Review* (July–August 1996), 69.

25. Cited in Ibid., 78.

26. Gary Hamel, *Leading the Revolution: How to Thrive in Turbulent Times by Making Innovation a Way of Life* (Cambridge, MA: Harvard Business School Press, 2000).

27. Mintzberg somewhat gleefully includes an embarrassing interview conducted by Hamel with Enron Chairman Kenneth Lay in *Strategy Bites Back.*

28. Hamel was not the only author to identify Enron as the model for the future. *The Financial Times* observed on December 4, 2001: "The books of various gurus have singled out the company as paragon of good management, for LEADING THE REVOLUTION (Gary Hamel, 2000), practising CREATIVE DESTRUCTION (Richard Foster and Sarah Kaplan, 2001), devising STRATEGY THROUGH SIMPLE RULES (Kathy Eisenhardt and Donald Sull, 2001), winning the WAR FOR TALENT (Ed Michaels, 1998) and Navigating the ROAD TO THE NEXT ECONOMY (James Critin, scheduled for publication in February 2002—and now, presumably being rewritten)."

29. Gary Hamel, *The Future of Management* (Cambridge, MA: Harvard Business School Press, 2007), 14.

30. Ibid., 62.

31. Gary Hamel, *What Matters Now: How to Win in a World of Relentless Change, Ferocious Competition, and Unstoppable Innovation* (San Francisco: Jossey-Bass, 2012).

32. Scott Adams, *The Dilbert Principle* (New York: HarperCollins, 1996), 153, 296. The strips which describe strategy are available on http://www.dilbert.com/strips/.

35 Deliberate or Emergent

1. Henry Mintzberg and James A. Waters, "Of Strategies, Deliberate and Emergent," *Strategic Management Journal* 6, no. 3 (July–September 1985): 257–272.
2. Ed Catmull, "How Pixar Fosters Collective Creativity," *Harvard Business Review*, September 2008.
3. Henry Mintzberg, "Rebuilding Companies as Communities," *Harvard Business Review*, July–August 2009, 140–143.
4. Peter Senge, *The Fifth Discipline: The Art and Practice of the Learning Organization* (New York: Doubleday, 1990).
5. Daniel Quinn Mills and Bruce Friesen, "The Learning Organization," *European Management Journal* 10, no. 2 (June 1992): 146–156.
6. Charles Handy, "Managing the Dream," in S. Chawla and J. Renesch, eds., *Learning Organizations* (Portland, OR: Productivity Press, 1995), 46, cited in Michaela Driver, "The Learning Organization: Foucauldian Gloom or Utopian Sunshine?" *Human Relations* 55 (2002): 33–53.
7. Robert C. H. Chia and Robin Holt, *Strategy Without Design: The Silent Efficacy of Indirect Action* (Cambridge: Cambridge University Press, 2009), 203.
8. Although Liddell Hart (as the prophet of the indirect approach) and Luttwak (as the celebrator of strategy as paradox) were called in aid, and both certainly argued against direct frontal approaches, neither suggested that somehow military success could be achieved by purposeless activity, seeing how the individuals in an army coped with the predicaments in which they found themselves (which without any direction would probably have been to surrender or desert). Indirect strategies in war required imaginative leadership and an ability to consider the world as it might appear to the enemy before embarking on maneuvers that could carry high risks.
9. Chia and Holt, *Strategy Without Design*, xi.
10. Jeffrey Pfeffer, *Managing with Power: Politics and Influence in Organizations* (Boston: Harvard Business School Press, 1992). His definition of power was "the potential ability to influence behavior, to change the course of events, to overcome resistance, and to get people to do things they would not otherwise do," 30.
11. Jeffrey Pfeffer, *Power: Why Some People Have It—and Others Don't* (New York: HarperCollins, 2010), 11. The best and certainly most amusing guide to organizational politics is F. M. Cornford, *Microcosmographia Academica: Being a Guide for the Young Academic Politician* (London: Bowes & Bowes, 1908).

12. Helen Armstrong, "The Learning Organization: Changed Means to an Unchanged End," *Organization* 7, no. 2 (2000): 355–361.

13. John Coopey, "The Learning Organization, Power, Politics and Ideology," *Management Learning* 26, no. 2 (1995): 193–214.

14. David Knights and Glenn Morgan, "Corporate Strategy, Organizations, and Subjectivity: A Critique," *Organization Studies* 12, no. 2 (1991): 251.

15. Stewart Clegg, Chris Carter, and Martin Kornberger, "Get Up, I Feel Like Being a Strategy Machine," *European Management Review* 1, no. 1 (2004): 21–28.

16. Stephen Cummings and David Wilson, eds., *Images of Strategy* (Oxford: Blackwell, 2003), 3. Their proposal: "A good strategy, whether explicit or implicit, is one that both orients a company and animates it," 2.

17. Peter Franklin, "Thinking of Strategy in a Postmodern Way: Towards an Agreed Paradigm," Parts 1 and 2, *Strategic Change* 7 (September–October 1998), 313–332 and (December 1998), 437–448.

18. Donald Hambrick and James Frederickson, "Are You Sure You Have a Strategy?" *Academy of Management Executive* 15, no. 4 (November 2001): 49.

19. John Kay, *The Hare & The Tortoise: An Informal Guide to Business Strategy* (London: The Erasmus Press, 2006), 31.

20. "Instant Coffee as Management Theory," *Economist* 25 (January 1997): 57.

21. Eric Abrahamson, "Management Fashion," *Academy of Management Review* 21, no. 1 (1996): 254–285.

22. Jane Whitney Gibson and Dana V. Tesone, "Management Fads: Emergence, Evolution, and Implications for Managers," *The Academy of Management Executive* 15, no. 4 (2001): 122–133.

23. Dilbert had an example: After the executive was told that he could gauge his success by the number of repeat customers, he proudly reported that "virtually every customer gets another unit within three months of buying the first one!" When asked what happened if he did not "count warranty replacements," he replied, "Ooh then we don't look so good." Adams, *The Dilbert Principle*, 158.

24. R. S. Kaplan and D. P. Norton, "The Balanced Scorecard: Measures that Drive Performance," *Harvard Business Review* 70 (Jan–Feb 1992): 71–79, and "Putting the Balanced Scorecard to Work," *Harvard Business Review* 71 (Sep–Oct 1993): 134–147. Stephen Bungay, *The Art of Action: How Leaders Close the Gaps Between Plans, Actions and Results* (London: Nicholas Brealey, 2011), 207–214.

25. Paula Phillips Carson, Patricia A. Lanier, Kerry David Carson, and Brandi N. Guidry, "Clearing a Path Through the Management Fashion Jungle: Some Preliminary Trailblazing," *The Academy of Management Journal* 43, no. 6 (December 2000): 1143–1158.

26. Barry M. Staw and Lisa D. Epstein, " What Bandwagons Bring: Effects of Popular Management Techniques on Corporate Performance, Reputation,

and CEO Pay," *Administrative Science Quarterly* 45, no. 3 (September 2000): 523–556.

27. Keith Grint, "Reengineering History," 193 (see chap. 33, n. 20).

28. Guillermo Armando Ronda-Pupo and Luis Angel Guerras-Martin, "Dynamics of the Evolution of the Strategy Concept 1992–2008: A Co-Word Analysis," *Strategic Management Journal* 33 (2011): 162–188. Their consensus definition: "the dynamics of the firm's relations with its environment for which the necessary actions are taken to achieve its goals and/or to increase performance by means of the rational use of resources." This has yet to catch on.

29. Damon Golskorkhi, Linda Rouleau, David Seidl, and Erro Vaara, eds., "Introduction: What Is Strategy as Practice?" *Cambridge Handbook of Strategy as Practice* (Cambridge, UK: Cambridge University Press, 2010), 13.

30. Paula Jarzabkowski, Julia Balogun, and David See, "Strategizing: The Challenge of a Practice Perspective," *Human Relations* 60, no. 5 (2007): 5–27. To be fair, the word had been around since at least the 1970s.

31. Richard Whittington, "Completing the Practice Turn in Strategy Research," *Organization Studies* 27, no. 5 (May 2006): 613–634. (Note the attractions of alliteration.)

32. Ian I. Mitroff and Ralph H. Kilmann, "Stories Managers Tell: A New Tool for Organizational Problem Solving," *Management Review* 64, no. 7 (July 1975): 18–28; Gordon Shaw, Robert Brown, and Philip Bromiley, "Strategic Stories: How 3M Is Rewriting Business Planning," *Harvard Business Review* (May–June 1998), 41–48.

33. Jay A. Conger, "The Necessary Art of Persuasion," *Harvard Business Review* (May–June 1998), 85–95.

34. Lucy Kellaway, *Sense and Nonsense in the Office* (London: Financial Times: Prentice Hall, 2000), 19.

35. Karl E. Weick, *Sensemaking in Organizations* (Thousand Oaks, CA: Sage, 1995), 129.

36. Valérie-Inès de la Ville and Elèonore Mounand, "A Narrative Approach to Strategy as Practice: Strategy Making from Texts and Narratives," in Golskorkhi, Rouleau, Seidl, and Vaara, eds., *Cambridge Handbook of Strategy as Practice*, 13.

37. David M. Boje, "Stories of the Storytelling Organization: A Postmodern Analysis of Disney as 'Tamara-Land,'" *Academy of Management Journal* 38, no. 4 (August 1995): 997–1035.

38. Karl E. Weick, *Making Sense of the Organization* (Oxford: Blackwell, 2001), 344–345. It appears in a number of versions in his work, starting in 1982.

39. Mintzberg et al., *Strategy Safari*, 160 (see chap. 30, n. 29).

40. This led to accusations of plagiarism. Thomas Basbøll and Henrik Graham, "Substitutes for Strategy Research: Notes on the Source of Karl Weick's

Anecdote of the Young Lieutenant and the Map of the Pyrenees," *Ephemera: Theory & Politics in Organization* 6, no. 2 (2006): 194–204.

41. Richard T. Pascale, "Perspectives on Strategy: The Real Story Behind Honda's Success," *California Management Review* 26 (1984): 47–72. *The California Management Review* 38, no. 4 (1996) had a roundtable to discuss the implications of this story which included Michael Goold (author of the original BCG report), "Learning, Planning, and Strategy: Extra Time"; Richard T. Pascale, "Reflections on Honda"; Richard P. Rumelt, "The Many Faces of Honda"; and Henry Mintzberg, "Introduction" and "Reply to Michael Goold." Pascale was challenging a report by the Boston Consulting Group commissioned by the British Government to explain the precipitate decline of the British motorcycle industry from a commanding market position. BCG blamed "a concern for short term profitability" in Britain while reporting on how the Japanese had managed to develop a massive internal market for small motorcycles. This meant that costs were low, so when they decided to export there was no way that British firms geared to large motorcycles could compete. Honda achieved stunning economies of scale: producing about two hundred motorcycles per worker per year compared with fourteen motorcycles in British factories. Boston Consulting Group, *Strategy Alternatives for the British Motorcycle Industry,* 2 vols. (London: Her Majesty's Stationery Office, 1975).

42. Henry Mintzberg, "Crafting Strategy," *Harvard Business Review* (July–August 1987), 70.

43. Andrew Mair, "Learning from Japan: Interpretations of Honda Motors by Strategic Management Theorists," *Nissan Occasional Paper Series* No. 29, 1999, available at http://www.nissan.ox.ac.uk/__data/assets/pdf_file/0013/11812/NOPS29.pdf. A shorter version appears in Andrew Mair, "Learning from Honda," *Journal of Management Studies* 36, no. 1 (January 1999): 25–44.

44. Jeffrey Alexander, *Japan's Motorcycle Wars: An Industry History* (Vancouver: UBC Press, 2008).

45. Mair, "Learning from Japan," 29–30. The debate is reviewed in Christopher D. McKenna, "Mementos: Looking Backwards at the Honda Motorcycle Case, 2003–1973," in Sally Clarke, Naomi R. Lamoreaux, and Steven Usselman, eds., *The Challenge of Remaining Innovative: Lessons from Twentieth Century American Business* (Palo Alto: Stanford University Press, 2008).

46. Phil Rosenzweig, *The Halo Effect* (New York: The Free Press, 2007).

47. John Kay, *The Hare & The Tortoise*, 33, 70, 158, 160.

48. Stephen Bungay, *The Art of Action: How Leaders Close the Gap Between Plans, Actions and Results* (London: Nicholas Brealey, 2011).

49. A. G. Laffley and Roger Martin, *Playing to Win: How Strategy Really Works* (Cambridge, MA: Harvard Business Review Press, 272), 214–215.

50. Richard Rumelt, *Good Strategy, Bad Strategy: The Difference and Why It Matters* (London: Profile Books, 2011), 77, 106, 111.

51. Ibid., 32. "Fluff" involved superficial restatements of the obvious, raised to a higher level by neologisms, or abstruse concepts which could give an appearance of profundity. It was reflected in a tendency to string abstract nouns together, each with a positive connotation. Rumelt blamed the academic world, where the manipulation of abstractions was often a way of making authors appear cleverer than they are, and could require constant translation with real examples to give meaning to the ideas.

52. Ibid., 58.

36 The Limits of Rational Choice

1. Cited in Paul Hirsch, Stuart Michaels, and Ray Friedman, "'Dirty Hands' versus 'Clean Models': Is Sociology in Danger of Being Seduced by Economics," *Theory and Society* 16 (1987): 325.

2. Emily Hauptmann, "The Ford Foundation and the Rise of Behavioralism in Political Science," *Journal of the History of the Behavioral Sciences* 48, no. 2 (2012): 154–173.

3. S. M. Amadae, *Rationalising Capitalist Democracy: The Cold War Origins of Rational Choice Liberalism* (Chicago: University of Chicago Press, 2003), 3.

4. Martin Hollis and Robert Sugden, "Rationality in Action," *Mind* 102, no. 405 (January 1993): 2.

5. Richard Swedberg, "Sociology and Game Theory: Contemporary and Historical Perspectives," *Theory and Society* 30 (2001): 320.

6. William Riker, "The Entry of Game Theory into Political Science," in Roy Weintraub, ed., *Toward a History of Game Theory*, 208–210 (see chap. 12, n. 19).

7. S. M. Amadae and Bruce Bueno de Mesquita, "The Rochester School: The Origins of Positive Political Theory," *Annual Review of Political Science* 2 (1999): 276.

8. Ibid., 282, 291.

9. See Ronald Terchek, "Positive Political Theory and Heresthetics: The Axioms and Assumptions of William Riker," *The Political Science Reviewer*, 1984, 62. Also on Riker see Albert Weale, "Social Choice versus Populism? An Interpretation of Riker's Political Theory," *British Journal of Political Science* 14, no. 3 (July 1984): 369–385; Iain McLean, "William H. Riker and the Invention of Heresthetic(s)," *British Journal of Political Science* 32, no. 3 (July 2002): 535–558.

10. Jonathan Cohn, "The Revenge of the Nerds: Irrational Exuberance: When Did Political Science Forget About Politics," *New Republic*, October 15, 1999.

11. William Riker and Peter Ordeshook, *An Introduction to Positive Political Theory* (Englewood Cliffs: Prentice-Hall, 1973), 24.

12. Richard Langlois, "Strategy as Economics versus Economics as Strategy," *Managerial and Decision Economics* 24, no. 4 (June–July 2003): 287.

13. Donald P. Green and Ian Shapiro, *Pathologies of Rational Choice Theory: A Critique of Applications in Political Science* (New Haven, CT: Yale University Press, 1996), X. One counterattack appeared in Jeffery Friedman, ed., "Rational Choice Theory and Politics," *Critical Review* 9, no. 1–2 (1995).

14. Stephen Walt, "Rigor or Rigor Mortis? Rational Choice and Security Studies," *International Security* 23, no. 4 (Spring 1999): 8.

15. Dennis Chong quoted in Cohn, *The Revenge of the Nerds.*

16. William A. Gamson, "A Theory of Coalition Formation," *American Sociological Review* 26, no. 3 (June 1961): 373–382.

17. William Riker, *The Theory of Political Coalitions* (New Haven, CT: Yale University Press, 1963).

18. William Riker, "Coalitions. I. The Study of Coalitions," in David L. Sills, ed., *International Encyclopedia of the Social Sciences, vol. 2* (New York: The Macmillan Company, 1968), 527. Cited in Swedberg, *Sociology and Game Theory,* 328.

19. Riker, *Theory of Political Coalitions*, 22.

20. Mancur Olson, *The Logic of Collective Action: Public Goods and the Theory of Groups* (Cambridge, MA: Harvard University Press,1965); Iain McLean, "Review Article: The Divided Legacy of Mancur Olson," *British Journal of Political Science* 30, no. 4 (October 2000), 651–668.

21. Mancur Olson and Richard Zeckhauser, "An Economic Theory of Alliances," *The Review of Economics and Statistics* 48, no. 3 (August 1966): 266–279.

22. Avinash K. Dixit and Barry J. Nalebuff, *The Art of Strategy: A Game Theorist's Guide to Success in Business and Life* (New York: W. W. Norton, 2008), x.

23. Anatol Rapoport, *Strategy and Conscience* (New York: Harper & Row, 1964). For Schelling's response, see his review in *The American Economic Review*, LV (December 1964), 1082–1088.

24. Robert Axelrod, *The Evolution of Cooperation* (New York: Basic Books, 1984), 177. The episode is covered in Mirowski, *Machine Dreams:* see Chapter 12, n. 11, 484–487.

25. Dennis Chong, *Collective Action and the Civil Rights Movement* (Chicago: University of Chicago Press, 1991), 231–237.

26. Robert Jervis, "Realism, Game Theory and Cooperation," *World Politics* 40, no. 3 (April 1988): 319. See also Robert Jervis, "Rational Deterrence: Theory and Evidence," *World Politics* 41, no. 2 (January 1989): 183–207.

27. Herbert Simon, "Human Nature in Politics, The Dialogue of Psychology with Political Science," *American Political Science Review* 79, no. 2 (June 1985): 302.

28. Albert Weale, "Social Choice versus Populism?", 379.

29. William H. Riker, "The Heresthetics of Constitution-Making: The Presidency in 1787, with Comments on Determinism and Rational Choice," *The American Political Science Review* 78, no. 1 (March 1984): 1–16.

30. Simon, "Human Nature in Politics," 302.

31. Amadae and Bueno de Mesquita, "The Rochester School."

32. William Riker, *The Art of Political Manipulation* (New Haven, CT: Yale University Press, 1986), ix.

33. William Riker, *The Strategy of Rhetoric* (New Haven, CT: Yale University Press, 1996), 4.

37 Beyond Rational Choice

1. Cited by Martin Hollis and Robert Sugden, "Rationality in Action," *Mind* 102, no. 405 (January 1993): 3.

2. Anthony Downs, *An Economic Theory of Democracy* (New York: Harper & Row, 1957), 5.

3. Riker, *The Theory of Political Coalitions*, 20 (see chap. 36, n. 17).

4. See pp. 153–154.

5. Brian Forst and Judith Lucianovic, "The Prisoner's Dilemma: Theory and Reality," *Journal of Criminal Justice* 5 (1977): 55–64.

6. For example, Nalebuff and Brandenburger granted that the "simple textbooks present a view of 'rational man' that doesn't apply very well to the mixed-up, real world of business. But that's a problem with the textbooks." For Nalebuff and Brandenburger, a rational person "does the best he can" depending on his perception, which is affected by the amount of information available and how he evaluates the various outcomes. This argued for remembering to look at a game from multiple perspectives. "To us," they concluded, "the issue of whether people are rational or irrational is largely beside the point." There is something refreshing about a book purporting to represent game theory to a wider business audience ducking so brazenly the fundamental conceptual issue that had shaped its methodology and potentially limited its application. Nalebuff and Brandenburger, *Co-Opetition,* 56–58.

7. Introduction in Jon Elster, ed., *Rational Choice* (New York: New York University Press, 1986), 16. Green and Shapiro, *Pathologies of Rational Choice Theory*, 20 (see chap. 36, n. 13) cite Elster to demonstrate the burdens strict criteria place on researchers. Elster was an early advocate for rational choice theory who later became disenchanted.

8. On the inability of individuals to manage formal reasoning and understand statistical methods, see John Conlisk, "Why Bounded Rationality?" *Journal of Economic Literature* 34, no. 2 (June 1996): 670.

9. Faruk Gul and Wolfgang Pesendorfer, "The Case for Mindless Economics," in A. Caplin and A. Shotter, eds., *Foundations of Positive and Normative Economics* (Oxford: Oxford University Press, 2008).

10. Khurana, *From Higher Aims to Higher Hands,* see Chapter 32, n. 10, 284–285.

11. Herbert A. Simon, "A Behavioral Model of Rational Choice," *Quarterly Journal of Economics* 69, no. 1 (February 1955): 99–118. See also "Information Processing Models of Cognition," *Annual Review of Psychology* 30, no. 3 (February 1979): 363–396. Herbert A. Simon and William G. Chase, "Skill in Chess," *American Scientist* 61, no. 4 (July 1973): 394–403.

12. Amos Tversky and Daniel Kahneman, "Judgment Under Uncertainty: Heuristics and Biases," *Science* 185, no. 4157 (September 1974): 1124. See also Daniel Kahneman, "A Perspective on Judgment and Choice: Mapping Bounded Rationality," *American Psychologist* 56, no. 9 (September 2003): 697–720.

13. "IRRATIONALITY: Rethinking thinking," *The Economist,* December 16, 1999, available at http://www.economist.com/node/268946.

14. Amos Tversky and Daniel Kahneman, "The Framing of Decisions and the Psychology of Choice," *Science* 211, no. 4481 (1981): 453–458; "Rational Choice and the Framing of Decisions," *Journal of Business* 59, no. 4, Part 2 (October 1986): S251–S278.

15. Richard H. Thaler, "Toward a Positive Theory of Consumer Choice," *Journal of Economic Behavior and Organization* 1, no. 1 (March 1980): 36–90; "Mental Accounting and Consumer Choice," *Marketing Science* 4, no. 3 (Summer 1985): 199–214.

16. Joseph Henrich, Steven J. Heine, and Ara Norenzayan, "The Weirdest People in the World?" *Behavioral and Brain Sciences,* 2010, 1–75.

17. Chris D. Frith and Tania Singer, "The Role of Social Cognition in Decision Making," *Philosophical Transactions of the Royal Society* 363, no. 1511 (December 2008): 3875–3886; Colin Camerer and Richard H. Thaler, "Ultimatums, Dictators and Manners," *Journal of Economic Perspectives* 9, no. 2: 209–219; A. G. Sanfey, J. K. Rilling, J. A. Aronson, L. E. Nystrom, and J. D. Cohen, "The Neural Basis of Economic Decisionmaking in the Ultimatum Game," *Science* 300, no. 5626 (2003): 1755–1758. For a survey, see Angela A. Stanton, *Evolving Economics: Synthesis*, April 26, 2006, Munich Personal RePEc Archive, Paper No. 767, posted November 7, 2007, available at http://mpra.ub.uni-muenchen.de/767/.

18. Robert Forsythe, Joel L. Horowitz, N. E. Savin, and Martin Sefton, "Fairness in Simple Bargaining Experiments," *Game Economics Behavior* 6 (1994): 347–369.

19. Elizabeth Hoffman, Kevin McCabe, and Vernon L. Smith, "Social Distance and Other-Regarding Behavior in Dictator Games," *American Economic Review* 86, no. 3 (June1996): 653–660.

20. Joseph Patrick Henrich et al., " 'Economic Man' in Cross-Cultural Perspective: Behavioral Experiments in 15 Small-Scale Societies," *Behavioral Brain Science* 28 (2005): 813.

21. Stanton, *Evolving Economics,* 10.

22. Martin A. Nowak and Karl Sigmund, "The Dynamics of Indirect Reciprocity," *Journal of Theoretical Biology* 194 (1998): 561–574.

23. Altruistic punishment has been shown to have a vital role in maintaining cooperation in groups. See Herbert Gintis, "Strong Reciprocity and Human Sociality," *Journal of Theoretical Biology* 206, no. 2 (September 2000): 169–179.

24. Mauricio R. Delgado, "Reward-Related Responses in the Human Striatum," *Annals of the New York Academy of Sciences* 1104 (May 2007): 70–88.

25. Fabrizio Ferraro, Jeffrey Pfeffer, and Robert I. Sutton, "Economics, Language and Assumptions: How Theories Can Become Self-Fulfilling," *The Academy of Management Review* 30, no. 1 (January 2005): 14–16; Gerald Marwell and Ruth E. Ames, "Economists Free Ride, Does Anyone Else? Experiments on the Provision of Public Goods," *Journal of Public Economics* 15 (1981): 295–310.

26. Dale T. Miller, "The Norm of Self-Interest," *American Psychologist* 54, no. 12 (December 1999): 1055, cited in Ferraro et al., "Economics, Language and Assumptions," 14.

27. "Economics Focus: To Have and to Hold," *The Economist*, August 28, 2003, available at http://www.economist.com/node/2021010.

28. Alan G. Sanfey, "Social Decision-Making: Insights from Game Theory and Neuroscience," *Science* 318 (2007): 598.

29. See Guido Möllering, "Inviting or Avoiding Deception Through Trust: Conceptual Exploration of an Ambivalent Relationship," MPIfG Working Paper 08/1, 2008, 6.

30. Rachel Croson, "Deception in Economics Experiments," in Caroline Gerschlager, ed., *Deception in Markets: An Economic Analysis* (London: Macmillan, 2005), 113.

31. Erving Goffman, *The Presentation of Self in Everyday Life* (New York: Doubleday, 1959), 83–84. Students of deception have sought to revive an old word *paltering*, which is defined as acting insincerely or misleadingly, creating a false impression through "fudging, twisting, shading, bending, stretching, slanting, exaggerating, distorting, whitewashing, and selective reporting." Frederick Schauer and Richard Zeckhauser, "Paltering," in Brooke Harrington, ed., *Deception: From Ancient Empires to Internet Dating* (Stanford: Stanford University Press, 2009), 39.

32. Uta Frith and Christopher D. Frith, "Development and Neurophysiology of Mentalizing," *Philosophical Transactions of the Royal Society, London* 358, no. 1431 (March 2003): 459–473. Responses to another's pain were found in the same area of the brain where individuals respond to their own pain. An individual's own pain, however, would lead to an effort to do something about it, and this required the activation of other parts of the brain. It was perhaps a legacy of the evolutionary process that by looking at others, important clues could be discerned about what to feel. In the faces of others could be seen warnings of an impending danger. T. Singer, B. Seymour, J. O'Doherty, H. Kaube, R. J. Dolan, and C. D. Frith, "Empathy for Pain Involves the Affective but Not Sensory Components of Pain," *Science* 303, no. 5661 (February 2004): 1157–1162; Vittorio Gallese, "The Manifold Nature of Interpersonal Relations: The Quest for a Common Mechanism," *Philosophical Transactions of the Royal Society, London* 358, no. 1431 (March 2003): 517; Stephany D. Preston and Frank B. M. de-Waal, "Empathy: the Ultimate and Proximate Bases," *Behavioral and Brain Scences* 25 (2002): 1.

33. R. P. Abelson, "Are Attitudes Necessary?" in B. T. King and E. McGinnies, eds., *Attitudes, Conflict, and Social Change* (New York: Academic Press, 1972), 19–32, cited in Ira J. Roseman and Stephen J. Read, "Psychologist at Play: Robert P. Abelson's Life and Contributions to Psychological Science," *Perspectives on Psychological Science* 2, no. 1 (2007): 86–97.

34. R. C. Schank and R. P. Abelson, *Scripts, Plans, Goals and Understanding: An Inquiry into Human Knowledge Structures* (Hillsdale, NJ: Erlbaum, 1977).

35. R. P. Abelson, "Script Processing in Attitude Formation and Decision-making," in J. S. Carroll and J. W. Payne, eds., *Cognition and Social Behavior* (Hillsdale, NJ: Erlbaum, 1976).

36. M. Lyons, T. Caldwell, and S. Shultz, "Mind-Reading and Manipulation— Is Machiavellianism Related to Theory of Mind?" *Journal of Evolutionary Psychology* 8, no. 3 (September 2010): 261–274.

37. Mirowski, *Machine Dreams*, 424.

38. Alan Sanfey, "Social Decision-Making: Insights from Game Theory and Neuroscience," *Science* 318, no. 5850 (October 2007): 598–602.

39. Stephen Walt, "Rigor or Rigor Mortis?" (see chap. 36, n. 14).

40. Jonah Lehrer, *How We Decide* (New York: Houghton Mifflin Harcourt, 2009), 227.

41. George E. Marcus, "The Psychology of Emotion and Passion," in David O. Sears, Leonie Huddy, and Robert Jervis, eds., *Oxford Handbook of Political Psychology* (Oxford: Oxford University Press, 2003), 182–221.

42. The designations System 1 and System 2 come from Keith Stanovich and Richard West, "Individual Differences in Reasoning: Implications for the

Rationality Debate," *Behavioral and Brain Sciences* 23 (2000): 645–665. Daniel Kahneman has popularized the terms in his *Thinking Fast and Slow* (London: Penguin Books, 2011). J. St. B. T. Evans, "In Two Minds: Dual-Process Accounts of Reasoning," *Trends in Cognition Science* 7, no. 10 (October 2003): 454–459; "Dual-Processing Accounts of Reasoning, Judgment and Social Cognition," *The Annual Review of Psychology* 59 (January 2008): 255–278.

43. Andreas Glöckner and Cilia Witteman, "Beyond Dual-Process Models: A Categorisation of Processes Underlying Intuitive Judgement and Decision Making," *Thinking & Reasoning* 16, no. 1 (2009): 1–25.

44. Daniel Kahneman, *Thinking Fast and Slow*, 42.

45. Alan G. Sanfey et al., "Social Decision-Making," 598–602.

46. Colin F. Camerer and Robin M. Hogarth, "The Effect of Financial Incentives," *Journal of Risk and Uncertainty* 19, no. 1–3 (December 1999): 7–42.

47. Jennifer S. Lerner and Philip E. Tetlock, "Accounting for the Effects of Accountability," *Psychological Bulletin* 125, no. 2 (March 1999): 255–275.

48. Daniel Kahneman, Peter P. Wakker, and Rakesh Sarin, "Back to Bentham? Explorations of Experienced Utility," *The Quarterly Journal of Economics* 112, no. 2 (May 1997): 375–405; Daniel Kahneman, "A Psychological Perspective on Economics," *American Economic Review: Papers and Proceedings* 93, no. 2 (May 2003): 162–168.

49. J. K. Rilling, A. L. Glenn, M. R. Jairam, G. Pagnoni, D. R. Goldsmith, H. A. Elfenbein, and S. O. Lilienfeld, "Neural Correlates of Social Cooperation and Noncooperation as a Function of Psychopathy," *Biological Psychiatry* 61 (2007): 1260–1271.

50. Philip Tetlcok, *Expert Political Judgement* (Princeton, NJ: Princeton University Press, 2006), 23.

51. Alan N. Hampton, Peter Bossaerts, and John P. O'Doherty, "Neural Correlates of Mentalizing-Related Computations During Strategic Interactions in Humans," *The National Academy of Sciences of the USA* 105, no. 18 (May 6, 2008): 6741–6746; Sanfey et al., *Social Decision-Making,* 598.

52. David Sally, "Dressing the Mind Properly for the Game," *Philosophical Transactions of the Royal Society London B* 358, no. 1431 (March 2003): 583–592.

38 Stories and Scripts

1. Charles Lindblom, "The Science of 'Muddling Through,'" *Public Administration Review* 19, no. 2 (Spring 1959): 79–88.

2. Gordon Wood, "History Lessons," *New York Review of Books*, March 29, 1984, p. 8 (Review of Barbara Tuchman's *March of Folly*).

3. Speech to the National Defense Executive Reserve Conference in Washington, DC, November 14, 1957, in *Public Papers of the Presidents of the United States, Dwight D. Eisenhower, 1957* (National Archives and Records Service, Government Printing Office), p. 818. He then observed "the very definition of 'emergency' is that it is unexpected, therefore it is not going to happen the way you are planning."

4. Hew Strachan, "The Lost Meaning of Strategy," *Survival* 47, no. 3 (2005): 34.

5. Timothy Crawford, "Preventing Enemy Coalitions: How Wedge Strategies Shape Power Politics," *International Security* 35, no. 4 (Spring 2011): 189.

6. Jon T. Sumida, "The Clausewitz Problem," *Army History* (Fall 2009), 17–21.

7. Isaiah Berlin, "On Political Judgment," *New York Review of Books* (October 3, 1996).

8. Bruce Kuklick, *Blind Oracles: Intellectuals and War from Kennan to Kissinger* (Princeton, NJ: Princeton University Press, 2006), 16.

9. Hannah Arendt, *The Human Condition*, 2nd revised edition (Chicago: University of Chicago Press, 1999), 200. First published 1958.

10. Steven Lukes, *Power: A Radical View* (London: Macmillan, 1974).

11. Charles Tilly, "The Trouble with Stories," in *Stories, Identities, and Social Change* (New York: Rowman & Littlefield, 2002), 25–42.

12. Naomi Lamoreaux, "Reframing the Past: Thoughts About Business Leadership and Decision Making Under Certainty," *Enterprise and Society* 2 (December 2001): 632–659.

13. Daniel M. G. Raff, "How to Do Things with Time," *Enterprise and Society* 14, no. 3 (forthcoming, September 2013).

14. Daniel Kahneman, *Thinking Fast and Slow*, 199, 200–201 206, 259 (see chap. 38, n. 44).

15. Nassim Taleb, *The Black Swan: The Impact of the Highly Improbable* (New York: Random House, 2007), 8.

16. Joseph Davis, ed., *Stories of Change: Narrative and Social Movements* (New York: State University of New York Press, 2002).

17. Francesca Polletta, *It Was Like a Fever,* see Chapter 27, n. 1, 166.

18. Joseph Davis, ed., *Stories of Change: Narrative and Social Movements* (New York: State University of New York Press, 2002).

19. Dennis Gioia and Peter P. Poole, "Scripts in Organizational Behavior," *Academy of Management Review* 9, no. 3 (1984): 449–459; Ian Donald and David Canter, "Intentionality and Fatality During the King's Cross Underground Fire," *European Journal of Social Psychology* 22 (1992): 203–218.

20. R. P. Abelson, "Psychological Status of the Script Concept," *American Psychologist* 36 (1981): 715–729.

21. Avner Offer, "Going to War in 1914: A Matter of Honor?" *Politics and Society* 23, no. 2 (1995): 213–241. Richard Herrmann and Michael Fischerkeller also introduce the idea of "strategic scripts" in their "Beyond the Enemy

Image and Spiral Model: Cognitive-Strategic Research After the Cold War," *International Organization* 49, no. 3 (Summer 1995): 415–450. Their use is, however, different with scripts considered as "hypothetical structures that offer a means to organize the totality of foreign policy behavior." Another approach is that offered by James C. Scott, *Domination and the Arts of Resistance: Hidden Transcripts* (New Haven, CT: Yale University Press, 1992). Scott describes how subordinate groups critique the "public transcript" promoted by the dominant group by surreptitiously developing a critique in the form of "hidden transcripts." He thus takes familiar arguments about paradigms, formulas, myths, and false consciousness and challenges them by suggesting that subordinate groups are not so easily duped.

22. Jerome Bruner, "The Narrative Construction of Reality," *Critical Inquiry*, 1991, 4–5, 34.

23. Christopher Fenton and Ann Langley, "Strategy as Practice and the Narrative Turn," *Organization Studies* 32, no. 9 (2011): 1171–1196; G. Shaw, R. Brown, and P. Bromiley, "Strategic Stories: How 3M Is Rewriting Business Planning," *Harvard Business Review* (May–June 1998), 41–50.

24. Valérie-Inès de la Ville and Elèonore Mounand, "A Narrative Approach to Strategy as Practice: Strategy-making from Texts and Narratives," in Damon Golskorkhi, et al. eds., *Cambridge Handbook of Strategy as Practice* (see chap. 35, n. 29), 13.

25. David Barry and Michael Elmes, "Strategy Retold: Toward a Narrative View of Strategic Discourse," *The Academy of Management Review* 22, no. 2 (April 1997): 437, 430, 432–433.

26. Robert McKee, *Story, Substance, Structure, Style, and the Principles of Screenwriting* (London: Methuen, 1997).

27. Aristotle, *Poetics*, http://classics.mit.edu/Aristotle/poetics.html.

28. Laton McCartney, *The Teapot Dome Scandal: How Big Oil Bought the Harding White House and Tried to Steal the Country* (New York: Random House, 2008).

29. Although the first senator to come out for Roosevelt and the New Deal, by 1939 he was known as a vigorous isolationist and for accusations that Jews in Hollywood were using the influence of the movies to stir up pro-war fervor. He denied Japan's hostile intent in the weeks before Pearl Harbor. This background led him to have a later literary incarnation, as Charles Lindbergh's vice president in Philip Roth's *The Plot Against America* (New York: Random House, 2004).

30. Michael Kazin, *American Dreamers* (see chap. 25, n. 51), 187; Charles Lindblom and John A. Hall, "Frank Capra Meets John Doe: Anti-politics in American National Identity," in Mette Hjort and Scott Mackenzie, eds., *Cinema and Nation* (New York: Routledge, 2000). See also Joseph McBride, *Frank Capra* (Jackson: University Press of Mississippi, 2011).

31. This self-regulating body for upholding proper moral standards in film was largely about sexual conduct, but Breen also imposed political censorship, for example preventing anti-Nazi films being made, at least until 1938.

32. Richard Maltby, *Hollywood Cinema* (Oxford: Blackwell, 2003), 278–279.

33. Eric Smoodin, " 'Compulsory' Viewing for Every Citizen: Mr. Smith and the Rhetoric of Reception," *Cinema Journal* 35, no. 2 (Winter 1996): 3–23.

34. Frances Fitzgerald, *Way Out There in the Blue: Reagan, Star Wars and the End of the Cold War* (New York: Simon & Schuster, 2000), 27–37.

35. The original script can be found at http://www.dailyscript.com/scripts/ MrSmithGoesToWashington.txt.

36. Michael P. Rogin and Kathleen Moran, "Mr. Capra Goes to Washington," *Representations*, no. 84 (Autumn 2003): 213–248.

37. Christopher Booker, *The Seven Basic Plots: Why We Tell Stories* (New York: Continuum, 2004).

INDEX

Allenby, Edmund, 182

America Can be Saved (Falwell), 444

American Civil War, 109–112, 262

American Federation of Labor, 381, 386

American War of Independence, 178,
    232

anarchism

    Bakunin and, 251, 269–273, 276,
        287–288, 392

    Conrad's depiction of, 278

    Luxemburg and, 288

    political strikes and, 287–288

    reluctance to take power and, 280

    Spain and, 279

    syndicalism and, 279

    terrorism and, 276–279

    Tolstoy on, 310

Andrews, Kenneth, 499–500, 521

Ansoff, Igor, 498, 500–504, 519, 521,
    539

ants, 6

Arab rebellion (1916), 181–182

Arab Spring (2011), 230–231, 412

Arab-Israeli War (1973), 199

Archidamus, 33

Arendt, Hannah, 392, 403, 614

Aristotle, 623

Arminius, Jacobus, 55–56

armored warfare, theories of, 129–132

Arms and Influence (Schelling), 166–167

Armstrong, Helen, 558

Aron, Raymond, xv

Arquilla, John, 229–230, 431

Arrow, Kenneth, 577

Art of Manipulation, The (Riker), 588

Art of War (Jomini), 84–85

Art of War, The (Machiavelli), 51

Art of War, The (Sun Tzu), 44–45, 509–
    510. *See also* Sun Tzu, strategic
    theories of

Association of Licensed Automobile
    Manufacturers (ALAM), 479

asymmetric wars, 220–225, 227

Atē, 29

Athens, 30–38, 46–47, 72

Athos, Tony, 545

Atlanta Compromise, 350

atomic weapons. *See* nuclear weapons

Attila the Hun, 506

attrition warfare

    Boyd on, 199

    compared to maneuver warfare, 201,
        206, 209, 242

    Delbrück on, 108–109, 180, 204,
        289, 332

    Liddell Hart and, 138

    Luttwack on, 203

    negotiations and, 243

Atwater, Lee

    on Baby Boomers, 447–448

    Machiavellian approach of, 445

    media strategies of, 446–448

    Southern strategies of, 447, 451

    Sun Tzu and, 445–446

    Willie Horton political ads and, 448

Augustine of Hippo, 55

Austerlitz, Battle of, 78, 100

Austria, 78–80, 93, 105, 254–255

Axelrod, David, 453

Axelrod, Robert, 584–586

Ayers, Bill, 455

Bach, Lee, 517

Bachrach, Peter, 373

Baker, Ella, 361

Bakunin, Mikhail

    anarchism and, 251, 269–273, 276,
        287–288, 392

    biography of, 268–269

    First International and, 270–271

    general strikes and, 287–288

    Herzen and, 268–269

    Marx and, 268, 270–272, 276, 474

    Nechayev and, 276

    on the Paris Commune, 271–272

    on philosophy of history, 273–274

propaganda of the deed and,
275–276
on revolutionaries, 273–276
Baldwin, Stanley, 126
Baratz, Morton, 373
Barnard, Chester, 471–473, 543, 563,
566
Barnouw, Jeffrey, 28
Barry, David, 622–623
Barthes, Roland, 428
Bassford, Christopher, 86
Batista, Fulgencio, 399
Battle of Britain (1940), 140
Battle of France (1940), 199, 210, 617
Battle of the Atlantic, 140
Baxter, Leone, 437–438
Beaufre, André, 193–194
Bebel, August, 284
Becker, Gary, 576
Beinhocker, Eric, 540
Belgium, 113–114, 123, 139
Bell, Daniel, 405
Bell, The (Herzen), 266
Benn, William Wedgewood, 348–349
Bergson, Henri, 328
Berle, Adolf, 489–490, 492, 526
Berlin (Germany), 172–174
Berlin, Isaiah, 98, 101, 265, 307,
613–614
Bernard, Jessie, 153
Bernays, Edward, 340–343, 414, 432
Bernstein, Eduard, 284–285
Berra, Yogi, 575
Bethlehem Steel, 463
Betts, Richard, 139–140
Bible, The
Aaron in, 13–15
Adam and Eve in, 11–12, 56–57
Book of Revelation in, 57
David and Goliath in, 10, 19–21,
617
Exodus story in, 10, 12–17, 21, 57
Garden of Eden account in, 11–12

Gibeonites in, 18
Gideon in, 18–19
God's role in human conflicts in,
10–21, 57
Israelites in, 12–20
Jacob in, 11, 13
Job in, 56
Joshua in, 17–18
Moses in, 13–17, 21
Pharaoh in, 13–17, 21
Philistines in, 19–21
Rahab in, 17
Samuel in, 20
Satan in, 56–57
Saul in, 19–20
Ten Plagues account in, 13–17
biē (strength), 23, 25, 42
bipolar strategy, 204
Birmingham (Alabama, US), 362–364
Bismarck, Otto von, 103, 106
Black Panthers, 394–395, 403–405
Black Power movement, 393–394
Blake, William, 57
Blanqui, Louis-Auguste, 251, 263, 271
blitzkrieg strategy, 139, 199–200, 210,
225, 617
Blumenthal, Sidney, 449
Bolsheviks, 180, 289, 292, 294,
296, 298, 466. See also Lenin,
Vladimir Ilych
Bonaparte, Louis-Napoleon, 258, 271
Bonaparte, Napoleon
French Revolution and, 249
influences on, 45, 76
Jomini on, 83–84
legacy of, 505–506
military strategies of, 70, 75–78,
93, 95, 109–111, 237, 613
personality cult of, 97
political objectives of, 93
Russia campaign of, 78–83, 90, 209
Spain campaign of, 90
Tolstoy's depiction of, 99–100, 617

Civil Disobedience (Thoreau), 347

Civil War in France, The (Marx), 271

civilian-military relationships, 241–243

Class Struggles in France (Marx), 258, 281, 286

Clausewitz, Carl von

  on center of gravity concept (*Schwerpunkt*), 91–92, 205–209, 243–244

  on coalitions, 90–92

  Engels on, 262

  on force, 89–90

  on friction, 87–89, 93, 164, 211–212, 540

  guerrilla warfare and, 179

  Jomini and, 85

  legacy of, 94, 106, 108, 117–118, 135–136, 160, 170, 181, 203–204, 221, 237, 250, 252–253, 262, 445, 504, 507–508, 608

  Liddell Hart on, 135–136, 204

  Marx and Engels and, 252

  on military intelligence, 89, 228

  military strategies of, 85–94, 118–119, 237, 240, 250, 426, 504, 507–508, 540, 613, xii

  Napoleonic Wars and, 82–83, 90–91, 237, 617

  on planning, 88–89, 641n21

  on politics, 86–88, 92–94

  on popular passions, 97

  Tolstoy's response to, 98

  on victory, 92–94, 209, 240

  von Moltke (the elder) and, 102–104

Clay, Cassius. *See* Ali, Mohammed

Clay, Jenny Strauss, 26

Cleaver, Eldridge, 403

Clegg, Stewart, 559

Clifford, Clark, 447

Clinton, Bill, 434, 450–453

Clinton, Henry, 232

Clinton, Hillary, 453, 455

Co-opetition (Nalebuff and Brandenburger), 523, 710n6

coalitions

  Carmichael on, 296

  Clausewitz on, 90–92

  game theory and, 582–583

  Hayden on, 376, 380

  Napoleonic Wars and, 90–91, 115

  Peloponnesian War and, 30, 32–35

  Riker on, 581–583

  Rustin on, 395

  Second World War and, 141–143

Coast of Utopia, The (Stoppard), 265

cognition, hot and cold forms of, 598–599

Cohen, Eliot, 141, 214

Cold War

  Berlin blockade crisis and, 172–174

  communication during, 167, 173

  Cuban missile crisis and, 173–176, 190

  deterrence theory and, 158–159, 165, 192

  nuclear weapons and, 156–159, 167–168

  origins of term, 145, 649n2

Cologne Workers Council, 257–258

Columbia University protests, 403–405

Command in the Air (Douhet), 125–126

Committee on Public Information (CPI, United States), 337, 340

communism. *See also* Lenin, Vladimir Ilych; Marx, Karl; Soviet Union

  origins of, 250, 254

  permanent revolution and, 256

  Spanish Civil War and, 279

Communist International. *See* Third International

Communist League, 254, 262

Communist Manifesto, The (Marx and Engels), 254, 256–257, 260–261, 270, 329

compellence theory, 163, 190–191

Delbrück, Hans
    on attrition warfare, 108–109, 180,
        204, 289, 332
    on Clausewitz, 204
    on First World War, 124
    on maneuver warfare, 205
    political activity of, 302
    Rosinski and, 195
Delian League, 30, 32
deliberate strategies, 554–556
Democratic Party (United States). *See
    also individual politicians*
    1968 Convention of, 406–408, 417
    political communication strategies
        and, 434–435, 441, 448–455
deterrence theory. *See under* Cold War;
    nuclear weapons
Detienne, Marcel, 28, 43
Dewey, John
    cause-effect relationships and, 320
    democracy and, 318–319, 338, 371,
        467
    Du Bois and, 351
    educational philosophy of, 316
    First World War and, 316
    Hull House and, 315
    League for Industrial Democracy
        and, 367
    legacy of, 371–372, 374
    political philosophy of, 315–316
    pragmatism and, 317–319
    Pullman strike and, 315
    on social reform, 316
    Tolstoy and, 318
    University of Chicago and, 315
    Weber and, 318–319
"Dilbert" (Adams), 552–553, 705n23
directive strategies and, 195
Discipline of Market Leaders, The (Treacy
    and Wiersema), 535–536
Discourse on Winning & Losing (Boyd),
    196
discourse traps, 235

Disney Studios, 565
Doctor Strangelove (Kubrick), 160
Donham, Wallace, 469–470
Douhet, Giulio, 125–129, 646n4
Dowding, Hugh, 126–127
Downs, Anthony, 577, 589
Dresher, Melvin, 154
Dreyfus Affair, 336
Drucker, Peter
    on business process reengineering,
        533
    General Motors and, 493–495
    on "gurus," 548
    on the management class, 493
    management theories of, 491,
        493–496, 498, 546, 608
    on planning, 493–494
    on scientific management, 464, 493
    on workers, 495
Du Bois, W.E.B., 350–352
Du Picq, Ardant, 112
Dühring, Eugen, 284
Dukakis, Michael, 445–446, 448–451
Dulles, John Foster, 157–158
DuPont family, 484, 495–497
Durant, William, 484
Durkheim, Émile, 300, 670n1
Dylan, Bob, 404

Eastman Kodak, 382–384
Eccles, Henry, 194
Echevarria, Antulio, 86–87
Economic Research and Action Project,
    376
Economic Theory of Democracy (Downs),
    577
economics, academic discipline of
    behavioralism, 576–577, 593
    business management's
        incorporation of, 516–517, 519,
        540–541
    Chicago school and, 515–516, 576,
        580

compared to other social sciences, 517–518

Cowles Commission and, 515–516

foundation funding for, 576

game theory and, 514–515

industrial organization and, 520

rational market theory and, 526

strategic management and, 513

Eighteenth Brumaire of Louis Napoleon (Marx), 258–259, 283

Einstein, Albert, 575

Eisenhower, Dwight, 150, 157–158, 502, 609–610

Eisner, Karl, 305

Elements of Pure Economics (Walras), 323

Elmes, Michael, 622

Elster, Jon, 591

Emancipation Proclamation, 111

emergent strategies, 554–555, 566

Emerging Republican Majority, The (Phillips), 440

Engels, Friedrich
on American Civil War, 262
Communist Manifesto and, 256–257, 260–261, 270, 329
disappointments of, 268
on electoral politics, 281–283, 285
on general strikes, 287–288
on guerrilla warfare, 180, 187
on insurrection strategy, 263–264
on military affairs, 261–262, 282
on petit bourgeoisie, 260
political theories of, 252, 254–255, 258, 272, 281–283, 286
Social Democratic Party (SPD, Germany) and, 281–282

"Engineering of Consent" (Bernays), 341

England, Hundred Years' War and, 48–49. *See also* Great Britain

Enlightenment, The, xii, 72–73, 77, 249, 308, 609

Enron, 531, 550–551

Equal Employment Opportunities Commission, 409

Erfurt Program, 284

Ermattungsstrategie (strategy of exhaustion), 108–109

escalation, 94, 170–171, 176, 652n44

Essai général de tactique (Guibert), 73

Essay on Liberation (Marcuse), 399

Etudes sur le combat (Du Picq), 112

Evolution of Cooperation, The (Axelrod), 584–585

Evolutionary Socialism (Bernstein), 285

ExComm (Cuban missile crisis), 174

Fabian Society, 313

Fall, Albert, 624

Falwell, Jerry, 444, 452

Fanon, Frantz, 392

Farmer, James, 354–355, 361

Fathers and Children (Turgenev), 266

Fawkes, Guy, 65

Fear of Freedom (Fromm), 369

Fellowship of Reconciliation (FOR), 354–356

Feminine Mystique, The (Friedan), 409

feminism. *See* women's liberation

Ferdinand, archduke of Austria, 278

Ferguson, Alan, 173

Field Manual 100–5: Operations, 200

Field Manual 90–8 Counterguerrilla Operations, 201

First International, 269–270, 295

First World War
air power in, 124–129, 647n11
Arab rebellion (1916) and, 181–182
Archduke Ferdinand assassination and, 278
France and, 114, 123–125, 127, 131
Germany and, 114, 123–125, 127, 130–131, 210, 333, 619–620
Great Britain and, 114, 118, 123–125, 130–131, 182
naval warfare in, 120, 123

First World War (*Cont.*)
  pacifism and, 347
  propaganda in, 337, 339
  Russian Empire and, 123–124,
    296
  socialists' response to, 295
  tank warfare in, 124, 129–130
  United States and, 123–125, 337
Fisher, Franklin, 528–529
Flacks, Dick, 375–376
Flint (Michigan) sit-down strike, 381,
    487–489
Flood, Merrill, 154
Florence (Italy), 50
FMFM-1 (U.S. Marine Corps), 201
Foch, Ferdinand, 112
foco, Guevara's concept of, 400–402
Follet, Mary Parker, 466–470, 473
Ford Foundation, 513, 516–517,
    576
Ford II, Henry, 501
Ford Motor Company
  antitrust case against, 489
  competitors to, 481–482, 484–486
  labor relations and, 479–483
  mass market strategy of, 479–480,
    486
  mass production strategies of, 480,
    483
  Model T and, 479, 485–486, 519
  "Whiz Kids" and, 501–502
Ford, Edsel, 482, 501
Ford, Gerald, 441–443
Ford, Henry. *See also* Ford Motor
    Company
  early business career of, 478–479
  management strategies of, 481–483,
    486
  successors to, 501
  Taylorism and, 483
Forman, James, 377
Forrest, Nathan B., 108
Fortune Magazine, 491

Foucault, Michel
  discourse and, 426–427, 430
  epistemes and, 424
  Kuhn and, 424
  New Left and, 426–427
  power systems and, 424–427,
    558–559
  sexuality and, 423–424
  strategy and, 425–427
Foundations of the Science of War, The
    (Fuller), 132
fourth-generation warfare,
    225–227
Fox, Justin, 526
framing
  concept of, 39, 415–416, 418
  decision-making and, 593
  political communication and, 422,
    434–436, 454, 461, 593, 615
France
  air power and, 127
  Algeria and, 188–189
  Dreyfus Affair in, 336
  Fifth Republic and, 403
  First World War and, 114,
    123–125, 127, 131
  Franco-Prussian War and, 105–106,
    112, 274–275
  Hundred Years' War and, 48–49
  Napoleonic Wars and, 78–81,
    116
  naval power and, 116
  New Left and, 403, 428
  Revolution of 1848 in, 254–256
  Second Republic of, 258–259
  Second World War and, 139–143,
    199, 210, 617
  student protests in, 403
  Third Republic of, 271
  Vietnam and, 186, 188
Franco-Prussian War (1870), 102–103,
    105–107, 112
Franco, Francisco, 142, 279

Frankfurt Institute for Social Research ("Frankfurt School"), 372, 399, 415

Frazier, Franklin, 351

Frederick the Great (Frederick I, King of Prussia), 75–76, 84, 109

Frederick William (crown prince of Prussia), 106–107

Free Speech Movement (Berkeley), 366, 406

free trade, 96–97

free-rider problem, 583–584, 595–597

Freedom is an Endless Meeting (Polletta), 377

French Revolution
  levée en masse conscription and, 76, 425
  Marx and, 259, 617
  military impact of, 70, 240
  populist aspects of, 97
  professional revolutionaries and, 249–250

Freud, Sigmund, 339–340, 602

Friedan, Betty, 409

Friedman, Milton, 515–516, 526

Fromm, Erich, 369

Frontinus, 43, 64, 72

Fujisawa, Takio, 567

Fuller, John Frederick Charles "Boney"
  on crowd psychology, 131–133
  Liddell Hart and, 134–135, 137–138
  military strategies of, 129–130
  Plan 1919 and, 130

Functions of the Executive, The (Barnard), 471

Future of Industrial Man, The (Drucker), 493

Gaither, H. Rowan, 516–517, 576

Galambos, Louis, 498

Galbraith, John Kenneth, 418–419, 491–492, 501

Gallup, George, 437

Galula, David, 188–189, 224

game theory. *See also* rational choice theory
  The Bible and, 11
  coalitions and, 582–583
  cooperation and, 584–587
  economics and, 514–515
  Fortune magazine and, 495
  free-rider problem and, 583–584, 595–597
  limits of, 514–515, 528–529, 580–581, 605–606
  minimax solution and, 151–153, 155, 165, 582
  nuclear weapons and, 155
  origins of, 151–153
  prisoner's dilemma and, 154–155, 585–586, 590, 596
  RAND Corporation and, 161–162, 513
  Schelling and, 160–162, 166–167, 515, 529, 585

Games and Decisions (Luce and Raiffa), 161–162

Gamson, William, 582

Gandhi, Mohandas
  assassination of, 350
  Du Bois and, 351
  Indian independence movement and, 348–350
  King Jr. and, 358–360
  nonviolent direct action and, 348–351, 354–355, 358–359, 385, 412
  pacifism and, 347, 352
  satyagraha and, 348, 355
  Thoreau and, 347, 675n4
  Tolstoy and, 347–348
  United States and, 351–352

Gantt, Henry, 464

Ganz, Marshall, 387

Garibaldi, Giuseppe, 179

Garstka, John, 217
Gat, Azar, 9, 126
gay liberation, 411
Gay, Edwin, 462
Gekko, Gordon (*Wall Street*), 508
Gell-Mann, Murray, 197
General Electric, 442, 494, 498,
    503–504
General German Workers' Association,
    284
General Motors
    antitrust issues and, 489, 494–495,
        497
    Chevrolet and, 486, 488–489, 495,
        497
    as competitor to Ford, 481–482,
        484–486
    Drucker and, 493–495
    Flint sit-down strike and, 381,
        487–489, 495
    labor relations and, 487–490, 495
    Sloan's management of, 483–486,
        496–498
    Toyota and, 523
general strikes, 287–289
geopolitics, concept of, 120–122
German Confederation, 255
German Democratic Party, 304
German Federation, 255
German Ideology, The (Marx and Engels),
    252
Germany. *See also* Prussia
    air power and, 124, 139, 143,
        157–158
    Berlin blockade crisis in, 172–174
    Federal Republic of, 211
    First World War and, 114, 123–
        125, 127, 130–131, 210, 333,
        619–620
    National Assembly in, 263–264
    naval power and, 116–117
    Revolution of 1848 in, 255,
        257–259, 261

Schlieffen Plan and, 113
Second World War and, 134,
    139–143, 157–158, 199, 210,
    213
socialist revolutionary failures in,
    298, 305
Gerth, Hans, 372
Ghamari-Tabriz, Sharon, 147
Ghoshal, Sumantra, 529–530
Giap, Vo Nguyen, 186–187, 191–192,
    401
Gilbert and Sullivan, 69
Gilbreth, Frank and Lillian, 464
Gingrich, Newt, 434
Ginsberg, Allen, 405–408, 683n48
Gitlin, Todd, 368, 388, 412–413,
    417–418
Gladstone, William, 73
Gödel, Kurt, 197
Goebbels, Joseph, 333, 340
Goethe, Johann Wolfgang von, 321
Goffman, Erving, 415–416, 418, 593
Goldwater, Barry, 439
Goodall, Jane, 7–8
Gore, Al, 448, 532
Gorgias, 36
Gorrell, Nap, 125, 130
Gottschalk, Andreas, 257, 261
Graham, Billy, 452
Gramsci, Antonio
    civil society and, 329–332
    hegemony and, 329–333, 415, 418
    Italian Communist Party (PCI) and,
        328, 332–333
    Machiavelli and, 330
    Marxism of, 331
    military analogies of, 331–332
    on political party organization,
        330–331
Grant, Ulysses S., 111, 506
Gray, Colin, 192, 237–238, 244
Great Britain
    air power and, 124–125, 157–158

American War of Independence and, 232

First World War and, 114, 118, 123–125, 130–131, 182, 647n11

free trade and, 96

general strike in, 287

Indian independence movement and, 348–349, 354

Liberal Party in, 345

Malaya and, 188

Napoleonic Wars and, 116

naval power and, 115–121

Second World War and, 134, 139–144, 147, 157–158, 349, 648n14

suffragette movement in, 344–346

Great Depression, 334, 441, 482

Great War. *See* First World War

Green, Donald, 581

Greenberg, Stanley, 433

Greene, Graham, 187

Gregg, Richard, 352, 355, 358, 412

growth-share matrix, 519–520

guerrilla warfare

American War of Independence and, 178

anti-colonial revolts and, 181–182, 240

Arab revolt (1916) and, 181–182

China and, 183–186

Clausewitz on, 179

Engels on, 179–180, 187

Lawrence and, 181–182, 227

Lenin on, 180

Liddell Hart on, 183

Mao and, 183–186, 191–192, 227, 400

Napoleonic Wars and, 179–180, 240

Peters on, 227

Russian Civil War and, 180

Spain and, 179–180, 240

strategic impact of, 179–180, 227

Trotsky on, 180

Vietnam and, 186–187, 191–192, 221

Guess Who's Coming to Dinner (film), 431

Guevara, Che, 188, 399–402, 404

Guibert, Jacques Antoine Hippolyte Comte de, 73, 76

Gulf War (1991), 214–215, 217–219

Gunpowder Plot (1605), 59, 65

Hadley, Arthur, 449

Haig, Douglas, 112

Halifax, Lord, 140

Halleck, Henry, 109–110

halo effect, 569–570

Hamel, Gary

on deregulation, 548–549

Enron and, 550–551

Honda and, 568

incorporation of Alinsky by, 549–550

incorporation of King Jr. by, 551

management theories of, 548–550, 556, 568

Hamilton, Charles, 393, 395–396, 449

Hammer, Michael, 533–534

Hammes, Thomas X., 226

Handy, Charles, 556

Hanisch, Carol, 410

Hanna, Mark, 438

Hanson, Victor Davis, 47

Harvard Business School, 461–462, 469–470, 517–518

Haushofer, Karl, 122

Hawthorne Studies (Mayo), 469–471

Hayden, Casey, 410

Hayden, Tom

Alinsky and, 388

campus protests and, 404

Chicago Democratic Convention protests (1968) and, 407

Jordan, Hamilton, 449
Joseph. *See under* Bible, The
Jullien, François, 46
Jungle, The (Sinclair), 312
Jutland, Battle of, 120

Kagan, Donald, 33
Kahn, Herman, 156, 159–161, 176
Kahneman, Daniel, 592–593, 604, 616, 622
Kai-shek, Chiang, 184
Kant, Immanuel, 316–317
Kaplan, Robert, 191, 561–562
Kaufman, Arnold, 374
Kautsky, Karl, 284–285, 288–289, 297, 332
Kay, John, 560, 570
Kellaway, Lucy, 564
Kelley, Florence, 314–315
Kennedy, John F.
    Berlin blockade crisis and, 172–173
    civil rights legislation and, 363–364
    civilian strategic advisers to, 149–150
    counterinsurgency and, 188
    Cuban missle crisis and, 173–176
    television debate with Nixon and, 438–439
    women's rights and, 409
Kennedy, Robert, 174, 386, 403, 407
Kerry, John, 433
Kershaw, Ian, 140
key performance indicators (KPIs), 562
Keynes, John Maynard, 513
Khomeini, Ayatollah, 424
Khrushchev, Nikita, 173–176
Kiechel III, Walter, 498–499, 501
Kilcullen, David, 224, 234
Kim, W. Chan, 537–539
King Jr., Martin Luther
    Alinsky and, 388–389
    assassination of, 403

Birmingham campaign and, 362–364
    on Black Power movement, 394
    Chicago and, 388–389
    economic issues and, 364, 395
    Gandhi and, 358–360
    March on Washington and, 364
    Montgomery Bus Boycott and, 357–358
    nonviolent direct action and, 344, 358–359, 362–364, 677n28
    plagiarism and, 359–360, 677n28
    Rustin and, 358–361, 389
    Student Nonviolent Coordinating Committee (SNCC) and, 391
    Wilkins and, 360–361
King Lear (Shakespeare), 64, 314
King, Mary, 410
Kingdom of God is Within You, The (Tolstoy), 347
Kissinger, Henry, 170
Kitzmiller v. Dover, 422
Kjellén, Rudolf, 122
Knights, David, 558–559
Kolakowski, Leszek, 11
Kornberger, Martin, 559
Kossuth, Lajos, 251, 260
Krepinevich, Andrew F., 215–216
Kubrik, Stanley, 160
Kuhn, Thomas
    Foucault and, 424
    paradigms and, 419–423
Kuklick, Bruce, 614
Kursk, Battle of, 143
Kutuzov, Mikhail
    Battle of Borodino and, 79–80
    Tolstoy's depiction of, 100, 102
Kuwait. *See* Gulf War (1991)

Laffley, Alan, 570
Lakoff, George, 434–436

on petit bourgeoisie, 260

political philosophy of, 247,
 251–261, 263, 272–274, 301

Revolutions of 1848 and, 253,
 255–259

socialist movement and, 284–285

Stoppard's depiction of, 267–268

Weber and, 302, 321

mass media and communication

agenda setting and, 417–418

conformism and, 416–417

limits to the power of, 436

nonviolent direct action and, 352,
 363–364

political strategy and, 438–439,
 450–451

mass publics. *See also* crowd psychology;
 propaganda

conservative theories about,
 325–326

Mosca on, 326

Pareto on, 323

socialist theories about, 250–251,
 253

master strategist, myth of the, 237–244

Matalin, Mary, 446–447

Matthews, Herbert, 400

Mauborgne, Renee, 537–539

Maurice (Emperor of Byzantium),
 47–48

Mauss, Marcel, 300, 670n1

Maximus, Quintus Fabius, 47

Maximus, Valerius, 43

Mayo, Elton, 469–472, 543, 563, 566

Mazzini, Giuseppe, 179, 251, 260, 328

McCarthy, Eugene, 407

McClellan, George, 110

McDonald, John, 152–153, 491,
 495–496

McFate, Montgomery, 231–232

McGinnis, Joe, 439

McGovern, George, 441

McGregor, Douglas, 543–544

McKee, Robert, 623, 628–629

McKinsey & Company Consulting,
 497, 544–546

McNamara, Robert

Cuban missile crisis and, 175

Ford Motor Company and,
 501–502

Luttwack on, 202

mutually assured destruction theory
 and, 170

quantitative analysis and, 149–150,
 199, 202, 501–502, 546

Second World War and, 501

Vietnam War and, 149, 502

McNaughton, John, 190–191

McNeilly, Mark, 509

Means, Gardiner, 490, 492, 526

Meckling, William, 526

Megarian Decree, 32–35

Melian dialogue, 31

Menand, Louis, 319

Mensheviks, 289, 292–294

mentalization, 598–600

Merriam, Charles, 576

Merton, Robert, 319–320, 416

mētis (cunning), 23–29, 42–44, 555,
 613

Mētis (goddess), 24

Metz, Steve, 229

Michaels, Jeff, 235

Michels, Robert, 321–322, 335

Micklethwait, John, 505

Military Strategy (Wylie), 194

military-technical revolution. *See*
 revolution in military affairs
 (RMA)

Mill, John Stuart, 96

Mills, C. Wright

analysis of power by, 372–373

influences on, 371–372

New Left and, 372, 399

on role of sociology, 373–374,
 685n4

Milton, John
    Arminianism of, 56
    on disobedience to kings, 63
    on guile, 64
    Paradise Lost, 54, 56–64, 617
Mind and Society (Pareto), 324
Mini-manual of the Urban Guerrilla
    (Marighella), 402
minimax solution, 151–153, 155, 165,
    582
Mintzberg, Henry
    deliberate versus emergent
      strategies, 554–555
    emphasis on storytelling by, 566
    on importance of community,
      555–556
    on strategic planning, 499–500,
      504, 550, 560
Mirowski, Philip, 148, 514–515, 600
Mitchell, Billy, 125
Modern Corporation and Private Property
    (Berle and Means), 490
Modern Strategy (Gray), 238
Mondale, Walter, 448, 449
Montecuccoli, Raimondo, 51
Montgomery (Alabama, US) Bus
    Boycott, 357–360
Moral Majority, 444, 452
Moral Man and Immoral Society
    (Niebuhr), 353
Morgan, Glenn, 558–559
Morgan, J.P., 476
Morgenstern, Oskar, 151–152, 154,
    161, 582
Morson, Gary, 102
Mosca, Gaetano, 321–323, 326, 335
Moses. *See under* Bible, The
Most, Johann, 277
Mr. Smith Goes to Washington (Capra),
    624–626
Ms. magazine, 430
Murphy Brown, 452–453
Murphy, Richard, 488–489

Musashi, Miyamoto, 510–511
Mussolini, Benito, 140, 142, 328
Muste, A. J., 354–356, 412
My Life and Work (Ford), 483
My Years with General Motors (Sloan),
    495–496, 616
myths
    Burnham on, 335
    Sorel on, 327–328

Nader, Ralph, 526
Nagasaki, atomic bombing of, 143,
    217
Nagl, John, 224
Nalebuff, Barry, 523, 710n6
Napoleon. *See* Bonaparte, Napoleon
Napoleonic Wars
    Clausewitz, and, 82–83, 90–91,
      237, 617
    coalitions in, 90–91, 115
    France and, 78–81, 116
    Great Britain and, 116
    guerrilla warfare and, 179–180,
      240
    international peace movement and,
      96
    naval warfare and, 119–120
    Prussia and, 78–79, 82
    Russia campaign and, 78–83, 90,
      209
    Spain and, 90, 179–180, 240
    Tolstoy's depiction of, 98–102
narrative
    business management and, 563–567
    qualities of, 621–622
    different notions of, 427–432
    information operations and,
      233–234
    political campaigning and,
      433–435, 437, 449
    problems with 615–618
Nash, John, 514–515, 594, 600
Nation of Islam, 391–392

National Association for the
    Advancement of Colored People
    (NAACP), 351, 357, 360–361
National Football League (NFL),
    522
National Liberation Front (FLN,
    Algeria), 392
National Liberation Front (Vietnam),
    397
National Organization of Women
    (NOW), 409–410
NATO (North Atlantic Treaty
    Organization)
    Berlin blockade crisis and, 173
    continental European defense and,
        199–200, 203, 210
    free-rider problem and, 583–584
    Turkey and, 175
Nazis. *See also* Hitler, Adolf
    ideology of, 122, 335, 343
    propaganda and, 336, 342–343,
        414
Nechayev, Sergei, 276, 392
neo-Machiavellians, 321, 329, 335
netwar, 229–230
neuroscience. *See* human brain, studies
    of
New Deal, 334, 441, 482, 487,
    489–490
New Industrial State, The (Galbraith),
    492
New Jersey, unemployment study in,
    472–473
New Left. *See also* Student Nonviolent
    Coordinating Committee
    (SNCC); Students for a
    Democratic Society (SDS)
    1968 Democratic Convention
        protests and, 406–408
    Alinsky and, 388, 408–409
    attitude toward electoral politics of,
        436
    campus protests and, 403–406

challenge to Western democracies
    by, 415
civil rights movement and, 375
community organizing projects and,
    376
conservative reactions to, 440
Cuba and, 398–399, 402
existentialist philosophy and, 368,
    370–371, 375–376
Foucault and, 426–427
France and, 403, 428
gay liberation and, 411
Guevara and, 402
hippies and, 405–406
legacy of, 411–412
liberation emphasis of, 367,
    369–370
media and, 417–418
Mills and, 372, 399
orthodox Left and, 367–368, 370
participatory democracy and,
    376–378
Port Huron Statement and, 367,
    374–375, 378
Third World and, 398–399
Vietnam War and, 396–399,
    405–407, 411
views of "technocracy" and, 370
Weather Underground and,
    403–405
women's liberation and, 409–411
Yippies and, 406–407
New Politics, The (Perry), 438
New School of Social Research, 415
New State, The (Follet), 468
Newman, James, 156
Ney, Michel, 84
Nicholas II (Tsar of Russia), 296
Niebuhr, Reinhold, 352–354, 358
Niederwerfungsstrategie (strategy of
    annihilation), 108
Nixon, Richard, 436, 439–441
Nono, Luigi, 176

nonviolent direct action. *See also*
   pacifism
   American civil rights movement
      and, 350–351, 354–365,
      386
   critiques of the limits of, 349–351,
      355–356
   Gandhi and, 348–351, 354–355,
      358–359, 385, 412
   King Jr. and, 344, 358–359,
      362–364, 677n28
   labor relations and, 352
   media aspect of, 352, 363–364
   Niebuhr on, 352–354
   Rustin and, 358–359, 362–363
   suffragette movement and,
      345–346
   Tolstoy and, 348
North Vietnam. *See under* Vietnam
Northern Alliance, 222
Norton, David, 561–562
nuclear weapons
   arms control and, 169
   Cold War and, 156–159, 167–168
   deterrence theory and, 157–160,
      168, 176–177, 194, 241
   escalation and, 176
   first-strike capability and, 167–169,
      171
   game theory and, 155
   Manhattan Project and, 147–148
   massive retaliation doctrine and,
      157
   mutually assured destruction theory
      and, 170, 218
   Schelling on, 164–165, 167–173
   Second World War and, 143, 156,
      217
   second-strike capability and,
      168–170
   Soviet Union and, 156–157,
      168–169, 177
   stalemate and, 177

   strategic impact of, 134, 145–149,
      155–160, 163–165, 167–171,
      176–177, 217, 219–220
   submarines and, 169
   thermonuclear weapons and, 156
   United States and, 147, 156–157,
      168–169, 171–172, 177

O'Reilly, Jane, 430
Oakland (California), 394
Obama, Barack, 453–455
Ochs, Phil, 406
Odysseus
   Homer's description of, xii, 22–27
   Sophocles' description of, 27–28
   Virgil's description of, 24, 42
Odyssey, The (Homer), 24–27
Offer, Avner, 619–620
Ogarev, Nicholas, 266
Oglesby, Carl, 397
Ohmae, Kenichi, 545
Olson, Mancur, 583–584, 586
On Escalation (Kahn), 176
On Thermonuclear War (Kahn), 160–161
On War (Clausewitz), 82–83, 86, 118,
      179, 203–204, 237, 445. *See also*
      Clausewitz, Carl von, military
      strategies of
One Dimensional Man (Marcuse), 399
One Step Forward, Two Steps Back (Lenin),
      293–294
OODA loops (observation, orientation,
      decision, action), 196–199, 201,
      217–218, 225, 451, 511–512
Operation Desert Storm. *See* Gulf War
      (1991)
operational level of war, 202–203, 205,
      207, 214
operations research. *See* quantitative
      analysis
Oppenheimer, Robert, 145
Ordeshook, Peter, 580
Organization Man (Whyte), 369

quantitative analysis. *See also* game
theory
limitations of, 150, 203
McNamara and, 149–150, 199, 202,
501–502, 546
RAND Corporation and, 147–148,
152–153, 513–514
Quayle, Dan, 452–453, 690n51
Quiet American, The (Greene), 187
"Quiz Kids." *See* "Whiz Kids"

radical Islamists, 222, 235–236. *See also*
al-Qaeda
Raff, Daniel, 616
Raiffa, Howard, 161–162, 514
Ramsey, Douglas, 506
RAND Corporation
game theory and, 161–162, 513
nuclear strategy and, 161–162, 168
quantitative emphasis of, 147–148,
150, 152–153, 513–514
rational choice theory and, 575–577
Randolph, A. Philip, 356
Raphals, Lisa, 43
Rapoport, Anatol, 585
Rapport, Mike, 250
rational choice theory. *See also* game
theory
bounded rationality and, 592
brain physiology and, 592
criteria for, 591
economics discipline and, 577, 580
experiments challenging, 594–597
heuristics and, 593
limits of, 575–576, 589–591,
594–597, 599–600, 605–606
political science and, 580–581
RAND Corporation and, 575–577
Rochester School and, 576–581
social contexts and, 594–597,
599–600
ultimatum game and, 594–596

Ratzel, Friedrich, 122
Reagan, Ronald
as California governor, 442–443,
448
political communication strategies
of, 442–444, 625–626
presidential campaigns of, 443, 447
religious right and, 443–444
Southern states and, 443, 447
realism doctrine, 30–31
red and blue oceans (Kim and
Mauborgne), 537–538
Red Queen effect, 536–537
Reengineering the Corporation (Hammer
and Champy), 533
Reengineering Management (Champy), 536
Reflections on Violence (Sorel), 327–328
Reformation of War, The (Fuller), 132,
135
Reid, Brian Holden, 130–131
Republican Party (United States),
political communication
strategies and, 434–436, 440–
441, 443, 447–449, 452–455.
See also Atwater, Lee; individual
politicians
Reveille for Radicals (Alinksy), 381
revolution in military affairs (RMA)
Afghanistan war (2001) and, 222
cognitive dimension of, 217–219
compared to fourth-generation
warfare, 226
definition of, 216
Gulf War and, 214–215, 217, 219
information warfare and, 215, 217,
222
land warfare and, 216
long-range missiles and, 219–220
precision warfare and, 219
"shock and awe" and, 217
United States and, 214–215,
218–219, 222–223

Savio, Mario, 366
Saxe, Maurice de, 48, 51
Scales, Robert, 231
Scammon, Richard, 441
Schank, Roger, 599
Schelling, Thomas
    Berlin blockade crisis and, 173
    compellence theory of, 163,
        190–191
    on focal points, 166–167
    game theory and, 160–162,
        166–167, 515, 529, 585
    Nobel Prize in Economics, 160
    nonviolent direct action and, 412
    on nuclear weapons, 164–165,
        167–173
    progressive risk and, 164–165
    RAND Corporation and, 162
    strategic theories of, 162–173, 190,
        198, 515
    Vietnam and, 191
Schlieffen Plan, 113, 198, 210
"Scholarship and Social Agitation"
        (Small), 315
Schwarzkopf, Norman, 215
Schwerpunkt. See center of gravity
        concept
"Science as a Vocation" (Weber),
        303–304, 307
Science of Revolutionary Warfare (Most), 277
Scott, James C., 716n21
scripts
    cognition and, 598–599, 619
    dramatic conventions and, 623–629
    honor script, 619–620
    plots and, 623–624, 626–627
    strategy and, xiv, 619–623,
        627–629
Seale, Bobby, 394
Second International, 295, 297, 329
Second World War
    air power and, 129, 140, 143,
        157–158

China and, 183–184, 186
France and, 139–143, 199, 210, 617
Germany and, 134, 139–143,
        157–158, 199, 210, 213
Great Britain and, 134, 139–144,
        147, 157–158, 349, 648n14
information warfare and, 228
Italy and, 142–143
Japan and, 143, 184, 186
nuclear weapons and, 143, 156, 217
Soviet Union and, 139–140,
        142–143, 145, 210, 213
tank warfare and, 143
United States and, 139–145
Secret Agent, The (Conrad), 278
Sedan, Battle of, 106, 112
Seeger, John, 520
Selling of the President (McGinnis), 439
September 11, 2001 terrorist attacks,
        222
Seven Pillars of Wisdom (Lawrence), 181,
        186
Shakespeare, William, 49–50, 64–65
Shapiro, Carl, 529
Shapiro, Ian, 581
Sharp, Gene, 412
Sherman Antitrust Act, 477
Sherman, William T., 111, 446, 506
Shridharani, Krishnalal, 355–356
Shrum, Robert, 433
Shy, John, 84, 185
Silberman, Charles, 383
Simon, Herbert, 517, 520, 544–545,
        587, 592, 598
Sinclair, Upton, 312, 379, 437
Sloan, Alfred P.
    compared to Ford, 486–487
    DuPont family and, 484
    management strategies of, 474,
        484–490, 494, 496–498, 608
    successors to, 502
    writings of, 495–496, 616
Small Wars (Calwell), 181

Sparta, 30–35, 38, 42
Spartacist League, 298, 305
Speier, Hans, 576
Spinney, Chuck, 226
Stalin, Josef
    Chinese Civil War and, 184
    purges by, 297–298, 334
    Second World War and, 142–143,
        213
    Taylorism and, 466
Stalk, George, 511, 568
Standard Oil, 475–477, 494, 523, 565
Stanton, Angela, 595
State and Revolution (Lenin), 297
Steffens, Lincoln, 312
Stewart, Matthew, 498, 523
Stonewall Inn (New York City), 411
Stoppard, Tom, 265–268
Strachan, Hew, 85, 92, 114, 209, 610
Strange, Joe, 208
Strategematon (Frontinus), 43, 72
stratēgike *episteme* (general's knowledge),
    72
Strategikon (Maurice), 47–48
stratēgōn *sophia* (general's wisdom), 72
strategy
    definitions of, x–xi, 72–75, 88,
        607–608
    etymology of, xii, 72, 635n12
    limits of, 609–612
Strategy and Structure (Chandler), 496
Strategy in Poker, Business and War
    (McDonald), 152
strategy of annihilation, 108, 204–205,
    215, 264, 332
Strategy Safari (Mintzberg), 560
Strategy: The Indirect Approach (Liddell
    Hart), 136
Stride toward Freedom (King Jr.), 360
Structure of Scientific Revolutions, The
    (Kuhn), 419
Student Nonviolent Coordinating
    Committee (SNCC)

Black Power doctrine and, 393–394
    Freedom Rides and, 361–362
    King Jr. and, 391
    militancy and, 366, 378, 393–395
    nonviolent direct action and, 391
    participatory democracy and,
        377–378
    women's issues and, 410–411
Students for a Democratic Society
    (SDS)
    Gitlin on, 412–413
    Port Huron Statement and,
        367–368, 374–375, 378
    radicalism in, 398
    Vietnam War protests and, 396–397
    violence and, 366
    Weather Underground and,
        403–404
suffragette movement, 344–346
Sumida, Jon, 613
Summers, Harry, 221
Sun Tzu
    business managers' use of, 508–511,
        549
    compared to Athenians, 46
    on deception, 42, 45–46
    on foreknowledge, 45
    Liddell Hart and, 135–138
    Mao and, 45, 185
    political consultants' use of,
        445–446
    strategic theories of, xii, 44–46,
        136–138, 185, 193, 382,
        445–446, 508, 549
Sun Tzu and the Art of Business
    (McNeilly), 509
Supreme Court (United States)
    abortion rulings and, 444, 452
    antitrust rulings of, 477
    desegregation rulings of, 356–357,
        359, 362
SWOT analysis (Andrews), 499, 521,
    561, 564

System 1 mental processes, 602–605, 612–614, 620, 622
System 2 mental processes, 602–605, 612, 614, 620, 622

tactics, definitions of, 72–74
Taleb, Nassim, 617
Taliban, The, 222
Tarbell, Ida, 464, 477
Tarde, Gabriel, 336
Taylor, Frederick. *See* Taylorism
Taylorism
    Drucker on, 493
    efficiency emphasis of, 463–465, 470, 546
    Ford Motor Company and, 483
    "Great Taylorism" and, 499
    labor unions and, 465
    legacy of, 132, 546, 551
    origins of, 462
    Progressives and, 465
    Soviet Union and, 465–466
    worker as machine principle of, 462–463, 470
Tea Party, 455
Teapot Dome scandal, 624, 626
Techow, Gustav, 263
Templer, Gerald, 188
terrorism
    anarchism and, 276–279
    assassination and, 277–278
    asymmetric warfare and, 222, 227, 230
    Far Left and, 412
    September 11, 2001 attacks and, 222
    theories of, 402
Tetlock, Philip, 604
Thaler, Richard, 593, 596
Theory of Games and Economic Behavior, The (Morgenstern and von Neumann), 151–152

Theory of Political Coalitions, The (Riker), 579
Theory of the Firm, The (Penrose), 496
thermonuclear weapons. *See under* nuclear weapons
Thiers, Adolphe, 271
Third International, 297
Thirty Years' Peace, 32–34
Thomas, William, 337
Thompson, Robert, 188
Thoreau, Henry David, 347, 358
Thorton, Charles Bates, 501
Thriving on Chaos (Peters), 548
Thucydides, 23, 30–38, 46–47, 50, 115
Thurber, James, 438
Tilly, Charles, 615–616, 622
Tirpitz, Alfred von, 117–118
Todorov, Tzvetan, 428
Tolstoy, Leo
    Addams and, 310–311
    on anarchism, 310
    Christianity of, 307
    Clausewitz depicted by, 98
    Crimean War and, 97–98
    Dewey and, 318
    Gandhi and, 347–348
    Kutuzov depicted by, 100, 102
    Napoleon depicted by, 99–101, 617
    nonviolent direct action and, 348
    on philosophy of history, 98–102, 274, 307–308, 320, 609, 617
    political philosophy of, 307–311
    Proudhon and, 274
    Sermon on the Mount and, 307
    strategy depicted by, 99–101
    on urban life, 309–311
    War and Peace and, 96, 98–102, 274, 307
    Weber on, 307
total quality management (TQM), 532

liberalism and, 301
Marx and, 302, 321
political activity of, 304–305
political philosophy of, 304–307,
    368, 413
on social science, 303–304
on the state, 305
Tolstoy and, 307
Wedge Project, 421–422
Weick, Karl, 544–546, 563–564, 566
Welch, Jack, 498, 504
Wells, H.G., 123, 128–129
West Germany. *See* Germany, Federal
    Republic of
Westen, Drew, 434–435
Western Electric. *See* Hawthorne
    Studies
Weydemeyer, Joseph, 262
Weyrich, Paul, 444, 452
Wharton School, 461
Wharton, Joseph, 461, 463
"What Is To Be Done?" (Tolstoy), 309
What is to be Done? (Chernyshevsky),
    266, 290
What is to be Done? (Lenin), 290
Wheeler, Burton, 624–625, 716n29
Whitaker, Clem, 437–438
White Collar Workers (Mills), 369
White, Margaret, 463
White, Thomas D., 150
"Whiz Kids," 501–502
*Who Governs: Democracy and Power in an
    American City* (Dahl), 372
Whole World is Watching, The (Gitlin),
    417
Whyte, William, 369, 491
Wiener, Norbert, 197
Wiersema, Fred, 535–536
Wildavsky, Aaron, 503

Wilhelm I (Kaiser of Germany),
    106–107
Wilkins, Roy, 360–361
Wilkinson, Ben, 235–236
Willich, August von, 262–263
Wilson, Charles, 495, 502
Winslow, Frederick, 462
Winsor, Ellen, 351
Wofford, Harris, 358, 361
Wohlstetter, Albert, 160, 168, 176
Wohlstetter, Roberta, 176
Wolin, Sheldon, 421
women's liberation, 409–411, 430. *See
    also* suffragette movement
Women's Social and Political Union
    (WSPU), 345–346
Wood, Gordon, 609
Wooldridge, Adrian, 505
Wordsworth, William, 178
World Crisis, The (Churchill), 139
World War I. *See* First World War
World War II. *See* Second World War
Wrangham, Richard, 7–8
Wrege, Charles, 463
Wretched of the Earth, The (Fanon),
    392
Wylie, James, 194–195

Xerox Corporation, 546

Yamaha, 567–568
Yarger, Harry, 238–239, 244
Yeats, William Butler, 391
Yippies, 406–407

Zarqawi, Abu Musab al-, 223
Zawahiri, Ayman al-, 665n54
Zeus, 24, 29
zhi, 43–44